M000072784

HARDENED TO HICKORY

THE MISSING CHAPTER IN ANDREW JACKSON'S LIFE

By

Tony L. Turnbow

ISBN-13: 978-0-692-19527-7

Cover design by FoxFuel Creative, LLC, Nashville, Tennessee.

Interior design by booknook.biz

Author's note as to spelling: Original misspellings have been used in quotations rather than corrections and without the use of (sic) to note errors.

CONTENTS

"He conquered . . . the conquerors of the conquerors of Europe; but he had to conquer his own government first, and he did it, and that was for him the most difficult of the two . . ."

—Andrew Jackson as described by
U.S. Senator Thomas Hart Benton on the presentation of
Jackson's sword to the U.S. Congress, Feb. 26, 1855[1]

"[T]his mutiny against supreme military authority, did more, I verily believe, than anything else to elevate the mutineer to the Presidential chair."

—Reverend William Winian

PROLOGUE

"It was columbia's true sons who had walked forth, awaked by the infringement of there independence, bequeathed to them by there Revolutionary parents."

—General Andrew Jackson, March 15, 1813

December 10, 1812—the day Tennessee became the "Volunteer State"—was one of the coldest days anyone could remember. An ominously strong northeast wind chilled farmers who arose before daybreak to milk their cows and begin other morning chores. It was no surprise when low-hanging clouds began releasing snow by 9 a.m. The storm quickly intensified and produced a blinding blizzard by noon. Snowfall would total over a foot before sunset.[2]

In normal times, men sheltered from the rare winter Nor'easter with their families around the warmth of their hearths for a well-earned rest from the work of the harvest.

The year 1812 was not a normal time. War-fever stirred Tennesseans from hibernation. For five years, Americans had railed at British challenges to a United States independence that they naively assumed had been established at the end of the last war. A war of revolution did not necessarily result in acknowledged independence.

In 1812, Britain still commanded the most powerful military in the world. Across the Atlantic Ocean, the United States' experiment in a democratic republic was struggling, and the fledgling nation stood on the brink of financial ruin. Commanders of its small standing army mainly were men either too young to have experienced war or those too old to be effective on the battlefield. Military leaders often were appointed based solely upon family and political connections among the elite rather than military skill. If Britain still viewed the American continent through its lens of empire or Americans as their colonists, there seemed to be little the U.S. could do to challenge that perception.

In private, British aristocrats often still referred to Americans as gutter trash and criminals, hardly worthy of their attention. The British *Morning Post* sniffed that Americans "possess all the vices of their Indian neighbors without their virtues."[3] American newspapers reported that British captains forcibly stopped American ships on the high seas. British guns even fired on the *U.S.S. Chesapeake,* when its commander refused British commands to allow British sailors to board the American vessel.

In addition to dominating the seas, Britain still controlled Canadian territory to the north of their other former colonies in America. If the British could establish a foothold on the Gulf Coast and gain control of traffic on the Mississippi River, most of the American continent might again fall under their dominance. The triumphant victory of the Revolution was becoming a distant memory for many Americans.

It was not just the American continent that teetered on the brink of change. The entire world had entered a period of transition. Spain had lost it prowess and stabilizing influence over Europe and the Caribbean. The recently crowned French emperor Napoleon Bonaparte had turned warrior and battled the British for domination of the globe. Economies were in shambles as an increasing international trade threatened old customs and cultures. Strong men who had learned to survive on their own without support from the old order would eventually rise to challenge its leaders.

Amid this turmoil, the U.S. federal government seemed divided and leaderless. President Jefferson had preferred diplomacy to war with Europeans, a novel experiment in a world where disputes ultimately were settled by brute force or a credible threat of force. Jefferson calculated that the new American nation of former colonies lacked the finances, unity, and sheer military power to oppose mighty European armies. But unintentionally compounding that weakness, Jefferson had ordered reductions in the number of U.S. regular army soldiers. He feared that the rival Federalist political party would use the army to depose him. Jefferson also could not guarantee a unified war effort among the states to oppose Europe. The interests of the New England states differed so much from those in the West that eastern leaders proposed secession from the Union if the U.S. went to war. Jefferson's weakness prompted a derisive order from Napoleon, who hoped to draw Americans into his world conflict. The emperor reasoned that if the American flag would not protect its ships against British searches and impressment, then American ships should also submit to the French.[4] Napoleon attempted to shame Americans into war by adding that it is the "duty of nations to resort to force, and to declare themselves against things which dishonor them and disgrace their independence."[5] A deeply divided new country appeared to its potential European enemies to be a land of cowards.

For Tennessee settlers, insults to national pride were overshadowed by a justifiable fear that the British were encouraging American Indians to rise and destroy western settlements. European enemies had often found it more effective to work through Indian proxies than to send their own invading forces across the Atlantic.[6] Two decades earlier, Tennesseans had supported the U.S. Army's defense of the Northwest Territory against northern tribes, only to spy British soldiers spurring Indians on from the rear. And it was no secret that Spain had once supplied weapons to southern Indians from Pensacola and Mobile to create proxy soldiers against American settlers.[7] Now rumors spread that the British were doing the same through their Spanish allies along the Gulf Coast.

If Tennesseans needed a reminder of the British Empire's abuses of authority against its former subjects, Andrew Jackson served as their icon. A scar on the Tennessee militia major general's head permanently recorded a British military officer's abuse of power against a then-fourteen-year old boy, who was thrown into a makeshift prison with criminals and nearly starved. The young Jackson's only offense was his refusal to stoop to shine a British officer's boot while the officer ransacked his cousin's home in the presence of his cousin's defenseless wife and small children. Worse, to a British soldier, the American Jackson demanded his rights. The boy instinctively raised his hand to defend against the answer of a British sword as it struck both his hand and head.[8] Jackson did not back down when challenged by overwhelming power. If anything, standing up for his own rights to an officer of the British crown—and surviving— steeled the young Revolutionary War messenger boy for greater challenges. It confirmed for Jackson, at an early age, his own sense of courage based upon strong-headed principles. It also revealed a common-sense intuition that Jackson would further develop into survival skills as a teenage orphan in the rough American backwoods.[9]

Andrew Jackson would never need medals on his uniform to demonstrate his bravery; the scar on his head bore an indelible witness to his courage. Jackson had smoothed some of the rough edges of his bootstrap frontier-like childhood and learned some of the social graces and political skills needed to succeed in a world led by gentry; however, his boundless ambition often still exceeded his experience and wisdom. Cautious military professionals, both British and American, who considered Jackson's impulsive and unorthodox actions too reckless, underestimated him to their own peril.

By 1812, reports of British abuses of American rights on the high seas prompted a visceral and determined response from Jackson. The British,

Jackson said, had taken everything from him that he held dear when he was child.[10] His mother and brothers died from causes he could attribute to British aggression.

Even prior to the official Declaration of War on June 18, 1812, Jackson had supported a group known as the "War Hawks." The group of federal legislators worked tirelessly to create a groundswell for military action to demand that Britain respect American rights. The Nashville *Clarion* backed the effort by publishing a regular column of the latest "British Intrigue." Though some settlers on the frontier could not read a newspaper, political leaders relayed news of British threats and added their own commentary. On muster days, when all male citizens between the ages of 18 and 45 were required by law to meet and train in the methods of war, citizen soldiers spent much of their obligatory training time listening to soaring speeches about military valor, mixed with denunciations of the most recent British outrage.

This generation had not been tested in war. Their fathers and grandfathers had entertained them many evenings with stories of their own sacrifices in the Revolution. The often-repeated accounts now formed a catechism that set the standard of patriotism. However, with an exception of occasional skirmishes with Indians, post-Revolution soldiers had exercised the opportunity to prove their valor only with words and musters. The *Clarion* mockingly described militia as men "who work themselves into fever, get upon their horses[,] gallop about in the woods for eight or ten days until they have eat up their provisions, and then come home and take upon themselves as if they had followed Alexander to the Ganges."[11]

But common Americans who faced the possibility of death every day on the frontier were not cowards. Now was this generation's time for action. Children and grandchildren of the American Revolution had been called to their duty in the tented fields, and even a foot of snow would not deter them.

Primed for months by Jackson's public orders to anticipate imminent action, more than 2,000 settlers from towns and hollows across Tennessee left the comfort of their cabins to answer the Call to Arms to what Cavalry Colonel John Coffee and other military men described as their "place of destiny." As frontier fathers and sons said their goodbyes to their families, young soldiers could dream of returning home as conquering heroes with stories of military glory to tell their children. Few of these Volunteers would ever know the extent to which their ultimate destiny would be to change the course of history.

No one foresaw that when the smoke of cannon fire had eventually cleared, large numbers of the American populace would view Andrew Jackson as the general who had "conquered... the conquerors of the conquerors of Europe."[12] Jackson had worked for years to prepare himself to become the next General George Washington to drive the British army from American soil. The Volunteer major general naively assumed that he could prepare his citizen troops to encounter the professional British army with little more than ten-days' additional training.

However, unknown to the even more politically inexperienced Andrew Jackson on December 10, 1812, his own storm clouds were forming. Jackson did not appreciate the challenge he faced from his nemesis, U.S. Army General James Wilkinson, who commanded American forces on the Gulf Coast. Jackson had long suspected that Wilkinson was a spy for an enemy power, but he did not appreciate Wilkinson's unparalleled powers of deception. Jackson never perceived the levels to which Wilkinson would stoop to destroy him. Nevertheless, anticipating that the fight with Wilkinson could become more than political, Jackson prepared for the encounter by planning to settle any unresolvable disputes of honor as he had with other enemies — by packing his dueling pistols.[13]

Wilkinson would set the fight with Jackson, however, on the field of federal bureaucracy, one that Wilkinson had spent a lifetime mastering. Wilkinson's blindside from within the United States Army transformed the Tennessee Volunteers' upcoming winter march into one of Andrew Jackson's greatest life crucibles, one that would have crushed almost anyone else. The unexpected challenges Jackson would face and overcome on the Natchez Trace would forge the backwoods duelist into a tested general and a new man, the man who would return from the Natchez Expedition as "Old Hickory."

CHAPTER ONE

TENNESSEE VOLUNTEERS

"We had taken the field raw and undisciplined with the intention of fighting the Battles of our country and experience had taught me to know that without discipline, courage alone would not do."

—Andrew Jackson to John Armstrong, April 24, 1813

On December 10, 1812, the Tennessee Volunteers met up with neighboring companies and formed increasingly larger groups along the primitive roads and trails to Nashville. By late morning, the paths were sometimes barely discernible through the snow. Citizen soldiers assured each other that no self-respecting man could rest comfortably in front of his hearth while their homes were threatened with destruction. Many recruits had already risked everything, including the lives of their families, to stake their claims to Tennessee land. They would not give them up without a fight.

Nashville had been designated only as the rendezvous point. A long march on the Natchez Trace lay ahead for the cavalry. Stories of its dangers were legendary. The new federal military wagon road ran a challenging 450 miles through the Chickasaw and Choctaw nations that settlers called the "Wilderness." Most Volunteers were yet unable to distinguish between friendly Indian nations and those they claimed to "thirst after American blood."[14] Soldiers were certain that in the long, forested expanse between settlements in Tennessee and Natchez, they would be vulnerable to attacks by tribes whose reputation for brutality had been embellished in newspapers and around campfires.

Volunteers' parents and grandparents could testify that life on the frontier could be brutal. Women and children were frequently shot, stabbed, clubbed, tortured, and hacked to death with whatever weapons were within an attacker's reach. Victims on both sides were often scalped as a final act of removing an enemy's dignity. Beyond the human threats, the infantry would travel an equally dangerous course down the untamed Mississippi River. While that route also presented dangers from Indians and pirates, the river itself was the greater danger. Unseen currents and below-the-surface snags could sink a boat loaded with soldiers in minutes.

As the Volunteers marched toward Nashville, cavalry officers hurriedly rode their horses past whole companies of infantry. Foot soldiers often grumbled that despite their fancy uniforms from Europe, officers were not professional soldiers. Except on muster days, cavalry commanders worked as storeowners, doctors, lawyers, and planters. Their incomes gave them the advantage of the ability to buy the horses, arms, uniforms, and accoutrements officers needed to command their units. Common militiamen sometimes thought that the sole function of some officers was to dress in embroidered uniforms and parade through town barking out orders to the common folk.[15] Lower ranks performed the real work. Rank-and-file perceptions were reinforced when someone noticed that a few officers were bringing along their own slaves to wash their clothes and cook their meals.

Unlike cavalry, the typical Volunteer infantryman trudged through the snow in his homemade farm shoes and homespun dark blue or brown hunting shirt. To the average man, hunting shirts were a military tradition that honored their ancestors who fought the Revolution wearing similar uniforms.[16] The outer shirts or frocks were often highlighted with white, yellow, or red fringe to distinguish companies from each other. Despite the homespun cloth that almost any man could afford, these company-specific details gave the troops a crisp military appearance that encouraged a sense of professionalism.

Most common soldiers' shoes and uniforms would wear out even before they had begun the return march. To travel light, the men would be able to carry no more than one change of clothes, including white vests and white pants for parade. If winter rains soaked through soldiers' knapsacks as well as their uniforms, Volunteers would have no choice but wear the wet clothing even if it froze on their backs. If the cloth tore beyond what could be mended in the field, the soldiers would be full exposed to the elements. Sleeping blankets rolled up to be carried on the soldiers' backs could be unrolled and worn around the shoulders for warmth, but winter coats were not part of the uniform.

In addition to a blanket, some Volunteers carried a rifle or musket and a small amount of food in their knapsacks. Others did not even own a firearm or a change of clothes, but their relative poverty did not deter them from service. They left home carrying what little food or equipment they could spare and found that other Volunteers were willing to share.

Many Volunteers were teenagers. Drummers could be as young as 12. Younger soldiers compensated for their lack of experience with optimism and energy. Despite the hazards that lay ahead, the boys could imagine themselves setting out on a grand adventure into the Indian territory settlers called the "Wilderness," an adventure that they would share with future generations, just as their grandfathers had entertained them with stories of the Revolution.[17] In addition to giving the boys a good reason to avoid daily chores at home, this war would provide a once-in-a-lifetime opportunity to prove their mettle.

Nashville citizens anxiously awaited the arrivals. The fledgling town bordered the United States southwestern frontier, a vast area that largely was still unknown and over which the young republic had little control. Only decades earlier, a hardy few had built a town of temporary log homes for families looking to start anew. Now, brick and stone buildings demonstrated that investors thought the frontier town would become permanent.[18] The state legislature had recently voted to move the state capital to Nashville from Knoxville, and plans were underway to construct the first bridge across the Cumberland River. There was talk that the first sidewalks would soon be built. A library was being organized for subscribers who could afford to pay a dollar.[19] For the few who had leisure time, a wax museum displayed figures of Washington, Jefferson, and Napoleon, as well as terrifying Indian warriors poised to attack.

The town of 1,200 extended westward only about seven streets. The small rise on the west side of the settlement at the edge of the forest was referred to as "the hills."[20] To the south, the long flat public field just north of the Davidson Academy property was called "the Green." The Green was where large public gatherings were held and troops were mustered.[21] A portion of the hills and the Green would become home to Jackson's new military family that winter. Just north of the town, David McGavock's more-than-mile-square plantation spread out north to the Cumberland River, and his bare corn fields would provide additional campsites.[22]

Weeks prior to the rendezvous, Jackson had ordered Nashville store owner William Carroll to study the best locations for campsites near Nashville and to lay out a plan for the temporary military cantonment.[23] Teams of oxen had pulled wagons loaded with rations for the men and forage for the horses into future camp sites for days. One-thousand ricks of firewood would be waiting when the men arrived, but it would not last beyond a day in the extreme cold. Fortunately, chopping new supplies from nearby woods and hauling it to the camps would keep restless soldiers busy and out of trouble. Business leaders also knew that clearing the woods so near to the town would help improve the value of Nashville land for settlement. The work of hundreds of soldiers, even during a brief encampment, would make a lasting contribution to the development of the town.

Despite the lack of equipment for a permanent army, the state had tents ready. Militia Deputy Quartermaster William B. Lewis had been at work for two weeks procuring 8,000 yards of cotton fabric from the Cairo Manufactory in neighboring Sumner County. There had been little time for contractors to sew the cotton into tents for 1,500 men.[24]

Tennessee Governor Willie Blount had traveled to Nashville to be present when the soldiers assembled. His reputation was at stake. Against the less-than-subtle suggestion of the War Department, Blount had responded to the directive to muster 1,500 troops in two regiments of troops under the command of a brigadier general by appointing his friend Andrew Jackson, a higher-ranking major general, to lead the expedition.

Jackson's political enemy Governor John Sevier had denied him the opportunity to lead the last military expedition down the Natchez Trace in 1803. Since then, Jackson had carefully positioned himself for this moment, when he could show the hapless professional generals and federal politicians what a leader with a little spine could accomplish.

Jackson had achieved part of his goal by winning the election to serve as major general of the Tennessee Militia, but that rank did not give him command of the entire state.[25] The election had been a tie between Jackson and Sevier, and prior governor Roane had no choice politically but to divide the Tennessee regiment in half. Jackson was forced for the time being to be satisfied with the command of the Western Division in what is now called "Middle Tennessee," and his opponent Sevier led the Eastern Division.

Because Jackson was one of the two ranking generals in the state, Blount assumed that he had authority to choose Jackson to lead the expedition. The appointment empowered Jackson for the first time to call on the resources of the federal War Department—or, at least, that was the assumption Jackson drew from the federal order authorizing the muster of volunteer troops and from the governor's written assurances based upon that order.

As Governor Blount and General Jackson met at the inn on the Public Square to discuss plans for the march, Jackson was feeling pressure to move with speed. A letter had arrived from East Tennessee with news that East Tennessee Militia Colonel John Williams had already marched for the Georgia southern border with 150 Volunteers.[26] That news meant that East Florida planters who called themselves "Patriots" were preparing to attack Spanish forces at Amelia Island and St. Augustine. Williams would be well-positioned to provide support to assure the transfer of the Florida peninsula to the United States, and his major general Sevier would, by implication, oversee the campaign and gain credit for the acquisition of new territory. If the real purpose of President Madison's call-up of Tennessee forces was to march troops to East Florida, Jackson had little time to waste in Nashville. This was an historic moment, and Jackson did not want public perception or history to relegate him to a support position for Sevier. Jackson's men would need to be assembled, supplied, and trained without delay.

But Jackson faced a more immediate crisis. He might first have to quell a mutiny of deserting Volunteers even before his regiments fully assembled. The War Department had not provided money to pay the men, and the young state government had none to spare. Ready currency in the U.S., particularly in the West, generally was still held in the form of European gold and silver pieces, and President Jefferson's embargo had virtually extinguished the supply of European currency on the frontier. The federal government could issue notes to be paid in currency on a later date, but there was not enough hard currency in Nashville to cash them. Under the terms of service customary for the time, Volunteers mustered in as they arrived in camp by signing a muster roll and accepting wages in advance. The newspaper advertisement announcing the call-up of troops had promised two-months' advance pay for privates and six for officers. Acceptance of those funds bound Volunteer soldiers to service. If soldiers deserted after accepting advance pay, the breach of their agreement subjected them to military discipline—even possible execution. However, if no funds were available to pay the men when they arrived, Volunteers could choose to return home without facing any penalty. The War Department's failure to supply funds in time for the troops' arrival undercut Jackson's authority for the first time he faced his troops as a federal Volunteer major general. It would not have been unreasonable to expect the lack of pay to turn Jackson's first significant attempt at military leadership into a career-ending failure before it even began.

Newly mustered soldiers also expected to receive equipment to begin training for the mission, but Jackson had only enough federal muskets for about half the men. One goal of the American militia system was that each citizen soldier would outfit and arm himself. Each Volunteer had been requested to bring his own rifle if he had one, but most frontiersmen could not afford a gun. Those who could were reluctant to leave their families back home without the protection of a firearm. Cavalry members generally were the only frontiersmen who had arms to spare. In fact, the prospect of receiving a rifle or musket was part of the incentive for enlistment. The lack of government weapons planted a seed of doubt in the Volunteers' minds as to the significance of their mission and the importance of their commander.

Few frontiersmen understood how unprepared the young, loosely organized nation had been for a declaration of war. The United States was almost half a year into the conflict, but their armed forces were still in tatters. If Tennesseans were needed to face the powerful British military, why had the War Department not followed through in fulfilling Jackson's anticipated requisitions? An overly cautious commander like those that filled the ranks of the professional army would sense impending disaster. Jackson did not allow room for doubt, and he was determined not to lose this opportunity to command.

The historic blizzard compounded the uncertainty. Jackson had no means of knowing how many men would answer the call to rendezvous. Tennessee had 40,000 men of fighting age in 1812, but large numbers were exempt from military service.[27] On lesser occasions, excuses of high waters and muddy roads had prevented companies from assembling for routine musters. And some men like militia Colonel James K. Polk were too ill or had other justifiable reasons not to answer the Call to Arms. As Jackson and Blount paced at the inn, the snowstorm produced a justifiable anxiety that there would not even be enough Volunteers to stage a mutiny.

Those early apprehensions may have heightened everyone's exuberance as companies of Volunteers began appearing from sheets of snow in numbers that overwhelmed even the most optimistic estimates. News of the Volunteers' arrival spread through the taverns, and patrons rushed out to see the arriving horde. Out-of-state guests were heard to comment that they had "often been where Volunteers turned out, but they had never seen such a turning out as that."[28] The editor of the *Clarion* Benjamin J. Bradford added that he had never seen anything like it himself. It convinced him to "turn out" as they called it, or volunteer to join their ranks. He wrote an article preparing his readers for his absence over the next few months.

Not every able-bodied soldier volunteered, but Tennesseans took pride in their patriotic sacrifice. Within a few weeks, Franklin resident Andrew Goff would pause in the middle of his letter to Virginian Robert Preston to brag about the number of Tennessee men who voluntarily turned out in defense of their nation.[29]

Years later, after Jackson had become a national hero, it would be suggested that it was only the power of Andrew Jackson's leadership that persuaded over 2,000 men voluntarily to rendezvous miles from their homes during a blizzard. Jackson had stated publicly that he thought he could raise 2,500 volunteers in what was then West Tennessee. Ultimately, Jackson did not achieve his goal, but it hardly mattered. As accounts of the war would later be written in the West, General Jackson would become the focal point, overshadowing the fact that comparable numbers of volunteers turned out during the war in Kentucky and in the southern Mississippi Territory.

Jackson would prove to be one of those commanders who seem willing to push his men to the limits and beyond to achieve victory. Such leaders often take their enemies by surprise. Their lives and decisions become key factors in victory or defeat, and if victorious, their own personal victories shape the public recollections of the war.

Any political enemy who had hoped for a sudden end to Jackson's potential rise in military leadership at the first rendezvous in Nashville was disappointed. By 4:00 p.m., Nashville streets were crowded with hundreds of citizen soldiers who seemed to have overtaken the entire town. It was no aberration of good fortune; Jackson had labored for years laying the foundation for this moment. Jackson positioned William Carroll and muster master Robert Hayes on the Public Square throughout the day as the designated officers to sign in Volunteers as they arrived.[30] After company captains met with the quartermaster, Carroll then directed companies to their campsites north on McGavock's plantation, west to the hills, or south to the Green.[31]

Jackson called his sprawling infantry encampments "Camp of Volunteers." Officers named them "Camp Necessity." Some wisecracking soldiers dubbed them "Camp Extortion."[32]

Spades and other tools were in short supply, and troops anxious to establish shelter from the cold resorted to using their feet to shovel snow to set their tent posts. Those not busy with setting up tents were assigned to chop trees for firewood or to bring buckets of water for campsites. Nashville citizens watched in amazement as the Green and the hills suddenly came to life with acres of human activity, the sights and sounds all enhanced in the reflection of a foot of snow.[33]

Despite frigid temperatures after sundown, General Jackson, the man who had orchestrated this first vast assembly of Tennesseans, walked through the camps accompanied by Governor Blount. Tension from months of what seemed intolerable handwringing was behind them; the time for action had finally arrived. Families no longer had to wait defenseless on their isolated farms for a surprise attack from British proxies. More than 200 tents and campfires lined the hills and extended beyond, and for the first time in Nashville, the music of many fiddles and laughter filled the cold night air.

Companies assembled at Nashville took comfort in the fact that they were part of a larger call-up of troops. The War Department had placed Jackson's former militia aide-de-camp Colonel William P. Anderson in charge of raising the U.S. 24th Regiment from Tennessee and Kentucky. Over 800 men enlisted and mustered in at a temporary cantonment near Nashville, probably one of the old fortifications built when Timothy Pickering had been Secretary of War and when settlers battled Creek Indians for territory. Another 1,100 militia in East Tennessee awaited orders to march south.[34]

As in every other encampment, soldiers waiting for orders to march speculated about their destination. The official call to rendezvous mentioned the march to New Orleans for defense of the Lower Country in general, but *The Nashville Whig* had already named the mission the "New Orleans Expedition."[35] Soldiers were needed to reinforce General Wilkinson's defense of the port city against a British attack.

News spread through the camps from the letter reporting that 150 infantry Volunteers from East Tennessee had marched for Georgia at their own expense, and it appeared that the Eastern Division's ultimate destination might be Pensacola. It was rumored that President Madison's true objective was to take preemptive action by invading East Florida, where the weakened Spanish government was thought to be at the point of collapse, opening the possibility for a British takeover of the peninsula. More troubling for Tennesseans, the Spanish were suspected of allowing British agents to arm Creek Indians from the ports at Pensacola or Mobile. One edition of the newspaper later seemed to confirm the talk that soldiers would march to Mobile, where it was said there stood a fort "garrisoned by black troops who have waded through blood for twenty years in the islands."[36]

Arguments could be made for immediate action to prevent Creek Indians from gaining superiority in arms. Soldiers could not help speculating whether they would face an alliance of Indian tribes on the upcoming march. Shawnee warrior Tecumseh and his spiritual prophet had stirred the Indian nations to unite against the settlers. The Tennesseans' march through the Wilderness would be their chance.

Other talk centered on how much better Tennessee had responded to a call to defend the Union than had New York. There, a debate over whether the relatively new and untested federal Constitution gave the federal government authority to call-up a state militia had resulted in a hesitation to provide a defense that produced disaster.[37] Tennesseans considered themselves more practical and less restrained on the frontier by the regulations that Easterners and Federalists embraced.

Some older teens no doubt also began to paint harrowing pictures to the younger boys of all the dangers they would face on the Natchez Trace. Storytelling was a chief form of entertainment at home. At bedtime, in particular, as one Tennessean recalled, adults commonly excited or frightened children with stories of ghosts, witches, wild animals, and Indians.[38]

Late-night campfire talk reinforced the fear that young Volunteers stood a good chance of being scalped or burned at the stake like French soldiers in the last military expedition on the Trace led by General D'Artiguette. Boys could imagine themselves as D'Artiguette's soldiers when hundreds of screaming Chickasaw women ran from the hills waving hatchets and knives as they trapped the invaders to torture them into slow, agonizing deaths.

Creek Indian hostiles were the men's greatest fear. Early Nashville settlers had described the sound of Creek war whoops as the sound of a "thousand devils." Veterans of Indian campaigns had told their sons about going into houses of Indian warriors and seeing scalps of their Nashville friends hanging throughout. The remainder of their friends' bodies had been chopped into mincemeat as food for wolves.

Indian warriors were not the only threat. Sixteen-year-old Volunteer William Campbell Love could attest to dangers from white bandits on the Natchez Trace. His father had been killed by members of the Harpe gang, cousins Big Bill and Little Mike, who ransacked the tavern in Kentucky where they were spending the evening.[39] Big Bill, or "Big Harpe," was captured. His head was cut off and impaled on a pole on the road that became known as "Harpe's Head Road" as a warning to other bandits who would think of entering the area. Little Harpe escaped to the Natchez Trace where he preyed on travelers. Though Little Harpe had been hanged near Natchez, and like his brother, his head had been impaled on a pole by the road, the gang's legend lived on. Travel on the Natchez Trace remained dangerous as other land pirates would follow their examples until after the War of 1812.

The Scots-Irish had no qualms spicing their stories with supernatural exaggerations so vivid that teens and even adults could almost picture scenes with their imaginations that their eyes would never see. Other campfire stories told of haunted places along the Natchez Trace, such as the field near Choate's Stand in the Choctaw Nation. Nighttime travelers were said to be met by horsemen without heads or find themselves being escorted through Choate's Old Field by hairy box-like creatures. If a traveler were riding on a horse, a creature might jump on the horseman's back and wrestle him until he had passed through the field. Those stories served a practical purpose for the locals, helping to deter the superstitious from searching for the gold that Choate was said to have buried in his field.[40]

More realistic and threatening were stories of a disease like the Black Death that rose from swamps of the Lower Country and claimed soldiers as they slept, taking them to graves in the wild area, never to see their families again. General Wilkinson had recently lost over 800 men to disease in the Lower Country, at least a tenth of the standing army at the time.[41]

After wide-eyed young teens listened to the older boys' hair-raising stories, only weariness from the day's march into Nashville would put them to sleep. Even Nashville town watchman Old Mr. Cruff's hourly crying of the time and weather conditions throughout the night would not wake them.[42]

For older Volunteers, a day that had begun with isolated marches into a blustery north wind ended in the warmth of fraternal and patriotic celebration. Men celebrated their loyalty to the cause for which their fathers had fought the Revolution. They celebrated their own willingness to surrender to the cause and drew courage from each other and their common mission, whatever it would turn out to be.

As the talk grew louder and the tales grew taller, jugs were uncorked and whiskey flowed. New soldiers became impervious to cold wind whipping through their tents. Young men freed from parental supervision for the first time drank too much. Fearing that several of his inebriated troops would freeze to death the first evening, Jackson and his quartermaster spent much of the night walking from tent to tent to make certain that all the men were safely inside, that their hands and feet were covered to prevent frostbite, and that campfires were kept burning to provide heat.[43]

Those awake and sober enough to see the apparition found it difficult to believe that the general whose anger was so legendary showed such personal compassion for low-ranking troops. Some young men soon began comparing Jackson to their own fathers, and it would become the first of many actions that would engender a devoted loyalty.[44] Often, people who had an opportunity to travel to Jackson's home, the Hermitage, to meet the man who was said to be "mad upon his enemies" were shocked to find that to the opposite extreme, Jackson was the "gentlest" and "tenderest" around his own family.[45] Jackson considered these soldier wards his new military family.

Jackson's father had died just months before his namesake Andrew, Jr. was born. The General understood what it was like to grow up without a father's support, protection, and guidance. In Jackson's formative early teen years, Revolutionary War military commanders had served as surrogate fathers to teach Jackson lessons in manhood that his own father would have taught him. They also gave him a sense of appreciation and affirmation that he needed to develop. Jackson's determination to demonstrate his skills as a military commander derived not just from the fact that military command was one of the primary ways men rose to political leadership; the Revolution-era military had served briefly to provide Jackson a nurturing family. Jackson could empathize with these young men now separated from home and dependent upon him. He would see to it that they would never have reason to doubt his concern. Jackson may even have surprised himself when he assured the soldiers publicly that he would act as a father to them.[46]

Many of the boys were sons of Jackson's neighbors and other supporters, and Jackson knew that his friends were looking to him to protect their sons' safety. Jackson had always taken care of family and friends who supported him with the same concern or intensity that he attacked enemies who opposed him.[47] Though the General recently had adopted a young nephew as a son and had taken in orphans to raise, the responsibility for the daily welfare of hundreds of men was a new challenge, and Jackson showed increasing maturity in his response. A death in the heat of battle could be accepted; however, at a minimum, a commander whose negligence caused an avoidable death or loss of limb faced public humiliation.

Jackson's cavalry set up camp separate from the infantry.[48] For obvious reasons, large numbers of horses needed additional space, and caring for them required different facilities. The young state could not afford to maintain a supply of its own horses for use of the militia, and no local source was large enough to sell the number needed. Cavalry Volunteers were asked to bring their own horses and accoutrements into camp along with enough forage for the horses until the march.[49]

The federal government allotted stands of arms for each state; however, Tennessee had grown so rapidly that the population had outgrown its allocation. Tennessee was apportioned a stock of 1,500 stands of arms,[50] and the War Department had provided an additional 1,000 stands in May 1812.[51] Because the state lacked firearms for many of the soldiers, Volunteers who brought their own rifles were asked to surrender them to the cause and accept muskets in exchange. An earlier tally had revealed that there were only enough firearms for one out of three militiamen.

Unaware of the advantage of loading muskets quicker than rifles in battle, officers assumed that rifles were superior battle weapons because of their aim. Soldiers who demonstrated the best marksmanship were chosen for a select group of mounted gunmen, and they would earn the right to carry rifles. General Jackson shared this assessment and praised the men for their willingness to cooperate in the swap. On the frontier, a man who owned a firearm depended upon it for survival. The weapon became part of his identity, and it was a significant sacrifice for a frontiersman to see another man carry his prized rifle.

Near daybreak, Jackson entered an inn to warm by the fire. A guest spotted the General and criticized him for hiding out in the warm building while his troops froze outdoors. Jackson angrily defended that he had not slept at all the prior evening while trying to keep the fires going to provide some heat for the men. Revealing his weary exasperation, Jackson then threatened to take the hot fireplace andiron and ram it down the man's throat if he said more.[52] The critic was a reminder that every decision the General took would be subject to second-guessing from people who did not know the facts and who would never have to see the human consequences of their suggestions.

Jackson faced more duties before he slept. A dispatch arrived early to inform him that an additional 500 men were making their way to Nashville, adding numbers to his command and placing more strain on limited resources. Because more men turned out than had been expected, groups of nine or ten were assigned to the four-foot-by-eight-foot tents designed for six. Three were required to share a blanket meant for one.[53]

The forced sharing of space was by design. It was common in the military at the time for a tent of six men to form a type of family unit that remained intact throughout the war. One person in each tent was responsible for cooking meals. That duty could be rotated unless one man showed a talent. Other duties were divided among the unit, known as a "mess." Not only did the arrangement lower the cost of providing housing and equipment for soldiers and allow them to travel lighter, it forced soldiers to learn each other's strengths and weaknesses as they would their own families. Camaraderie generated by the confined space and overcoming a common challenge produced an effective team that acted as a single unit in the field.

The bitter cold at the camp persisted for three days, covering the exterior of the tents with a heavy frost at dusk. Men awoke to find frost on the canvas inside the tents and on their blankets from a crystallization of vapor from their breaths in the cold. Smoke from campfires hugged the ground and sometimes created a fog. Any activity that required walking was difficult. As troops oriented themselves to their outdoor winter quarters, additional companies continued to pour in.

In the excitement of the arrivals, no malcontent succeeded in spreading concern about the breach of protocol due to the lack of advance pay.

The Volunteers understood that under their new experiment of self-government, citizens bore the burden of protecting their own homes. No large standing army shielded their families from the British or Indians who wanted to drive them from Tennessee. At first, the men bound themselves to service by their own collective honor and sense of duty. *The Nashville Whig* noted, "Every man feels that his country has been most viley insulted and abused by unprincipled British and Indian savages; and every man is fixed with an holy enthusiasm to spend to the last drop of his blood in maintaining the precious inheritance of his fathers!"[54] Tennesseans were ready to go to war, and they gladly endured the momentary hardships. Soldiers also understood that the federal War Department rather than Jackson bore the responsibility to provide funds to pay Volunteers and weapons to outfit them. The young republic's bureaucratic inefficiencies were well known, even if not fully appreciated.

Jackson may have used the men's lack of trust in the federals to tamp down concern over lack of payment, but he was too quick to brush off his own concerns about the War Department's failure to deliver some of the most important resources he would need for the expedition. He had already ignored an ill omen from the wording of the order that required men who had already enlisted as state militia to re-enlist as federal Volunteers and officers elected under his direction to stand again for election. It made no practical difference. Under either order, Jackson controlled the outcome.

The General had encouraged the election of a staff of officers whose varied talents he needed, but foremost from men he knew and trusted. John Coffee was named as colonel commandant of the cavalry. As Jackson's business partner, Coffee was the man of fighting age Jackson trusted most. Though business operations had seldom proved profitable for the two, Jackson knew that Coffee understood him.[55] Physically and temperamentally opposite from the thin, irascible Jackson, Coffee was described as tall, broad-shouldered, and quiet or gentle.[56] At 216 pounds when most men were thin, Coffee was a physical force by his bulky size and quiet determination. The lanky Jackson exuded force by his determined stare and words. Together, their differences forged a good team. Further binding the two together, Coffee had become family to Jackson, having recently married Mary Donelson, the niece of Jackson's wife Rachel, in a small ceremony at Jackson's Hermitage.[57]

Thomas Hart Benton served as first aide-de-camp to Jackson and colonel commandant of the Second Regiment of Infantry. Benton was a thirty-year-old lawyer from Franklin, Tennessee, whose mother had founded the adjoining town on the Natchez Trace known unofficially as "Bentonville" (now Leiper's Fork). Jackson had befriended Benton's parents early in his life when Jackson was living in North Carolina. Like many young Nashville men who admired Jackson, Benton probably had been inspired by Jackson's example to seek political success by first becoming a lawyer and military leader.

Benton offered a combination of the backwoods toughness required for survival on the frontier and the intellectual brilliance to rise to the highest levels of power. And he shared Jackson's ambition. When Jackson asked Benton about his interest in serving as an officer in the expedition, the young judge and state legislator replied that he would always be happy to exchange a judge's robe for a sword. Benton assured Jackson only that he could offer a young man's ambition to succeed, and if Jackson wanted him to raise a regiment, then he would commit not just to raising a regiment, but he would raise the largest regiment possible.[58] In his biography of Benton, Theodore Roosevelt noted Benton's traits of vanity and boastfulness.[59] But then, in 1812, when even wealthy Americans owned few physical possessions, men attempted to distinguish themselves by their reputations, and boasting was one way to appear to excel.

Jackson recognized many of his own qualities in the young Benton. However, the two strong personalities were so similar that in just a few months, their friendship would be interrupted in a bloody brawl on the streets of Nashville. Jackson would suffer the effects of the bullet Benton put in his arm during the brawl throughout much of the War of 1812 and into his presidency. After Jackson's death, Benton attempted to claim credit for the organization of the call-up of troops for the Natchez Expedition as well as other Jackson accomplishments.[60] Senator Benton would overlook the brawl when attempting to revise his role in Jackson's biography.

At the other end of the spectrum, the slight, fair-haired, well-mannered, and well-dressed William Carroll was elected brigade inspector. The young businessman had moved from Philadelphia to Nashville to open a hardware store.[61] His father had been a partner in a store operation with Albert Gallatin, who became the U.S. Secretary of the Treasury. Carroll, who impressed Jackson as sober and discrete, won Jackson's respect in business and demonstrated organizational talents needed for his new position. The *Clarion* editor saw the future war hero that Carroll would become and bolstered his reputation, stating that he was gallant, highly promising, prompt, and decisive in character, and like Jackson, he "is fond of military life and thirsts after fame."[62] Those characteristics made him one of Jackson's favorites. Though Carroll commanded a militia company in Nashville, it would take time for the young eastern city man to earn the respect of the Tennessee woodsmen soldiers from outlying areas. They considered Carroll too much of a delicate dandy to give him their full respect.

As in the selection of Coffee, Benton, and Carroll, an early test of Jackson's leadership was his ability to match available talent to the task. John Reid, a young lawyer from Franklin, Tennessee, who was known for his attention to detail and who would later write much of Jackson's first biography, was named as second aide-de-camp. When Jackson asked Reid to join his military family, Reid replied that he had no military command experience, but he could assure Jackson that if Jackson perished, he would perish with him.[63]

William Hall, a seasoned military leader and sheriff of Robertson County, Tennessee, served as colonel commandant of the First Regiment of Infantry. The older, wiser man would serve as a good counter-balance to Benton.

Jackson's business associate James Henderson, selected as brigade quartermaster, had the difficult job of supplying Volunteers with provisions and equipment from limited resources. Henderson would travel ahead down the Natchez Trace to make provisions for the men, while his assistant William B. Lewis remained in Nashville to serve as a conduit with the government. Many staff members would later see their service rewarded by the naming of new counties in their honor.[64]

Once Governor Blount had officially approved Jackson's election of officers, the General was ready to begin training the Volunteers. Through Benton, Jackson warned the men that it would take more than courage to prevail against British disciplined opposition.[65] Like commanders before him, Jackson's job was to turn what he called "raw recruits" into soldiers. They would need to be trained to act instinctively as a team when overwhelming force gave them no time to think.

From the first days of encampment, enlisted men who would serve Jackson faithfully throughout the war also began to distinguish themselves. Nineteen-year-old ensign Andrew Jackson Edmonson reflected the talent and lack of experience that many of the boys brought to the effort. Edmonson was said to have been the first child in West Tennessee to be named for Andrew Jackson. His father Robert survived the Battle of King's Mountain during the Revolution, only to be seriously wounded by an Indian attack at Neelly's Bend not far from Jackson's future Hermitage home. Edmonson, like many in his ranks, wanted to prove to those heroes of the Revolution that their offspring carried the same courage in their blood.

Officers elected Edmonson to serve as sentinel of his company.

Knowing little about sentinel duties, Edmonson devoted time to studying the manual of military tactics, and he learned the routine: *"Q. Who goes there? A. Rounds Q. What Rounds? A. Grand Rounds Q. Stand Grand Rounds,"* then *"Advance Sergeant with the Countersign, Countersign Right, Pass Grand Rounds, and Present Arms."* When Ensign Edmonson felt confident that he was ready for inspection, he presented himself to Benton, who was serving as officer of the day. Benton drilled Edmonson and complimented him on how well he had learned the manual. Benton then offered to show Edmonson the Bonaparte method of presenting arms. Edmonson started to lower the muzzle of his rifle to hand the gun to Benton, when he remembered that contrary to camp orders, he had loaded the weapon in camp. As an excuse not to reveal his mistake, Edmonson also remembered something his father told him about a sentinel never allowing anyone to touch his firearm. The young ensign cited the precedent and refused to surrender his weapon to Benton. Benton protested that Edmonson should know that his superior officer was not an enemy; this command was for practice. Edmonson's father's campfire advice trumped. Benton moved on to the next man, shaking his head in disbelief. Edmonson had demonstrated that he could think fast on his feet and hold firm to his convictions, but it occurred to him that he would never learn the Bonaparte method.[66]

Unlike Edmonson, Private Oliver Bush distinguished himself as one of the first deserters, and one whose punishment would serve as a lesson to the others. Military infractions could be punished severely. Until Congress outlawed the practice in 1812, soldiers were often whipped as punishment like slaves or prisoners. Cattails could be used, and 60 lashes spread out over hours to increase suffering could be followed by fellow soldiers pouring and pounding salt into the wounds. As guards brought Bush forward, the men were ordered to fix their bayonets and surround the private. Each direction Bush looked, he saw only the sharp points held by his former comrades. Fife-drum-music was played as a signal to march Bush to the head of the company to face his sentence. As the prisoner reached Captain Carroll, the music stopped, and Carroll used a long silence to prolong the punishment. Then the sentence was solemnly pronounced, "By this crime, the most infamous which a volunteer could commit, he has rendered himself unworthy of associating with the voluntary defenders of their country."[67] He was then marched a mile and a half out of camp and told not to return. The remainder of the Volunteers were ordered never to associate with the deserter to ensure that his shame followed him.

Jackson may have hoped that similar public embarrassments would deter future desertions, but it would be the first of several punishments that grew in severity. Citizen soldiers were unaccustomed to taking orders from commanders, who were often their neighbors and whom they had elected. Militia service was normally for short durations, and when the time of service expired, most men simply returned home. Jackson and his officers were challenged in establishing discipline among men who were accustomed to taking charge of their own military defense of their farms. By nature, tough and independent citizens often judged their own manhood by their unwillingness to submit to the instruction of another man. Jackson was reluctant to approve severe punishment for his military family, but that reluctance lessened each time his attempts to find humane deterrents failed. Compared to men that Jackson later ordered to be shot for mutiny during the Creek campaign, Bush received a light sentence.

To convert this group of independent men into a cohesive unit, Benton decided it was time to deepen the soldiers' understanding of their roles. Unstated, Benton was attempting to shape Jackson in the image of the revered General George Washington.[68] Jackson had studied General Washington's actions through newspaper accounts, but he was not a scholar who pored over dusty military manuals. The studious Benton likely had rendered that service for several months to help Jackson establish a professional command structure that would take him to a higher level as a general.

Though Jackson had worked to train his militia to be as professional as any in the young nation, the civilians were not the battle-hardened professional soldiers they would face soon. Neither was Jackson. But in his unlimited ambition, Jackson was taking the first steps to become the next general who would save his nation from a British invasion.

Benton used terms any soldier could understand. Starting at the top, Benton informed the men that General Jackson's relationship to his soldiers was to be that of a father to his children.[69] Benton reminded Volunteers that they owed their military father the respect of obeying his commands. As Jackson's sons, the soldiers were to act as a "band of brothers" within their military family. The term "band of brothers' was probably coined by Shakespeare in *Henry V*, but Washington often had used the term to describe the bond military service had created in the Revolution and like other American soldiers, Volunteers adopted the name to best describe their own bond. Some of the more educated who had been taught passages from Shakespeare through recitations may have recited it to the others:

> "We few, we happy few, we band of brothers;
> For he to-day that shed his blood with me
> Shall be my brother; be he ne'er so vile
> This day shall gentle his condition;
> And gentlemen in England now a-bed
> Shall think themselves accursed they were not here
> And hold their manhoods cheap whiles any speaks
> That fought with us....".[70]

The name also reminded Volunteers that they were part of a long chain of military tradition, and the men would often repeat the term as they sacrificed their own comfort and safety for the welfare of their compatriots. Volunteers accepted their new identities and sometimes referred to each other as "brother," even when complaining about the actions of another soldier.[71] It was now their responsibility to learn their duties as brothers in that family.

Infantry training consisted of teaching men to form, maneuver, and hold lines as they marched shoulder-to-shoulder to create an impenetrable human wall to overwhelm the enemy by force. Those in the front were expected to hold the line even when facing certain injury or death. Parades were held to demonstrate the soldiers' abilities on the line.

The second objective was to teach the men to fire their muskets or rifles in unison to provide a larger firepower.[72] After basic instruction for the troops, Jackson determined that it was safe to open the stone storehouse in Nashville being used for its arms magazine. Detachments were to march into town to obtain the supply.[73] The small number of firearms available was an embarrassment, and it gave Jackson the idea that the U.S. government should place a large arsenal in Nashville to help guard the frontier.[74]

Throughout their encampment, the men were instructed to be on their best behavior toward the townspeople. No soldier was to abuse his position to insult a citizen or think that he had any right to take a citizen's property. To avoid conflicts from either soldiers or civilians, Volunteers carrying loaded weapons were ordered to encircle the camp at all hours, and permission would have to be given to enter or exit. All civilians were to be escorted out of camp at dusk. No woman was to be seen in camp at dark.[75]

Jackson re-enforced the need for discipline in his general orders:

"Troops have been seven days encamped and during that period experiencing the unusual rigor of the season. The small proportion of this time to attend to discipline. The orderly and military conduct of both officers and men on all actions is a sure pledge that your General but hopes will be realized that in this detachment will be verified the expectation of the worthy patriots of the Revolution who framed the Constitution, that a well organized militia in the same defense and the grand Bulwark of the nation. Your general expected all officers and soldiers in the detachment to continue their allegiance to discipline and let it ever be kept in mind that the materials conforming the detachment when full disciplined can never _____ _____ equal numbers. That without discipline our valor may be vanquished by superior military skill, tho directed by inferior force."[76]

The cavalry required separate training and equipment. Cavalry soldiers were ordered to ride their own prized horses into Nashville for appraisers to assign a value to the horses and equipment. The state purchased Volunteers' horses with only an exchange of government promises of payment. After their arrival at the encampment, Colonel Coffee ordered the cavalry to march into town to train, naming the new camp "Good Exchange."[77] No doubt the name was chosen to assure the men that there would be a good exchange for their horses and equipment.

By December 16, 60 swords had been located for the cavalry's use and delivered to Childress' Inn.[78] Unlike the few rifles, muskets, or even the knives that every man carried, swords were not needed by average civilians in their everyday work. Muster days did not provide enough training to make the cavalry proficient swordsmen. They had little time to prepare to face their British counterparts.

Few men openly discussed the fact that General Jackson had never commanded a battle or that he had engaged in few hostile conflicts other than a skirmishes with small Indian parties and duels of his own making. No one challenged his training orders. Many successful professionals including physicians and lawyers were self-taught at the time. Like their commanders, some newly minted military men also thought nothing of teaching themselves military regulations and strategies from books just prior to battle. West Point, the first American academy for training military professionals, was only 10 years old, and graduation from such a program was not a prerequisite for leadership.

It was true that Jackson had no command experience to know how to prepare his men to face the British, but the General had never allowed his lack of position or training to cause him one moment of hesitation in pursuing any goal he sought. He had agreed to serve as Tennessee Superior Court Justice even though he could not read or write as well as other lawyers. He had served as U.S. congressman and senator before he had learned political skills and customs of the nation's capital. Jackson believed that democracy was a great equalizer and that the heroes of the Revolution had produced a nation in which any citizen could go as far as his talents, initiative, and courage would take him.

Jackson's civilian success had come in the business of training champion racehorses.[79] The trainer's objective was to instill enough discipline in the horse to keep it under control while maintaining and spurring its competitive spirit. Because non-professional soldiers' lives were concentrated mainly on civilian affairs, Jackson focused first on creating fighting spirit and confidence. Jackson watched his soldiers closely until he saw that, like racehorses pushing against the fence, they were primed for action.

The drummers began to practice the tune to which the soldiers would march, "Victory or Death:"[80]

"To arms! To arms: ye brave.
The avenging sword unsheath!
March on! March on! All hearts resolved.
On victory or death!"[81]

26

To show the people of Nashville that citizen companies had been pulled together as one unit, Jackson took advantage of the cavalry's march into Nashville to their new encampment to organize a grand march of troops through the town. The infantry joined the cavalry's procession from camp at the home "Bellview" and then all three regiments marched toward the Public Square.[82] Governor Blount appeared at the front of Bell's Tavern to review the troops. The blaring of martial music from fife and drum acted as a siren to announce the procession and a crowd assembled along the route.

Major General Jackson was centered at the head of the march with his aides-de-camp Thomas Hart Benton and John Reid at his side. Colonel Coffee appeared next, leading a procession of mounted cavalry dressed in sharp uniforms and carrying sabers and other military accoutrements. The new cavalry officers were generally better suited to serve as the focal point for small town parades, but the lines of 670 uniformed men and horses produced an image of power that had to impress even the most skeptical.

Colonel Hall followed with a march of the First Regiment of Infantry. Then Benton's Second Regiment appeared. The sounds of the synchronized marches, horse hoofs, and the calls of the orders reverberated through the streets. A common pride swelled as it became clear that in just a few days, the average man had been transformed into something more. These were, as one spectator described them, "Sons of the West" bound together in a common cause.[83] The only words the awestruck observer could find to describe the effect on the citizenry were that "every heart beat in unison."[84]

Securing support from the home front is one of the foundations for protracted action. Citizens remaining at home also would be called on to sacrifice in money and supplies, but more importantly to sacrifice the lives of their men of fighting age. Women and children would be left behind. Though Governor Blount politically had assured the soldiers that they could count on civilians at home, it was important for Jackson to secure the full support of Tennesseans and to convince his neighbors of his ability to lead an effective force, so that there be no hesitation when he called for additional men or materials.

The Call to Arms had the effect of pulling together small bands of settlers for the first time as Tennesseans. Tennesseans would now be dedicated to sacrificing their lives not only for their own farms or communities, but for their state. For many citizens, the march of over 2,000 Tennessee soldiers through Nashville to military music was the first time they had witnessed such power from the State of Tennessee.

Jackson had planned to march the Volunteers from Nashville by mid-December, and he had only ordered enough provisions to feed the men in camp until the 20th.[85] The General preferred to end his grand parade by marching his men at their peak of readiness out of town and on down the Natchez Trace and Mississippi River.[86] Though the State of Tennessee was verbally bound to the effort, the federal bureaucracy had still not provided funds to pay the men or supplied additional weapons needed to mount a respectable defense.

After convincing the citizens of Nashville and the politicians that he had assembled a fighting force and after stirring his own men to march to the Gulf Coast, Jackson had no choice but to march the men back to their camps to wait in Nashville. Challenges of the Natchez Trace and Mississippi River would grow with each day's delay.

CHAPTER TWO

ROAD OF PEACE

"The road from Nashville to Natchez, was asked by the United States and we gave a grant that it should be so, and to be a road of peace – no bloodshed was to be made on it."

—Chickasaw Chief George Colbert, May 1812

"The President [Jefferson] is extremely anxious for the increase in the population on our South Western frontier and will give every encouragement in his power to so important an object."

—Secretary of War Henry Dearborn to Mississippi Territory Governor W.C.C. Claiborne, December 6, 1802

In retrospect, the Natchez Trace had been a North American proving ground for centuries, and its challenges continued through the War of 1812, when it became Andrew Jackson's proving ground. From the time of early human activity, the convenient trail through the forest and across the shallows of the wild Tennessee River had drawn people from different areas of the continent, and its confines forced human interaction. It became a place where warriors and cultures clashed, resulting either in the forging of new civilizations made stronger by the mixture of the hardiest of peoples or the absolute defeat of rulers who had outlived their time.

The Natchez Trace as an Indian trail was a footpath, rarely wider than a few feet. To the untrained eye, the path appeared to be no more than an opening through the forest and prairies. The common path originated as a series of trails hewn through the wilderness by people traveling on foot between the Gulf of Mexico and what is now Canada. Such trails often appeared where animals had developed migration routes. The strongest and most clever animals staked out their territories and took on challengers for the right to feed on weaker animals drawn down the trail. Humans followed the paths to hunt those animals and then found the paths convenient routes for their own travel. Like nature's fiercest predators, sometimes stronger humans used the paths to hunt and trap weaker humans. Often, tall cane grew so thick that it created what appeared to be walls along the route, providing places for attackers to hide within reach of travelers.

Indians developed an early form of sign system to mark the path by bending small trees, their bent shape pointing toward the path ahead. The trail normally followed a ridge path that provided a more commanding view and drier surface. But in dry weather, travelers sought out alternate lower trails along streams where they found less undergrowth to wade through along creek beds as well as access to drinking water.

Chickasaw and Choctaw tribes discovered the paths when they moved their nations east to the southern portion of the continent. Legend holds that the two brothers Chicsah and Chata led their people east but then disagreed where they should settle. Chicsah settled his clans near the modern-day site of Tupelo, Mississippi. Chata led his people south to the present-day Philadelphia, Mississippi area. The Natchez Trace became a path that linked their nations for peaceful purposes. The Chickasaw called it their "peace road." For Choctaw, it also doubled as a warpath.

Carefully studying animals that were the best hunters in their new homeland, Indians adapted their warfare tactics to the thick southern forests. Warriors attempted to blend into the environment and take their enemies by surprise. They stripped and painted their skin with red and black stripes, then covered themselves with bear grease. To move with rapid speed, warriors hid weapons along the path and retrieved them just prior to attack. They also learned to move almost silently until just moments prior to attack, when they shouted war whoops to make their forces seem larger than they were. Indian guerilla-warfare tactics kept later colonial Natchez Trace travelers in a constant state of unease. White settlers never knew whether what appeared to be a peaceful natural landscape also included camouflaged warriors ready to attack.

Despite their unmatched abilities as warriors, by the late 1700s, the Chickasaw recognized that the world was changing and that European firearms provided overwhelming superiority. Like other Indian nations, the Chickasaw's trading of hundreds of thousands of pelts for European goods had depleted much of their wild game. Indians then began to capture members of enemy tribes and sell them to Europeans as slaves. The result was a series of Indian wars that wiped out large numbers of warriors and took the lives of even women and children.

Chickasaw reached out to British colonists for an alliance against their common French enemy during the French and Indian War. Soon, trade developed from port cities along the Southeastern Seaboard to inland Indian villages. Several British traders found Indian lands and cultures to their liking. Young colonial settlers generally found a friendly reception. As Chickasaw Chief George Colbert's son-in-law John McCleish would later describe the Indian hospitality, Southeastern American Indians warmed the settlers by their fires and welcomed them into their homes.[87]

Traders not only settled in Indian nations but took Indian wives. In the Indian matrilineal society, leadership rights passed down through the woman's lineage; therefore, it was not uncommon for the sons of

American colonial settlers to become American Indian chiefs. Mixed-blood chiefs were more accepting of the customs of the settlers and willing to abandon ways of the Indian ancestors. Men who had a foot in both worlds could work with each to the advantage of the Indian nations, and often to their personal advantage.

Indian trade encouraged by mixed-blood chiefs gave Europeans a growing influence on the Trace and in Indian villages. Indians sought the European arms for an advantage over their enemies even as an increasing dependency on the European trade altered Indian culture and placed them at a long-term risk. The adoption of European customs also created unease among the Indians as the bedrock customs of their culture softened. Divisions erupted within tribes between those who wanted to hold fast to the culture and teachings of their ancestors and those who were willing to adapt to European culture.

Indians and settlers both recognized the strategic importance of intersections of the Indian trail and river crossings. The widest Trace crossing was at the sometimes mile-wide Tennessee River, where rock formations created shallows that allowed people to ford the river in shoulder-high water during dry seasons. The shallows also slowed down river traffic, making voyagers vulnerable to attack and as the settlement party led by Jackson's future father-in-law John Donelson described it, "the river current running to in every direction from piles of driftwood which were heaped high upon the points of the island. The deflection of the stream made a terrible roaring, which might be heard for many miles. At some places the boats dragged the bottom, while at others they were warped and tossed about on the waves as though in a rough sea."[88] Indians called it "Muscle Shoals." Whoever controlled the Muscle Shoals controlled travel over a vast region.

George Washington also recognized the strategic importance of the Great Bend area in the Tennessee River to the defense of the southwestern U.S. territory. As president, Washington negotiated with Indians for territory five miles in diameter near the Natchez Trace at the mouth of Bear Creek where the U.S. government wanted to establish a fort to control the river. Indians, however, understood what such a military presence would mean in their nation.[89] They met any attempts to establish the outpost with attacks. John Donelson and associate John Gordon attempted to enforce the treaty on their own by setting up a colony on the river through the Tennessee Land Company, but they barely escaped their new Muscle Shoals settlement with their lives in a retreat to Nashville.[90]

Just 20 years prior to Jackson's grand march from Nashville, attack-weary settlers often sheltered in their fort on the Cumberland River at the northern end of the Chickasaw Trace. Though the Cumberland Settlement at Nashville was just far enough from major Indian villages that it posed no immediate threat to Indian nations, Indians frequently killed Nashville settlers and kept the settlement in a constant state of unease.

Indians generally had not inhabited the Nashville area since the Chickasaw defeated its Shawnee villagers. Nevertheless, several tribes considered it a common hunting ground. Chickasaw still hunted the land up into the area that is now Paducah, Kentucky, and Cherokee had not given up their claim to what they considered the "middle ground." Of all tribes, Creek and their Shawnee relatives were the most aggressive in attacking American settlers who threatened to take any Indian land. The Creek knew that the white settlers would deplete the game they hunted for food and pelts, and some Creek warriors used their villages on the Tennessee River not far from the Natchez Trace crossing as a staging area to attack Nashville settlers.

In an effort to make peace between the settlers and the Indians, the Chickasaw were invited to a meeting at Sulphur Springs just north of Nashville's fort.[91] James Robertson led the delegation of Cumberland settlers. Robertson was a large man, and his bushy eyebrows were said to overshadow his light-blue eyes. More significantly, Robertson projected the impression of a man who was serious, honest, and thoughtful.[92] Indian leaders could relate to a man who considered his thoughts carefully before he spoke.

Robertson followed a Chickasaw messenger to Sulphur Springs, but when he arrived there seemed to be no delegation awaiting him. Slowly, Indians began to appear from the forest. Robertson may have wondered whether his party was surrounded and whether he had fallen into a trap. Then, Chickasaw Chief Piominko, or "Mountain Leader" appeared and invited Robertson to smoke the pipe with him.[93] Robertson obliged. As a fire was built in the center of the open grounds, a circle formed, and talks began. Piominko made it clear that his intentions were friendly, and Robertson responded in kind.

Confidence built slowly, and the talks stretched over a few days. Satisfied that Robertson was a man who could be trusted, Piominko presented gifts as proof of friendship and respect. The Chickasaw warrior handed a leather string to Robertson to represent a tie that would bind the two peoples. The chief next presented a bag made from doe skin to symbolize that the Chickasaw placed their trust in Robertson. Finally, Piominko presented a pair of moccasins that were placed on Robertson's feet. He called Robertson "Little Father," and the Chickasaw said that the moccasins symbolized that they would follow Robertson's leadership. Piominko told Robertson that Chickasaw would give the Cumberland Settlement the right to occupy their land down to the ridge that divided the waters of the Duck and Elk rivers from the waters of the Cumberland River, a ridge just south of the town that would become Leiper's Fork. Chickasaw wanted only to retain the right to hunt the territory. Robertson welcomed the unexpected development that at least one tribe would allow the Cumberland settlers to occupy the land in peace.

Piominko then reached the real purpose of his agreement to talk. He proposed that the Nashville settlement and the Chickasaw Nation work together to build a new path between the two.[94] It would become a road of peace, both symbolic and literal. The new path, more direct than the old Chickasaw Trace, would be created merely by cutting limbs and briers and marking the way to increase traffic by travelers on foot or horseback. Piominko hoped that trade would increase by making the path more direct between the two peoples.

Unstated, Piominko also hoped that an alliance with Nashville settlers would counterbalance Spain's influence on his nation. Chickasaw, like other American Indian nations, were caught in a vice of pressure from competing European powers who hoped to gain a beachhead on the North American continent. Piominko's rival Chickasaw chief Uguluyacabee ("Wolf's Friend") had responded to threats from outside powers by making a pact with the Spanish and pledging Spain the allegiance of the Chickasaw. Piominko had abandoned trade with the Spanish in Natchez to the south, and he needed a northern trade partner and a northern path to facilitate that trade.[95] The British had proved more trustworthy, and Piominko was willing to chance that he could also trust their former subjects.

Relieved at the prospect of an alliance, Robertson quickly accepted Piominko's proposal. For Nashville, an alliance with the Chickasaw would begin to help secure the southern border of the settlement. And as allies, Chickasaw could provide the settlement with intelligence and early warnings of attacks by the Creek, whose nation was located south and east of the Chickasaw Nation.

The new path—which the settlers called "Piomingo's Trace" or "Mountain Leader's Trace" and later "Natchez Trace"—became more popular than the older main trail and replaced the series of trails.[96] It shortened the distance from Nashville to Chickasaw settlements about 80 miles south of the Tennessee River, but more importantly, it served to build a friendship between the two men and two peoples. Robertson called on Piominko to send warriors to join him in helping U.S. Army General Anthony Wayne defend American settlements in the Battle of

Fallen Timbers up in the Ohio Territory. Robertson then disobeyed War Department orders by sending two companies of militia from Nashville to help defend Piominko from a Creek attack on the Chickasaw. Robertson also supplied food to Chickasaw when a poor planting threatened starvation. In turn, the new Chickasaw allies warned Nashville settlers of imminent attacks by Creek Indians. Though Nashville settlers did not trade with the Chickasaw as much as Piominko had hoped, the new road and the friendship it fostered laid a foundation to provide security for both.

One of the first American military excursions on a portion of the new path was led by a young militia private, who was described as "bold, dashing and fearless, and *mad upon his enemies.*"[97] The early historian should also have added "ambitious." Andrew Jackson had recently moved to Nashville to serve as attorney general for the Western District of the territory and to develop a law practice. A call to form a posse to pursue Creek attackers down the Natchez Trace provided Jackson an opportunity to develop a reputation as a military leader who was not afraid to fight. On the frontier, the public turned to the brave for defense and then gladly rewarded their own warriors with public office.

Early Tennessee resident and historian J.W.M. Brazeale described the allure of military service for ambitious young men on the frontier:

> "In old, wealthy and densely populated communities, family rank, and opulence, exercise an influence which bears down and over-rides the poor, obscure and indigent, however talented and enterprising they may be. Hence, the bold, talented, intrepid and aspiring amongst the lower ranks, many of whom are frequently the most virtuous and highly gifted individuals in the community, will seek a theatre for the display of their energies, and the exercise of their genius where they can be useful to their country, and acquire rank and honor

for themselves. It, therefore, frequently happens that men of the most brilliant and lofty genius leave the country of their nativity, to seek a field in the exercise of their talents . . . in new and thinly populated regions, where they can rise to distinction with the growth of community of official rank and station. And hence it is, that we often see the most wonderful feats of military skill and valor . . . where experienced general would expect to see nothing but a jumble of blunders, miscarriages and misfortunes."[98]

Jackson's chance to prove his eagerness to fight arrived at age 22 when Indians overpowered and attacked men guarding workers in James Robertson's field. Robertson was shot in the foot. The alarm sounded in Nashville and a posse formed. The posse tracked the Creek to the McCutcheon Trace, then over to the highlands of the Duck River Ridge and to the Natchez Trace. They surprised the Indians who were busy preparing breakfast and killed one of the party.

Despite dangers on the Natchez Trace, foot traffic and horseback traffic increased as economic interests between Natchez and Nashville grew. Chickasaw chiefs and brothers George and Levi Colbert began to operate a small ferry to transport travelers on the Natchez Trace across the Tennessee River. The intersection of river traffic and one of the main north-south paths became a landmark, and the Colberts grew in influence with both the Chickasaw and settlers even as they angered neighboring Cherokee Chief Double Head, who viewed the Colberts' ferry as a threat to his own territory. Double Head threatened to scalp George Colbert and go to war against the Chickasaw, as well as to begin the operation of his own river ferry in competition for settlers' money.[99]

The Natchez Trace also increased in importance to commerce for American settlers as people moved from the colonies westward to the Ohio River Valley. No roads existed to transport settlers' farm goods for sale to ports on the Gulf Coast, and farmers in the Ohio Territory turned to the Mississippi River to deliver their products to port. Boatmen were hired to float the farm goods south on rafts or flatboats to sell to European traders at ports in Natchez. Unless boatmen also had been hired to transport goods from Natchez back upriver, poling smaller canoes or pirogues back upstream on the Mississippi took too long and was too expensive. For about half of the boatmen, walking home on the Trace was the quickest and cheapest way.[100]

Traffic on the Natchez Trace increased only so long as ports along the Gulf Coast were open to American trade. Spain controlled the port towns Natchez and New Orleans. The Spanish government viewed new American frontier settlements as a long-term threat to their claims of land in North America, particularly to their valuable silver mines in Mexico. Attempting to halt the expansion of American settlers into the Ohio River Valley, the Spanish governor exerted his control over the river by declaring the ports off-limits to all but Spanish citizens.[101] Farmers and merchants who depended upon access to ports for trade suddenly were unable to sell their goods. The new Ohio River Valley territory was of little value to settlers unless it would support a farm economy. Land speculators risked losing a market for their land.

Though early western settlers honored the memories of their colonial ancestors who forced a British retreat, those who fled the American colonies along the Eastern Seaboard for freedom in the West did not necessarily feel bound to the new government. The interests of western farmers who relied upon river access to southern Mississippi River ports and a coordinated defense from western Indian enemies differed from those of Americans who lived east of the Appalachians and who relied more directly upon Atlantic shipping and European trade. Political leaders in the Southwest questioned whether settlers could count on the weak distant central government in Washington City and its small professional army to protect them from Indians or from invasion on the frontier.

Western land speculators also entertained the idea that an alliance of newly formed states with Spain, Britain, or France might offer better chance of survival. The possible divisions posed such a threat to the union of states that George Washington discussed it in his farewell address. The divisions only increased when the federal government negotiated Jay's Treaty that limited the right of people west of the Appalachians to ship their farm goods by the Mississippi River while assuring easterners the right to trade on the Atlantic.

The Spanish governor Esteban Miro, who was given charge of New Orleans and Natchez, played on the uncertainty by offering to open his ports to any American settler willing to pledge loyalty to the King of Spain. Like Tennesseans willing to name their Cumberland settlements "Mero District" in honor of the Spanish governor Miro, Jackson toyed with the idea that an alliance with Spain might offer Tennesseans protection from the Indians and the British that a distant and weak United States federal government could not.[102] Passage of a new federal constitution in 1787 to replace the Articles of Confederation, a looser confederation of independent states that had failed, had renewed debate about the government under which states west of the Appalachians would prosper. Though such discussions are now perceived as somewhat treasonous, they had been part of the accepted debate of the day when citizens in the West wondered whether a distant federal government would ever be able to protect them.[103]

But in 1789, an impulsive, young Andrew Jackson traveled to Spanish-controlled Natchez to sign his name on the roll, "subjecting himself to all Spanish laws, obeying all orders, proclamations, and edicts of the Kingdom, as the rest of the vassals of His Catholic Majesty."[104] It was not an inconsequential act. Spain had been accused of supplying Indians with the weapons they used to kill settlers in Nashville. Like Nashville founder James Robertson, Jackson may have promoted Spain's help to stop the attacks on Nashville, but his pledge of loyalty allowed Jackson to open a trading post in the Spanish-controlled Bruinsburg just north of Natchez, to avoid paying a small ransom to men who had authority to ship goods on the Mississippi, and for Jackson personally, to make it possible to obtain Spain's consent for his future wife Rachel Donelson Robards to secure a divorce in Spanish territory a year later.[105] Jackson even lived at times in the Spanish territory in a cabin near the trading post, where he also operated a racetrack.[106] General James Wilkinson told the Spanish governor that most men who signed the roll did so only to avoid paying Spanish agents a surcharge to transport their goods, and that they had no intention of becoming Spanish citizens.[107]

Jackson shared attitudes in common with many people who eventually crossed over the Appalachians to settle the southwestern frontier of the United States. They valued their independence, and they were tough. There was no alternative. The weak did not survive long on the frontier. Jackson had not only survived in what was then the American Wild West, but he had done so as a teenage and young-adult orphan. Jackson navigated backwoods and frontier dangers using only his own intellect, instincts, and courage, driven by an intense will to survive and boundless ambition.

As part of his survival, Jackson developed a reputation for being fearless, but also rash and unpredictable. It may have been a defense mechanism. Young upstarts anxious to prove their own courage by attacking someone known for courage were less likely to challenge an erratic man whose reaction could not be predicted. Challengers could not determine how much of Jackson's actions were based upon courage and how much were bluff, however, the intense stare of his steely blue eyes forced them to err on the side of courage.[108]

Jackson became familiar with boating on the Mississippi River and travel on the Natchez Trace when he sought financial success by opening a store in Nashville. Farmers bartered for ready-made goods from Philadelphia or New Orleans in his store by paying with cotton, corn, and other farm products. Jackson and his partners hired boatmen to load the farm goods onto flatboats and float them to Bruinsburg for sale at his trading post. Jackson would later deny it in his presidential campaign, but he also bought and sold slaves in Natchez.[109]

Though overseeing trade through dangerous Indian territory and down the Mississippi River offered more than enough risk for most men, it may not have made the mercantile business challenging enough for Jackson to devote his full attention. He and business partner John Coffee were forced to close the operation within two years.

Horse racing was a different matter. The "gentleman's game" offered players immediate gratification of risk, the thrill of victory, and public adulation from men with means. Newspapers gave fame to the names of victorious horses, and their breeders and trainers shared in the fame by association. Jackson took to the sport with passion.[110] Jackson raced his horses in quarter races in Nashville and Franklin on the north end of the Natchez Trace, as well as in Spanish territory in Bruinsburg on the southern end. Through his frequent journeys on the Natchez Trace, Jackson developed relationships with people who lived along the trail.

On one of his trips on the Natchez Trace, Jackson was said to have been entertained by George Wilson Humphreys at his home "The Hermitage" near Gibson's Port. Perhaps Jackson admired the front columned porch and wide-center hallway and dreamed of his own plantation of the same name and style when he had made his fortune.[111]

Jackson's travel on the Natchez Trace between Natchez and Nashville fostered his reputation for bravery.[112] Mississippi River boatmen who returned on the Trace carrying large sums of money from goods sold in Natchez attracted cutthroat bandits, and the Natchez Trace became known as a haven for land pirates or highwaymen. Settlers traveling south on the road often waited in Nashville until other travelers could join them to form parties large enough to ward off potential attackers.

But there are no references to the well-armed Jackson ever fearing to travel on the Natchez Trace.

Despite the dangers, the United States began regular mail delivery from Natchez to Nashville on the Trace. Bandits rarely accosted post riders, however, the occasional exceptions led Secretary of State Timothy Pickering to suggest the construction of an official post road and stations along the route to protect mail riders.[113] His request was ignored. Improvements to an established mail service was a luxury that a nation on the brink of insolvency could not afford.

Thomas Jefferson's election as president in 1801 and his vision for the future of the continent changed everything. Mountain Leader's Trace was created to be a road of peace, but Thomas Jefferson redesigned it to become a war road. It would become one of the first, if not the first, wagon highways significantly improved by the U.S. federal government.[114] For public purposes, it was called a "mail route" or "post road.[115]" In private, Jefferson would refer to the proposed wagon highway as a "military road."[116] It would become one of Jefferson's most consequential internal improvements as president, but one that few people attributed to him, because its true purpose had to be kept secret.

On January 18, 1803, President Jefferson sent a message to Congress marked "confidential."[117] It revealed the motive for Jefferson's plans that had been in the works since his inauguration and possibly earlier. The nation did not yet have the military capacity to defend a public disclosure of its contents – Jefferson's vision to acquire much of the North American continent from the Indians and European powers. The message would later become known for Jefferson's request for funding for the Lewis and Clark Expedition. The significance of that request has since obscured the second half of the message. Jefferson's vision required acquisition of Chickasaw lands in the Mississippi Territory to secure control of the Mississippi River.

New Orleans was key to Jefferson's transcontinental plan. Jefferson believed that in an age when river traffic and shipping lanes were the main arteries for commerce and warfare, whoever controlled New Orleans and the Mississippi River would control the future of the North American continent. Jefferson explained to his Ambassador to France Robert Livingston:

> "There is on the globe one single spot, the possessor of which is our natural and habitual enemy. It is New Orleans, through which the produce of three-eighths of our territory must pass to market, and from its fertility it will ere long yield more than half of our whole produce and contain more than half our inhabitants."[118]

Jefferson could not hope to acquire the Far West on the American continent until he had secured the old Southwest Territory, land which would later become Alabama, Mississippi, and Louisiana. Control of the Mississippi River was so crucial that Jefferson initially had even suggested that the United States should ally itself with its former enemy Britain as the lesser of two evils if France took control of New Orleans.

Jefferson was not alone in recognizing the strategic significance of New Orleans. British military planners assessed that control of New Orleans would give Britain control of the continent, a strategy revealed in letters during the War of 1812. British Captain John Stirling wrote his superiors in March 1813, noting that the United States economy depended upon Mississippi River shipping for its goods, and that dependency made the U.S. vulnerable because it did not control the ports at Mobile, Pensacola or East Florida. He added that the New Orleans area was populated with immigrants from various nations who might be willing to side with the Spanish.[119] Their large slave population might be encouraged to rebel against their white masters, and the eastern Gulf area had a high concentration of Creek Indians who did not support United States expansion. Stirling calculated that all that was necessary for the

British Empire to regain territory was to enforce a blockade along the Gulf of Mexico, create a rebellion in Louisiana, and then with a small force, the British could take Kentucky, Tennessee, Ohio, and parts of Virginia. That assessment continued throughout the War of 1812. Reverend Jonathan Jones, who grew up on the Natchez Trace, reflected the locals' understanding of the significance, "If the British forces captured New Orleans, it would be breaking the lock and opening the door of the Valley of the Mississippi."[120]

American military commanders had long since reached the same conclusion. New Orleans lay more than 600 miles from Tennessee and from settlements north where most citizen militia lived. If British forces chose to invade the continent along the Gulf Coast, mobilization and movement of enough troops to repel an invasion would be almost impossible. Building a road would be just the first step. Because the nation relied upon a defense from local militia, the U.S. government also needed to encourage large settlements to be developed on or along the Mississippi River.[121]

The lean federal government was not in the business of road building. Politicians strictly construed Article I, Section 8, of the U.S. Constitution that permits the federal government to build roads to transport mail as the only authority for federal roads. Secretary Pickering's request in the 1790's that the U.S. government improve a mail route between Nashville and Natchez had been ignored, however international conflicts had changed the landscape by the time of Jefferson's election. Napoleon and other European powers threatened a greater military presence along the Gulf Coast. The U.S. needed soldiers to defend the coast, and in an era of a small standing army, it needed to encourage settlers to move southwest where they could provide militias. Secretary of War Henry Dearborn confided, "The President [Jefferson] is extremely anxious for the increase in the population on our South Western frontier and will give every encouragement in his power to so important an object."[122]

Jefferson used mail delivery as the pretense for improving the Natchez Trace as a wagon road. But the new road known officially as the "Columbian Highway" would be built along the Natchez Trace to permit the hauling of supplies for troops and a future immigration route for settlers. In part, because the true purpose of the road was military, Jefferson tasked the U.S. Army to build it.

In 1801, Jefferson placed U.S. General James Wilkinson in charge of construction of the Natchez Trace and negotiation with the Chickasaw and Choctaw to permit the United States government to build the wagon highway through their nations. Wilkinson may also have encouraged Jefferson to build the highway for Wilkinson's own purposes.

Chief George Colbert negotiated the treaty for the wagon highway on behalf of the Chickasaw.[123] Wilkinson assured Colbert that the new road would be a road of peace; no bloodshed would be allowed on it.[124] Wilkinson claimed that the government's only goals were to improve the delivery of the mail and to provide better passage for boatmen returning from Natchez. To emphasize the peaceful intent, Wilkinson gave Colbert a Jefferson Peace Medal for his role in the negotiations. Though the presentation of such medals was common when presidents' representatives met with Indian chiefs, the Colbert family long considered the chief's medal a prized possession.[125]

Colbert would later state that the government also asked him to move to the highway to operate a ferry for Natchez Trace travelers at the Tennessee River, but more likely, he made that term a condition of his support.[126] Businessmen often spoke of Colbert's negotiating skills as "cunning," in a derogatory description, because he frequently obtained the better bargain. Treaty negotiators secretly praised his business skills, and they singled him out as the man who prevented them from taking more land from the Chickasaw in the early 1800's. As part of his price for agreeing to allow the U.S government to open the road, Colbert also insisted that Chickasaw operate the ferries at the Duck and Tennessee rivers as well as all inns on the road in the Chickasaw Nation. American settlers thought Colbert abused his monopoly and became wealthy charging 50 cents for each traveler and one dollar per horse, compared to other ferry-men who charged only 12½ cents, but more likely, the white men could not believe that an Indian possessed the skills and intellect to develop the cattle, cotton, and fur industry that Colbert created on the future lands of the Old South.[127]

Wilkinson and the War Department were so anxious to begin con-struction of the road that work began on the first section just south of Thomas Hart Benton's farm before negotiators had even completed trea-ties with the Indians. Army surveyors set out making a survey of the ex-tant Piomingo's or Mountain Leader's Trace and the proposed Columbi-an Highway beginning at the Nashville Court House.[128] The two routes split just south of Benton's farm and the straighter wagon road would run along the ridge tops several miles east of Mountain Leader's Trace until the two roads merged again near Brown's Bottom in the Mississippi Ter-ritory. Despite Wilkinson's assurances to Colbert, Wilkinson revealed the true purpose of the road on the bottom of the survey, "This road being completed, I shall consider our Southern extremity secured the Indians in that quarter at our feet and the adjacent Province open to us."[129] Rather than a road of peace as he had promised, Wilkinson designed the wagon highway to become military road.

Military logistics dictated that the road be built to accommodate trains of wagons needed to haul food, equipment, and even wounded sol-diers over long distances. The roadbed was to be cleared eight feet wide, the width necessary for wagon travel. Four feet either side of the road bed were to be cleared of overhanging brush. Ramps for wagon wheels were to be dug at small streams. Larger streams were to be bridged. Swamps were to be drained, logs placed to firm the surface of wet areas, and cause-ways built when possible. Ferries were to be built to transport travelers and their horses, carriages, and wagons across the rivers.[130] At first, the road would be marked with mile markers by notches axed in trees along the route. Settlers unfamiliar with the Spanish name "Natchez" would mistake the name of the road as the "Notchy Trace."[131]

Road construction provided an opening to build federal agencies in the Indian nations. The U.S. government constructed a Chickasaw Agency south of the Chickasaw Old Town near what would become Old Houlka, Mississippi. The Choctaw Agency was moved to the area that would become Ridgeland, Mississippi. Agencies in Indian nations were complexes of buildings comparable to foreign embassies. Their large granaries provided food for travelers but also indicated to Indians the abundance they could enjoy in association with the Americans. Large brick buildings, built for agents' work, also were designed to convey a sense of American power and permanence in the Indian territory.

Jackson and his silent land partner John Overton understood the business opportunities the new road created. Overton lobbied for funding for the road, assuring politicians that its construction would enhance land values.[132] As the federal receiver of property and tax collector in Nashville, Overton would also be responsible for payment of U.S. soldiers charged with building the road.[133]

With Overton's help, Jackson obtained a War Department contract to build the first U.S. government ferry boats for the Tennessee River crossing in 1803.[134] Jackson associate John Gordon entered into a partnership with George Colbert's brother William Colbert to operate the ferry, inn, and trading post at the Duck River crossing. It was not considered a violation of the Chickasaw Treaty for settlers to operate on the road when a Chickasaw was a partner or spouse.

Jackson also arranged to operate a commissary on the new road at the Natchez Trace Camp Columbian near George Colbert's ferry. George Colbert did not hesitate to show his opposition to Jackson's intrusion into his nation and his market area. Colbert refused to trade with Jackson and took his animal pelts to Mobile to sell them to Spanish traders at half the price that Jackson offered.[135]

Colbert's cunning surfaced as surveyors began laying out the road across the Tennessee River. The parties had agreed that all Tennessee River army ferries boats and buildings were to be turned over to Colbert, who would gain full rights to operate the buildings on Tennessee River. Colbert claimed that building the road along the Piomingo Trace Tennessee River crossing near present-day Eastport and Waterloo would leave the road prone to flooding.[136] He insisted that the army move the road five miles east. Part of Colbert's real motivation may have been to remove Jackson's foothold in his nation and to create greater competition for Double Head's trading post. In any event, the building in which Jackson conducted his commissary business likely became Colbert's when all army buildings were given to Colbert as part of the treaty.

Though treaties with the Chickasaw and Choctaw provided that only Indians would be permitted to operate inns along the highway, when bandits killed travelers on the road near Swan Creek in 1803, the Tennessee governor suggested that the army begin building additional stations to protect travelers.[137] President Jefferson agreed, and a federal program was established for the government to lease land from the Indians and build public stations, stands, or inns the distance of about every 20 miles, the distance most travelers with wagons would be expected to travel in a day.[138] The inns would include a cabin, a separate kitchen, a corn crib, and stables. Up to 300 acres were also leased for many inn operators to raise food to feed the travelers and corn to feed their horses. Most often, enslaved African-Americans were used as labor to raise food and operate the stables and kitchens. Inns also maintained a supply of goods to sell travelers. In settled areas, inn keepers held licenses to sell liquor and supplies to travelers, therefore, like inns along the east coast, inns often were called "taverns." The federal program was also extended to the Cumberland Road and Federal Road with the hope that by adding safety and convenience for travelers from the East, the government could encourage settlers to migrate farther west to build new settlements and provide militias to guard the frontiers.

Jefferson's plan was threatened when Napoleon indicated that France would retrocede New Orleans to France. After Napoleon attempted to conquer Europe, he sent about 40,000 troops to the Caribbean with a view toward retaking land on the American Gulf Coast. Napoleon's new interest in land on the American continent, accompanied by another closing of the right to ship goods down the Mississippi River, set off a panic in American military circles. Jefferson said, "Perhaps nothing since the revolutionary war has produced more uneasy sensations through the body of the nation."[139] Jefferson concluded that war was inevitable unless the U.S. could assure control of New Orleans.[140]

The Natchez Trace Columbian Highway took on a different perspective. A wagon road that could be used to transport large numbers of troops southward toward the Gulf Coast could also be used by an invading power to move troops northward deep into the interior. In 1802, army road builders were removed from highway construction and put to work building forts at strategic points on the road. Fort Dearborn, which was later renamed "Cantonment Washington," was built just north of the Mississippi territorial capital in Washington, Mississippi Territory; Camp Columbian was fortified at the Tennessee River crossing at Colbert's Ferry; and the Wilkinson Cantonment was built or fortified at the Duck River crossing at Gordon's Ferry.[141] A garrison built south of the Benton farm in the late 1700's remained in operation.

As Napoleon focused on conquering Europe, his soldiers in the New World tropics met a stronger enemy of yellow fever and altered his plans for the American continent.[142] After the disease wiped out thousands of Napoleon's troops encamped in the Caribbean, the French Emperor lost interest in the New World. In 1803, Napoleon gave the United States a document transferring ownership of a large swath of the continent known as the "Louisiana Purchase," however, it was no secret that the American military was not large enough to defend it.

Spain was not expected to honor the French bargain, and Jefferson ordered 500 Tennessee militiamen down the Natchez Trace to enforce the transfer.[143] Jackson had just received his appointment from the governor as major general after he tied in the election by officers of the Tennessee Militia.[144] Jackson's friend U.S. Congressman William Dickson had advised Jackson that Congress would be expected to take action.[145] As the militia major general in charge of the defense of West Tennessee, and closest to the anticipated scene of confrontation, Jackson assumed that political leaders would recognize him to be the military commander best suited to lead such an expedition to Natchez. However, President Jefferson and Tennessee Governor John Sevier passed over him for more-experienced professional military commanders. Jackson reached out to Secretary of War Dearborn seeking to override the governor's decision by arguing that he was the man his militia had chosen to lead the troops and the governor was known for acting out of his own selfish purposes rather than the public good.[146] The War Department was not moved by Jackson's self-serving criticism of his superior. Jackson received only the contract to build the boats for the expedition.[147]

Undeterred, when it became clear that Spain would not send an armada to challenge the transfer and Tennessee troops returned home, Jackson next petitioned Jefferson for an appointment to serve as Governor of the new Louisiana Territory.[148] Jackson's political enemy William Henderson cautioned President Jefferson that Jackson was "violent, disputatious and arbitrary," compelling Jefferson to deny Jackson's advancement for the second time by appointing instead a young W.C.C. Claiborne, a fellow Nashville resident, as Louisiana Governor.[149] Jefferson also appointed General James Wilkinson as Governor of the new Upper Louisiana Territory, the portion of the Louisiana Purchase to the north and west of New Orleans.

The third denial of Jackson's ambition, particularly the appointment of Wilkinson, stung. Jackson's biographer Robert Remini wrote that from the moment Jackson learned that Jefferson had rejected his offer to serve as Governor of Louisiana, Jackson became increasingly anti-Jefferson.[150]

Jackson set out to position himself to lead the next military expedition down the Natchez Trace. But he became so driven to lead a military campaign that his boundless and sometimes reckless ambition threatened the United States general and War Department whose support he would need. Jackson first would have to conquer his own government before he could set his full attention to defeating the British.

CHAPTER THREE

MARKING TIME

"there is not an individual among the volunteers who would not prefer perishing in the field of battle, who would not cheerfully yield his life in the defense of his country, than return to the bosom of his family and his friends, covered with shame, ignominy and disgrace…"

—Andrew Jackson, December 21, 1812

Though Jackson was eager to begin the long-awaited expedition that would bring him glory and advancement, he could not ignore the precarious situation of his Volunteer army. If these men could not be paid for their service, a full-on mutiny was not out of the question.

General Jackson and Governor Blount publicly ignored the lack of War Department support and worked to build morale by instilling in the men a sense that they were part of a noble mission based on the foundation of the Revolution. On December 18, Governor Blount dictated an address to be read to the men to express the appreciation of the state. The governor's address was delayed for a day to allow Jackson to attend the funeral service of a Revolutionary War veteran at Talbot's Tavern, and for his Company of Guards to serve as honor guards at the funeral to allow the old hero to be buried with the honors of war.[151] The funeral of the man who preceded the Volunteers in battle would serve as a reminder of the sacrifices of their fathers, and Jackson could use it to give a foundation to his own address to the men.

The following day, the General ordered his men stand in formations of perfect squares with their arms presented to show respect while the governor's address was read:

"Citizen Soldiers, Your prompt attention to the call of your government to enter into the service of the republic, your manly conduct in bearing without a murmur, the severity of the severest cold experienced here for years proves your patriotic exertions to arm, equip and clothe yourselves at your own expense as volunteers. Your ready exchange of your rifles for muskets in order to complete rifle companies for the good of the service, at the mere request of your general are sure pledges of your love for country and affords certain proof that you are not only lone citizen soldiers in principle, but further proves that you are the patriotic sons of the patriots of the revolution, now at your post ready to defend your rights and privileges, which the heroes of the revolution obtained for you. This heroic gratitude you are _____ of the many toils, dangers and difficulties which were ___ by the immortal Washington, and those who fought by his side during the Revolutionary struggle and you duly appreciate them. You well understand the blessings of liberty, and the right of self- government. You inhabit the government given by the wisdom and exertions of those who went before you and who established it for the benefit of making defended it as the greatest good your neighbors and expect you to receive their grateful acknowledgment for your good ___. They are satisfied of your bravery. They look to you as so many defenders ... Go forth and make a manly stand against your enemies wheresoever they may be found. Your enemies are the enemies of peace, liberty, independence and of every comfort. Your families and friends rejoice with you.[152]

Governor Blount sensed what the men needed to hear for inspiration. The Volunteers were no longer individual frontiersmen, but they had now become part of the historic movement begun by their fathers and grandfathers in the Revolution. The power of the state was behind them, as well as the power of the nation—even though the men had not yet seen any proof of their nation's support. Many men would no doubt remember this moment a few months later as they were trudging through the Wilderness at the point of starvation. But for the moment, the governor's words stirred patriotic sentiments with all who heard them.

When the address was finished, General Jackson took the opportunity of his reply to the governor's message and to burnish his reputation for aggression by subtly threatening anyone who would consider disobedience:

"The volunteers have drawn their swords, and shouldered their muskets for no other purpose than that of defending their country against the hostile attacks of their enemies the British and their _____ allies, the Indians, and may they never be returned to their scabbards until the enemies of America of every denomination be humbled in the dust and constrained to acknowledge, that which has so often and so long demanded by amicable negotiation. Justice. We flatter ourselves that your Excellency will do us the justice to believe that there is not an individual among the volunteers who would not prefer perishing in the field of battle, who would not cheerfully yield his life in the defense of his country, than return to the bosom of his family and his friends, covered with shame, ignominy and disgrace – Perish our friends, perish our wives, perish our children, the dearest pledges of heaven may perish all terrestrial considerations, but let the honor and fame of a volunteer soldier be untarnished and un_____.... When the volunteers say that it is their full determination to return covered with laurels, or die endeavoring to receive them in the bloody field of war – accept from the General himself and the volunteers the homage of the highest confidence and respect."[153]

The two addresses also prepared the men for the sacrifices that lay ahead. The deprivations and even the potential loss of life were no greater sacrifices than those asked of every generation to protect its liberty.

Whatever enemies and battles soldiers faced, disease was often the deadliest enemy. It was common knowledge that nearly seven times as many men died from disease on marches or in camp as died on the battlefield. The fear of disease was so great that whole towns were quickly abandoned on just a rumor that a neighbor had contracted a communicable disease. Not understanding the causes of many diseases, the public knew only that warm weather in the Lower Country produced fevers that killed. Jackson understood the fear, and he promised his recruits that he would do his best to protect them from disease by returning them home prior to summer weather.[154]

Nevertheless, when soldiers left their homes, they knew that there was a reasonable possibility they might not live to return, even if they never met a British soldier or hostile Indian warrior. In an age when a man lived by his reputation for courage, if the threat of death caused any hesitation, it must never be voiced.

By December 22, General Jackson confidently announced that the Volunteers who would defend the Lower Country had been assembled.[155] It was two days later than he had planned to march from camp, but the War Department had still not provided the funds to pay them. Jackson wrote to U.S. Lieutenant Deputy Quartermaster Alpha Kingsley to create a record that he had met his timeline and that the War Department had not met its obligations to supply him with funds and supplies. The General noted that military morale depended upon movement—certainly Jackson's did—and he was concerned that the lack of purpose would produce indolence in camp. As he understood, "slothful indolence in camp" would break down discipline.[156]

In one respect, the delay temporarily worked to Jackson's advantage by giving him additional time to train and prepare for the march. Now that the cavalry had been supplied with additional swords, sword practice was conducted each day at 8:00 a.m., 10:00 a.m., noon, 2:00 p.m. and 4:00 p.m.[157] Drills and parades kept the troops busy, but also sharpened effectiveness. By the time the Volunteers camped in Natchez, they would be able to form a line on a ten-minute notice.

The daily sounds of fife and drum comforted and entertained Nashville townspeople. But as civilians watched the camp activities from a distance, there was some apprehension about what effect 2,000 troops with time on their hands would have on their town. Older citizens who had migrated from the colonies still remembered how British soldiers had disrespected their civilian rights and the virtue of their daughters during the Revolution. Those abuses were one reason Americans opposed supporting a large standing army. Volunteers assembled in Nashville, however, were drawn generally from West Tennessee town leaders and their sons. The *Clarion* marveled that soldiers had not damaged any property.[158] No one had even reported any brash young soldier's insult to any citizen. Campfires had been so well-patrolled that a private wooden rail fence located about 30 yards from the campfires had not even been scorched.

Thick cedars on the western hills bowed with heavy snow and hid farms scattered beyond. Other than cutting firewood, feeding farm animals, or hunting, there was little work that farmers could perform until a thaw. Fathers often used bear skins for sleds to pull their small children in the snow. Sounds of young laughter and the occasional sighting of children accompanying their parents to town reminded soldiers of their own families enjoying the rare holidays from work without them.

Nevertheless, camp discipline was becoming part of a new psyche for the men. An order had been issued not to fire guns in camp, since misfires and accidents were likely to cause injuries in the close quarters.[159] Loaded weapons also increased the chances that an angry soldier could challenge authority. One sick soldier lying in his tent spotted a squirrel and asked a tent mate to kill it to make a soup for him. Hot squirrel soup was a frontier remedy when chickens were unavailable. Rather than disobey the order against firing, the soldier walked about a quarter mile down the line to find Colonel Benton to ask permission to shoot. Benton consented but ordered that the firing be properly supervised.[160]

The lack of infractions demonstrates not only the character and discipline of the men, but also how seriously they prepared for their mission. When fires were reported at a stable, in a building behind the stone tavern, and at a warehouse, no one accused rowdy soldiers of starting them, and after a fire ladder was finally loosened from the court house, the fires were quickly extinguished.[161]

On Christmas Eve, an early test of discipline arrived as temptation in the form of an old man.[162] Thought to be preacher, the visitor appeared at camp and asked to see his son and friends. His sole mission was to encourage them to return home. He may have been one of the ministers who had complained that young men in their congregations had too easily been taken in by military recruiters' appeals to their vanity for military glory.[163] The old man assured the Volunteers that because they had not yet been paid, Jackson could not stop them from leaving. The preacher had even brought along his wagon to haul away whatever baggage the men had accumulated. What he failed to realize, however, was that a few days in camp had already transformed the young men from civilians to soldiers. Rather than returning home, the Volunteers reported the civilian to their superiors and had him arrested in camp to face Jackson's punishment.

Jackson used the old man as an example to steel the Volunteers' resolve, while carefully avoiding the substance of the man's argument. Jackson scolded that it was bad enough that this man had refused to volunteer his own service to protect his country, but his encouragement of willing defenders to desert was a greater crime. When someone pointed out that the old man was the father of a young son in camp, Jackson announced that he would commute the man's sentence based upon the bravery his son had exhibited in volunteering. It was all bluster; Jackson knew that he had no authority to impose any sentence on the civilian. The old man was then escorted out of camp as hundreds of men stood silent.[164]

As the governor and the General cajoled the War Department for the funding needed to march, it would prove a tougher test of leadership to keep discipline and readiness at a high level without an immediate challenge. Nashville offered its own temptations. A notorious old tavern called the "Red Heifer" stood by the Spout Spring on the bluff near the Public Square. In Nashville's earliest days, the tavern distilled its own whiskey, and when the hot brew was ready to flow, a worker blew a buffalo horn to alert patrons. Adding to the tavern's rowdy atmosphere and primitive marketing, drinks were served from cattle horns suspended from the tavern ceiling by leather strings.[165] Men such as Davy Crockett, like those of earlier generations, would take up the habit of drinking spirits from a buffalo's horn. Despite Nashville father James Robertson's encouraging the legislature to pass a bill outlawing on-site distillation, the tavern's owner William "King" Boyd was undeterred. Word spread through camp that when the bell rang at Red Heifer, the old cow was ready for "milking."[166] If the temptation of the Devil's brew were not enough, customers could also find games of "Rattle and Snap," "Seven Up," "Old Sledge," and "Dodge the Devil." Those stepping outside for fresh air could bet on cockfights in the small pens kept for that purpose just off the Public Square.[167]

Like most tavern keepers of the day, King Boyd entertained his guests with stories such as the one of Chickasaw Chief Piominko's mountain warriors who frequently entered the tavern carrying a gallon jug and asking for whiskey:

"How much?"

"Jug-you fill him—young warrior—snake bite him—die soon—whiskey cure him."

"A gallon is too much."

"No—snake very big."[168]

King Boyd added through the laughter that they never killed that snake.

It was soon unnecessary for soldiers to obtain leave to go to the tavern for libations. Whiskey-peddling vendors were drawn to the camps of soldiers.

Students at the Davidson Academy just south of Nashville were also attracted to camp to watch the military parades. For many boys, it was one of the most exciting events they had witnessed. Schoolmasters did what they could to hold the students in their three-story classroom and dormitory building, but boys intent on being part of the camp adventure, broke windows to escape. Like students at the Harpeth Academy south in Franklin, Tennessee, they were tempted to enlist. Fortunately for the school, muster rolls were already complete.[169]

Jackson had rushed training to prepare the men to march as quickly as possible, but the motivation that created soldiers ready to fight only made it more difficult to keep morale high when there was no battle. Training created a need for action that Jackson could not fill. Waiting became the more immediate enemy. Captains increasingly found that soldiers in their companies were absent from camp. Jackson issued an order that any soldier outside camp without a pass was to be considered a deserter. Furloughs only seemed to lead to opportunities for gambling outside camp, and they were suspended.[170] Also, any peddler or anyone else who sold spirits to a Volunteer was to be arrested. By Christmas, card playing was prohibited as it led to gambling, and gambling led to fights and a breakdown of discipline.[171] Enterprising soldiers soon discovered that dice could be made from lead bullets, prompting an order that gambling with *any* object was prohibited.[172] Minor discipline cases were punished with courts-martial, sentences of confinement to camp, and additional clean-up duties.

Heightened routines were required to create challenges to keep the men focused. The cavalry was ordered to parade in their camps at morning trumpet. Rolls were called. Morning reports were written to be given to the sergeant major of each battalion at sunrise. A camp guard was to be appointed to select and supervise appropriate numbers of subalterns to enforce discipline. Those not busy with other duties were put to work cleaning camp both out of necessity and to keep the men occupied.[173] Run-away horses provided Colonel Coffee's dragoons frequent diversions. Coffee obtained approval to send detachments to track down and return strays.[174] Minor missions and time away from camp proved as important for cavalry rank-and-file as for the horses.

Continued threats of discipline went only so far; moral leadership was needed to provide positive encouragement. Jackson sought a chaplain to encourage proper conduct and to minister to the spiritual needs of the men. The General's first choice, Reverend Robert Henderson, apparently declined the appointment with its generous salary of $120 per month, almost as much as the governor's.[175] The salary should have made no difference, because ministers were expected to live in a constant state of poverty. When Jackson submitted his official list of officers for commissions, he left the position of chaplain blank.

After further consideration, it was decided that a typical New England city parson would have little effect on frontier soldiers away from the constraints of home. Jackson's knowledge of the Natchez Trace then produced an obvious choice. Methodist evangelist Learner Blackman's ecclesiastical career had developed one of the most challenging circuits—the Mississippi Territory and the Natchez Trace. On the frontier, evangelists often were required to prove their manliness by fighting their prospective congregants before they could preach to them.

Blackman began his ecclesiastical career at age 19. He had trained by riding the Natchez Trace with the legendary Methodist minister Lorenzo Dow, who was considered a wild man in appearance for his long stringy hair and unusual mannerisms.[176] But Dow was a man who had learned how to work with the strong-willed and sometimes eccentric settlers on the Trace, and Blackman benefited from Dow's experience. Blackman understood the hardships the men would face on the road; he had experienced them many times during trips between Nashville and Natchez. Blackman was also no stranger to Jackson. In fact, Blackman had lodged with the Jacksons at the Hermitage just a few months earlier. During that visit, Blackman noticed that Rachel was seeking religion, and he prayed that the General would do the same.[177]

Though Blackman had read as much as possible to prepare himself to preach, congregations were put off by his youth and lack of formal education until he began to speak. His powerful oratory quickly won their respect. Blackman was described as "dignified without stiffness, a fluent conversationalist without levity, he could associate without embarrassment with the high officials of the Territory and with the most refined, intelligent and elevated classes of society, and at the same time make himself so agreeable in the cabins of the poor and less cultivated..."[178] After helping to grow congregations in Natchez, the young man was made presiding elder of the Nashville District.

Now 31 years old, Blackman took a leap of faith to assume the challenge of the ministry of 2,000 soldiers, and he admitted to hesitating at first when Jackson's messenger approached him with an offer to serve.

Though churches found the young Blackman effective, the Methodist minister William Winian, whose writings reflected that he often formed a quick, critical assessment of the people he met, considered Blackman's talents "merely adequate."[179] Winian may have expressed that opinion to Blackman, whose own writings reveal that Blackman had a deep sense of humility in his own abilities. As Blackman considered Jackson's offer, he weighed his own sense of inadequacy with the opportunity to change the moral climate in the county.

Though Methodist ministers at the time avoided involvement in worldly affairs such as politics and matters of government, some Protestant ministers drew comparisons between the Promised Land given to Israel and their new country, which they also saw as a gift from God. Blackman reflected, "How much like old Canaan is the wilderness of America. Saccharine fluid flows from the maple and when the inhabitants lack salt it pours in watery particles from the mountains. So the Lord takes care of his American Israel. Our country abounds with milk and honey or with things that can equally incorporate with the staff a life."[180] But Blackman had read the newspapers and followed the political talk. The American "Promised Land" was no longer prospering. Americans had divided themselves into two bitter political camps, and European powers threatened. Blackman also thought that threats from the Indians and British as well as natural disasters likely were brought on by God's displeasure at how Americans failed to create a more religious nation. "The earth has been made to shake under our feet and the mountains to tremble about our heads. Jehovah seems to have a controversy with our nation. The cloud blackens."[181] Maybe, Blackman concluded, he had been called in some way to help set things right. He accepted Jackson's offer.

Concerned about how other ministers such as Winian might criticize him, Blackman determined that he would use the salary only for necessary expenses. He would keep an accounting and submit it to the annual conference of Methodist ministers for their approval. With some accountability, Blackman hoped that no one could accuse him of greed.

Before setting out to join the camp, Blackman stopped to offer a prayer:

> "O! my God. I am about to enter in to a new Scene. I need much grace to shield me, much zeal for thy great name—Go with me, O, thou God of Armies & direct my course. Make me useful. May I do good and git good."[182]

Blackman would soon conclude that none of the officers were religious, but then only pockets of the population west of the Appalachians were religious at that time. The preacher pictured himself as Daniel entering a den of lions. He would learn, however, that the officers were gentlemen and that they would treat him with respect. Jackson set the tone by showing Blackman deference and the freedom to minister to the men as he saw fit.

Colonel Coffee shared Reverend Blackman's reluctance for war. Unlike the younger men who spoiled for a fight to win military glory, Coffee preferred the whole enterprise to end as soon as possible so that he could return home. He had left behind his bride of two years, a young daughter, and a farm operation. Coffee was a businessman by nature, as his later fortunes in Alabama would prove. Many nights in Coffee's camp near Nashville, his home seemed tantalizingly close.

Though a sense of patriotism initially had encouraged Volunteers to overlook the technicalities of their enlistment, the enhanced work and discipline highlighted the fact that the men were truly serving as volunteers. Every day it became more obvious that citizen soldiers were working hard from sunrise to sunset without pay. Jackson could sense the growing restlessness. When federal paymaster Kingsley replied to Jackson's letter of December 22 that he would be happy to cooperate in supplying funds, Jackson asked that payment be made without delay.[183] As Jackson ordered, captains marched their companies to Kingsley's office in town over two days.[184] There they formed lines to sign the roll to officially muster in and receive their pay in exchange for a pledge of service.

Kingsley, however, had not anticipated that Jackson was a man of action, and he was unprepared. The Nashville Bank did not have enough specie to pay all the men. Instead, soldiers were to be paid by bank notes that promised to honor payment with specie or hard money at a later date. Kingsley placed advanced advertisements in the newspaper to make merchants aware that he would begin paying the men in notes, hoping that merchants would not object to accepting them for payment.

Soldiers realized that bank notes were not hard currency, particularly after the newspaper had also just reported that someone was passing counterfeit notes on the Nashville Bank.[185] Even if soldiers avoided getting phony notes, if the bank failed, its notes would be worthless. Several Volunteers made a run on the bank with their notes demanding that they be redeemed for currency.[186]

After consulting with friends who were directors in the Nashville Bank, Jackson learned that the bank had enough currency on hand to pay a third of the amount needed to muster in the soldiers. He arranged for the bank to pay a third of the wages in specie and two-thirds in bank notes to be redeemed in 90 days. Bank directors informed the General that they had persuaded Nashville merchants to accept the notes as cash, particularly because the arrangement might encourage some soldiers to spend all their funds before they departed. Jackson assured his soldiers that it was the best arrangement that could be made.[187]

Yet grumblings within the ranks remained. Private Corbet was one of the first to refuse to perform fatigues without payment. He declared that Jackson's officers were a bunch of rascals or scoundrels, and he threatened to kill Coffee.[188] With discontent growing, Jackson faced the crisis he had feared from the beginning. Officers spotted what Jackson called the "seeds of mutiny." Jackson had to put a stop to it quickly.

The title "Volunteer" was not exactly what the name implied. As part of the American political compact, American soldiers chose to volunteer in exchange for compensation from those they defended. It was the British who impressed soldiers into service against their will. Colonists had considered British recruiters no better than abductors, and the impressment of American sailors continued despite the country's independence. Jackson's refusal to pay the men in full in advance reminded some soldiers of the British enemy that political leaders railed against.

The General needed a significant diversion to avoid a spreading mutiny. Perhaps a change of campsite in anticipation of the march would mollify the men. Besides, just three weeks in camp had already depleted available firewood and changed the landscape of Nashville. Jackson determined that the infantry would move their camp to the area near the ferry landing on David McGavock's plantation.[189] There the soldiers could see the river and anticipate boarding boats for New Orleans.

Jackson's order produced the opposite effect than intended. Word that Volunteers would move camp toward the landing and begin loading the boats for the voyage to the Lower Country made some soldiers even more concerned that Jackson's officers were attempting to force them from their homes to serve without pay.

The mutiny became real. Captain Williamson refused to strike his tents. He said that he could not move to new camp if his men would not support him. Sergeant Samuel Goode insisted that he be paid before he moved. Jackson heard the sergeant boast that he would rather lose his life than work without pay, and the General witnessed him stepping out of ranks and holding his firelock in defiance as he said it. Goode's rebellion inspired a small group to refuse to move and insist that they also be paid before moving. Captain McEwen and large numbers of Volunteers stepped in to put it to an equally quick end, and Sergeant Goode was arrested to face court-martial.[190]

Private John Wise and a group of men from Captain Hewlitt's Company saw no need to wait for pay. They deserted camp to return home. Benton was ordered to lead a detachment to return them.[191] Another soldier insulted his officer when his request to go home to make a new pair of shoes was denied.

Private Corbet's court-martial jury hoped to make him an example to stop further infractions. They chose the old British and U.S. army punishment of "riding the wooden horse." Corbet was seated astride an inverted v-shaped wooden sawhorse with weights tied to his legs as his regiment marched by him to witness his shame.[192] Depending upon the height of the horse, the punishment could inflict serious pain and injury to sensitive areas.

It was becoming clear that without movement toward a mission, the discipline that Jackson had successfully coordinated could unravel. He had to make a move toward marching out of camp, even if he had no funds. Jackson ordered Colonel Bradley to inspect the boats that had been delivered to the upper and lower wharfs of Nashville and to report their fitness for duty. But Jackson warned that he did not have time for inspection results to delay departure. If repairs were discovered to be needed, soldiers were to perform the work rather than waiting for the contractors. At the same time, the General informed Nashville contractors Cantrell & Read that he was ready for them to begin issuing provisions for 60 days to be loaded onto the boats while they were still tied at the wharfs on the Cumberland River.[193] A few soldiers from each regiment would be tasked to help with the loading on December 30. Those men were then ordered to drop the boats down to the best harbor they could find below (down river of or north of) Nashville.

Maybe the parson could calm the men. Reverend Blackman was ordered to preach to the infantry at noon on December 31. He may have hesitated. [194] Blackman already worried how he would relate to soldiers, but to step into the middle of a mutiny made the job even more difficult.

Blackman did not record in his journal that he fulfilled the General's order, and no soldiers made mention of the reverend's sermon.

Adding to the stress of command, Jackson was also forced to mediate a dispute between his two aides-de-camp. Benton and Reid were friends as well as fellow lawyers from Franklin, and it was said that Benton had recommended Reid's service to Jackson. Through a misunderstanding, it had been announced that Reid would take Benton's position as first aide-de-camp rather than second aide-de-camp under Benton. The ambitious Reid did not want second, and Jackson offered Reid the opportunity to withdraw his service. It is unclear whether Reid accepted Jackson's offer or whether he became too ill to march as rumored. In either event, Benton remained first aide-de-camp, and Reid did not follow Jackson to Natchez.[195]

Governor Blount finally certified the commissions for Jackson's officers and issued the final order for Jackson to march his men just as soon as they had been paid and were bound into service: "You will as soon as practicable after the Troops are paid, move with the Detachment of Tennessee Volunteers under your command . . . to New Orleans for the defence of the lower Country. . . . On your arrival at New Orleans, you will await, the order of the President of the United States."[196] The "place of destiny" was no longer considered a mystery. The march would lead to New Orleans.

Knowing that Jackson eventually hoped to move against the Creek, Blount ordered Jackson to take great care in marching through the Indian nations that he not give the Indians any justification to attack the Volunteers. Based upon the number of times Jackson's subordinates later reinforced the order, Blount must have emphasized the point to Jackson in no uncertain terms.

Jackson was aware of the significance of the moment. He finally had the order in hand he had awaited for so long. Jackson prayed, "that the

God of Battles may be with us, and that high Heaven may bestow its Choice Benedictions on all engaged in this Expedition."[197]

The governor's order injected Jackson with new inspiration. Now he had the task of inspiring the men whose fighting spirit had waned in the weeks awaiting pay and particularly those who had threatened to abandon him. Jackson carefully worded an order to be read on January 1 at the morning formation.[198] He began by stating that he had promised to act as a father to the troops, and sometimes it was necessary for a father to chastise his children. He reminded the soldiers of the severe penalty for mutiny. Jackson was their commanding officer, and his subordinates had an obligation by law to obey his orders. Cleverly, he singled out those who stirred trouble due to the lack of pay by asking who among them had volunteered for monetary gain. Would they want their families to think that they were simply mercenaries? No one was willing to admit that money was more important than patriotism. He reminded the men that he had no control over the War Department's payments and added a personal plea for patience. Building on the enlisted men's desire to keep officers in their place, Jackson threatened a court-martial for any soldier, including officers, who caused division within the ranks. The disgruntled were perfectly within their legal right to insist that the promised money be paid, but Jackson changed the discussion to his strengths—patriotism and the power to punish.

Civilians were permitted to attend the ceremony to support the troops, and local ladies presented Carroll's company with their hand-sewn banner emblazoned with "GOD ARMETH THE PATRIOT" along with their prayers that they would "prove victorious." Carroll seized the moment to improve morale, "Who would not fight in his country's cause under colors painted with such taste . . . Under this banner, what foe dare we not encounter? What valorous deeds can we not achieve? It shall float in triumph, or be surrendered only with our lives . . . This is the signal for heroic exploit . . . Under the snow white wave of this banner we 'conquer or die."[199] Victory or death.

Jackson's address and the patriotic ceremony, rather than a religious one as planned, diffused a potentially explosive situation. The move to a new camp, along with the work needed to set it up, temporarily distracted the men's attention. Soldiers who refused to move to the new camp were court-martialed. After testimony, sentences of imprisonment and fines of half-pay were rendered and then sent to the General for confirmation. Jackson remitted only portions of the sentences.[200] He balanced demonstrating the need for discipline and preventing further loss of morale. Jackson understood the men's frustration. He felt it himself.

At midnight on January 2, the duties of the day behind him and with the camp asleep, Coffee's thoughts turned toward home. He would have preferred to visit his wife in person, but particularly after participating in trials of other men who attempted to return home, he could not afford to exercise a privilege of his command. Instead, he sat down to write a letter to his wife Mary:

> "When duty requires it, all who wish to act justly, will and must obey, although our private interest, as well as our most tender wishes, would dictate otherwise, when I parted with you last, I flattered myself if detained here thus long, I would have had the gratification of seeing you again before I left the State, but in this I am and must be disappointed, when I am absent from my command all appears to be wrong, it's hard to get along with my business when present, but worse, much worse, when away-therefore have resolved to do my duty at the sacrifice of my dearest interest and wishes, and I know you will, like a true patriot, applaud my resolution, notwithstanding your fond desire that I could be with you, - but the time will soon roll away when, I hope, the situation of the

country will not require the service of her citizens- and then my love we can sit down in peace and enjoy the comforts that are laid in store for us and which we shall so fondly enjoy... when we can sit down with our dear little infant daughter and spend our days in each other's tender embrace.[201]

CHAPTER FOUR

FORWARD

"[W]e trust in the righteousness of our cause, and the god of Battle and of Justice will protect us."

—Andrew Jackson, January 8, 1813

The march finally in sight, Jackson began to set final plans for logistics in motion. Though it had been reported that all boats had been completed, the newspaper continued to advertise for them. Governor Blount also issued an order for Jackson to obtain the necessary horses, blankets, swords, and other equipment needed for the cavalry's overland trip down the Natchez Trace.[202]

Quartermaster Lewis was still unsure how to determine what food, forage for the horses, and equipment would be needed for the cavalry and how to transport it. With the last opportunity to obtain supplies from the contractor in Franklin, cavalry with packhorses could carry only enough provisions for 10 days, enough for the men to reach the Tennessee River. In good weather, the cavalry might expect to reach New Orleans in 25 days. But if there were delays, soldiers would need additional food and forage for each day. It was determined that the cavalry would need 46 packhorses and tents for the sick and for storage of supplies.[203] The cavalry would travel with only 28 light linen tents and the remainder of the heavier cotton tents would be transported by the infantry in flatboats.

Contractors would leave provisions for the men at trusted inns along the Natchez Trace. Lewis suggested providing the brigade quartermaster with enough money to purchase additional provisions along the road, but there were few funds. Government vouchers would have to serve as payment. If officers could find anyone to accept them, the promises of reimbursement could be sold to the U.S. deputy quartermaster in Natchez. But if the government contractors failed to provide supplies, the cavalry was authorized to obtain supplies wherever they found them. Jackson ordered Coffee not to halt the cavalry's march at any point to wait for delivery of supplies. After all, Jackson assured that Tennessee Volunteers were marching to save the country.[204]

The following day, Jackson ordered a dispatch rider to rush down the Natchez Trace to deliver a message for the U.S. army assistant deputy quartermaster in Natchez.[205] The General's message advised the quartermaster that Jackson was preparing to march toward New Orleans with 400 infantry soldiers, 670 cavalry troops and an unspecified number of mounted infantry.[206] The infantry actually totaled 1,400, and Jackson's own orderly book recorded the number as 1,400 in its handwritten copy of the letter. If the duplicitous Wilkinson did not create a forgery of Jackson's letter to understate the number, perhaps the difference was an error by the letter's scribe. However, if the main purpose of Jackson's letter was to make certain that adequate food and forage awaited his arriving troops, the understatement of his numbers by a thousand was a serious error. Alternatively, if Jackson deliberately understated the number to add an element of surprise to his old enemy General Wilkinson, Wilkinson's spies along the Mississippi River and Natchez Trace should have been expected to alert him to the higher number prior to Jackson's arrival.[207]

Jackson then directed Wilkinson's Natchez federal quartermaster to make plans to provide forage for the Volunteers' horses upon the cavalry's arrival. Jackson's Volunteers were in service to the federal government based upon President Madison's order to call up the troops as federal volunteers. If there should be any doubt whether the federal government should provide supplies for Jackson's troops, the War Department had refused to accept Jackson's tender of troops as state militia and insisted on a reorganization of the forces as federal volunteers when it attempted to deprive him of command. Jackson therefore never doubted his authority to draw supplies from the War Department, particularly when Governor Blount's order seemed to delegate that authority to Jackson.

Whether Jackson intended his order to the U.S. quartermaster, General Wilkinson's subordinate, to be his first shot in a battle for command of the southern forces is unclear. Jackson later claimed that he thought Wilkinson had taken quarters at Fort Stoddert hundreds of miles east of Natchez and that Jackson's requisition for forage and supplies in Natchez would be more efficiently sent directly to the deputy quartermaster in Natchez. Whatever Jackson's true motive, Wilkinson would interpret Jackson's order as a direct challenge.

Proof of Jackson's scheming seemed to be that he sent the order unsealed directly to his good friend Washington Jackson in Natchez and requested that he deliver it in person to the deputy quartermaster.[208] Jackson claimed that he did not know the name of the deputy quartermaster and that he was forced to rely upon his civilian friend to assure delivery. Washington Jackson's brother James was one of the directors of the Nashville Bank, and Washington was an influential merchant in Natchez. Jackson more likely used Washington to pressure the deputy quartermaster, as Wilkinson suspected. The pressure worked. The deputy quartermaster would spend thousands of dollars for forage for Jackson's cavalry that had not been approved by his army superiors.[209]

A few weeks later, when Wilkinson carefully studied the wording of Jackson's order, he noticed that Jackson had stated that New Orleans would be only his *first* destination.[210] That meant that Jackson intended to march his troops east toward Florida without Wilkinson.

And he did. On the same date that Jackson drafted his order to the Natchez U.S. deputy quartermaster, Jackson wrote his friend W.C.C. Claiborne, Governor of Louisiana, to ask him to give enclosed letters directly to the U.S. deputy quartermaster and government contractor at New Orleans to tell them to prepare for the arrival of Jackson's men. Jackson confided that his real goal was to march along the coast to Mobile, Pensacola, and St. Augustine.[211] He also asked Claiborne to use his influence with the U.S. quartermaster in New Orleans to persuade him to honor Jackson's requests. Like his use of Washington Jackson, Jackson used Claiborne to side-step Wilkinson.

Confident that he soon would command areas along the Gulf Coast, Jackson was ready to issue the order everyone understood as a signal that troops would soon march: the cavalry was ordered to have horses shod.[212]

Colonel Henderson took a detachment and rode in advance to make arrangements for provisions on the Natchez Trace. He would plan to ride about 100 miles ahead and make certain supplies were available for the cavalry when they reached designated inns along the road. The first day, Henderson traveled only as far as Bentonville and camped near William Neelly's farm at Beaver Springs before heading farther south.[213] During his march or sometime later, some of the troops took time to carve their names into the logs on the White's farmhouse just off the Natchez Trace to assure that their role in the war would not be forgotten.[214]

Jackson grew characteristically impatient when federal firearms requisitioned from Harpers Ferry in Virginia had still not arrived. He decided to wait for the weapons only an additional two days, but no more. If the guns had not been sent to Jackson's troops by then, Jackson would send troops to the guns. When the guns did not arrive two days later, Jackson ordered Lt. Colonel James Bradley to take a detachment and to march toward Knoxville on the Cumberland Road until they met the wagons hauling firearms and then march back, escorting the wagons to make certain that there was no delay.[215] "Escort" was understood to give Bradley authority to do whatever was necessary to make certain the arms were delivered as soon as possible.

If the requisitioned weapons still did not arrive in time for the departure, plans were made to transport them separately in a keelboat to Natchez so that departure would not be further stalled.

The sudden rush of activity in a military structure was foreign to Reverend Blackman. He had no fear of another journey to Natchez or of dying. But the military reordering had changed everything he had known as the frontier. It was an unnatural state-of-affairs that he described as "jarring," and the prospect of so many men killing and dying at the end of the journey was more than reason would settle.[216] Many people speculated that the great upheaval going on around the world proved that the end of time was near. They would expect to see an apocalypse before the end. Perhaps these men were marching off to face it. Blackman comforted himself with the assurance of Heaven and the faith that at some point there would be an end to whatever troubles the world now faced. Blackman first had to reassure himself before he could convey that faith to 2,000 men preparing to leave their state for possible battle and death.

Jackson ordered all regiments to unite for a pre-departure religious service at Dr. Sappington's racetrack near the camp and ferry on the Cumberland River.[217] Blackman had not shown the confidence Jackson needed for the task, and the General assigned the job to Cavalry Chaplain Gideon Blackburn (whose name is often confused with the infantry Chaplain Learner Blackman). Just as Shawnee warrior Tecumseh had used his spiritual Prophet to speak to the Indian warriors' hearts as he spoke to their heads, Jackson counted on Blackburn's powers of persuasion to inspire the men before setting out.

Troops were ordered to form a circle around a platform placed in the center of the camp. Mounted soldiers remained on horseback at the rear to listen to Blackburn's address as the infantry stood in front.[218] Due to an old injury that he had suffered when working with the Cherokee, Blackburn likely sat in a chair to deliver his sermon. His oratory was so powerful that audiences quickly overlooked the fact that he sat when he spoke. If any troops were unable to hear Reverend Blackburn, additional men had been ordered to form a separate square to the east of the formation, where infantry chaplain Reverend Blackman would address them. Blackman's journal, through its silence on the day, suggests that he again avoided the opportunity to speak.

Once Blackburn's stirring sermon had given soldiers renewed motivation, it was time to present orders for departure. Because cavalrymen were more likely to encounter hostile Indians, the infantry was ordered to deliver their arms to the cavalry in preparation for their march through the Indian nations.[219]

It was then announced that the infantry would strike their tents the next day at noon.[220] Three companies that had not yet been paid would march into Nashville formally to be mustered in. Bank directors had contributed more money to make sure the men would be paid. After signing the rolls, the men would march overland to Robertson's Landing west of the town where they would expect to meet their boats.

The cavalry was ordered to strike their tents on January 10 at 8:00 a.m.[221] Those who had not been paid would be compensated prior to departure. Jackson resolved his quartermaster's question of how much to supply the cavalry by accepting his recommendation to order contractors in Nashville to supply the troops with ten-day's rations in Franklin and providing notes to purchase any additional provisions needed along the road. The Volunteer quartermaster would attach himself to the cavalry and ride with them to be certain the troops had supplies when needed.

The cavalry's order of march was set from Franklin, to Columbia, and then to Captain Dobbins' Stand on the Natchez Trace, and down to Colbert's Ferry to cross the Tennessee River. The cavalry's destination would be Cantonment Washington near Natchez, where they would wait for the arrival of the infantry by river.[222] Infantry and cavalry would then proceed on to New Orleans.

Exuberance was tempered by a warning from aide-de-camp Hynes, based upon the order from Governor Blount:

> "You will use great care in passing through the Indian nations, that no insult be offered to the Indians but if offered to be immediately punished. Although the tribes of Indians through which you pass are thought to be friendly, still you are to conduct yourself as if you were in the heart of an enemy's country expecting attacks daily. You will therefore keep out patrols, strong guards, and encamp in regular order."[223]

The order was a reminder that the men would first have to survive their encounters with hostile Indian warriors before they faced the British. Hynes also warned the cavalry to anticipate finding the British or their proxies near the southern end of the Natchez Trace. An invasion was expected at any time. The cavalry was to assist local forces if needed while waiting for Jackson's arrival.

Officers had reached the final stages of preparations. There would be no further requests for furloughs.[224] Rolls were to be called each morning to make certain that all soldiers were in camp. Soldiers who had taken ill during the rendezvous encampment would have to be left at home to recover at the military hospital in Nashville.[225] The departure-preparation formation accomplished all its objectives. Tennessee Volunteers were again primed to march.

Returning to headquarters in Nashville, Jackson attended to last-minute communications with the federal capital. He asserted the independence of his command by challenging a second protocol established by Wilkinson and sent a letter directly to the Acting Secretary of War James

Monroe rather than through Wilkinson. Jackson alerted the War Department that he was preparing to march toward New Orleans as ordered by Governor Blount.[226] Indirectly, Jackson took the opportunity to make Monroe and the War Department aware that Tennessee Volunteers lacked firearms. Most importantly, Jackson proffered that though his troops had been directed to march toward New Orleans to lend aid to General Wilkinson, Jackson was perfectly ready to lead them under his own command to Mobile, Pensacola, and St. Augustine to take control of East Florida and the Gulf Coast. In anticipation that Monroe, whom Jackson had supported in the previous presidential election, would accept his offer, Jackson told his own men that his orders were to defend New Orleans *and* the Lower Country.[227] Jackson did not know that plans had already been arranged for his friend James Monroe to be removed as Secretary of War and for John Armstrong to take his place.

The *Clarion* also was unaware of the political maneuvers in the capital. It accepted Jackson's request as a near certainty, reporting for re-publication across the country that Jackson was likely to use his troops to take Mobile and Pensacola.[228]

General Wilkinson would have other plans for Jackson. In his camp in New Orleans, Wilkinson was busy laying the groundwork for his own capture of Mobile. For Wilkinson, the mission would provide the only military command victory of his career—if Jackson did not steal his thunder. Contrary to newspaper editors' characterization of Mobile as heavily fortified, the installation was a lightly defended Spanish fort that could be taken without much effort or loss.

Prior to Jackson's arrival in the Lower Country, Wilkinson would have learned of the newspaper reports of Jackson's plan for Mobile. He would have seen the need to devise a plan to stop Jackson's advance before he reached the Gulf Coast. If Wilkinson also had intelligence that Jackson's cavalry had been ordered to halt near Natchez until Jackson sent further orders, Wilkinson could build on those orders to advance his strategy. The cavalry would plan to set up camp at the town of Washington outside Natchez for an extended duration, not knowing when Jackson's boats would reach Natchez. Jackson would have to ration his resources each day to determine where to house his men. From a logistical standpoint, it would take fewer resources for Jackson's infantry to quarter near an encampment that his cavalry had already established, particularly if the duration was expected to be brief in anticipation of official orders to march to Mobile. The challenge for Wilkinson would be to make Jackson conclude that the halt at Natchez was his own idea.

At daybreak on January 7, William Carroll received a copy of Jackson's order for the men to depart. Apparently, Benton was to oversee the departure, but when Benton failed to arrive, Carroll gave the order for Hall's First Regiment of Infantry of 700 soldiers to strike their tents and board boats waiting near their camp at McGavock's ferry landing. Volunteers were less than assured to see that one of the boats was already sinking. Lieutenant Pillow was ordered to do what he could to preserve it.[229]

Many young soldiers had never seen a flatboat or taken a ride on a river. To men who rarely left their farms, the boats must have resembled floating chicken coops or barns. In fact, on the march down the river two years later, someone named one of the boats "The Barn."[230] Teenager William Love, who would make his home on that boat for the next month, later described it as a "large old salt boat covered with slats like a house and steered from on our inside in wind. She went where she liked."[231] He said that the boat proved so difficult to steer that it often rammed into other boats, and the men feared her.

On the outside, most flatboats were little more than wide floating platforms about 15 feet wide and 60 feet long, with planks tied together with cable and pitched or coated with tar underneath.[232] A square box was built on top for shelter. The roof might be slanted slightly to shed rain, but it was flat enough for boatman to walk on top. Horses and cargo could be transported on the bottom portion that was not enclosed. Broad oars on either side could be raised and lowered to help guide the boat, giving it the appearance of a steer and the name "broadhorn."[233]

Some boats, at least those for the officers, were partitioned into rooms, furnished, and equipped with wood-burning fireplaces. Benton later wrote that his boat was comfortable, and that unless the room had a window, travelers often did not even realize they were moving.[234]

Mounted infantry had to persuade their horses to walk the swaying ramps. Equally apprehensive, some boys stepped off the firm surface of the Earth for the first time and the unsteady rocking of the wooden platforms under their feet added to the sense of unease. It was symbolic of the uncertainty of their lives in wartime. Boatmen who made their livings floating goods on flatboats on the Mississippi River often returned home with stories of adventure. To the more daring Volunteers, the impending sense of danger only added to the thrill.

Benton claimed that he did not receive Jackson's order to oversee the departure until the 8th. When Benton arrived at the camp to lead the march, he found that the tents had already been struck and the men had been waiting at McGavock's ferry landing since the previous day.[235] Benton finally arrived at the river midday to order the boat captains to slip the cables. Benton reported to Jackson that every man appeared happy to move, without adding his disobedience of Jackson's order as part of the reason. The winter river current picked up the boats and silently propelled the first group on their journey toward the Gulf Coast to meet the enemy.

The first day, boats in the lead traveled about 17 miles to Robertson's Landing, which, because of the bends of the river, was only about six miles west of Nashville by land. Captain Martin, who was familiar with the river, was given charge until Carroll arrived.[236]

About 1:00 p.m., the order was given for Benton's Second Regiment of 700 soldiers to depart.[237] Despite assurances that the boat contractor had given Benton and those Benton had forwarded to Jackson, several boats had not been delivered. Hundreds of men waited to board the nonexistent boats. Again, Benton's attempt to establish his leadership reputation before he left Nashville was challenged, and he faced a moment of decision. Should Benton order that the men already traveling on the river halt or should they be allowed to proceed and hope that the remainder would catch up? There had already been too much delay that had taxed the fighting spirit they had worked to achieve. Keeping troops confined to the camp any longer would only worsen their morale and risk desertions.

Benton decided that the first group would proceed by river and the second would march by land an additional 13 miles to the mouth of the Harpeth, near present-day Ashland City, Tennessee, to wait on completion of the boats.[238] Benton purchased or rented one boat that he found along the river and a captain spotted a second boat that might be secured if they could locate the owner. Both groups would meet first at Robertson's Landing before reuniting downriver to continue the voyage as one unit.

As his Second Regiment left camp, Benton not only chose to lead the march; he ignored tradition by choosing to march on foot with the soldiers rather than leading the procession on horseback.[239] Quartermaster William Lewis would later accuse Benton of sacrificing his horse for the march solely for the purpose of being *gazateered*," that is for public appearances to receive favorable newspaper articles rather than out of necessity.[240] It was said that even as a lawyer, Benton preferred political stump speeches to legal arguments on behalf of clients.[241] Benton was already living up to his acknowledged ambition.

After being confined to camp for almost a month, the men were so anxious to march that Benton had to order them to slow their speed.[242] Soldiers did not even seem to mind that they had to march an additional three miles on the south side of their camp, likely back to Nashville and down Cedar Street and the Old Chickasaw Trace, to avoid a swamp. It took them exactly two hours and six minutes to reach Robertson's Landing on foot. Contractors had been hired to provide food for the men when they arrived, but no food awaited. After marching for nine miles, the men went to sleep hungry. Food was finally delivered at 3:00 p.m. the following afternoon.[243] As an unintended training exercise, it would be the first of several days on the expedition that Volunteers would go without adequate rations.

The first evening, as the First and Second regiments met at Robertson's Landing, officers took advantage of what might be the last opportunity to parade the men together as a unit before encountering the British.[244] The next morning, the First Regiment boarded their boats for the next leg of the journey to the mouth of the Harpeth. Benton gave Captain Martin command of the flotilla and Captain Reynolds command of five companies of his Second Infantry on their march overland to the same destination. Benton's companies whose boats had not been finished waited at Robertson's until fireplace chimneys could be completed.[245] All Volunteers were to halt ahead at the mouth of the Harpeth and wait until Jackson arrived to lead the voyage downriver.[246]

Jackson had planned for all infantry to remain together during the southern voyage. But because the boats were delayed, once the first soldiers departed from the mouth of the Harpeth, some of Benton's Second Regiment would not see Hall's First Regiment for almost a month. When Jackson learned that boats were not ready for the advance and that troops were already scattered before all had even departed Nashville, Benton heard rumors that he would face a court-martial. Nevertheless, even though Jackson had put Benton in charge of the lead boats, rather than remain with the men in the lead or proceed on to the mouth of the Harpeth to speed delivery of boats, he returned to Nashville to make his excuses to Jackson and to take part in the anticipated officers' public departure ceremony.[247]

Jackson still waited at headquarters in Nashville, holding out hope until the last minute for the arrival of the muskets he would need to make his Volunteers a fighting force. The General retired at 1:00 a.m. on January 8. With his candle almost out, he took time to write a final letter to his wife Rachel before departing. She had sent him a locket with a miniature of her image. He promised to wear it over his heart. Then his mind quickly returned to his mission:

> "Let us not repine, his [God's] will be done, our country calls, its rights are invaded, the innocent babe, and helpless mother, massacred by the ruthless savages, excited to these horrid deeds, by the infernal engines of British policy, and British depravity recollect then, that the god of Battle cries aloud for vengeance, we are the means in the hands to punish the impious Britains, for their sacraligious Deeds, we trust in the righteousness of our cause, and the god of Battle and of Justice will protect us."[248]

Jackson was sure of his mission and confident in his own abilities to lead. His historic victory over the British would occur exactly three years from the date of that late-night letter to Rachel. In the interim, Jackson would face obstacles that would nearly destroy him, but victories over those obstacles would toughen him to a man who had reason to be confident.

On the Cumberland Road east of Nashville, Lt. Colonel Bradley located the teamsters who were slowly driving teams of wagons loaded with the firearms that Jackson had requisitioned. Bradley relied upon the broad interpretation of his order to "escort" the wagons to resort to the threat of using his saber against the drivers to increase their speed. Jackson later discovered the reason for the delay. Though the government kept its commitment to deliver the arms, it had contracted to pay the wagon drivers by the day rather than by the mile. The drivers had no incentive to travel more than five or six miles per day rather than the 20 daily miles or so most wagons traveled.[249]

Hall's First Regiment of Infantry on flatboats made an overnight landing on the north side of the Cumberland River.[250] Snow continued in the cold. The next morning, they set out for the mouth of the Harpeth where they would wait for General Jackson's arrival.

A few companies still had not been paid. Jackson would have no choice but to leave them behind in Nashville until funds arrived, unless he could think of creative alternatives. Blount, Jackson, and several prominent Nashville citizens turned to directors of the Nashville Bank to lend the state money to advance the pay.[251] By January 9, bank directors had made new preparations to pay the cavalry. With no reason left to delay, Jackson urged Coffee to proceed as soon as possible, "The threatened invasion of the Lower Country as I am advised by Col. Jno. Bullock, makes it necessary that we should be in motion."[252]

Jackson worked through the evening on January 9 until the early morning hours the following day, making plans for departure.[253] He would lead the march with little sleep.

About noon on Sunday, January 10, large numbers of spectators assembled at Jackson's headquarters to witness the departure ceremony that everyone had anticipated for a month. Inside, Jackson prepared to perform his public role as general for his supporters in Nashville. Jackson had followed George Washington's example in establishing a small group of his best and most-trusted troops as his Company of Guards. Also known as "Lifeguards," the soldier's job was to protect the General's life but also to give him an aura of command by being surrounded and followed by elite troops. Washington's soldiers had even worn special uniforms to distinguish their honored service, and Jackson's guards may have followed their example. Signaling to the crowd that the ceremony was ready to begin, Company of Guards Commander Lieutenant Deaderick, dressed in full uniform, made a formal entry to headquarters to receive their general.

Governor Blount, the Tennessee Secretary of State, and Tennessee's Superior Court Judges arrived to symbolize the support of Tennessee's political leadership. Robert Searcy recorded that the mood was solemn, mixed with respect for the occasion and the sorrow of separation from family members.[254]

After allowing anticipation to build, Jackson appeared from his headquarters. He acknowledged the soldiers and then began leading the procession. Field officers, state officials, and Reverend Blackman followed him to the Cumberland River. Flying flags and fife-and-drum music added to the pageantry. The crowd was not disappointed, and they followed the procession to the river to give Tennessee's sons a proper send-off.

Rather than boarding a boat near one of the two wharfs near the Public Square, Jackson chose to march on foot two miles north to McGavock's ferry landing where his headquarters boat *Phereby* waited on the river.[255] Unlike Benton, Jackson was not accused of grandstanding by walking. The martial ceremony was one the public would not forget as they waited for Volunteers to return home.[256]

The procession moved past the public burying ground at the French Lick stream that had first attracted buffalo and other animals to create a trail that became the Natchez Trace. Jackson would have been aware that the cemetery contained the graves of his predecessors who had commanded the defense of their homes. Moving on through the area where the Shawnee Indians had lived when they controlled the same land, the parade crossed the stone bridge near the landing on the riverbank. Dignitaries waited as provisions were loaded onto the boat. The drummer signaled the departure with taps of the drum. Someone shouted "*huzzah!*" The crowd followed with three additional shouts, "*hip, hip, huzzah!*" A cannon fired, and Jackson descended to the boat.[257]

As cables holding the *Phereby* were slipped and Jackson's boat began to move from shore, small arms fired up to 17 rounds to mark Jackson's departure. The cannon repeated its fire, and each time, the crowd matched the boom with three additional "*hip, hip, huzzah's.*" The cannon fire, shots, and shouts echoed from the rock cliffs on the east bank and reverberated downriver, amplifying the sounds and announcing to anyone ahead that General Andrew Jackson was on the march.[258]

The grand ceremony was a welcome relief from the gloom of what had become routine news of military failures by the U.S. Army near Canada. To those overlooking the Cumberland River at that moment, Andrew Jackson personified Tennessee, and he took with him the aspirations of the young state. Onlookers optimistically assessed that when their Volunteers had defeated the British, Tennessee would take its place among other states as respected partners in the American experiment, and its leaders, including Jackson, would grow in influence and respect.

Four flags were raised as Jackson's boat cast off. Citizens watched the boat slowly disappear into the icy winter landscape. It was just after 3:00 p.m.[259] The winter sun had already begun to sink, and its low rays shimmered off ice floating in the river. Over the northern horizon, large, quick-moving ice floes would make the river journey as potentially treacherous as the land route the cavalry would follow down the Natchez Trace.

The departure ceremony may have given the public visions of soaring military power through spectacle, but field officers and staff remaining on the riverbank were grounded with logistical problems. Benton's failure to assure that the remaining boats had been completed left several of Jackson's officers stranded on land. Some officers banded together to impress unoccupied public boats. Even though none of the officers had experience with navigation, a few took their chances in the short trip to Robertson's Landing. Others preferred to walk the six miles to the rendezvous site at the landing.[260] There, they hoped to find the finished boats and experienced captains waiting.

Later in the evening, Carroll, Benton, and the newly commissioned U.S. Colonel William P. Anderson found an unoccupied boat to commandeer to follow Jackson and the infantry down the Cumberland River. No one onboard knew how to navigate. Anderson, who had the highest rank, stood at the helm as captain. Benton recorded that the skittish land commanders frequently and jokingly repeated a phrase from one of Caesar's battles when he traveled on a boat in a storm, "*Quid times,*" or "why fear when Caesar is here?" The "captain" finally decided they would do just as well to allow the boat to float wherever the river current carried them, and everyone went inside to take some shelter from the cold. They would risk the consequences.[261]

As Jackson had led the formal procession of the remaining infantry through Nashville, the trumpet sounded at Camp Good Exchange, and the remaining cavalry began their own march southwestward out of Nashville.[262] Nashville citizens, whose attachment to the colonies had lagged, sensed a nationalistic pride. The soldiers felt that pride and good wishes go with them. Optimism ran high as the cavalry began their march. Now inspired by a month of patriotic speeches reflecting on their assuming the mantel of the heroes of the Revolution, Volunteers could imagine a grander ceremony as Nashville townspeople welcomed them home from victories over their old enemy Britain.

CHAPTER FIVE

AGENT 13

"[A] man [is] as much disgraced by serving under Genl Wilkinson as by marrying a prostitute"

—Winfield Scott

A ndrew Jackson may never have served well as anyone's subordinate, but General James Wilkinson incited Jackson's insubordination. Wilkinson embodied everything that Jackson detested about professional military leadership and government politics of the time. Under either system, a common man like Jackson had little opportunity to rise to the highest command.

Early-American military and political leaders were generally appointed to high rank based upon family or social status rather than merit, like the British aristocracy that colonists had thrown off in the rebellion. It was generally understood that Wilkinson's appointment had come from social connections and political feats rather than his battlefield triumphs.

Physically, Wilkinson was described as being "heavy" and "squat."[263] Though Wilkinson compensated for his lack of a warrior appearance by wearing self-designed, outlandish military uniforms, decorated with wide sashes and gold spurs, and by riding on a leopard skin saddle with leopard claws attached, the French minister Tureau repeated the common perception that Wilkinson's "military capacity is small."[264] Jackson considered such ineffectual military leaders to be products of a corrupted system rather than the meritocratic republic the founders intended.

For Jackson, Wilkinson might as well have been British. In fact, Wilkinson boasted about his British ancestry.[265] And like the British, Wilkinson represented an enemy who stood between Jackson and the military success and recognition that he craved.

Jackson openly referred to Wilkinson, the highest-ranking commander of the United States Army in a time of war, as the "publick villain."[266] Military historian Robert Leckie identified Wilkinson more benignly as a "general who never won a battle and never lost a court-martial." British enemy commanders assessed that Wilkinson, "is reported to be a man of much expence and considerably in debt. His principles are not considered very firm and he has been treated very harshly by the American government."[267] A brash, young Winfield Scott described him as an "unprincipled imbecile,"[268] one "who merely wants a splendid uniform to satisfy his peacock vanity."[269] Most significantly, to the United States' enemy Spain, Wilkinson was known on its payroll as its spy, "Agent 13."[270]

The best evidence of Wilkinson's unrivaled powers of duplicity is that no one confirmed Wilkinson's treason until decades after his death when records from the Spanish archives in Havana became public.[271] Convinced of Wilkinson's guilt, however, Jackson devoted endless hours trying to expose the top U.S. general as a spy.

Wilkinson's and Jackson's personalities had more in common than Jackson preferred to admit. Wilkinson was ambitious, and, like Jackson, federal politicians assessed that, "General Wilkinson would act as lieutenant to no man in existence."[272] Like many men of the period, both Jackson and Wilkinson had been taught from an early age to defend their reputations at all costs. Wilkinson, who had also lost his father at a young age, remembered that his father's last words to him were, "My son, if you ever put up with an insult, I will disinherit you."[273] Similarly,

Jackson recalled last words from his mother as, "for slander . . . Settle them cases yourself."[274]

Though like Jackson, the untimely death of Wilkinson's father also left his family financially strapped, Wilkinson grew up among the Maryland gentry, and he easily learned the social manners and developed connections that would make his path to military command easier than Jackson's struggle as an orphan on the frontier.[275] Wilkinson shared with Jackson the desire to prove himself both in business and as a military commander.

The Revolutionary War provided him that opportunity. Wilkinson was six years older than Jackson when he began military service. But where Jackson worked to gain the support of the common militia soldiers as well as officers to be elected to militia leadership, Wilkinson used his connections from Maryland to build the support of a small group of the elite commanders in what he considered the more prestigious Continental Army.[276] Using his connections among men with far greater military influence, Wilkinson secured an appointment as a United States general at age 20, though he had never led a military campaign.

Men who thought military rank should be earned saw Wilkinson as a social climber. Those who knew the details of his rise would have an even harsher assessment. During the Revolutionary War, Wilkinson served briefly as an aide to the traitor Benedict Arnold, and despite his apparent involvement in a conspiracy among army officers to remove General George Washington from command, Wilkinson used his affability and extraordinary powers of persuasion to retain Washington's support. Washington was not completely fooled. He supported a promotion for Wilkinson only because it would "feed his ambition," "soothe his vanity," and keep him involved with the army.[277] At the same time, Washington tasked army officer Andrew Ellicott as his own spy to keep an eye on Wilkinson to attempt to obtain evidence of Wilkinson's corruption.[278] Rumors of Wilkinson's duplicity also reached John

Adams when he served as president, but no one was able to present actionable proof.[279]

Wilkinson soon married a wealthy widow in the influential Prevost family, whose money and social standing would be needed to expand a poor young man's influence. Jackson also married into a prominent family in Nashville; Rachel Donelson's father had been one of the founders of the town. However, frontier social standing meant little to Eastern Seaboard society, where social position within that small group was considered an important qualification for leadership at the highest levels.

When social standing did not provide the business success Wilkinson needed to sustain an aristocrat's lifestyle, Wilkinson briefly accepted an appointment as clothier for the army. Wilkinson did not succeed in endeavors that did not feed his need for social affirmation, and like Jackson's store operation, Wilkinson's time as a clothier was a failure. But Wilkinson's work as an army supplier gave him the opportunity to learn the intricacies and the weaknesses of the procurement system for military supplies. That knowledge of the military bureaucracy would give Wilkinson a tool to use against his enemies.

Wilkinson supported the supremacy of the standing army over the militia, a system that played to his political skills. Professional soldiers could be better trained and more capable of providing a defense on short notice, and those selected for highest rank could be vetted by men with command experience. At least, that is how the limited army was designed to operate. It would be some time before the nation had the resources to provide the training, equipment, and soldiers to achieve that goal. In the interim, as militia commanders like Jackson would realize, militia units often were better equipped, and their commanders may have had just as much experience as professional soldiers. Despite beliefs among many that a militia system was superior to a professional army because it harnessed a spectrum of citizen soldiers who often served of their own free will, weaknesses of that system in the Revolution convinced Congress that the country needed both.[280]

After the Revolution when land speculation became one of the few ways for Americans willing to take risk to create wealth, Wilkinson saw financial opportunity on the western frontier in Kentucky. In addition to acquiring land, Wilkinson opened a store in Lexington, where he supplied goods to settlers in Nashville and began to develop a personal relationship with its leaders.[281] Like Jackson, Wilkinson's farm operations were threatened by the Spanish governor's closing of access to the Mississippi River ports at New Orleans. But unlike Jackson, Wilkinson not only added his name to the lists of farmers willing to pledge loyalty to the King of Spain; Wilkinson took a flotilla of boats loaded with Kentucky products south on the river to New Orleans and audaciously sought an audience with the Spanish governor. For political purposes in Kentucky, Wilkinson railed publicly against Spain's closing of the ports, but privately, Wilkinson encouraged Spain to deny shipping rights on the Mississippi River to U.S. citizens to force settlers west of the Appalachians to seek their support from Spain.[282] He assured the Spanish governor that politicians in Kentucky would follow his lead and agree to secede from the Union and serve under the Spanish crown. All Wilkinson wanted in exchange for his support for rebellion was the ability to ship goods from the Ohio River Valley to Natchez and New Orleans ports. Of course, as the only authorized shipper, Wilkinson could set higher prices for his own goods and obtain a percentage of all other goods shipped. The Spanish governor accepted the proposal on a trial basis, contingent upon Wilkinson paying him a percentage off the top.[283]

Wilkinson confessed to the Spanish Governor, "When a distinguished person intends to expatriate himself, he should weigh carefully the obligations between himself and his country. The policies of the United States having made my own happiness impossible, I am resolved to seek it in Spain. I love my reputation infinitely more than life. I hope it may never be said of me that in changing my allegiance from the United States to His Catholic Majesty, I have broken any laws of nature or nations, nor of honor and conscience."[284]

Wilkinson returned to Kentucky and promoted a Spanish Kentucky Association to encourage settlers to join their state to the Spanish. Rumors spread throughout Tennessee that the Kentucky Spanish Association even went so far as to encourage Indians friendly to the Spanish to attack Nashville.[285] When agents of the movement attempted to recruit followers in Tennessee, those rumors, whether true or not, prevented the agents from finding a receptive audience.[286] Farmers understood Wilkinson's connection to Spain when they were asked to pay Wilkinson's boatmen high prices to ship goods that few others were permitted to ship. Connections between Wilkinson and Indian attacks convinced Tennesseans that Wilkinson was not to be trusted.

Jackson would never mention his own rash act of signing the roll at Natchez to pledge loyalty to the Spanish crown when accusing Wilkinson of treason. Jackson no doubt rationalized that Wilkinson's direct payments from the Spanish were far worse than the exercise of his natural right as an American in transporting his goods to Mississippi River ports. If Wilkinson's Spanish employers ever made their spy aware of Jackson's name on their enrollment list, he too must have concluded that Jackson's true weakness was acting on impulse.

Wilkinson's spying operation began on a limited basis until it became clear that Wilkinson would be unable to persuade fellow Kentuckians or Tennesseans to cast their fortunes with Spain. When his business ventures failed, it seemed that he would be of no further use to the king. Creditors stepped up pressure, and Wilkinson desperately needed money to avert financial ruin.[287]

Just in time, Wilkinson proved far more valuable to Spain in military intelligence, and his treason went beyond mercenary. In 1790, Wilkinson was informed of President Washington's plan to send U.S. Army

Major John Doughty and a small detachment south to Muscle Shoals to negotiate with the Southeastern Indian tribes.[288] Based upon a warning from Secretary Knox that Indian tribes in the South were likely to band together to make war against the United States unless Indians learned to assimilate into the settlers' culture, President Washington hoped to encourage Indians to develop agriculture and trades.[289] Unstated, reducing Indians' reliance on hunting would also open Indian land for white settlement. The "Great Father" would even provide a cotton gin and supply farm tools. Washington also wanted to build a military installation at the mouth of Bear Creek on the Tennessee River. More threatening to Spanish power on the Gulf Coast, one historian believed that President Washington also wanted to build a federal road from Kentucky to New Orleans to circumvent Spain's control over the Mississippi River.

Wilkinson's main work for Spain was to provide intelligence and advice on how to prevent the United States from extending its territory westward into Spanish territory. A strong United States military presence on the Tennessee River would undermine Spain's influence among Indian nations, as well as on his own ability to extract money from Spain. Wilkinson rushed information about Major Doughty's mission to the Spanish with the suggestion that the Spanish Governor use proxy Indian warriors to destroy the mission "in the bud" and that Doughty's party be "cut off."[290]

When Doughty's troops arrived at Muscle Shoals, Spain's Shawnee, Chickamauga, and Creek Indian proxies surprised them with bullets and tomahawks. Out of 15 U.S. soldiers on the mission, five were killed, and six were injured.[291] Wilkinson's espionage, resulting in the death of U.S. soldiers under his command, would not be known by anyone but the Spanish until after his death. When Wilkinson heard the rumor that Doughty was one of the fallen, he wrote Spanish Governor Miro, "I have long known and esteemed him, and therefore sincerely regret his fall. Let us waive the painful subject," before quickly moving on to business as to how he could "advance his Majesty's interest and glory."[292]

Wilkinson received the opportunity to renew a military command in a reorganized "New" U.S. Army. Wilkinson assumed that he would be appointed first-in-command as its major general. Those who had spotted defects in Wilkinson's character and noted the irregularity in Wilkinson's accounts during his time as clothier objected, and General Anthony Wayne was given the appointment. Wilkinson was relegated to second-in-command as brigadier general, a position his ambitions would not permit.[293] Wilkinson first attempted to outmaneuver Wayne politically using passage of legislation in Congress to battle for the position that a brigadier general rather than a major general would lead the command of U.S. troops.[294] That fight would provide Wilkinson other lessons he would use against Jackson.

Jackson could have learned much about how Wilkinson worked to destroy a rival, and perhaps in the small world of American leaders at the time, he did. As Wilkinson plotted to have his rival general Wayne removed from command, Wilkinson carefully wrote letters that if later used as evidence in a tribunal, made him appear to be polite, professional, and even anxious to be of assistance. But behind the scenes, Wilkinson undermined Wayne at every turn.

In 1794, as General Wayne was attempting to set up a massive army outpost at Fort Greenville, far from the logistical support of the settled areas, he found the War Department and its army contractors unusually slow to provide pay and supplies to his men.[295] Wayne could have assumed that the delays were the result of routine inefficiencies. But after Wilkinson sent an anonymous article to a newspaper accusing Wayne of being an incompetent drunkard, Wayne's allies realized that Wilkinson was behind the delay.[296] Wilkinson secretly admitted to his Spanish paymasters that he worked to disgrace Wayne to obtain his command.[297]

The lack of resources for Wayne to move his soldiers forward forced the regiment to remain camped in close quarters. Wilkinson, who originally trained to become a physician, observed that the containment of soldiers in close spaces resulted in the spread of influenza and other communicable diseases "beyond anything" he had ever seen.[298] Disease and a breakdown of morale from a lack of pay, food, and supplies also resulted in a degrading of discipline and division of troops that made Wayne appear unable to command.

As Wilkinson stepped up his political campaign against his rival general, Wayne retaliated. He launched an investigation with suspicions that Wilkinson was a spy for Britain and pronounced Wilkinson a "vile assassin" to the Secretary of War.[299] Wayne intentionally removed Wilkinson's command responsibilities with the hope that Wilkinson would resign his commission in search of success elsewhere.[300] Wayne also learned that Robert Newman, who served as courier for Wilkinson's payments from Spain, had been caught and claimed that Wilkinson was under Spanish pay, but more spectacularly that Wilkinson intended to separate territory from the United States.[301] That allegation seemed too outlandish for anyone to believe. Wilkinson produced his associate Phillip Nolan to contradict Newman, and a simple character witness proved to be all that was needed to end the charges.

However, in reviewing the evidence, Wayne told Secretary of War Henry Knox that there was something about Wilkinson that was not what it seemed, using a phrase from Shakespeare's *Hamlet*: "There is something rotten in the State of Denmark."[302] Jackson must have heard the report, because the phrase was used as a running joke among Jackson and his friends whenever they suspected Wilkinson of being involved with an unexplained action from Washington City.

After surviving the crash of a large tree on his general's tent that a few have suspected to have been an assassination attempt, Wayne began to suffer extreme inflammation of his joints and excruciating abdominal pains that were diagnosed as stomach ulcers. He died suddenly at the age of 51. Wilkinson wrote to President Adams to shed crocodile tears that, "The Death of General Wayne silenced an Investigation... Prosecution is in the grave with General Wayne."[303] Wilkinson did not deny that he wanted to "injure General Wayne"[304] by attacking his reputation, but he claimed to suffer a greater loss that Wayne's death cheated him of the opportunity to prove his innocence of Wayne's charges. Wilkinson's offense-tactic bluff paid off. Wilkinson was promoted to Wayne's vacant command.

The position as commander of U.S. forces also provided Wilkinson the opportunity to make a more valuable offer to the Spanish governor in exchange for payment—his inside knowledge of American military intelligence. Wilkinson's offer was quickly accepted, and Wilkinson officially was entered the Spanish payroll as "Agent 13."[305]

Wilkinson's efforts to destroy the Lewis and Clark Expedition were less successful. With information that Wilkinson obtained from President Jefferson and passed on to the Spanish in his "Reflections" memorandum on how Spain could thwart U.S. attempts to expand westward, Spanish soldiers were able to track the explorers to within 60 miles, but they never came close enough to capture or kill them.[306] It is unknown whether one of Wilkinson's associates was the source of an article in the Nashville newspaper that prematurely reported that Indians had defeated Lewis and Clark and killed all but one member of their Corps of Discovery.[307]

Though Wilkinson hid his treason and his role in the death of American soldiers, rumors followed him. Future decorated general Winfield Scott would later be court-martialed at Cantonment Washington near Natchez for declaring that the only two traitors he ever saw were the liar General Wilkinson and Aaron Burr. He also stated that if he were called to serve in battle under General Wilkinson, he would sleep with two pistols—one for the enemy and one for Wilkinson. More colorfully, Scott was accused but acquitted of referring to the rumors of Wilkinson's spying in allowing that "he considered a man as much disgraced by serving under Genl Wilkinson as by marrying a prostitute or in words to that effect."[308]

Like much of the establishment that Jackson detested, Wilkinson was seen to be protecting his own selfish interests at the expense of the people he served. The line between self-promotion and public sacrifice was a blurry and subjective one that Jackson also later would be accused of crossing.

General Wilkinson attracted Jackson's fire as early as 1803 when Wilkinson court-martialed Jackson's friend Colonel Thomas S. Butler and refused to honor Jackson's request to dismiss the matter. When President Jefferson placed Wilkinson in charge of surveying and building the Natchez Trace military highway, Butler was selected as Wilkinson's second-in-command with direct responsibility for construction.[309] Jackson's silent land partner John Overton encouraged Butler to extend the highway from the northern 1801 Chickasaw boundary through Franklin, Tennessee to Nashville. Indirectly, Overton admitted that building the extension would aid speculators such as Overton and Jackson who owned land in the area.

At first Butler declined, because the federal government was thought to have authority to build the road only in the Indian nations, and Butler's orders specified that construction would end at the northern boundary.[310] The order was modified to allow the road to be cut to Nashville on the most-direct route, which was about five miles west of the town of Franklin. After lobbying, likely by Overton and Jackson, the War Department agreed to build the road through Franklin if the local governments would maintain it. Cash-strapped local governments refused; however, Butler's soldiers busy cutting the road west of Franklin stopped their work and began making highway improvements on the old Natchez Trace Indian trail through Franklin to Nashville. No order authorizing the move has ever been found.[311] Butler would later call on Jackson to repay the favor.

Butler was a hero of the American Revolution. He and his four brothers were dubbed the "Fighting Butlers," to whom General George

Washington offered a special toast at a post-war victory party.[312] The Butlers were among a small band of soldiers who remained with Washington at Valley Forge when many others were ready to surrender. President Washington rewarded Butler's service by giving him command of Fort Southwest Point in East Tennessee with the mission of protecting settlers from attack by the Indian nations.

Beginning in 1801, Butler marshaled soldiers from Southwest Point and Wilkinsonville on the Ohio River to begin the survey and construction of the Natchez Trace military road. But soon after Butler's soldiers improved the road to Franklin, Butler was transferred to command Fort Adams south of Natchez, closer to Wilkinson's New Orleans headquarters where Wilkinson could keep a closer watch on his second-in-command. Fort Adams was about 600 miles from Butler's wife and young children near Nashville. Butler attempted to resign and waited a year to travel south while he appealed to friends for help.[313]

What finally undid Butler seemed to begin as a trivial matter. Like some of his compatriots of the Revolution, Butler wore his hair shoulder-length and tied at the back of his head with an eel skin in a queue or "pony tail." Those military men, primarily Federalists who opposed Jefferson, prized their queues as a Samson-like symbol of strength. Wilkinson determined from his medical training that queues offered a breeding ground for lice, and he and Jefferson were aware that short-cropped hair in the Roman fashion was the rage among military men in Europe. Either out of a sincere effort to protect the soldiers' health or less nobly, to make his mark on the army's appearance to impress Jefferson, almost immediately after Jefferson became president, Wilkinson ordered that all army soldiers cut their queues.[314]

Butler had little respect for Wilkinson, and he flatly refused to cut his hair. Butler argued that a man's right to wear his hair as he chose was a natural right that citizens had not relinquished to the government to control, picking up on Jefferson's natural rights arguments in the

Declaration of Independence and his own service in enforcing those rights at considerable sacrifice in the Revolution.[315] Butler was not alone in his reaction. Some officers' refusals to comply with the order were so acerbic that they were almost considered to be in mutiny.[316]

At first, Wilkinson seemed to make an exception for Butler as a hero of the Revolution. Later, Wilkinson came to believe that Butler's pony-tail was a symbol of defiance. Wilkinson withdrew his mercy, approved Butler's arrest, and ordered the soldier to appear at a court-martial in Maryland.[317]

In fighting back against Wilkinson, Butler raised an issue that would be of interest to Jackson: Was an officer in the U.S. Army required to follow a patently illegal order? Butler said no. James Robertson and other Nashville pioneer leaders whom Jackson admired had disobeyed orders from the federal government when they determined it to be in the best interest of their settlement to do so. Frontier leaders saw the power of the state governments being equal to or sometimes greater than the rights citizens and states had granted to the federal government, and they were forced to deal with the realities of making decisions regarding the defense of their settlements without the ability to obtain immediate communications from a central command.

But Butler's refusal was a test of the limits of obedience due within the army chain of command.[318] Relying upon historical precedent from other officers who had refused to obey illegal orders, Butler replied that there was no need to appear at his court-martial, because he would state flatly that he would not cut his hair.[319]

Butler appealed to Jackson to ask his friends in Washington City to intervene. Jackson rarely refused an offer to help a friend, and Jackson did not hesitate to make Butler's enemy his own. Rather than stoop to dealing directly with Wilkinson, Jackson took up Butler's case directly with President Jefferson beginning in August 1803.[320] Jackson did not name Wilkinson but suggested that Wilkinson's order was issued outside the normal course of procedure and that its effect might be to discourage state militias, such as Jackson's, from offering to serve if called. Jackson's position over the militia at the edge of the western frontier and the nation's first line of defense in the Southwest should have been his leverage to override Wilkinson's order.

Despite Jackson's intervention, in November 1803, the court-martial ordered that Butler be officially reprimanded.[321] Jackson was furious. Jefferson attempted to resolve the dispute between generals diplomatically by assuring Jackson that Butler had been called to account because he had refused to appear for duty at Fort Adams rather than for refusing to cut his hair. Butler would not be punished for failure to report at Fort Adams, and it appeared at first that no additional action would be taken on the hair-cutting order. Jackson seemed to have won.[322]

Wilkinson may have been given information to conclude that Butler flaunted his queue in an open act of rebellion.[323] A year after the first court-martial, Wilkinson wrote Butler to consider himself under arrest for refusal to obey the order to cut his queue, despite Jefferson's assurance to Jackson that Butler had not been tried for the haircutting order.[324] Jackson realized that Jefferson had misrepresented the court's decision to him. Butler was ordered to report to New Orleans for another court-martial. Wilkinson stepped up his attack by adding the personal insult that if Butler agreed to continue to serve in the army, he hoped that he left his "tail" behind.[325]

For Jackson, the fight was not just a matter of what was best for the country or a veteran of the Revolution. Wilkinson had not honored a fellow general's intervention in the matter. Jackson attacked Wilkinson's "base and vindictive mind" in a letter to Butler.[326] Jackson also interpreted the second order for Butler's arrest as an attack of his own judgment, and he expressed his anger in a letter to Jefferson to protest Wilkinson's persecution of Butler.

More ominously for the future, Jackson protested a second Wilkinson order that any army officer who objected to Wilkinson's actions first must obtain Wilkinson's approval to send those objections on to his superiors at the War Department. Jackson argued that Wilkinson was attempting to shield himself from criticism.[327] Jackson considered Wilkinson's actions as the "buds of oppression" and saw an opening to punish Wilkinson by appealing directly to the commander-in-chief. He argued that the Tennessee militia might be called into the field and they would need to know whether they had a general they could support.[328] Jackson prepared a draft of the letter, but it is not known whether Jackson mailed it to Jefferson.[329] If Jefferson received the letter, he did not honor it with a reply. Nevertheless, in formulating his argument to aid Butler, Jackson had decided to push the argument that his command over Tennessee troops was independent of the command structure of the standing army. To Jackson, Wilkinson's attempt to limit the right to criticize an army general set a dangerous precedent that could give room for a military man to act as a local dictator without proper supervision from civil authority. That misstep might give Jackson a second opening to have Wilkinson removed.

Wilkinson continued to give Jackson's objections no consideration in demanding that Butler travel to New Orleans to appear for a court-martial to answer for his disobedience. Butler pleaded that yellow fever was rampant in New Orleans and that he would unnecessarily expose himself to the disease.[330] But receiving no support from his friends in the military command, despite Jackson's assistance, by late December 1804, Butler finally relented and traveled to New Orleans to face Wilkinson's tribunal.

Jackson saw no point in appealing directly to the Secretary of War Henry Dearborn. Many commanders called Dearborn an "old granny," but Jackson would later suggest that even an old granny had more courage than Dearborn, and he did not expect Dearborn to stand up to Wilkinson.[331] Both Dearborn and Wilkinson would have to be circumvented.

Even though the founders had created a republic, Jackson knew that ultimately the representatives in power had to answer to the citizens. Jackson appealed directly to the people to pressure their representatives. He obtained the signatures of 75 citizens to protest Wilkinson's actions directly to the president and to the Senate.[332] In his citizen's protest, Jackson branded Wilkinson a despot and suggested that the militia would worry whether such abuses of power would shackle them with similar "humiliating conditions."[333] Jackson further informed the president that Wilkinson had suggested that Jefferson approved the haircut order.[334] Jackson, maybe tongue-in-cheek, was certain that Jefferson would not approve such a serious change in military code based solely upon a fashionable European hairstyle.[335]

It was a jab at Jefferson. Jackson knew that the common folk thought Jefferson gave more attention to European fashion than to military defense. Jefferson apparently ignored the letter, however, and Jackson's intrusion into the matter of military discipline and the personal criticism of the president did nothing to earn Jefferson's confidence.

Butler was far from home awaiting Wilkinson's court-martial in New Orleans when he received news that his wife had died in Tennessee.[336] Though one of Butler's sons lived in New Orleans, the Revolutionary War hero languished far from home and far removed from the direct support of family and friends. Because none of his old friends in Washington City would come to his aid or even reply to his letters, Jackson was the only influential man Butler could turn to, and the colonel poured out his personal feelings to Jackson. Jackson's anger against Wilkinson kindled with each letter, and eventually it spilled over to the War Department and even to the president who refused to assure that the system treated Butler fairly.

When the time for Butler's trial arrived, Butler said it was clear that Wilkinson had appointed judges predisposed to render the verdict Wilkinson wanted.[337] Butler had not even been furnished with a copy of the charges against him at the time he was ordered under arrest. Making matters worse, as Butler had been warned, yellow fever raged in New Orleans, and the tribunal rushed through Butler's hearing to leave town. One judge even heard testimony from his sick bed to give Wilkinson a verdict. Butler claimed that Wilkinson had "tortured" the language of a letter he had sent the general to claim that he had made insubordinate threats. Wilkinson also broke protocol by intervening in the supposedly neutral proceeding by sending a letter to the judge not only offering evidence outside the proceeding that Jefferson had approved his order that soldiers cut their queues, but that Jefferson himself had set the standard by cutting his own queue.[338] Jackson protested to the president that the only explanation for such unjust treatment of a hero of the Revolution must be that Jefferson did not know about Wilkinson's actions.[339]

But Jackson knew that he did. Jackson suspected that Wilkinson had some power over the decision makers in the federal city.

And he did. Jefferson knew of the rumors of Wilkinson's espionage that dated back to Washington's administration.[340] However, the president feared that Wilkinson had so much control over Federalist officers in the army that he could use those officers to organize a coup. Just as Jefferson preferred to avoid confrontation with foreign adversaries, he chose diplomacy over confrontation with Wilkinson and attempted to control him through rewards. Jackson seemed to suspect as much, and he considered it weakness.

Shortly after receiving the verdict of the court-martial and suffering the humiliation of his conviction and sentence, Butler died suddenly. However, the veteran's campaign was not finished. Washington Irving wrote, maybe exaggerated in satire, that Butler left instructions that a hole be cut in the bottom of his coffin to allow his queue to dangle in full public view as it was carried to his grave.[341] If true, that final assertion of natural rights would show the public the character of the soldiers who threw off British rule. They would not surrender their unalienable rights to King George or to a dictator like General Wilkinson.

Even if Jackson was unsure whether the fight with Wilkinson had hastened Butler's death, the fight created a crevice that quickly deepened into a canyon. Proving their genuine friendship with Butler, Andrew and Rachel took Butler's young orphaned children into their home to raise.[342] The children served as constant reminders of Wilkinson's disregard for the welfare of the men he commanded.

Jackson's backwoods survival schooling would have turned pain into a lesson. From observing how Wilkinson had crushed his rival second-in-command, Jackson would have noted that he would have to be careful never to find himself in Butler's vulnerable position under Wilkinson's control, far from his supporters at home and detached from his friends in Congress.

CHAPTER SIX

THE BURR CONSPIRACY

"[Burr is] *as far from a fool as I ever saw, and yet as easily fooled as any man I ever knew.*"

—Andrew Jackson, June 17, 1812

As Jackson worked to rescue Colonel Butler by destroying Wilkinson's command, Wilkinson began fighting back in ways Jackson did not yet appreciate. In May 1805, Vice President Aaron Burr arrived in Nashville and pulled Jackson into a scheme that he would regret the rest of his life.

Aaron Burr had almost been elected president in 1804, having received the same number of electoral votes as Thomas Jefferson. Under the relatively new and untested Constitution, early political leaders, both Federalists and Republicans, did not trust the other party to respect the outcome of elections for a peaceful transfer of power. Both sides thought the future of the country hung in the balance with each election. Burr, whom a relative commented was "somewhat overstocked" with ambition, devised a plan to give Jefferson and himself the highest number of votes and then to garner support of the opposition Federalists to snatch victory from Jefferson. It was only through a deal struck in the House of Representatives that Jefferson was declared the winner and that Burr had to settle for the vice-presidency.[343]

The vice-presidency did not satisfy Burr's political ambitions. He grew restless without real power, particularly after Jefferson marginalized him, and he chose to make a run for Governor of New York. When Burr heard that his longtime rival Alexander Hamilton was said to have made defamatory statements about him during the campaign, the two dueled. Dueling was often more about proving a point and testing the courage of an opponent, and Hamilton apparently threw away his first shot, firing at a tree instead of Burr. Hamilton might have expected the same courtesy. Instead, Burr's return shot fatally struck Hamilton directly in the abdomen. Burr claimed that he intended to throw away his shot but that he stumbled, and the pistol misdirected. The public in the East accepted no excuses and turned on Burr. When Burr was indicted for murder in New York, he continued serving as Vice President of the United States and simply avoided traveling home to New York.

When it became clear that Burr had lost all hope of political success in the East, he directed his ambition to the southwest frontier where his political views remained popular.

Burr's ultimate objective continues to be debated. Opponents argued that his elaborate plan included raising a militia, starting a slave rebellion as a diversion, robbing the Bank of New Orleans, and using the money to fund an invasion of Mexico. If successful, Burr would install himself as emperor of Mexico and build on the western settlers' frustrations with the federal government to pull the Mississippi Territory, Tennessee, and maybe Kentucky into his new nation.[344] Eventually, states along the Eastern Seaboard could be expected to abandon their new federal constitution and submit to Burr's western government seated near New Orleans and near the mouth of the Mississippi River that was thought to control the future of commerce and transportation on the North American continent.

Others suggested that Burr's planned Mexican invasion was merely a diversionary tactic and that Burr ultimately intended to attack Washington

City, disband Congress, and assassinate Jefferson. In uncertain times, more people preferred to believe the latter.[345] That rumor likely originated with Wilkinson, who warned Jefferson of the "deep, dark, and widespread conspiracy," because it gave Wilkinson the opportunity to play the role of Jefferson's protector to ensure his continued loyalty.[346] It was not the first time Wilkinson had created an assassin only to inform the victim and then play his defender; Wilkinson once had hired an cutthroat to attack a British agent in Kentucky on behalf of Spain, only to seek rewards from both the intended victim and Spain after the fact. Jefferson seemed to believe the Wilkinson rumor, taking the details as a personal threat that Burr wanted him dead. He reacted by stretching the boundaries of the law to use the powers of the presidency to prosecute Burr.

Burr's defense was straightforward, if unconvincing to most. He claimed that his intention was to support the U.S. government in its efforts to take control of additional territory between U.S. and Spanish territory along the Sabine River that joined Louisiana and the Mexican Texas. Once occupied by Burr and his forces, the new territory could then be added to the United States by negotiating with its new friendly occupants without a declaration of war. Burr suggested that his plot had the support of the highest government officials, but that they would have to deny all association with the plan publicly to avoid an international crisis.[347] Burr's rise almost to the highest level of government gave him some credibility. Besides, everyone knew that Jefferson wanted to add territory and that he was negotiating with Spain to purchase East Florida. Jefferson's own preference to rely upon diplomacy rather than war made Burr's argument more plausible.

Even as Burr completed his term as vice-president, he reached out alternatively to Britain and Spain to request that they support him in a plan to divide the American states.[348] European powers still occupied adjoining territory. Like Indians in the uncertain time, U.S. leaders were forced to use diplomacy to negotiate with stronger opposing European governments for survival on their own continent. Spain could be used to counter Britain. Britain could be used to counter Spain and France.

Burr's plot to separate the West was not the first such effort. Jefferson and Wilkinson had been thought to have participated in a conspiracy with British leaders in Canada to oppose the French by separating the western territory from the U.S.

Whatever Burr's true goal, Wilkinson would have recognized that Burr's willingness to pursue his ambitions outside the bounds of the law made him a man Wilkinson could manipulate. Burr lived almost in a fantasy world that he created for himself, and he cast the people he met in the roles he wished them to play rather than as they were. Jackson called Burr "as far from a fool as I ever saw, and yet as easily fooled as any man I ever knew."[349]

In May 1804, just prior to Burr's duel with Hamilton, Wilkinson renewed his early military friendship with Burr with typical flattery, writing, "I think of you always my handsome and dear devil" and then called on Burr at his home.[350] During that first meeting, Wilkinson may have suggested that Burr pursue plans for an invasion of Mexico. Burr then met with Wilkinson in Washington City where the two are said to have spent days behind closed doors studying maps of the Southwest and the Spanish territory beyond.[351] Wilkinson also encouraged influential and disaffected New Orleans businessmen who were part of a group known as the "Mexican Society" to call on Burr when in Washington City. They would help foster Burr's fantasy of the feasibility of a southwestern secession.[352]

Burr, in turn, took advantage of Jefferson's attempt to curry his support in the Senate to demand Jefferson's appointment of Wilkinson as Governor of the Upper Louisiana Territory.[353] Wilkinson would remain the general in command of U.S. troops, and the combination of the two positions would give Wilkinson unique influence over events in the West. Jefferson consented. Possibly to lay a foundation for his plans with Burr, Wilkinson attempted to take advantage of his new position by suggesting that Jefferson move the main U.S. military command away from the East Coast to Fort Adams near New Orleans.[354] Certainly, Wilkinson's motives were far greater than settling a score with Jackson; however, Wilkinson's unique talents included the ability to manage multiple schemes simultaneously.

Wilkinson would never have been able to gain control over Jackson directly. Jackson distrusted Wilkinson too much and his own ambitions rivaled Wilkinson's. Wilkinson often found more success by acting indirectly through people his marks trusted. Burr's opposition to Jefferson and his apparent understanding of the needs of people in the Southwest made the like-minded Jackson a logical ally. Wilkinson would be able use Burr, as Burr hoped to use Jackson. To the extent that Jackson would show any natural skepticism, Wilkinson could count on Jackson being blinded by the opportunity to achieve what he wanted most—military command success and the reputation as the commander who finally made the southwestern frontier safe.

Burr crossed Jackson's Hermitage cabin doorstep in Nashville on May 29, 1805.[355] The visit did not seem out of the ordinary. Everyone of note was expected to pay a visit to Jackson when traveling through the area. Burr was the highest-ranking U.S. official to travel to Tennessee, and Jackson was taken with the flattery that Burr honored him with time at his Hermitage. Burr asked to board his horses and coachman at Jackson's house as he took a river trip to New Orleans and then returned to Nashville on the Natchez Trace.[356] Jackson offered the hospitality of his home, and he even supplied Burr with a boat for his river voyage.[357] Jackson never suspected that one purpose of Burr's river trip was to meet with Wilkinson.

Burr had planned to travel together with Wilkinson down the Ohio River on his visit to Nashville. When Wilkinson apparently failed to keep his rendezvous with Burr, Burr had left his own boat north on the Ohio at Fort Massac before taking a land detour across Kentucky to Jackson's Hermitage in Tennessee. When Burr left Jackson, he immediately returned to Fort Massac where he recorded in his journal that he had met with Wilkinson.[358] Wilkinson then arranged for Burr to travel on a grand boat with 10 military guards for the remainder of his river voyage to New Orleans, perhaps to reward him for establishing Jackson's confidence, and certainly to feed Burr's illusions of the power that awaited a future emperor. Jackson would have been doubly offended had he known that Burr's guards on the boat were in fact officers that Wilkinson was sending to New Orleans to court-martial Colonel Butler.[359]

As Wilkinson awaited news of the progress of Burr's connections, he wrote a letter to U.S. Army accountant William Simmons enticing him in vague terms to join a great project for which plans were still in progress.[360] Wilkinson took other army officers into his confidence, giving them hints of the scheme that some would use to inform Jefferson, but stopping short of giving evidence of an actionable threat. In New Orleans, Burr used an introduction letter from Wilkinson to meet with businessman and congressman Daniel Clark, who was part of the Mexican Society. Clark followed the meeting with Burr by visiting Spanish territory to evaluate Spain's military defenses.[361]

Wilkinson arrived in St. Louis to begin his work as Governor of the Upper Louisiana Territory, and he reached out to Seth Hunt to consider participation in a new venture with the promise, "if certain great events take place that are in agitation, I shall have it in my power to give you a situation by which you may make your fortune."[362] Hunt, who would soon help found Huntsville, Alabama, refused to join in the scheme and discovered that it was dangerous to cross Wilkinson. Indian agent John McKee found Hunt deathly ill at Fort Pickering.[363] Hunt later alleged that Wilkinson had attempted to have him assassinated.[364]

On his return from New Orleans, Burr traveled on north to the Hermitage to talk with Jackson for several days, and then continued north to meet with political leaders and Jackson allies such as U.S. Senator John Adair in Kentucky to gauge their support. Following what appears to have been a recruitment campaign, Burr then traveled to St. Louis to meet with Wilkinson.[365] There is little doubt about what they discussed. Artillery officer Major James Bruff would later testify that Wilkinson suggested that the American Republic was not the proper form of government for Louisiana and that during Burr's time in St. Louis, Wilkinson attempted to recruit Bruff to join a large enterprise. Bruff was convinced that Wilkinson was a spy and in league with Burr.[366]

After seeing that Jackson was willing to be taken into his confidence, Burr began working his plan in early 1806. Burr informed Jackson that President Jefferson had secretly requested two million dollars from Congress to purchase East Florida from the Spanish. That much was true. Then Burr added supposedly confidential information that if negotiations did not go well, Jackson's Tennessee militia might be needed to defend the southwestern frontier from Spain.[367] The U.S. government had to deny any connection with the effort to prevent possible war. Spain had the ability to use its armada to seize American ships in foreign ports, and there was little the small number of United States naval ships could do to defend themselves.

Burr established common ground with Jackson's distrust of the professional military, telling him not to rely upon professional officers who held commissions unearned through military victories. Then Burr flattered Jackson, "your country is full of fine materials for an army and I have often said that a brigade could be raised from West Tennessee which would drive double their number of Frenchmen off the Earth."[368] The vice-president was comparing Jackson favorably with Napoleon, the conqueror of Europe.

Burr's compliment was exactly what Jackson needed to hear. It reflected on how well he had trained his soldiers and his own military leadership. Burr then suggested that Jackson forward a list of his best

Tennessee soldiers and promised that he would recommend the men to the War Department.[369] Burr's unusual offer to help Jackson influence army officer appointments outside official channels should have been a warning signal to Jackson, but Jackson saw only the opportunity to place his own officers in positions of influence by going around Wilkinson. Once Burr had the list, he could recruit Jackson's soldiers directly if needed.

Perhaps Burr knew Jackson well enough to see the desires of his heart and to know how best to influence him, but the expert of character study and manipulation was Wilkinson.

By fall, when Burr was ready to execute his plan, Jackson was even more vulnerable to Burr's manipulation. He needed Burr's public support to save his reputation. Jackson had just killed a fellow Nashville resident Charles Dickinson in a duel, and the public support Jackson craved suffered. Dueling, though illegal, was accepted at the time in Tennessee. However, a violation of the *code duello* removed any facade of respectability. Jackson and Dickinson's representatives had agreed in writing that each would fire one shot simultaneously.[370] Dickinson shot first and his bullet struck Jackson in the chest. When Jackson attempted to return fire, his pistol clicked but did not fire. Jackson said that under the agreement of rules the parties had made, the attempted shot was not considered a shot if the gun misfired.[371] He reattempted his shot, and the second bullet fatally wounded Dickinson.

Immediate public outrage stunned Jackson. Several people were unafraid to call Jackson's shot "murder." Newspaper editors even placed black mourning borders around their papers to announce Dickinson's death.[372] It was an unusual acknowledgment of public respect normally reserved for high officials.[373] Criticism isolated Jackson. If Jackson accepted the public verdict, his career would have been at an end. He might have lost power to fend off charges should officials choose to prosecute. James Robertson had counseled Jackson against wasting his influence by engaging in careless duels. Jackson could not expect his help. It was the opportunity Jackson's enemies had awaited.

At first, Jackson fought back without any political sophistication. Jackson obtained and published general statements from the duelists' seconds that Jackson had followed the agreed rules of engagement without specifically addressing the issue of the second shot.[374] He then set out to attack the group of people who had persuaded the newspapers to run the mourning border. Jackson's land partner John Overton, who also served as his lawyer and counselor, warned Jackson not to lose the respect of friends he still retained by taking on a rabble of hotheaded young men or "puppies."[375] Jackson should show the public the wisdom of his age and experience by conducting a more political and sophisticated offensive to regain public support.

Aaron Burr seemed to provide that opportunity. Jackson learned that Burr would be returning to Nashville on the Natchez Trace from another trip to New Orleans. Rather than shunning an infamous duelist to avoid further discussion of the Dickinson duel, Jackson shamelessly announced that he would host a public dinner for Burr at Talbot's Tavern in Nashville. True, Burr had fled the East because he had killed Alexander Hamilton in a duel. That duel was less controversial in Nashville. The Federalist Hamilton, who hoped to form a government run by families of eastern aristocrats, was not very popular on the frontier, and Burr's populist positions still received wide support. In the West, women still swooned for the dark-haired politician, and several families named their children in Burr's honor. Jackson could hope to regain respectability by showing the public that he still had Burr's support.

The scandal over Jackson's duel normally would have prevented leaders from attending the dinner, but politicians would not risk offending Burr. Curiosity added to the attraction, and Tennessee leaders packed the tavern. Guests anxiously awaited Burr's arrival, one remembering years later the "hush and thrill" of the entrance.[376] When Burr appeared, Jackson was at his side, dressed in his full Tennessee major general uniform. Jackson took Burr's arm so that the men could be seen walking arm-in-arm as they greeted guests.[377] Jackson then toasted Burr and gave approval to Burr's plan. Only Burr knew which of several rumored schemes were the plans Jackson gave his public approval.

Privately, Burr had told Jackson of modified plans for an expedition south on the Mississippi River.[378] This expedition would be directed west of the Mississippi as well as East Florida. Burr would need Jackson's help to raise a volunteer militia of about 2,000 men to secure the Texas and Santa Fe territory of Mexico. It was an easy sale. Jackson believed that acquisition of Texas was necessary to control New Orleans.[379]

Burr could expect Tennessee to be among the first states to pull away from the Union with Jackson's support. The western states and territories had often expressed their displeasure with federal power centered along the East Coast, and the new constitution written to salvage their Union was not even two decades old. Burr's rebellion would test its strength, and he calculated that Jackson's influence in the West was key to dismantling it.

Burr assured Jackson that the expedition had the private support of the U.S. government, which was anxious to acquire the territory. However, to make Jackson even more likely to support the effort without much investigation, Burr hired the cash-strapped Jackson to build boats to transport soldiers to Natchez and gave Jackson notes payable to Burr in lieu of currency to begin construction. Jackson accepted the notes and endorsed them, leaving written evidence of his connection with the plot.[380] Jackson would place his associate John Coffee in charge of construction.

Burr's expedition offered Jackson the command opportunity he craved. Making the deal even sweeter, Burr paid Jackson more money than was needed for boats. Jackson also used some of Burr's funds to recruit mercenary soldiers to support the expedition.[381]

To Jackson's disappointment, respected U.S. Army General James Winchester refused to attend the dinner for Burr. Undeterred, while Burr was still Jackson's guest at the Hermitage, Jackson sent Winchester a letter suggesting he had seen evidence that the United States and Spain were on the brink of war after Spain had rejected the U.S. offer to purchase East Florida.[382] Jackson calculated that the U.S. military could take East Florida and all remaining Spanish territory, including Texas, for less money than Jefferson had offered to pay for peaceful acquisition. Jackson also reported his understanding that Wilkinson was dealing directly with the Spanish conflict in Natchitoches, west of Natchez. Jackson's knowledge of Wilkinson's activities no doubt came from Burr. Jackson's normal skepticism of anything involving Wilkinson, and especially any business involving Spain, should have made him question the operation from the outset.

But Jackson was hooked. In addition to the opportunity to demonstrate his military leadership, this expedition might be the opportunity to prove to the nation that Jackson was more effective than Jefferson in pursuing national interests.

As soon as Burr departed, Jackson published an order to the Brigadier Generals of the 2nd Division of the Tennessee Militia alerting them to prepare their units for an order to march.[383] He hoped to raise two to three thousand troops.[384] Business partner John Coffee would be his second-in-command. Jackson told Winchester that the military action offered young men the opportunity to acquire fame.[385] That admission may also have been insight into the opportunities Jackson also thought the action offered their general.

Neither the Tennessee governor nor the president had authorized the call-up of troops. Washington City politicians would later conclude that Jackson was pledging the loyalty of his West Tennessee militia to Burr's rebellion. The weight of evidence was to the contrary. Believing Burr's deception that Jefferson had authorized the mission, Jackson wrote a letter to Jefferson to report his actions directly to the president.[386]

On November 10, 1806, before Jackson's letter to Jefferson was delivered by mail to the President's House, Captain John Fort arrived as a guest at the Hermitage. Fort casually mentioned Burr's expedition. When Jackson asked for details, Fort said that Burr's true plan was to rob the Bank of New Orleans, invade Mexico, set up a new government, and pull the western section of the country away from the U.S.[387] As if Jackson needed additional evidence of how his ambition had blinded him, Fort reported that Wilkinson was to lead command of the military action for the rebellion. Captain Fort had enough information about the plot to be credible.

Immediately, Jackson saw Wilkinson's handiwork behind Burr's plans. He suspected that Wilkinson's objective was not to set up a small rival government. Instead, he concluded that Wilkinson was using Burr as a pawn to foment an attack on the southwestern frontier to make New Orleans and Louisiana vulnerable to an invasion by Spain.[388] France had no legal right to sell the former Spanish New Orleans or the territory west of the Mississippi to the United States. This was Wilkinson's opportunity to return the territory to his Spanish masters. All Wilkinson needed was to push the U.S. government to go to war with Spain, and then as commanding general of U.S. forces, he could control the outcome. The conspirators' new American government centered in New Orleans would be subservient to European powers.

What also seemed clear, as Jackson had warned, Wilkinson could use the precedence set in Colonel Butler's case to demand that no soldier reveal what was taking place without Wilkinson's consent. Wilkinson would have the power to stop delivery of the mail from New Orleans to make certain that no citizen could warn anyone about the plot. By the time the federal government in Washington City learned what was transpiring in New Orleans, it would be too late. Spain would have regained

New Orleans and the Louisiana Territory that Jefferson had purchased from France.

Jackson's speculation was not without foundation. William Eaton later testified that Burr confided to him that part of the plan was to make New Orleans vulnerable to attack by Britain or Spain, prompting the Mexican Society group of New Orleans leaders to pledge their loyalty to the new rebel government defended by an army led by Wilkinson.[389] Seeming to provide confirmation of Wilkinson's involvement, the November 8th edition of the Nashville *Impartial Review* reported that Wilkinson had just dismissed the local New Orleans militia.[390] That action left Wilkinson's remaining troops as the only soldiers in control of New Orleans.

Jackson realized that rather than going down in history as the western commander who made the Southwest safe for settlement, he could be portrayed as a traitor who had allowed European powers to nullify the results of the Revolution.

Springing into action, Jackson immediately wrote President Jefferson to inform him of the plot and to assure that his Tennessee militia was ready to march in defense of New Orleans.[391] He also wrote Louisiana Governor Claiborne, among other reasons, to create a public record to distance himself from Wilkinson's conspiracy. Advising Claiborne that there was "something rotten in the State of Denmark," Jackson warned about the plot and told the governor to guard against "our General" [Wilkinson] and to expect an attack from within the country as well as Spain."[392] To make it clear where he stood, Jackson stated his hatred of the Spanish Dons, adding, "I love my country and government . . . I would die in the last ditch before I would see the Union disunited."[393] He also wrote to New Orleans Senator Daniel Smith to encourage him to keep an eye on Wilkinson and see if he could uncover evidence of the plot.[394] Having first established his loyalty to the Union in writing to several witnesses, Jackson next wrote Burr to ask directly whether his intentions were contrary to U.S. interests. Burr replied with a denial.[395]

Surprisingly, when Jefferson replied to Jackson's warning letter, he did not express shock that a call-up of troops was contemplated.[396] Major Bruff had also warned the federal government that Wilkinson was in league with Burr.[397] With information that Wilkinson's Spanish masters had released to attempt to force him to initiate his plot, newspapers in both the East and West printed accusations that Wilkinson and Burr were plotting a rebellion to divide western states. Jefferson was finally forced to take some action to appear to defend the nation.

Jefferson's cabinet met in emergency session. They determined that officials in the southwestern states should be sent confidential letters to be on watch for any movement of rebellion by Burr or his conspirators and arranged for gunboats to be sent to the Mississippi River. What about the other conspirator? Their minutes noted: "General Wilkinson being expressly declared by Burr to Eaton to be engaged with him in this design as his lieutenant, or first in command, and suspicions of infidelity in Wilkinson being now become very general, a question is proposed what is proper to be done as to him."[398] Two days later the cabinet determined to send out a spy to follow Burr but reversed the decision to send gunboats.[399]

A new rumor that Burr's plans included an eventual attack on Washington City and the president got Jefferson's attention. Jefferson finally released an official proclamation on November 27 alerting the public to a treasonous conspiracy in the West.[400] He then sent out additional spies to gain information as to how far the rebellion had spread.[401]

Within a few days, an express rider carrying a confidential letter from Washington City made a dramatic entrance into Nashville. Though the courier was rushing to New Orleans, he was forced to stop from exhaustion before riding down the Natchez Trace. The "confidential" letter said that it was suspected that two regiments were being raised in Tennessee to support Burr.[402]

When news of Burr's plot spread throughout Nashville, a state of public alarm was sounded. The *Impartial Review* editor proclaimed that Burr should be hanged, prompting an outraged mob to meet on the Public Square and hang Burr in effigy.[403] The ringleaders were Jackson's enemies, who used the occasion to strike out at Jackson.[404] If emotion spiraled out of control, Burr's local supporters such as Jackson could be forced to appear in person for the genuine "honor."

Distancing themselves from Jackson, his friends in Franklin held a special patriotic meeting in his absence to proclaim publicly that they were loyal to the Union.[405] Thomas Hart Benton served as secretary for the meeting.

At the same time, trusted Father of Nashville James Robertson side-stepped Jackson's militia command in moving to organize and rendez-vous local veterans of the Revolution as the "Corps of Invincibles" to put down the rebellion. Jackson thanked the men for their patriotism at the same time he begged them publicly to return home before the mostly elderly men overexerted themselves.[406]

When the *Tennessee Gazette* editor added to the consensus that Burr was a traitor, Jackson saw the danger for his own leadership, and he moved quickly to get ahead of the wave of outrage.[407] He used his po-sition as Tennessee militia major general to allay any suspicions of his own loyalty by calling his troops to readiness as defenders of the Union. Jackson published orders and letters in the newspapers for several weeks to re-enforce that image.

Jackson wrote his friend, U.S. Congressman William Campbell, with the expectation that his letter would be shown to Jefferson, "One thing is generally believed, that if Burr is guilty Wilkinson has participated in the treason."[408]

Unknown to Jackson, when Wilkinson had learned that someone had leaked information about Burr's invasion plan and, fearing his own expo-sure, Wilkinson had immediately turned on Burr and made the former

vice-president the scapegoat. Wilkinson had ordered Burr's arrest and demanded that he be brought to New Orleans where Wilkinson would have
full control over him.

Wilkinson also turned the tables on Jackson by using Jackson's letter
to Louisiana Governor Claiborne that warned of a potential conspiracy
threatening New Orleans as legal justification to impose an extraordinary
martial law in the city.[409] Wilkinson arrested some of the people involved
in his plan and used those arrests to silence others.[410] To prevent witnesses from implicating himself, Wilkinson ordered some of his prisoners
including Kentucky General and U.S. Senator John Adair taken to sea
aboard ships, with the cover of having them taken away for trial. Once
it became clear that there was no rebellion, anyone who wanted to complain about Wilkinson's martial law could blame Jackson for stirring a
needless loss of liberty.

Just as Jackson had worked fast to use his position as Major General of the Tennessee Militia to get ahead of public outrage in Nashville,
Wilkinson rushed as General of the U.S. Southern Command to create
his own image as guardian of the Union in New Orleans. With typical
Wilkinson political drama and duplicity, he proclaimed to his subordinate, "the plot thickens . . . what a situation has our Country reached.
Let us save it if we can."[411] In another, like Jackson, Wilkinson assured
that he hated the Spanish Dons, and he added the flourish that he would
kill his own father to protect the Union.[412] Those who knew Wilkinson
knew better.

Taking advantage of his situation at the center of the chaos, Wilkinson
wrote to Jefferson boldly requesting that Louisiana Governor Claiborne be
replaced with one of Wilkinson's friends, that officers loyal to Wilkinson
be sent to support him, and that the U.S. government increase his pay. At
the same time, Wilkinson wrote to his Spanish paymasters asking for money to compensate him for protecting their interests against Burr's invaders.
In retrospect, it appeared to be a bidding war for his loyalty.[413] Wilkinson

attempted to use the uncertainty that he had helped create to solidify his position in control of the pivotal New Orleans, whatever the outcome.

Nashville newspapers breathlessly followed developments in Kentucky, Natchez, and New Orleans, and editors did not restrain in portraying Wilkinson as an enemy of the state. Wilkinson's actions to round up and imprison citizens were said to be those of a despot who was attempting to hide his guilt.[414] Nashville citizens joined the outrage when news arrived that Wilkinson had arrested Senator Adair, presumably to keep him from revealing what he knew about Wilkinson's work as a spy for Spain. The *Impartial Review* brought those accusations and potential outrage back to Nashville when it reprinted a report from another newspaper that suspicions about a conspiracy had fallen upon two people: Wilkinson and a Tennessee general.[415] In Pittsburg, John Read wrote the Secretary of War to allege that Jackson was leading Burr's army as a conspirator.[416]

Jackson learned that the U.S. Attorney Joseph Daviess had brought Burr before a grand jury in Kentucky, but he was probably unaware that Daviess was also evaluating Jackson's role in the rebellion. The incriminating evidence was a letter that Jackson had sent to Jefferson stating that "Mr. Burr would eventually prove to be the savior of this Western country."[417] News that the Kentucky grand jury refused to approve an indictment when a witness disappeared and that Burr had been released was welcomed at the Hermitage. Jackson did not want to believe that the vice-president whose interests aligned with his own would have been duplicitous. More than that, Jackson did not want to believe that he so easily had been duped.

When Burr returned to Nashville on December 14 and paid a call to the Hermitage, Jackson made certain to be away from home to avoid being seen with Burr. Rachel's greeting made it clear that Burr was not welcome, and he did not attempt to lodge with Jackson.[418]

But Jackson's frontier-survival intuition and ambition fought. Amazingly, Jackson told Coffee to complete two of the boats under construction for Burr and to refund only the payments for the remainder.[419] Burr remained in Nashville until the boats were ready. Jackson's friend Patton Anderson had succeeded in recruiting only 75 men for Burr's expedition. On December 22, with just a small band of would-be invaders including Rachel's nephew Stokely Donelson Hayes aboard those boats, the eternal optimist Burr began his voyage on the Cumberland River toward Natchez. Jackson later claimed that he had sent his nephew to spy on Burr and gave him instructions to report Burr at the first sign of illegal activity.[420] The *Gazette* editor criticized that young men like Jackson's nephew had been led astray by Burr, and with tongue-in-cheek asked in criticism pointed toward Jackson, "Was there no old men in the plot?"[421]

Jefferson seemed to make little effort to use military forces to stop Burr's advance, leading to some speculation that Jefferson supported Burr's invasion as Burr had claimed. Jefferson may have thought Jackson's warning referred only to an invasion of East Florida, which he may have supported as a bargaining chip in his negotiations to purchase the peninsula, without knowledge that Burr now wanted to seize the opportunity to take Texas and Santa Fe. Or perhaps, the expansionist Jefferson also shared that goal.

Jackson wrote Secretary of War Dearborn to offer support of the Tennessee militia and to blame Wilkinson for the conspiracy.[422] Jackson told the secretary that he feared that Wilkinson's conspirators may have taken control of the U.S. Fort Massac to the north and lead mines that were used to produce bullets for the army. Jackson said that he had arranged to use private boats to transport soldiers to help defend New Orleans if necessary, careful not to reveal that he had made Burr's advance possible by building two boats for him.[423]

That omission may have deepened Dearborn's suspicions about Jackson. Jackson soon learned that the Secretary of War was accusing Jackson not only of building Burr's boats, but of planning to command them in helping lead the rebellion.

Jackson could not let the perception take root. He lashed out at the Secretary of War in a letter he copied to President Jefferson.[424] Jackson accused Dearborn of providing the order authorizing Burr's mission and of being part of the plot to use the office of Secretary of War to allow Wilkinson to arrest people without cause in New Orleans. Jackson cited the "persecution" of Colonel Butler as evidence that the War Department was complicit in Wilkinson's actions. By initiating a new system that gave Wilkinson authority to stifle dissent, the groundwork had been laid for preventing suspicious army officers from sending official notice to the Secretary of War of Wilkinson's actions in New Orleans. Dearborn had been complicit in the change of protocol that now gave Wilkinson power to hold New Orleans under martial law until Spain arrived to take control. Jackson's charge was a bold and rash allegation against the Secretary of War from a general who wanted a military command more than anything else.[425]

Jackson penned his real anger in a supplement to his January 8 letter to Dearborn in which he protested that if it had been proved that Burr was a traitor, "I would cut his throat with as much pleasure as I would cut yours on equal testimony."[426] Either Jackson's temper cooled, or wise counsel prevailed on him not to send such a veiled threat to the Secretary of War. His final draft was more diplomatic.[427]

Once Senator Adair arrived as a prisoner in Washington City, and convinced a judge of his innocence to obtain his release, he began a public campaign against Wilkinson that re-enforced rumors that Wilkinson could not be trusted.[428] But Wilkinson calculated that he only had to give his supporters in Washington just enough grounds to defend him. As it turned out, he again was the master of manipulation and deception.

Jefferson refused to accept the Kentucky grand jury's dismissal or there was no evidence that Burr had engaged in a conspiracy. He ordered federal prosecutors to arrest Burr for treason and to bring him as a prisoner to Richmond for a very public trial, one that could have implicated Jackson. Supreme Court Chief Justice John Marshall, who served as presiding judge in the trial, ruled early in the proceeding, "all those who perform any part, however minute, or however remote from the scene of action, and who are actually leagued in the general conspiracy, are to be considered as traitors."[429] Jackson's construction of the boats to be used in the rebellion was more than a small act. His receipt of Burr's money to hire mercenary soldiers was even more egregious, but that fact was not yet known. Jackson's reputation and possibly his freedom were now tied to Burr's fate.

The trial of a former vice-president for treason attracted a variety of the country's notables, including author Washington Irving and Winfield Scott. Spectators crowded into the courtroom during sessions and then met in the streets and in taverns afterward to offer their observations. It was one of the first criminal trials that captivated nationwide public interest. Irving wrote about the trial to amuse the public.[430]

Jackson was subpoenaed to testify as a witness.[431] In addition to putting Jackson at the scene of action, the trial was his first opportunity to interact with such a wide number of leaders since he had served in the Senate.

Unlike most spectators who carefully guarded their observations and reputations using polite and political social norms, Jackson took advantage of gatherings to defend Burr with passion to anyone who would listen. He also denounced the president for using the justice system to prosecute a political enemy. When news of the British attack on the *U.S.S. Chesapeake* arrived in Richmond during the trial, Jackson delivered an hour-long address from the steps of the State House. Jackson branded Jefferson a coward, and added, "Mr. Jefferson can torture Mr. Burr while England tortures our sailors."[432]

Jackson seemed to persuade no one. Critics claimed that Jackson's forceful defense of Burr bordered on the irrational, but they understood his message: Jackson claimed that the President of the United States was prosecuting an innocent man for political reasons and that the primary commander of U.S. forces, a spy, was the real culprit. Such an outrageous claim made the frontier Jackson an easy butt of jokes among the eastern aristocrats.

Some onlookers also may have sensed a hint of desperation in Jackson's harangues. They can only be explained by his intense, competitive desire to prevent his new enemy from getting away with another fraud—as well as to save his own hide. Federal prosecutor George Hay reported to Jefferson that Jackson described Wilkinson in the "coarsest terms," because only by encouraging Wilkinson's prosecution could he hope to salvage his own reputation.[433]

Jackson welcomed news that the "publick villain" had also been subpoenaed to testify in Richmond. A rumor spread that Jackson bragged that he would "make the ground tremble round Genl. Wilkinson for 20 miles, if he ever met him."[434]

During Burr's trial, the focus of the government prosecution took an unexpected turn toward implicating Wilkinson as a part of the conspiracy, as Jackson had suggested. Wilkinson and Burr had used a cipher device to communicate in code, and Wilkinson had sent Jefferson a translation of a message that implicated Burr, conveniently omitting the portion of the message that implicated himself. Grand Jury Foreman and Jefferson enemy John Randolph broke the code and discovered the omission. Speaking of Wilkinson, the federal prosecutor confessed to Jefferson, "My confidence in him is shaken, if not destroyed."[435]

Though Wilkinson had been called as chief witness for the prosecution, the grand jury came within two votes of indicting Wilkinson. John Randolph assessed, "Wilkinson is the only man that I ever saw who was from the bark to the very core a villain."[436] But Jefferson's prosecutors could not allow Wilkinson to be charged, because proof of Wilkinson's treason would only damage the reputation of the president who empowered and protected him. Winfield Scott declared that only Jefferson's influence prevented Wilkinson from being indicted for treason.[437] Randolph went further and attempted to point out the connection between Jefferson and his general, "W. [Wilkinson] is the most finished scoundrel that ever lived . . . Yet this miscreant is hugged to the bosom of government."[438] Jackson agreed and repeated the accusation.

Jefferson would later explain that he was loyal to Wilkinson because he saw him as the one general who could assure control of New Orleans for the United States. Helping Jefferson achieve that objective would cover a multitude of sins.

Wilkinson's Spanish paymasters also watched the spectacle from a distance and seemed amused that their man had turned on Burr only to save himself, but the public believed him, adding, "Wilkinson detests this government, and the separation of the Western States has been his favorite plan . . . Wilkinson is entirely devoted to us. He enjoys a considerable pension from the King."[439] They bragged that Wilkinson had even improved his value by gaining popularity in creating the false appearance that he was the savior of the Republic.

Jackson received no credit for having the insight and courage to declare Wilkinson a traitor and co-conspirator. To the eastern crowd, Jackson's erratic conduct only confirmed the reputation as the wild man that he had worked hard to foster on the frontier.

As Jackson's friend John Overton had subtly counseled in handling the matter of dueling, Jackson needed to develop his skills as a politician and statesman for his more valuable skills of courage and insight to be useful to the country. He needed to play within the rules of the system and hold his fire for the right moments. Overton certainly felt his close friend's embarrassment, even if Jackson did not admit to any. There would have been a conversation or two of wise counsel.

Overton would spend his last hours directing his correspondence to be burned in the fireplace as he supervised from his death bed.[440] No letters between Overton and Jackson about the Burr trial have been found. Overton fixed more than one of Jackson's errors, and Jackson's missteps during the Burr trial were public enough that they would have required counsel if not a fix from Overton.

When Justice Marshall defined the crime of treason to require proof of an overt act rather than a conspiracy to commit an act, Burr was found not guilty. Burr had not been present when the alleged traitors acted to plot their departure.

Though Jackson also escaped prosecution for his involvement in Burr's alleged crimes against the State, the Burr trial only diminished Jackson's reputation in Washington City. Jackson's reappearance on the national stage was a wasted opportunity to demonstrate his wisdom and leadership as a political general. Some in the permanent political class would use Jackson's behavior to link Jackson to Burr and argue that Jackson could not be trusted with the command of soldiers.

Wilkinson took advantage of the public criticism of Jackson to pile on his own character assassination. Samuel Swartwout, a friend of Jackson and Burr, had embarrassed Wilkinson in Richmond by publicly haranguing him and forcing him with his shoulder into the street.[441] Wilkinson had heard the rumor that Jackson threatened to attack him if they met in Richmond. Once Wilkinson was safely back at his post, he bragged that when he was in Richmond, he saw Jackson standing in the street talking with a friend and that he walked up between Jackson and the man and began his own conversation to Jackson's friend, while ignoring Jackson. Wilkinson alleged that rather than standing up to the insult, "Jackson sneaked off like a cowardly dog who had lost his ears."[442] No one reported witnessing the public incident that would have been as much the talk of the town as Swartwout's attack on Wilkinson.

Jackson returned to Tennessee at the end of the Burr affair politically bloodied both in the East and at home. Jackson's biographer Parton noted that Jackson withdrew from public life to seek solace in the relative privacy of his Hermitage.[443] Someone recorded that Jackson was drunk when he appeared in public in Franklin at the trial of the man who had killed Patton Anderson, one of Jackson's best friends and one of the Tennesseans who had joined the Burr expedition.[444]

But Jackson's retreat was not a surrender. His insight into Wilkinson's involvement had been correct even if his tactics had not, and it frustrated him even more that no one respected him enough to listen. He still did not doubt his own judgment or his destiny to lead. One of the older boys who had wrestled Jackson as youth later reflected, "I could throw him three times out of four . . . but he would *never stay throwed*. He .. . never *would* give up."[445] From the time of his youth, Jackson always responded to defeat by fighting back.

Jackson used his Tennessee base of support to keep up the fight against Wilkinson's machinations. As discussions of war with Britain began to heat up in 1809, Jackson called a meeting of officers of the 2nd Division of Militia in Nashville. Acting as president of the meeting, Jackson promoted one of the resolutions, "And whereas, the success of an Army depends much upon the confidence the officers and Soldiers repose in the patriotism, honor, fidelity and talents of the commander in chief, Resolved therefore unanimously, that the officers composing the 2nd Division of Militia of the State of Tennessee have not confidence in James Wilkinson the present commander in Chief in the event of War between the United States and any foreign power."[446]

By early 1810, Jackson thought he had found the evidence needed to prove Wilkinson a spy. Jackson sent Tennessee U.S. Senator Jenkins Whiteside a letter he had received from a man claiming to have seen letters between Wilkinson and Louisville Postmaster Michael Lacasange documenting Wilkinson's payments from Spain. He added that having such a "publick villain" at the head of the army was a stain on the government. Jackson asked Whiteside to show the letters to President Madison, adding his contempt for Wilkinson in his own letter to the president, "What my Dear Sir Just on the eve of war, and a Treator at the head of the army--a commander in chief in whom the citizens that is to fight your Battles have no confidence--."[447]

Jackson also corresponded with Wilkinson's former business partner U.S. Congressman Daniel Clark who had published accusations of Wilkinson's treason in newspapers in New Orleans and in a book *Proofs of the corruption of Gen. James Wilkinson and of his connection with Aaron Burr: with a full refutation of his slanderous allegations in relation to the character of the principal witness against him.*

Wilkinson's false arrest of Senator Adair during the Burr "crisis" in New Orleans led to Wilkinson's own court-martial before a committee of the House of Representatives. In February 1811, Governor Blount wrote Jackson, "--I have heard nothing of Genl. Wilkinson's trial of late except that he is writing a book with the hope of washing away his sins--he will have hard work to effect his purpose."[448] The book, *Burr's Conspiracies Exposed and General Wilkinson Vindicated*, was written in the style of a third-party making a defense of the patriotic general, though most people figured out that Wilkinson was the author. Wilkinson made a point to attack Jackson, "General Jackson of Nashville, who has been by Burr's emissaries very frequently mentioned as having engaged in the project with two regiments, is nevertheless confided in, and has orders to secure all boats, provisions, or persons, which may appear to be destined for the conspiracy."[449]

Wilkinson admitted that he had corresponded with Burr in code through a cipher device, but he argued that the use of a cipher should not have raised any suspicion about Burr's intent. He finally claimed that he was informed of the conspiracy by a note from Samuel Swartwout, though the note was found to be in Wilkinson's own handwriting. Wilkinson, the general who made thousands of dollars from the sale of U.S. intelligence and who would use his position in the military on the Gulf Coast to acquire Dauphin Island off Mobile Bay for himself, pleaded in his apology that the only crime in his career was his failure to look out for his own selfish interests.[450]

The court-martial was the battleground where Wilkinson could display his true skills, and he gave a masterful performance. Wilkinson convinced the tribunal that any suggestions he was on the payroll for Spain were mere attempts from his enemies to destroy his character. Wilkinson then methodically undermined the reputations and credibility of those formerly well-respected accusers, presenting facts that revealed the wide range of his own intelligence operations within the army. Wilkinson pleaded that he had established connections with the Spanish governor merely to help open the Mississippi River for American farmers. Several witnesses testified to seeing large shipments of gold from the Spanish to Wilkinson, but Wilkinson claimed that those payments were his rightful receipts for transporting goods on the Mississippi River. Wilkinson also claimed that his conversations about recruiting people to join him in a grand project related only to a possible construction of a canal on the Ohio River rather than an attempt to separate territory. His meetings with Burr were only to propose that Burr run for Congress.[451]

Wilkinson was far better prepared than the prosecution. The tribunal found him not guilty. Though after reading the findings President Madison concluded that Wilkinson had acted improperly, he accepted the verdict.

Again, Wilkinson won.

Wilkinson knew of Jackson's continued public accusations against him and Jackson's seemingly full-time mission to destroy him. The perceptive Wilkinson may have realized that one of his equally egregious crimes in Jackson's eyes was that he used political power to cling to the command Jackson wanted most and thought he was much better suited to hold.

Jackson's assessment of Wilkinson as an inept general and unmatched spy was correct. But even if Jackson never knew of Burr's true mission, his willing involvement in the matter raised questions about his judgment. Jackson spent years trying to obtain proof of what had actually transpired in the Burr matter and that the whole affair had been masterminded by Wilkinson. Jackson could only blame himself for his lack of judgment, but instead, he turned his anger toward Wilkinson.

The Natchez Expedition would provide an opportunity for both Jackson and Wilkinson finally to settle old scores.

CHAPTER SEVEN

TECUMSEH'S WAR

"[Tecumseh is] one of those uncommon geniuses which spring up occasionally to produce revolutions and overturn the established order of things."

—William Henry Harrison

Indians believed that war resulted when the balance of nature was disturbed. They deliberated carefully before choosing war, because forces strong enough to produce war could not be controlled. Those forces would not settle easily, and the new natural balance at the end of the conflict would likely not resemble the old.

In Indian culture, nature would signal when the natural order had become so unbalanced that people should prepare for war. Chickasaw Chief Piominko told early Nashville settlers that the Chickasaw had interpreted a great earthquake in East Tennessee as a sign from the Great Spirit to make war on the Shawnee and drive them out of the Cumberland River area that became Nashville.[452]

Another harbinger of war was the appearance of a comet.

The comet that appeared in the summer of 1811 left a tail that stretched 132 million miles and traveled close enough to the Earth that it shined as bright as a second moon in the night sky, visible even in daylight.[453] At a time when most people still viewed the atmosphere for signs to predict weather, the strange light in the heavens was not a passing oddity. It was an omen of things to come.

Adding to the unusual natural occurrences in 1811, the ground throughout the Cumberland Valley produced a rumbling that sounded like rolling thunder. Thousands of squirrels rushed in from the north toward the source of the sound.[454] Tennessee settlers interpreted the squirrel invasion as a plague sent to persecute them like the plagues that God sent to persecute the Egyptians. Nature seemed to be out of joint, and dire times could be expected.

Indians that held to their ancestors' beliefs would have reacted to the abnormal occurrences by becoming apprehensive and defensive. They could be expected to replace their white kings, those suited to peacetime leadership, with red kings more skilled at mobilizing a nation to battle. It would have taken little provocation for tribes disturbed by the phenomena to go to war.

North in the Indiana Territory, Shawnee leader Tecumseh, whose name also meant "Shooting Star," hoped to be that provocation. The rumbling earth had been felt since January. The comet had been visible in Tecumseh's village in Indiana Territory by early June. Tecumseh's British ally astronomers and scientists may have alerted the warrior to how long the comet would be visible in the sky in the Southwest as well as the meaning of rumbling. Tecumseh could use the strange appearance of the celestial light to create the impression that his appearance on the Natchez Trace at the same time as the comet was a sign from the Great Spirit that the time had arrived to restore the natural balance to the American land.[455] Like the earthquake that had prompted the Chickasaw to go to war against the Shawnee years earlier, nature was signaling now that it was time for Indians to drive out the white settlers.

Tecumseh, true to his Shawnee ancestors, protested that the Great Spirit had created American land for Indians, that Indian land belonged

138

to all tribes, and that no tribe had the right to surrender it through treaty with the United States.[456] European explorers, traders and American settlers had disturbed a centuries-old balance by taking Indian land. Up in the Northwest Territory, encroaching settlers had forced tribes to take their subsistence from smaller tracts, and Tecumseh's own Shawnee people had been forced to live in the homelands of other tribes. Tecumseh had met at least twice with U.S. Territorial General William Henry Harrison to demand that Americans withdraw from Indian territory.

Tecumseh both impressed and threatened Harrison. The Shawnee warrior, he said, was "one of those uncommon geniuses which spring up occasionally to produce revolutions and overturn the established order of things."[457] Methodist minister William Winian, who witnessed one of Tecumseh's councils with Harrison, described Tecumseh as "Nature's true nobleman."[458] In a time of transition, uncertainty, and discontent, with a Napoleon, and soon a Jackson, upsetting the old order, Tecumseh represented the Indians' best hope for a strong leader to assure that their culture survived the current political earthquakes.

Like Jackson, Tecumseh recognized almost instinctively that international struggles for power would soon determine control of the American continent. The British Governor-General of Canada had reached out to Tecumseh and other Indian leaders in the Indiana Territory to ask for help if the United States chose war with Britain.[459] Soon, there would be a brief window of opportunity for the Indians to take advantage of conflict among the Anglos to reassert dominance.

As Tecumseh traveled hundreds of miles to consult with leaders of other tribes, he had witnessed the same sufferings his own people were experiencing. Sickness, death, and war had left the tribes' numbers depleted as white settlers continued to pour in from the East. Nearly all tribes had been forced to cede rights to their homelands and to live as transients. Tecumseh understood that Indian nations were at a precipice. No one nation had enough warriors to oppose the Americans. Tecumseh was certain that unless the northern and southern Indian nations banded together, their cultures would be vanquished. European settlers had successfully divided the Indian nations and were on the verge of completely conquering them. Only by uniting against their common enemy did they have a chance at halting the American advance.

American firepower and numbers were formidable, but Americans could be divided too. Tecumseh may have been aware of political divisions that were already threatening to tear the American government apart, but he clearly understood the significance of dividing American military forces. British envoys could inform him that Americans hoped to take advantage of the British war with Napoleon in Europe and strike to remove the British from the continent before they could mount a proper defense. Indian nations could prepare themselves for the following stage when many of the already limited numbers of American troops were sent to the northern frontier to battle the British, leaving southwestern American settlements unprotected. That moment would be the Indians' best opportunity to strike.

Tecumseh's warriors in the Indiana Territory stood no chance to oppose overwhelming numbers of white settlers unless he recruited tribes from other areas.[460] The British offered to help supply what Tecumseh needed to counter American weapons. It might be the Indians' last chance to drive Americans back to the sea where they first invaded.

As Tecumseh could have calculated, the timing of events, occurring at the same time as unprecedented natural phenomena, seemed so perfect that some tribes could be persuaded to accept the plan as spiritually guided. Younger warriors already sensed that their ancestors had lived lives more in line with their spiritual beliefs. Now, like white settlers, rather than hunting and killing, warriors more often spent hours sitting and talking of their ancestors' past glories. The European calico they wore, the manufactured tools they used, and the growing agricultural uses of the land might satisfy older warriors' needs for comfort, but they did not provide younger men the opportunity to prove themselves in war. To the younger idealists, their shrinking nations reflected the loss of balance that resulted from their failure to follow their beliefs. The uncertainty of transition produced a longing to return to the certainty of earlier times.

Tecumseh's message was crafted to reach an audience of young purists eager to restore their place in the balance of nature. A few years earlier, Tecumseh's brother Tenskwatawa, the "Prophet," had created a spiritual revival among tribes in the North. Like Christian evangelists, the Prophet denounced fornication and drinking whiskey, and he promoted the care of the old and infirm. The Prophet also assured Indians that the Great Spirit would support Tecumseh's cause.

Tecumseh's plan was bold, but overly optimistic. It counted on tribes putting aside generations of conflicts for which revenge had still not been fully exacted. Tecumseh also relied upon proud chiefs acknowledging that he was a superior warrior and relinquishing their leadership to him. Tecumseh may not have known that some of his suggested white victims had sometimes risked their own lives to help defend tribal leaders. And his plan relied upon cooperation of chiefs who benefited from their relationships with the Anglos to act counter to their own financial interests.

In August 1811, Tecumseh set out to meet with the southern tribes to build his great confederation. He selected six Shawnee warriors, six Kickapoo representatives, six deputies of another Northern tribe (likely Delaware), and his cousin Seekaboo to accompany him as his "company of guards." Seekaboo, a preacher of Tenskwatawa's message, would speak to the warriors' hearts as a disciple of the Prophet. Seekaboo had Creek blood like Tecumseh's wife, and he spoke Creek, Choctaw, and other Muskogee languages that enabled him to act as an interpreter.

Before traveling south, Tecumseh warned Harrison of his mission to the southern tribes. Just as Tecumseh used his communications with the British as leverage to oppose Harrison's power, he may have expected the report of his recruiting mission to build negotiating leverage with Harrison rather than to undermine the element of surprise for an attack. But a Kickapoo Indian chief warned Harrison that the true purpose of Tecumseh's confederation was to harm the United States.[461] Other Indians had reported that Tecumseh was in league with the British. And coming on the heels of rumors that the Indians were preparing for a final war with the whites, Harrison was alarmed. He reported Tecumseh's recruiting mission to the War Department.[462] Whites living in the Southwest should be on alert that if they spotted Tecumseh in their area, they should interpret it as a sign that southern Indians were preparing to make war.

To avoid conflict with the settlers, Tecumseh's party likely traveled though Tennessee in western Chickasaw territory along portions of the old Chickasaw Trace and Glover's Trace, and then crossed the Tennessee River at the traditional Chickasaw Trace crossing at East Port or the mouth of Bear Creek. The party of warriors turned toward the new Natchez Trace military highway and toward Chickasaw Chief George Colbert's house on the Natchez Trace to request a meeting.[463]

The Natchez Trace looked vaguely familiar to Tecumseh as he rode southward. He had spent time in the South in his earlier years where he may have participated in attacks on Nashville. It is said that he may have joined the Chickamauga and the Creek on the attacks on the Doughty party at Bear Creek in 1791.[464]

Now, just as Tecumseh had feared, the Indian path had been replaced by a wagon road similar to other new roads that had recently been built in what the white men called the "Indiana Territory." Construction of a wagon road meant that settlers would soon follow. They would demand land—and then more land—as they competed with Indians for dwindling supplies of wild game. There would soon be no land left for Indians unless the white settlers' advance was stopped.

The Shawnee passed through Chickasaw land frequently. From their reports, Tecumseh knew that Chickasaw leader George Colbert worked with Americans to operate a ferry for the Natchez Trace across the Tennessee River. Tecumseh was prepared to be rebuffed, but he may not have anticipated the extent to which Colbert had developed his own empire around the new United States road operation.

Unlike smaller ferries that many settlers operated at river crossings, Colbert's operation had become its own town that travelers named "Georgetown" in his honor. Colbert's enterprise even included the remains of the Camp Columbian fortification and commissary that the U.S. army had built when it constructed the highway. Colbert's ferry storehouses sometimes held U.S. army gunpowder and lead for bullets that the military transported by river.[465] Colbert charged the United States government for his services just as he charged everyone else.

Georgetown consisted of numerous roads, Indian houses, and stands set up to sell travelers produce and handmade goods. Passage could even be booked there for flatboats traveling the Tennessee River north to river towns Smithland and Eddyville, Kentucky.[466]

Colbert's own house, perched on the hill overlooking the ferry, looked like a white man's house—and for good reason. The U.S. Army began construction of the house when they built the ferry. The builders used a common design similar to King's Tavern in Natchez, perhaps one they were familiar with as a tavern. Numerous glass window panes stood out as a luxury for homes in that area at that time, and they revealed that Colbert benefited from his commerce with the Americans. Slave cabins were so numerous that they formed their own village. Exotic peacocks ran around his yard.[467]

Acres of fields planted in cotton or used to graze cattle and worked by Colbert's slaves revealed to Tecumseh that Colbert had bought into Washington's and Jefferson's schemes to encourage the Indians to assimilate. In traditional Indian culture, only women practiced agricultural work; it was shameful for a warrior to put his hand to a hoe or plow.[468] Though Colbert would not have found any shame in using slave labor for women's work, his success in agriculture revealed a perspective different from his ancestors.

What Tecumseh would not perceive through his philosophy of cultural purity was that Colbert had leveraged the right to operate a ferry across the river into an opportunity to build a commercial center that had become a landmark in the Southwest for both Indians and the United States. Military men who constantly assessed how they could allocate their limited resources to protect the frontier knew that Colbert was an important partner in establishing the United States west of the Appalachians. Colbert did not depend upon the white man as much as the white man depended upon him. And through that influence, Colbert helped the Chickasaw remain independent and prosper. It was a temporary American success story that would be lost years later when the Chickasaw were forced to move to Oklahoma.

George Colbert would not have been taken in by Tecumseh's warlike appearance. Colbert appeared equally striking. At 48, Colbert was considered handsome by his contemporaries; he was tall, slender, and had straight black hair that he wore down his back.[469] Colbert often wore a combination of the finest European fashions mixed with the clothes of his Indian people. If Colbert felt the need to create the effect of a military presence, he had no problem dressing in full U.S. military uniform with epaulets, hat, and sword.[470] It may not have been the first time Tecumseh and Colbert had met. Colbert had achieved his rank of major when aiding the U.S. army against the Shawnee in the Battle of St. Clair, a clear victory for the Shawnee when the Chickasaw withdrew their support from inept U.S. army commanders.[471]

When Tecumseh began his council with the Chickasaw, he likely recited the same speech he would give to several tribes. Southwestern Indians had not yet felt the full effects of white settlements. Tecumseh could describe from his travels in the north the bleak future that awaited southwestern tribes if they did nothing. Tecumseh believed that southern tribes had a duty to help those in the North who had lost the power to resist.[472] His objective was either to halt the American advance onto Indian land or to build a confederation of Indian nations to exterminate American settlements on former Indian land. The Chickasaw had a reputation as fierce warriors who had never been defeated, and Tecumseh needed those warriors now. Because the American military had committed most of its forces to military action in the North, now was the perfect time to strike and gain the advantage in the Southwest.

It may have surprised Tecumseh that Colbert did not speak well of his contact with white people. In addition to well-respected settlers, the American western frontier attracted a rough assortment who had escaped the law as well as charlatans who took advantage of frontier liberty to take advantage of others. Colbert had seen plenty. Colbert made it clear to anyone who talked with him that though he had met an American president and had even served as tour guide for Louis Philippe, the future king of France, he did not particularly respect white men. Colbert was quoted as saying, "Ah, Natchez people great for preach, but they be poor, lazy, thieving, bad people . . . Kentuckians are bad people, and white men are worse than Indians everywhere, though they have much preaching and much learning The Indians never know how to steal, get drunk, and swear until the white men learned them."[473] Colbert's wife Tuscahootoo was even more adamant. She would not allow white travelers to spend the evening in their home. Travelers who needed to remain at the ferry overnight either camped or boarded in separate apartments that the Colberts maintained for non-Indians.

Many white settlers had appeared at the Tennessee River crossing ragged, hungry, sick, and penniless after underestimating the difficulties and expense of traveling on the Natchez Trace. Though Colbert charged rates higher than those of other ferry operators to white travelers who had funds, he showed poor white travelers mercy by giving them free passage across the river, feeding them and seeing that the sick were given care.[474]

The Chickasaw understood that maintaining a distance from Americans would help preserve their people's independence. Chickasaw Chief Wolf's Friend had warned that American soldiers had hard shoes—if they were not careful they would step on the toes of the people they promised to protect.[475] Diplomatically, he acknowledged that Chickasaw and Americans were friends and brothers, but he stated plainly that they would remain friends only if they maintained some separation.

Nevertheless, the Colberts were enterprising, and they did not allow personal feelings to interfere with business. It was not necessary for them to respect or even like the settlers to understand where the future of their people lay. Europeans had slowly introduced their culture through trade. Indians favored European firearms, farm implements, and even blankets, for which they traded fur pelts, cattle, and slaves. Now the Indians had been changed. They relied upon trade rather than their old traditions, which were being forgotten. Americans had even brought in weavers to teach the Indians how to weave again.

The Colbert family did not fight inevitable change. They realized the importance of Chickasaw land in the future cotton industry. The soil and the climate made it some of the best-suited land for growing cotton, an increasingly lucrative commodity, and the land was bordered by rivers that enabled easy transport to European markets. Early on, Colbert had accepted George Washington's offer of a cotton gin and farm implements to become one of the early major cotton producers, and since then his nation had been constantly fending off both proposals and threats. Attacking Americans would destroy the economy on which the Chickasaw had come to depend, and one in which they were positioning themselves to lead. With new demand for American cotton from Europeans, cotton wealth could be expected to give the Chickasaw

Nation international leverage, particularly as Europeans still vied for control of the American continent.

Tecumseh, as he should have expected, would find no support from the Chickasaw. Chickasaw were now influenced more by economic concerns than natural omens. Chickasaw and the Americans were at peace, and the Colberts intended to use their influence to see that peace continued. Undeterred, Tecumseh met with other Chickasaw leaders, but found that their responses all mirrored Colbert's. The Chickasaw would not become Tecumseh's warriors.

Chickasaw leaders knew that Tennessee settlers were already uneasy over the prospects of Indian attack, and they worried that even their council with Tecumseh would raise American suspicions. Travelers may have spotted northern Indians talking with the Chickasaw, and it was thought to be better that Americans learned of Tecumseh's visit directly from the Chickasaw. A Chickasaw chief gave messages to northbound travelers on the Natchez Trace to inform American leaders, particularly the president, that Tecumseh's delegation had visited their nation. The chief wanted the president to know that Tecumseh and northern tribes were seeking a confederation of all southern tribes to join them in attacking American settlements. He also wanted the president to know that the British were encouraging Tecumseh's actions.[476]

That message was sent to Nashville, and from there, to points north. Contrary to the chief's intent, his message did not instill confidence of Chickasaw loyalty. As the minko, or Indian leader, suspected, a traveler had reported that he had seen Tecumseh's party meeting with George Colbert at Colbert's Ferry. It is what Harrison had warned. With a whiff of panic, the Nashville newspaper reported that Shawnee warrior Tecumseh was traveling through the Indian nations to encourage the Indians to band together to attack.[477] Though the editor suggested that Colbert would have the wisdom to reject Tecumseh, he encouraged settler families to begin preparing to defend themselves.

Various accounts of Tecumseh's visit would soon become lore and then lore-based history, and historians have questioned the accuracy of the details. What is clear is that the lore was based upon an impression that settlers took from Tecumseh's visit and that spread to create a greater panic. On September 9, 1811, 250 regular army soldiers were ordered to march from Cantonment Washington near Natchez to Colbert's Ferry in anticipation of coming attacks.[478]

After their meeting with the Chickasaw, by one account, George Colbert's brother Levi escorted Tecumseh out of the Chickasaw Nation.[479] The Shawnee party continued south and crossed into Choctaw territory

The reception was unexpectedly cool. Choctaw chiefs greeted Tecumseh, but no one showed any support.[480]

Tecumseh sought out Hoentubbe, an influential Choctaw warrior. The Shawnee warrior assumed that he could reason with Hoentubbe as a fellow warrior, who would not appreciate the loss of war and the hunt, and who would not want to lose his independence. If Tecumseh could gain Hoentubbe's support, Hoentubbe would be able to persuade other warriors to follow him. Warriors in turn would influence reluctant chiefs.

Tecumseh had considered the impression he needed to make on warriors and young men who aspired to become warriors. The warriors who accompanied him painted and dressed alike to show their solidarity as a fighting force. War paint was applied in semi-circles under the eyes and extending to the cheekbone. Red dots were painted on each temple and a large red circle on the chest. Tecumseh's war delegation carried rifles and tomahawks. Scalping knives hung from their belts. The warriors wore silver bands on their arms and large silver gorgets around their necks. Their moccasins and garters were fringed with long beaded tassels. Each subordinate wore the feather of an eagle and a hawk, but Tecumseh wore larger crane feathers—one red and one white. The white feather symbolized peace toward the Indians and the red symbolized war for their enemies.

The entourage displayed Tecumseh's message of strength and prosperity for those who followed him.

Tecumseh's warriors were guided to Hoentubbe's village, and messengers were sent throughout the nation to gather leaders to hear Tecumseh's talk. Minkos of many of the districts responded. Their villages were likely to be impacted by the war that was rumored to be pending. Tecumseh's talk would be an opportunity to learn what was likely to happen in the North.

As Choctaw leaders assembled, Tecumseh displayed his warriors with a Shawnee war dance called "Dance of the Lakes." Weapons of war were brandished. Indian warriors also often performed a scalping dance, as they imitated the final blows on their victims. Knowing that Choctaw had heard of his reputation as a fighter, Tecumseh used the dance to show that the leader who had the power to deliver the Choctaw from the Americans was now in their presence.

When the dance had worked its effects on the crowd, a council assembled near Hoentubbee's house. Tecumseh began his talk. The white men had taken their lands and treated them badly. It should be clear to them now by their present circumstances that white men hoped to reduce them to poverty.

The Choctaw responded that they could agree that Americans had encroached on their hunting land. Unlike the Chickasaw, Choctaw had not developed their own cotton plantations. Instead, many of them worked on the white men's plantations near Natchez, and the menial wages planters paid could not support them.

Tecumseh declared that to become a strong fighting force, Indian nations first had to establish peace among themselves. If they continued to war with each other, they would only reduce their collective strength against the American settlers. The Choctaw's wars with the Chickasaw and the Creek wars with the Chickasaw had not produced any lasting benefit. Choctaw leaders could agree on this point as well.

Having established some common ground, Tecumseh centered on his objective. The time was right now for action, because the British were ready to make war on the Americans. All Indian nations should ally themselves with the British. If they failed to take advantage of this opportunity to remove Americans from their soil, they might never have another.

Tecumseh paused. It was clear that Tecumseh was proposing that Choctaw begin a war with the settlers and their army, and the response was muted.

Choctaw Chief Pushmataha began his reply. Pushmataha claimed not to have known his parents or admitted to having a likely humble upbringing.[481] He was thought to be an orphan whose parents had been killed by the Creek. When Pushmataha appeared at a bear hunt as a child to prove himself to be a good hunter, he claimed to have raised himself. After taking opportunities to demonstrate his bravery as a warrior fighting Osage Indians while competing for their Arkansas hunting grounds and against Creek Indian enemies nearer home, Pushmataha had embellished his warrior reputation by claiming, maybe with some humor, that he had not been born as a mortal man. Rather, one day when lightning struck a mighty oak tree and broke it apart, the full-grown warrior Pushmataha had popped out.[482] Choctaw gave him a name that meant "brag" when he was a young man, until he proved that he could back up his brags. At first, Choctaw leaders were dismissive of the abilities of the young man because he could not establish his family ties. Like Jackson, Pushmataha told his war leaders that a warrior should be given rank by the merits of his deeds rather than his lineage.[483] In time, the warrior's actions matched his brags and they gave Brag the name "Pushmataha," their most respected name.

Pushmataha reminded his brothers that Choctaw had always been at peace with their white neighbors. They had never shed the blood of a white man. Americans had proved to be their friends. They had given the Choctaw no reason to go to war. Why would the Choctaw attack their friends on behalf of the British? Who knew what British motivations were for wanting to destroy the Americans? Should Choctaw believe that the British wanted to help the Choctaw? Most likely, if Choctaw allied themselves with the British and attacked their friends the Americans, whichever side prevailed, the Choctaw Nation would be destroyed in the end.[484]

And what were Tecumseh's true motives? If southern tribes bore the brunt of settlers' attacks, would Tecumseh's warriors be left in a dominant position among Indian nations? There was no question that the upcoming battle between the British and American settlers put Indians in a unique position. But was it an opportunity for southern tribes or opportunity for Tecumseh? Pushmataha made it plain that he did not trust Tecumseh, and he encouraged Choctaw warriors to take no more of Tecumseh's talk.[485]

With Pushmataha's strong rebuke, Tecumseh's spell was broken. The council abruptly ended as Choctaw rose to leave without giving Tecumseh an opportunity to respond.[486]

After unsuccessfully attempting to persuade other warriors, as a last-ditch effort, Tecumseh asked for a final grand council of all Choctaw leaders at the home of Moshulitubbe. In addition to Pushmataha, Hoentubbee and Puchshenubee, who was minko of the entire western section of the nation, Choctaw leaders included David Fulsom, who operated the inn *Pachi anusa* or Pigeon Roost at a crossing of the Black River stream on the Natchez Trace.

A council site was selected beneath the shade of a large red oak tree on the top of a hill overlooking the surrounding countryside. Many in the audience had seen the dance and heard Tecumseh's speech more than once, but he still went through the motions of the same dance and the same talk. All eyes glanced toward Pushmataha as the presentation ended. Pushmataha gave his reply additional weight by refusing to give an immediate answer and indicating that he would give his reply the next day.

Pushmataha may have discussed the proper response with his brothers the first evening to assure that he had their support for action. When he rose the following day, he gave a reply like those he had already given in response to Tecumseh's talk, but this time he added a warning to give emphasis to an answer Tecumseh had refused to accept: If any Choctaw man left the nation to fight with Tecumseh, the Choctaw should put him to death upon his return.

Following Pushmataha's lead, one minko after another spoke to agree that the penalty for following Tecumseh should be death. Tecumseh had his answer from the Choctaw, and it was final.

Adding to the insult, another Choctaw leader spoke to inform Tecumseh that if he did not leave their nation, he would be put to death as well. Other minkos voiced their approval of the decision to kill Tecumseh if he remained. In fact, to make certain that Tecumseh left the Choctaw Nation, Fulsom was directed to form a party to escort the Shawnee men out. Hoentubbee joined them.

Tecumseh had intended next to visit the Seminoles and Lower Creek farther south. He persuaded his escort to follow him in that direction. The party traveled east toward the Tombigbee River, and camped until they could build rafts to float the men and their horses across the river.

Sometime in the night, Creek Chief Black Warrior's men came across the river and took Shawnee and Choctaw horses. When the theft was discovered the next morning, Shawnee warriors were sent to follow the Creek trails. Creek spotted the Shawnee and opened fire.

Tecumseh, who had already been embarrassed in the eyes of his warriors by the rejection of two nations, would not permit an unanswered attack. He directed his warriors to cross over the river and pursue the Creek. Choctaw too joined the action to recover their horses. Men who were directed to kill Tecumseh if he did not leave the Choctaw Nation found themselves fighting with him for their lives.

The conflict was fierce. Men died on both sides. Fulsom was shot in the shoulder, and Hoentubbee was shot in the chest. Hoentubbee, certain that a shot to the chest would be fatal, cried out "I am dead!" The blow was glancing, and warriors laughed as the "dead" man stood to fight again.

At the end of the battle, Creek fighters disappeared back into their nation, taking most of their dead from the field to prevent Choctaw from scalping the bodies. Tecumseh and his warriors proceeded on toward Creek territory. Fulsom returned to seek aid of additional warriors to attack the Creek villages in revenge for stealing horses. They set fire to several houses belonging to Creek leader, Black Warrior. As the Choctaw were leaving, someone spotted the Choctaw and Shawnee horses that had been taken at the Tombigbee. It was the confirmation they needed that Black Warrior was responsible.

Now free of their Choctaw escorts, Tecumseh's party moved deep into the Creek Nation, his mother's people. Tecumseh sought out Menawa, a chief who had earned his reputation as a warrior attacking the Nashville settlement, likely when Jackson was part of the militia defense.[487]

Tecumseh found that Creek leaders were more divided, and it gave him an opening. Younger leaders did not approve of the cultural changes brought by trade with Europeans. Their people were failing to follow the old ways. The slaughter of game for pelts to trade with settlers was wiping out their hunting grounds, and without hunting or war, young men had no way bring honor to themselves. Young warriors were receptive to ways to create a spiritual renewal that would lead them back to the ways of their ancestors.

As word of Tecumseh's visit spread, large crowds gathered to watch the dance and to hear his talks. On September 10, 1812, the Creek then gathered for their annual grand council, a large assembly of over 5,000 people that included white traders and leaders of other Indian nations. As usual, the United States Agent to the Creek Nation Benjamin Hawkins was invited to attend. Hawkins was particularly anxious to hear Tecumseh's message and to determine whether the British were implicated in Tecumseh's efforts.

Tecumseh waited until the second day of the council to make his appearance, a move that built suspense for his presentation. Knowing that he was likely to find a friendlier reception among the Creek, Tecumseh and his warriors arrived in the town square painted for war. They were pleased to find that a large cabin had been prepared as their accommodations. It meant that their message would find a warm reception.

Each day of the grand council, Tecumseh's warriors danced around the circle, and some people said that Tecumseh appeared and shook the hand, or took the arm, of each representative. But Tecumseh did not speak. Instead, one of Tecumseh's warriors announced each day that the sun had gone down too far and that Tecumseh would speak the next day at midday. After waiting several days and deciding that Tecumseh was not planning to speak, Hawkins left the village.

Hawkins's departure was Tecumseh's cue. Grand ceremonies were held in the roundhouse as a prelude to the talk, and once the people were worked up to a fever, Tecumseh finally rose to deliver the message Creek had waited to hear. Tecumseh reminded the Creek of their noble past, when men hunted and fought as men. Now, like other Indians, they had adopted the ways of the white men, and their farming caused them to sit and talk rather than fight. It was an unmanly departure from the ways of their ancestors. Tecumseh reminded his audience that the white man had taken their lands and had shown their true motives in the spirit in which they had done so. If nothing was done to stop them, Indian nations would no longer exist. It was the message that confirmed the young purists' beliefs. Now the chiefs could hear that message from a proud warrior they respected.

Mississippi historian J.H.C. Claiborne gave a summary of the speech as:

"Brethren of my mother! Brush from your eyelids the sleep of slavery, and strike for vengeance and your country . . . Their bones bleach on the hills of Georgia. Will no son of those brave men strike the paleface and quiet the complaining ghosts? Let the white race perish! They seize your land; they corrupt your women; they trample on the bones of your dead! Back where they came, upon a trail of blood, they must be driven! Back—aye, back into the great water whose accursed waves brought them to our shores! Burn their dwellings—destroy their stock—slay their wives and children, that the very breed may perish. War now! War always! War on the living! War on the dead! Dig their very corpses from their graves. The redman's land must give no shelter to a white man's bones."[488]

That version of the speech was one of the first published by Claiborne, and it became widely accepted. But the historian H. S. Halbert, who supplied his notes to Claiborne, wrote that Claiborne's account was fiction.[489] More likely, Tecumseh's speech mirrored those he gave in the presence of Harrison. His intent was not to declare war on the Americans, but to build a confederation to take a stand that the Americans should proceed no farther.[490]

Nevertheless, the whites and probably the Indians present, caught up in the moment, took away the impression that Tecumseh proposed war on existing settlements. Claiborne claimed that hundreds of men waived tomahawks in the air to show agreement as Tecumseh spoke. Even Big Warrior clutched his knife as he apparently got caught up in the talk.[491] Within a year, what most settlers remembered was that Tecumseh had encouraged the Indians to take up the tomahawk on behalf of the British and declare war on the Americans.[492] Ceremonies in the Creek Nation went on until midnight.

As in the Choctaw Nation, older minkos in the Creek Nation rejected Tecumseh's overtures, and Tecumseh focused his appeal to younger warriors who might challenge their leaders.

Stories of Tecumseh's talks no doubt became exaggerated with time. It is said that on one occasion Tecumseh gave men sticks painted red for war, and he told them to take a stick for each day and begin their attacks when they had reached the last. Another account claimed that Tecumseh made a final appeal to Big Warrior at his village in Tookabatcha that resulted in an explosive and colorful confrontation.[493] When Big Warrior told Tecumseh that he wanted none of his talk, Tecumseh pointed his finger at Big Warrior and said, "Your blood is white... You do not believe the Great Spirit has sent me. You shall believe me. I will leave directly and go straight to Detroit. When I arrive there I will stamp my foot upon the ground and shake down every house in Tookabatcha."[494] With that angry curse, Tecumseh, the "Shooting Star," departed the Southeast just as the comet faded from view.[495]

CHAPTER EIGHT

SHOOTING STARS AND SULPHUR PITS

"In all the hard shocks mentioned, the earth was horribly torn to pieces—the surface of hundreds of acres, was, from time to time, covered over, of various depths, by the sand which issued from the fissures…some of which closed up immediately after they had vomited forth…"

—Elyza Bryan to Lorenzo Dow

Like Indians, white settlers also interpreted a comet as sign of impending calamity. In early summer 1811, two years before Jackson's troops began their expedition, near Clarksville, Tennessee, northwest of Nashville, Baptist Elder Reuben Ross was attending an unusual nighttime burial of a neighbor, and as dirt was being shoveled into the grave, the horizon of the dark sky lit up with the appearance of the comet. Ross never forgot the unsettling effect of the comet on the already-jittery mourners.[496]

Over the next months, Ross said that when the comet was followed by the northern lights it sometimes created "a dark red hue, many thought that the movements of armies and bloodshed were portended, and lost heart altogether, but the worst was not yet."[497]

By late fall, Tennesseans also noticed that the constant rumbling of the ground became louder. Farmers discovered that they could place their hands on the tops of fence rails and literally feel the ground move.[498] Finally, an earthquake centered near New Madrid, now New Madrid, Missouri, struck with such force that water in the Mississippi River rose 20 to 30 feet and flowed backward. An eyewitness reported that the violent shaking produced "a complete saturation of the atmosphere, with sulphurious vapor, causing total darkness" and forming "a scene truly horrible."[499] More graphically, she said it was as if the Earth had vomited. Other witnesses said that the ground opened crevices like jaws, before spewing sulfur and then closing again, as if it had become a beast ready to eat them.[500] The formerly firm ground near New Madrid moved like the sea for days. People watched in amazement as valleys of treetops rose and fell like waves on an ocean. The frontier town that white settlers were building to become the "Metropolis of the New World" on the Mississippi River lay in ruins. Its inhabitants ran from its buildings and sought refuge in the woods. For weeks, pieces of houses, boats that had lost their passengers, and decaying corpses of horses and cattle floated downriver past the landing south in Natchez.[501]

The powerful quake was felt throughout the eastern continent, ringing church bells as far as New England. In Nashville, as chimneys and scaffolding collapsed, some black slaves celebrated that the end of time had arrived and that God would bring judgment on their masters, finally rewarding religious slaves their anticipated freedom in Heaven.[502]

Elder Ross related the story of one Tennessee woman who felt powerless to change the sudden disruption of everything she had known. As the woman prayed on her knees, a tremor caused a hillside to collapse behind her and covered her back with sand. The poor woman rose, brushed herself off, and exclaimed in frustration, "Well! What is this world a-comin to?"[503]

When the earth shook in Tookabatcha in the Creek Nation, Creek ran out of their houses shouting that Tecumseh had returned to Detroit.[504] To some Indians looking for spiritual confirmation of the power of Tecumseh's message, nature provided what seemed to be unquestionable evidence. It might even have been significant to them that as a constant reminder that everything had become of balance, the earthquake opened a fountain of water near Jackson's Hermitage.[505]

A few young Creek warriors followed Tecumseh back to the Wabash in the Indiana Territory for further indoctrination. Tecumseh's Prophet's disciple Seekaboo remained behind in the Creek Nation to proselytize dispirited young Creek warriors, but his message went beyond even the Prophet's. He preached to the Creek that the Great Spirit would give them power to control nature by changing the course of bullets. Seekaboo assured that if Creek warriors followed Tecumseh's talk, they could attack settlers and no harm would come to them.[506]

Tecumseh had failed in his mission to create an Indian confederation, but his talks had planted seeds. Some groups of young, disaffected Creek searching for the foundations of their culture and the former glories of their ancestors, were willing to pick up the red war clubs. They would become known as the "Red Sticks" who would eventually cause a civil war that would lead to Andrew Jackson's destruction of their nation.

As settlers also speculated that the end of the world was near, ministers in the Southwest noted that people who had no interest in religion prior to the earthquake suddenly began attending their sermons.[507] The Lexington, Kentucky newspaper that reported the earthquake observed, "The great scale upon which Nature is operating should be a solemn admonition to men, (or those ANIMALS in the shape of men) to abandon the pitiful, groveling schemes of venality and corruption in the prosecution of which they are so ardently engaged. An HONEST heart alone can view these great events with composure . . . Nature appears, in spasmodic fury, no longer [t]olerate the moral turpitude of man."[508] Ross would call those with temporary fear-based, newfound religion "Earthquake Christians."[509]

The steamship *New Orleans* was making its inaugural voyage down the Mississippi when the earthquake struck. Passengers saw steam rising from the ground, and someone suggested that the comet must have fallen into the river.[510] Based upon newspaper reports and the violence of quakes in Nashville, Jackson speculated that the Mississippi River had become too dangerous for travel.[511]

The unusual comet, northern lights, and earthquake brought notice to all the other extremes of 1811: a hurricane, scorching summer, torrential rains, and widespread tornadoes. Those events may have gone unnoticed by themselves, but when nature suggested that God was upset, natural phenomena seemed to provide additional evidence.[512] Tecumseh had also timed his visit well to create a heightened unease among the settlers as to whether the Indians would prove to be the final instrument of their destruction.

On November 29, Chickasaw Agent Major James Neely reported the Shawnee's visit to Secretary William Eustis:

> "The Shawnee Indians and some of the Kickapoos solicited the king of this Nation for men to join the Prophet's party, but the old king told them that if they killed all his white brothers that he would die too – I am told that there are some Creek gone to join the Prophet's party, how many: I have not heard . . . The Choctaw I believe are engaged in a war with the Osages which keeps them employed. I do not _____ that many of them will join the Prophet. I have been constantly advising this nation against and showing them the consequences of joining the Prophet."[513]

If Tennesseans had known how quickly most Indian leaders had rejected Tecumseh's call for attacks and the value they placed on friendship with Americans, events might have followed a different course. News of Tecumseh's visits only further undermined confidence in the settlers' friendship with the Indians. Settlers did not know which tribes had agreed to join the Shawnee confederation, and the uncertainty clouded their view of ordinary events.

Governor Blount reported to the Secretary of War that Tecumseh was in the Southwest meeting with the Creek and other southern Indian tribes attempting to recruit warriors.[514] George Colbert acted quickly to quash any rumors that the Chickasaw had anything to do with Tecumseh.[515] Rather than using flattery, he appealed to logic— the Chickasaw knew they did not have power to go to war against the United States. Blount replied with flattery that he knew the Chickasaw had too much good sense to listen to bad talk.[516]

Meanwhile, as Wilkinson put his latest court-martial behind him and planned to regain command of the South and Southwest, he wrote a defense plan for the Gulf Coast for the consideration of the Secretary of War. Wilkinson had presented his Spanish masters a similar evaluation in a long paper entitled "Reflections" of military conditions and plans for Spain to defend against the United States' expansion. Though Wilkinson titled the U.S. military plan "Thoughts," he inadvertently began by describing the plan his "reflections."[517]

In his "Thoughts" for the U.S. Secretary of War, Wilkinson concurred with Jefferson that New Orleans, at the mouth of the Mississippi, was the most important "pass on the globe"—or perhaps Jefferson had taken the idea from Wilkinson. He agreed that "the power which commands the Mississippi must ultimately control the politics of the people who depend on its navigation for the sale of the ____ of their labors." New Orleans, then, should be expected to be attacked by a foreign enemy, and the small United States navy would be no match. Among

Wilkinson's suggestions was that the "yeomanry of the country should be organized, armed, equipped and arranged for co-operation without delay." Wilkinson suggested that militia be recruited from Louisiana and the Mississippi Territory, and that the interior states only be used to supply equipment for his soldiers.[518] Notably, he did not suggest that Jackson's Tennessee militia or its generals participate in the effort.

Tennessee was populated with a large number of Revolutionary War veterans. Though most were now too old to offer a practical defense, they still felt obliged to serve. James Robertson again revived his Nashville veterans this time called the "Silver Greys" company. If nothing else, the old soldiers could offer some military presence at home while the younger men were battling on one of the fronts.

For men still of fighting age who wanted to prepare themselves for war, the *Clarion* editor and printer Benjamin Bradford published additional copies of the *Military Instructor*, Von Steuben's Revolutionary War military standard of practice and tactics that had created an American army from a group of volunteers. Von Steuben's manual had been written with the encouragement and help of General Washington, and it set the standard for the American military. The newspaper announced that copies were available free of charge to company commanders, though the State of Tennessee provided a free copy to each County Clerk to distribute to the citizens.[519] An overly eager Nashville commander William H. Shelton took the manual to heart and began drilling his company in the methods so strenuously that his men began to refer to him as "Baron Steuben."[520]

Politicians took news of frontier developments to Washington City. Some leaders in Congress began to question whether the United States should rely upon a volunteer defense. For Jackson, the debate was more political than military. If only professional military leaders were selected to lead the army, militia leaders such as Jackson would be stalled in rising through the ranks to the highest levels of command.

Like his feudal European ancestors, every able-bodied American citizen was expected to serve in a local militia unit and muster with fellow citizens several times a year to train in the methods of war.[521] Tennessee muster days were typical of those from other areas. Men met in the morning to run through drills as musicians played "Yankee Doodle" and "Jay Bird Died of the Whooping Cough."[522] Drills were interspersed with inspirational speeches from commanders. The rare assembly of a large crowd in the community attracted peddlers, politicians and preachers. As soon as drills were concluded, festivities began. Ladies brought pies, cakes, and cider. Whiskey and beer also could be found in abundance, and by afternoon, wrestling matches, shooting contests, and fist fights ensued.

In the early United States, qualifications for political leadership and military command were synonymous. Men who wanted to rise through military ranks carefully studied Henry Knox's treatise on the future role of the military in the United States. Knox declared it the duty of those who had the power to choose political leaders with their vote to share in the burden of defense by risking their lives. Military service gave citizens the right to be "FREEMEN," the highest honor. Similarly, he suggested that men who demonstrated success as military commanders should be the only men who had earned the right and gained the experience to lead the government.[523] In practice, those leaders were selected only from elite families.

Conversely, according to Knox, the ultimate power in the country lay in the citizens who had the ability to uphold rights by arms.[524] Laws and rights were meaningless without the power to enforce them. Though people understood the practical benefit of maintaining a large standing army, with limited police enforcement in the United States, early leaders feared that politicians could use that army to abuse their power. Certainly, the power of the federal government over its citizens would be limited as long it relied upon those citizens to enforce the laws it enacted. To ensure that the real political power was left in the hands of the people, the practical power to enforce their rights was also left to the people through service in state militias. The people only grudgingly accepted a small standing army for its practical benefit of mounting an immediate defense in an emergency.

Some politicians disagreed and argued that the time had arrived to establish a large professional army. Jackson accepted the challenge to prove the militia system, the one in which a common man like himself could rise to command, was more effective than a standing army. It was said that Jackson considered the militia so important that he almost matched from his own funds the amounts that the state provided to assure that men under his command were properly outfitted.

That preparation could now return Jackson's investment. If war was imminent, Jackson could win the race for preparedness and be ready to strike the enemy earlier than any challenger. Jackson published the names of the commanding officers of his Volunteers, with an eye to what he described as an inevitable war.

In days, news arrived that while Tecumseh was traveling through the southern Indian nations, Shawnee, with the help of the British, had attacked General Harrison's camp in the Battle of Tippecanoe, near Prophetstown, the center of Tecumseh's proposed confederacy. After hearing of U.S. Army losses, Jackson wrote Harrison offering to lead 500 or 1,000 Tennessee militia to back up the Harrison's soldiers.[525] Jackson told Harrison that Jackson's militia would stand ready to receive Harrison's request for assistance. Governor Blount reported the offer to the Secretary of War to bolster Jackson's position.[526] Jackson did not consider that Harrison might view his letter as an insinuation that the professional army was not up to the task of defending the Northwest. If Harrison ever acknowledged Jackson's letter, no copy has been found.[527]

The effects of the U.S. Army's losses and loss of deterrence ominously spread south toward Tennessee. Creek disciples of Tecumseh who had followed him north for further indoctrination fought alongside the Shawnee at the Battle of River Raisin, and on their return home, the emboldened young warriors killed settlers near the Ohio River. The attacks were reported in the Nashville newspaper, giving credence to Harrison's unheeded warnings that Indians were planning war.[528]

Congress had avoided passing a war resolution to prepare the army for mobilization, but pressure for action was building. Jackson was not far from the center in stirring the forces of war. He worked through his old friend U.S. Congressman Felix Grundy to push for a resolution. In November 1811, Grundy had told Jackson that "we shall recommend" authorization for troops, assuring Jackson that before the Congress adjourned, the nation would have either war or an honorable peace. A month later, Grundy was pleased to report that the Volunteer Bill authorized recruitment of 50,000 volunteers. Ranks of honor would be conferred. Congressman Grundy gave Jackson an early notice, stating, "I name these things to you, believing that you can turn them to your Country's service."[529] In other words, Jackson should use that information to position himself to lead the forces ahead of any other commander.

Grundy overlooked an important point in the wording of the bill as it worked its way through Congress. It stated that a general no higher in rank than a brigadier general would command the Volunteers. Neither man may have known that Wilkinson had fought some of his previous battles for command in Congress through directing the wording of legislation as to which rank was to command. Wilkinson was a brigadier general. Jackson was a higher-ranking major general, and both Jackson and Grundy must have assumed that the final bill would name a major general who would command the brigadier generals.

Grundy knew that "Shall we have War?" was the question Jackson most wanted answered.[530] By January, Grundy could report to Jackson that the bills had passed; however, by that point, he noticed that there was something "rotten in Denmark."[531] The bills did not state who was to command the Volunteers that the Secretary of War was authorized to recruit. Because General Wilkinson had been found not guilty in his court-martial, rumors circulated in Washington City that Wilkinson would lead the new Volunteer forces that Jackson had worked so hard to lobby to create. For Jackson, the rumors confirmed that Wilkinson's influence within the War Department had not waned.

Just as the northwestern frontier was heating up, the Southeast became a threat. Napoleon's attempt to install his own king on the Spanish throne had met with opposition, and the Spanish government looked to be on the verge of collapse. What would happen to East Florida if Spain was no longer able to control it? The most likely scenario was that Britain would move its military forces in and establish a base from which it would become a permanent threat to the United States. East Florida and Georgia planters were convinced that the United States should act before Britain seized the opportunity and focused its attention on Florida. It would be easier to win by surprise attack. As a bonus, control of the Florida peninsula would add security to the southern boundary of the nation, which would have the incidental benefit of aiding land speculation by increasing land prices.

President Madison was notified of the plans, and he supported them. Like businessmen in the East who invested capital wherever higher profits could be achieved, Madison is said to have dabbled in land speculation on the southwestern frontier.[532] He could be persuaded that control of Florida was worth the risk of war. But profit was not the only motive. Following on Jefferson's plans to make the frontier safe and profitable for settlement, the government would provide settlers an incentive to move to generally uninhabited territory where they would form a population base for militias to defend the borders.[533]

Attacks on Spanish fortifications at Fernandina and Amelia Island were set to begin on March 15, 1812 as the Patriot Movement of Georgia and East Florida planters coalesced around a plan. U.S. Navy

Commodore Hugh Campbell along with army officers just north of the Georgia border promised to back the attack. Discussions had already been held with President Madison about a peaceful surrender of the territory once Spanish troops had been defeated.[534]

Jackson's land speculation in Georgia and continued contact with his old friend Senator William Crawford kept him in touch with businessmen and leaders who were familiar with concerns about a British incursion along the Gulf. In mid-February, Congressman Felix Grundy notified Jackson that Congress had passed authorization for a mobilization.[535] Building on passage of the bill and knowing of Madison's support for acquisition of Florida, Jackson may have revealed his own knowledge and approval of the East Florida Patriot Movement with the timing of his *Volunteers to Arms* from the Hermitage on March 7, 1812:

> "Citizens! Your government has at last yielded to the impulse of the nation. Your impatience is no longer restrained. The hour of national vengeance is now at hand. The eternal enemies of American prosperity are again to be taught to respect your rights, after having been compelled to feel, once more, the power of your arms.
>
> War is on the point of breaking out between the United States and the King of Great Britain! And the militia host of America are summoned to the tented fields! . . . No drafts or compulsory levies are now to be made—A simple invitation is given to the young men of the Country to turn out for their own and their Country's rights."[536]

Jackson went on to explain the causes of war:

> "Who are we? And for what are we going to fight?

Are we the titled slaves of George the Third? The military conscripts of Napoleon the great? Or the frozen peasants of the Russian Czar? No we are the free born sons of America; the Citizens of the only Republic now existing in the world; and the only people on earth that possess rights, liberties, and property which they call their own.

For what are we going to fight? To satisfy the revenge or ambition of a corrupt and infatuated ministry? To place another and another Diadem on the head of an apostate Republican General? To settle the balance of power among an assassin tribe of Kings and Emperors? "or to preserve the Prince of blood, and the Grand Dignitaries of the Empire" their overgrown wealth and exclusive privileges? No. Such splendid achievements as these can form no part of the object of an American War. We are going to fight for the re-establishment of our national character, misunderstood and vilified at home and abroad, for the protection of our maritime citizens, impressed on board British Ships of War, and compelled to fight the battles of our enemies against ourselves; to vindicate our right to a free trade, and open a market for the productions of our soil, now perishing on our hands, because the mistress of the Ocean has forbid us to convey them to any foreign nation; in fine to seek some indemnity for past injuries, some security against the future aggressions by the consequence of all the British Dominions upon the continent of North America.

Here then is that true and noble principle on which the energies of the nation should be brought in action: A free people compelled to reclaim by the power of their arms the right which God has bestowed upon them, and which an un-fulated King has said they shall not enjoy.[537]

Jackson appealed particularly for young men who were not tied down with domestic concerns and who yearned to prove their bravery, "the period of youth is the season for martial exploits; and accordingly, it is upon the young men of america that the eye of the nation is now fixed."[538] The General ordered the militia to muster and officers to read the Act to each company.

Jackson's *Volunteers to Arms* was the culmination of months of behind-the-scenes stirring of the forces for war and lobbying for a formal call-up of troops. It was also premature. Divisions developed within the Patriot movement and the numbers expected to join the effort never materialized. President Madison found resistance in Congress from shipping interests that feared that war with Spain or Britain would imperil business already suffering from federal embargoes. A bill authorizing seizure of East Florida would make its way to the floor of the Senate before being narrowly defeated.

American ships remained off the East Florida coast in the event reluctant senators could be persuaded to change their minds. The State of Georgia even strengthened its infantry forces along the border. Despite unexpected setbacks, East Florida was not yet considered a lost cause.

Though Jackson's *Volunteers to Arms* did not have support of a direct order from the War Department, it was the only authorization state militia leaders needed. John Coffee and other militia officers began riding through towns to enlist future volunteers and place them in a state of readiness. Jackson wanted to be prepared to offer his services the moment war was declared. Until he had federal authority, though, Jackson would be required to draw legitimacy from a series of his own public pronouncements, each with even more immediacy to keep fickle public attention focused on war.[539]

The *Volunteers to Arms* from the major general in charge of defense, coming on the heels of news of Tecumseh's visits, set vulnerable settlers on edge and in turn gave Jackson the support he needed. In Huntsville, a small group of Indians walked into a store and bought 15 rounds of ammunition. After they departed, settlers began to speculate what the Indians were planning. The consensus was that hostilities would break out at any moment.

Some mischievous young men overheard the exaggerated conversations and thought they could have some fun seeing what reaction they could provoke. After sunset, the youths painted themselves as Indians, approached the settlers' houses and fired from the woods, imitating Indian war-cry sounds.[540] To the rascals' delight, jittery settlers reacted by abandoning their cabins and running for their lives. Wagons were quickly loaded with whatever household goods and furnishings settlers could carry. Those who remained sheltered with other families in common cabins to add numbers to their defense. Doors were chained shut. Men used cracks between the cabin logs as portholes for rifles. Women who did not have firearms armed themselves with butcher knives. In some cases, women and children were sent to hide in the cane breaks as packs of their farm dogs encircled them and barked to protect them.[541]

The young men had a good laugh, and there were accusations that the youths planned the panic to rob abandoned homes. The incident demonstrated how even a small ripple in serious times can create a wave.

The imagined attack became more menacing each time fleeing settlers told their stories. The near-victims reckoned that the Indian party that attacked them must have been 1,500 in number. By the time the rumor spread north to Columbia, Tennessee, about 20 miles south of Franklin, the imaginary Indian party had grown to 2,000. Someone gave the rumor urgency by reporting that Indians had just attacked and killed 25 families on Bradshaw Creek in Giles County, just north of Huntsville, and that a Creek Indian attack party was headed north to Columbia. Alarms sounded, and riders took the message to farms as far north as Franklin. By 10:00 a.m., more than 200 men had gathered in Columbia, ready to defend the town from the Creek. It was rumored that 3,000 men had also rendezvoused in Nashville, and militia captains in other counties called their companies to action.[542]

Without waiting for objective evidence, a justice of the peace sent a message to Jackson by express rider certifying the massacre of families on Bradshaw Creek. As Major General of the Militia of the Western Division, Jackson ordered companies to muster and march south toward the Creek Nation on the Fishing Ford Trace to make a defense.[543]

General James Winchester was visiting with Jackson at the time, and he or other cooler-headed leaders questioned the supposed signs of an imminent attack. It was wisely suggested that troops wait for further information. The next day, Jackson rescinded his orders, acknowledging that he had just received an express mail that reports had been baseless.[544] One boy later recalled witnessing streams of settlers' wagons returning home loaded with their household possessions.[545] Without a hint of embarrassment, the Nashville newspaper that had participated in the hyperbole suggested that the exercise only proved that 10,000 citizens were ready at any time to fight for their liberty.[546]

General Winchester joined in the praise for the citizen soldiers' willingness to volunteer on a moment's notice. Though Jackson needed no prodding, Winchester also re-assured their major general, "knowing the path of honor of a soldier is not strewed with flowers. Peace is always desireable, when it can be maintained on honorable terms. But war, dear general, with all its evils are preferable to the present state of things in these United States: then honorable peace without delay, or war should be the watch word."[547]

Tennesseans were not alone in their reactions to rumors of an attack by Indian neighbors. North of Natchez, settlers at Grindstone Ford heard reports that nearly 600 Creek were ready to attack. Like neighbors in Alabama, the Mississippi Territory settlers fled taking whatever possessions they could carry. A storeowner in Gibson's Port who was known for his stinginess passed out ammunition free to his neighbors to encourage them to remain to help defend their homes—as well as his store.[548]

Indian attacks might have been illusory for the moment, but public reaction was real. Politicians were forced to act. Governor Blount publicly supported Jackson and his actions, giving an indication that it was only a matter of time before the northern and southern Indian tribes joined together and Jackson would be needed to push them out of the state.[549] He overtly suggested that the government should give Jackson authority to pursue the Indians.

As the public sensed that attacks were imminent, Nashville storeowner William Carroll published a notice to settle all debts with William Carroll & Co.[550] He expected to be called to duty any moment. He had good reason. Three days earlier, a party of hostile Creek Indians had arrived silently in 14 canoes at an outpost settlement on the Sandy River west of Nashville near the Tennessee River.[551] The settlement was several miles distant, but it was situated on the old Chickasaw Trace that led to Nashville. The Indians burned buildings and stole livestock as encouraged by Tecumseh's Prophet to deprive settlers of the ability to support themselves and to force them to abandon Indian land.

First reports seemed harmless compared to rumors of the prior month. The Indians had not taken any lives. Chastened by reporting the march of the Creek that never materialized, the *Clarion* editor for once seemed reluctant to exaggerate. Other papers reported that that 300 Tecumseh disciples from various tribes had built a new town in the Chickasaw Nation but given the false report of massacres near the Tennessee River, the burning of the buildings on the Sandy River seemed little more than a nuisance by Indian "banditti."[552] Only seven militiamen were sent to investigate.

Tragically, it was the one attack settlers should not have ignored. The hostile Indian party would return a month later to kill members of two families and unknowingly help provide U.S. Senate War Hawks additional ammunition to push President Madison to declare war.[553]

George Colbert added to the growing angst when he reported that he had heard rumors again that the Creek were preparing to burn Huntsville.[554]

As rumors of a potential Indian invasion swirled, Natchez Trace post rider Elmore returned to Tennessee and excitedly announced that he had met a Quaker preacher on the road who claimed that he had witnessed a council of Indians at George Colbert's house.[555] Four nations had sent deputies. Elmore said that the Indians had debated the question of how they should respond if the United States and Britain went to war. According to the traveler, Colbert had made it clear that he would not forfeit his friendship with the Americans; however, the Choctaw, Cherokee and Creek delegates indicated that if war gave them an opening to succeed in rebelling, they would likely oppose the Americans.

Elmore's report accelerated growing unease. If the British had succeeded in forming an alliance with three Southeast tribes, they had made even more progress than suspected. Tennesseans could be attacked from several fronts simultaneously, and they could not muster enough men to defend such a wide area. Consequently, it was critical to know whether the story was reliable. The Quaker preacher was ordered to be detained for questioning as he rode into Tennessee.

A man fitting the description was spotted on the Chickasaw Trace, and he was placed in custody in Stewart County. The inquisition drew a crowd as excited war-speculation settled for the moment on one spot. Everyone was anxious to know how close four tribes were ready to declare war against them, and they were eager to get every detail about the enemies they might soon face. Officials arrived and forced the man to answer questions under oath.

At first, the witness pretended to be a lunatic, and he answered questions in an intentionally irrational manner. A spectator from the audience stepped forward and claimed that he recognized the witness. He said that the man was not a Quaker preacher, but Simon Gerty, a half-Irishman who had traveled the area in the early days as a British trader and scout. More recently, Gerty had fought with the Shawnee against the Americans in the Battle of St. Clair. Gerty was alleged to be a spy on the British payroll. Gerty would have been elderly by 1812, and if he had traveled down the Natchez Trace that year, Americans reasonably would have concluded that he was at work for the British. Blount reported that the witness was raised in the Creek Nation and was now a spy for the British.[556] However, nothing further was said about the bogeyman of the Revolution. Just the rumor of his presence created the intended effect.

Natchez Trace travelers seemed to confirm the post rider's report by claiming that they had witnessed a group of hostiles encamped at the mouth of Bear Creek in the Chickasaw Nation, along with parties of Chickasaw, Creek, and Choctaw. When Colbert heard those rumors, he assured Governor Blount that the travelers had mistaken a council held with the U.S for a hostile meeting. The Chickasaw had held no councils with the hostiles.[557]

Governor Blount consulted with Jackson about the risks that Tecumseh's followers were using the remote western areas of Tennessee as a staging area to build coalitions of hostile Indians. The first attack of settlers at the mouth of Duck River suggested that possibility. At a minimum, hostile Creek were using the old Glover's Trace branch of the Chickasaw Trace as a communication route between the northern and southern tribes. Blount gave Jackson authority to investigate and to act to prevent the Creek from initiating attacks from the remote area. The governor also asked the Secretary of War for authority to use Tennessee militia as U.S. Rangers to range and scout in the area between the Duck River and Tennessee River.[558]

In Nashville, the *Clarion* published a poem "Farewell To Peace" that included:

"Our Country Calls—freemen AWAKE!
Rise like the Lion from his lair,
Though Comets glare, and Earthquakes
Shake,
What men can do, that bravely DARE!

Tell the proud Tyrant of the waters,
That this is FREEDOM'S dear bought land,
That rather than England's slaves,
We'll, fight, and die upon the strand.

Guard then these blessings from the foe;
Unfurl the standard—plant it high!
Strike, strike, one great, one common blow,
Life free, or in the "last ditch die!"

SPIRITS OF FIRE! Awake! Behold
The traitors on your vitals prey!
Tis British fraud—'tis British gold,
Which steals your liberties away."[559]

On the Duck and Sandy Rivers on the Chickasaw Trace west of Nashville, the Crawley and Manley families, neighbors of the settler whose farm had been destroyed by renegade Indians, banded together in one cabin for safety.[560] When days passed without incident, militia captain and boatman John Crawley and his neighbor Jesse Manley felt safe leaving their families to go to the mill for corn. But with the recent attack on the neighbor still fresh, Mrs. Manley and her children took shelter with Martha Crawley. A boarder Mr. Hayes also remained behind to protect the women. It was thought there would be safety in numbers.

On May 12, a few of the Creek who had participated in the first Sandy River attack returned. Sudden war cries startled the women. Mrs. Crawley had allowed two of her children to play outside. The Creek killed them first. Mrs. Crawley opened puncheon boards that served as a trap door in the floor of her cabin and threw one or two of her children into the potato cellar to hide them under the cabin floor. The women then rushed toward the cabin door and attempted to force it shut with their bodies, but the Indians overpowered them and broke through. One of the Creek attackers snatched Mrs. Manley's nine-day-old child from her arms, grabbed the infant by the heels, and crushed its head against a wall. Mrs. Crawley's young son ran outside to escape, but the Indians' dogs chased him and caught him. Four Creek danced around the boy and then, according to one account, allowed the dogs to tear him apart. Mrs. Manley was shot in the knee and jaw, scalped, stabbed, and left for dead with arrows in her body. She suffered other indignities that the newspaper chose not to print. When the attack ended, Mr. Hayes, and six Crawley and Manley family members, mostly children, were killed.[561] The attackers kept Mrs. Manley's neighbor Martha Crawley alive and took her as a hostage, often forcing her to walk behind them.

A neighbor found Mrs. Manley and carried her to Squire Morton's on Richland Creek where she recovered long enough to describe the horror of the attack that had killed all her children. She soon died from an apparent heart attack brought on by the trauma. Neighbors sent a party back to Duck River to bury the dead. One of the Manley family was still missing.

Captain Crawley returned home from the mill five days later to find what was left of the gory scene. He sent for help to locate his wife, and news of the attack rippled throughout the state.

John Bennett of Williamson County was at the Hickman County Court House at Vernon when news of the attack arrived. He rode to Humphreys County with 25 militia and met Colonel Phillips who provided details of the massacre.[562] Scouts acknowledged that they had spotted no Indians, but based upon the conditions they saw, they speculated that the Indian party must have numbered between 500 and 600. Part of the hostile Creek strategy was to use terror attacks to make the strength of their forces seem greater than it was. They had succeeded.

Thomas Johnson, Brigadier General of the 6th Tennessee Militia Brigade, arrived at the Humphreys County courthouse the next evening and was met with reports of the attack. He ordered 42 men to travel to the Crawley house about 12 miles away to investigate.[563]

As news of the massacre spread, companies from Franklin and Rutherford County met and marched toward the Duck River together with offers to help. Within a short time, the posse's ranks had grown to 700 or 800. General Johnson found that most men were not as well armed as he had hoped, but he concluded that they were as well or better equipped than the militia had been in many years. He sent out scouts to the Chickasaw Nation to determine where the captors had fled. Johnson's spies attempted to follow paths on the opposite side of the river but found that the earthquake had created fissures and had fell trees that made the terrain difficult to negotiate.[564] When scouts returned, they reported finding a Chickasaw man who mentioned the new rebel town that had been reported in the newspapers. The man told the scouts that Tecumseh was encamped in their nation with some of his best Shawnee warriors and that he was waiting for the Americans. News that the infamous Shawnee warrior was so close gave Johnson pause. He delayed his pursuit.

Rumor of the existence of the hostile Indian New Town had power over a state already on the edge. In fact, the town more likely was a camp of 350 Creek that had formed at the mouth of the Duck River in 1808.[565] Its inhabitants had committed a few depredations against settlers before disbanding.

Settlers in Huntsville spread rumors that Colbert again had sent messengers with warnings that Creek were preparing to attack their town. It would not be the last threatened attack. A young soldier later joked that

Creek burned the same Huntsville several times if all the stories of attack were true.[566] To people living near the Indian nations far from militia protection of any size, the threat of attack was no joking matter.

The *Clarion* reported the Duck River attack in gruesome detail in a special supplemental issue on May 19.[567] John Coffee vouched for the truthfulness of the witness who swore to the facts. Other newspapers spread the account across the nation. The *Pittsburg Gazette* added, "Language cannot pourtray nor imagination scarcely conceive this unequaled scene of Hellish barbarity."[568]

Tennesseans in a panic over the Duck River attacks could relate to the victims' families. From details of the stories, the attack could have happened to any of them, and it still could. In addition, Martha Crawley gave the story a face that related the news to settlers on a human level. Some settlers sheltered with other families for safety in numbers, and they told their children not to make a sound until the danger had passed.[569]

Governor Blount reported the attack to the Secretary of War as grounds to request that the Volunteers that Congress had authorized be mobilized as quickly as possible. He relayed that General Jackson was more than ready to lead them. However, Jackson's ambitions were greater than the defense of West Tennessee. Undermining the argument for an urgent defense of Tennessee, Blount passed along Jackson's assurances that he would be just as happy to invade Mexico or fight the British in Canada.[570]

Bravado notwithstanding, Jackson and Blount would first have to motivate the militia to volunteer for a fight outside the nation when the average Tennessean was more concerned about risks closer to home. Indian attacks had been common just 20 years earlier, but this generation had grown up in a relative time of peace.

After the Creek terror attacks west of Nashville, vivid descriptions of the event changed perceptions of everyday sights and sounds that unnerved settlers. People living on the north side of the Tennessee River reported hearing dogs and guns firing in the Indian nations on the south side, sounds that had often gone unnoticed, but which now seemed menacing in the heightened unease from the recent attack.[571]

Captain William Carroll called his militia company to parade through Nashville.[572] The presence of a defensive force was designed to help settle townspeople's nerves, as well as to put the militia in a heightened state of readiness. Colonel Thomas McCrory followed suit and ordered his company to assemble for parade. A few days later, their militias were ordered to begin filling their cartridges for a possible march into Indian territory.[573]

About 80 miles southwest, as Mrs. Crawley's abductors continued homeward with their prize hostage, they uncovered bark canoes that had been stashed on the Tennessee River on their northern journey. Paddling the frightened mother across the Tennessee River, they took her deeper into Chickasaw territory.

The first evening, the captors tied Mrs. Crawley to a tree by her hands and neck as they debated what should be done with her. Occasionally they approached her and threatened to kill her if she attempted to escape. The next morning, they continued south through the Chickasaw Nation, again forcing Mrs. Crawley to walk behind them.

Chickasaw leaders were still in council, and the rebels found little resistance. When the abductors reached Bear Creek, they camped for a day. Occasionally, passing Chickasaw men stopped to smoke the pipe and drink with them.

Chickasaw runners rushed to George Colbert to inform him that Creek camped at Bear Creek had brought a woman hostage from Tennessee. The Creek wore white people's scalps around their waists.[574] To Colbert, it was another attempt by the Creek rebels to pull him into the fight with the settlers. For months, Creek had stolen horses from the whites and taken them to Chickasaw land, hoping that the settlers would attack the Chickasaw, who would then be forced to align themselves with the Creek for defense.

Colbert rode to Bear Creek where he spotted the captors. He asked to talk with their prisoner, and the Creek did not refuse. Though Colbert did not describe what he saw, he took pity on "the poor woman."[575] Colbert said that after interviewing her, if he had any authority to act on behalf of the government, he would have ordered her release even if it cost him his life.

Colbert questioned the Creek about the scalps. The hostiles said that they had taken the scalps at the place where the Buffalo River empties into the Duck River. That area was where the Sandy River or Duck River attacks had taken place. They had also taken about 18 horses from the settlements. When Colbert returned from the Creek camp and spoke to larger groups of Chickasaw men, he ordered that the Creek rebels be forced from the nation. He had already confiscated two of the horses that he suspected to be stolen, but he had not insisted on Mrs. Crawley's release.[576]

Mrs. Crawley later remembered Colbert speaking in a friendly manner to her captors, but she did not later recall speaking to him. She noticed that the Chickasaw men outnumbered her captors, and she could not understand why Colbert had not forced the Creek to free her. Mrs. Crawley did not explain how she recognized Colbert by sight, as she claimed.[577]

Chickasaw Agent Neelly reported to Secretary Eustis, "I have also been under the Necessity of sending another express to Fort Hamilton to notify Capt. Sevier of a party of Creek passing thro a part of this country with six white scalps and a white woman prisoner. George Colbert saw the woman and talked with her."[578] Major Neelly did not know that the scalps were from the victims of the Duck River attacks.

Neelly sent a second warning to Secretary of War Eustis that some of the Creek were working harder to persuade other nations to attack the settlers, "There has been a number of Creek Indians in this nation dancing with three or four white scalps and have been trying to persuade this nation to join them in killing whites but the people of this nation have steadily refused."[579] Indians walking around wearing white settlers' scalps challenged the authority of the U.S. and if they were not stopped, they would only encourage others to do the same.

A more imminent threat from the north distracted Colbert. Blount had used his power under the Tennessee state constitution to prevent an invasion by sending militia to pursue invaders south into Chickasaw territory.[580] Colbert received news that General Johnson's militia posse planned to track and chase the captors across the Tennessee River into his nation.[581] Colbert knew that a group of angry and lightly trained citizen soldiers was unlikely to take time to distinguish between Creek and Chickasaw. The Creek might be successful after all in pulling the Chickasaw into a fight with the settlers.

If the captors were taking Mrs. Crawley into the Creek Nation, Governor Blount would need authority to pursue them that far from the borders of Tennessee. Blount also needed to calm fears by demonstrating that Creek rebels from the south would be cut off from traveling through the area to join tribes in the north. He anxiously awaited a response to his letter to the Secretary of War asking for authority to send a militia unit either to rescue Mrs. Crawley or to punish her captors. Blount's constituents were looking to him and Militia General Jackson for justice. The governor reported that the incident had so outraged citizens he could "barely contain them."[582]

Once Colbert left Bear Creek, the captors took Mrs. Crawley off the Natchez Trace to avoid being followed. After forcing her to walk behind them for four days, the group reached Creek towns on the Tombigbee River and set up camp. Other Creek stopped at the camp to smoke and drink with the captors. Mrs. Crawley said that her abductors told the other men that they had taken her from the Battle of Tippecanoe and that they planned to return there again in four moons. The Creek explained that they planned to stir up Indians to fight whites. They hoped that they could recruit additional followers, but they were doubtful. Mrs. Crawley never explained how she understood the language.

After moving on, the abductors took Mrs. Crawley to a Creek town at the Falls of the Black Warrior River at Tuscaloosa, likely the village of Creek chief Oceocehemotla, who had persuaded the Choctaw to let him live close to their villages. Soon, Mrs. Crawley noticed that the men were digging a hole. One of the Indian women told her the hole was a grave, and she knew that she was no longer useful to them.

The men loosened Mrs. Crawley's restraints and ordered her to stir a pot of hominy. It was her only opportunity to escape. Mrs. Crawley picked up a tin cup and pretended to walk to the spring for water. Instead, she ran into the darkness, with the abductors on her heels. She found a hollow log and crawled inside to hide until morning.[583]

Colbert's fear that Johnson's troops would not take time to distinguish between Creek warriors and Chickasaw hunters prompted him to appeal directly to the settlers through the *Clarion* on May 22:

> "Brothers and Friends, We the Chickasaw now we must explain what we always thought, there is but one God who have made all things that is on earth and of course we have one father who have made us all, however we look to the President of the United States as father and guide, know that the government have been at a great deal of trouble and expense for our people welfare, endeavoring to procure a better living and comforts, to supply us with present goods every year, which, we know it must cost a great deal . . . .
>
> Brothers and Friends, We know we have got women and children to support and whish to live in peace—we have not doubt but that all the Indian tribes that ever have any intercourse with the U. States, has a good right to know the intention of the United States as well as we the Chickasaw

from the friendship that government have acted towards the Indians, yet it is not only this tribe of Indians that government have supported, but all that live, so if any tribe wishes to be in peace they can live in peace,

Brothers and Friends, The road from Nashville to Natchez, was asked by the United States and we gave a grant that it should be so, and to be a road of peace—no bloodshed was to be made on it. In the treaty, the United States requested we should settle on the highway; accordingly we done so, and have been much troubled thereby; but our greatest [concern] is, that white people have stolen our horses and robbed our houses, and burdensome; that has scared our women and children, but we are in hopes that it [is no] more than some of the bad people that does it. . . . We understand by travelers that general Johnson's army were out in pursuit of those offenders, and intend to cross the Tennessee river; you ought to give us notice before you cross the river, because there is many innocent Chickasaw hunters down that way therefore you might destroy your friends."[584]

The next day, Colbert clarified his position:

"Relative to my talk yesterday, no sooner had I finished the other talk, some runners came to my house and said that there was a company of the Prophet's, near Bear Creek, with a white woman prisoner, and I was obliged to go and examine them; I held a talk and after examining them, they said in the first place they have been at some houses at the mouth of Sandy Creek, and had killed cattle- and in the second place they destroyed five little children, and one man, & caught this woman below the mouth of Duck river, where there is some pine trees on the banks of the Tennessee river. I have had a chance to talk with the white woman and she says her name is Mrs. Crawfort; there I saw them with my own eyes. Mrs. Crawfort says her husband and one of her sons were gone to mill, while these savages broke upon the poor woman. And they say when they get home with the prisoner and other property if their head men should disapprove, they will turn in and serve the leading men in the way that they have done the white people, Big Warrior, in particular. Had I the least power from the government, I should have taken the prisoner from them at the risqué o my life. But I have only to grieve at the poor woman's fate, it is truly sorrowful to any feelings; so the sooner after you see this letter, you lodge a complaint with Col. Hawkins the United States' agent to the , the better. The commander of this company, his name is Ellipohorchew. Anything that lays in my power to inform the public, I will do it with haste, these people are in a very great haste and have gone this day."[585]

What more could he do to prove his friendship to the settlers? It was not the first time that Colbert addressed the public directly through the newspaper, but it was clear that he did not want to rely upon Jackson, Blount, or anyone who was trying to stir war to interpret his motives to the public.

In early June, the War Department authorized the rangers Blount had requested, but it did not limit his authority to use them by specific orders. Taking advantage of that opening, Blount called out 100 militia rangers, the advance force of Indian scouts, under the command of Captain David Mason to ride or range through Tennessee between the waters of the Tennessee and Mississippi Rivers.[586]One of the first advance spies, John Clifford, took a boat and floated the Buffalo River from the Tennessee River to the Natchez Trace, but he saw no signs of Indians.[587]

Captain Mason ordered the remainder of the rangers to rendezvous at Captain David Dobbin's Stand on the Natchez Trace, where they may have met Clifford for his report. From there, rangers rode up to where the Crawley attack had taken place at the mouth of the Duck River and crossed over the Tennessee River.[588] Reserves were left at their headquarters north on the Natchez Trace at Gordon's Ferry.[589]

Rangers heard a rumor that the party of Creek that had attacked the settlers were just across the Tennessee River near the location of the Crawley farm. After a search, they found evidence of two former large encampments, but there was no sign of the mythic New Town.

Rangers expected Creek to jump out from behind every tree or through the thick cane breaks. Adding to the tension of riding near the massacre site, the effects of the earthquake had created deep fissures that covered large areas with white sand and that still spewed steam, giving the landscape an otherworldly appearance.

Near a cross path, likely Glover's Trace, known to be used by Creek traveling to Shawnee territory, rangers fell in with a party of four Indians they thought to be Shawnee pretending to be Chickasaw. One of the Indian men turned and ran down the path. Rangers followed and shot the man they assumed to be a hostile Indian.[590] They discovered later that the man was Choctaw and that the suspect Indian party was a peaceful group of Choctaw who were searching for a hunting campsite. The only fatality in the ranger force was a horse belonging to Thomas Hart Benton's brother Jessie. The horse had died from friendly fire.

Suddenly, a wave of terror broke out on the Natchez Trace as travelers came under constant attack from unseen fighters. Rangers assumed that the man they had killed must have been an important Choctaw leader and that Choctaw warriors were exacting revenge. Mason's rangers could worry whether their actions may have inadvertently pushed the

Choctaw to side with Tecumseh. When attacks led to the death of a traveler Thomas Haley, an investigation was ordered. It was then discovered that the terror from revenge came from just one person—the ten-year-old or twelve-year-old brother of the fallen Choctaw man.[591]

Separate militia detachments continued their search for Mrs. Crawley south in Chickasaw Territory. Despite Colbert's warnings, militia colonel Pillow took about 80 men and began crossing the Tennessee River eight miles west of Fort Hampton. An express letter was delivered from General Roberts conveying a report that Creek were encamped on Bear Creek with a woman prisoner. General Roberts ordered Pillow to meet him at Levi Colbert's Natchez Trace inn "Buzzard Roost" about 10 miles from the mouth of Bear Creek. They could plan an attack from there.

On the way to Colbert's, the detachment passed a Cherokee town. An Indian man named "Big John" greeted them, claiming to be Cherokee. Joseph Brown, a Maury County resident, began a conversation with the man in Cherokee. When the Indian could not answer him in Cherokee, the impostor ran. Soldiers pursued him and brought him back to the town for questioning.[592]

Soldiers then showed the prisoner to Cherokee at Chief Double Head's village. Cherokee recognized him and called him by name. They described him as a "bad Indian" under Tecumseh's influence. The prisoner had just returned from Shawnee country at the Wabash area, and he had brought stolen horses into the camp. The militia decided to tie up the Indian man and take him with them to Buzzard's Roost, where he would be held in a possible exchange for Mrs. Crawley.

The Indian prisoner began to complain that the restraints were too tight. When soldiers loosened them, the man broke free and began to run. Five soldiers fired, and the man fell.[593]

General Roberts was waiting for the party at Buzzard's Roost. He said that reports of Creek camping at Bear Creek were no longer accurate, but Levi Colbert had more troubling news. He had been informed that the

Creek had already killed settlers in their area. They were now carrying 17 scalps.[594] The Creek party, rumored to be 40 or 50 in number, approached some of the Chickasaw and joined them in their dances. Creek displayed the scalps of their white victims and encouraged Chickasaw to join their fight against the settlers.

Rangers had been unable to track the Creek hostiles.[595] On June 12, Neely wrote to Secretary of War Eustis that the renegade Creek were elusive, "I have been under the necessity of applying to Captain Sevier for a detachment of the troops under his command at Fort Hampton in order to take those Creek Indians who had the white scalps, but the Indians hearing of the troops being on their way to apprehend them, made their escape from this nation three or four days before the troops arrived and the troops have returned to Fort Hampton."[596] The Creek hostiles, he reported, were causing trouble especially for the Chickasaw, and the Chickasaw were attempting to resolve matters diplomatically.

Neely confirmed that the Indians had held a council, but it was a Chickasaw council, adding, "The Chiefs of this nation held a Council on the 12th Inst. Respecting some straggling Creek that are hovering about this country stealing horses and committing depredations on travelers, and other white people settled on the frontier, the result is they have ordered the Creek home and have wrote to the Creek nation to call them home. These stragglers say they have joined the Shawnee Prophet and his party which accounts for the depredations committed by them on the whites. The Chiefs of this nation has wrote to the Creek wishing to know whether or not the whole nation had joined the Prophet and his party against the whites naming at the same time that they have no intention to go to war, but if possible to maintain peace and friendship with all nations."[597]

The only encouraging news was, as Neely reported, that friendly Creek chiefs had answered Colbert's request by showing their support for Americans when their runner appeared and ordered all Creek visiting other nations to return home. But before they returned, horses were stolen from several Chickasaw leaders' farms.[598] The Natchez Trace was becoming as dangerous for Chickasaw who befriended the settlers as it was for the settlers.

Governor Blount needed a tally of soldiers who could be counted on if war erupted. He ordered Jackson to have militia commanders determine the number of men willing to volunteer.[599] Officers were instructed to ride through the counties and enroll additional recruits. The war that Jackson had wanted for so long finally seemed close.

CHAPTER NINE

LEADING
THE CHORUS OF HAWKS

"[T]o have waited untill a blow was struct, and then give...
orders to apply a remedy—This is sending for a Phician after the
patient is dead."

—Andrew Jackson to Willie Blount

As tensions grew exponentially in the West, Congress debated the merits of war. Tennessee representatives influenced by Jackson joined the voices of the "War Hawks." Some easterners had long thought that western settlers provoked Indian attacks as an excuse to take Indian land. Now they also challenged that it was easy for westerners to push for war from the safety of hundreds of miles from the eastern seashore the British were expected to target. Westerners countered that citizens on the frontier faced just as much, if not more, risk from the British and their agents due to their proximity to hostile Indians. The recent attack of settlers and abduction of Mrs. Crawley proved their point. The British supported Tecumseh, and Tecumseh had stirred the Creek hostiles to attack. What additional proof did easterners need that the British were attacking settlers through Indian proxies?

As the primary military commander who had felt the responsibility for the security of Tennesseans on the frontier for a decade, Jackson had been forced to consider risks of Indian attacks and to evaluate defenses. Growing up in an area that faced Indian attacks had already established Jackson's view of Indians in general as the enemy or at least a potential enemy. His responsibility to protect Tennessee homes from attack had no doubt altered even more how he viewed Indian nations. He saw risks others did not see, just as his experience as a land speculator no doubt also caused him to consider benefits in removing those risks to profit from Indian land.[600]

Though George Colbert and Jackson had worked together as "friends" when their interests coincided, Colbert knew Jackson well enough to know that his threats signaled this was not a time they could reason together. Whether Jackson believed that Tecumseh's threat was real or whether he saw opportunity in the threat, their relationship had been changed. Colbert sought peace. Jackson wanted war.

Rather than turn to Jackson, Colbert sent a plea to his old friend James Robertson to appeal to Governor Blount to call off the militia. As Colbert feared, militia soldiers had assumed that Creek renegades were hiding everywhere, and they were terrorizing the women and children by entering Chickasaw houses to search for them. Colbert had held a council at Bear Creek to explain the situation in his country, but it had not helped.[601]

Robertson responded quickly to Colbert's request by publishing a letter to the editor of a Nashville newspaper. In it, he disputed the notion that the Chickasaw were giving aid to the Creek or making any preparation for war. He said that he had just visited with several of the Chickasaw chiefs and that they were just as "exasperated" with the Creek as Tennesseans were. Robertson assured Tennesseans of George Colbert's loyalty. He said that Tennesseans should understand that Colbert was in a delicate situation as leader of his own nation and there were limits on the actions he could take against the Creek. More pointedly in a possible jab at Jackson's war prodding, Robertson urged Tennesseans to be careful of those who wanted to create tension with the Chickasaw when none existed.[602]

Though Congress continued to debate what course to take, a war resolution looked more certain. Congress authorized the purchase of almost 90,000 uniforms. The Militia Act was passed, authorizing the President to organize and equip a militia detachment of the United States Army and hold them in a state of readiness should they be needed. The militia so organized would be entitled to the same pay as regular army. However, continuing to fear the consequences of establishing a large standing army, Congress limited the militia's term of service to six months.[603]

The Regular Army, downsized during the Jefferson administration, also began recruiting. A regiment of the "New Army" in Tennessee organized under the command of Andrew Jackson's militia aide-de-camp William P. Anderson.

General Jackson might have reacted to the Crawley attack and the wave of public outrage by summoning his militia and taking matters into his own hands with the justifiable basis of a state of emergency, but he was in Georgia when the attacks occurred. For public purposes, Jackson had been required to travel to Georgia to settle legal disputes over his sales of investment lands.[604] From the vantage point of Georgia, however, Jackson was positioned to learn of events taking place in East Florida. He needed to know when forces from Tennessee might be called on to support the taking of the territory from the Spanish and ensure that British forces did not move in to fill the vacuum.

Jackson took time to talk directly with the Cherokee, and particularly one of the Cherokee ferry operators who told him there was no doubt the Creek were preparing for war. The Cherokee informant understood that a few of the Chickasaw and Choctaw would join with the Creek in attacks, but he gave Jackson solemn assurances that the Cherokee would join with the Tennesseans.[605]

Cherokee chiefs had sent a letter to the Creek through their American interpreter, warning the Creek that if they joined the British they would lose. For public purposes, Cherokee also assured the Creek that if they joined the Americans, the Americans would also be their friends. The Cherokee's letter, which was sent through their American interpreter, was probably written more for the benefit of the Americans than the Creek. The Cherokee, like all other Indian nations, were caught in an uncertain struggle for survival among competing interests. The main effect of their diplomacy was that in their attempt to strengthen their own relationship with Jackson and the Americans, the Cherokee undercut Tennesseans' confidence in the loyalty of the Chickasaw and Choctaw. Even then, Jackson did not accept the Cherokee's assurances. He reported to Blount that Cherokee and Creek would join the British in an attack against Americans if the British chose to invade from the Gulf Coast.[606]

Already troubled by the Cherokee's assessment of southern Indian neighbors, Jackson was greeted with the grim news of the Duck River attack when he returned to the Hermitage on June 4. He said that his "heart bled" when he heard the account.[607] Jackson was acquainted with Martha Crawley's husband Captain John Crawley, who had transported goods for Jackson by river.[608] Jackson could show genuine outrage as a family friend.

Agitated town leaders were no doubt anxious to give Jackson every detail of the story. The Crawley attack had left many settlers feeling vulnerable on the frontier. The public was in a panic and no leader seemed to know what to do. What the public really wanted was a plan of action.

Jackson suspected that the British had instigated the attack at the Duck River and that it would be only the first of many. The fact that the Creek did not fear taking Mrs. Crawley to the Chickasaw Nation might mean that Chickasaw were becoming supportive of Tecumseh's efforts. Jackson's intelligence from the Cherokee that some Chickasaw were thinking of joining Tecumseh's confederation clouded Jackson's trust of the Chickasaw.[609]

Jackson's first order of business was to learn what Tennessee Militia Brigadier General Thomas Johnson's men had accomplished. After some inquiry, Jackson discovered that rather than pursing the attackers, Johnson was still encamped near Nashville with 500 men, and that he had done nothing to follow the Creek party or to recover Mrs. Crawley.[610] Johnson should not expect people to believe that a little rough terrain caused by the earthquake made it impossible to locate the Indian tracks or camp. Jackson would accept no excuses.

Jackson quickly developed what seemed a commonsense plan of action that the public demanded. The militia should be called to arms and march into the Creek Nation to rescue Mrs. Crawley and to remove the threat of the young rebels and their supporters. Tennessee leaders and possibly federal leaders would realize too late that Jackson's plan might have avoided a wider war with the Creek.

Jackson appealed to Blount first with an emotional argument and then followed with three reasons the governor should be compelled to act. Jackson described the Duck River massacre as an attack on all their "innocent, wives and little babies."[611] What responsible Tennessee leader could sit idle while women and babies were under attack? Jackson relayed that the public not only wanted protection from the Creek, but they demanded revenge. Second, the British were certainly the instigators and their threat had to be nipped in the bud. Third, if Tennesseans acted quickly to show a strong defense, wavering Indian nations would be compelled to join the Americans rather than the British and increase the chances of victory. Anticipating that the governor would be concerned about logistics, Jackson offered to raise 2,500 men in a short period and scrape up limited supplies and munitions to prosecute the action.

As additional pressure, Jackson told the governor that even prior to receiving the governor's reply, Jackson would issue an order to prepare the militia to march. The only thing preventing just punishment of the attackers that the public demanded and the obliteration of the threat forever was merely the formality of the governor's signature on the order. Jackson assumed that he had made it impossible for the governor to say "no," as 2,500 Tennessee town leaders demanding action were practically saddled up and ready to go.

To ensure that his command would not be challenged by Tennessee Militia Brigadier General Johnson, Jackson used the newspaper to undermine Johnson's leadership. Jackson publicly accused Johnson of being nearby the Duck River area when the attacks on Crawley and Manley had taken place.[612] The frightened public should know that Johnson had done nothing to defend the settlement. And the governor should conclude that the obvious choice to command a defense was Jackson.

Jackson had done everything possible to make it easy for the governor to give him authority to lead the military campaign, except for literally drafting the governor's order for him. He was so close to achieving the command he wanted, why should he hesitate for protocol? Jackson took the liberty of writing the governor's official order to call the men to arms, and he enclosed the suggested order with a letter reemphasizing the British involvement with the Indians.

Revealing just how important Jackson thought this moment was finally to achieving the command he wanted, Jackson carefully considered the draft of his letter and decided to call on his friend and former aide-de-camp William P. Anderson to re-write it to make the wording stronger:

"Now Sir the object of tecumpsies visit to the creek nation is unfolding to us. That incendiary, the emissary of the Prophet, who is himself the tool of England, has caused our frontier to be stained with blood, and our peaceful citizens to fly in terror from their once happy abodes."[613]

Jackson urged swift and overwhelming revenge that would get the Shawnee and Creek attention before they had the opportunity to persuade other tribes to join them. In his hyperbole, Jackson went on to describe plans to lay waste to the Creek Nation. Given Jackson's ultimate war on the Creek, it would be reasonable to conclude that he intended that outcome from the beginning. However, even Jackson knew that when the Creek were facing a civil war, he only needed to remove the threat from the side that was hostile to the United States.[614]

Confident that he had left Blount no choice but to sign the order immediately, Jackson took it upon himself to deal with rumors of potential Chickasaw involvement. He penned a letter to George Colbert, addressing him in the customary salutation "Friend and Brother," and assuring the Chickasaw chief of his friendship.[615] Jackson reminded Colbert that the Cumberland settlers had once joined the Chickasaw to repel the Creek from the Chickasaw Nation. Jackson promised that if the Chickasaw Nation joined with the Tennesseans again and helped stop Creek attacks, his Tennessee militia would defend Chickasaw from the Creek.

But Jackson showed the limits of their friendship by making it clear that Colbert would be held accountable for allowing the Creek to operate out of the Chickasaw Nation.[616] If Colbert had taken two stolen horses from Mrs. Crawley's captors as he had claimed, why had he not used that same power to rescue Mrs. Crawley? Jackson added the threat he hoped would be conveyed to the Creek: If Creek chiefs did not surrender Mrs. Crawley, Jackson would see that their nation was destroyed. Then he warned that if the Chickasaw did not prevent the Creek from continuing to travel through their lands to attack the settlements, Jackson would assume that the Chickasaw were in league with the Creek and the Chickasaw might suffer the same fate.

Jackson summed up his message bluntly, "Friend & Brother! You tell us you are the friend of the whites. [N]ow prove it to me."[617]

Jackson's threat to Colbert violated the spirit of the governor's order to Ranger Commander Mason. Because Colbert had assured Blount of the Chickasaw's friendship, rangers were to assume that all Chickasaw were friendly unless evidence proved otherwise. All other tribes found in the Chickasaw Nation were to be presumed hostile unless evidence proved otherwise.[618] Though Jackson was not technically bound by the order to Mason, Jackson pushed the bounds of his command authority over the rangers by forcing the Chickasaw Colbert to prove his loyalty.

Chief Colbert did not appreciate the paranoia that was now charting the course of events. Chickasaw had lived with the threats of attacks from hostile Choctaw and Creek for decades. How could Tennesseans so soon forget the Chickasaw's long friendship? But Colbert took Jackson's threat seriously. The Chickasaw chief reluctantly accepted the role enforcing Jackson's demands for the Creek rebels. But Colbert was also motivated by his own self-preservation. Creek rebels had shown no reluctance to use his nation as a staging area to attack whites. The teachings of the Prophet also were beginning to have an influence on a few of the Chickasaw, and the cotton trade that Colbert was developing ran counter to such teachings.[619] Unless Colbert took some action, the hostile Indians might soon place him in the same category as white invaders, just as the whites lumped him together with hostile Indians. Colbert sent a letter to the Creek that he shared with settlers to let them know he was complying with their requests:

> "We held a council yesterday at the king's house, in which
> it was discussed the depredations committed by some strag-
> gling people of your nation on the whites; they have killed
> and robbed some white people & have stolen horses from the
> whites and brought them here for sale, and on this subject we

called the council in order to have stop put in such proceedings as we have a desire to live at peace with all nations—but we may be blamed by the whites for mischief done by your people in our land, it may be probable that you nor the good people of your nation knows nothing of what their stragglers do here,

Friends & Brothers,

We have been informed by a flying report that you and your nation had joined the Shawnee Prophet & his party against the whites—we could not believe it until we can hear it from your own mouth.

Friends & Brothers,

You will be so good as to let us know whether or not you have joined the Prophet.

Friends & Brothers,

These people of your nation that are here say that they have joined the Prophet, & that is the reason they commit the murders & robberies on the whites.

Friends & Brothers,

It would be well for you & your nation to call these stragglers home. If they do any more mischief to white people they may take satisfaction in killing them & we don't wish any blood to be spilt on our land but want to be in peace and friendship with all nations,

Friends & Brothers,

We see the way these people of your's manage here and have advised them to go home, but they will not take our talk & if they get killed by the whites we cannot save them. We are but a small nation and wish to remain at peace."[620]

Tecumseh's efforts, which seemed at first to produce the seeds of an Indian confederation, now resulted in divisions that Americans could exploit. Martha Crawley's abduction not only drove a wedge between Creek families, the Big Warrior faction of the Creek and the Little Warrior faction and younger purists, but it also pitted Indian nations against each other. For decades, Chickasaw had protected their nation diplomatically by balancing the interests of opposing nations on the American continent. Looming war between the British and the Americans—and more directly between the Creek and the Americans—made it impossible to continue that strategy. Each needed to use Chickasaw land for staging attacks or moving troops or warriors. Each called on Colbert to choose sides. In fact, Colbert had already chosen to side with the settlers, but Creek actions and Cherokee rumors undermined the settlers' confidence in his pledges of loyalty.

Colbert understood the pressure that settlers put on Jackson or maybe how Jackson created that pressure to justify war. Colbert followed Jackson's example and again appealed directly to Tennessee citizens by pleading his nation's defense in the newspapers:

"Friends and Brothers !
I find you are very jealous of the Chickasaw Indians, and I do not know why you should be so without reason; we have given no cause of offence.
Friends and Brothers,
This we all know—the strong man is often ready to find fault with the weak man, because he knows he is unable to help himself.
Friends and Brothers,
It is not only you the whites who know that we the red people are weak. We ourselves know it; we do not know how to make ammunition, guns and other necessaries for war—when the

whites discover in our nation preparations of a warlike kind I presume it will be time enough then to suspect us; but you find nothing of the kind.

Friends and Brothers!

Therefore I hope some of the leading men in Tennessee will endeavor to find out the authors of the reports going about, of our supporting the Creek who are doing mischief—I do not think the printer was altogether right in putting such reports in the papers without the authors name. We are anxious to know his name, as there has been but very few whites amongst us.

Friends and Brothers!

The whites are jealous of us, also the Creek are jealous of us on the other hand, and say we are upholding the whites, so we are afraid on both sides. we have reason to be afraid of the whites, they have come and burnt some houses, shot at the doors, robbed and stole horses, &c Also the Creek kill our cattle, steal from us, &c and I understand some of you should say, why did I not take the woman from the Creek—About 15 years ago the whites promised every assistance if our nation was invaded, but when it took place, we had to fight without any help—When we experience a thing, we generally recollect it. This the old settlers of Cumberland know.[621]

Colbert demonstrated the cunning for which he was known. He expressed the humility his audience wanted to hear, all the while using the Tennesseans' inaccurate perceptions of the Indians as weak to prove his inability to make war against them. Older Nashville citizens would know that Colbert's portrayal of their alleged failure to honor their pact of defense with the Chickasaw was inaccurate. Robertson even had directly disobeyed an order from the federal government to march his soldiers to their defense.

Colbert capped off his argument by showing his insight. The Tennesseans' suggestion that the Chickasaw were listening to the words of the Prophet was fallacious. Colbert said that the Chickasaw knew that if the Prophet truly had God on his side, Tecumseh would not be asking the Chickasaw for help.[622]

But Colbert's efforts to appeal directly to the people were blunted quickly by Jackson's influence. The newspaper editor turned Colbert's communication skills back on him. If the chief could make such a persuasive case to excuse his failure to stop the Creek from attacking, why had he not used that same skill to convince the Creek to release Mrs. Crawley?[623]

Tennessee citizens reacted to the Duck River massacre by pointing fingers of blame in all directions. Why had Colbert not used his position to inform Tennesseans of a potential attack? Why had the federal Chickasaw and Creek Indian agents not anticipated and prevented the attack?[624] Why was Governor Blount still in Knoxville when he needed to be in Nashville directing a defense? The only reason the United States Army was not brought into the criticism is that westerners had long since given up on the federal government to protect them from Indian attack.

Public criticism of Colbert demonstrated the power the Indian leader wielded on the frontier. Settlers assumed that Colbert could impose the same influence over other tribes that he had in their affairs. The whites simply did not understand how Indian culture differed. In issuing the challenge to Colbert, Jackson made the same mistake in diplomacy that U.S. government agents would make in issuing demands to Creek leaders to bring the Crawley captors to justice. It may have seemed prudent to expect Indian leaders to take responsibility for administering justice on their own people on behalf of the settlers, but forcing specific Indian leaders to side with the white man against other Indians only created further divisions within the tribes. Some people in Washington City understood the importance of avoiding disruption of stability at that crucial time. However, the U.S. government through its Indian agent Benjamin Hawkins would make the same mistake in dealing with the Creek. Jackson's rash challenge to Colbert had taken the first step toward undermining a delicate diplomatic balance among the southeastern Indian nations.

The *Clarion* stirred anxiety further by reporting that the Creek were preparing for war by making special bows and arrows that they could use to attack settlers at night when lookouts would be useless. It was also reported that Creek Indian Agent Colonel Hawkins had been advised to leave the Creek Nation to save his life.[625] The Pittsburg *Gazette* relayed stories of the Duck River attacks and gave life to the rumored hostile "New Town" by suggesting that Tennessee rangers had evidence that Indian rebels from various tribes had built a new town about 160 miles southwest of Nashville. Tecumseh was said to be in the area with 600 men.[626]

Closer to the Natchez Trace, a traveler reported seeing white scalps when passing though the Choctaw Nation, those who had never taken the life of a white man. The story confirmed the impressions that Indians were becoming so antagonistic toward the settlers that they were beginning to refuse to provide any supplies to travelers on the road.[627] The reports also raised concerns that settlers were beginning to lose support of their few remaining Indian friends.

Tecumseh and the British seemed to be winning through their Indian proxies' terror attacks. The most significant proof of their campaign: Settlers began to leave their farms on the edges of the frontier and move back toward the interior.[628] The future for Tennessee to take its place among other states looked bleak.

In frustration mixed with fear, the Nashville newspaper considered relationships between the state and Indian tribes in the area. Though acknowledging that Chickasaw had always been friends to the whites, the writer linked together all tribes and bragged that it would not take two months "for the Tennesseans to sweep all these tribes from the face of the earth."[629]

Tennesseans followed Jackson's lead in demanding retaliation against the Creek, but Blount resisted Jackson's political pressure. Indian nations were the federal prerogative. Blount would have to answer to the president and the War Department if Jackson acted recklessly and started an Indian war that he could not contain. Such an effort would require money only the federal government could raise. It was not as simple as sending news to Washington City of an Indian attack on a settlement. Until Blount was assured of federal support, he had no power to grant Jackson's request and could not sign the order Jackson had so proactively drafted. The War Department would make the final decision.[630]

Jackson did not back down. He was too close to achieving his dream of command of a military mission. Jackson pressed the governor to reassess the situation, and Blount conceded that he was dubious about the Cherokee's recent overtures and pledge of support. Perhaps remembering years earlier how the Cherokee had assured Southwest Territory governor William Blount of their loyalty at the same time they were making plans to attack, he said frankly that he did not trust any Indians.[631] The Cherokee had a large contingent of Tories living among them, and it was clear that Tories were still sympathetic to the British. Even the Chickasaw and Choctaw had large numbers of former British citizens and British sympathizers who had settled in their nations during the Revolution. In fact, the only areas in the Indian nations they could count on were the agencies. Blount asked whether Jackson had noticed that all the Indians suddenly seemed restless. The only answer must be that British agents were hard at work among all the tribes.

Jackson proposed a strategy of forcing the Cherokee Nation to war with the hostile Creek.[632] In addition to using Cherokee men to weaken the Creek defense, the Cherokee would find the Creek an overpowering opponent and discover a need for Tennessee militia protection. That need would assure their loyalty. Jackson repeated a common saying among westerners of the time, "fear is better than love with an Indian."[633] If Tennesseans were uncertain of the Indians' professed loyalty out of friendship, they could be assured of their need for self-preservation. It would be a mistake to allow the Cherokee to remain neutral where they would be easier to sway to side with the Creek or British.

Still, Washington City was not prepared to support the attack on Creek hostiles that Jackson demanded. Even if the federal government decided to act, the U.S. Army numbered only about 7,000 standing troops and only about 3,000 untrained recruits for the New Army.[634] The few who were making provisions for war were certain to continue to focus their efforts on the lightly defended northern boundary and the East Coast.

President Madison attempted to use threats of military action to bring the British to the bargaining table for a peaceful resolution. At the same time, Federalist politicians opposed to war undermined the president by revealing to the British that the American threat of war was just a bluff. They must have convinced many Americans as well.[635] As Federalists and Republicans fought in Congress to use the war debate to political advantage, no one seemed to be making any preparations for supplies needed for wartime. And the government was already near the point of defaulting on its debt. Recruiters even had difficulty finding fifes and drums.

Despite the success of the American Revolution that leaders would recall in public pronouncements, they knew that this war would be the first fought under the new United States Constitution.[636] The ability of the former colonies to lay aside sectional and political differences to combine their war efforts under a republican form of government was untested.[637] No one in Washington City seemed to know how to work within the new federal system to pull the states together to mount a defense against a foreign enemy.

Jackson said that waiting for the federal government to defend people on the frontier was comparable to sending for a physician after the "patient is dead."[638] As political leaders in Washington City floundered about with the enemy at their door, Jackson argued that it would be up to Tennessee to defend the southwest frontier and that the governor needed to make his own provisions for the militia to be prepared to defend the state.

Jackson's repeated arguments finally wore down Blount's resistance. The governor authorized Jackson to build his militia to prepare a defense, but he stopped short of giving approval for military action and directly challenging the authority of the War Department.[639]

A small cover of political authority was all Jackson needed to begin motivating citizens to join him. Jackson used the limited authority that the governor gave him and began building an army he would eventually lead to war. He published his Division Orders on June 19:

"The General of the Second Division of Tennessee Militia having been commanded by His Excellency Willie Blount Governor of the State, forthwith to detach from the Second Division one thousand four hundred men (,) officers included (,) – To consist as nearly as possible in the following proportion of Artillery, Cavalry, and Infantry, viz: one twentieth part of Artillery, one twentieth of Cavalry, and the residue of Infantry- There will be no objection to the admission of a proportion of Riflemen duly organized in distinct corps, not exceeding one tenth part of the detachment."[640]

Jackson's subordinates complied. Advertisements appeared in newspapers offering to provide individual training in military procedure to men who hoped to excel at the challenge. Recruiters again rode through towns assembling potential recruits with the sounds of fife and drum. As a subordinate waited with an open recruitment book, the future company commander gave an inspiring speech about the duty of the men to defend their freedom and opportunities for military glory.

James Henderson later gave an example of the speech that lured young men anxious for glory from their farms:

> "Let the love of liberty and independence inspire our souls. And when called on to act we will be like a band of brothers—always willing to obey the lawful commands of our superior officers—conducting ourselves like gentlemen, as well as soldiers so that if we fall our fall will be glorious—if we live to return home let it be with laurels on our brows."[641]

Not every community leader was susceptible. Religious ministers did what they could to counter the effects of the speeches on impressionable young men. Their sermons criticized the recruiting tactics designed to appeal to the men's vanity rather than logic. The young men, it was said, were misled *"by the pomp and circumstance of glorious war."*[642] Ministers preached that the recruiters were pied pipers who encouraged young men to leave serious responsibilities to their families, their farms, and their church congregations to run off following a promise of vain military glory.

Despite the efforts of the peacemakers, Jackson did not have to wait long until it seemed that the War Department's interest aligned with his own. Overcoming Federalists accusations that the whole purpose of war was to gain territory in Florida and Canada, and despite threats that some northeastern states might secede from the Union, Jackson's friend

Congressman Grundy and other War Hawks won the debate in Congress. On June 22, 1812, Madison signed the Declaration of War:

"AN ACT

Declaring war between the United Kingdom of Great Britain and Ireland and the dependencies thereof, & the United States of America and their territories.

Be it enacted by the Senate and House of Representatives of the United States of America in Congress assembled, That war be and the same is hereby declared to exist between the united kingdom of Great Britain and Ireland and the dependencies thereof, and the U. States of America and their territories, and the president of the U. States be, and he hereby is authorized to use the whole of the land and naval force of the U. States to carry the same into effect, and to issue to private armed vessels of the United States commissions of letters of marque and general reprisal, in such form as he shall think proper and under the seal of the U. States, against the vessels, goals and effects of the government of the same united kingdom of G. Britain and Ireland and the subjects thereof.

Approved.

James Madison"[643]

It would take about 10 days for news of war to reach Tennessee, and it would not arrive too soon for Governor Blount. The *Clarion* stepped up pressure on the governor to act. The editor said that the governor had statutory authority to order his militia to prevent an invasion and Indian nations had invaded that State of Tennessee. Governor Blount could direct Major General Jackson to lead an expedition into the Creek Nation to demand that they return Martha Crawley along with her captors to answer to American justice. Yet, the governor had done nothing in the weeks since the attack.[644] The article ignored that Blount had already pushed the limits of his authority by sending militia and federal rangers into the Chickasaw Nation.

South in Huntsville, Federal Receiver John Brahan, likely for his own financial interests, attempted to generate a contract from the War Department to purchase gunpowder and salt peter from a cave near Huntsville by reporting that the Indians were buying up large quantities of gunpowder in the area and taking it to the Creek Nation.[645] Reminding everyone of the rumor that had generated false stories of an imminent Indian attack, the account added to speculation that the Indians were preparing for war.

Out of public view, Blount worked to seek federal approval to act on a larger scale. He wrote the president on June 25 that General Jackson and his Volunteers tendered their service to the President.[646] It was also a preemptory move to make it more difficult for the War Department to choose a commander other than Jackson.

A few weeks later, Jackson would be elated when Secretary of War Eustis replied that the president had accepted Jackson's tender of service "with peculiar satisfaction."[647] Jackson would assume that the deal had been struck and that the president was pleased, particularly when Eustis went on to praise Jackson's "zeal and ardor" in organizing his command even *before* formal orders for organizing troops had been sent. In retrospect, Eustis's letter could be interpreted as sarcastic praise for an overly eager general, but it did not matter to Jackson. Andrew Jackson's war had arrived.

CHAPTER TEN

WAR

"It is a bitter pill to have to act with him, but for my countries good I will swallow [it]."

—Andrew Jackson, November 29, 1812

The headline in the next issue of the Nashville *Clarion* was one Jackson had long awaited: WAR.

The July 4, 1812 edition noted how appropriate that the story should be published on the nation's day of independence, though it appears that the 4th was printed only on the story of the declaration of war for symbolism and that the newspaper was in fact published on the 7th. The editor proclaimed, "We are highly gratified to find this second declaration proves that the people of the present day have still some of the spirit of their forefathers, and are determined to fight for the rights acquired by them."[648] Whatever date the paper was published, the connection of the Revolution to the present conflict would not be lost as a basis to build support. In Nashville, Captain Hobbs called together his militia company and fired several rounds to welcome news that war finally had been declared.[649]

Just below the announcement of the declaration of war in the Nashville newspaper was a news story of equal interest to Jackson. The Patriot group in East Florida had engaged in battle with the Spaniards. Patriots were offering Florida land to military men who would join them.[650] Jackson knew that Madison wanted to take control of East Florida, and if Jackson could show that his Tennessee troops already mustered were prepared to deliver it, the president would be unable to turn down Jackson's command.

Independence Day already had been set as an opportunity to use heightened patriotic spirit spurred by memories of the Revolution to inspire militia leaders to push for war and to support Jackson as their commander. Jackson had arranged for a Fourth-of-July meeting of several of his future officers at Dr. Sappington's racecourse on the Cumberland River that was frequented by most of the men, a setting that gave Jackson an opportunity to emphasize an area of public success in his civilian life. Nashville's first physician Dr. Sappington supplied a fine dinner and abundant spirits to prime the audience. He also lent Jackson the currency of his fame. Sappington was well-known to the public as the inventor of "Sappington's Pills," pills of unknown content that were coated with sugar and given as a cure-all throughout the settlements.[651]

As predetermined, Jackson was quickly elected president of the meeting, and his aide-de-camp William P. Anderson was named vice-president. The two old friends took their places on a stage set up to position Jackson in prominence as the leader of community leaders.[652]

The abundance of fine food in a time of embargo austerity provided a mood of celebration and shored up confidence that anyone lacked. As a series of toasts was offered, the strategy became clear. First came a toast to the patriots of the Revolution. Then to "June 18, 1812, a second era of American Independence." Finally, to the real purpose: "The war with England, may it never terminate until the Mistress of the ocean has been taught to respect our rights."[653]

If the food, spirits, and speeches were not enough, as toasts were read, Captain Carroll's militia company shouted cheers and fired their muskets in approval. Few could resist the collective pressure to support Jackson. As the major general looked down from the stage to assess the reaction of the men who would follow him into his first battle command, he knew that he could count on their support.[654]

The *Clarion* was quick to publicize the troops' support for Jackson's command, while also reporting a recent account about Martha Crawley's abduction that was certain to stir passions. Rumors had spread that Mrs. Crawley had been burned at the stake. A part-Cherokee man refuted that claim but reported that Mrs. Crawley had been severely beaten and that she was being paraded naked to warriors.[655] At that very moment, the young Tennessee mother was said to be serving as a virtual slave to the Indians. Like Colbert, the Cherokee man reported that the leader of the abductors was prominent Creek leader Tippe- hor-chew, and Mrs. Crawley had been taken to a major Creek town Tookabatchee. The suggested conclusion was that the abduction was not the work of wayward young rebels.[656] It had been sanctioned by Creek leaders, which meant that settlers should expect more attacks.

The newspaper editor also reminded the public that no action had been taken to rescue the hostage or to punish her captors. Rangers were too few to prevent further attacks or administer justice, and the federal government so far had refused the militia's offer. The newspaper even suggested that if the federal government did not act, Tennesseans might have to take matters into their own hands. Then it ended the editorial with the point of the entire issue: "Are you ready to follow your general to the heart of the Creek nation?"[657]

Jackson could not have orchestrated the groundswell of support for his command of Tennessee troops to take on the British and their purported Indian allies with any more efficiency.

Thomas Hart Benton was not one of the select officers who joined Jackson for the officers' meeting at Sappington's. He wrote from Franklin to inform Jackson that Ranger Captain Mason and his militia were ready to attack the Creek even if the federal government refused to declare war. Benton told Jackson about Mason's rangers killing the Choctaw man, and boasted, "I am glad he has got some blood. It will keep the war alive."[658]

Tennessee and Mississippi Territory military leaders waited impatiently for the order to assemble troops. A thousand stands of arms were supposed to have been made available for Tennessee, but it was discovered that bureaucrats had sent them to Newport, Kentucky on the Ohio without any funds to get them to Tennessee. Not to be stalled, Jackson persuaded friends to advance funds to have the arms delivered to Nashville by special delivery and sent Eli Hammond to secure the firearms from the federal installation. Eighteen thousand cartridges were also to have been available. Hammond found none.[659]

Nashville storeowners sensed that troops would soon be called out. Merchant George Deaderick stocked up on swords and silver epaulets. A competitor James Hanna ordered swords and fifes.

Jackson hoped that the declaration of war would free him to take immediate action. On July 9, he issued an order for his men to be ready to march into the Creek Nation either to punish Mrs. Crawley's captors or to lay waste to their nation. Referring to the Crawley massacre and probably to politicians who opposed him, Jackson said, "The wretch who can view the massacre at the mouth of Duck River, and feel not his spirit kindle within him and burn for revenge, deserves not the name of a man; and the mother who bore him should point with the finger of scorn, and say 'He is not my son.'"[660] Jackson argued that it would not be prudent for his militia to march off toward Canada to fight the British until the Creek no longer presented a threat to their homes in Tennessee.[661] However, when Jackson finally received the orders to march to defend against the British on the Gulf Coast months later, he would not let the threat of a Creek attack on Tennessee towns stand in his way.

News of the declaration of war reached Natchez by July 11. Citizens who had worried about attack by Creek Indians lit bonfires and celebrated. Reverend William Winian watched from a distance and declined to join. He reflected, "the terrible calamities always incident to war, as seemed to me, rendered rejoicing in its declaration a matter of bad taste, as well as an indication of defective, if not of corrupt moral principle. The consequences of war will soon be felt in our portion of the Country, in the severe pressure upon every species of interest."[662] In a few months, Winian would have the opportunity to preach his reflections on war directly to General Jackson.

Rumors of Mrs. Crawley being beaten and paraded naked turned out to be false. After escaping her captors, Mrs. Crawley planned to walk toward "Bigby Creek"—more likely the Tombigbee River, a known trade route from Mobile Bay to the Tombigbee Mississippi Territory settlement of whites—hoping to find a traveler who would rescue her. She wandered through the woods for days, sometimes hiding in swamps. Not having the opportunity to take food with her when she escaped, she foraged blackberries. Finally, out of hunger, cold and desperation, she returned toward a town on the Black Warrior in Creek territory to increase the likelihood that she could find an American trader who would rescue her.

Mrs. Crawley approached some of the Indians she hoped would prove friendly. One told her that there was someone in the village who spoke English. She should go with them to the house where the American was visiting.[663] She found the house and entered in an expected sense of relief to find a trader and other settlers to take her home. Her relief turned to panic as she realized that everyone in the house was Creek. Her presence drew attention and she sensed by their sudden talk that they were plotting to kill her. She made a sign with her hand to tell one of the women that she needed to go outside. As soon as she was out of the house, Mrs. Crawley again made an escape into the woods.

On the second day of running, Mrs. Crawley was startled by the sudden appearance of a Creek man in front of her. He carried a gun slung over his shoulder. The Creek made it clear that he was there to take her back to the Tuscaloosa town on the Black Warrior. She refused. He made a sound that was answered by another Indian in the woods. Mrs. Crawley concluded that a party of Creek surrounded her just out of sight, and reluctantly, she submitted to her new captors.

As the men led her near the Tombigbee, the English-speaking traveler Mrs. Crawley had hoped to find appeared. Tandy Walker was a blacksmith sent by the U.S. government years earlier to live in the Creek Nation. Mrs. Crawley would understand that Walker was in the Creek town to purchase beef. In truth, Walker had heard reports about Mrs. Crawley's capture and that the Creek had taken her to the village of Chief Oceocehemotla on the Black Warrior. When Walker discussed the reports with Fort St. Stephens commander George S. Gaines's wife Ann, the sixteen-year old woman pleaded with him to attempt to rescue Mrs. Crawley. Walker knew that he would be risking his life, but he was willing to make the effort.

Chief Oceocehemotla trusted Walker. As Walker made his way through the Creek Nation, he had pretended that he was making a journey to Tuscaloosa to discuss other business with the chief. Walker offered the Creek men 25 dollars for the prisoner. The men agreed, then discretely left Walker with the white woman he had just purchased. Mrs. Crawley did not know that Walker paid her ransom.

When Walker first had a chance to observe Mrs. Crawley, he saw a woman in mental and physical distress.[664] Her bare feet and legs were injured from days of running. She had been forced to walk hundreds of miles after witnessing the slaughter of her children. Her "feeble condition, her mind a good deal impaired by suffering," as he described it, would affect her recollection of events.[665]

Walker spoke to her kindly and secured a canoe to take her to Fort St. Stephens. When the pair arrived at the fort, the young Mrs. Gaines immediately took Mrs. Crawley into her home and nursed her back to health. After a few days, Mrs. Crawley seemed to have recovered her faculties and was fit for travel. Commander Gaines arranged for Mrs. Crawley to return to Tennessee with William Henry and other friends who were traveling in that direction.

As the Henry party crossed the Chickasaw Nation, Mrs. Crawley said that she again spotted George Colbert, who talked with the men of the village and smoked and drank with them. In Mrs. Crawley's mind, George Colbert had it within his power to have her released, and he had instead acted as a friend to her captors. She would make a public accusation against Colbert when she returned to Tennessee, but she may have imagined seeing him at so many places on her return through the Chickasaw Nation.

George Colbert had been successful in heading off a full-scale invasion into his nation, however, as he feared, many settlers and now their leaders grouped all Indians together. Jackson was set to pursue the Crawley captors and to use that opening to prime his militia to lay destruction to the villages of hostile warriors that had attacked Nashville for decades. Public outrage over the Crawley attack should have been the opportunity he needed, but the American government was tied down fighting in the North. The federals discouraged Governor Blount from opening another front. Rather than authorizing Blount to use Jackson's militia to attack the Creek Nation, the Secretary of War preferred to use diplomacy. He told the Indian agent to work through peaceful means to obtain Mrs. Crawley's release and to deliver the attackers for justice.[666]

Jackson fumed as he waited, and he worried about losing the public momentum for action that he had built. He issued an order to the militia to reassure them that he had not given up on the idea of a war with the Creek.

The momentary calming of the unrest came too late for Chickasaw Agent James Neelly. Chickasaw Chief and Natchez Trace inn owner James Brown raised allegations against the agent, including a charge that Neelly had sent a servant to attack the chief with violence and that he had self-dealt on transactions with Indians that he was to protect.[667] Those allegations combined with the War Department's growing concerns over Neelly's ability to maintain Chickasaw loyalty prompted the War Department to make a change. Major Neelly was dismissed in June, and James Robertson was reinstated as Chickasaw Agent.

Southwestern Indians had dealt with Robertson for years and generally they trusted him. They respected him as a proved fighter who now sought peace. If anyone could persuade Indians to remain loyal to the Americans, it was James Robertson. Robertson, at 68, was an elderly man for the time. Though he suffered like everyone else in the economic downturn, he looked forward to more relaxed years in the comforts of the young town he had helped found. These were uncertain times, though, and if the Indians in the Southwest sided with Britain, everything they had worked for would be lost. Robertson had written a perfunctory letter to the War Department to offer his services, probably knowing that he would undermine Neelly, and the offer was readily accepted.[668]

Friends counseled Robertson that at his age, he was unlikely to return from the mission. He acknowledged that he was tired and that long rides were now difficult for him. Nevertheless, the elderly Robertson agreed to leave his wife and a peaceful life behind to set out down the Natchez Trace to take up residence at the Chickasaw Agency house.

Robertson's appointment also undermined Jackson's stirring of the forces of war. Before traveling south into the Chickasaw Nation, Robertson decided that his first duties were to work in Tennessee to attempt to prevent a conflict with the Indians. Robertson rode south of Nashville on the Natchez Trace to Mason's ranger headquarters at Gordon's Ferry on the Duck River. Robertson had heard rumors that Mason had been ordered to pursue Mrs. Crawley's captors into the Chickasaw Nation under state authority rather than wait for federal approval. It made no sense to Tennesseans that the militia had to stop at arbitrary and constantly changing state borders in pursuit of attackers. Robertson countered that the Indian nations were sovereign nations under the protection of the federal government and that whoever ordered Mason to ride south into Chickasaw territory had no authority to do so. The person who issued the order remained unnamed, but Robertson probably suspected that person to be Jackson.[669]

A few days later, Blount informed Robertson that he had used his authority as governor to authorize the rangers to range in Indian territory.[670] Blount had asked the War Department for approval to call out rangers, and though the War Department had not specified where the rangers could ride, they were officially federal soldiers and he had directed them into the Chickasaw Nation to attempt to cut off the hostile Creek. Robertson had no choice but to acquiesce. He would prove to be more effective negotiating with the Indians than with Blount or Jackson.

George Colbert wasted no time renewing an alliance with Robertson that he could use to counter Jackson if the major general threatened a larger invasion or occupation of the Chickasaw Nation. He wrote Robertson to let him know that he would join the new agent as he passed by his house and that he would ride with him past the Chickasaw King Chinnubbe's house all the way to the agency. Colbert would use the journey to remind Robertson of the Chickasaw's longstanding friendship and assure him that the friendship had not weakened. Colbert wrote that he was "overjoyed" that Robertson would again be agent to the Chickasaw, proclaiming that Robertson had been the "life of this nation."[671]

Though Jackson had already organized his men and appointed officers under the militia system, an organization that Jackson assumed the president had accepted, the War Department seemed to undermine the advantage of Jackson's preparation. It made it clear that under the terms of a new act passed on July 6, state militia recruits would serve as federal Volunteers and that officers elected by the state militia would have to stand for election again by newly recruited volunteers.

Jackson ignored the slight. Undaunted by the potential loss of face of acknowledging that the previous election of officers had been pointless, Jackson issued another order to explain the delay caused by uncertainty over appointments and to maintain a zeal for going to war, "The War has now begun. Your Brothers in arms from the Northern States are passing into the country of your enemies; & (I know your impatience) you burn with anxiety to learn on what theatre your arms will find employment. Then turn your eyes to the South! Behold in the province of West Florida . . . the asylum from which an insidious hand incites to rapine and bloodshed, the ferocious savages, who have just stained our frontiers with blood..."[672] He urged recruits to consider that they would be extending the boundaries of the United States to the valuable waters of Florida, which could prove beneficial to the western states. To the family man, Jackson appealed to fear and the need to protect his home and hearth. To men without those ties, he appealed to the fortunes that would be made once both West Florida and East Florida were in the control of the U.S.

Throughout the summer of 1812, factions of Creek who had been stirred by Tecumseh's message asked for councils with the Choctaw. Pushmataha made it a point to attend the councils to continue to remind the Choctaw of the friendship of the whites. At one, it is said that he spoke for almost two days as he counseled against any alliance to make war on the Americans. Pushmataha protested that the Indians might have temporary success, but attacks would only lead to the destruction of both nations. Other Choctaw minkos supported Pushmataha's message.[673]

Just when Mrs. Crawley's plight had worked the public to a fever pitch for war against the Creek, news of her rescue removed a main justification for action. William Henry, one of the party who escorted Mrs. Crawley back to her family, reported her release. Though Henry described the murder of the Crawley and Manley children on Duck River as an account that would "chill the blood," he called into question whether Mrs. Crawley was ever in danger of being killed as she thought."[674] The Creek he talked with all appeared friendly and loyal to the United States. Mrs. Crawley challenged that the chief at Black Warrior had bought her from the kidnappers, apparently for his own use. The Creek leader denied it, protesting that he had sent men out to apprehend Mrs. Crawley's captors. But United States agents questioned whether the chief had ever apprehended the men.[675] Facts were left in enough of a muddle that proponents and opponents of war could select those that helped their own case.

Creek chief Big Warrior appreciated the significance of the calls for vengeance. He traveled to Fort St. Stephens to purchase an American flag that he intended to fly over his house throughout the anticipated conflict to demonstrate that he was not an enemy of the United States.[676]

Robertson arrived at the Chickasaw Agency on July 25. After conferring with other Chickasaw leaders, Robertson quickly summed up the situation. Despite the Cherokee's rumors, Chickasaw would remain loyal. Colbert's lobbying was successful. Robertson assessed, "There cannot be a people more determined to observe peace with the United States than the Chickasaw."[677] Robertson hoped that conditions had cooled enough that Jackson's expedition would be unnecessary. The Choctaw were still upset with the killing of one of their men by Tennessee rangers, but they were keeping vengeance under control. Robertson had seen enough bloodshed in his lifetime. At the same time Jackson worked to stoke the fires for war, Robertson was throwing water on the flames.

Robertson went to work immediately to form an alliance among the Indians nations already friendly to the U.S. The British could use their influence on the Creek to set one nation against another, and if the Indian nations were tied up in a war among themselves, they could not lend support to the settlers.

Robertson praised the Chickasaw council to push the friendly Creek chiefs to avoid war:

"it is said to be the greatest council ever remembered in the Chickasaw Nation, more order could not have been observed in Congress hall—never a nation of Indians more firmly attached to any government than the Chickasaw are to the United States, they are determined to execute the Creek law in the most rigid manner on all thieves and murderers."[678]

Creek minkos friendly to the U.S. asked Robertson to publish their letters in Nashville newspapers to explain their actions. They said that the men who attacked the Duck River settlement were not representatives of their nation, but rebels who would not listen to the counsel of the chiefs. Loyal Creek leaders had seen that justice was carried out on the attackers. There would be no need for Jackson to administer his justice on their whole nation.[679]

Creek leaders, pushed by the Chickasaw, had executed the attackers to satisfy Jackson's call for justice. Young Creek rebels were so angered by the executions that they began a fight against older chiefs, and when the divisions were further heated by additional executions, the Creek Nation exploded into civil war. A divided nation would be unable to defend itself against Jackson's troops. Little ripples again caused major waves.

Robertson could hope that punishment of Red Stick rebels would calm threats of war against the Indian nations, but now he also found himself embroiled with the Choctaw. The United States demanded that Choctaw leaders turn over the boy who had killed the traveler Thomas Haley in retribution for the rangers killing his brother. The Choctaw king wrote Robertson and offered to comply with the request. However, in return, he insisted that the United States turn over to him the rangers who had killed the Choctaw man. If Choctaw submitted the member of their nation to face United States justice, the rangers should submit themselves to Choctaw justice.[680]

Robertson investigated the Choctaw man's death. He determined that rangers found the man on a side path that the Creek and Shawnee used to travel between their nations, and he concluded that rangers were justified in suspecting that the man was part of the party that had attacked settlers at Duck River.[681]

Robertson also worried that the Choctaw man may have been a member of a powerful family that would persuade the king to attack settlers in retribution. He decided to stall. Robertson told Choctaw messengers that there would be an important state meeting in Nashville a month later and that they should accompany him there to receive an official reply. He hoped that the delay would give Choctaw passions time to cool.

Chief Colbert also highlighted the rangers' killing of the Choctaw man.[682] It was the result he had warned would be produced by Tennesseans' rash reactions. The soldiers had not taken time to separate the innocent from the guilty.

South in the Mississippi Territory, Governor David Holmes announced the formal declaration of war and that men in the territory should begin preparing to be called up under the command of Colonel Thomas Hinds. The Mississippians would be ordered to rendezvous at Cantonment Washington before moving on to march south to Baton Rouge to provide re-enforcements for General Wilkinson.[683] For Jackson, news that Hinds was preparing his troops for action re-enforced his intuition that he needed to work harder to secure authorization for a command.

Even though a draft would eventually be used in the war, one weakness or strength of the militia system was that politicians could not recruit men willing to go to war without compelling justification. Just as Robertson hoped that Mrs. Crawley's rescue would remove the need for the Tennessee militia to march, a calming of tensions posed a threat to Jackson's war campaign. Jackson had worked since issuing the *Volunteers to Arms* from the Hermitage on March 7 to propel public sentiment to go to war with himself at the lead. In a candid letter to his friend Governor Blount on November 11, Jackson admitted that he had worked hard to "Excite them to assume a proper attitude as americans" and to keep the men motivated to move when called to action.[684] Though Jackson was ready to call his men to the field by September, the War Department did not officially request their services until late October.

For Jackson, the danger had not ended, and the public was likely to turn their attention elsewhere. Jackson had to find some means to keep the public excited, and he determined it necessary to issue numerous orders to keep the men motivated. The *Clarion* provided help. Having already expressed concern that the public outrage over the Crawley and Manley family massacres was subsiding without producing a result, it now claimed that about half the people in each tribe were supportive of a new Indian confederation as an enemy to the United States. The editor then asked why the United States was still paying annuities to the tribes.[685] Jackson picked up on the tenor of the article, and his September 8th order bordered on the frantic:

> "Citizens! Let not the rumored armistice relax your exertion. It will be an armistice on one side alone. For while the American army shall sheathe its sword, the tomahawk and the scalping knife will redouble their activity, and mingle together the blood of the grayheaded age, of the tender mother, and the infant babe.
>
> Disastrous intelligence is received from New Orleans the hand of Providence has smote that city; the approach of the enemy adds to the horror of its situation . . . Citizens! Be ready! You must and will be employed and how scandalous to be found unprepared, when you are ordered to march to the assistance of your brethren."

There seemed to be enemies on every front, and the government should find some use for Jackson and his troops for one of them. Jackson noted, "These are the times which distinguish the real friend of his country from the town-meeting-brawler, and the sunshine patriot. While these are covering their conduct with the thinnest disguises, and multiplying excuses to keep them at home, the former steps forth, and proclaims his readiness to march."[686]

The pronouncements were effective. Following weeks of newspaper articles headlined "British Intrigue" and "Indians," on September 15, a large meeting was held in Nashville to determine how to deal with the threat from the Creek. Respected Methodist Minister Thomas B. Craighead, who served with Jackson on the board of the Davidson Academy, presided. Someone moved that General Jackson be directed to raise 5,000 men to march against the Creek.[687] It seemed clear that the citizenry was tired of waiting for the federal government to act. Jackson had rallied his militia and the public to prepare for war, and from his continued public orders, it appeared that he was determined to lead his men into war on someone.

On the same day, the United States called for a council at Itala with the Cherokee, Choctaw, and Chickasaw nations, which Robertson helped convene.[688] Disputes between the Cherokee and Choctaw had the chance of leading to retaliation that could spiral out of control. Just as important for Robertson, he could gauge support for the Americans. Chickasaw support now seemed assured, but doubt remained about the loyalty of other tribes.

After a week, Choctaw chief Tootumastubbe spoke to General Robertson, "My heart is straight, and I wish our father the President to know it. Our young warriors want to fight. Give us guns, and plenty of powder and lead. We fight your enemies; we fight much; we fight strong." Recalling the killing of a Choctaw man by the Rangers, the chief said, "I do not like white rangers; make trouble in our country. Our Father don't want to make us trouble. Our warrior good Americans—fight strong. You tell him so. You, General Robertson, know me; my heart straight. Choctaw soldiers good soldiers. Give epaulettes and guns and whiskey— fight strong."[689]

Robertson determined that American Indians were better suited than regular U.S. soldiers to be rangers and scouts.[690] They were more familiar with the territory and the customs of other tribes. Indians would be able travel easier unnoticed and have more access to information. Choctaw spies could be assigned to help secure a barrier between the Creek hostiles and American settlements.

Creek minkos that were friendly to Americans made a futile attempt to regain control. Chief Bark assured that he had put to death the nine men and one woman who took part in the Duck River massacres. Explaining the unusual execution of a woman, Bark said that she had stabbed the victims with a sharp pole as the men were killing them.[691]

The executions did not deter other hostiles. Though Creek chiefs had first assured that they would bring the rebels under control, the chief now wrote to Robertson with regret that taking the lives of the attackers had not stopped the rebels' efforts to spill white blood.[692] The group of peace chiefs wanted to make it clear that the actions of some warriors did not reflect the will of all. The friendly Creek also asked the Chickasaw for a council, but George Colbert refused. He could not chance that Tennesseans would think that he was in league with any Creek.[693]

Robertson returned to Nashville to use his personal influence to help cool passions toward the Indians.[694] Though Robertson asked the *Clarion* to publish the friendly letter from the Creek minkos, he had already lost the political war. The newspaper waited until January, after the Volunteers were ready to march, to print the letter that showed not all Creek were the settlers' enemies.

News arrived in Nashville that Kentucky had mustered its volunteers under the new act. So many more men offered their services than authorized that over 1,200 citizens were sent home. It led one Kentucky soldier to brag, "Well, Kentucky has often glutted the markets with flour, hemp, pork and tobacco, and now quite in this manner, the[y] has done it with VOLUNTEERS!!!"[695]

When the War Department finally sent the order to muster Tennessee troops, it was ambiguous. It began, "should the Volunteers offer [to serve] . . ."[696] Effectively, Jackson's tender of the Tennessee militia under his command had not been officially accepted. No one in the Madison administration had forgotten Jackson's blunt criticism of Jefferson at the Burr trial, nor the fact that Jackson had supported Madison's opponent Monroe in the presidential election. Worse, Aaron Burr had promoted Jackson's appointment as a federal general to his friends in New York, which may have worked only further to undermine the War Department's confidence in giving him command of troops.[697] Just as the message to Jackson should have been clear that officers tied to his command would have to stand again for election by Volunteers, the message to Governor Blount was clear: He was free to appoint a commander other than Jackson.

Adding insult to injury—and perhaps to dampen Jackson's enthusiasm for commanding the force—rather than being directed to help free Florida from European control, the Tennessee Volunteers were to be sent to the Lower Country area that General Wilkinson commanded. The Secretary of War instructed Governor Blount to keep Wilkinson informed of the number of troops raised and the details of their march.[698] Though the order did not specifically state that Tennessee Volunteers would serve under Wilkinson's command, Jackson understood that it could be read with that interpretation.

In addition to Jackson's own knowledge of Wilkinson's shortcomings, Wilkinson had begun to receive ridicule in the press. One of Wilkinson's enemies Humphrey Marshall had just published a scathing critique of Wilkinson in his 1812 *History of Kentucky*.[699] Serving under Wilkinson would bestow no public honor.

Congressman Grundy's assessment that something was "rotten in Denmark" had been correct. It seemed that Wilkinson had somehow hijacked all Jackson's efforts for an authorization of volunteer troops by limiting the action to the support of Wilkinson's command. The order also directed that a brigadier general be appointed to command the Volunteers. Tennessee Militia Brigadier General Johnson would fit the bill. Blount's relationship with Jackson and Jackson's own undermining of Johnson in the press put that change out of the question.

Jackson carefully studied the War Department's order, which stated that *if* volunteers were raised, *then* the troops were to go to New Orleans in the region where Wilkinson was headquartered. War Department commanders knew Jackson had already assembled Volunteers.

More disturbing, the order did not mention Jackson's name. Jackson noticed the jab, "There appears to be something in this thing that carries with it a sting to my feelings that I will for the present suppress."[700] Jackson claimed for public consumption that he could put his pride aside for the good of his country and serve wherever needed and under another's command if necessary. Probably not even Andrew Jackson believed that statement.

But Wilkinson's scheming against Jackson suffered from his reliance upon the same bureaucratic inefficiencies that he attempted to mobilize to his advantage. In particular, Wilkinson relied upon Secretary of War William Eustis, who was considered incompetent. Wilkinson later blamed Eustis for creating the confusion of command apparently by not stating directly that Jackson could not be appointed. Jackson was a higher-ranking major general who would have federal authority as a federal Volunteer. Wilkinson was a lower-ranking federal brigadier general but tasked with lead command of the southern forces. Because the orders did not specify which general would command the other, if Blount appointed Jackson and if Jackson pressed the opportunity to command, the two foes would be left to determine the command structure by resorting to their own means. People who knew both Jackson and Wilkinson recognized that a battle of titans had been set.

It may have been that no one in Washington City knew how to resolve the issue. Sometimes boys on the frontier threw two hostile animals into a sack to see what would happen when neither could escape. The War Department had effectively played the same cruel trick on two commanders it needed. If any good resulted, the exercise would prove which of the two was stronger or cleverer.

Even without an affirmative prohibition, Governor Blount understood the significance of the War Department order. The War Department encouraged him to select a general other than the one who had already organized his troops and tendered their service to the president. But Jackson was the general who had mounted the campaign in the newspapers to build public support for organizing troops. He was also one who had worked through his friends in Congress to support a war resolution to give those troops a mission. Jackson exerted his own pressure personally on Blount, who held his position with Jackson's support. By this point, Blount would have committed political suicide had he appointed anyone but Jackson, and more seriously, he would have risked creating divisions in the militia at a time when the nation faced war. Though Blount knew that he was not following the letter of the order by appointing a higher-ranking major general to lead the forces, Blount could rationalize to the War Department that the most expeditious means to respond to the call-up of troops in Tennessee was to appeal to the forces already assembled for that purpose. It was certainly more expeditious for Blount personally.

That issue resolved, Governor Blount provided Jackson the order he had requested for months, and for Jackson, putting the most significant part at the end:

"Division Orders

Sir, I am required by the President of the U.S. through the Sect. of War to call out. Organize, arm and equip fifteen hundred of the militia of Tennessee detached comfortably to the acts of April the 10th, 1812, for the whole or such part of the required detachment as may be deemed expedient, to be rendezvoused at such parts of the state as may be judged most convenient for their march to new Orleans, for the defense of the lower country to be organized as far as practicable, according to the laws of the United States, under the command of a Brigadier General—I am authorized to assure the volunteers that they will not be continued in service in the lower country during the next summer. Commissions are forwarded for Officers to command the volunteers as selected—When said volunteer corps may be commissioned and organized, the fifteen hundred will be ordered to New Orleans, either by land or water as shall be most convenient; to go on all together or by detachments of four or five hundred according as the necessary arrangements therefor can be made. They are the volunteers under your command who are to perform this service, whose services with yours have been tendered to and accepted by the president. You will command them."[701]

Blount directed Jackson to order officers to meet in Nashville for preparations for the march. The War Department had authorized the Tennessee governor to delegate to the appointed general the power to draw expenses from the War Department. Blount delegated that authority to Jackson and gave him specific authority to acquire boats needed to transport the troops to New Orleans if a march on the Natchez Trace was determined to be impractical.

Blount's order set the wheels of war in motion in West Tennessee. Officers were to rendezvous in Nashville on November 21 to advise the governor who should be appointed as field officers.[702] Basic plans for the expedition would be outlined. Any companies that lacked 66 men were to recruit additional volunteers.

On November 14, Jackson followed up on the governor's order by issuing his own order for the officers to rendezvous in Nashville on November 21 to elect field officers. Jackson's order was also to be read to individual militia companies to keep the future lower-ranking troops motivated by laying the foundation justifying the need for action:

> "The Maj. Gen. has now arrived at a crisis when he can address the volunteers with the feelings of a soldier. The state to which he belongs is now to act a part in the honorable contest of securing the rights and liberties of a great and rising republic. In placing before the volunteers the illustrious actions of their fathers in the war of the revolution, he presumes to hope that they will not prove themselves a degenerate race, nor suffer it to be said that they are unworthy of the blessing which the blood of so many thousand heroes has purchased for them. The theatre on which they are required to act, is interesting to them in every point of view. Every man of the western country turns his eyes intuitively upon the mouth of the Mississippi. He therefore beholds the only outlet by which his produce can reach the markets of foreign nations, or of the atlantic states. Blocked up, all the fruits of his industry rots upon his hand; open, and he carries on a commerce with all the nations of the earth. To the people of the western country is then peculiarly committed by nature herself, the defence of the lower Mississippi and the city of New Orleans. At the approach of an enemy in that quarter the whole

western world should pour forth its sons to meet the invader and drive him back into the sea. Brave Volunteers! It is to the defence of this place, so interesting to you, that you are now ordered to repair. Let us show ourselves conscious of the honor and importance of the charge which has been committed to us. By the alacrity with which we obey the orders of the President, let us demonstrate to our brethren in all parts of the union, that the people of Tennessee are worthy of being called to the defence of the Republic."[703]

Recruiters built on Jackson's public pronouncements by continuing to add to the number of Volunteers to reach the 1,500 authorized. Presbyterian Reverend Gideon Blackburn was not one of the ministers who worried about impressionable young men being led astray by military recruiters. He had served as a soldier on the East Tennessee frontier at the same time as he ministered.[704] Jackson would have been impressed that, like himself, Blackburn had essentially grown up as an orphan on the frontier. And Blackburn had shown ambition by riding to Washington City to persuade President Jefferson to appoint him to work as a federal schoolteacher and missionary to the Cherokee Nation. Blackburn's main income came from making whiskey, which was the currency of the day in many areas. Blackburn's confrontation with several tribes over some of his whiskey stolen by the Creek almost led to war, and he had been accused of using his position to sell whiskey to the Cherokee.[705]

Blackburn had organized the Franklin Tennessee Presbyterian Church in 1811, and he had just become headmaster of the Harpeth Academy in Franklin when the Volunteers were called to duty. Contemporaries described him as a "logical thinker and forceful speaker."[706] Those talents shined when Blackburn responded to Jackson's *Call to Arms* by addressing the citizens of Williamson County on the importance of turning out for the mission.

At a little over six feet tall and with a model soldier's athletic build, Blackburn did not disappoint recruiters who stood in the center of a gathering with flags and a recruitment roll as Blackburn delivered his fiery address:

> "Leave, for a few months, your frugal board—your cheering firesides, and your agreeable connections. Step into the field of glory. You will be followed by the prayers and best wishes of all your acquaintances . . . Step forth then at your country's call—erect your forts near Orleans, and plant your cannon on their batteries...Return in triumph, the joy of your friends will be heightened by the recital of your victories, and the sight of your trophies. Need I advise you not to return inglorious? You are Tennesseans—sons of Columbia—children of the heroes of the Revolution . . . Your hearts are palpitating—your sinews are strung—you already anticipate the desired success. Behold the Eagle is waiving in the air. Behold the flame of liberty is painted on the cheek of your brothers. See! The heroes are collecting around the standard of liberty—the sound of the drum invites you to your station. Let the true patriot set a gallant example to the tories of the day."[707]

It was an effective camp-meeting altar-call sermon for recruits for Jackson's Volunteers.

Blackburn's powers of persuasion impressed Jackson, and he was willing to overlook the whiskey-selling allegations. Blackburn's genuine concern for and close relationship with the Indians could prove to be an important asset on the Volunteer's march through the Indian nations. Jackson appointed Blackburn chaplain of the cavalry. So many of Blackburn's pupils were stirred by his speech and followed his call to enlist that the academy was forced to close until the end of the war.[708]

As planning began in earnest, uncertainties about the Indians added challenges. There was no question that factions of the Creek were loyal to Tecumseh, and therefore likely aided by the British. The loyalty of the remainder of the Creek could not be assured. How many would join the rebels? The Cherokee too had been loyal, but it was unclear how they could react to Americans whose defense was spread over long distances. The Chickasaw and Choctaw had long been friendly. But in the paranoia of impending war, rumors that some of the Chickasaw and Choctaw people supported the Prophet gave room for doubt. Even rumors of involvement of the Shawnee and Kickapoo tribes made the threat potentially worse. Jackson's Volunteers would march into an area far from support, and it was impossible to calculate the risk that hundreds of warriors from a supposedly friendly tribe would attack. The march to New Orleans was becoming more complicated.

When officers assembled in Nashville in November to begin formal planning for the expedition, the enemy that consumed their thoughts was not the British or their Indian proxies, but the U.S. general encamped 600 miles south. It was falsely rumored that James Wilkinson had been promoted to Major General of the Seventh Division.[709] Had it been true, that promotion would have placed Wilkinson on the same level of rank as Jackson and in complete command of the defense of the entire Gulf Coast. Officers knew that Jackson had no intention of serving under Wilkinson. Jackson, who had learned to survive based upon his own instinct and skills, was not a natural subordinate. If Jackson were required to submit to Wilkinson's inferior leadership, his own reputation as a military leader would rise no higher than Wilkinson's incompetence. Jackson's ability to demonstrate his talents as a general would depend upon his ability to separate his leadership from Wilkinson's.

As the discussion about Wilkinson continued, some officers got carried away and proved their loyalty to Jackson by swearing that they would refuse to serve under Wilkinson. Later, when the officers worried that their conversation could be interpreted as insurrection, Benton pointed his finger at Coffee and suggested that it was all Coffee's idea. Benton would profess that he objected to Coffee's suggestion the officers refuse Wilkinson's command and that no more was said about it.[710] Jackson would challenge Benton's revisionism and would later claim that Benton expressed the same disgust for Wilkinson as all the other officers.[711] Jackson, in turn, unconvincingly took credit for softening opposition to serving with Wilkinson.[712] If he did, his argument to his officers was not that Wilkinson was worthy of commanding the men; it was that Jackson would be their immediate superior who would protect them from Wilkinson.

Jackson was confident that once the troops and the public had an opportunity to compare the leadership of the two generals, they would acknowledge Jackson as the better commander. That comparison would begin with Jackson's extraordinary willingness to march his troops hundreds of miles in winter, while Wilkinson sheltered in a southern fort like so many professional generals who were rumored to be afraid to fight.

Jackson had clearly thought about the upcoming battle with Wilkinson, and he offered a surprise to his officers—instead of marching only about 75 cavalry troops along with two regiments of infantry as authorized, he would add a full regiment of cavalry and march them separately. The plans for a separate cavalry regiment also would come as a surprise to Wilkinson as something different from the War Department plans that Wilkinson had orchestrated. Perhaps that was Jackson's intention. A mobile unit of 670 men on horseback was in many ways a more formidable force than 1,500 men on foot. The cavalry would give Jackson military power of his own right if he had to battle Wilkinson to lead the command of the Gulf Coast.

Just like positioning troops for an attack on an enemy position, Jackson would also divide his forces and approach Wilkinson's camp from two sides. The infantry would be transported by river and the cavalry would march by land down the Natchez Trace. If Wilkinson had plans for containing the infantry soldiers arriving by river, the cavalry on the Natchez Trace could be Jackson's ace-in-the-hole. But the element of surprise would work only if Jackson mobilized and marched his forces quickly.

Jackson could justify his decision to divide his forces, in part, based upon the challenges in supplying his troops. Each day of the march, the men would need about three tons of food, and each horse would need about eight quarts of corn.[713] Though Jackson initially had planned to march all his men down the Natchez Trace in a unit, the freezing and thawing dirt road, commonly called the "badness of the road," would not support the long trains of wagons needed to haul supplies. Army units on the northern front found that they could not depend upon wagon transportation except in seasons when conditions were dry or roads were frozen. It would be impossible to transport the food needed for large numbers of troops without wagons.

Men on horseback were better suited to make the march on the Natchez Trace. Companies of mounted militia in the regular army on the northern front herded cattle along with their march to have a ready source of fresh beef.[714] But the condition of the Natchez Trace and the sensitivity of the Indians would make that source of food impractical. The cavalry would be able to carry some food with them in saddlebags on horseback to reach the Tennessee River, and from that point southward, government contractors could be hired to lay out deposits of food and forage along the route.[715]

The infantry would be better served by floating down the Mississippi River on flatboats. The decision was not taken lightly. The Mississippi, running a mile wide in most areas, presented unknown dangers. A few Nashville men had made frequent river voyages to float farm goods from Nashville to Natchez or New Orleans or to pole, row, or sail boats back up current to bring goods from New Orleans to Nashville.

Their stories of dangers were enough to raise concerns about untrained boatmen transporting soldiers. However, marching on foot in January was typically avoided when possible. Exposure to rain and cold would only increase the numbers of deaths from disease when the men lacked changes of uniforms. By transporting the infantry south on flatboats, Jackson could order enclosures constructed to protect the men from the elements. Fireplaces could be built to keep the troops warm.[716] Jackson would order Benton to arrange for 33 flatboats.

Fortunately, Zadok Cramer had published a book for travelers, *The Navigator*, in which he had attempted to reveal the mysteries and dangers of the Mississippi and Ohio Rivers. Cramer made a point to describe and number islands boatmen could use for landmarks, and more importantly, to describe known dangers and areas where the currents were safe. In 1811, Cramer had revised the book and added maps.[717]

Cramer claimed that river traffic was generally safe in a good boat, except when ice was flowing on the rivers. It would be safer for Jackson to wait until spring. The late fall weather in 1812 had been cool but warm enough that peach trees were still blooming south in the Mississippi Territory, and Cramer noted that in warm winters, ice did not form on the rivers to present any hazards. Both may have factored into Jackson's decision to march in December. Cramer also noted that if captains wanted to make extra time and if they trusted the river current, it was safe to float at night on the Ohio River when there was a full moon.[718]

Cramer warned, however, that river travel on the Mississippi could be more treacherous. Captains should expect risks from riverbanks collapsing, unseen strong currents flowing into the Mississippi from intersecting rivers or currents that would spew boats out of the river into bayous or swamps along the river. More dangerous were trees growing from the river bottom but not visible above water level, and floating trees just below the surface of the river.[719] Because of all the risks, it was unsafe to float on the Mississippi at night even under a full moon.[720]

Cramer advised that boats designed for a voyage on the Mississippi River needed to be specially designed with strong timbers, additional caulking, and heavy cables.[721] Captains were encouraged to take at least one canoe alongside the boat to navigate shallow waters that would not allow the boat to land at shore.

Jackson did not have time to build heavy-duty boats. He advertised in the newspaper to purchase regular boats. Cantrell & Read, the local merchandise company that had been awarded the contract to supply food and equipment to the Volunteers, was authorized to pay cash for whatever boats could be obtained.[722]

Contractors also advertised to purchase 2,000 gallons of whiskey, 330 barrels of flour, and 30,000 pounds of pork to feed the troops until they arrived in New Orleans.[723] Whiskey was commonly meted out to the troops in small rations to provide a concentrated form of calories.

As officers left the planning meeting, they were still unsure how they would coordinate the divided forces. But one thing was certain: Before they fought the Creek or the British, there would be a fight between Jackson and Wilkinson.

For his part, Wilkinson was confident that he had outmaneuvered Jackson based upon the final wording of the legislation authorizing the call-up of troops and the order from the Secretary of War that a brigadier general was to command the Tennessee troops, knowing that stipulation disqualified Jackson. Wilkinson was anticipating the arrival of Tennessee troops to serve under his command by building temporary barracks in New Orleans to house them.[724] Though he had received no communication from Governor Blount, Wilkinson included Tennessee Volunteers in the 4,000 troops he bragged that he would have under his command to defend against a supposed British attack.[725] Just a few weeks later, Wilkinson would plead the lack of supplies in New Orleans as a pretense to keep Jackson from marching his troops to the city, but availability of supplies was not an issue when Wilkinson thought he would command those troops, despite a fall hurricane. Wilkinson even took the liberty of ordering coats for his men without waiting for approval to spend the funds.

On the northern end of the Natchez Trace, Jackson attempted to use his new position as a federal Volunteer general to rid the West, if not the country, of Wilkinson. Leaving nothing to chance in his anticipated *tete-a-tete*, Jackson struck a fatal blow before he bogged down in the details of logistics. Eastern aristocrats may have dismissed Jackson, but he still had powerful western friends in Congress. On November 29, Jackson wrote his friend, Tennessee Congressman George Washington Campbell, who would later decline President Madison's offer of the position of Secretary of War, to request that he use his influence to have Wilkinson removed from command in the South and West.

Jackson told Campbell about the planning meeting in Nashville and confided to the congressman:

> "There is but one thing I fear, Should we be ordered to join Genl. Wilkeson, he is so universally disliked by our citizens, that something unpleasant may arise—It was whispered that he was to command—It raged like wild fire—and it was only laid by the governor stating positively in his order that I was to command them—as to myself, you know my sentiments—It is a bitter pill to have to act with him, but for my countries good I will swallow [it]. I go with the true spirit of a soldier to defend m[y count]ry and to fight her battles— and should anything [come] between him and myself to put a speedy end to it without injuring the service or disturbing the Public . . . It is much to be wished that he should be moved from the South and west."[726]

Unless Campbell should see Jackson's hand behind the officers' disgust with Wilkinson, Jackson passed along a rumor from an officer in the Mississippi Territory that the militia in West Florida also had flatly refused to serve under Wilkinson.[727]

Jackson, who likely motivated his officers to question the propriety of serving under Wilkinson, then used those officers' concerns as a pretext to question whether Wilkinson could command them. Although Jackson was now a federal Volunteer major general and his men were federal Volunteers, he suggested to the congressman that men who were essentially Tennessee militia would have constitutional qualms about serving under Wilkinson as a general in the federal regular army and that they then might refuse Wilkinson's commands That reluctance could put the nation's defense at risk, as the New York militia's reluctance had proved on the northern front.

Jackson boldly suggested that if the Secretary of War would simply appoint Jackson as a major general in the regular U.S. army to command his militia as federal Volunteers, that grave risk would be avoided. More importantly, Jackson suggested that the War Department should remove Wilkinson from command of the southern coast to clear the way for Jackson's service as a federal major general.

When Congressman Campbell received Jackson's letter, he made a note to follow up with a discussion about Wilkinson with the Secretary of War.[728] Later, when the War Department responded to Jackson's letter acknowledging concerns that Tennesseans would face the same issues as the New York militia, it became clear that Jackson had struck on the proper argument. The War Department acknowledged that maybe a major general should be appointed after all, but it did not go so far as to suggest that major general should be Jackson.[729]

Jackson's request that the War Department move Wilkinson raised the fight to a new level, though the nuances of bureaucratic infighting were Wilkinson's *forté*. News would arrive soon in New Orleans that someone had suggested that Wilkinson be moved to the northern front. Wilkinson wrote in his defense that he should not be separated from his family or bear the expense of a move.[730] Colonel Butler had made the same pleas to him, which he had rejected. Nevertheless, Wilkinson had no reason to doubt that he could still control his destiny.

Once Wilkinson learned that it was Jackson who had encouraged the War Department to consider his transfer to the northern front, he would make Jackson eat his own words, using Jackson's argument that his federal Volunteers were still Tennessee militia as the basis of a campaign in the War Department to destroy the upstart Tennessee general on the Natchez Expedition.

The titans' final contest of wits and wills had begun.

CHAPTER ELEVEN

JACKSON'S FLOTILLA

"We go to conquer our enemies—to reap laurels, not to tarnish our reputation."

—Andrew Hynes, January 15, 1813

The enemy waited at the end of a difficult winter's march as the Volunteers departed camp on January 10, 1813. Logistics and daily routines would keep them occupied until that moment arrived, and like courageous men before them, the new soldiers would learn to appreciate the joys of the moment. But in the back of their minds, the Tennesseans knew that each mile they marched from Nashville brought them closer to the enemy—whether it be the British, their Indian proxies, or the myriad camp diseases that normally claimed most soldiers' lives. Not everyone would return home to their families.

For Andrew Jackson, the enemy at the end of the march was General Wilkinson. Jackson's ability to overcome that enemy depended upon how well his Volunteers arrived in the Lower Country as a fit, disciplined military force with Jackson clearly in command.

Jackson's headquarters boat was commanded by Lieutenant David S. Deaderick, trusted son of Jackson's friend, merchant, and banker George Deaderick.[731] The boats carrying Jackson's Company of Guards, were lashed together with the General's boat to float together as one. The river waves sometimes collided the boats together, then tugged them in opposition.

The command boats had barely left the shore in Nashville when officers began planning. Survival tactics were no longer a training exercise. Officers opened Zadok Cramer's *The Navigator*, and carefully studied his maps and descriptions of river currents and dangers to plan the voyage. As helpful as the guide was for captains who had never navigated the Mississippi, the 1811 earthquake had altered the river, changing its course and currents. Though Cramer had attempted to update the maps to reflect changes, unmapped dangers lay where trees continued to fall into the river from the collapsing banks and where new islands had been formed. The river current also altered its course so often that even recent maps were not completely reliable.[732]

Officers had brought along their own copies of accounts of military sieges to study when they were not performing their official duties. But the first day of the voyage was Sunday, and Reverend Blackman thought it was his responsibility to speak to the officers. Blackman was still unsure about how to minister to soldiers, almost to the point of embarrassment. The preacher rose, faced the wall of uniforms, and haltingly fired the first salvo in the war he was there to fight. Searching for a way to connect to military men, Blackman chose to emphasize *duty*. He explained that as chaplain of the infantry, it was his duty to admonish the men on Sunday, implying that it was their duty as soldiers to pay respectful attention to his message.[733]

Blackman's associate minister once described him as tall and slender with dark, flashing eyes and a "silvery" tongue that demonstrated a brilliant mind.[734] Blackman was unsure of himself and humble, nevertheless, he projected a forceful presence that compelled the officers' attention. Whether preaching to himself or speaking to what he sensed the soldiers needed to hear, Blackman selected Matthew 10 as his text, and he related that soldiers should not fear those who can destroy the body, but the one who can destroy the soul in Hell. Rather than duty, what most of the officers took from the first message was courage.

Though Jackson's men were not religious by Reverend Blackman's standards, the serious nature of their mission weighed their thoughts to issues deeper than logistics. To Blackman's surprise and relief, the men put aside their planning and listened. At first, Blackman credited the officers' deference to him to common politeness. But they were also following the General's orders. Though the public knew more about Jackson's sins than his virtues, his mother had made certain that he spent hours in church services and religious training when she was alive to guide him. That training formed more of Jackson's foundation than he may have recognized or admitted until later in his life, and it became apparent in the respect he gave to the work of the chaplains. Still, the men's attentiveness to the parson's message revealed more than obedience to their major general. One soldier noticed that several officers carried handsome pocket Bibles from Baltimore in their trunks. The soldiers did not talk of it in their typical camp banter, but Blackman spoke to more serious concerns on their minds, heightened by the possibility of death.

Blackman abbreviated the sermon from his typical hour's length both due to the officers' pressing work and his own insecurity. He ended by praying "for the success of the Expedition, and for the Individual happiness of the General, Officers and men."[735] Officer Robert Searcy recorded that it was a "very affecting" prayer.[736]

Planning resumed. Travel and supply logistics are as crucial as battle tactics in war. The best military tactical plans are worthless unless troops arrive on the battlefield healthy and prepared to fight. Moving 2,000 men 800 miles by river or 450 miles by land in winter through undeveloped areas was no common challenge. Even General Wilkinson would later acknowledge the unusual feat, or possibly as a backhanded compliment designed to emphasize Jackson's inexperience, eagerness, and arguable recklessness. Clearly, Jackson had undertaken a winter movement of troops designed to impress even the most seasoned American military leaders—if he succeeded.

The voyage by night was slow. Cautiously following the advice of Cramer's *The Navigator* for the Mississippi River, most captains only felt comfortable moving on the Cumberland River when moonlight was bright enough to reveal hazards.

And it was bitterly cold. Fireplaces did not keep the boats as warm as planned on the river where the open channel funneled wind through cracks in the wooden plank walls. Several officers found that their blankets were not heavy enough to keep warm.[737] Though the lapping of small waves rocked Volunteers' berths as gently as their mothers' cradles, the boats were colder than their tents had been, and men would not sleep well until they had adapted.

Early Monday morning, the sun rose to reflect from tree branches covered with frost that had accumulated in the night.[738] Steam also rose from the warmer water. Sunlight quickly dissipated both and gave the men the first warmth they had felt in several hours.

Jackson's flatboat headquarters had traveled through the night only to Jonathan Robertson's Landing. The boat stopped for soldiers to load the cavalry's cotton tents to transport to the Lower Country. Embarrassingly, in another logistical error, the tents had been sent instead to David McGavock's ferry landing, arriving in wagons just as Jackson was departing.[739]

Not to waste the delay of the stop, the General went ashore at 9:00 a.m. to assess the progress of boarding soldiers on the remaining boats. The news was frustrating. Boats lagged miles behind. Captain Moore reported that chimneys had not yet been constructed on his boat. Captains McFerin, McEwen, Moore and Hewlitt's companies did not even have boats. They were still waiting for them to be completed.

Jackson could not afford to wait. Chimneys could be completed on the river to avoid delaying departure. He ordered Captain Moore to have bricks for his chimneys loaded on his boats and then to advance at the earliest possible departure. The men would have to endure the cold until the bricklayers had finished their job. Jackson was already three weeks beyond his original planned departure date, and they could expect ice floes to be increasing north on the Ohio River.[740] Captain Anderson took news of the General's displeasure of the slow advance seriously. He risked floating his boat four hours in darkness to catch up with Jackson's headquarters.[741]

As Jackson's boat departed, Captain Moore ordered his platoons to fire a salute. Jackson's soldiers responded with beats of the drum and cheers.[742]

Soldiers waiting for Jackson's arrival farther downriver at the mouth of the Harpeth took the time to hunt and made their first kill of two deer. The anticipation of fresh venison was cause for celebration, until an angry settler named "Davidell" claimed that the great hunters had killed two tame deer he kept as pets.[743] Making such claims posthumously for deer in the wild might have been the settler's real source of revenue on the river. Nevertheless, Jackson did not want to take the chance that anyone would claim that he had allowed his men to act improperly toward civilians as the British had when he was a child. The soldiers would be forced to pay the settler 10 dollars for his claimed loss. Jackson used the incident to teach a lesson in discipline and respect for the rights of American citizens. Benton exaggerated his account of the event to claim that the hunters' actions had "disgraced the army."[744]

To avoid future conflicts, it was further ordered that each time the boats halted at a town, soldiers allowed to go ashore were to be on their best behavior toward the townspeople. Sentinels were to be posted to make certain that others remained onboard.[745]

Jackson's orders also reinforced some of the sermons soldiers would now hear on a regular basis. The war would have a profound influence on the way the men viewed religion. Though much of the nation was undergoing a spiritual revival known as the "Great Awakening," many

West Tennesseans had experienced little regular contact with parsons or churches. One soldier's grandson later described how the soldier's life had been influenced by the "fiddle, card playing and drink" until his grandfather developed relationships with the religious men during the war. Afterward, in a visit with a fellow veteran, the officer underwent a religious conversion and became a changed man and a pillar of his community.[746] Reverend Blackman and Reverend Blackburn's work would have a similar effect on many Volunteers.

The next morning, Jackson started the day's voyage an hour before sunrise with five additional boats floating along with headquarters. The weather cleared, and as Jackson's boat approached the mouth of the Harpeth, someone spotted Volunteer infantry boats waiting ahead downriver. It was a momentary glimpse of the command Jackson had envisioned with an almost dreamlike effect. Soldiers in uniform could be seen walking on the flatboat rooftops. Rays of the early morning sun highlighted flags flying above the boats. Martial music could be heard playing from a distance. The whole scene presented a professional military appearance that inspired confidence in the hastily assembled militia.[747] Capping off the moment of personal satisfaction, as Jackson's boat approached, drummers honored him with ruffles, and 18 companies fired a salute in his honor.

Reality spoiled the surreal glow when a soldier reported that five of the boats needed for the voyage were still 20 miles upriver on the Harpeth. Only two companies of the Second Infantry could fit on the boats that were ready to depart. Though Benton had been charged with completing the boats, he shifted blame to Captain Newsome. Newsome had been given orders to command the boats down the Harpeth River to meet the infantry, and it was rumored that Captain Newsome's religious beliefs prevented him from traveling on Sunday, the Protestant's day of rest. Someone else suggested that the Harpeth River was frozen over and that no boats were moving, and another claimed the boats had run aground.[748]

The angry Jackson threatened to sue the boat contractors, but it did nothing to speed his advance. The Nashville newspaper reported the delay and noted that Napoleon had the power to march his army across Europe so quickly because the emperor was not forced to deal with the government bureaucracy that constrained American generals.[749]

Jackson ordered Major Martin to take a detachment of a hundred men and march to wherever the boats were waiting and bring them down to the Cumberland River. If Martin still found it impossible to move the boats, he was to march all the men overland and to meet Jackson for further instructions downriver at the next halt at Clarksville.[750] Benton had been ordered to take charge of the lead march to make certain that there would be no delays, but instead he had returned to Nashville. Jackson consoled himself that if all else failed, he could always commandeer more private boats they would expect to meet on the Cumberland.

Jackson was also informed that a few men in Captain Nash's company had deserted. Militiamen were unaccustomed to the prolonged rigors of camp routine, but the General could not afford to allow discipline to slip as the boats spread out on the voyage. The march was only in its second day, and he could not halt the advance every day to hunt down stray soldiers. Lone hunters were known to perish in the uninhabited areas along the river. Jackson would have to provide an account for the welfare of every man on the expedition, even those who deserted. Jackson ordered that the deserters be apprehended.

The General had made his plans based on the best technical knowledge and resources of his day. Though the boats likely would float through ice floes, they were expected to provide sufficient transportation and shelter. War Department contractors had been hired to provide food for the troops at Clarksville, Tennessee, a town that had become a Cumberland River port to transport Tennessee's farmers' goods to market. Ammunition from War Department contractors and additional equipment would await the Volunteers in Natchez. Nevertheless, even under the best circumstances, all of Jackson's resources would be stretched. There was little room for error in the unusually harsh winter environment. And ultimately, Jackson would be in almost complete reliance upon a distant War Department over which he seemed to have no influence.

That vulnerability became apparent when Jackson reached Clarksville with Hall's First Regiment just after sundown on January 13. Contractors were to have met the flotilla at the Clarksville Landing to deliver 160 barrels of flour and cured pork as food for the infantry from that point until they reached New Orleans. As boats pulled up to the wharf, Jackson found only 60 barrels waiting in warehouses, and no contractors. When the suspicious general ordered flour barrels opened, he saw that many were only half-full. He opened pork barrels and discovered that the pork had not been well salted to cure the meat, and the carcasses had not been properly butchered. The men even found pigs' skulls stuffed with the pork in the barrels.[751] In a few days, the meat would have been useless, or worse, it would have made the men ill, and left them starving downriver. Jackson was forced to halt the momentum of his advance for two nights and a day while soldiers that should have been preparing to meet the British pulled pork from the barrels and completed the contractor's job in the cold.

The standard for civilian relations that Jackson had established in compensating the settler for his "pet" deer was short-lived. Jackson could not lead the men into unknown territory without stores of food. The General ordered soldiers to impress flour for the good of men. It was a longstanding right of soldiers to forage for needed food and materials from civilians, but that power could be abused. Jackson assured that he would arrange later to compensate the owners.[752]

When even the number of impressed barrels was inadequate, the General ordered soldiers to go out into the countryside north on Red River to the old Renfroe Station settlements with authority to offer to purchase flour from farmers.[753] The party returned empty-handed and reported that farmers refused to sell.

Jackson was dumbfounded. It was difficult to believe that all the farmers who had often complained that they had no market for their products during Jefferson's and Madison's embargoes could not be persuaded to sell their flour. But he had no ready cash to pay them. The farmers would have to rely upon his written promises of future payment, and flour was ready currency for farmers in a barter-system economy. Government promises from a nearly bankrupt nation were not.

Jackson had every right to be furious about the contractors' gross negligence when his soldiers' health depended on reliable supplies. His anger was blunted for the moment by the need to devote attention to advancing his march, and more significantly, by the fear that some of his friends may have held the contracts.[754] Besides, War Department bureaucratic inefficiencies were common, and all commanders suffered under the army's contractor system that required little accountability from providers.

If Jackson began to worry about whether the bizarre incident was Wilkinson's greeting card, he did not pass those concerns on to his officers.

In addition to the growing risk of ice floes, the amount of food and supplies needed to reach the destination increased with each delay. Increased costs had to be justified. Delay also made it more likely that men in confined spaces would become ill and desertions would multiply. Volunteers were already more than two days behind the planned travel time, not including the three-week delay in beginning. The boats that had been stalled on the Harpeth had still not been delivered. The General ordered that the two companies of the Second Infantry that had boats ready to board join him in the advance. Jackson saw no choice but leave the remainder of the troops behind at the mouth of the Harpeth until their boats arrived.

Jackson did not allow Benton to escape responsibility for the failure to have the supplies and equipment ready for the march. He ordered Benton to remain behind to make sure the dilatory boats caught up to the flotilla. And while Benton was waiting, he could take advantage of the time to find additional flour to add to their supplies.[755] Jackson's order revealed his anger and gave the rumors of a possible court-martial of Benton some credence, "We have been too long detained, and no further detention is to be permitted for want of boats or provisions. They must be had."[756] The General underlined for emphasis.

Captain Carroll noticed that a Tennessean named Isaiah Hayes had managed to enlist in the place of one of the Volunteers before they departed. Hayes was a notorious gambler and swindler, and Jackson called the matter to Benton's attention, as Benton was Hayes's superior. Benton acted surprised and claimed that if Hayes were not drummed out of camp, he would "swindle the soldiers out of every thing they had."[757] Jackson understood from Benton's reaction that Benton would send Hayes home, and the General moved on to more pressing decisions.

With a little over half the provisions needed to reach New Orleans loaded onto boats, Jackson and Colonel Hall's First Regiment cast off from Clarksville at daybreak on January 15. Jackson's boat passed the small Tennessee frontier town of Palmyra, where a settlement had grown up around an iron furnace operation that James Roberson had started. Jackson stopped just long enough to send a dispatch to report their progress to Governor Blount.[758]

The General soon discovered logistical weaknesses in his plans. Each captain had been given charge of his own boat, and one of the main challenges was to keep the captains focused on the larger mission of moving forward as a unified force. Without a good communication system, boats scattered as each captain met the individual needs of the men on his own boat. Boats needed firewood at different times. Individual soldiers left boats to hunt or chop wood, only to disappear when they had trouble reconnecting with boats downstream. Each captain had to navigate the river channels using his own judgment and to different results. Captains apparently claimed they could not hear a horn that was blown to let everyone know that boats were advancing or halting. A stray group of Captain Moore's soldiers was spotted on land just below Palmyra, and Jackson ordered them taken aboard.[759] The march by river was not the orderly process Jackson had envisioned.

The stress and lack of sleep in the cold that Jackson attributed to a cold began to take its toll. Severe pain in Jackson's neck and head revealed the tensions that were mounting.[760] Jackson awoke on January 16 with a new resolve to make corrections and gain greater control. Rather than blowing trumpets to announce that boats were ready to proceed, four minute guns fired in rapid succession would be the signal. If the boats were to land on the right bank, three minute guns would be fired. Two guns would be fired for a landing on the left bank. Captains would have no excuse that they could not hear guns, and those who found that their boats were too far ahead of the others were to wait for the lagging boats to catch up.[761] With no established military protocols to use as a guide, Jackson set his own standards.

When Jackson's boat met a Nashville-bound keelboat loaded with merchandise for Andrew Hynes's store, Jackson impressed 260 blankets for the Volunteers.[762] He wrote out receipts and sent a letter to his quartermaster in Nashville, telling him to make payment.[763] Jackson and Carroll personally distributed the blankets to the men to show their concern for their soldiers' welfare.

As Benton was left in command out of Jackson's direct supervision, Benton's own ambition he had warned Jackson about began to surface. Jackson's challenge to procure flour was a test of Benton's leadership. Benton's orders were to purchase flour from farmers at prices far above value if necessary, and if farmers still refused to sell, Benton could purchase additional supplies from contractors Cantrell & Read in Nashville.[764]

Benton ordered that farmers be paid eight dollars per barrel, even though the going rate was five or six dollars. But Benton exceeded his authority. Perhaps taking a cue from Jackson's order to Bradley to "escort" arms wagons at the point of saber, Benton armed his men with fixed bayonets and sent them out to the countryside to add additional persuasion for farmers to part with their flour. The higher price and threat of bayonet were sure to produce results. Finally, Clarksville merchants Elder and Poston agreed to risk reimbursement and sold Benton another 70 barrels of flour.[765]

Benton also took advantage of the time away from Jackson to pen a journal of the expedition from Nashville to Clarksville for publication in a Nashville newspaper, no doubt with his own political future in mind.[766] The accounts titled "Journal of a voyage from Nashville to New Orleans, by the Tennessee Volunteers" often featured Benton at the center of action, but they referred to Benton in the third-person as if written by another officer who was impressed by Benton's leadership.[767] The accounts also offered a gratuitous comparison to the high quality of Benton's military manuals with U.S. Colonel Anderson's, a less-than-subtle suggestion that the organization of the troops had operated under Benton's plan. Once it was discovered that Benton was the author of the journal, an enemy published a comical version in a similar style titled "A Journal of the Perigrinations of my Tom-cat."[768]

Even after the delayed boats had been delivered to Benton, Volunteers waited a few additional days at Fort Massac.[769] Benton may have taken seriously rumors of a court-martial over his failure to have the boats completed and intended the publication to lay a backup plan for his career. Months later, in a public dispute with Quartermaster William B. Lewis, Lewis charged that Benton, despite the self-proclaimed "almost incredible feats" recounted in his published journal, not only failed to see that the boats had been constructed on time, but that his dallying at Fort Massac caused a further delay in the boats under his command reaching Jackson.[770]

In addition, rather than drumming Hayes out of the company at Clarksville, Benton apparently had allowed the notorious gambler and swindler to accompany him to Fort Massac. Gambling with the soldiers stationed at Fort Massac seemed to be a second motive for the delay, and Hayes may have been a ringer. The plan did not work. While at Fort Massac, Benton had Hayes arrested and discharged for stealing a game chicken from Colonel Anderson. It is not known what happened to Hayes, but Lewis would later accuse Benton of taking Hayes across the river from the fort for "punishment" and leaving Hayes to die there in the winter wilderness.[771] Benton did not report the manner of Hayes's dismissal to Jackson.[772] He later claimed that he had ordered Hayes dismissed at Clarksville, and he did not know that Hayes was still on the boats until they arrived at Fort Massac.[773]

The men also waited as Benton took time to complete another chapter in his anonymous journal for the Nashville newspaper. The new installment alerted readers that Benton was leading the command of the rear flotilla, after the previous edition had made it clear that that Benton had never commanded flatboats.[774] If the boats wrecked and men were lost, Benton had laid the groundwork to shift the blame to Jackson for leaving an inexperienced boatman in charge. If he succeeded, his reputation would be burnished by his ability to learn quickly in the field.

Ahead in the lead, Jackson was given a report that without his knowledge, Captains Hamilton and Moore of Hall's First Infantry had stayed behind at Clarksville with Benton who commanded the Second Infantry. It was the second time that Moore had delayed, and he had not been able to keep his men together. Whether Benton had approved the detachment made no difference; it was an act of insubordination and a breakdown of the command structure. Benton was commander of the Second Infantry captains, not the First. Jackson directed Sergeant Horne and two others to return to Clarksville and give the delinquent captains orders that their men were to row continually until they caught up with Jackson's boat.[775]

Even attempts to take control over logistical details could not prevent the unexpected. Jackson would have to allot some time each day to deal with unexpected problems caused by 1,400 men, each making what seemed minor decisions that affected the whole force. Lieutenant Glendenin allowed a lit candle to fall into a bucket of gunpowder.[776] It caused a flash that severely burned the soldier's face and hands and blinded him. A handkerchief covering a bucket of gunpowder also caught fire. A large explosion could have resulted, but a quick-thinking soldier put the fire out with water.

Sunday, January 17, brought new challenges. Early in the morning, Hynes and Carroll were awakened with the alarming report that a boat was sinking about a half-mile upriver behind them.[777] They quickly dis-patched in a smaller boat to row upstream to find that it was the quar-termaster Alexander's boat that had begun to list, endangering needed supplies. Fortunately, Alexander had acted quickly, and his men were saved. Alexander had also managed to transfer the horses and some of the corn to Bradley's boat just before his own boat sank. Alexander's men would have to be scattered among the remaining boats for the remainder of the voyage.

Captains Hamilton and Moore finally caught up to Jackson. The captains had watched their own men row constantly for miles as a price for their decision to remain behind with Benton.[778] Now they had to take their own medicine from Jackson in person.

Early afternoon, boats were lashed together for Reverend Blackman to deliver the Sunday sermon.[779] Men crowded on the roof of the boat among the barrels of re-packed pork to allow larger numbers to hear the address. At some point, the combined weight of soldiers and pork barrels became too much for the support beams, and the ceiling collapsed. Edmonson and 11 other soldiers fell through the roof, though the ceiling dropped slowly enough that no one was injured. Blackman had faced more surprising interruptions on the Natchez Trace.[780] He simply moved over to Captain Renshaw's boat and resumed preaching.[781] Fortunately, Colonel Matthew Lyon's large shipyard and lumber mill lay just ahead at his settlement Eddyville, Kentucky.[782] The damaged boat would stop there for repairs, and it would provide Jackson an opportunity to obtain information about Wilkinson.

Once Jackson's flotilla was some distance from Nashville and growing more reliant upon the army for support with each mile, General Wilkinson began working his plan to halt Jackson's advance short of his camp at New Orleans. Governor Blount had forwarded Wilkinson the Secretary of War's letters of October 23 and 24 to advise him that Tennessee Volunteers had been approved; however, the letters somehow had been delayed in reaching Wilkinson until December 29.[783] Even then, possibly defensive of his decision to appoint Jackson, Blount did not make Wilkinson aware that Jackson would command the Tennesseans. On January 6, Wilkinson had sent a letter to the nameless "Officer Commanding the Militia and Volunteers from the State of Tennessee" offering to provide every comfort to the soldiers upon their arrival.[784] Wilkinson did not know who would command the Volunteers. Apparently, on January 19, Wilkinson wrote to the Secretary of War that he had heard nothing about the march of the Tennessee troops except a rumor that some would be traveling by water and some by land. And he welcomed the news, because the Tennesseans might prove helpful in his upcoming invasion of Mobile.[785] At the same time, Wilkinson complained to the Secretary of War that Governor Blount had not advised him of the progress in sending the Volunteers.[786]

Later in the day, Wilkinson was advised of Jackson's direct order to Wilkinson's quartermaster.[787] That order was Wilkinson's earthquake; despite Wilkinson's best efforts, Major General Andrew Jackson would be commanding the Tennessee Volunteers.

Referencing Jackson's letter ordering the Natchez deputy quartermaster to prepare supplies to provide for the Tennessee Volunteers, Wilkinson wrote Jackson to establish his territory and to confirm his command.[788] Without saying so directly, Wilkinson asserted that Jackson had no authority to order the U.S. quartermaster to do anything. Wilkinson had been given charge of U.S. army supplies, and he made it clear that Jackson would receive no food or supplies from the army unless Wilkinson approved. Wilkinson implied that Jackson's direct request to the quartermaster had broken protocol; however, Mississippi Territory Governor David Holmes had also sent orders for provisions for his men directly to Wilkinson's quartermaster, apparently without prompting any objection or threat from Wilkinson.[789] To Wilkinson, Jackson's real breach of protocol was in taking command of the Tennessee Volunteers.

Wilkinson also wrote to Jackson that he had received no orders from anyone as to Jackson's mission, other than copies of letters directing the officer commanding the Tennessee Volunteers to consult with Wilkinson and to alert him as to the movement of his troops. From the appearances of those letters, Wilkinson would insist that Jackson serve under his command.[790]

Wilkinson and Jackson both knew the orders were vague as to whether Jackson would be Wilkinson's subordinate. Wilkinson could argue that Jackson had unwittingly conceded the point, since it was Jackson who had argued to Congressman Campbell that Wilkinson should be reassigned away from the Gulf Coast because Wilkinson was a federal general and Jackson would command men who were essentially state militia. Using Jackson's own words, Wilkinson would ignore Jackson's new status as a federal Volunteer and emphasize Jackson's command of a state militia. Wilkinson pointedly referred to Jackson's men as "auxiliary forces," meaning auxiliary to Wilkinson's command.

Most significantly, Wilkinson advised Jackson to halt his advance at Natchez, where Jackson and his soldiers would pose no threat to

Wilkinson's command of the Gulf Coast. Natchez was about 250 miles, or a two-week march, north of New Orleans. Wilkinson knew from Burr's intelligence that Jackson's real interest was to invade Florida. Using the carrot of the assignment Jackson wanted most, Wilkinson implied that if Jackson halted at Natchez, he would be better prepared to march to Mobile.

As a stick, Wilkinson warned Jackson that there was not enough forage farther south for Jackson's horses or supplies for the men.[791] Of course, Wilkinson knew that statement was untrue. Even under his quartermaster Bartholomew Schaumburg's stingy allocation of supplies, Wilkinson had prepared to house and supply the Tennessee troops under his own command at New Orleans. In addition to constructing temporary barracks, he had requisitioned 3,000 stands of arms, 500 pistols, and 500 swords just a few days earlier.[792] Wilkinson's plans changed when he learned that Jackson would be leading those troops. Wilkinson knew that if he did not stop Jackson short of New Orleans, his months of preparations would have provided Jackson a headquarters and beachhead in the heart of what was believed to be the most important spot in the future in the nation.

Wilkinson assured Jackson that most of the Tennessee Volunteers would find comfortable accommodations near Natchez at Cantonment Washington, adjacent to the territorial capital Washington, Mississippi Territory. The fort had been built and operated by the U.S. Army, and even further developed under Wilkinson's command there. The offer of quarters in a U.S. fort should be expected to stroke Jackson's ego to suggest that he would join the ranks of U.S. commanders. Wilkinson added that if Jackson determined that Cantonment Washington could not accommodate all his men, 400 or 500 of the excess troops would be welcome to make camp in Baton Rouge with Wilkinson's own troops—and of course, under Wilkinson's sole command.

As additional incentive for Jackson to halt at Natchez, Wilkinson pledged that though he had received no authorization from the War Department to provide for Jackson's troops, he had ordered his paymaster and inspectors to meet Jackson's men at Natchez to pay them. He admitted that he had been in contact with the government contractor but assured that the contractor would be "prepared with a competent supply of provisions."[793]

Jackson should have been able to decipher Wilkinson's not-so-subtle message: cooperate and your troops will receive pay and food and you will position yourself to receive the Florida mission you want; refuse to cooperate, and your men will mutiny from lack of pay and disease and starve in the Lower Country. To wrap the package in classic Wilkinson duplicitous prose should anyone question his intent, Wilkinson added, "and if it is in my power to add to the comfort and accommodation of the band of patriots under your orders, it is only necessary to point out the mode to me."[794]

Near the same time that Wilkinson wrote Jackson, he also wrote to the Secretary of War to reveal his supposed reason for stopping Jackson short of New Orleans: "I will not avert to the probable consequences of two thousand undisciplined militia far removed from those social restrains in which they have been bred, turned loose on this licentious community, made up of all kinds of countries and colors."[795]

But neither was the true reason Wilkinson wanted Jackson to halt at Natchez. Wilkinson went on to reveal his real motive his letter to the Secretary of War: Wilkinson wanted Jackson removed from his territory, and he wanted Jackson's troops to be ordered to serve under his command. Wilkinson complained that the Tennessee general's failure to write him as to his location or plans demonstrated that Jackson would not be willing to subordinate his command. Because of the urgency, Wilkinson requested the Secretary of War to send an order by express rider "to the Tennessee Volunteers and that I should be instructed for their government."[796]

Before Jackson had time to receive General Wilkinson's January 22nd letter, Wilkinson fired off a second three days later. He said that he had just received a letter from Governor Blount that Jackson was marching south with 1,400 infantry troops—not the 400 that Wilkinson later claimed that Jackson wrote the assistant deputy quartermaster that he had mustered—and a full regiment of cavalry without any authority from the War Department.[797] A second letter sent so soon after the first revealed that Wilkinson was surprised and concerned. Two thousand soldiers, including a cavalry, meant that Jackson did not intend to serve under Wilkinson, and he expressed shock that Jackson had not communicated his intent. He said that he had suggested to Jackson that he camp at Fort Dearborn because he thought Jackson had only 400 infantry soldiers. Nevertheless, Wilkinson was even more adamant that Jackson halt at Natchez.

Wilkinson would have to be less polite about the question of the chain of command. Again, he used Jackson's breach of the command structure to make his point. He emphasized more pointedly that Jackson should have requested provisions from him as commander of the southern forces rather than treating Wilkinson's quartermaster as Jackson's subordinate, adding directly, "under the orders which direct my conduct, my personal honor, my public obligations and the national interests forbid that I should yield my command to any person, until regularly relieved by superior authority."[798] Wilkinson had a better understanding than Jackson of the importance of access to supplies. Even if Jackson never acknowledged that Wilkinson had superior command of the Tennessee Volunteers, once Jackson acknowledged Wilkinson's control over food and supplies, Wilkinson would control Jackson.

Now that Wilkinson had made it clearer that he was challenging Jackson's authority, he would need to deflect Jackson's well-known anger with a diversion. Wilkinson added to the enticement of a possible

Pensacola operation by suggesting that Jackson keep his boats in ready for the anticipated order.[799] He knew that order would never be given.

Wilkinson had thrown down the gauntlet directly at Jackson's feet. Did Jackson plan to seize command of southern operations, or would he agree to subordinate himself to Wilkinson? Whether Jackson halted his advance in Natchez would prove his intent. The letter was dispatched toward Natchez to reach Jackson upon his arrival.

Andrew Jackson, the crude frontier brawler who had made Wilkinson's political destruction one of his life's missions and who now had the audacity to attempt to take over command of the Mobile-to-East Florida campaign, was entering Wilkinson's domain. Wilkinson would enjoy this opportunity to repay Jackson for all his inconsiderate efforts. If all went as planned, the backwoods Tennessee militia general would be shown to his own men and political base to be nothing more than a hot-headed lawyer playing soldier. Jackson would finally be destroyed.

CHAPTER TWELVE

COFFEE'S CAVALRY ON THE WAR ROAD

"[A]*lthough the nations immediately claiming the country on which we pass over have long since been friends, yet we know there are savage tribes adjoining who thirst after American blood.*"

—Colonel John Coffee, January 29, 1813

South on the Natchez Trace, the cavalry expected to face their own challenges traveling overland. Their last opportunities to obtain fresh food and supplies were in the towns of Franklin and Columbia just south of Nashville. The mounted soldiers would then plan to take enough food and forage to reach just beyond the Tennessee River, where government contractors would deposit supplies at some of the inns along the road.

John Harding's Natchez Trace inn, just a few miles southwest of Nashville, served as a reminder that they were headed toward hostile Indian nations. Creek Indians had killed the cabin's first owner Daniel Dunham and his family when they were among the first settlers in the area.[800] Recollections of the frequent deaths of early settlers reinforced Jackson's primary instructions to avoid Indian attack on the march.

Jackson also likely knew Jefferson's dual purpose for the Natchez Trace wagon highway. Ultimately, it was to be used to settle immigrants from the East who would claim land in Indian territory, form militias, and control the Mississippi River area. The Indians may have suspected the true purpose by this point, and no one could guess how already apprehensive tribes would react to 672 mounted soldiers riding through their land. Jackson knew that Coffee's men could find themselves quickly outnumbered.

Coffee carried an order from Andrew Hynes to take care not to insult the Indians. Given the potentially explosive results, Coffee could not simply read the order at morning formation. The least-disciplined soldier held the safety of the company in his hands. One wrong move, such as a shot fired by mistake, might be interpreted as hostility. If newspaper accounts had not already instilled a fear of the Indians in the minds of the troops, Coffee had to make the men think of all Indians as the enemy. He would not risk a reliance on former friendships with the Chickasaw and Choctaw.

South of Nashville, the cavalry crossed over the Harpeth River and set up camp just outside Franklin, likely near the spring at the stone bridge on the River Road just northwest of town.[801] The cavalry would remain in Franklin for a week while they made final arrangements for travel.

Franklin was a well-heeled frontier town by 1813. Travelers from the East were surprised to find that Franklin townspeople bathed and dressed in their finest clothes on Sundays. Gurdon Squires had just opened a large retail building. Thomas Sappington had just completed a new two-story hotel off the Public Square. White's Tavern, which both Jackson and Benton frequented during peacetime, was closest to the camp. Jackson was known to race horses on the road leading from the tavern to the Natchez Trace wagon highway.[802]

Near the town center, Benton's law office reflected the growing significance of the Natchez Trace town. Adventurous businessmen such as Andrew Jackson and John Coffee had created a connection between Franklin and Natchez, where entrepreneurs traded horses and drove cattle to market. Disputes arose, and lawsuits often were tried in one of the two towns where the first judge could be found.

Gunsmiths were also in demand. Andrew Crockett and his son James built and repaired firearms in a shop on the Public Square, though the Crockett forge was located several miles north out of town on the Fishing Ford Trace.[803] Taking advantage of the Crocketts' gunsmith skills before leaving the last settled areas, Coffee ordered that all muskets and cartridges that needed repair be gathered.[804] James Crockett could also provide important warnings about the upcoming march on the Natchez Trace. He had served as one of Mason's Rangers who patrolled the road in search for Martha Crawley.

Coffee ordered that each company select two men best suited to fill cartridges.[805] They would make good use of their time in Franklin preparing ammunition for the march ahead.

Planning had kept Coffee so focused that he had taken little time to reflect on the responsibilities he had undertaken. Franklin provided a break, and for the first time since the cavalry had left Nashville, he felt the full weight of command. Coffee realized that he was now solely responsible for leading almost 700 men safely across the Tennessee River and through the Chickasaw and Choctaw nations in time to meet Jackson's troops. He was also responsible for maintaining a level of discipline and assuring that the men could operate as a fighting force when they arrived. The colonel could no longer pass the final decision to Jackson. Coffee wrote his wife:

> "I am not disposed to complain or shrink from the task I have undertaken, but will only observe, that it is a laborious one, it requires all the Philosophy, all the energy and firmness I am master of, to keep things going on in a proper train.

One hour's absence will take days to regain the former order of things. I am now left to the entire command of my
Regiment, and the eyes of my men and those of the world
are upon me, and one small piece of neglect would never be
regained by me during my life."[806]

To men like Coffee, Jackson never seemed self-conscious of what others thought and rarely seemed to fear making a mistake. Jackson had the
benefit of always thinking he was correct, later stating, "I care nothing
about clamors . . . I do precisely what I think is just and right."[807] Or at
least Jackson always gave the impression that he had right on his side,
trusting that "Providence" would provide the ultimate support for his
decisions.[808] From the powerful general's persona that Jackson created,
it was not clear to his subordinates whether Jackson thought he could
divine the will of Providence or whether he thought even God would
recognize his decisions.

At 40, Coffee, like Jackson, was considered an old man in an area
where many people did not live beyond their thirties. Coffee's years in
business had made him an astute observer of people, but like most of
his contemporaries, he had no reserve of fighting experience to give
him confidence. That confidence first had to be gained in overcoming
the challenges of the Natchez Trace. The health and safety of hundreds
of men now rested on his decisions. Halting the march, a full week in
Franklin demonstrated the care Coffee took to make sure no detail was
left to chance before he left the security of the settled area.

It was not as necessary for cavalry officers to find make-work activities to keep the soldiers busy. Caring for the wellbeing of each horse
occupied much of the cavalry's time. If a horse went lame days from
home or from the destination, the march could not be halted. The
rider could not remain behind to care for it, and if the horses were
not fit, several men could find themselves walking hundreds of miles

if packhorses were unavailable. But the connection between horse and soldier was more than functional. The cavalryman's horse was the soldier's personal horse, and a relationship of trust had developed between horse and man. Volunteers' horses were more than farm animals—their horses had names.[809]

The quartermaster secured the best bacon and flour that could be obtained in Franklin. Soldiers were ordered to go to the contractor's tent and draw rations for 10 days to pack in their saddlebags. With the additional supplies, rations were expected to last until the cavalry crossed the Tennessee River.[810]

Transporting the common camp supplies presented its own challenges. Without wagons, packhorses would have to be used to haul more limited supplies. To make certain that the horses did not go astray with provisions that could mean the difference between life and death, a commissioned officer was assigned to the team of packhorses and non-commissioned officers were assigned to groups of horses within the team. Individual soldiers were assigned to lead the packhorses at the end of the procession.[811]

Just prior to departure on January 23, muskets and cartridges that had been repaired were distributed. The men were given two hours to shoe any horses that needed shoes. At 10:00 a.m. sharp, the trumpet sounded to provide a one-hour warning to pack up and be ready to depart. At 11:00 a.m., the trumpet sounded again, and each man mounted his horse and paraded in front of the encampment. Sixteen advance guards armed with swords were ordered to ride 100 yards ahead of the regiment, and 16 rear guards armed with muskets were to ride behind. As Franklin citizens gave the Volunteers their best wishes to whipping the enemy, the troops marched south toward Columbia.[812]

Coffee's wife had begged him to return home for one final visit before he departed, but he felt a greater duty in planning for the care of his men. Coffee worried about what would happen to his farm in his absence and whether his wife would be able to supervise the operation. For many soldiers' wives, the expedition would allow them their first opportunity to demonstrate their own abilities to operate farms in absence of the men. Mary Coffee would have no choice but step to up and perform farm management that had always been conducted by her husband. Coffee took time to write to encourage his wife that she had "resolution enough to do anything."[813] But as a fallback, he also wrote to his father-in-law to ask him to check in on her to make certain she was not overwhelmed by the responsibilities.

Colonel Henderson continued his advance about a hundred miles ahead of the main body. By January 20, his detachment had reached Bear Creek south of the Tennessee River.[814] Two days later, he would arrive at James Colbert's inn, and he would remain four days in the Chickasaw Agency area. Henderson sent messages to provide Coffee with updates on where he had arranged for provisions, but he said little about his reception among the Indians.

On the same day that Wilkinson began his own campaign to halt Jackson's advance, Colonel Coffee led the Cavalry west along the Columbia-to-Natchez Road in Tennessee. The road then rose to follow the ridge lines, ending at Dobbins's Stand at the intersection of the Natchez Trace, at present day Gordonsburg, Tennessee.[815]

Arriving late in the day on January 23, the cavalry pitched their tents in the flat field near the cane breaks. The men carried their own provisions in the saddlebags, but they had to make certain the horses had enough forage to reach the Tennessee River. Typically, in cavalry encampments, as soon as the evening meal was completed, soldiers set out preparing the camp for the next morning's activities. The soldiers were ordered to draw 25 ears of corn for each horse from the quartermaster and to have their corn shelled and in their bags before morning.[816]

As part of a new small frontier settlement, Dobbins's Stand was situated in the picturesque Swan Valley at Big Swan Creek.[817] There, the

Natchez Trace meandered up a steep hill to the north and a smaller rise to the south. The temperature in the valley runs about five degrees cooler than the surrounding areas, which made a cold January night even more uncomfortable.

The Volunteers had now reached the southwestern edge of American settlement north of the lower Mississippi Territory, and the next day they would pass the last legal settler's house into the Chickasaw Nation. Campfires would be kept burning through the night not only for warmth, but also to act as a deterrent to the panthers, bobcats, and bears that stirred through the valley on such evenings, if they had been prodded out of their winter quarters in the caves in the hill overlooking the valley by the uncommon sound of 670 men and horses. Those same caves had served as hideouts for bandits on the Natchez Trace, and they would produce more campfire stories to keep the younger teens awake. Several Natchez Trace travelers had been killed on that very spot as they returned to Tennessee carrying bags of gold after selling goods in Natchez.[818]

Inn owner Captain David Dobbins was a Revolutionary War veteran who had settled in Tennessee near a colony of Episcopalians that included the Polk family. Dobbins would also join the Volunteer ranks before the end of the war. The well-known ornithologist Alexander Wilson stayed at Dobbins's house in 1810 when traveling to New Orleans, and he commented that during his visit the inn was so crowded that ten to twelve travelers slept on the floors.[819] Like other taverns along the Natchez Trace, Dobbins's provided opportunities for men to spend their advance pay.

On January 24, the cavalry began the morning routine they would follow on the southward march. At 5:30 a.m., an hour before sunrise, the bugle blew reveille. Soldiers rose and fed their horses as a man from each tent cooked breakfast for his unit. The scents of frying bacon and coffee boiling in pots over the campfires were the real morning wake-up. Water was added to flour create a dough that the men speared on the end of their bayonets and baked over the fire to make a type of bread or biscuit. At 7:00 a.m. the bugle blew again to give the men a thirty-minute warning to prepare to depart. When it blew the third time at 7:30, the tents were to be struck, the supplies loaded, and the men mounted on their horses in formation in front of their ground.[820]

Lines of cavalry began a slow ascent up the south hill as the men then entered the Natchez Trace to commence their remaining four-hundred-mile march to Natchez. The cleared bed of the wagon road was just wide enough for two men to ride side by side. The 672 soldiers, officers' servants, and the horses would have stretched out for about a mile. By 1810, over 10,000 people traveled the Natchez Trace each year; however, the threat of impending war, fear of attack by the Indians, and the growing embargo slowed traffic.[821] Nevertheless, soldiers would still encounter travelers and post riders traveling north with news from the direction they were heading.

As the Natchez Trace descended the ridge and crossed Little Swan Creek before rising again, the cavalry rode past the grave of explorer Meriwether Lewis and Grinder's Inn where he died. One soldier noted that the door of Grinder's Inn was about 10 steps from the commonly accepted border of the Chickasaw Nation.[822] A visible small rise was also a watershed. The waters to the north flowed to the Duck River and to the south to the Buffalo River. It was a natural boundary that needed no demarcation. Natchez Trace travelers called it the "Line" or "Tennessee Line." To be certain, however, likely a sign on the Natchez Trace made travelers aware that they were leaving Tennessee and entering the area controlled by the Chickasaw. On occasion, passports had been required for Americans to travel through the Chickasaw Nation as well as the Choctaw Nation, as the Indians had been promised when the road was built. Jackson protested that no American citizen should be required to produce a passport on the United States road.[823] His cavalry would not be concerned about passports as they crossed the watershed into the Chickasaw Nation. They had been careful not to alert the Chickasaw or any other Indians that soldiers would be traveling south.

From Grinder's Inn southward, the soldiers were uncertain what dangers they might face. Parties of Creek had often traveled north to attack settlements. Some Volunteers may have expected to see large scalping parties around each bend as Hynes had warned.

As the cavalry descended the ridge to the Buffalo River crossing, the group tested the reaction of one Chickasaw. John McCleish, who would be granted his own Indian reservation on the Natchez Trace in the 1816 cession treaty, operated a stand, a mining operation, and a mill at the Buffalo River crossing.[824] McCleish was the son of a Chickasaw mother and an Irish trader or interpreter who settled in the Chickasaw Nation. McCleish's wife was Chickasaw Chief George Colbert's daughter Susan, and if asked, he could have given assurance that Coffee's cavalry would find a good reception south of the Tennessee River. McCleish and many of the Chickasaw eventually would choose to join Jackson's forces to repel the Creek and British threats. Hynes's instructions were clear, however. There was to be little contact with the Chickasaw, and there is no record that Coffee took the opportunity on this march to seek McCleish's help. The troops passed without incident.

The cavalry continued southward toward the next Chickasaw stand, Young Factor's. The distance the men aimed to march each day approximately coincided with the locations of stands that had been established along the Natchez Trace, though stands were not always chosen as campsites. Springs that provided a large flow of healthy drinking water were more important destinations. Even with limited scientific understanding of bacteria, experience had proved that contaminated drinking water could turn a healthy fighting force into a dehydrated hospital unit in short order. Frequent travelers on the Natchez Trace knew the locations of safe springs.

Young Factor's inn had been established by the son of a Chickasaw chief referred to as Old Factor, who lived in the northern Mississippi Territory. General James Robertson vouched for Young Factor's, calling it a "fine house of entertainment," another term used for the taverns and lodges of the day.[825] By 1818, Young Factor's inn owners would boast fine furnishings from Nashville, and they served guests from china.[826] It is not clear how advanced Young Factor's inn was in 1812, but the soldiers would likely have found it not too different from taverns they visited in Nashville. Just as the cavalry passed by McCleish's inn, it does not appear that soldiers were given the chance to make contact with the Indian Young Factor.

On the Natchez Trace, Coffee's troops were oblivious to the latest power struggle just beginning between Jackson and Wilkinson. The cavalry was concerned with the more immediate challenge of surviving the march through Indian nations. As troops approached the deafening roar of the water running through the shoals on the Tennessee River, they separated into companies spaced so that everyone would not arrive at the crossing at the same time. An individual traveler could spend up to two days waiting to cross the river if ferry boats were not manned. It would take time to transport the 672 men and their horses across the river on the small boats.

The Tennessee River was the landmark that would separate the soldiers from the area they knew as home. Standing on the north bank on January 26, the cavalry looked across the almost-mile wide wild river that they all had to cross.[827] It was a physical barrier that would place them firmly in the Indian nations; there would be no quick retreat across it. Someone dubbed the temporary camp on the north side of the river "Camp Tennessee."[828]

Three to five of Colbert's slaves normally pulled the chains to draw the floating platforms loaded with travelers and their horses across the river. Soldiers may have helped with the physical labor necessary to pull so many people across the river in a short time. Coffee ordered the men to cross in the same order of the march.[829] Major Gibson was given command of the troops as they landed on the south bank until Coffee had crossed. Gibson was to enforce strict discipline, keep pistols ready, and make certain that guards were posted. He was reminded of Hynes's order; the men were to be strictly instructed to make no insults toward the Indians that could lead to an attack. If Colbert or his servants could not be located to ferry the men across the river, Coffee had been instructed to keep a record of the crossing so that Colbert would be compensated for each man, as Colbert had retained the right to ferry all travelers across the river. Coffee was to give the Chickasaw no grounds to lessen their loyalty to the United States.

The cavalry would be more vulnerable to attack when their forces were divided by the river, therefore Coffee instructed the men to cross as quickly as possible. As the first groups landed on the south bank and waited for the remainder, they began to set up camp and a defense position they named "Camp Jones."[830] The temporary camp was located near the former army "Camp Columbian," and with its elevated views of the river and the surrounding area, it was easily defensible. The Tennessee River served as an important transportation corridor and the intersection with the Natchez Trace made that spot even more crucial. Eventually, U.S. regular troops would be sent to Colbert's Ferry to guard the crossing for the remainder of the war.[831]

Soldiers began cutting trees to build campfires to generate some warmth along the breezy winter's Tennessee River, and they extended their camp some 460 yards in length along the riverbank.[832] If Creek warriors unfriendly to interests of the U.S. floated down the river and saw the encampment, Coffee made it appear from the river that he had a much larger force by stretching out the camps in a line. It was a subterfuge to deter potential attacks.

The cavalry took the opportunity of the lengthy crossing to rest in camp two days before proceeding farther south. The long journey was challenge enough, but if troops faced hundreds of Creek or Shawnee warriors, rested soldiers stood a better chance of defending themselves.

Coffee also used the respite to write his wife for the first time since leaving Columbia.[833] He was growing more confident in his command, "being now convinced all is not a bubble."[834] He described his men as carefree and anxious to meet the enemy. Cavalry troops were easier to organize and command than the more diverse infantry, who had less experience and training. Coffee would later tell his father-in-law that the march down the Natchez Trace was about half the trouble of supervising the troops in Nashville, though it may have seemed easier only because Coffee was becoming more experienced and confident in command.[835]

Coffee was assured that Colonel Henderson continued laying out supplies a hundred miles in advance.[836] When calculating the quantity of food supplies he would need and where food deposits would need to be laid, Coffee estimated that troops would march up to 20 or 25 miles per day. Just south of the Tennessee River, the procession was nearing the point where Coffee had calculated that the cavalry would begin to exhaust their supply.

By January 29, the cavalry's advance reached Bear Creek, within a few miles of where the Creek Indians had camped with their hostage Martha Crawley. As Volunteers neared Underwood's Village, they anticipated encountering Chickasaw families who had moved near Colbert's Ferry to sell food and supplies to travelers on the Natchez Trace.[837] That point was also the intersection of Bear Creek and a trade route by water to Mobile. They could expect that Chickasaw traders would walk out to the road to engage them in talk and to bargain with them to sell beef, pumpkins, beans, and other products. There were opportunities for misunderstandings that could lead to a full-scale battle.

Coffee warned, "We are now passing through an Indian country. The eyes of the people we are among are upon us. Let it not be said that the uncivilized savages shall ever have it in his power to reflect on our conduct. Touch nothing belonging to them. Mingle as little as possible with them. Let not your honor that you at home protect at the risk of life and all that is sacred to you be now forgotten and tarnished."[838]

Scouts apparently added to the tension by reporting that the food to be supplied by the government contractor was nowhere to be found. They did not yet know that the infantry had also encountered problems with War Department contractors. The pelt trade and new settlements in the area had long since exhausted the rich supply of game, forcing the Chickasaw to turn to agriculture for survival. It did not take the Tennessee hunters long to notice the lack of wild game and begin to wonder where they would be able to obtain the next meal.

Coffee had to keep morale high. He assured the troops that he had heard from the quartermaster that Henderson was successful in laying out supplies and that the men would find food as they neared the Chickasaw Agency.[839] The men would need to ration their remaining provisions for a sixty-mile march to the Agency over the next three days.

Despite Coffee's attempt to keep up spirits, he began preparing his troops for the possibility that they would face stretches without food. He warned the men that he would not tolerate the spectacle of some men enjoying a feast while others were starving. Coffee reminded the men of Benton's orientation, "We are a band of brothers who are all to share and share alike."[840] Coffee's admonition was also a reminder of the noble quality of their mission, a way to focus attention on the need for shared sacrifice and away from the deprivations of the moment.

Once hunger set in, men might be encouraged to approach friendly Indians for food, or worse, take what they wanted at gunpoint. Coffee again charged the Volunteers to be on their best behavior in the Indian nations. As the cavalry pressed on even deeper into the Chickasaw Nation,

Coffee warned: "Volunteers, we are now in the heart of an Indian country surrounded by people we know not whether friend or enemy, although the nations immediately claiming the country on which we pass over have long since been friends, yet we know there are savage tribes adjoining who thirst after American blood."[841]

Coffee discovered additional reason for concern. A man had attempted to prompt a Chickasaw attack on the cavalry by not only giving the Chickasaw advance-notice of the march, but by telling Colbert that Coffee's mission was to assassinate the Chickasaw leader. The agitator had also told the Chickasaw that the soldiers would take everything they wanted from their villages.[842] The warning had come on the heels of Colbert's complaints a few months earlier that white rascals had raided his storage sheds and taken what they wanted.[843] If Colbert could be convinced to push the Chickasaw warriors to attack Coffee's cavalry to protect his own safety, the Creek might not even be forced to fight the Tennesseans. But from the description Coffee later gave, the man who attempted to stir the Chickasaw to attack the cavalry was a white "gentleman." Soldiers traveling north from southwestern forts commanded by Wilkinson to Fort Massac frequently traveled Natchez Trace. Colbert did not state whether the "gentleman" was in any way connected to General Wilkinson.[844]

Colbert's experiences had taught him to be cautious. When Colbert was a younger man, his brother William had killed a Cherokee man at the mouth of Bear Creek when it was falsely rumored that the Cherokee had killed Chickasaw Chief Piominko.[845] Colbert had learned from the mistake.

Regular travelers on the Natchez Trace would have vouched for Chickasaw's friendliness to settlers. Journals often reflected that the Chickasaw waved to travelers to join them and insisted that they take meals with them and sleep in their houses.[846] Settlers who had regular contact with Indians were less likely see them as a threat. Reverend Blackman was among those who accounted for the existence of Indian tribes of different appearances and habits than the white man by speculating that Indians were part of a lost tribe of Israel.[847]

With each mile that the cavalry passed without incident, it became more apparent that the men did not have reason to fear attack by the Chickasaw. As they neared the center of the Chickasaw Nation in the area known as Old Town, soldiers began to relax and look forward to finding the U.S. Agency house.

The relief was short-lived. Coffee faced a crisis. It was reported that the government contractor obligated to provide food and provisions for the men at the Chickasaw Agency had also not performed, and the men had already exceeded the time allotted for their provisions.[848] Commanders would later attribute the contractor misfeasance to government regulations and a bidding process that took too long. But Colonel Henderson had assured Coffee that the provisions were in place at inns along the road.[849] Coffee had no time to worry about making recriminations against Henderson or starting an investigation as to whether the food had been taken.

Starving troops and horses required a quick assessment and plan of action. The men had already marched about 10 days from the last source to purchase food from settlers' stores. There were no storehouses or settlements between the Tennessee River and Gibson's Port just north of Natchez—over 300 miles—other than the regular limited supplies they might find at the agencies or what the Indians may have stored for winter. Men could be detached to hunt for fresh game, but they could not be expected to find enough to meet their needs. Dividing the men into hunting parties also presented too much risk in an area where Indian attacks were likely. If the troops aborted the mission and returned home, they would leave Jackson short-staffed when the British attacked from the coast.

Jackson had anticipated a shortage of supplies as well as Coffee's thoughtful hesitation and had explicitly ordered Coffee not to halt his march. The only option appeared to be to move forward. It would take less time for the cavalry to meet up with supplies sent from the south if they moved ahead. Coffee wrote Louisiana Territory Governor W.C.C. Claiborne to request emergency aid.[850]

The cavalry would need to travel faster to reach access to food sources sooner, but the winter rains and melting snows made swamps out of flatlands. Rising waters transformed even small creeks into barriers. The colonel reflected that he had never known of such bad weather or poorer travel conditions along the Natchez Trace.[851] Just ahead, Henderson waited for swollen streams to recede. Once, taking a chance to swim a creek, one of his men lost his coat, pistol, and sword in the current.[852]

George Colbert was not present when the cavalry approached his farm, nevertheless Colbert's wife and son gave them a friendly reception.[853] When Colbert appeared, the Chickasaw leader was apprehensive at first, however once it became clear that Coffee had no intentions of assassinating him or raiding his nation as rumored, the tension faded. Colbert challenged Coffee on why Governor Blount had not made the Chickasaw aware that he was sending troops through their nation, though the answer was obvious: Blount did not trust any Indian.[854] Coffee quickly turned the discussion to the need to purchase food and fodder from Colbert. Henderson had already laid a foundation for a deal. Apparently discovering that the contractors had not performed, Henderson had offered to pay 25 cents more per bushel for corn than Colbert normally charged if Colbert could spare food for the troops and horses.[855]

A better offer to farmers at Clarksville had not produced flour for the infantry and providing corn to the troops was even riskier for Colbert. Those were stores of corn his nation needed until their summer harvest. But Jackson had insisted that Colbert prove his friendship, and Colbert had assured the militia that they would find that the Chickasaw were their friends as they crossed the Tennessee River. This was an opportunity for the Chickasaw to demonstrate their loyalty and cement their relationship with the militia for the course of the war. It would also put them in a better position to seek the Volunteers' help in defending against the Creek.

Though Henderson had made the arrangements, if Coffee accepted Colbert's proffer of food he would be in clear violation of Jackson's order to avoid Indian contact and interaction. Paying for the ferry crossing was to be expected; accepting food and interacting with the Indians to procure supplies was another matter. But Coffee had no choice. Jackson had told Coffee that he should do whatever was necessary to procure food on the march. The men and horses could not be allowed to starve to enforce the technicality of an order.

As the men continued their march south, Chickasaw began appearing beside the road with their backs loaded down with corn and fodder.[856] Coffee surmised that some Indians were giving the troops all they had, and their sacrifices made an impression.[857]

Crisis averted for the moment, Coffee expressed his relief: "I find that all the Indians on the road, and particularly the Colbert family, are all very accommodating to us, we shall be tolerably well supplied in passing through the nation."[858] A few days later he wrote, "We do very well, get plenty of corn and fodder, meat, etc. I find we shall not want for anything while passing through this country."[859]

Travel conditions also improved. The Chickasaw routinely burned the undergrowth in the forests and grass in the open plains to herd game and to make it easier to see approaching enemies. As the men neared the Black Prairie area, the forest gave way to wide-open grassland.

Just as one crisis subsided, another seemed to arise. Northbound Natchez Trace post riders and other travelers on the road reported that the Indians farther south were disturbed by news of the cavalry marching in their direction and that they were abandoning their houses.[860] Henderson sent Coffee a message that like the mysterious man who told the Chickasaw that Coffee's cavalry was a threat, men from Mississippi had told the Choctaw that Coffee's men intended to wipe out their nation.[861] There had also been reports that some Choctaw had become disciples of Tecumseh. Coffee could not know whether the Indians who were leaving their houses feared his forces or whether they were preparing to blend into the woodland along the road for a surprise attack.

Coffee was anxious for any news of British sightings as he marched south. Northbound riders reported no signs of an invasion.[862] Coffee had expected the British to be on the brink of invading the coast, and Jackson had mentioned news of an imminent invasion to spur payments just before the men departed Nashville. Where were the British soldiers that supposedly had been massing on the coastline? Jackson apparently had not confided his true purpose of the mission even to Coffee. Though the threat of British ships was reliable, Jackson knew that New Orleans was not the real purpose of his mission. It was Florida. But Jackson did not temper the officers' speculation of a British threat. He needed men ready for a fight on the Gulf, whoever the enemy, and the imminent threat of a British invasion kept his soldiers on ready.

By February 4, the cavalry had reached the Chickasaw Agency.[863] While the Chickasaw had more than proved their friendship, it was still comforting to the troops to enter the official U.S. compound. The Chickasaw Agency house was the first brick building the men had seen since they marched through Columbia. Even more comforting was the sight of the large storehouse and granary built for providing supplies for travelers; however, the supplies would not have gone far for 672 men and horses.

In fact, rather than relying upon corn from the agency, Henderson had made a contract with George Colbert's brother James for supplies, and he had repaired an old horse-drawn mill at the agency to grind the corn into meal for the men.[864] James Colbert had also agreed to sell beef, pork, and other products.[865]

Nearby Pontotoc was also a large settlement at the crossroads on the Natchez Trace of Indian trails to Fort Pickering (modern-day Memphis) to the west, Charles Town (Charleston, South Carolina) to the east, with access by river to Mobile to the south. Trade goods and people were in abundance, but orders prevented the soldiers from interacting. Even Indians who had built a village around the agency grounds were off-limits.

For the first time since the cavalry left Nashville, the intense cold weather broke, lifting spirits, even as it left a soft surface on the thawing road.[866] Several soldiers also recognized the friendly, reassuring face of James Robertson. To Tennessee soldiers of every age, Robertson was the epitome of a military hero and a wise, battle-tested leader who had led Cumberland settlers though perilous times.

Coffee welcomed the opportunity to confer with Robertson, whose experienced assessment of the Chickasaw and Choctaw was critical. From Robertson's perspective, the situation had stabilized for the moment. Unlike his predecessor Major Neelly, Robertson had not been required to send letters to the Secretary of War to report that the Prophet's disciples were making inroads among the Chickasaw. Robertson could confirm that the Chickasaw generosity Coffee had experienced was genuine.

As Coffee later informed his wife, "As yet I have been fortunate, the Indians through which I have passed, have been remarkably kind. I suffered for nothing when among them, they fed my men and horses bountifully and showed every mark of respect, to us they could."[867]

Coffee could not rest at the agency. His troops were only halfway to Natchez. He told his wife that he had so much work to do in making preparation that he barely had time to send her a "scrawl" and, as unintentional proof, Coffee admitted that he almost forgot to write her.[868]

CHAPTER THIRTEEN

RIVERS OF ICE AND SNOW

*"Those men were our country men—they were citizens of the
same state; they were the Patriots that stepped forth voluntarily at
the call of their country to defend her rights, and to have viewed
them perish near their colleagues in arms, without the privilege
of contending with an Enemy, would have been too distressing.
But Providence held the destiny of those men by a hair..."*

—Robert Searcy, February 3, 1813

North on the Cumberland River, Jackson's boats neared Eddyville, Kentucky. The boat with the collapsed roof was repaired at Lyons's shipyard, and Jackson ordered his own boat pulled alongshore with the announced purpose of sending letters back to Nashville.[869]

The true purpose was to visit with his old friend Matthew Lyon. The two had much to discuss. Jackson became friends with the former Revolutionary War soldier while serving in Congress. Lyon had earned Jackson's respect by standing up to the Federalists in government for the interests of the common man and suffering the consequences. The Adams administration prosecuted and imprisoned Lyon under the Alien and Sedition Acts for making political statements in opposition to President Adams and the political aristocrats. Escaping an attempt to re-imprison him by asserting his constitutional rights as a congressman not to be arrested while in travel for assembly with the Congress, Lyon had the privilege of casting the deciding vote that made Thomas Jefferson president and removed the Federalists from power.[870] Lyon, who later contracted to oversee delivery of mail on the Natchez Trace, likely had continued his relationship with Jackson, assessing that Jackson "only wanted opportunity and that [he] would always be ready to force luck."[871] Jackson's appearance with a flotilla of military boats headed for New Orleans proved that Lyon had been correct.

Like Jackson, Lyon had been caught up in the recent Burr scandal, and Jackson likely halted his advance for information on Wilkinson and Burr. Lyon's Eddyville, perched on the bluff above a turn in the river, gave the colonel knowledge of the boats that traveled on the Cumberland. As Burr had made his way south to meet with Jackson in 1805, he had met up with Lyon on the Ohio River and the two tied their boats together to confer.[872] As they continued to talk, Lyon began to suspect that Burr had nefarious plans and refused to help him further.[873] Wilkinson and Burr also had met at nearby Fort Massac to plot their schemes. Lyon could answer questions about their activities.

Rather than visiting Lyon's home, Jackson summoned Lyon to his boat. He may have felt the need to prime his guest to encourage the free flow of details. As Jackson and Lyon continued their conversation, Ensign Edmonson noted that Lyon helped himself to as much whiskey as he could hold. Lyon became loud and egotistical.[874] Jackson did not record the information he obtained, but he sent Lyon back to land once his mission was accomplished.

On January 18, Jackson took advantage of a brief period of fair weather to speed his advance toward the mouth of the Cumberland River on the Ohio River. He ordered the men to row.[875] Near dark, about 10 miles from the destination, captains noticed that eddy water was rising from the Ohio. Trusted officers Deaderick and Hynes were sent to scout conditions. When they neared the proposed landing site, a traveler in a keelboat promised that if the scouts would wait, he could travel ahead to provide information about the condition of the Ohio River farther west. Though the information was what Jackson needed, it was not what he had ordered. When the scouts did not return at their scheduled time, Jackson chose not to wait and proceeded on toward the Ohio. Finally, scouts met up with the boats and reported that there were heavy ice floes on the Ohio. If Jackson had continued on his present course, the boats could have been sunk. He ordered the boats to halt until morning when they could make a better visual assessment.

The next morning, Jackson directed boat captains to proceed cau-tiously and ordered Hynes and Hall to determine whether conditions were safe to cross.[876] The scouts returned to report that they had seen the flow of the Ohio River opposite the island at the confluence of the rivers. This was a year when the ice was running. The Volunteers would pay a price for the delays, because the chunks were already large and rapidly moving. There had been no traffic on the river in almost three weeks. Seasoned boatmen knew that conditions were too dangerous to proceed. Those boatmen usually pulled their boats out of the water when the ice began flowing and lived inside them until the thaw.[877]

A traveler from Tennessee approached Jackson's boat and invited Jack-son to follow him, bragging that he was not afraid of a little ice. Jackson wisely declined. The traveler's boat did not travel more than three miles before it wrecked.[878] Jackson's impatience and impulse were guarded by some temperance after all.

Cramer's *The Navigator* gave the position for an island that lay ahead near the confluence with the Ohio.[879] Jackson ordered the flotilla to halt near the island, where the bend and northward flowing water from the Cumberland would direct the ice floes away from their boats. It was the site of Smithland, Kentucky, a settlement of 160 houses and 27 stores.[880] Along with Eddyville, Smithland was one of main river towns north of

Colbert's Ferry. Though the two-story Bell's Tavern on top of the hill was as fine as any in Nashville, Ensign Edmonson was unimpressed. He called Smithland "a poor apology for a town."[881]

The temperature was still uncomfortably cold, but the men had been cooped up on the boats for days, and they needed to be exercised physically and psychologically. Jackson ordered the men to go ashore and parade in the snow while they waited. At noon, Jackson went outside to review them, then he had lunch back onboard with unnamed guests who were traveling to St. Louis from Fort Massac. Messengers brought news that the group of Volunteers who had deserted at the mouth of the Harpeth had been apprehended. Jackson ordered that a court-martial be set for them the following day. He had one day to decide how to deal with his failure to prevent desertion.[882]

Cramer's *The Navigator* described the Ohio River as one of the most beautiful rivers in the "universe" and claimed that the French called it "La Belle Riviera."[883] Edmonson and some of the solders must have read Cramer's description and went down to the confluence of the river at sunset to see for themselves. The view was not a disappointment. The setting sunlight on the ice gave the young men visions of an Arctic landscape, one Edmonson would remember in his advanced years.[884] The enemy was still days away, and the constantly changing landscape provided new sights that made this portion of the trip the grand adventure the young men had anticipated.

Jackson did not have time to enjoy the landscape. Boats stalled by ice floes created new challenges of command. Soldiers confined to close quarters with no work to focus their attention were likely to create their own diversions, which could lead to a breakdown of discipline. On January 20, Jackson ordered the boats to cross the Cumberland and anchor opposite Smithland to a forested bank so that men could make use of their time cutting wood and parading on the beaches.[885]

Inside, the court-martial for the deserters began. Whether the prospect of death or the pursuit of a greater adventure was the motivator is unclear, but Jackson could not ignore the challenge to his command or to the collective duty to serve. After being duly convicted, the deserters were first humbled by a full regimen of punishment that included limited rations, a drumming along the line, and wearing a ball and chain.[886] Then they faced an angry general, who was quick to use them as an example. Jackson scolded, "I am surprised to see here men and likely men who turned out Voluntarily in defence of their injured Country after having endured all the cold weather with cheerfulness and patience now tarnish their honor by deserting their posts."[887] The men would face a final day of drumming on January 21, with additional encouragement from the top. When it became clear that the deserters were penitent, the remainder of the punishment was declared satisfied.[888]

As a deterrent to future offenders, Jackson insisted that his patience had been exhausted. The men already had plenty of time to learn their duties, and they were too far from home for Jackson to be delayed searching for deserters. Delays endangered all lives. Jackson announced that from that point forward, desertion would be considered a capital crime, and offenders would be used as examples to the full extent of the law.[889] He wanted there to be no uncertainty that in the future anyone who violated their muster oath by deserting would be shot.

As the men went onshore for drilling on the third day that they had been iced in at the same location, Reverend Blackman added a diversion. He mounted a stump and delivered a fifty-minute sermon on the evils of swearing, something he noticed had become popular among the men. Blackman cited Isaiah 1:19-20 as his text: "If you are willing and obedient you will eat the good things of the land. But if you resist and rebel, you will be devoured by the sword."[890] Blackman was referring to obedience to God. Searcy thought Blackman was encouraging the men to be subordinate to their officers in camp, and he complimented the sermon.[891] Military regulations prohibited swearing, but the officers practiced it, and officers' violations made it impossible for them to hold their subordinates accountable. Blackman had noticed that the regular U.S. troops were even worse at swearing. The minister preached that the country faced perilous times, and practices such as swearing could be a cause. It was time for the men to take control of their speech or risk being destroyed by an invading enemy's sword.

Despite the confidence that Blackman demonstrated through the message he preached, he wrote in his journal that he still felt inadequate to the task of ministering to military regiments.[892] Nevertheless, Blackman found that the men listened respectfully as he pointedly challenged their conduct. Blackman's confidence grew with each sermon.

Impatient to continue the march after being confined to the same location for several days, Jackson was willing to take greater risks. On January 22, Jackson ordered scouts inspect the river again, likely unintentionally suggesting that he did not want them to report that ice would prevent their advance. When the scouts allowed that the ice floes seemed to have lessened, Jackson did not seek any verification. He ordered the boats to advance by 8:00 a.m.[893]

As the flotilla approached the confluence of the Ohio and entered its cross waters with no opportunity to reverse course, captains were startled to discover that the scouts' reports of the river had greatly understated the rapidly moving ice floes. Large chunks of jagged ice were primitive torpedoes, and as they began pounding the boats, captains immediately recognized the danger. Cramer's *The Navigator* provided advice:

"If at any time you are obliged to bring to on account of the ice, great circumspection should be used in the place to lie in, if you wish to preserve your boat; there are many places where the short projecting to a point, throws off the cakes of ice towards the middle of the river, and forms a kind of harbor below."[894]

As an indication of the intense effort captains made to avoid being wrecked by the ice, it took an entire day to move a few miles. At first, captains attempted a landing in the evening at Fort Massac on the north side of the river, but they discovered that this position put them directly in the trajectory of the ice. Captains finally determined that the ice was deflected away from the south bank, probably by the large sand bar in the middle of the river and ordered the boats to move across the river to the south side opposite the fort until conditions improved. The maneuver itself was risky. In addition to avoiding hits by ice as much as possible, the crews had to push against a strong head wind and river current.

The weather only worsened. High wind brought snow and rain mixed with freezing ice that coated the wooden flooring, making it dangerous to walk on the decks.[895]

Blackman's next challenge was to comfort a dying soldier. The stress of the prolonged cold began to take its toll on Private John Rogers of Nashville. His labored breaths in the extreme cold aggravated a preexisting heart condition.[896] Blackman visited the private on Captain Wallace's boat and did his best to comfort the young man, but he knew that the soldier's condition was grave. About 1:00 p.m. on January 23, after three days of struggled breathing, Rogers became the first Tennessee Volunteer to die in active service.

Several men had fallen ill, and Blackman was asked to console them. Rather than providing the usual encouragement that the men would recover no matter how serious the illness, Blackman thought it better not to lie. With pure Protestant pragmatism, if the soldier's condition appeared to be fatal, Blackman told him so and suggested that he prepare for eternity. Jackson learned about Blackman's approach and told Blackman that he preferred the men to be encouraged that they would recover, even when there was no hope. Any loss of morale would influence the whole regiment. Jackson was obviously unaccustomed to following someone else's directions, but Blackman thought that chaplains should take their direction from a higher authority and said so. Blackman recorded in his diary, "I find the Gen. cannot bare much opposition. He is a good General but a very incorrect Divine."[897] Blackman kept that assessment to himself and his diary.

Jackson was informed of Private Rogers' death. Hynes announced that Rogers had *"paid the debt of nature."*[898] Because the boats were not far from the U.S. Fort Massac, Jackson thought it appropriate that Private Rogers's body be buried near the fort. The General knew that the soldiers would closely watch how he managed Rogers's burial. Jackson had assured the men several times that if any of them died during the expedition, they would be buried with the full honors of war. The General's directions for Rogers's burial gave him an opportunity to live up to that promise.

Jackson ordered that Rogers was to be given a full military service. Sergeant Armstrong and a detachment of Captain Carroll's company would perform the ceremony. Rogers's body was to be dressed in his best dress uniform, and if he did not have one, a uniform was to be made for burial. Soldiers were ordered to obtain a coffin at Fort Massac, but the ice flow made it impossible to complete that mission for two days until rains began a thaw.[899]

Benton and his smaller rear flotilla still lagged eight days behind Jackson's, and they had traveled only a mile beyond Clarksville when Benton's boat met up with Captain Martin's. The field officers had assembled over a meal of biscuits and vegetables to discuss how to increase their speed to catch Jackson's boats.[900]

They were still ahead of the cold-front rain that covered Jackson's boats in ice. That evening, the front approached with a squall line and winds so strong that even the lookouts had to leave their posts and let the boats float where they would. Soldiers lashed the boats together so that none would get lost. As could have been predicted, with no lookouts or steerage, the boats came to an abrupt stop.[901]

Soldiers rushed outside to see what they had struck. It was so dark that candles were ordered to be brought out and lowered to the water's surface for light. Someone observed that they had just run aground on a river bank. Poles were brought out to push the boats off the rocks and sand and proceed on in the night.[902]

The boats had not traveled far before lookouts spotted two additional boats tied together and moored waiting for light. Benton ordered their captains to cast off at the rising of the moon and follow him.[903]

A warmer rain on the morning of January 24 began a thaw. The ice flow on the Ohio subsided enough that Jackson's boat could cross the river to Fort Massac on the north side. Jackson accompanied the burial party for Private Rogers up the steep hill to the fort.[904]

The palisade wall was perched on the north bank of the Ohio, and its four corner blockhouses provided a commanding view for 11 miles upriver and four downriver. It was the fourth fort on the same location. Explorer Hernando De Soto is said to have built a fortification there. Later, the French built a fort they named "Fort Ascension" on the site. Tennessee soldiers heard a story that an Indian dressed in a bear skin lured pelt-greedy French soldiers from the palisade walls. Once the French were in the open, the Indians massacred them. Fort Massac, they were told, got its name from an abbreviation of the word "massacre" and referred to the death of the French troops.[905] It seemed to make sense, and it became one of the stories that gains traction the more it gets passed around. No one explained to the soldiers that the fort was named in honor of the Marquis de Massiac when France controlled the position.

On the north side of the fort, trees had been cut to provide a three-acre graveled parade field. Many Tennesseans who had also volunteered for service in the U.S. New Army were temporarily stationed at the fort, and even though it rained all day, Jackson's presence was the impetus for parades in his honor.

The funeral party's strains of "Logan Water" brought the fort to solemnity. The tune was traditionally used for military burials. The familiar sound told soldiers who did not know Rogers that one of their own had died. Searcy described the service as solemn and impressive.[906]

Colonel Anderson was still at Massac, waiting to travel to the northern front. Anderson ate breakfast with Jackson and his officers before the General crossed the river to return to his boat.[907] Perhaps Anderson also shared what he had learned there about Wilkinson and Burr's meeting.

As it was Sunday, Reverend Blackman found shelter from the rain in a shed and began to preach to anyone who would listen.[908] Blackman had overheard talk on the voyage from citizens who had been transformed to soldiers about the lives of professional soldiers. Often their descriptions were seasoned with a hint of jealous admiration, but as Blackman observed the lives of the professional soldiers at Fort Massac, he determined that they were little more than slaves who worked for their commanders. He noted, "O the evils of war who can enumerate them."[909] Blackman would also use the subject of Rogers's burial in a sermon to the Volunteers the following Sunday to ask the men to consider the brevity of life.

That evening, another storm pelted the boats. Jackson's boat sprang several leaks. The following day was no better. High winds forced the boats to halt about noon, then rain, hail, and snow fell and continued through a second night.[910]

Still days behind and some 110 miles downriver from Nashville, soldiers on boats under Benton's command also had reason to contemplate the brevity of life. At noon, they passed the small cluster of islands known as "Line Islands" that marked the line between the states of Tennessee and Kentucky.[911] It was a near a risky passage that boatmen called the "Devil's Shoe." Rolling thunder in the distance to the west sounded a preview of another evening of storms.

Rain squalls hit about dark. The boats were so far behind Jackson's schedule that they nevertheless risked floating for two hours through the storm. Finally, not being able to justify the danger, Benton ordered that the boats halt until the rising of the moon.[912]

Two hours later, there was still total darkness. Captains consulted *The Almanac*, which showed that the daylight could be expected in about an hour. It was thought safe to move forward, and the boats moved slowly as soldiers put their hands in the water to attempt to feel what dangers might lie ahead. When it felt as if they were running aground, all soldiers rushed to grab oars to steer away from shore.[913]

At daylight, two boats that had run sideways onto gravel banks were spotted just ahead. The soldiers said that they tried to push them off, but in the excitement, everyone pushed in opposite directions, working against themselves. Captain Reynolds told soldiers to bring hand spikes, and under his immediate supervision, the soldiers were finally able to coordinate to push the boats off the bank.[914]

Not far downriver, the men spotted the wreck of Captain Alexander's boat from Jackson's lead flotilla. Speculation among the troops as to how the boat wrecked and whether anyone was injured likely dominated conversation for a few days. They also saw the boat of the Tennessee traveler who asked Jackson to follow him into the Ohio. Benton described the boat as being "smashed into atoms," and it made the men wary of the power of the ice.[915]

About noon, Benton's rear flotilla arrived at Eddyville. The boats were lashed together for 13 companies to conduct a religious service. The minister stood at a makeshift pulpit and noted the significance that he was preaching the "gospel mortality of Christ" on the very spot a few years earlier occupied only the buffalo, Indians, and an occasional white hunter. Now, their presence represented progress that would change the landscape forever. The sermon sparked a secular conversation for the voyage as soldiers speculated on the changes that the Mississippi River would soon bring to the nation and how their expedition was part of that progress.[916]

In the evening, the cold front finally arrived, and rain turned to freezing rain. One of the steersmen came down from the roof to warm up. His clothes were frozen stiff with ice. Benton decided to halt the boats until the storm had passed. About three in the morning, captains attempted to set out again but were soon met with blizzard conditions. Benton recorded that his men had not seen sun, moon, or stars in many days.[917]

Jackson's pronouncement of the death sentence for desertion proved to be an ineffective deterrent. A young fifer in Captain Carroll's company had deserted on January 22 at the mouth of the Cumberland.[918] Recalling Jackson's order that deserters would face capital punishment, the fifer showed extreme penitence. His trial forced Jackson to reveal that his gruff demeanor was just a facade to those he considered his friends or family, and these soldiers were now his military family. Given the deserter's youth and penitence, the tribunal would not consider capital punishment despite Jackson's prior announcement. Instead, the court sentenced the young man to five "cobbs"— paddles on his posterior with a cob stick—and to wear a ball and chain. Even then, when the sentence was handed to the General for approval, he rejected it because Congress had just made flogging soldiers illegal. The youth was simply reminded that desertion was a capital crime, and he was admonished that he had passed "the confines of redemption." If he was wicked enough to desert again, he would surely pay with his life.[919]

The winter storm intensified on January 25. Wind gusts rocked the boats so hard that the men could barely stand. Edmonson's boat almost came loose from its anchor. Lightning threatened those exposed. First hail pelted them, and then snow covered them. The storm was followed by another period of extreme cold.[920] The steersmen decided they were doing little to determine the course of the boats and that they should go inside and let the boats follow their own courses.

Finally, at sunrise, the storm passed as suddenly as it had arrived, and a bright blue sky appeared. Without clouds to hold what little heat remained, the temperature plummeted.[921]

The cold front also pounded Benton's flotilla, and then passed briefly to show the sun.[922] Despite Benton's apprehensions, his first command of boats was proving successful.

Ahead, with clearer weather, Jackson's boats proceeded on toward the Mississippi River on January 26 and advanced all day.[923] Just west of Fort Massac, the boats passed a farm now called "Wilkinsonville" near chains of rocks.[924] Wilkinson had amassed large numbers of troops there in 1801 and built a fort to replace Fort Massac. As in many chapters in Wilkinson's life, his true motives are not entirely clear. Butler had pulled some soldiers from the fort to build the Natchez Trace military road in 1801.[925] The fort was soon abandoned and dismantled. Soldiers did not even leave a plank behind to reveal what had been located there. If Jackson had not already been so far behind schedule, he might have stopped to gain additional intelligence.

Canoes that had dislodged in the storm the previous evening were spotted. A detachment was sent to capture them. The canoes were lighter than the flatboats, and despite frantic rowing, the detachment could not catch the heavier flatboats. The detachment was forced to carry the canoes on foot through the snow and ice until the boats made their next stop. After almost getting lost, the recovery party barely caught them.[926]

By evening, the lead boats landed at Cash Island, about nine miles from the mouth of the Ohio at the Mississippi.[927] It was the last island the Volunteers would pass in the Ohio River. Despite the heavy snow, hunters succeeded in taking eight deer to provide fresh venison. Reverend Blackman thanked God for the provision of fresh food, but after apparently watching the pride the hunters took in their kills and butchering of the deer, he observed that man spent so much time taking the lives of God's creatures for food, taking a man's life in war was not such a far step.

Death was part of everyday life on the frontier. To Blackman, it seemed no wonder that wars were so common.[928]

Upriver, Benton's boats were just arriving at Smithland. Townspeople still talked about Jackson's arrival and about how professional his troops had acted. Ensign Edmonson's views of the town had not circulated. Likely at Bell's Tavern, Benton took delivery of the orders that Jackson had left for him. The message was direct. Jackson pressed Benton to move his boats on to meet the remainder without delay.[929]

But ice floes were again so perilous that almost no one was traveling on the river. Someone told Benton about the traveler who had wrecked eight days earlier as Jackson had waited.[930] Now, after passage of the storm, the weather was even colder, and the risks were greater.

Everyone Benton talked with at Smithland told him that it was too dangerous to proceed until the ice floes ceased. Benton consulted with his own experienced officers. Pillow and Reynolds favored proceeding, given Jackson's orders to meet his boats as quickly as possible.[931] Under normal conditions, non-officers in the militia who elected their leaders from among their ranks saw no need to hold back their own opinions as to what their leaders should do. This time was different. The men appreciated the dangers and that the decision to proceed could put men's lives at risk. When even the rank and file were afraid to offer an opinion, Benton knew the conditions were dangerous.

Benton walked the riverbank and studied the ice. The decisions he had made on his own at Clarksville had seemed easy compared to this one. Under other circumstances, there would have been no question that waiting was more prudent, but Jackson was already angry with him. Benton described the choice as "painful"; his decision would determine whether "a multitude of fine men should perish in the ice, or live to see their friends again."[932] As political cover, he recorded for publication that he would have preferred to have waited until river conditions improved, but that in the end, he deferred to the decision of more experienced boat commanders who thought it was safe to proceed.

As the only rudimentary defense Benton could imagine, he secured long poles with iron attached to the ends for soldiers to use to push away chunks of ice.[933] Captains demonstrated their growing skills by navigating the floes without disaster.

Jackson's lead boats began movement early on January 27 in anticipation of finally arriving at the Mississippi River. Cramer's *The Navigator* naively speculated that the confluence of the Ohio and Mississippi was destined to become "one of the most considerable places in the United States."[934] The General was disappointed to see that ice floes in the Ohio had actually increased during the previous night as the temperature had dipped. Jackson sent Hynes to scout, but ice kept him from reaching the Mississippi River.[935] Too far behind schedule, Jackson took a chance to proceed on with caution.

As the boats neared the Mississippi River, lookouts sounded an alarm to halt. The surface of the Mississippi was frozen solid. Some boats landed at a bank on the Ohio, but others could not find a safe location to anchor. Ice chunks threatened them from behind and the Ohio River current propelled them toward a crash ahead into solid ice. *The Navigator* suggested that if all else failed, boatmen could fell trees and use them to build a small dam to push ice away from the boat.[936] But there was no time to stop to fell a tree. Captains improvised. A nearby sand bar would serve the same purpose to deflect ice and provide a safe harbor for the evening.

The next morning the surface of the Mississippi was flowing, yet large quantities of ice peppered the water. The men were ordered to go ashore on the sandbar to practice several maneuvers. William Campbell Love's account of the journey two years later probably also described the brief diversions on shore. If the boats stopped at night, soldiers ran into the river cane and conducted mock battles. After the battles, if the weather allowed, soldiers spread their blankets and slept on the riverbanks by the fires. At the call of the second trumpet in the morning, just before boarding the boats to continue the advance, the young men cut loads of cane and threw them into the fires. When the cane heated, it created popping sounds like gunfire. Love reflected, "We gained a splendid victory without the loss of one man."[937] It was a reminder that many of the soldiers were young boys on an adventure. Unlike Jackson and his officers, who were burdened by the concerns of leadership and logistics, Love spoke for the privates and said, "We had a merry time."[938]

The river rose about 10 feet in 24 hours, but ice floes slowed enough that it was decided the boats could venture on.[939] On January 30, news that the boats could finally move south on the Mississippi to a warmer climate was met with shouts described as "Salutations of Joy."[940] Cramer's *The Navigator* promised, "After you enter the Mississippi you begin to wind considerably southward. . . The climate becomes mild and warm, and the winter gives but a trifling check to the growth of vegetation."[941]

The rising water overnight had cleared most of the ice, leaving only floes of driftwood. Jackson had intended to make an early start, but it was reported that a drummer had crossed the river the night before, and he had not returned. He did not appear until shortly before 7:30.[942] The drummer's joy at finding his way back was tempered by learning that he was responsible for keeping the boats from moving forward. Rather than showing anger, Jackson was probably relieved that he did not have to wrestle with another potential capital offense.

The confluence of the Ohio and the Mississippi formed a triangle that Cramer called the "Willow Point." Strong currents from each river approached rapidly from both sides. If captains were not careful to keep boats in the center of the two swift currents, boats would be forced into a spin.[943] Captains showed their growing skills by successfully maneuvering the pass.

The ice mysteriously disappeared, so the passage was slightly easier than it could have been.[944] Finally in the Mississippi and heading south, the river current became more rapid. The captains felt Jackson's prodding and made up for lost time by traveling more than 40 miles. They passed the old United States Fort Jefferson on their left. It was the one site where Chickasaw Indians had attacked American soldiers, and a reminder that they were moving away from the settled areas.[945] The island identified as No. 6 on Cramer's map was selected for the evening's landing. Volunteers would pass an additional 94 numbered islands before they reached Natchez. Soldiers who hoped that their southerly route had put winter behind them were disappointed. Another heavy snow fell overnight.

Nevertheless, travel improved the mood of the infantry and the mighty Mississippi made an impression. This was the river of legend for most of the Volunteers. Some thought its name was taken from the Indian *Meschacebe*, meaning "Old Man Far Off," which whites interpreted as "Father of Rivers."[946] Tennesseans were seeing in person what they considered one of the Wonders of the World, and it provided them visions of the scale of their future nation. Robert Searcy reflected the conversations in his journal, "Ought we not to believe that the God of Nature, intended our civil institutions to be formed on a large scale of Empire, to be in uniformity with his mighty works of Nature? The Rivers, the mountains and the Lakes of America surpass every other country in the world in their extent and greatness."[947]

The river lived up to its reputation. Soldiers could sense that the Mississippi was almost living, as if they were riding a slow-moving serpent. The untamed river was dynamic, constantly changing course by up to a mile or more. It undermined riverbanks that came crashing down into the water, at one point exposing chalk deposits on one side and iron deposits on the other. Sometimes isolated cabins could be spotted dangling from the sides of the banks where unsuspecting settlers had built too close to the changing course. Local legend held that Jackson's own cabin in Bruinsburg eventually fell into the river.

For the curious, New Madrid (now New Madrid, Missouri) provided the experience of seeing the effects of a great disaster. Volunteers arrived about 4:00 p.m. and a few men asked the captains to stop so that they could disembark to observe the scene they had heard so much about.[948] The massive 1811 earthquake had caused deep ridges in the streets of the town that once boasted a thousand inhabitants, and now held on to only 300.[949] Large trees on the fault line had been split in two and pressure from the earth had blown sand through limbs. The ground even continued to shake at times more than a year after the main quake.

Blackman used the scene for a sermon from the text from the Gospels to pose the question of what a man gains by acquiring the whole world and losing his own soul.[950] Town ruins were a stark reminder of the impermanence of life. Even cocky young bucks in his audience were struck by the power of nature and the limits of human achievement. This site was where land speculator George Morgan had started his new town that he hoped would become a rival for control of the Mississippi. Morgan had even been willing to deal with their enemy Spain to make money. The ruins seemed to mock Morgan's vain human search for glory and legacy, the same reason many soldiers had signed up for this mission. The parson noticed some soldiers listening with more than a little interest. He was beginning to make an emotional connection.

Cramer's map could not account for recent changes after the quake. Sand bars seemed to rise from nowhere to present new hazards. Wise-cracking Davy Crockett would be known to suggest that river captains send up to New Madrid for a "boatload of earthquake" to sink a particularly large river sandbar.[951]

Perhaps to avoid unexpected hazards from the "shakes," Jackson chose not to remain overnight at New Madrid. His boats floated about three miles past the town and moored on the east bank of the river.[952] Despite Cramer's assurances of warmer weather, additional snow continued to pile up along the riverbanks and on the boats. The weather finally cleared on February 1, but winter continued with "unusual severity" for days.[953]

The seemingly endless Mississippi River was one of the primary reasons the soldiers were making the expedition, and they knew it. Blackman speculated that in 60 years, more than twenty-million people would populate the West. But that time of progress could not seem more distant. As boats passed by the Little Prairie near the epicenter of the earthquake, Volunteers noticed that the river ran through streets where a town once stood.[954]

Captains landed the boats opposite Island No. 23 near Hale's Point at the mouth of the Obion River. Volunteers were making progress. They had moved 50 miles in one day, and they were now 136 miles south of the mouth of the Ohio. Though the soldiers had finally adapted to the cold, the men looked forward to warmer weather as they headed south to the Gulf Coast.

The next day the voyage resumed at dawn. Because of the bends of the river, Volunteers found themselves floating eastward into the morning sun. Searcy recorded the "splendor" of the early morning light on the water.[955] Captains continued to increase their speed with the flow of the river. Searcy watched the riverbanks and observed that many people who had lived near the Mississippi had abandoned their homes after the earthquake. Few remnants of American civilization remained. Those who had returned made their livings hand-to-mouth from hunting and fishing. It was a seemingly carefree way of life, but he preferred at least the amount of civilization that the frontier in Nashville offered.[956]

People living along the river probably had no appreciation for the danger the young republic faced or the sacrifices the soldiers were making to protect it. But then, the lives of people so far from civilization might have changed little whatever the outcome of the war. It would matter to their children and grandchildren. Like soldiers before them, Volunteers were sacrificing for people who did not even know the risks they were taking and for future generations whose lives would be forever changed by the outcome of their efforts.

The boats traveled 50 miles and came to a hazardous passage near an island called "Flour" because of all the flour boats that had been wrecked miscalculating the treacherous passage and crashing into it.[957] Captains worked to avoid a similar landing as they made their harbor there for the evening. Cramer's *The Navigator* showed that the Chickasaw Bluffs lay ahead. The men were almost back to Tennessee from their northern river course.

On February 3, the lead flotilla passed the Second Chickasaw Bluff and Island No 35. At Jackson's prodding to make up for delays upriver, boatmen became less cautious, allowing the boats to move at greater speed each day.[958] They ignored large trees that had fallen into the water from the side banks, their roots dropping below the surface so the tops lay unseen, just below the surface.

One of those trees that soldiers called "sawyers" snagged Captain Wallace's boat and it began to sink rapidly. Panic struck the men on board. They shouted for other boats to come to their aid as they waved their arms to draw attention. Some boat captains responded by dispatching canoes. When captains saw men in the sinking boat reaching out to the canoes, they warned the canoe captains to be careful that drowning men overcome by their survival instincts not pull their boats under.

As Captain Newland's boat passed the wreck, Newland refused to take any of its men aboard his boat, apparently fearing that they would overweight it. Captain Martin's years of experience told him otherwise. Though his boat was not the closest to the sinking boat, he ordered his men to row toward it as quickly as they could. By the time Martin arrived, the wrecked craft had sunk, and soldiers were standing on its roof as the current and waves of the cold Mississippi threatened to carry them under. Searcy recorded:

"the Scene was most awfull and distressing. Every one who witnessed the fate that portended those men, mingled their sympathies with the apparent sufferers. Those men were our country men—they were citizens of the same state; they were the Patriots that stepped forth voluntarily at the call of their country to defend her rights, and to have viewed them perish near their colleagues in arms, without the privilege of contending with an Enemy, would have been too distressing. But Providence held the destiny of those men by a hair, and made Capt. Martin the Instrument of their salvation."[959]

As the men were taken into canoes, the lightened boat rose in the water. Martin had the wreck towed to shore, and men began removing valuable supplies and firearms that would have been lost to the Mississippi. Martin more than repaid his debt to Jackson for remaining behind with Benton at Clarksville, and he proved that Jackson correctly assessed that he needed Martin with the lead flotilla.

Memories of the wreck added to the men's anxiety as they almost immediately entered a swift and hazardous channel called the "Devil's Race Ground," followed in a day by a sharp bend where an island in the middle of the river made a sharp left point called the "Devil's Elbow." Reflecting on a trip down the Mississippi River, Davy Crockett remembered how hard the boatmen worked to maneuver through the same bend without wrecking, "if any place in the wide creation has its own proper name, I thought it was this."[960] Cramer's *The Navigator* warned that trees below the surface lay on one side of the river and that the captain would have to be careful shifting to the opposite side because the river current could throw the boat into the island.[961] Colonel Bradley led the way, and all ships passed safely. Captains were more careful, fearing they could face the same fate as Captain Wallace.

Soldiers who had been on Captain Wallace's boat told Reverend Blackman that men prayed as the boat began to sink. They even encouraged one man who was thought to have stolen coffee to confess before he died.[962] Blackman took that unexpected reaction as an indication that his efforts were bearing fruit. God had heard their prayers and answered with a rescue.

Blackman did not wait for the few occasions to preach when most men were together. He tagged an early Tennessee pioneer John Carr to take a canoe and row him to various boats to address the men, both during the day and at night. Blackman and Carr typically pulled up to a flatboat and asked the Captain for permission to board to speak to the men. As the boat continued its flow downriver, the oarsman did the best he could to keep the boat steady. Blackman found a place in the center of the boat and asked the 80 to 100 men to surround him as he talked to them about their sins against God.[963] Blackman took so many risks in canoes on the water to perform his mission that Volunteers never suspected that the parson could not swim.

Jackson's flotilla passed the Middle Chickasaw Bluff of Tennessee about noon and landed on the east side of Island No. 36. As they had moved southward, the weather gradually improved and snow began to disappear.

With scenes of drowning men fresh on their minds, the next day the captains reduced speed, traveling only about 10 or 12 miles. The boats stopped for men to go ashore to cut firewood.[964] Soldiers were still stunned at how close they had come to drowning, and the men who had not been known for their religious practices thanked God for saving them.[965] Blackman's job became easier.

News arrived that Benton's boats were only a day behind Jackson's.[966] The slower speed of the lead boats allowed Benton to shorten the distance between them. Despite the reduced speed, Blackman recorded in his journal, "We float with great swiftness on the bosom of the great

River [.] The Mother of Rivers fed with ever flowing springs & streams bursting from a Thousand Hills."[967] They halted just above Fort Pickering at the Fifth Chickasaw Bluff.

Reemphasizing the point of the Blackman's sermon of a few days earlier, on February 5, as the boats approached the Chickasaw Bluffs near present-day Memphis, Volunteers noticed the ragged appearance of the old federal Fort Pickering.[968] The once-impressive structure had been allowed to fall into disrepair as soon as the Spanish were no longer considered an immediate threat. A cannon from the fort fired a salute as flags from Jackson's boats came in view.[969]

General Carroll and Reverend Blackman disembarked and walked up the 150 log steps on the steep embankment to the fortification. Designed to accommodate 500 soldiers at the Chickasaw settlement, the deteriorating fort now only housed 40 and served primarily as a trading post with the Chickasaw. Traders' temporary shacks added to the squalid appearance.

Blackman started to preach to the federal soldiers and chastise them for their swearing, card playing, and worldly activities, then he noticed that the soldiers' uniforms were ragged and that one federal soldier did not even have shoes to wear in the winter weather.[970] These unpolished federal regulars confirmed the officers' impressions of the state of the United States military, particularly under Wilkinson's command. Washington Irving wrote that Wilkinson's federal troops had a reputation of being "a handful of hen-stealing, bottle bruising ragamuffins," stealing food from areas surrounding their camps.[971] It would be up to state militias to save the country. As Jackson presently served as a militia commander with temporary "Volunteer" status, he did not discourage such comparisons.

CHAPTER FOURTEEN

RENDEZVOUS AT NATCHEZ

"I fear the difficulties, which will stare me in the face, will baffle all my best efforts."

— General James Wilkinson, February 19, 1813

Back on the land route, Coffee's troops navigated their own hazards as they rode their horses over the "Devil's Backbone," another name for the Natchez Trace wagon highway that ran along the ridges. Though Coffee had been well-supplied with food in the Chickasaw Nation, he did not know whether he would find similar accommodation from the Choctaw. Henderson would ride ahead to arrange for food and forage when possible, but despite Henderson's letters, Coffee knew that he had no assurance that food would be waiting.[972] Coffee asked that Mississippi Territory Governor Holmes persuade the quartermasters at Cantonment Washington to meet his men at the lower Choctaw line at Grindstone Ford with supplies. Governor Holmes attempted to use his influence, but Commander Leonard Covington wrote to Henderson that he had no authority to supply Coffee.[973] He suggested that Coffee rely instead upon the Mississippi militia. Jackson's friend Robert Purdy wrote to Coffee to urge that the cavalry travel to Cantonment Washington without any delay, because no food would be waiting at the Choctaw line.[974]

Though the Chickasaw could not have done more to prove their friendship, Coffee was still unprepared to let down his guard. The men could expect to return home through the Chickasaw Nation, and it was critical that the Chickasaw's last impressions of the soldiers be ones that assured a safe return passage. No soldier was to take any action that the Chickasaw might perceive as a threat. Coffee ordered that the procession would be formal. At 5:30 a.m., the trumpet would sound, and the men would form their lines. No one was to speak. The sergeants and officers would call the roll, and the men would prepare to leave at the sound of the next trumpet. The first company would commence the march. The second would allow about 100 paces and then proceed. The distance would ensure that if one company stopped briefly the others could continue to proceed and not hold up the line of march.[975]

About 60 miles, or three days below the Chickasaw Agency, Volunteers left their new Chickasaw friends and crossed over the border into the Choctaw Nation. It was rumored that Tecumseh still had disciples among the Choctaw. That was where the lone Choctaw boy had attacked travelers to create a wave of terror. Chickasaw and Choctaw had been fierce enemies over the years, and just a hundred years earlier, Choctaw had even slaughtered a large group of Chickasaw returning home from Mobile. The soldiers' friendship with the Chickasaw might be taken as a threat to the Choctaw.

The cavalry found that Henderson had arranged for them to purchase 2,000 pounds of bacon at Lefleur's inn called "Frenchman's Camp" or "French Camp." He had also contracted for corn. Additional corn that would fuel their horses should be waiting farther south at Anderson's Stand.[976]

After marching two days without incident, troops reached the Choctaw chief David Fulsom's inn "Pigeon Roost" at a crossing of a branch of the Black River near present-day Mathison, Mississippi. The blustery winter conditions returned. The men had endured the weather well, but the cold and rain were beginning to show effects. Soldiers were getting sick, and a few had reached the point where they would no longer be able to travel.

Coffee could not afford to stop the march until the sick recovered. In addition, though Henderson had arranged for Fulsom to supply the cavalry with corn for their horses, by the time Coffee arrived at Fulsom's, he was already short on food.[977] He had no choice but to further countermand Hynes's order that he keep a distance from Indians. Coffee decided that the sick men would be safe at the Choctaw leader Fulsom's inn. Fulsom had fought with Tecumseh against Creek rebels as he was escorting him out of the Choctaw Nation, but army officers, post riders, and businessmen knew all the inn owners along the Natchez Trace. They knew who could be trusted.

Coffee assigned surgeon's mate Henderson and cornet Harris to remain with the sick men and nurse them back to health.[978] Harris was given money to purchase food and forage from Fulsom as needed. Once the soldiers were well enough to travel, the detachment was to keep the men together in good order and march them to their companies down the road.

Necessity had forced a clearer assessment of the threat Choctaw might pose. Even though Coffee trusted Fulsom, he could not be certain that the small number of troops would be safe from attack by overwhelming numbers of Indian parties, either at Pigeon Roost or on the march to join their companies. Coffee may have been forced to acknowledge that taking the risk of losing a few men was the least-worst option. In any event, in the paranoia whipped up against all Indians in the months before the war, Coffee had taken what some at home would consider a risky decision of trusting Indians potentially at war to safeguard sick Tennessee soldiers in the heart of the Choctaw Nation.

All but one soldier would recover under Fulsom's care. Henderson later wrote Coffee that Fulsom's treatment of the soldiers deserved the "applause of the American people."[979] Developing a working relationship with Fulsom was important, because the Choctaw also trusted Fulsom. As with the Chickasaw, a partnership with the Choctaw in the war effort had begun from what appeared to be necessity. Tennesseans had not appreciated that the partnership had existed all along.

* * *

By February 6, conditions also improved for the infantry on the river just south of Fort Pickering. The weather calmed. As the boats passed the mouth of the Wolf River, Council Island, the Grand Cutoff, and the St. Francis River, troops spent their time continuing their sightseeing of the riverbanks. They ogled at prairies unlike anything they had in their portion of Tennessee.[980] Occasionally they encountered a lone pioneer. One man from Pennsylvania told the soldiers that he had lost five children since moving to the river and had only raised one acre of corn, hardly enough to sustain his family.[981]

Indians that they encountered were doing little better. Volunteers stopped at a settlement of Arkansas Indians, hoping that they could spare fresh venison. Much of Arkansas's game had been wiped out by Chickasaw and Choctaw hunters, and the Indians could offer only to share the artichokes and potatoes that sustained them.[982]

There seemed to be little fear of attack from western tribes. The Osage had given up their claims to land along the western banks of the river. Though the Osage were still dissatisfied with their treaty with the Americans, they liked Tecumseh even less. The Osage still remembered the Shawnee's brutal attacks on their people years earlier, and Tecumseh had found a cool reception when he attempted to recruit them to his confederacy.[983]

Riverbanks were also sparsely populated with men who cut cypress logs and floated them to New Orleans where they were sawn into planks for shipment to the Caribbean or beyond. These colonies of men had been removed from society for so long that they had lost whatever social habits they had ever learned. They grew none of their own food but lived off whatever they could earn from river traffic. Some of the outcasts from society would eventually become river pirates, as dangerous as the land pirates that preyed on travelers on the Natchez Trace. Soldiers spotted one abandoned farm that was said to already be a pirate hideout.

South of the mouth of the St. Francis stood Fort Pike, which the soldiers commented was built by explorer Zebulon Pike. The men who dared to gossip about the Burr affair near Jackson would remember that Wilkinson had sent Pike on an expedition to Santa Fe during the Burr crisis. Pike was taken prisoner by the Mexicans. Some people speculated that Wilkinson planned Pike's capture as a pretext to invade Mexico for Burr. However, discovery of Burr's plot left Pike to fend for himself as a Spanish prisoner in Mexico. The boats did not stop at the fort but continued farther south to land just below the Big Prairie.

Rising before daybreak the next morning, the men stared up at the stars in the clear winter sky, stars which one soldier commented "glittered in the firmament."[984] Jackson, in a moment in which he let his gruff facade slip, encouraged the soldiers to think about the beauty of the heavens, and particularly the Morning Star, as they began each day. By implication, their general did the same.

By February 8, as captains felt more confident that they had traveled beyond the greatest dangers, they put anxious memories of Captain Wallace's wreck behind them and increased their speed, making up to 53 miles in a day. They passed the White River—careful, as Cramer warned, to avoid the current of the sudden flow of side rivers. The men saw abandoned cabins along the riverbanks. That area was also said to have been a criminal hideout, and a couple decades later, the Natchez Trace bandit John Murrell's band of a supposed thousand criminals would use the same area as its headquarters. Anchor would be set for the evening not far from the mouth of the Arkansas River.[985]

In Nashville, the additional federal arms Jackson had requisitioned finally arrived, almost a month after his departure, though they were delivered to the point where Jackson departed rather than to Robertson's Landing where he ordered. When Quartermaster William B. Lewis opened the crates, he discovered that many of the weapons were rusty. Whether through government inefficiency or deliberate action to deprive Jackson of weapons he needed to take command of the Lower Country, the nameless bureaucrat had assured that Jackson would lack the arms he needed to present a threat to the British — or to Wilkinson. Probably due to the poor condition of the weapons, Lewis decided to store them rather than send them to Jackson.[986] Additional weapons were to be waiting when Jackson arrived in Natchez. Lewis could only hope that War Department contractors there were more efficient.

Though it had been rumored that Benton's boats were only a day behind Jackson's, Benton sent dispatches by Major West by land to meet Jackson's boat and inform him that ice floes had detained them.[987] Benton had written to Jackson on February 1 to assure him that his delay was justified, given that his regiment did not have enough boats and some boats were damaged in the ice.[988]

Jackson was not persuaded. Was Benton intentionally delaying to exercise a separate command? Jackson wanted no more excuses. He ordered the lead boats to halt until Benton's flotilla caught up. A boat in the distance from the U.S. army fired a salute with small arms, but no one could see it.[989] It was not Benton's.

As soldiers waited, they read that Cramer's *Navigator* promised travelers they would see pelicans, and the men were excited to spot the first one.[990] One of the hunters shot it to get a better look. Its beak was said to hold three to four gallons of water. The sight of a pelican, the first for most Tennesseans, was a good sign that the Volunteers were finally moving south. Based upon Cramer's descriptions, soldiers looked forward to seeing millions of pelicans, swans, and geese in the unsettled areas along the river.[991]

Finally, shots from boats upriver signaled that Benton's boats were just behind. Arrangements were made to make Benton aware of the locations of Jackson's boats. A messenger reported that a soldier in Benton's regiment had died, but his name was not given.[992] It was never reported whether the soldier was the gambler Hayes.

Benton's boats overtook Jackson's late on the evening on February 10, and the flotilla proceeded. The rumor that Benton was only a day behind had proved correct. Jackson expected Benton to report early the next morning, but Benton avoided facing the General for a few more hours. Benton sent word that his men had been on fatigue until late the prior evening and that he would be unable to meet with the General. Jackson told his officers that he would halt his advance again that evening and advance no farther until Benton reported to him.[993]

River traffic kept the soldiers' attention as they continued to wait. A keelboat loaded with goods from New Orleans making its way north to John Young's store in Nashville approached them. Going against the often-swift stream, teams of boatmen put down poles to the river bottom and tied ropes to trees to pull the boats against the current or used wind sails when they caught a southerly breeze. The intense effort required to move upstream explained why many travelers returning to Nashville from New Orleans without goods to transport would choose the land route of the Natchez Trace instead. Larger barges such as those operated by Rapier and Stump's company now made regular trips north to Nashville. Boat captains were apparently unaware of the hazards of the ice to the north, or they may have planned to harbor until conditions improved. Occasionally, Volunteers spotted other boats floating south loaded with settlers escaping society for Arkansas.[994]

Benton continued to delay before finally facing Jackson and giving answer for his failures and lateness. But to his apparent relief, there would be no court-martial. All Jackson apparently needed was reassurance that Benton understood that he was subordinate to Jackson's command.[995]

Reverend Blackman may have watched Jackson and Benton's conflicts and been reminded of Proverbs 27:17, "Iron sharpeneth iron; so a man sharpeneth the countenance of a friend." The parson could almost hear the scraping sounds of two metal objects when the two men tested each other. It was not yet clear whether both would survive the conflict and prove to be iron.

When evening arrived, Jackson halted his boats at a sunken island that Cramer's *The Navigator* called the "Crow's Nest." Prior to the shakes, the Crow's Nest formed a notorious inlet where two caves provided shelter for river pirates. Four years earlier, about a hundred rough boatmen had decided that they had suffered enough from the pirates and attacked the hideout by surprise at night, breaking counterfeit printing presses and hanging bandits. Within a short time, other pirates returned, defeated only when the island disappeared in the great quake.[996]

The serpentine course of the river made wind both friend and foe. Sails could catch a friendly breeze in one direction, only to face a headwind just a few miles ahead. On February 11, headwinds slowed progress to only 38 miles. The Volunteers landed not far from Island No. 94.

After Reverend Blackman preached to the men on Captain Martin's boat, he finished reading the Books of Moses. He reflected on the changed attitude that he now observed, "Preaching or something has had some effect to prevent profane swearing among the company in a great degree. I do not hear half as much of this as I did when we embarked."[997]

* * *

Henderson continued his advance preparations on the Natchez Trace. By February 11, he had reached Claiborne County in the Mississippi Territory, and had arrived at Cantonment Washington near Natchez two days later.[998] Henderson had suggested that Coffee could buy enough corn at the Choctaw Agency to last until he reached the destination as well and apparently had no knowledge that Coffee was not finding the deposits of food or arrangements with contractors along the Natchez Trace.[999]

Still 150 miles north of Cantonment Washington, Coffee's cavalry approached a settlement known as "Redbud Springs," now Kosciusko, Mississippi. Some people called it "Earthquake Springs." Four springs appeared on a knoll soon after the massive 1811 earthquake that some Indians attributed to the Shawnee Prophet's prediction. To the younger soldiers' relief, none of the rumored headless horsemen or boxlike creatures met them as they rode past Choate's Old Fields.

* * *

On February 12, Congress finally authorized the occupation of West Florida and the taking of Mobile.[1000] Jackson would have used news of that authorization to insist on commanding the mission, but Wilkinson was already at work to be certain that by the time that news reached Jackson in the Lower Country, he would no longer be able to take advantage of it.

At last, with Benton's lagging boats now moving with the lead and signals for advancing and halting coordinated, Jackson's flotilla moved as one unit. Soon, they would begin nearing the settled areas in the Lower County. The confusion in working out logistics had taken place out of the view of the public, and more importantly, out of the view of Wilkinson's spies.

As the boats passed Walnut Hills, now Vicksburg, Mississippi, the infantry was only three-days voyage from Natchez. Jackson would need to halt at Natchez long enough to meet with messengers from the cavalry and to make arrangements for the continued march south to New Orleans.

Jackson ordered the boats to halt for a day just below Walnut Hills. Jackson's march into Natchez would be a chance to re-create his image in the minds of federal officers who would be certain to report to Wilkinson. The Volunteers were ordered to wash their uniforms before appearing in Natchez. High southerly winds in advance of an evening thunderstorm would help the uniforms dry.[1001] The first impression his troops made on the townspeople would be critical if Jackson eventually took control of operations on the Gulf and had to rely on logistical support from Natchez.

As Jackson conferred with his officers, he could not understand why the War Department had made no attempts to communicate with him. Army express riders could have met his boats at any point along the river. Jackson should already be making preparations if he was to be ordered to march his troops to Mobile or elsewhere along the coast.

Resuming the voyage a day later, Jackson's flotilla neared Warrenton, a settlement of 20 farms along the river. So long as captains avoided the suck of Bayou Pierre that could take them inland and the "Devil's Punchbowl," where currents could force boats of unsuspecting travelers out of the river channel into a swirling muddy mire and a nest of river pirates, they had successfully navigated the winter river hazards. Jackson could now focus on the final phase of his march before his temporary halt at Natchez.

On the east bank, boats approached Pine Ridge Road that led to both Natchez and Cantonment Washington. Ahead, a large bend in the river would take the boats about 18 miles west away from Natchez before turning south again. Just below the bend, the boats would pick up a known river current that would lead them effortlessly the final three miles to the crescent-shaped Natchez Landing. This spot would be ideal to halt to make final arrangements for the grand arrival.

Jackson ordered Carroll to take a small boat to Natchez to pick up any dispatches and send them back directly on land by special rider.

Carroll was ordered then to ride ahead to meet up with the cavalry that should be approaching Cantonment Washington.[1002] It also made sense for the mounted infantry to disembark at that point. The horses could be exercised on the ride to Cantonment Washington, and they were likely to find forage growing wild along the way. Reverend Blackman was given permission to take a pirogue to go ashore at Warrenton to visit old friends near the Pine Ridge church and then to meet the Volunteers in Natchez.[1003] Blackman persuaded Carroll to deliver a letter for him to a fellow Methodist to set up a speaking circuit for him in the Natchez area.[1004]

The next morning on February 14, Jackson was so anxious to get news from Natchez that he rose at 2:00 a.m. and gave commands for everyone else to be awakened and prepared to advance within an hour.[1005] His boat stopped briefly in Warrenton to call on the postmaster to see if any letters from the War Department were waiting for him there in transit. There were none. Refusing to return empty-handed, Jackson had to settle for a newspaper and read his news like everyone else.

Jackson's boat continued past the Mississippi Territory Palmyra, a settlement of about 15 farms, and landed at Island No. 109. For the first time, Volunteers saw magnolia trees covering riverbanks. Their deep green leaves were a welcomed sight to Tennesseans in winter. Natchez was not far.

* * *

East on the Natchez Trace, Coffee's cavalry also began to sense that they had survived most of the dangers of the march. Once the riders passed Redbud Springs, Choctaw plantations appeared more frequently. Finally, as Volunteers passed Woolridge's Tavern and crossed Bayou Pierre on February 16, the Wilderness began to recede. Daniel Burnett's Grindstone Ford inn and gristmill welcomed them to a settlement that looked more like the ones at home. Instead of Choctaw plantations, settler farms and plantations became more numerous. The road improved. Excited farm boys ran out to see lines of troops passing on the road.[1006]

The cavalry rode through the middle of Gibson's Port along the Mississippi River, then Greenville. Houses lined the hillside overlooking a valley as well as a hollow known as the "Gallows Hollow," where justice was administered by hanging criminals, and where Little Harpe's head had been impaled on a post as a warning. Now the booming town attracted future leaders, including the Territorial Governor Cowles Meade and the future founder of the University of North Carolina.

The procession finally neared the Mississippi territorial capital of Washington, just six miles east of Natchez. Washington had been built quickly after being selected as the second territorial capital in 1802. Rural farmers opposed the influence of the Federalists and Natchez moneymen voted to move the territorial capital east to the new town.

A spring on the eastern end of Washington had served as a refuge for George Washington's spy and army surveyor Andrew Ellicott, and by 1812, an enterprising businessman had taken advantage of the water to offer hot and cold baths at a price. The Assembly Hall and three taverns dominated the town, and the county also had erected a small courthouse and a jail. About 30 houses lined the six streets.[1007] Though the town had progressed barely beyond the stage of a new settlement, a stagecoach ran daily between Washington and Natchez. Most importantly for young soldiers, the town was filled with young ladies who would delight at watching the soldiers march and train.[1008] They would prove to be a boost to morale that many boys needed after the long journey from home.

Northeast of the town, the fort palisade was visible on the hilltop. Ravines on three sides provided additional protection from invaders. Cantonment Washington, formerly called "Fort Dearborn," was 143 square feet, and at one time, it housed up to four companies.[1009]

Cantonment Washington Commander General Leonard Covington had built a stately two-story house adjacent to the fort. Covington christened his home "Propinquity" because of its proximity to the installation.[1010] The Natchez Trace ran only a few yards from his front door.

As the Cavalry neared St. Catherine's Creek, Coffee's anticipations for the comfort of permanent army quarters were disappointed. Even at first glance, the U.S. army fort looked dilapidated. The cavalry would have to make the best of the situation until Jackson arrived near Natchez with the infantry, and then he could decide what to do.

* * *

They did not have to wait long. As Coffee's cavalry reached Cantonment Washington, a few miles west, Jackson's flotilla passed Island No. 110. Even more anxious than the previous night, Jackson woke the soldiers at 11:30 p.m. with orders to proceed in only half an hour.[1011] The early advance was futile as a heavy storm slowed the boats as they rounded the great bend just north of Natchez. The storm set the mood for stories of death when the boats traveled near the Greenville area of the former plantation of Natchez Trace mail contractor and territorial leader Abijah Hunt, and men could recount stories of the duel that took George Poindexter's life a little over a year earlier.

The storm and stories of the fight among such powerful men also reminded the Volunteers that they would reach General Wilkinson's camp by water in New Orleans in less than a week. Anticipating the upcoming meeting between Jackson and Wilkinson, it was also a reminder that their own general was a duelist who had always defeated his opponents. If bets were taken, it is doubtful that many wagered against Jackson.

Captains Smith and Humphrey of the cavalry met the boats and presented Coffee's report of the cavalry's successful passage through Indian country on the Natchez Trace.[1012] Jackson was relieved. Indians had not attacked. He sent a note to Coffee telling him to assure the cavalry officers and men of his affection for his military family, as a father would express affection for children who had concluded a long trip.[1013]

February 15 was a momentous day for additional reasons. As all Jackson's troops neared Natchez, Congressman Grundy heard a rumor in Washington City that Jackson and the Volunteers had been recalled.[1014] Despite the Secretary of War's formal compliment of Jackson's leadership of the Volunteers in a letter to Governor Blount only seven days earlier, the rumor indicated that the decision had been taken some time ago.[1015] Why would the secretary compliment the Volunteers' continued service if he had already ended that service?

It made no sense to Grundy that the War Department would recall Jackson's troops now. Only three days earlier, Congress had voted to approve the army's occupation of Spanish-controlled West Florida.[1016] The timing of Jackson's arrival in the Lower Country would be ideal to position him to command such a mission. Certainly, the addition of the Tennessee Volunteers to the number of U.S. regular troops in the Lower Country would ensure military success.

Apparently unable to confirm the rumor with the War Department, Grundy questioned other Tennessee representatives in the capitol, and no one from Tennessee had been consulted or informed as customary on decisions affecting such large numbers of military leaders from their state. Grundy would again have spotted "something rotten in Denmark" or Washington City in the dismissal order. Jackson relied on Grundy to protect his command from the top levels of the federal government. Grundy said, "I cannot account for this proceeding—I know of no cause, which can justify the ordering them out, withdrawing them so suddenly, I hope the government has sufficient reason for its conduct.—I shall endeavor to obtain the necessary information on this subject and communicate it."[1017]

Grundy immediately may have suspected that Wilkinson was the instigator of the order, as the Senator had previously surmised when it appeared that Wilkinson was working behind the scenes to take command of the Volunteers. News of the outcome of his work and of Jackson's continued secret campaign against Wilkinson would not arrive in Natchez in time to give Jackson any comfort.

At the mouth of the Yazoo River, Carroll's rider Allen returned to the flotilla with letters from Natchez.[1018] Jackson stopped the advance to review the mail. He made the decision to halt the flotilla upstream and delay the final landing to allow local speculation and interest to grow.

Leaving nothing to chance for the important first impression of the troops in Natchez, just after daybreak on February 16, Jackson and his aides Carroll and Hynes, took a small boat to the town to assess conditions. As Jackson ascended the steep hill at Natchez Landing, local soldiers greeted him with a booming salute by a field piece.[1019] Unexpectedly, Wilkinson's messenger Brigade Inspector Captain Hughes also greeted him with delivery of Wilkinson's January 22nd letter.[1020]

The letter was expected. Jackson anticipated that Wilkinson would protest his command, and he could expect that Wilkinson would be afraid to face him general-to-general, or even man-to-man. Nevertheless, Jackson may have been surprised at how acutely Wilkinson had assessed the Tennessee general's vulnerabilities. Wilkinson made it clear that he controlled Jackson's access to supplies through the contractors and quartermasters, and Jackson would find no provisions if he chose to continue his march south from Natchez. Food waited only at Cantonment Washington.

Wilkinson also knew that Jackson's influence depended upon his base of support in Tennessee. By mentioning the possibility of disease in Baton Rouge, Wilkinson played on Jackson's understandable fear of dealing with an outbreak of sickness among the troops so far from home without any means to care for them. Jackson could not afford to return to Tennessee with his forces ravaged.

Though Wilkinson added the incentive of promising Jackson that he had instructed the Brigade Inspector Captain Hughes and District Paymaster Lieutenant Knight to go to Natchez to pay the soldiers, he never had any intention of following through. And, in typical Wilkinson manner, despite Wilkinson's insistence that Jackson serve under his command, he had carefully worded the letter with enough promises and niceties to give Jackson the initial impression that the communications were "of the most friendly kind."[1021]

It was a key moment of decision. Should Jackson stop his advance at Natchez as Wilkinson suggested or should he proceed on to New Orleans as ordered by Governor Blount? *The Nashville Whig* had proclaimed its confidence that Jackson's soldiers would not halt until they "crossed over the borders of the country."[1022] Jackson sought the counsel of Thomas Winn, who now kept the tavern "Traveler's Hall" in brick and frame buildings on Front Street at the bluff in Natchez.[1023] The General took his breakfast at Winn's and talked over the situation.

Clearly, Wilkinson did not want Jackson anywhere near his command in New Orleans. He would want to avoid a personal confrontation that could end with dueling pistols. But from Jackson's perspective, that fear may have provided reason for Wilkinson to use his influence to urge the War Department to send Jackson toward East Florida, where he would not interfere with Wilkinson's comfortable command at New Orleans. Wilkinson even anticipated Jackson's suspicion by suggesting that a Pensacola campaign for Jackson was "very probable."[1024]

Jackson gave no consideration to Wilkinson's suggestion that if Jackson had 400 or 500 infantry soldiers more than he could feed, he could send those to Baton Rouge. Jackson certainly would not entrust any of his men to Wilkinson's command or give Wilkinson the opportunity to recruit them. Wilkinson made it clear that Jackson would have to find his own provisions for those troops if he kept them.

Jackson knew that his quartermasters were not immediately prepared for housing and feeding more than 2,000 Volunteers and at least 1,000 horses without support from the army. Unless Jackson was prepared to take United States Army supplies by force, he had no option but halt at Natchez. And if he had any hope that the War Department would assign him to march to Pensacola, he would have to convince the War Secretary that he could be trusted to cooperate with Wilkinson. After all, the federal government considered Wilkinson the professional. Jackson had no battle-command experience to provide a convincing counter-argument to federal leaders who already distrusted him.

Though Jackson was suspicious of whatever Wilkinson proposed, the lessons that Jackson had learned from earlier embarrassments now forced caution. This was the chance he had wanted to lead as a general and to gain public respect. It would be necessary to play by the political establishment's rules to gain their confidence.

It ran against Jackson's nature to halt his advance based upon Wilkinson's wishes, but any suspicion was overcome by the promise of the East Florida mission. Even if Jackson did not take command of the New Orleans area from Wilkinson, he could maintain his separate command on an equal footing and then upstage Wilkinson in Florida.

Jackson penned his reply to Wilkinson—polite on the surface but peppered with his own subtleties.[1025] He acknowledged that for the moment he would halt his advance in Natchez and quarter his men at Cantonment Washington, six miles east of Natchez. He would wait for further orders from the government, not Wilkinson. Jackson left open the possibility that he would move his troops when *he* determined it necessary to defend the Lower Country as required to fulfill his mission. Wilkinson's letter referred to Jackson's men only as a "band of patriots," a term commonly used to refer to citizen soldiers. Jackson's reply described his men as "Troops," using a capital "T" for emphasis and further emphasizing that he too was a general. Jackson sent the letter to Wilkinson by steamship before returning to his own flotilla.[1026]

As Jackson was leaving Natchez, he received the letter from Wilkinson dated January 25, which stated in even stronger terms that Jackson should halt his advance at Natchez. It also questioned Jackson's authority to act independently of Wilkinson.[1027] Jackson certainly could not concede that he would serve under Wilkinson's command.

Formal concession would prove unnecessary. Cantonment Washington was the spider's web Wilkinson had weaved for Jackson. And like a spider, Wilkinson would entangle, paralyze, and torture Jackson before moving in for the kill.

CHAPTER FIFTEEN

CANTONMENT WASHINGTON

"To be without funds medicine and a number sick is an unpleasant situation—we are here without any orders or advises, from any quarter, fed some times on the poorest beef on earth—and without an[y] necessity for us being here."

—Andrew Jackson, March 13, 1813

General Wilkinson had arrived in Natchez a few years earlier, observers recalled, with "all the pomp and style of a conquering hero."[1028] Andrew Jackson would carefully stage his formal entrance to let the public know that an even greater general had arrived.

Volunteer captains caught the river current to take the boats to their final descent to the Natchez Landing. The approach, though carefully choreographed, did not allow for the unexpected. A small family boat crossed the path of Jackson's boat just as it neared the landing.[1029] Even when steered by the best captains, flatboats were difficult to maneuver, and his larger boat could not stop. The civilians on board the smaller vessel cried out in fear that they would be the first fatalities in Jackson's advance on the British, but no injuries resulted. It was only a momentary distraction, but it was the first omen that Jackson's command in Natchez would not go exactly as planned.

Natchez citizens nonetheless were impressed by the flotilla. The presence of so many military boats brought crowds to the bluff as word spread through town.[1030] Despite the excitement of the moment, Jackson's frontier intuition nagged him. Wilkinson's second letter strongly warning Jackson not to advance was troubling. Though he had already sent Wilkinson a pleasant reply offering to cooperate, it was now clear that Wilkinson was issuing a challenge.

Jackson understood that he was more likely to obtain the War Department's approval for a campaign at Mobile and Pensacola if he played by their political rules and complied with Wilkinson's request to halt at Natchez. But once the boats were anchored at the landing, Jackson returned to Traveler's Hall to discuss the matter with Winn and local friends who could provide more information about Wilkinson's activities in the area. With townspeople now clearly interested in Jackson's movements, the Company of Guards accompanied him.[1031] Natchez friends could inform Jackson that when the Mississippi Territory militia had prepared to rendezvous at the nearby Cantonment Washington a couple months earlier, a steamboat promptly delivered U.S. arms, ammunition, and equipment to the Natchez Landing.[1032] Those soldiers under the command of Ferdinand L. Claiborne had agreed to march south to Wilkinson's camp at Baton Rouge. Jackson might expect the same consideration if he halted at Natchez.

Natchez townspeople could also confirm stories that when Wilkinson commanded Cantonment Washington four years earlier, his soldiers became so destitute that they routinely resorted to raiding Natchez for food and supplies.[1033] Wilkinson was too weak a leader to stop the violence, and courts-martial became an almost daily occurrence. By taking command at Cantonment Washington, Jackson would have an opportunity to prove that his militia was superior to Wilkinson's professional soldiers.

True, Jackson's orders from the president and the governor directed him to march on to New Orleans, and he had no intention of following any command from Wilkinson if he could avoid it. But as much as Jackson distrusted and despised Wilkinson, the Mobile-to-Pensacola campaign offered the chance to deliver Florida to the United States, and finally bring the Creek Nation hostiles to heel. Those accomplishments were what Jackson wanted most. Wilkinson's letters hinted that he could have them.

Ambition again distracted Jackson from his normally clear evaluation of Wilkinson and the need to comply with the governor's order.[1034] Blinded by ambition and pride, Jackson halted his advance at Natchez. He would quarter his men at Cantonment Washington as Wilkinson requested. Jackson assured himself that the decision to halt was his own, not Wilkinson's.

The decision to remain may also have been influenced by the false comfort Natchez brought after weeks away from what he considered civilization. Because of its location on the Mississippi River, Natchez was well on its way to becoming one of the wealthiest cities in the world as cotton increased in value. Farmers from the Ohio River Valley floated corn, pork, and other farm goods to market there, and the town held vast supplies of fresh food. The embargoes instituted by the last two presidents had made Natchez even better stocked. As Jackson would soon learn, however, warehouses stocked with food were worthless to him unless the War Department was willing to authorize purchases.

Natchez would prove to be an important source of materials and services to the troops later during the Battle of New Orleans. For now, it was a town wealthier and more international than most of the Tennesseans had ever seen. Atop the bluff overlooking the Mississippi River, brick mansions were being built among the wooden shanties and cabins.[1035] The access of the town to international ports and its former French, Spanish, and British control gave it a cosmopolitan culture for its time.

Physicians and tradesmen were also plentiful. The comforts it seemed to offer compared quite favorably to the sparsely inhabited winter environments the Volunteers had endured for more than a month.

As the Volunteers prepared to go ashore, a few officers were assigned to go into town to obtain wagons to haul the equipment. Troops remaining on the flatboats were left to study the landing area that they had long heard about—the notorious "Natchez Under the Hill." Even before the town of Natchez had been built on the bluff, the Under the Hill district sprang up to cater to frontier boatmen and relieve them of their hard-earned wages through every vice known to appeal to them.

Under the Hill itself was not much to see. The wooden shacks built on stilts over streets of raw river mud looked as rough and impermanent as the games and other diversions that went on inside. Some stilts had given way during the 1811 earthquake and a chunk of the hillside had collapsed.[1036] Under the Hill gave Natchez the reputation of being so wicked that when the great earthquake struck, even a newspaper in the worldly New Orleans pointed its finger at the more sinful Natchez as the cause of the vengeance of God.[1037]

Despite the rough appearance of the buildings, music, shouts from games of chance, and fights offered excitement to young men far from home. Adding to the allure, half-naked women who greeted newly arriving boatmen from the upper-story windows of the bawdy houses were the first women the men had seen in weeks. Some Volunteers had likely seen such establishments, even if from a distance, but never so many crowded together in one place and none that felt free to elevate their vices to such a level. Young farm boys received a sudden education in the ways of the world.

Natchez Landing proprietors had honed their marketing, and Jackson's soldiers were just the latest boatmen to arrive at their doors with pent-up energy and money to spend. After the infantry had been surrounded by uninhabited river banks for weeks, Natchez Under the Hill began working its temptations on four officers, who later were arrested by a patrol in one of its brothels.[1038] In just two days, it would become necessary to issue an order that all men outside camp without permission were to be rounded up.

As the men disembarked from the flotilla, Reverend Blackman no doubt recalled stories of Sodom and Gomorrah and warned the men about even casting their eyes on the evils of the place. If spiritual warnings were not enough, soldiers traded rumors that some houses built with rear walls hugging the bluff contained secret rooms tunneled into the hillside. Those establishments used the allures of fleshly pleasures to trick young men to enter their realm, then robbed them of even the shirts off their backs, killed them, and dumped their bodies through trap doors underneath.[1039] Young boys would be tempted to stay awake looking for dropping corpses. Older teens kept watch for more tempting sights.

Despite—or perhaps because of—these temptations, General Jackson warned his men to be on their best behavior as they entered Natchez. Subordinates were instructed to reinforce the order. The first impression the men would present to Natchez was crucial to the image Jackson projected of his ability to command.[1040]

Colonel Benton complied. He had observed the refinement of the town on the hill and he pictured the image his soldiers would create as they marched through on parade. The men had just spent a day washing their uniforms, and now they also had to clean up their behavior. Some of the younger soldiers had taken up all the bad habits of the older men to prove their manliness. The officers had banned gambling, but despite Reverend Blackman's optimism, swearing had become a second language. Benton issued an order declaring that swearing was both ungentlemanly and unchristian, and it would reflect badly on the good reputation the men had already earned. Swearing was to be punishable.[1041] One of Reverend Blackman's first sermons to the infantry had been on the evils of swearing. Now that officers were willing to punish swearing, he could assume that his sermon was bearing fruit.

To make certain there was no infraction of the General's order, Hynes also issued an order just prior to going ashore to tell the men that they were to pass through a "well polished" area.[1042] It was not just Natchez townspeople who would take notice. Like the publisher of the Nashville *Clarion* the same day based upon Jackson's General Orders of December 17, Hynes reminded the men that the nation relied upon its citizen militia, "The eyes of the American nation is upon us. We are the forlorn hope of the militia of the union. On us depends the lost reputation of the bulwark and defense of a free people a well-organized militia."[1043]

It was important that the people who relied upon citizen troops for their defense know that Volunteers were respectable. Hynes wanted to hear only polite language and if the soldiers had forgotten how to speak in that manner, they should remain silent. Even if the men did not care how Natchez viewed them, the Natchez Trace created close connections between Natchez and Tennessee, and friends at home would soon know how they performed.

The order seemed unnecessary to the lower ranks. From the cursing that Volunteers overheard at Under the Hill, if the sole purpose of Hynes's order was to impress onlookers, there was little reason to watch their language.

The Volunteers disembarked and proceeded up the steep climb of Silver Street. Rambunctious sounds and pungent odors from Under the Hill faded 200 feet up as the soldiers paused at the top of the Natchez bluff to form a line for a military parade through the town. The bluff also provided a commanding view of the river upstream from where they had arrived. The Volunteer infantry could congratulate themselves on their first victory. The mighty Mississippi River had not defeated them.

As Tennessee Volunteers began their march down the main street, they found that citizens were well-polished as promised. Searcy recorded that they were met with "distinguished politeness" by the citizens, and particularly by the local authorities.[1044]

Buildings that remained from Spanish occupation gave the soldiers the impression that they had entered a different world. Ladies wore perfumes and dressed more like earlier French settlers than women back in Tennessee. Scents of food cooking in the taverns drifted through the streets and mixed with Creole spices hanging from shop porches. Doors opened, and people filled balconies and galleries to see the Volunteers from Tennessee in lines longer than Natchez had ever witnessed.

One man stood out. There at the lead was the Andrew Jackson many Natchez townspeople had seen as a younger man at the race tracks and in taverns, but now impressively uniformed with all the accoutrements of an army.[1045] He commanded a procession of 1,400 infantry soldiers as their major general. It was a moment of personal triumph and transformation, the culmination of years of political work. Like his rival Wilkinson, Jackson now entered Natchez with the appearance of a conqueror, empowered by military command.

For Natchez residents, beneath the excitement of watching the march lay a realization that the talk of war must have gone beyond the rumor stage. Just a few months earlier, their own Mississippi territorial militia company, the "Natchez Rifles," had marched south to Baton Rouge to provide support for General Wilkinson.[1046] If the British or Creek rebels attacked, Jackson and his Tennesseans were there to protect them.

Jackson could take a moment to drink in the wave of public support. His grand entrance was proceeding as planned, and he wanted to give Wilkinson's spies ample time to witness the arrival of a new general. Perhaps the conqueror's performance was as much to stake out territory from Wilkinson as it was to reassure Natchez.

Soon after passing the brick church and the public burying ground, the train of soldiers passed St. Catherine's Racecourse, the scene of some of Jackson's smaller victories as a civilian. Even those thrills did not compare to the satisfaction he now experienced as a general.

The procession soon left the refined areas of Natchez and the sounds of the town. As houses became sparse, Volunteers neared the point Natchez called "Forks of the Road." The north road was the Natchez Trace that led to Cantonment Washington and back home to Nashville. The southern route was the old Spanish trail that led to Fort Stoddert near Spanish Mobile and on to Pensacola. Jackson would have preferred to take the southern route to military glory by wresting West Florida and East Florida from the Spanish. It was literally a "fork in the road" in Jackson's life. The General may have assumed that he would have the power to choose the southern route whenever he wanted, but by choosing the Natchez Trace to Cantonment Washington, Jackson sealed his future.

The same fork had already become the place where Jackson had made decisions that would haunt him. The Forks of the Road was the slave auction site for Natchez. Tens of thousands of men, women, and children had been forced to walk from as far as Virginia to be sold at that spot. Jackson had brought slaves from Nashville to Natchez to sell for friends.[1047]

The mood changed as the freshly polished soldiers began a long, six-mile slog through mud on the new dirt road, made worse by the storm that pounded Natchez the night the flatboats approached the town.[1048] Only 10 years earlier, the Natchez Trace military road had been diverted from the old Indian trail to connect Natchez to the new territorial capital of Washington. Noticing the rough appearance of the town, as the infantry passed through Washington, they could see the full impact of the great earthquake; the ground had opened and swallowed a house and barn whole.[1049]

Washington was the last semblance of civilization, and it was nearly 4:00 p.m.[1050] The winter sky was darkening, and an unsettling appearance greeted the Volunteers. In winter, white Spanish moss hanging from barren tree limbs can give the Deep South woods a ghostly appearance. Travelers called the moss "Spanish beard." Somewhere in the midst of it, soldiers spied 800 to 900 tombs containing the bodies of Wilkinson's soldiers, men who had died from the fever in the area less than three years earlier. It was an unexpected and startling scene that could not help but raise questions. Were those the men who had lived in the same quarters where Jackson planned to house the Volunteers? Had the soldiers now lying in those tombs rested on the same racks where Volunteers would sleep? Had they too made this same march into the fort thinking that they would soon return home? The soldiers in the tombs did not die in the glory of battle, but owing to the poor judgment of their general, they had encountered the enemy they most feared—disease—and wasted away in sick beds in the southwestern wilderness. That enemy had been at this spot and might be lurking here still. Would General Jackson allow that enemy to defeat the Volunteers?

Any natural hesitation was overcome as the rear lines pressed the whole body forward to the edge of the woods. The very appearance of the fort confirmed reason for gloom. A dilapidated Cantonment Washington stood on top of a steep hill overlooking the territorial capital. The hillside had been denuded by Wilkinson's feverish soldiers searching for firewood.

Behind the palisade wall built to guard against attack and beyond the central block house stood rows of officers' quarters and huts built by Wilkinson's dying men when they arrived there in November 1809. Old six-foot-by-ten-foot latrine huts used by sick soldiers lined the rear of the camp, not far from Ellicott's Spring that would supply their drinking water.[1051] Whatever disease Wilkinson's army brought to this place had passed from the latrines to the spring. The more superstitious Volunteers took the scene as a bad omen of things to come, and they would prove prescient. Imaginative and superstitious young Scots-Irish soldiers may have looked out into the darkening woods and pictured ghosts of Wilkinson's men greeting them to join their ranks.

Infantry were surprised instead to be greeted by the friendly faces of live Volunteers, Coffee's cavalry who had marched into Washington to greet them.[1052] The melancholy spell was broken. As the procession moved into the fort walls, so many men packed the space that the structures became less noticeable. Colonel Coffee greeted Jackson, and Jackson quickly reviewed the cavalry.

The reunion of the regiments for the first time since departing Nashville was a cause for celebration. Infantry recalled harrowing experiences on the Mississippi River and the sinking of captains Alexander's and Wallace's boats. Cavalry matched the stories with their searches for food and successful evasion of Creek scalping parties and bandits in the Wilderness.

Wilkinson's lure of food and pay at Cantonment Washington had been part of what attracted Jackson into the fort. Despite careful planning, the infantry food wagon train lagged in Natchez. The cavalry shared their food, and Cantonment Washington's commander Leonard Covington made sure that every man was well-fed.[1053] Even General Wilkinson's subordinate Inspector Hughes was helpful in providing food.[1054] Wilkinson wanted to make certain that Jackson did not find the need to continue his advance south before he had unpacked to make camp. The abundance of food and the excitement of reuniting friends helped the men forget their surroundings for the moment.

Colonel Coffee was not in the mood for a reunion party. Now that Jackson had arrived to take command, life-and-death logistics did not consume every second of Coffee's day. He missed his wife and took time to write her.[1055] The persistent cold only added to his misery. It had followed them down the Trace even to Natchez where he had expected some relief. Now as the sun set, snow again filled the air to welcome the men to their new camp. It was the coldest weather Natchez had experienced in years.

As Jackson struggled to overcome the damp chill in his quarters, he also worked to deal with the implications of the ramshackle condition of the fort. The warm glow of the public reception in Natchez faded quickly as his brief inspection produced disgust. There would be no honor in commanding Cantonment Washington. The central blockhouse built in 1803 had not been maintained after Secretary of Treasury Albert Gallatin's cutbacks. The sixteen-square-foot wooden sleeping huts were even worse.[1056] Decaying buildings only added to Jackson's low opinion of the ability of the federal government to manage any operation west of the Appalachians.

When the name of the fort had been changed from Fort Dearborn in late 1809, it must have lost some of its prestige that was reflected in its upkeep. Jackson found a "collection of filth" that he said would cause a plague after being in the sun for one week.[1057] Making matters worse, wood for campfires was scarce in the immediate vicinity. Much of the soldiers' time would be consumed by hauling wood from distances up the steep hillsides to the fort. The hilltop was too small to house all the men as one unit for any length of time. Additionally, there was inadequate space for all the men to parade.[1058] Dividing the forces would not create the *esprit de corps* that Jackson aimed to achieve to attack the enemy. On top of everything, the large numbers of Wilkinson's soldiers' graves near the fort had a detrimental effect on morale.[1059] The tombs served as constant reminders that illness could quickly ravage an army in a climate thought to breed disease. Rather than providing the comfortable accommodations that Wilkinson had promised, Jackson recognized Cantonment Washington as a site better suited to wear down, divide, and then destroy his command.

Conditions of the fort must have disabused Jackson of any thought that he could place enough trust in Wilkinson to work with him. Jackson wrote his own letters to General Wilkinson and to Governor Blount describing the old houses as rotting.[1060] The more Jackson considered it, the wave of evidence was compelling: Wilkinson had laid a trap and Jackson had stepped right into it. Jackson's first major decision as a general in the Lower Country was a major error.

If Jackson conducted a quick evaluation of his predicament, an unsettling feeling became his new companion. Whether his men could move on to their "place of destiny" was now beyond his power to determine. More immediately, whether his troops survived this encampment for any mission was also to some extent out of his hands. Wilkinson controlled food supplies. Wilkinson controlled medicines. Wilkinson controlled arms and ammunition. Wilkinson could keep Jackson's men holed up in this disease-ridden, rotting death trap of a fort until Jackson begged for mercy.

The one factor Jackson still controlled was his own men. The Volunteers had not yet succumbed to Cantonment Washington's conditions. U.S. Army brigadier general or not, Wilkinson would not conscript Andrew Jackson's Tennessee "sons" to the ranks of the dead buried just outside the fort.

Jackson resolved to take matters into his own hands and move his troops as soon as possible. He wasted no time in ordering scouts to begin looking for an alternate location.[1061] He would need tents to replace the wooden huts at the fort. Because most of the cavalry tents had been left behind by accident in Nashville, Jackson would need to request that Mississippi Territory Governor Holmes allow him to use his allocation of tents from the U.S. quartermaster.

If Jackson ever allowed a moment of self-doubt, he might have wondered whether his own actions had contributed to this situation. He had known the War Department did not trust him after the Burr affair, yet in the hubris of organizing the rendezvous for the march, Jackson had published orders to his men promising the acquisition of West Florida territory.[1062] Could Jackson be trusted to follow orders not to invade Spanish East Florida if his men were stationed nearby? Jackson would later prove that the answer was no. If Jackson conquered East Florida, could the U.S. government trust him to relinquish control to the United States rather than set up his own country? Certainly. But it would take time for Jackson to prove to the powers in Washington City that he was no Aaron Burr.

Before Jackson had marched from Nashville, out of frustration of having to wait on delivery of arms, he had suggested to Secretary of State James Monroe that the federal government establish a storehouse of arms in Nashville.[1063] He had not taken time to consider how that request would be viewed. Only five years earlier Nashville had been considered a hotbed of Burr's supporters who were suspected of plotting to pull Tennessee away from the Union. The Secretary of War had considered Jackson a ringleader. Most Nashville residents had even voted against Tennessee's statehood in the United States and subjecting themselves even more to control by people east of the Appalachians. An already suspicious War Department could only speculate at what Tennessee General Jackson would do with access to a full arsenal of arms in Nashville.

Even the combination of names "Wilkinson" and "Jackson" reminded everyone of the unpleasant Burr affair. Wilkinson knew how to play those fears to advantage. Just as had been planned for the Burr rebellion, here was Jackson in charge of 2,000 men in the Lower Mississippi Valley with Coffee in charge of a cavalry. The Secretary of War could see too many similarities. The failure of the War Department to accept Jackson's tender of troops and to name Jackson specifically as their commander led to ambiguity that Wilkinson could manipulate.

Jackson had even greater cause to be disappointed in the War Department, but he would not know it for a month. A letter dated January 5, 1813, January 6, 1813, and February 6, 1813, on various copies from the newly appointed Secretary of War John Armstrong was waiting to be handed to Jackson:

"The causes for embodying & marching to New Orleans the Corps under your command having ceased to exist, you will, on the receipt of this Letter, consider it as dismissed from public service, & take measures to have delivered over to Major General Wilkinson, all articles of public property which may have been put into its possession.

You will accept for yourself & the Corps the thanks of the President of the United States.

Very Respectfully I am Sir your most obt. Humble Servant.

John Armstrong"[1064]

Jackson would justifiably see the work of Wilkinson when the version dated January 5 appeared to be signed by Armstrong and ordered Jackson to turn over his equipment to "Major General" Wilkinson. Whoever wrote it had not taken account of the facts that Armstrong had not been appointed Secretary of War until after February 5, and that Wilkinson would not be appointed Major General until March 5.[1065] Or perhaps the writer had known that Wilkinson was still a brigadier general but wanted Jackson to believe that Wilkinson had been promoted the same rank as Jackson to give the impression that Jackson was required to follow Wilkinson's orders.

The order was unprecedented in its failure to make use of men whom even Wilkinson conceded should be honored for marching in the dead of winter. Regardless of whether the need for Tennessee Volunteers to march into Florida had ended when Congress refused to approve Madison's plans, the government that ordered the men to march hundreds of miles from their home had an unwritten duty to return them to their homes. Moreover, the need for the soldiers had not ended. Congress had just authorized the Mobile campaign.

No military or political official would ever give a satisfactory explanation for the order and its errors. As Wilkinson may have anticipated, the well-known War Department bureaucratic incompetence would successfully cloak the true motives from everyone but Andrew Jackson. The order and its potentially deadly consequences would only confirm his instinct not to rely upon a government bureaucracy that he did not control.

Wilkinson's contemporaries described him as "wonderfully tenacious of his authority."[1066] When Wilkinson had learned that Jackson had received the appointment to lead the march toward New Orleans, he had acted quickly. The dismissal order was most likely a forgery—for which Wilkinson was known—though Secretary Armstrong would cover it up. If Wilkinson did not forge the order, he almost certainly intercepted it and held it until Jackson's position was sufficiently weakened for the order to cause the most damage.[1067] Jackson's copy of the order would arrive first from New Orleans enclosed in a letter from Wilkinson.

Without a clear demarcation of leadership, Jackson and Wilkinson began a game of bluff, played out in a series of letters between the two men.[1068] Wilkinson, in his January 25 letter, had asserted that he would not surrender his leadership to Jackson without a direct order from Washington. He pointedly emphasized that an army could not have more than one head; therefore, he, Wilkinson, needed to remain in control until the War Department decided otherwise. Jackson may have taken some comfort in Wilkinson's defensive tone. But despite hearing a rumor from Washington City that he might be recalled, Wilkinson was unafraid. Jackson, in his reply, agreed it best that the two generals work in cooperation, subtly refusing to acknowledge Wilkinson's leadership.[1069] Wilkinson continued to assure Jackson that his men could find adequate shelter at Cantonment Washington, though he clearly knew by this point that Jackson had more men than it would quarter.

On the surface, the two enemies knew that they were being watched and that their written correspondence could be used as evidence in future proceedings.[1070] Jackson also knew that Wilkinson had spies in Mississippi Territory reporting on his every word and act.[1071] Cantonment Washington commander Leonard Covington and quartermasters Hughes and Andrews were just three known informants.[1072] Wilkinson was their superior, and it was their duty to report Jackson's moves to Wilkinson.

The rival generals created an illusion of cooperation with an almost cloying affability. As both worked behind the scenes to destroy the other, Jackson promised that he would keep Wilkinson duly advised of his activities. Wilkinson expressed his pleasure at Jackson's safe arrival and his willingness to provide support.

Jackson soon discovered that he was in an even more vulnerable position than he first thought. The War Department contractor responsible for delivering ammunition to Jackson on his arrival at Natchez had not performed, just as contractors had not delivered food to the soldiers on the Natchez Trace, or if they had, it had disappeared by the time the troops arrived at deposit points.[1073] Jackson did not accuse Wilkinson of orchestrating the debacle, but without ammunition, Jackson had no power even if he commanded soldiers. He would be forced to beg Wilkinson for ammunition.

Jackson also needed swords. Only about half his men had been outfitted. Using a foppish comparison to Wilkinson's public success as a dance master in Philadelphia as a veiled insult, Jackson later pointed out to Wilkinson, "A soldier without arms is like a Beau in a ball room without shoes, each being unprepared for action."[1074] Jackson was that soldier; Wilkinson had earned greater notoriety on the dance floor.[1075] Without equipment, it would be impossible for Jackson to win the confidence of the War Department.

More seriously, Jackson also lacked basic medicines to prevent his troops from dying. He also would be forced to beg Wilkinson for those.

Everyone knew of the seething hatred between Jackson and Wilkinson. Many expected an explosion other than British shells when the two came into proximity. Even *The Nashville Whig* found it newsworthy to report that Jackson and Wilkinson were both behaving with prudence because of the greater good.[1076]

But no matter how much Jackson despised Wilkinson, for the time, Jackson was expected to use his forces to back up Wilkinson's defense of the Lower Country. Jackson's counselor Overton had warned him to check his passions and play the role of statesman to win public support. The eyes of the public were not on his soldiers as much as they were on him. This was his opportunity for redemption in the public eye. Though Jackson's instincts told him to fight, he would follow his counselor's advice and play by the rules as much as possible.

One of the Tennessee officers wrote home to let soldiers' families know that the men had arrived at Cantonment Washington. The soldiers did not yet know whether they would be assigned to march to Mobile or Pensacola. It was possible that the enemy would not materialize, and if so, Volunteers would be disappointed to "come home without taking a little brush."[1077] One fact was clear to the young officer, the men loved Jackson, and the soldier was not ashamed to refer to Jackson as "beloved" in his letter. The Tennessee boys, as he called them, were motivated to show good behavior to earn Jackson's respect more than out of fear of his discipline.

Lower-rank Volunteers also worked to keep up spirits among the troops. Sam Bains in Captain Martin's company wrote to his wife that the "boys" were attempting to boost his morale despite his helplessly sick state. In Bains's fevered delirium, he imagined seeing his wife visit him and attempt to provide help for him, only to be turned away.[1078]

Jackson and Coffee's own letters to family back in Tennessee painted rosy pictures that differed from the reality reflected in their own records. Jackson's reports for public consumption were designed to show the success of the mission and his own leadership. His correspondence would also suggest a position of strength if Wilkinson should intercept any of the messages. Jackson and Coffee wrote that everyone arrived in Natchez in good health, yet official morning reports showed that the numbers of cavalry who arrived healthy enough to report for duty had been reduced by about a tenth.[1079] Even when Jackson later became ill, he continued to report good health to his wife Rachel.[1080] Coffee reported to the Nashville newspaper that his troops never ran out of food on the southward march on the Natchez Trace, without mentioning the near-panic effort to find food when supplies ran low.[1081] Nashville newspapers dutifully performed the job of publishing Jackson's reports for public consumption.

Despite uncomfortable camp conditions, Jackson refused to concede to Wilkinson's command. He replied to Wilkinson's letters unconvincingly that though he had received Wilkinson's "orders," of January 6 and 22, he had halted the advance at Natchez only because he had already arrived at the conclusion that halting would be prudent.[1082] He implied that halting was his idea and that it was certainly convenient that Wilkinson had concurred with his decision. Jackson threw out what he may have seen as his own bait by offering to leave the Natchez area. His eyes were focused on potential campaigns to the East, and he was ready to march.

Though Wilkinson confidently used the full power of his command in the U.S. Army, he began to see Jackson as a greater threat. From his camp in New Orleans, Wilkinson complained to the Secretary of War that Jackson and Blount had exceeded their authority by sending more troops than authorized by the War Department. Wilkinson also suspected that Jackson intended to march on toward Mobile.[1083] Wilkinson conceded, "I fear the difficulties, which will stare me in the face, will baffle all my best efforts."[1084]

If Jackson continued his advance through New Orleans where Wilkinson was encamped with his forces, superior numbers or reckless determination would determine which man prevailed. Wilkinson had good reason to fear. When Jackson had packed his dueling pistols for the expedition, knowing that Wilkinson was a man of fine tastes, Jackson had bought the finest gunpowder to impress Wilkinson before he shot him.[1085]

Jackson still had access to about 25 to 30 boats, and when conditions in Natchez proved too difficult, the unpredictable Jackson might still decide to dispatch large numbers of his men south toward Wilkinson.[1086] Attempting to remove Jackson's lifeline, Wilkinson wrote to Jackson to suggest that the Volunteers' boats would be more secure if tied at the west bank of the Mississippi River, opposite the shore from the side where Jackson was encamped.[1087] Jackson knew that the more isolated location would make it easier for Wilkinson to see that the boats disappeared, and he did not fall for the deception. Jackson replied with his regret that expediency made it impossible to move the boats to the west bank.[1088] It would take longer to move his men across the water to the boats if he needed to move them suddenly to march. He would leave reliable officers in command of the boats to make sure of their safety. An escape to New Orleans via Baton Rouge was one of the few options that Jackson could still threaten.

Jackson went around the deputy quartermaster and sent an order directly to the army contractor to tell him to make a delivery of food to his camp.[1089] Food was delivered, but as Wilkinson anticipated, without supplies and access to medicines, Jackson had no choice but submit to the realities of sick soldiers living in cramped quarters.

By February 20, Jackson had run the bluff of a competing command for as long as he could. Men were falling ill, and supplies were short. Jackson forced himself to do what went he never anticipated. So soon after his triumphant march into Natchez and his refusal to serve as Wilkinson's subordinate, Jackson swallowed his considerable pride and begged Wilkinson for help. He needed ammunition, and he needed swords. His troops knew that they were not a fighting force without them. Jackson tried to make the request appear as an inconsequential afterthought by inserting it as a postscript to a letter. Wilkinson recognized Jackson's plea as the main point of the letter, and he relished it nonetheless.[1090]

Making matters worse, a letter from Jackson's quartermaster William Lewis arrived from Nashville alerting Jackson that people in Tennessee were talking about the anticipated fight Jackson would have with Wilkinson.[1091] Before he left Nashville, Jackson had bragged that the country was not big enough for Jackson and Wilkinson. Jackson was losing a fight he had picked, and Nashville was watching. So was the War Department. Jackson's enemies were ready to witness Wilkinson get the better of him.

Jackson sent a reply for public consumption in Nashville by putting the best face on the anticipated conflict that he could, but a careful reader would sense that Jackson knew he was in trouble. Lewis should tell the public that Jackson "marched with the true spirit of a soldier that I come to fight the battles of my country, and not to contend for rank but to harmonize—that if any dispute should arise between me and the Genl—the Public service should not be interrupted thereby, if I had the power to controle it, but that the genl and myself would settle any dispute if any should arise without injury to the publick service or disturbance to the public."[1092]

Jackson did not specify that he planned to settle the dispute with pistols. That letter may have been one his aide-de-camp Benton later took credit for suggesting. It was the political defense.

An unnamed officer under Jackson's command, and presumably with his authorization or at his suggestion, followed up with a letter to *The Nashville Whig* to confirm that Jackson had put his personal feelings aside to work with Wilkinson for the greater good. The officer said that he was unaware of any clashes between the two. On the same day that Jackson moved his camp away from the unhealthy Cantonment Washington quarters Wilkinson had provided, the officer reported that Wilkinson had been so accommodating that he had earned the officers' respect.[1093] That unnamed officer may also have been Benton, who worried that

Wilkinson would challenge Jackson's attempt to exercise a superior command. Again, statements made for publication bore little resemblance to private communications. Jackson could now only hope that the public would lose interest in his anticipated fight with Wilkinson before his enemies understood the true tar pit in which he had placed himself and his men.

Adding to Jackson's melancholy, the weather had not improved. The temperature stayed extremely cold, and snow and sleet continued to fall. Despite the unnamed officer's public assurances about the remarkably good health of the men, a serious chest cold was beginning to infect many men in camp, and Jackson's body was beginning its own fight against the contagion.[1094] There were still no medicines.

Wilkinson played his next card. Jackson had argued that his direct superior was the Tennessee governor rather than Wilkinson. Wilkinson turned the argument against him. Wilkinson wrote Jackson that after examining the letter from the Tennessee governor, it appeared after all that the two commanders were to act independently in the administration of their own affairs.[1095] He suggested that they keep each other informed of every order so that they could act in concert against their common enemy.

Jackson could see that Wilkinson was placing him in the horns of a dilemma. If Jackson acknowledged that he and Wilkinson were to work in concert, he would have to accept Wilkinson's command to obtain supplies. However, if Jackson continued to assert that he was to act independently, Wilkinson could deny any obligation to provide him any supplies or medicines. In case Jackson did not understand the power that Wilkinson wielded through his control of army resources, Wilkinson taunted: "I forbear to trespass on you further at this time, because you must be much occupied in providing for the accommodation, comfort & Health of the patriot soldiers Intrusted to your care; and would to god! It were in my power to contribute effectually to either, in a country without means & without resources."[1096]

Jackson now saw the dagger in the monogramed calfskin glove he had always warned was Wilkinson's *modus operandi*. Wilkinson was applying to Jackson the lessons he learned from attempting to destroy his rival Anthony Wayne. From his spies at Cantonment Washington, Wilkinson knew that men were falling ill, and a growing number of sick would affect overall morale. The healthy did not want to become one of the infirm, and they would hold their commander responsible for their misery. Wilkinson should expect soon to see signs of divisions within Jackson's ranks.

Wilkinson then moved to cut off any further tools Jackson could use against him. Jackson's cavalry could make their own advance on Wilkinson's camp. Wilkinson had his quartermaster Bartholomew Schaumburg send an express rider to Nashville to demand an explanation for whether Jackson's cavalry was properly called into service.[1097] The cavalry was the third regiment that had not been authorized. It was the beginning of a foundation to refuse to supply any additional forage and force the cavalry to abandon Jackson.

The cavalry was still getting food, but complaints arose that the government contractor pork they were given to eat was rotten. Men apparently were developing digestive ailments, and Jackson's surgeons suspected that the foul pork was the cause. The local sub-contractor Mr. Cowan was brought in for questioning. He assured that he had used only fresh pork, and he asked for an appeal of the surgeon's decisions to an *ad hoc* tribunal. Colonel Bradley and a citizen inspected the rations and found no problem.[1098]

Cavalry solders continued to complain.[1099] It was not forgotten that foul beef had been one of the explanations for the 800 soldiers who had died under Wilkinson's command in 1809.[1100] Following on Jackson's inquiry, the army contractor conducted his own examination and discovered that "old pork" had been substituted in the rations without his knowledge.[1101] After Jackson's experience with the improperly cured pork in Clarksville, it was plausible that the two instances were more than coincidence. The contractor was released with a promise that he would do a better job of supervising delivery in the future. Jackson said that he believed that the contractor was innocent. As a precaution, however, Jackson ordered that sentinels guard the storage houses to prevent anyone from tampering with food supplies.

Jackson would not "stay throwed" in Wilkinson's web. He had wanted to move his campsite from the moment he arrived. In the short time the troops had been at Cantonment Washington, men were already showing signs of illness. They could also not escape the psychological effect of the overwhelming presence of hundreds of graves near the fort to remind them of the risks of disease. Jackson was determined that his men would not suffer the fate of Wilkinson's soldiers in those tombs they were forced to look at each day.

At first, Doctor Thomas Claiborne's farm looked promising as an alternate campsite, and Jackson was prepared to issue the order to move camp. Then, someone pointed out that Doctor Claiborne did not own the land and could not authorize the encampment.[1102] Scouts then found a suitable spot on the plain on Joseph Perkins's farm on Perkins Creek, about a mile west of the fort, near the ruins of an old French tavern.[1103] The flat fields where soldiers could be properly exercised were located near two good springs that would supply plenty of fresh water.

Jackson hoped to move to the new site as early as February 21, but pouring rain made the roads impassable.[1104] Materials had already been moved to the new campsite, and Jackson had to make an emergency request for a day's supply of food and firewood for the cavalry.[1105] Camp conditions were quickly deteriorating, and he could not wait long.[1106] Jackson was concerned enough about worsening morale that he declined an invitation to dine at General Claiborne's house. Though Jackson had dined at Secretary Dangerfield's house two nights earlier, conditions had worsened, and he would not be seen feasting in the comfort of an elegant home while his men were essentially trapped in cold, wet filth.

Blaming the bad condition of the roads, Jackson directed Benton and Searcy to attend the dinner in his place. Benton extended General Jackson's apologies to General Claiborne, then enjoyed a fine Virginia-style dinner that had been prepared for Jackson. The dinner also provided an opportunity for a conversation with territorial secretary Cowles Meade.[1107] Likely, the true purpose of the meeting for Jackson was to bolster local support should Jackson need local assistance.

On George Washington's birthday, February 22, the sun shined for the first time in days and both the national holiday and weather were taken as good signs to issue the order to strike the tents and march to new quarters, putting the gloom of the old cantonment behind most of them. The roads were still muddy, but Jackson did not want to spend an hour more than necessary at Cantonment Washington.[1108] Only a few of the cavalry would remain and care for the horses there. Coffee left the march long enough to visit the post office to mail another letter to his wife.

CHAPTER SIXTEEN

CAMP JACKSON

"To see him, who is worthy to command a nation, reduced to the necessity of quarrelling with petty agents of government, to make them do their duty, was too much to be born with."

—Tennessee Volunteer, March 24, 1813

The new camp on Perkins's farm was christened "Camp Jackson." After a week at the dreary, dilapidated fort, Ensign Edmonson thought that Camp Jackson was "a beautiful place."[1109] The forest provided an abundance of firewood just outside their tents.

The entire day of February 23 was devoted to setting up the new camp, lifting the spirits of the men as it provided a break from the drills. With morale less of an issue and with rumors that the army quartermaster was threatening to cut off forage supplies, Jackson and Colonel Henderson left camp early to return to Natchez to determine what supplies could be obtained if the quartermaster made good on his threat.[1110] The officers inspected their boats at the landing and calculated that a large quantity of corn remained available. Jackson and Coffee also discovered that they could purchase corn from boats floating produce to market in Natchez and at ports farther south, but they had to pay a high price.[1111]

And they would still need to find a way to tap the larger supplies needed from the government.

The change of scenery at Camp Jackson also provided an opportunity to re-establish a strict routine, which in turn would build morale and preparedness. An order was issued to establish the camp schedule: Reveille was to be at daybreak and the men were to stand at arms for roll call. The retreat was to be beat at sundown, and tattoo would be beat at 8:00 p.m. each evening.[1112]

As the troops waited for orders to move south or east, time would be spent bringing the forces back up to peak condition so that they would be ready to engage the British. There had been little time for sustained training on the march. Coffee ordered that cavalry officers were to parade for two hours and then to train the men in forming and wheeling. Now that the Volunteers were camped in wide-open fields, they would train in the use of the musket. The Master of the Sword also drilled them.

Reverend Blackman noted the improved morale and took the opportunity to leave camp to travel into Natchez, where he confirmed that the lifestyle had changed little since he had left his clerical circuit there. He reported: "In the City of Natchez the Devil's kingdom is divided against itself. They have had one playhouse burnt down—Torn down by the mechanics. They have erected a new one. Mechanics are not allowed to attend hence it is supposed that they burnt down the former & that they will burn the latter likewise—so we may hope the Devil's kingdom will fall."[1113]

Blackman also walked into the town of Washington and to an old friend's house on Pine Ridge to preach to the communities north of Natchez, however, he observed that he had never seen an area less interested in preaching. The students at Washington Academy in the territorial capital provided better prospects.[1114]

The resources of the new camp relieved some immediate pressure, and Jackson allowed time to receive several guests including Kentucky General John Adair.[1115] The two men were old acquaintances, but there was more going on beneath the surface. Adair was the Kentucky Senator whose arrest by Wilkinson in New Orleans had led to Wilkinson's trial before the House of Representatives. Like his visit with Matthew Lyon, Jackson's social call was more likely a continued search for information to prove Wilkinson's responsibility for the Burr affair and to push for Wilkinson's removal from command. Jackson's fight against Wilkinson behind the scenes seemed to be a shadow fight. Jackson would receive no encouragement from the nation's capital that his plan was gaining any traction.

Reverend Blackman again was permitted to travel from camp to meet with old friends in the area and to conduct religious services. Blackman attended a quarterly Methodist Church meeting at the Selsertown Meeting House north of Camp Jackson, where he met with Reverend Winian, who was working in the Natchez District.[1116] Blackman's new position as military chaplain likely prompted a discussion of the ministers' impressions of soldiers and war. Though Winian professed not to support the war, he was intrigued about the nature of military commanders. What kind of men could encourage 2,000 ordinary citizens to leave their homes and risk their lives to go to battle? Unlike the humble young Blackman who had presumed that his own meager talents would never measure up to the needs of soldiers, Winian considered himself wiser and qualified to evaluate them on a human, if not a spiritual, level. Blackman invited Winian to visit Camp Jackson and offered to introduce him to General Jackson and his officers.[1117]

On his first encounter, Winian formed immediate impressions that he recorded in his journals. Jackson and Carroll struck him as plain and unpretentious. Like Jackson, Winian assessed that Carroll's talents were superior to all the officers, but he also thought Carroll more talented than Jackson. Knowing little about Jackson's life's struggles, Winian quickly assumed that Jackson, like Wilkinson, must have risen to higher rank only through circumstances that the non-religious would call "good fortune." Coffee apparently said little and impressed Winian only by the sheer force of his physical size and presence. Winian failed to perceive that Coffee was not enjoying the grand adventure and that he preferred to be back home with his wife and family. Winian confused Coffee's melancholy attitude and quietness for lack of intelligence and wrote that he found Coffee dull.[1118]

Winian reserved his sharpest criticism for Benton. Though Benton's social talents and intelligence were obvious, Winian recorded that in his whole life he had never seen a more perfect specimen of the "detestable qualities" of "pride, superciliousness and self-conceit."[1119] During Winian's visit, he overheard Benton attempting to impress Jackson's officers with his own criticisms of Napoleon's military strategies. It was, Winian observed, as if "The chirping sparrow might as reasonably criticize and pronounce upon the performance of the mocking-bird."[1120]

Winian protested war, but he revealed a fascination with military life by returning to Camp Jackson several times. Despite continued interactions with the officers, Winian's frequent visits only changed his opinion of Jackson.

By late February, the bitter cold finally retreated north, and a brief period of the warmer southern weather lifted spirits but also added to a new restlessness. The British enemy had not appeared. Men had left home and family because they were told the country was threatened with imminent attack, but they found none here.

Many of Jackson's soldiers earned their livings on their farms, and militia service was generally limited to a few months to give citizen soldiers time to return home to keep the farm operations productive. Warmer, spring-like weather almost instinctively reminded the farmers among them that planting season was nearing at home. Some Volunteers began to look longingly homeward up the Natchez Trace. Even Coffee's thoughts turned to what would be needed to prepare the soil for the year's crops, and he observed that the warm weather made men anxious to return.[1121] A crop failure would prove a financial disaster for men who had bought their farms on credit. Officers would be able to rely upon farm supervisors or servant labor, but most of the men did not have that luxury. With spring advancing day by day, soldiers were increasingly torn between duty to their country and duty to their families.

As Jackson had anticipated, "Indolence breeds disquiet."[1122] He could lose support quickly without a threat from the enemy to focus discipline to duty. The General issued orders to keep the men ready to march as well as to keep them busy. On February 25, parades began to be held each day. Bayonets, swords, and musket barrels were to be shined as bright as could be, even if they had not been bright in a generation or so. The corn house could stand to be raised, and men were detailed to raise it.[1123] Men could always be directed to clean camp, whether it needed it or not. Increased activity could also be expected to give encouragement that the soldiers would soon face action.

If Jackson had not fully comprehended Wilkinson's last veiled threat, he would soon appreciate that Wilkinson was beginning to turn the screw. Wilkinson's quartermasters had already begun discussing how to undermine Jackson's authority to draw on government supplies. Bartholomew Schaumburg, the deputy quartermaster in New Orleans who was in direct contact with General Wilkinson, protested Jackson's latest order. Following Wilkinson's lead, Schaumburg referred to Jackson's Volunteers as *state militia* rather than *Volunteers organized under federal orders*.[1124] Did Jackson as a state militia commander have authority to call on the credit of the U.S. government to order supplies? Schaumburg offered the opinion that without a direct order from the War Department, it would be risky for the federal quartermasters to supply materials pursuant to the orders of Jackson, a state militia major general.

If the state-versus-federal question were not enough, Wilkinson's subordinates pointed out that the official order under which Jackson's troops were mustered required that the troops be commanded by a brigadier general. It provided no authorization for a major general such as Jackson. Jackson and Governor Blount seemed to have ignored that important distinction. The order also authorized only 1,500 infantry soldiers. It said nothing about the additional third regiment of 670 cavalry troops that arrived in Natchez.[1125] What gave quartermasters authority to turn government provisions over to men who were not properly serving under an official order?

If the British were ready to attack as Wilkinson had claimed a few months earlier, the army would have been grateful for the additional troops who volunteered to serve. Now that it appeared nothing would be gained by the expedition and that costs would become an issue, army bureaucrats could justify caution.

Unless Jackson would be willing to act as an independent contractor and place his own credit on the line, Deputy Quartermaster Andrews decided that army quartermasters should not go out on the limb of giving away government property to someone unauthorized to requisition it. His superior Schaumburg had consulted with Wilkinson, and Wilkinson had said that because Jackson had refused to serve under Wilkinson's command as the Commander of Southern U.S. Forces, Wilkinson would not certify that Jackson had any authority to call on the credit of the government. If the quartermaster provided the forage on Jackson's order, and if Jackson had no authority, the quartermaster would be forced to pay the bill from his personal funds. Consequently, the quartermaster made good on his threat that he would reject all of Jackson's future requisitions for forage for horses.

Despite Wilkinson's continued assurances to Jackson that his quartermasters would honor Jackson's requests, just as Jackson had raised objections in his officers' minds to serving under Wilkinson and then used those objections as the basis to oppose serving under Wilkinson, it was becoming clear that Wilkinson was acting to increase his quartermasters' concerns, and then hiding his directions behind those concerns. Jackson had argued in his request to have Wilkinson dismissed from the southern command that he wanted to act independently of Wilkinson, and Wilkinson had made it clear to his quartermaster that Jackson's orders would not be honored unless he served under Wilkinson. Wilkinson could blame Jackson for his decision to maintain an independent command and would see that Jackson paid a price for his independence.

With no mission in sight and no immediate threat to focus their attention, as Wilkinson could have anticipated, camp discipline became a greater challenge. Jackson was forced to send out guards to round up wayward soldiers every few days.[1126] Another officer found in a brothel was court-martialed. Jackson directed that he be severely reprimanded as an example with a hope that no officer in the future would be seen with the soldiers in places of "ill fame."[1127]

Benton intervened for his subordinate Captain Hewlitt who was found drunk and asked Jackson to overrule his arrest, just as Jackson had requested that Butler's arrest be overturned. Jackson did not honor Benton's request. Seeming to follow Wilkinson's example, Jackson argued that the matter had already been submitted to the court-martial and that he should not intervene.[1128]

On February 27, Colonel Covington invited Jackson and his officer "family" to dine at his home "Propinquity," adjacent to the Cantonment Washington. Mississippi Territory Governor Holmes and Secretary Dangerfield would join them. Jackson did not relish the idea of explaining his situation in person and he chose not to accept. But he could not pass completely on the opportunity to build support of the territorial government as a source of supplies, and he sent Carroll, Hynes, and Coffee in his place. When the officers returned to camp, they reported that after dinner they "passed the glass" and had a good time with their hosts.[1129] Their true mission was accomplished among the frivolity. Jackson would be able to count on the support of the territorial government.

Jackson had another reason for remaining in camp. Despite improved weather, the late-winter chest infection passing through camp had spread in his own body. Jackson may have attributed its onset to exhaustion, but the chest cold suddenly worsened and sapped his strength. Even in good health, Jackson still felt the effects of the wound from Dickinson's dueling bullet in his lung.[1130] The cold had to be taken seriously. Jackson had sent a request for medicines for the camp on February 26.[1131] None had arrived. The last thing Jackson needed was to become an invalid when Wilkinson waited for any sign of weakness to pounce and when so many men depended upon him to deliver them from the quagmire he had created. Camp surgeons were called. After examining the General, they recommended the fallback routine cure of the day. Surgeon Butler, likely the son of Jackson's old friend Colonel Thomas S. Butler, produced a lancet, slit an opening into one of Jackson's veins, and began to bleed him.[1132]

The treatment was expected to work, and Jackson duly reported to be feeling better—at least physically.[1133] Emotionally, the fact he had received no communication from the War Department was disconcerting, particularly as he was now at Wilkinson's mercy. The lack of any response from friends in Washington City had been the first warning sign of more serious trouble for Colonel Butler, just before Wilkinson crushed his career as a soldier.

Carroll and Jackson's aide-de-camp Andrew Hynes visited with the sick men in the camp hospital to assure them of the General's concern and to boost morale.[1134] They also took an assessment of the condition of the horses and the old cantonment. Blackman followed the officer's visit to the hospital with one to provide spiritual comfort. Taking advantage of an empty wagon, Blackman mounted it and began preaching to a company of cavalry, men who were under Chaplain Blackburn's charge and accustomed to Blackburn's more powerful oratory. As a boost to his confidence, Blackman found that the men listened and seemed responsive to his sermon.[1135]

Jackson was having less success, and he would have to take more desperate measures. He pressed a response from the Secretary of War. On March 1, Jackson wrote to the secretary explaining his decision to move his men from Cantonment Washington. After staring at Wilkinson's soldiers' tombs, his men feared the enemy of disease more than the British. Then Jackson moved on to the real purpose of the letter: Jackson asked for medicines for the Volunteers, and he sought an escape. Jackson had marched south as the War Department had wanted (though not where it had ordered), but he assumed that his real mission had been to take Florida. He had since heard news that Congress had not approved an attack on the Spanish territory. Jackson admitted that he was embarrassed to have command of the troops without direction from the War Department. If his assistance was not needed in the Lower Country, he offered to lead his men to Canada to help with the prosecution of the war in the North.[1136] Showing the urgency of the plea, Jackson apparently sent the letter by express rider a portion of the distance to Washington City to arrive within three weeks.

At the same time, Jackson wrote a separate letter to Wilkinson, acknowledging that he was aware of his predicament and hinting ambiguously that he might finally concede his complete cooperation — the plan to move his men out of the reach of Wilkinson's command would be for the secretary's eyes only.[1137] Jackson admitted to Wilkinson that he had received no information from the War Department about the destination of his own men. Jackson noted that, "An inactive life is not well suited to the genius or disposition of the troops that compose my detachment."[1138]

An inactive life certainly did not suit their general. Jackson also admitted that he was concerned about the health of his men, but he bluffed that he wanted to move them while, "Their constitutions are glowing with health and vigor."[1139] He offered that he would be happy to receive Wilkinson's "advice" as to where to march, because Wilkinson had maps of the topography of the country. Jackson may have wanted Wilkinson to believe that he would be willing to serve under his command in support of a march to Mobile and Pensacola.

Jackson began hinting that he would consider concessions, but he knew that Wilkinson now faced his own challenges. The six-month terms of the Mississippi Territory militias that had been called up to provide support for Wilkinson on September 29 were expiring.[1140] Recruitment efforts for replacements were failing. If Jackson were not faced with the growing illness of his troops and had time to wait out Wilkinson, he would soon compete for command with a general who led few troops.

Wilkinson was pleased to see that Jackson was conceding. It gave him an opening to strengthen his own weakening position. Wilkinson wrote to Secretary of War Armstrong, blaming Armstrong's predecessor Eustis for creating the confusion of his competing command with Jackson but falsely assuring the secretary that he was working with Jackson to divide his command. The Secretary of War had ordered Wilkinson to send recruiters 300 miles to muster new soldiers to fill the positions of his disappearing ranks. Wilkinson replied that there was no need to send recruiters anywhere when he could take that number from the best of Jackson's men. Contrary to Wilkinson's prior representations that Jackson's soldiers could not be trusted in the Lower Country, he now vouched that "I am assured that they are the finest men ever assembled."[1141] And if the secretary would just authorize the use of federal uniforms for Jackson's men, Wilkinson assured that he would make good use of the Tennessee Volunteers. He also asked the Secretary to write to Jackson to "sooth him into acquiescence, for the present to prevent irritation, ill blood and _____ consequences."[1142]

Wilkinson had thought he could make use of the Tennessee Volunteers before he knew Jackson would command them. Now, based upon the lack of new recruits from the Mississippi Territory, Wilkinson had begun to view them as a necessity. First, he had to remove Jackson from their command.

In Wilkinson's reply to Jackson, he flattered Jackson's troops as he toyed with his victim, seeming overly conciliatory. He honored the sacrifice of Jackson's Volunteers, "For the march of two Thousand Free men, a thousand miles in the dead of winter, for the public defense, is a novel scene, which much call forth the sympathies of every Patriot Bosom, and entitle the actors to an extraordinary indulgence."[1143] And though Wilkinson knew that Jackson had little ammunition, he again promised to provide Jackson old muskets that were stored at Washington, likely those carried by the troops who died there under his command.

Did Wilkinson know that the federal arsenal had provided Jackson several boxes of worthless rusted muskets in Nashville? Was that proffer a message that Wilkinson had been undermining Jackson's command from the start? Wilkinson's offer, if accepted, would serve no purpose but to emphasize to Jackson's men that their general had no ammunition. Wilkinson, of course, assured Jackson that ammunition would be forthcoming just as soon as practicable.

Wilkinson shamelessly asked Jackson to rely upon his word as a "fellow soldier" that he wanted to do everything within his power to help Jackson's men. He assured Jackson that he would put a stop to any attempt by his officers to recruit Jackson's Volunteers into his army regiments. That assurance on Wilkinson's signature was for the public record.

But to make the point that he had authority to recruit Jackson's men, Wilkinson enclosed for Jackson's edification a copy of the statute that gave Wilkinson authority to recruit state militia. Jackson immediately noted the fallacy. Possibly to thwart Jackson's command, the War Department had required the reorganization of Jackson's troops as federal volunteers. Recruitment of volunteers organized under a federal order from one federal unit into another was prohibited by law. Wilkinson should have been defeated by his own scheming.

Beneath the veneer of feigned cooperation, Wilkinson continued to apply pressure. Without acknowledging that he had suggested Jackson quarter his men at Cantonment Washington, Wilkinson commended Jackson for taking action to move his camp from the fort. Then Wilkinson warned, "But Sir, let me advise you to be regardful of your Health, for disease begets discontent, and a Sickly camp afflicts every feeling & enfeebles every faculty."[1144]

The National Intelligencer's "Military Maxims" as printed in the Nashville *Clarion*, stated, "The first of all military qualifications is valor; the second is ambition, the third is health."[1145] Wilkinson added to Jackson's concern by telling him of the camp disease horrors he had witnessed to be sure Jackson understood the power he had to destroy his command as he had undermined General Wayne. Having highlighted one of Jackson's greatest fears that disease would take his men, Wilkinson said that he also regretted that he could not authorize medicines and hospital stores for the sick men. Jackson would have to rely upon his own authority or credit to keep his camp well.

Wilkinson also feigned regret that he could not find some mission for Jackson's men, because keeping them in camp without a mission would just breed more discontent.[1146] Jackson would learn only later that at the same time Wilkinson claimed that he had no mission, Wilkinson was busy making plans to invade Mobile using Jackson's troops. If Wilkinson were genuinely concerned about the morale of Jackson's troops, he could have sent already Jackson's forces east to aid the invasion under Jackson's command. Wilkinson could not give Jackson that opportunity for military success. His immediate objective was to crush Jackson.

Jackson could read between the lines and see Wilkinson's threat. Jackson may have escaped the Cantonment Washington trap, but all Wilkinson had to do was keep Jackson's Volunteers holed up in camp near Natchez until enough men became sick that they threatened mutiny. Wilkinson's recruiters would then step in to rescue the best soldiers from Jackson's failed command, leaving Jackson and the remainder to be rescued by Tennessee or to die 450 miles from home.

When Jackson had first recruited his Volunteers, he used the governor's assurance that the soldiers would not serve through the summer in the Lower Country, the time of year when it was believed that they stood the greatest chance of facing disease.[1147] As more men fell ill, and the weather warmed, that promise would now further embolden anyone who wanted to foment discontent.

In the meantime, Wilkinson's Deputy Inspector Hughes said that he would send inspectors to review Jackson's troops and to report back to Wilkinson.[1148] The promise of inspections could raise anticipation of a mission among Jackson's soldiers and make Jackson more vulnerable to be crushed by the Secretary of War's dismissal letter. It would also drive a wedge between Jackson and his men, particularly officers such as Benton who sought to make their fame from military glory, by suggesting the opportunities of more consequential service under Wilkinson.

Jackson defensively objected that Wilkinson's deputy assistant had no right to review his troops. However, the inspection would be an opportunity to show Wilkinson and the War Department how Jackson had successfully organized, trained, and now commanded 2,000 citizen soldiers. Taking the bait that inspections were a sign that War Department orders to march were in motion or out of pride to show Wilkinson how well he had trained his troops, Jackson approved an order that the men were to appear in formation looking their best, clean-shaved and dressed in uniform with their hair powdered to present their arms for formal inspection.[1149] To further sharpen their appearance, while on parade, the troops were ordered to refrain from spitting, moving their hands, or shuffling their accoutrements.

Of course, Jackson would not take Wilkinson's word even for things he could see with his own eyes. With increasing numbers of troops falling ill, Jackson needed an immediate fallback plan. He had no choice but to turn again to his old friend Washington Jackson, whose Nashville bank had helped supply funds for arms and payments to muster men into the expedition.[1150] He needed money for medicines, and if he lost his own battle with Wilkinson's War Department quartermasters he would need money for food and forage. Not anticipating the recalcitrance of the War Department, Jackson had not brought funds for basic provisions that he assumed the army would supply under his orders. As Wilkinson pointedly advised, Jackson was in an area "*without resources*" from the government— except for those Wilkinson commanded. General Jackson, Washington Jackson, and Washington's brother James had joined in business transactions, and the General expected them to know that his personal credit would stand good for the debt.

If the Jackson brothers were cautious bankers, however, they would have known that Andrew Jackson was in deep financial trouble. Like many men who had attempted to make money from land speculation, Jackson had been burned by faulty titles and a crashing real estate market. If this expedition became a public failure, what hope did Jackson have of gaining public support necessary to recover in business? He certainly could not prosper in business in Nashville if large numbers of soldiers died while under his command.

Whatever strategy Jackson used, his gamble paid off. Washington Jackson and his brother James would lend General Jackson money, but not because his personal guaranty removed the risk of the loan. They were Jackson's friends, and the Tennesseans camped nearby were sons of their family and friends. The note would be drawn in a couple of days.[1151]

After the war when fathers, including Indian leaders, chose to name their sons "Andrew Jackson" in honor of the victorious general who saved their independence from new British rule, few men would remember Washington or James Jackson's names, and they may never have known how much the Jackson brothers' generosity altered the course of their own lives. Had the Tennessee bankers refused the General's request, large numbers of Tennessee Volunteers would have suffered, and many more would have died.

Friends would provide the support needed, but friends would expect much from the General in return. Years later, when Jackson's friends pressured him to open Alabama and Mississippi Indian lands for settlement, one factor in his decision would be the obligation to repay the favor.

Volunteers labored through the additional preparation for inspection only to be disappointed when no army inspectors arrived.[1152] Jackson could not afford to let morale slip. He proceeded with inspections of his own. To give the inspections more than routine importance as the men had anticipated, Jackson improvised by inviting Mississippi Territory Governor Holmes, Cantonment Washington Commander Leonard Covington, and important local citizens to join him in reviewing the troops.[1153]

Volunteers began preparing at 10:30 a.m. By noon, companies were in formation. Jackson first approached the right of the cavalry and inspected the regiments. Covington completed his inspection and congratulated Jackson. Jackson then mounted the review stand that had been placed on the highest ground and troops passed in review.[1154]

On March 3, Assistant Deputy Inspector Captain Hughes finally arrived in camp to inspect the troops. Despite his earlier protests, Jackson allowed Hughes to conduct inspections, though he insisted that his officers be drilled by his command tent.[1155] The General would allow no speculation that his officers would serve another commander.

After Volunteers had properly impressed spectators with some new evolutions and after U.S. inspectors were safely out of view for the day, less honorable business had to be conducted. Another officer, First Lieutenant Gambrill, had used his liberty to go to a brothel at Natchez Under the Hill. The guards brought him to the front of the camp for Benton to reprimand him:

> "I am sorry to have to address an officer belonging to my regiment on such an occasion as this. For an officer to go contrary to orders and besides as you have done to go to such as place as "Under the Hill" as it is called—the place where Hell reigns on earth, where the refuse of creation assembles, This Sir, is a thing that pains me to think about and which I never want to talk [about] in public again."[1156]

Perhaps Volunteer Bains worried about whether news of such infractions would travel home. He wrote his wife to assure her that though washer women were allowed in the camp during the day to collect clothes to wash for pay, no woman was allowed in camp after dark. In fact, he said, the camps were the most "moral" places in the world. He even assured that anyone who swore was required to pay a fine.[1157]

The whole camp was involved in the reviews. The inspection of the First Regiment was completed on March 4.[1158] The cavalry would be inspected the following day. As both Jackson and Wilkinson planned for different purposes, the excitement of heightened activity and formality gave the troops the sense that a mission was finally imminent.

General John Adair and Colonel R.C. Floyd returned to camp to inspect the troops on the final day and then dined with the officers. Searcy recorded that General Adair "conversed on the Expedition of some americans who had" but the remainder of the entry was torn out.[1159] Whether he discussed the purpose of Pike's expedition and how it related to Wilkinson and Burr can only be speculated.

Despite Wilkinson's promise that Jackson would receive better cooperation from his army quartermasters, Jackson was served with a list of interrogatories from Assistant Deputy Quartermaster Robert Andrews to answer under oath whether he had been called to service by competent authority and whether he would personally guarantee payment if the War Department refused to honor the payments for reimbursement.

Jackson was incredulous. An *assistant deputy* quartermaster now had the audacity to challenge the major general and demand answers under oath! Jackson proclaimed the interrogatories unusual and contrary to the military chain of command. It was as if he were being court-martialed by a junior officer. Jackson knew that Wilkinson must be behind the disgraceful act, and though he had no choice but answer the junior's interrogatories if he wanted to continue to receive food, he said that his answers were calculated to "make the old satellite of duplicity sc[ream] with rage."[1160] Jackson reminded the assistant deputy quartermaster that he and every officer under his command were serving under orders directly from the President of the United States, and the president did not need a guaranty. Jackson said that Andrews's superior Schaumburg, who had spent years in the army, must have been ignorant not to know proper military requisition procedure.[1161]

Jackson also demanded to see the deputy quartermaster's order under which he issued the questions to a general. Then, Major General Jackson warned the younger man that he had issued an order for supplies and that he intended to obtain those supplies by whatever means he needed to take.[1162]

Jackson also had a few questions for Assistant Deputy Quartermaster Andrews. Under what order had he already provided provisions to the cavalry? Andrews had already gone out on a limb by allowing Washington

Jackson to pressure him into supplying the cavalry. Jackson suggested that Andrews would not want to risk exposing that error if the provisions were illegal. Jackson demanded that Andrews appear in his camp to give his own answers to Jackson's questions in person. Andrews wisely failed to keep Jackson's appointment.[1163]

Privately, the challenge by a junior officer of the regular army showed that Jackson was losing the bluff of control. Jackson began to worry that the Tennessee governor would hold him accountable for an embarrassing and wasted expedition of 2,000 men. If the growing numbers of sick soldiers died, even his political friends might not be able to save him. Jackson confided to his own quartermaster William B. Lewis:

> "I am here without any advice orders or directions, as to my future operations—no enemy to face—or any thing to do—no medicine chest, or medicinal supply for the troops. I shall on tomorrow purchase out of my own funds and depend on government—for payment—my men cannot nor shall not die for the want of medical supply."[1164]

Compounding concerns, the 450 miles between Jackson's troops and their Tennessee homes were heating up with an imminent war between the Chickasaw and Creek. James Robertson wrote to Captain John Davis:

> "The Chickasaw are in a high strain for war. They have declared war against all passing Creek who attempt to go through their nation. They have declared, if the United States will take a campaign against the Creek, that they are ready to give their aid. They consider the United States at war already with the Creek nation, and they say that, to their knowledge, one of the ten who did the mischief near the mouth of the

Ohio has been a principal leader for upwards of up to twenty years, and that there was another chief present; so that the Creek can no longer say that it is their young men only who are at war."[1165]

Creek rebels threatened ferry operations to hinder the march and re-supply of troops. Colbert's Ferry would be a rich target. Chickasaw were so concerned about imminent attacks that they requested two companies of U.S. Army horsemen to protect them.[1166]

It was Jackson who had ordered the Chickasaw to stop the movement of Creek through their nation, without considering the consequences to the Chickasaw or friendly Creek for placing responsibility on the Indian leaders rather than U.S. troops. His orders had unintentionally ensured conflict among the Indians and divisions within their nations. Now those orders threatened to lead to an outbreak of an Indian war. Jackson had also promised Colbert that if he stopped the Creek from using his nation as a staging area for attacks, Jackson would help defend him. Jackson was certainly in no position now to honor that promise.

Worse, if Jackson's men were forced to return home on the Natchez Trace, he would have to lead them through an Indian conflict of his own making without adequate transportation, food, firearms, or ammunition to have any control over the outcome.

Only Reverend Blackman remained optimistic. He was beginning to think about how he could build on his work with the men when they returned home. The minister was clearly growing more confident. On March 8, Blackman's sermon focused on the need to set up Bible societies in West Tennessee, where work with the men would continue.[1167] Jackson's overabundance of ambition may have influenced him. As Ensign Edmonson observed, soldiers were not the most receptive audience.

Wilkinson followed the movements of the British in the Caribbean and sent a letter to the Secretary of War to lay the foundation for his march on Mobile and then to Pensacola. Wilkinson no longer bragged that he would command 4,000 troops and acknowledged that recruitment numbers continued to disappoint. The territorial government had authorized 1,500 new recruits but finding men willing to serve under Wilkinson was proving more difficult. Wilkinson conceded that, "Jackson's Corps will be required," but professed, "I dare not command."[1168] The letter implied that Wilkinson would permit Jackson to command his own troops in coordination with Wilkinson, but Wilkinson was careful not to say so explicitly. Wilkinson could not take the chance that the secretary would send an approval of the plan with Jackson in charge of the Tennessee Volunteers. If Wilkinson could persuade the secretary to send a general authorization for action, Wilkinson could appeal to Jackson's junior officers and use the order of dismissal to maneuver Jackson out of the way. He had already seen evidence that Benton appeared to be more concerned about his own future than Jackson's.

When Wilkinson first learned that Jackson would be marching to the Lower Country with cavalry, he had protested to Jackson and Armstrong that there were not enough supplies. Now that Wilkinson determined that he could use those forces, he told Armstrong that he wanted 120 horses and would need ample forage for them.[1169]

By March 8, Jackson began to lose even his limited patience to keep up his charade with Wilkinson. He wrote Wilkinson to thank him for his offer of old muskets. Knowing that only a third of the Volunteers had firearms, Jackson falsely claimed to have made sure to arm his cavalry officers with good muskets before they departed Nashville.[1170] Jackson rejected Wilkinson's suggestion that he submit requisitions for supplies under his own authority. He would not fall for Wilkinson's invitation to expose himself to the War Department's rejections of his requests for reimbursement because he had not followed proper protocol. Wilkinson could be expected to have undue influence over the outcome, and he could not afford to pay the expense on his own. As Jackson noted, the whole purpose of the quartermaster system was to provide supplies to troops when requisitioned by their commanders, and he had followed the proper procedures.

Jackson assured Wilkinson that he was perfectly content to keep his troops in Natchez, but if Wilkinson would care to certify that he was no longer needed in the Lower Country, he would be happy to lead his men to serve in Canada or wherever they were needed.[1171]

With timing a little too close for coincidence, one of Jackson's officers bolstered Jackson's case by writing a letter home for publication in the newspaper. The officer's letter claimed that the men were all healthy and that they had spent their time in Natchez becoming a highly disciplined military force. Their only regret was that they had been sent so far from the scene of battle rather than to the front lines with the British in Canada.[1172] Jackson could expect other newspapers to print the story. As newspapers also continued to report a series of defeats by the regular army, the letter advertised that Jackson and his highly trained Volunteers were available for action.

Privately, the growing number of sick men was becoming serious, and Jackson was troubled that he had still received no communication from the War Department or even the Tennessee governor whose order he had disobeyed by halting in Natchez.

Bills were coming due for the forage for the march south and for provisions for the sick men left along the Natchez Trace. Coffee attempted to draw from limited funds to pay the debts, but Jackson had no funds to spare.[1173] Refusing Coffee was humiliating for the general who took pride in taking care of family and friends. The junior officer Coffee was forced to pledge his personal credit to obtain supplies to help care for the sick men of the cavalry and the horses.[1174]

As Wilkinson had anticipated, the longer Jackson's troops remained in camp without a mission, the more difficult it was for Jackson to enforce discipline. Courts-martial occupied nearly all of March 9. One soldier was sentenced to the wooden horse, but had his punishment remitted. Others were sentenced to four days at hard labor for the same offense.[1175]

Worse than reports of an increase of disciplinary infractions, Jackson was informed that Private John Drum died late in the afternoon the previous day.[1176] Drum would be buried with full honors even if another formal burial ceremony would heighten concerns about the number of men who were falling ill.

Natural instincts continued to drive some healthy men to escape from the confines of boredom, sickness, and death in camp to seek the sounds of life in Natchez. Jackson ordered the cavalry to ride into Natchez to round up stray soldiers and bring them back to camp.[1177] He further ordered that the lines of sentinels on the perimeter of camp were to be increased. The order was necessary to enforce discipline; however, Jackson knew that once the men began to feel that he was holding them prisoners in their own camp, he had begun to lose the battle with Wilkinson. It was becoming obvious that the Volunteers were now primed to welcome any opportunity to engage in some action, even if Wilkinson commanded them.

Heavy rain on March 13 soaked through the linen and cotton canvas of the tents and dripped inside.[1178] Cold and damp conditions took a heavy toll on the troops' health, and the close quarters provided an environment for the diseases to spread quicker. More than 150 men were now sick. Fifty-six of those were unable to walk.[1179]

Jackson was informed of another death, trumpeter Benjamin Darnell.[1180] Captain Smith's company was ordered to provide the coffin. The sounds of its construction were unmistakable to sick and dying men confined to camp with little to occupy their thoughts other than questions of whether they would face a similar fate. The burial party assembled for a full military burial near dusk at 5:00 p.m. Soldiers carried the body to the grave with solemn precision. As the soldier was buried, troops fired volleys to honor their brother. Immediately, they marched away from the grave in a brisk march to upbeat music as if returning to life. Reverend Blackman spoke after volleys were fired.[1181] Reverend Winian attended the service and provided a critique. He was impressed with the ceremony but found the uplifting ending in "bad taste—the transition from grave to gay, from solemn to merry measures being so sudden as to jar offensively upon the sense of congruity."[1182]

The soldier's death, the second in four days, added urgency, and Jackson's growing weariness and exasperation showed through in his letter to his quartermaster Lewis as he realized that almost the whole camp was getting sick, "To be without funds medicine and a number sick is an unpleasant situation—we are here without any orders or advises, from any quarter, fed some times on the poorest beef on earth—and without an[y] necessity for us being here."[1183]

How did the nation expect to win a war if it placed so many of its soldiers far from action to be forgotten? Jackson began to blame Governor Blount for sending him on a mission where there was no enemy and then forgetting him. In his frustration, Jackson did not recall that he had literally extorted the appointment for the command of the Natchez Expedition from the governor and that he had gladly accepted it, knowing that the real mission in Mobile and Pensacola had not yet been approved by Congress. Jackson also overlooked the detail that his soldiers were trapped by Wilkinson in Natchez only because he had disobeyed the governor's order to march to New Orleans.

To make matters worse, in addition to holding his command together in Natchez, Jackson was forced to deal with a growing public dispute in the Nashville newspapers between his own quartermaster Lewis and aide-de-camp Benton. Lewis revealed that Benton was the author or supporter of the anonymous journals of Jackson's voyage that had appeared in the Nashville newspapers, in which Benton had attempted to shift blame for the delayed construction of the boats to Lewis.[1184] Lewis defended that he had not even been appointed when the contracts were let for the boats, and he suggested that Benton had been dilatory in bringing the boats to Jackson.

Lewis did not consider how his allegations against Benton reflected on Benton's superior. If newspapers from across the country reported the story, the fight would do nothing to bolster Jackson's reputation or encourage offers for service. Despite Jackson's best efforts to create a newspaper campaign about the success of his abilities to organize and command a successful military operation, the dispute between his subordinates became one additional problem that he had to attempt to influence, without resources and far from home.

In New Orleans, General Wilkinson reviewed the inspector's reports of the readiness of Jackson's troops. Seeing that Jackson indeed commanded the quality of troops Wilkinson could use and knowing that his request to inspect the troops had raised false expectations, Wilkinson determined that the time had arrived to deliver the War Department dismissal order. To add an additional blow, Wilkinson penned his own letter to Jackson to be delivered with the secretary's order. Like a surprise explosion of thunder from a clear, blue sky, the order, Wilkinson gloated, "will come like a thunderclap on Jackson."[1185]

On Sunday, March 14, Wilkinson's letter enclosing the Secretary of War's order of dismissal arrived at Camp Jackson by mail.

A second copy of the order had been delivered in the mail in Nashville just prior to March 9.[1186] Governor Blount had forwarded it to Jackson by mail, and that copy would not arrive for another week. If Jackson considered the timing of the deliveries and the time that it took for mail to travel from Washington City to Nashville, and then to New Orleans, it would not have made sense that Wilkinson received his copy of the order in New Orleans just a few days after Blount had received his copy in Nashville.[1187] Making the timing of the delivery even more suspicious, on the prior day, March 13, someone in the Mississippi Territory passed along "intelligence" to Lt. Colonel Carson, commander of the Mobile District, that Jackson had been ordered to return to Tennessee. Jackson again would have concluded that there was "something rotten in the State of Denmark."[1188]

Jackson was seated in a camp church service listening to Reverend Winian preach when a soldier handed him Wilkinson's correspondence.[1189] Jackson politely dismissed himself from the service to step outside to review the order. Jackson would have instinctively greeted news of the arrival of orders with relief. Finally, he had his orders and the Volunteers would know their mission.

When Jackson opened the letter, Wilkinson's prediction came true. An unexpected bolt of lightning from a clear, blue sky would have not had a greater surprise or physical force, and Jackson was understandably stunned.

Wilkinson's note read:

"Sir, I had the honor yesterday to receive your favour of the 1st. Jany and agreabley to my engagements I enclose you a copy of a note received from the Secretary of war by yesterday's mail, which exhibits every word I have received on the interesting subject. It is our duty to be satisfied with every arrangement of those whom we are bound to obey, and __ unlooked for measure, before us, in no doubt founded in sound Policy. It appears to me to be the Harbinger of peace, a blessing which you and the Gentlemen of your command have manifested a willingness to purchase for your country, at the points of swords."[1190]

As Jackson then read the order supposedly penned by the Secretary of War, his reaction was what Reverend Winian described as "violent indignation."[1191] Winian later reflected that General Harrison once cursed almost as much as the General.[1192]

Jackson carefully studied the letter and order. By yesterday's mail? The enclosed letter from the secretary was dated January 5.[1193] That could not be possible. Wilkinson's protestations that the secretary's order was the only information he had received on the "interesting" subject belied guilt. Wilkinson then went on with his flowery prose to regret that he and Jackson would not have the chance to shake hands at Mobile or Pensacola, where Wilkinson said he "gladly" would have given Jackson command of the troops. The letter revealed that Jackson's coveted mission to Mobile and Pensacola had been in the works all along.

Wilkinson's words, no doubt as designed, poured salt in Jackson's fresh wounds. Wilkinson wrote that he was certain Jackson would eventually serve on the "*staff*" of the army, which this dismissal was calculated to guarantee would never happen. Wilkinson further suggested that Jackson serve his country by encouraging his men to enlist under Wilkinson's command, and he asked Jackson to let him know what would happen to the Volunteers. Finally, Wilkinson renewed what had always proved to be a false offer to do everything in his power to make the Volunteers comfortable.

The Secretary of War's undated letter to Wilkinson postmarked February 8 was brief:

> "Sir, The Militia force organized by Govr. Blount under command of Genl. Jackson expedited to new orleans early in the last month is discharged from further service. The General is required to have delivered over to your direction such articles of public property as have been committed to them."[1194]

Jackson recognized an error immediately. Forgetting the point that he had made to seek Wilkinson's removal, Jackson noted that the Volunteers were not a state militia force but called into service as federal Volunteers by orders of the president.

As Jackson's shock quickly turned to fury, he suspected a plot. The secretary's erroneous statement implying that Jackson's men were a state militia force was the one Wilkinson had used to deny provisions. Was that error a clue to another Wilkinson forgery? Now the arrival of Wilkinson's inspectors on March 3 took on new meaning. Wilkinson had been so neglectful of the care of his own troops that many of them had died, the terms of service of the Mississippi Territory militia were expiring, and few new recruits wanted to serve under him. Wilkinson needed troops, and this was his plot to confiscate Jackson's Volunteers and equipment to command the fight against the British on the Gulf.

Jackson's biographer Parton later related many of the questions that flooded Jackson's mind.[1195] He had asked 2,000 men to march hundreds of miles in winter, through extreme deprivations and risk their own lives and fortunes only to be told the march was unnecessary? Worse still, he was to dismiss those men 450 miles from home without any provision to get them back? He was asked to turn over to the U.S. Army all arms that the men had brought from their homes and that had been provided by the government, guns that would be needed to fend off an attack on a return march through a possible Indian war? Guns they expected to keep as additional compensation for their services? He was even asked to return the tents men would need to shelter them from the rain and cold? No, he was not asked. Wilkinson's inclusion of the secretary's order made it clear that Jackson's forced abandonment of his men and equipment was an order under penalty of punishment from the U.S. government.

Jackson only had to survey the camp to see faces of the young men who looked to him for protection and guidance. He had told them he would be a father to them, and now he had been ordered to abandon them. These were the sons of his neighbors and Tennesseans who had elected him as head of the militia. Those neighbors trusted him with the lives of their families. How did the War Department expect him to go back to Tennessee and explain to his supporters that he had left their husbands, sons, and brothers to fend for themselves without any medicines, food, weapons, or supplies near territory that was threatened by the British and their Creek Indian proxies?[1196]

As if Jackson required any additional reminder of the need to act quickly, he was interrupted with news that Private John Wise had become ill and died.[1197] The General may have remembered that before the Volunteers marched from Nashville, Wise had attempted to return home and that Jackson had ordered him brought back and tried for desertion.[1198] As it turned out, it seemed at the moment that Wise had given his life for no benefit to his country. Wise's family and friends would be expected to ask that Jackson give an account for his actions. It was a particularly poignant moment when Jackson signed the order for the former deserter to be buried will full honors. Jackson confided to William B. Lewis that despite his public assurances of the soldiers' glowing health, the entire camp was sick.[1199] They had now experienced the third death in four days. Whatever the General decided, he had to act soon.

News of the secretary's order spread like a wildfire through the camp. Recruiters had been wrong. There would be no glorious battles against the British under the leadership of General Jackson. The Volunteers had been told to disband in the field and get home the best they could without provisions or even weapons to defend themselves.

The soldiers noted that the secretary's letter to Jackson was dated five days before they had marched from Nashville.[1200] How could that be genuine if they were ordered to turn over equipment to General Wilkinson, who was not in Nashville or even at Fort Massac in January?

To the older men, this order just confirmed their suspicions that the government in Washington City had no interest in the common folk on the frontier. The younger men could not imagine what future awaited them 450 miles from home with no means to return. Would they ever see their families again? Those too sick to walk had even greater reason to worry. Jackson's biographers Reid and Eaton wrote that the young soldiers who were sick looked at Jackson with tears in their eyes and begged him not to abandon them.[1201]

That was the heaviest blow. One soldier wrote that when Jackson thought he would not be able to obtain the wagons he needed to transport the sick soldiers home, the crusty General also shed tears.[1202] If Jackson could figure a way out of this web, all those responsible would pay a heavy price.

CHAPTER SEVENTEEN

ESCAPING
THE SPIDER'S WEB

"I led them into the field, and I will at all risqué and hazard
lead them home*"*

—Andrew Jackson, March 15, 1813

Jackson had suspected Wilkinson's plot to destroy him from the moment he saw the condition of Cantonment Washington. The strategy was now even more painfully obvious. Wilkinson had used the lure of food and pay to maneuver him into a trap near Natchez where his men would remain idle, removed all means of support, and left Jackson with a regiment of sick and dying soldiers and no access to medicines. Jackson had played right into Wilkinson's hands. Two thousand of his best supporters would suffer from his decisions, and those who survived would tell the story to people at home. As all his friends and enemies watched, Jackson was firmly in Wilkinson's crucible and the pressure was crushing.

Jackson had to make his decision. He was forced to choose between abandoning his entire force, his 2,000 "sons" who had followed him into the field or committing insurrection against a government he believed was the only one on Earth that provided liberty to its citizens.[1203]

Communication with the War Department would take at least three weeks even using express riders for delivery. There was no opportunity to make a defense or determine whether there had been a mistake. Of course, based upon Wilkinson's reputation, there was a good possibility that the secretary's letter and order were forgeries. The War Department might have no intention of dismissing Jackson. If that were the case and if Jackson abandoned his men and his command hundreds of miles from home just when he was needed to defend the Gulf Coast, he would appear to be unreliable at best or a coward at worst.

Whatever Jackson decided would also have long lasting consequences on his family and friends. Either choice bore unthinkable consequences. What would happen to the Volunteers if he obeyed the order? Wilkinson wanted 400 or 500 of the best men, but what of the others? The sick and the poor who had no means of their own would starve and die. Wilkinson could claim that many of those soldiers were the ones whose number exceeded the official recruitment order and that Jackson was solely responsible for the consequences of that violation. Did government aristocrats have no feeling for the ordinary man who was willing to give his life for his country? Did they not believe that all citizens deserved the government's respect?

If Jackson chose to return the men home now, he would have to overcome difficulties in supplying food to the troops. As the Nashville newspaper would note, late winter was the worst season for marching on the Natchez Trace. Early spring rains, swollen creeks and swamps, and the thawing dirt road surface would make it almost impossible to transport trains of supply wagons. If Jackson could just wait another month, the road would firm up and there would be less chance that the men would starve on the march.[1204] But his men were sick, and they were beginning to die. If just a few more Volunteers became ill, finding the wagons for transport would become almost impossible. Jackson may have suspected that Wilkinson timed delivery of the dismissal to limit his options.

A soldier in Captain Renshaw's company died, adding more urgency to Jackson's decision.[1205] As Jackson weighed alternatives, his frontier survival skills rushed to the fore. His mind would not accept defeat. The scar on Jackson's head bore witness that he would not back down when he thought he was correct, no matter what authority told him otherwise.

From instinct and a sense of right rather than logic, Jackson reached the decision that would change his life, "I led them into the field, and I will at all risqué and hazard lead them home."[1206]

But more than that, Jackson would not only return to Tennessee in command of his men, he determined not to leave even one man behind. Jackson likely knew that some companies of soldiers serving under the "Swampfox" Francis Marion in the Revolution had followed the same principle, but he could not appreciate that he was helping confirm a standard that all future American military commanders would follow. Just like refusing to leave a soldier behind to be mistreated in enemy territory, Jackson refused to leave men under his protection behind to be neglected or mistreated by a cold-hearted commander.

The lawyer in Jackson began searching for a legal justification. He reviewed the statute passed by Congress on January 11, 1812, which read in part, "that whenever any officer or soldier shall be discharged from the service, he shall be allowed his pay and rations or an equivalent in money for such term of time as shall be sufficient for him to travel from the place of his discharge to the place of his residence."[1207] Jackson could argue that because his men had not been provided that pay, he had a duty under the law to keep them together until he returned them home. The former Superior Court Judge Jackson acknowledged the interpretation of the statute for the first time, and he would claim it and follow it.

More than statutory authority, though, no matter what the Secretary of War had ordered, a higher duty compelled Jackson to follow the age-old common law precedent of returning troops to their homes.

The decision was confirmed. Before midnight, Jackson drafted an order to Assistant Deputy Quartermaster Andrews demanding wagons and supplies to return his men to Tennessee. The order should have calmed Jackson's anger by directing him toward a course of action. But he could not sleep.

Jackson did not internalize his anger. Just after midnight, he vented rage to everyone, starting at the top.[1208] He wrote to President Madison, enclosing a copy of the Armstrong dismissal, notably not allowing time for an aide to polish his text. In it he said that December 10:

> "was the proudest day of my life it was the proudest for West Tennessee. . . Why I cannot beleave it is after inviting us to rally round the Standard of coutry in its defence, accepting our Services as tenered, and orderin us to the lower Mississippi (an inhospitable clime) you would Dismiss us from Service Eight hundred Miles from our Homes, without Money without supplies and even strip our sick of every covering, and surrender them victims to Pestilence and famine, and if any of my Detachment escape this there arms are to be taken from them. They have to pass thro' a Savage wilderness and subject to all these Depredations. I cannot Beleave that you would reward thus, the tendered support of the purest patriots of America, to beleave it would be to belave that you were . . . to all sence of humanity and love of Country."[1209]

Next, Jackson penned a letter to Secretary of War John Armstrong.[1210] He began by undermining the secretary's dismissal letter by its date January 6. Armstrong did not take office until February, Jackson said. Was the dismissal legal if the secretary wrote it before he took office? Jackson restated the order to make certain that Armstrong would have a chance to deny that he wrote it if he had not. And if the order was legal, how could the secretary order soldiers called to service under the president's command to surrender all their equipment hundreds of miles from home? Did the secretary expect soldiers to travel without shelter, arms and any equipment through a hostile Indian territory? Jackson added more vividly the image in his mind: "must our band of citizen soldiers wander and fall a sacrifice to the Tomhawk and scalping knife of the wilderness our sick left naked in the open field and remain without supplies without nourishment or any earthly comfort."[1211]

If Armstrong's dismissal was genuine—which Jackson doubted—it seemed clear to Jackson that the order proved the superiority of the militia system. No militia commander who served with his neighbors in the field would ever issue such a careless order. Jackson would fulfill the government's duty of returning the men to their homes, even when the professional military led by the privileged failed to acknowledge that duty. He informed Armstrong that he would march his men back to Tennessee to their homes and families. Emboldened by the rightness of his decision, Jackson defiantly added that when he returned his men to Tennessee, he expected the federal government to pay them for their service.[1212]

Jackson called Benton into his tent to read the draft that he had penned without Benton's help and to test his reaction. The aide-de-camp was shocked. The letter made it appear that Jackson was issuing orders to the Secretary of War rather than the other way around. Benton no doubt considered how his own service to an insubordinate general would be viewed and strongly encouraged Jackson to soften the language.[1213]

Benton was correct. Jackson *was* issuing orders to the Secretary of War, if not to the President of the United States, claiming a higher statutory and common law authority on behalf of the common soldier he commanded. And like his friend Colonel Butler, Jackson was following precedent in refusing to follow an order he believed to be illegal.

With a few hours to consider the matter, Jackson now believed that if the secretary's order was genuine, it was so far afield from common decency that the public would come to Jackson's defense if the government attempted to punish him. One of the few bills Jackson that had promoted in his brief term as a U.S. Congressman was to secure reimbursement of expenses for Tennessee military men who led a campaign against the Cherokee in violation of an order from the federal government.[1214] He even promoted a bill to reimburse Chickasaw leader George Colbert for his help in the earlier joint campaign with Tennesseans against the Creek that also violated War Department orders.

Ultimately, the American people were in control through their representatives, and if Jackson failed to persuade the bureaucrats in the War Department, he again could go over their heads and chance appealing to the public through Congress. Jackson, the survivalist, the politician, the lawyer, and the judge was now backed by a re-awakening of Jackson the brawler.

Jackson had tried to play within the accepted rules of the establishment bureaucracy, and this was the result. Wilkinson and his political cohorts in the War Department were trying to use those rules to destroy Jackson. Worse, they were willing to waste the lives of hundreds of poor Tennessee men just to maintain their own power. It would not stand! He turned loose the frontier fighter Jackson that had been restrained by Overton's advice since his duel with Dickinson.

Wilkinson could have calculated that Jackson—housed in a cold tent 450 miles from home, sickened and weakened from near-pneumonia, removed from his base of political support, forced to watch men in his protection die from disease and hunger, ordered by the Secretary of War to turn over all his equipment, arms, and even his troops' tents to his political enemy, and then faced with a remaining life of public humiliation and financial ruin if he lived to return home, would finally accept defeat and surrender. But Wilkinson had failed to calculate that Andrew Jackson "the quitter" did not exist. Jackson would not "stay throwed."

This attack went to the heart of Jackson's concept of his own identity, both as a general and as the protector of his extended family. If Jackson allowed Wilkinson to prevail, he would not only have failed to command a battle, he would have abandoned the poor and sick soldiers to die. No doubt Jackson had publicly criticized Wilkinson's incompetence that led to the death of hundreds of soldiers under his command. Wilkinson's revenge would now give Jackson the same reputation.

Until this point, Jackson had sought his purpose in business, gambling, law, and politics, but he had failed at business and had quickly given up on other pursuits when he did not find his purpose in them. And though Andrew Jackson had always fought back no matter the enemy, often he fought as the boy who had lacked a father's guidance to mature into a man. Like a teenage orphan trying to survive, Jackson had fought only for himself and his friends.

Not only did Jackson's command suddenly have a purpose—to save himself and his military family—he had discovered a mission greater than himself. Jackson had not been born a political aristocrat; however, from this point forward, he would not fear taking on any eastern politician, even the President of the United States, on his own level for the common citizen who could not fight for himself.[1215] Jackson would balance his attempts at political savvy with his no-holds-barred frontier-style grit. In the pain of an agonizing decision in his cold tent on the Natchez Trace, a new Andrew Jackson was born.

The mightiest human winds had shaken him to his firm core. Though his soldiers had not yet given the "tough-as-hickory" general the name, in making the decision to fight back against Wilkinson and aristocratic bureaucrats for Tennessee Volunteers who were being neglected and abused by their government, all Jackson's life-earned characteristics surfaced and reconstituted a new man. A more focused and mature man.

An even tougher, hardened, and seasoned man. A man who was being reborn as "Old Hickory."

Fittingly, the day was Jackson's 46th birthday, and Old Hickory was born from Jackson's strong will as a full-grown fighter. Wilkinson's "*thunderclap*" was almost like the lightning in Choctaw Chief Pushmataha's self-reputed mythical birth that struck a mighty oak tree and produced a fully formed warrior.

The General's decision would alter the course of the remainder of his life. Old Hickory's enemies and the enemies of the common citizen were entrenched beyond Tennessee in Britain, New Orleans, and the federal capital. The new Andrew Jackson would not stop fighting until he had defeated all of them.

Once as a teenage orphan on a trip far from home in Charleston, South Carolina, Jackson overspent his resources and had no means to pay his bills or fund the long return home. Undaunted, he walked into a game of "rattle and snap," one he had never played. The teenager's self-assured manner enabled his bluff as he bet 200 pounds and rolled the dice. He won, paid his bills, and returned home.[1216] Now, as a more experienced racehorse gambler, Jackson bet the lives of 2,000 men that his principles and strategy were correct.

The letter to Wilkinson would need careful crafting. Wilkinson still held the power to supply him with the food and wagons Jackson needed to return his men home. He could not afford to anger Wilkinson before he obtained what he needed if there was any possibility of requisitioning supplies. Even then, he could not help mentioning that it appeared the government was trifling with the men's patriotism. Jackson chose to run a bluff based on whatever authority Wilkinson may have believed he still retained.

Jackson said that he would comply with the secretary's order to relinquish his equipment to Wilkinson, however, he would retain the army tents released to Governor Holmes and the few supplies he needed for the sick.[1217] Wilkinson had challenged Jackson's right to order the quartermaster to dispense federal property. Jackson offered to send an express rider to New Orleans to obtain funds to assist the deputy quartermaster in making payments for his men. He asked that Wilkinson see that the order was followed. Of course, he would encourage his troops to enlist under the U.S. forces, but only once he had returned them to Nashville. That statement would let Wilkinson know that his machinations did not fool him, but he could still dangle the proposition of Wilkinson commanding his troops even if he had no intention of following through on his promise. Then, just like Dr. Sappington's famous pills, a coating of sugar was added to encourage Wilkinson's cooperation: "I have only time to tender to you the sentiments of my high consideration."[1218]

To his friend Willie Blount, Jackson could be more honest. The War Department had "abandoned" his men in a strange country. He wrote the governor that he was thunderstruck at the order "to be divested of all public property. There is no reservation, not even a tent for the canopy of a sick man's bed."[1219] In the third letter of the day, Jackson explained that if he complied with the War Department order and dismissed his men near Natchez, they would have been a "fine harvest for petty recruiting officers to have taken advantage of their necessities, which would constrain them to enlist, in order [to] get the means of subsistence."[1220] He would need Blount's help in getting the men home.

Jackson quickly devised a plan to draw on the army quartermaster for twenty-days' rations and march the men as far north as Colbert's Ferry. If he could secure no other assistance, he would have to pledge his own credit to pay the quartermaster. He needed the governor to arrange to deliver food to Colbert's Ferry to get the Sons of Tennessee from Natchez back to their families. Jackson threatened that he would have to use his position as Tennessee Major General to resort to taking food by the force of arms if the governor did not comply.

Jackson next turned to U.S. Congressman Felix Grundy. As Tennessee's representative to the federal government, Grundy would be called to account for why the men had been sent 450 miles with no mission to accomplish and why they were forgotten, neglected, and forced to return home without even a tent to cover them from the elements:

> "These questions will be asked of you as their representative; of the President, and this new incumbent who must have been drunk when he wrote it or so proud of his appointment as to have lost all feelings of humanity & duty, that he commenced by anticipation on the duties of his office a month before he was really in office, such treatment as this [is] well calculated, to bring about disgu[st] which will never gain the object in view. Is the whole purpose to discredit the militia system to bring about a standing army?"

Jackson claimed that even "Barbarous Europe" never did anything parallel. He had been forced to choose between an outrageous and possibly illegal order and the men under his charge. His loyalty would be with his men: "As long as I have friends or credit, I will stick by them. I shall march them to Nashville or bury them with the honors of war. Shoud I die I know they will bury me."[1221]

If Jackson could not directly pressure the War Department, he could use his influence to pressure Congressman Grundy to do so on his behalf.

Emboldened by his own arguments in each letter he wrote, Jackson now felt confident in threatening that he would not disarm the men when he returned to Tennessee, and he would not dismiss the troops until they were paid. The threat would remind the government of Revolutionary War soldiers who refused to disband until they had been paid.

To his wife Rachel, Jackson felt free to reveal his personal feelings. He correctly assessed that he saw the dismissal as a plot to encourage his men to enlist in the army. He would not turn them over to Wilkinson to neglect. He had assured his men that he would be a father to them, and he would stay with them until they returned home. He wrote, "it is only by and through me, that these things can be [done] the sick shall be taken back as far as lif[e] lasts, and supplies shall be had—altho their Patriotism has been but illy rewarded by an ungratefull officer, (not Country) it is therefore my duty to act as a father to the sick and to the well and stay with them untill I march them into Nashville."[1222]

By inserting, "(not Country)," Jackson wanted to make it clear to anyone who might see the letter that his loyalty to his country was unwavering. His dispute was with the aristocratic politicians who ran it.

Jackson's mind was whirling from the logistical challenge of getting the men home without the army's support. After assuming that Governor Blount would honor the request for funds for emergency provisions, Jackson wrote Quartermaster William B. Lewis in Nashville to have provisions and forage delivered to meet the troops at Colbert's Ferry as they marched northward on the Natchez Trace. Even in giving Lewis orders for food, Jackson found himself railing again at the War Department who would order him to abandon sick soldiers, but then said that he had to force himself to change the subject, "*I bring home my sick or perish in the at[tempt].*"[1223] Having thought through what he would do if help did not arrive to feed the men in the four-hundred-fifty-mile Wilderness, Jackson concluded that if all else failed, the men could eat the horses.[1224]

The long evening and early morning of venting through his pen was finished. Jackson indeed now found himself in the position his old friend Colonel Butler had faced. He had disobeyed an order he thought was illegal. He was far from home, and though he was sending letters to the federal city, he had no assurance that anyone would lend support. If any consolation helped Jackson sleep, it was that he would not give up without a fight.

Jackson held a council of his officers to announce his decision. Though Benton would later write that the officers stood behind Jackson to a man, Benton's recollection was another of his revisions of history.[1225] The officers only voiced support when Jackson first gave them his decision. Jackson was still angry, and no one wanted to become the focus of that anger.

After Jackson retired for the evening, officers met in what Jackson's biographers Reid and Eaton called a "secret caucus" where they could be freer to voice opposition.[1226] Benton clearly worried that they would all be viewed as committing mutiny against the government, and he apparently attempted to generate support among Jackson's officers to pressure Jackson to reconsider.

Benton's objections were logical, "Wagons were wanted, and many of them, for transport of provisions, baggage, and the sick—so numerous among new troops . . . The wagons were ten dollars a day, coming and going . . . the amount to be incurred was great . . . The troops had received no pay . . . the clothes and shoes were worn out; the men were in no condition for a march so long and so exposed."[1227] As Wilkinson may have suspected, it seemed that Benton could be persuaded to surrender.

Even in the improbable event that Jackson's plan worked, the War Department would likely consider it mutiny. Every officer would be forever tainted by his involvement. Jackson was considered advanced in age. He would not be expected to live long with the consequences. Younger men with a full life ahead would pay the price. They must somehow talk the General out of this course of action and dismiss the men at Natchez as ordered.

Reverend Winian, again loitering in camp, overheard the officers' conversations, which gave him the impression that Jackson addressed his superiors "in the most violent terms—declaring his determination to disobey." Winian reflected the officers' concerns that, "All this was high-handed mutiny; and in ordinary cases, would have been followed by execution, under sentence of a Court-Martial."[1228]

Benton's brother Jessie would later revive Benton's views of the events that Jackson "manifested great violence on the occasion, inflamed the troops with a view to render the government odious, and himself popular."[1229] Thomas Hart Benton, who was concerned about his own career in the military, already had made the mistake of suggesting to Jackson that Wilkinson outranked Jackson, because Jackson was only a militia general and Wilkinson was a U.S. Army general.[1230] Jackson may have surmised that Benton opposed returning because he preferred to serve under Wilkinson.

When the officers reached a consensus to suggest that Jackson reconsider, the General met their suggestion with the same fury he still harbored for Wilkinson. It was easy for the officers who had money to decide they would pay their own way back to Tennessee, Jackson reminded his officers. But most of the 2,000 Volunteers were common men who did not have that option.[1231] Jackson did not appreciate the lack of confidence in his judgment. He had made his decision, and he expected it to be followed and supported. Unless officers had confidence in Jackson's abilities, the men would not survive the return march. From all practical appearances, Jackson would have to pull the means he needed to return his troops home from thin air.

Old Hickory ignored Benton's advice and ordered the letter sent immediately to the Secretary of War. The die was cast. Now Jackson would have to survive long enough to enforce the decision he had made.

Jackson could not leave arrangements for food to chance. In a few days, he would order Aide-de-Camp Andrew Hynes to ride to Nashville with five linemen to make sure his requests were followed.[1232] If Jackson could obtain enough food, forage, and supplies to march the men to the Colbert's Ferry, he did not doubt that Tennessee governor Blount would sent supplies to meet them there. Jackson would also send letters to the

U.S. Paymaster Kingsley to prepare to have funds to pay the men. If there was not enough specie available, the cavalry should be paid first.[1233]

In the space of a few hours, the shock of the secretary's dismissal had been replaced by a plan of action. It was risky, and Jackson would need all the help he could get from the support he had fostered with friends and territorial leaders in Natchez, and he counted on the Tennessee governor to provide what the federal government refused. Jackson issued additional orders for officers to begin planning the return. Cavalry officers were to prepare horses and packhorses for the march. Officers were to ask the assistant deputy quartermaster to fill their cartridges for their weapons.[1234]

Jackson now held no illusions that he could place any trust in Wilkinson, but he could not pass up any chance that the army would provide food. Besides, Wilkinson should have no authority to overrule the long-standing practice of dismissing troops near their homes so as not to leave them exposed to the hazards of a distant area. Jackson sent His officers to deliver an order to Assistant Deputy Quartermaster Robert Andrews at Cantonment Washington with instructions to obtain enough supplies to reach the Tennessee River and to have contractors lay out supplies on the road.[1235] The request included 21 wagons that Jackson calculated he needed to transport sick men and supplies, and one wagon to haul the officer's baggage.

Perhaps Jackson followed his own advice to the soldiers on the river journey to Natchez and took time the next morning to stare into the predawn firmament to look for the Morning Star.

Knowing how Jackson reacted to the dismissal order was paramount for Wilkinson, and almost immediately one of his spies in Natchez reported to him. Wilkinson was advised that Jackson flew into a rage and threatened that if the quartermaster and contractor would not provide him the supplies he needed, he would take them, ostensibly by force.[1236]

On the same date of Jackson's receipt of the secretary's letter, Wilkinson issued his own order to assure that Jackson interpreted the order correctly and, by putting that interpretation on record, to place a nail in General Jackson's coffin: "The Asst. Dept. Qr. Master Genl. Is to receive and receipt for whatever public property, Genl. Jackson may order to be delivered to him, and will have the same put in order and well secured."[1237]

Though the secretary's full order stated that Jackson was to turn over equipment only if he had not yet descended the Mississippi, Wilkinson interpreted the order to direct Jackson to turn over to Wilkinson's quartermaster the soldiers' tents and whatever firearms and little ammunition that had been provided. Soldiers who had volunteered with the prospects of keeping their firearm could be expected to turn on Jackson. And once the soldiers had no shelter, Jackson could not keep his men together as a unit.

For public purposes, Wilkinson also included provisions for the troops that he would be expected to make: "The President having been pleased to discharge from further service, the patriotic intrepid Volunteers of Tennessee, encamped near Natchez, under the Order of Major Genl. Jackson, they are to be mustered up to the day of their discharge, and in addition to the pay due them, are to receive from the District paymaster the usual allowance of mileage in returning home, and the Contractor will furnish provisions for the same period."[1238]

It was no more than any commanding general would be expected to do, and Jackson said so, but Wilkinson had no intention of following through.

Certain that the dismissal order had overwhelmed and defeated Jackson, Wilkinson wasted no time following up with a letter to gloat over Jackson's failure as a general. Wilkinson said that he regretted that the secretary's dismissal would prevent the two of them from serving together as generals. He wished Jackson a pleasant trip home and back to "civilian life."[1239] He enclosed the order that the quartermaster pay Jackson's men and honor requests for supplies for the return march. For public purposes, the letter showed Wilkinson as being the fairer man. Privately, Wilkinson had already planted enough seeds of doubt with the army quartermasters that they would refuse to provide Jackson's troops with the pay or all the supplies he needed.

As days of late-winter rain added to the gloom, even Reverend Blackman's optimism faded. Blackman stared at the small number of people who braved the weather to attend his third attempt to hold a religious service in Washington and concluded, "It seems as if Providence was saying 'Do not preach to the people of Washington; let them alone, they are joined to their idols.'"[1240]

Andrews greeted Jackson's men with surprise. He said he knew nothing about Wilkinson's new offer to provide supplies, and he was unpersuaded by Jackson's novel legal argument. He simply had no authority to provide Jackson with U.S. government provisions, and that was that.[1241] Volunteers again returned to camp empty-handed.

As a steady heavy rain continued to confine troops to their tents and collective misery, Wilkinson struck his final blow. On March 22, he sent a letter advising Jackson that he had received Jackson's letter of March 15. He was certain that Jackson must be embarrassed by the situation in which he found himself.[1242] Though Wilkinson had led Jackson to believe his troops would be supplied, he regretted he could do no more than he had already done. The army would not bear the expense of Jackson's march back to Tennessee. There would be no more charades to offer false hope. The announcement of that decision should have been the checkmate move. Wilkinson expected Jackson just to leave his soldiers and return home "like a cowardly dog that had lost his ears" as he had described Jackson in Richmond.

Instead, Jackson defiantly wrote Secretary Armstrong, knowing that he would need to move his men before the order even reached Armstrong, but creating a paper trail he planned to publicize if he returned home.[1243] Jackson enclosed a copy of the order that was undated but postmarked to Wilkinson on February 8 that the command organized under General Jackson was to be dismissed. He relied upon the law that a soldier discharged is to be given money and rations or the equivalent to return home. No provision having been made for his forces, "No direction to pay the troops here" and "no compensation," he called on the quartermaster to provide rations and cover his expenses.[1244]

Then came the accusations that would have power only in future publications:

> "Your note of the 5th. Of Jany. 1813 directs that two thousand well organized volunteers under the acts of congress of Feby the 6th. And July 6th. 1812 are to be dismissed at New Orleans without pay or a compensation for rations. Is this yr. impartial rule. And this reward to whom? Men of the first character patriotism and wealth of the Union; who left their comfortable homes and families for the tented fields, to support the Eagles of their country at any point ordered by the constituted authority—"[1245]

Next, Jackson replied to Wilkinson's final refusal to supply provisions. This time, there was no pretext of being respectful or cooperative. Those tactics had been fruitless. He wanted Wilkinson to know that his plan to make his troops hapless conscripts had failed. Jackson was ready to make his escape up the Natchez Trace.

Using the only political ammunition that remained, Jackson issued a threat. Wilkinson should be on notice that Jackson planned to make an issue of the dismissal before the whole world. Jackson wanted Wilkinson to know that he was aware of Wilkinson's involvement in the dismissal order. He pointed out that the Secretary of War's letter had said the he expected his order would reach Jackson before he left Fort Massac, but Jackson had sent a letter on January 4 advising the secretary that he would be marching south. The handwritten copy of the secretary's letter apparently forwarded by Governor Blount with a February 5 date was just Wilkinson's attempt to claim ignorance of the January 4 date. Jackson said he could not help but smile as he read it. Jackson accused, "This gauze is too thin, too flimsy to hide the baseness of the act."[1246] He went on to declare that either the letter he received dated January 5th was in Armstrong's handwriting or "every word, letter and figure " was a "forgery."[1247]

The failure of the secretary's dismissal order to provide instructions for return of the soldiers to their home and payment upon mustering out was a glaring omission. Wilkinson may have left out that provision because he knew that the secretary had not issued the order and Wilkinson had no funds or authority to pay the men. Or if the men received their pay, they may not have remained in the Lower Country to serve under Wilkinson.

Jackson warned Wilkinson that he had reported the dismissal directly to President Madison, certain that he had not approved the order.

Jackson then facetiously thanked Wilkinson for directing to be done no more than the law required in payment of his troops. Jackson would not surrender the military leadership he had worked so hard to orchestrate by permitting his men to join the regular army. He was certain that Tennessee forces would be needed in the Northwest, and he planned to keep them together until he reached Nashville. His trip back home would not be to civilian life as Wilkinson had hoped. It was a promise or a threat that Wilkinson would hear from him again when the two were on more equal terms. Finally, after accusing Wilkinson of forgery, Jackson then returned some of the syrupy prose that Wilkinson had included in his letters, Jackson thanked Wilkinson for his "offer of friendship" and noted that he had the "highest consideration of respect" for Wilkinson.[1248]

Jackson might have expected another "thunderclap" from the sky for that statement.

Unlike his false praise for Wilkinson, Jackson next wrote Mississippi Territory Brigadier General F.L. Claiborne to give genuine thanks for all his assistance and moral support. The news shocked Claiborne. Was the war over? Had the British just given up without a fight and sailed away? That could be the only meaning of the dismissal. Claiborne was as surprised as Jackson that the War Department would dismiss, "At this perilous crisis so respectable a reinforcement of men whose patriotism and valour are so well established would have given security to this exposed Section of the Union, from all attacks from without, & commanded from the savages in our vicinity an adherence to the most pacific course."[1249] Even in his expression of gratitude, Jackson's mind was still focused on Armstrong and Wilkinson. He noted his disgust, "This will long be recollected by Tennessee and her sons."[1250]

The decision made it clear that Volunteers would not be advancing to New Orleans. Jackson ordered detachments to go into Natchez to turn over the boats to Andrews.[1251] The boats had been Jackson's last lifeline, and now he was handing them over voluntarily. To deprive Andrews of gaining too much satisfaction from the handover, Jackson also ordered that the detachment leave Andrews all the horses too lame to make the return trip. Wilkinson could decide what to do with that property.

Who knew what Wilkinson would attempt once he knew that Jackson was planning to lead the troops back to Nashville? Jackson had already violated the Secretary of War's order (or, more likely, Wilkinson's forged order). He could not stop there if he had any chance to prevail. Jackson issued an order that any army recruiter who entered the camp was to be arrested and drummed out of camp. No Wilkinson recruiter would divide Andrew Jackson's forces.[1252]

Lingering doubts over Jackson's connection to Burr's plots had already made the War Department reluctant to trust Jackson with leadership of federal forces; this outright rebellion would only confirm their suspicions.

It was a major gamble, but Jackson was confident he could ultimately expose Wilkinson if he could first get his men back home.

Marching 670 men on horseback down the Natchez Trace had already taken a major effort. The challenge now would be to march 2,000 men through the same territory. A good number of those soldiers were too sick even to walk. It was calculated that 2,500 men and their horses would need 10 wagon loads of food each day; a ten-day's march would require up to 20 tons of meat and a thousand bushels of corn.[1253] Food supplies at the stands had already been tapped, and Jackson's funds were limited.

Jackson had no hopes of buying additional weapons. He made an argument for retaining the weapons in hand— the Natchez Trace was too dangerous even for 2,000 soldiers to walk it unarmed.[1254] It is not clear that he had ammunition for all of them, but he knew that some men had volunteered into service to obtain a firearm and he risked another mutiny if he made them leave the firearms behind.

Under normal circumstances, any funds Jackson spent during the march back to Tennessee should be reimbursed by the federal government. Given Jackson's disobedience, reimbursement would be unlikely. In addition to the embarrassment of not accomplishing anything on an expensive expedition, Jackson likely faced financial ruin when he returned home.

Washington Jackson offered additional help. He was aware that many soldiers had already worn out their shoes in the southward march and in the wet encampment. Foot soldiers would not survive the four-hundred-fifty-mile march without shoes. Washington Jackson arranged for his store in Natchez to supply 100 pairs of shoes to the Volunteers.[1255] Other Natchez merchants followed his example and supplied what they could to the troops who had been willing to defend them.[1256] It was an act of charity to the troops of a general who had entered Natchez as a conqueror a month earlier.

Though the weather was warming, Jackson could not risk the march without some shelter from the elements. He appealed to the Mississippi Territory governor David Holmes to allow him to retain the U.S. Army tents that had been charged to Holmes.[1257] Holmes stood personally liable to the federal government for the value of the tents, and he risked becoming classified as an accomplice in Jackson's insubordination. Jackson had carefully maintained his relationship with Holmes, and Holmes agreed to supply what Jackson needed. Jackson's return of some of the tents he brought from Tennessee would give him the appearance of some cooperation.

With equipment except for wagons arranged, Jackson carefully planned his address to the men to prepare them for the return march. He also needed carefully to consider which officer would read the address to the men to properly motivate them. Jackson chose Coffee over Benton:

"The 10th December 1812 with pleasure will be recollected by every patriotic bosom, you with the spirits of free men whose rights were invaded bore without murmur the snowy blast. You entered the camp with order of good citizens. You bore privations like good soldiers... You are now about to return to your country and it remains for to unfold whether you have been treated by the agents of government with that attention your patriotism entitles you to expect and whether you have not been shamefully forgotten by representatives in Congress . . . The Major Genl having pledged himself that he never would abandon one of his men and that he would act the part of a father to them has to repeat that he will not leave one of the sick nor of the detachment behind. He has led you here. He will lead you back to your country and friends. The sick as far as he has the power and means shall be made comfortable. If any one dies, he will pay to them the last tribute of respect. They shall be buried with all honors of war. Should your General die, he knows it is a respect you will pay to him. It is a debt due to every honest and brave soldier of the detachment.[1258]

Reverend Winian again was present in camp, and though he was no Jackson admirer, he observed the soldiers' reactions: "[the address] appeared to find an echo in every bosom, and to swell almost every heart with gratitude and devotion to their brave and sympathizing General, who did not hesitate to step between them and the power of the General Government, with so much risk to himself. The General carried out his magnanimous determination, risking at the same time the whole expense and the personal danger incident to such an act of disobedience."[1259]

An evening parade was planned to boost morale and confidence. Instead, heavy rain forced the men inside their tents. The canvas leaked so much that the troops were forced to sit in huddles and wrap themselves in their blankets. With nowhere for rainwater to drain on the saturated ground, cold water covered the soldiers' feet.[1260] The misery was compounded by the lack of a mission to make the sacrifice worthwhile.

Coffee wrote his wife:

"We have had a fatiguing trip and as things have turned out will be for nothing, but that was to us unknown. Our men would have gone home better satisfied could they have had one stump of a fight, but perhaps better so than worse, yet I flatter myself had we been put to the test, a good account would have been rendered from the Volunteers, we had just begun to learn how to do duty when we shall be discharged."[1261]

Cracks appeared in the base of support Jackson needed to return the men home. Soon pressure began to surface among the less experienced officers. Tempers frayed in a sign of deteriorating morale. Benton returned to camp and fired off his gun in violation of camp regulations, which prompted an angry response from General Jackson. The general who was in open rebellion against the War Department wanted no more insubordination from his own officers.

Jackson's anger with Benton had been building since the departure in Nashville. Rather than ignoring the latest infraction or discussing the matter privately with his aide-de-camp, Jackson ordered the alarm sounded and once the troops had assembled for an emergency, reprimanded Benton in front of the men. Coffee heard the commotion and jumped on his horse wet and without a saddle to see who was causing the disturbance, only to discover that it was the General himself.[1262]

The troops' growing eagerness to return home put additional pressure on Jackson. Without even the prospects of a mission for inspiration, the lower ranks also grew restless as the delay dragged on. Each day they expected to receive orders to march home, and each time they were told they might march "tomorrow" they interpreted it as an excuse. To pass the time, Volunteers put on their knapsacks and practiced marching with them to get accustomed to the feel and the weight.[1263]

Volunteer Baines wrote his wife that his coat and socks had worn out. Even his trousers had worn thin. He could not afford to replace them. The small amounts of money he had kept were almost spent. "I shall be tolerably ragged by the time I get home," he told her.[1264]

The sooner Jackson could get the Volunteers back to Tennessee, the more likely he would retain their loyalty. However, without wagons to transport the sick, and refusing to leave the sick behind, Jackson was trapped in the web of deteriorating morale that Wilkinson had weaved.

On March 19, Jackson wrote directly to the army contractor Brandt that he would be sending Hynes for army wagons and provisions he had requested.[1265] Brandt replied to ask for at least another week. He said that he had 15 wagons under contract, but he had not yet arranged for the additional 20 wagons. Provisions would be ready to be distributed the next day, though Brandt knew that Jackson had no way to transport them.[1266] It made no difference; Quartermaster Andrews would override Brandt's offer.

Having anticipated another rebuff, Jackson was already at work on his final plan. On March 23, he wrote Andrews that he had made a request for forage and wagons to transport the sick and baggage.[1267] He had received word that Andrews had refused his order. Jackson attempted to bluff that his order could not legally be refused, arguing that he was still authorized to draw on the federal government, because there was no order from the Secretary of War for the dismissal and payment of his men to effectively terminate his service. That statement was only partially true. The order supposedly written by the secretary had ordered the dismissal, but not the normal payment due on discharge from service.

Andrews was not taken in. He knew that Jackson was struggling to maintain any control over the situation. Andrews replied the same day that he had contracted for wagons as Jackson requested, but that he had heard Jackson delayed his departure.[1268] He said that he would have complied with the request, but he had learned that Jackson had been dismissed from service. In effect, the bureaucrat nonchalantly informed the already frustrated general that his first request had been too early and the second had been too late.

Jackson might receive the twenty-days provisions for the infantry, but Andrews could supply nothing for the cavalry. It was just as well. Pork that the cavalry was supplied again was unfit to eat.[1269] Convinced that Jackson's hands were tied, Andrews not only renewed his rejection of Jackson's order, but he took pleasure in revealing to Jackson that the quartermaster had always doubted whether Jackson was ever properly called into service. The comment was a threat that Jackson might bear the entire expense of the expedition if Wilkinson was successful in promoting that argument. In any event, Jackson now held no official position; therefore, the quartermaster could not legally supply him with any government wagons or additional supplies.[1270]

Jackson intensified his pressure. A few wagons rolled into camp, apparently to retrieve equipment from Jackson.[1271] The following day, Jackson issued an order for 30 men to take whatever wagons Andrews supplied to go to Natchez. Half the wagons would be loaded with corn and the other would be taken to the contractor's store near the church at Natchez for supplies.[1272] Officers would safeguard the provisions and dispense them in the usual course to make certain they lasted. But Andrews supplied no wagons to transport the sick, and Jackson would not march until he has secured transportation to take every man with him.

Jackson set out to assess Andrews's own vulnerabilities. As assistant deputy quartermaster, Andrews made payments for official government expenses and then relied upon the federal government for reimbursement. Jackson knew that overly cautious bureaucrats at the War Department would not issue payments for reimbursements when someone contested them. They did not want to risk the challenge. Wilkinson had played that game by highlighting every irregularity to prevent quartermasters from paying Jackson. If the War Department delayed reimbursing Andrews for legitimate expenses, Andrews might find himself personally liable for official obligations and unable to pay his personal creditors.[1273] Governor Meriwether Lewis had suffered the same fate when his personal secretary turned on him and sent letters challenging his expenses to the War Department.

Jackson wrote Andrews to acknowledge receipt of his refusal to supply basic provisions and to respond by threatening to contest Andrews's reimbursements.[1274] Jackson's letter made official demand that Andrews settle all his accounts with the Volunteer quartermaster. If Andrews refused to make settlement, Jackson told Andrews that he would ask the

War Department not to settle any of Andrews's accounts until all matters with Jackson had been cleared.[1275]

Though a clever tactic to take advantage of Andrews's only vulnerability, Jackson's threat was just subterfuge to divert a cautious quartermaster's attention. The real purpose of the letter was made to appear secondary. Jackson could assume that Andrews was under Wilkinson's orders to retrieve the Volunteers' tents the moment Jackson relinquished them, and Jackson knew that Andrews would need to bring wagons to haul the tents. Jackson added a passing note in the letter to advise Andrews that he would surrender his tents to Wilkinson if Andrews would arrange to have wagons at Camp Jackson on March 25 to take possession.[1276]

Andrews fell for it. When 11 of Andrews's army-contracted baggage wagons arrived at Camp Jackson, Jackson ordered his men to commandeer the wagons and compel the drivers to transport the sick men home to Tennessee.

Andrews arrived at Camp Jackson to supervise taking possession of the tents. When he saw his wagons under Jackson's control, he hurriedly attempted to dismiss the drivers. Jackson made it clear that the wagons and drivers were in his lines of camp and that he was in command.[1277] Jackson had threatened to take needed supplies by whatever means necessary, but Wilkinson had not expected even Andrew Jackson, led to believe that he had been discharged from service, would have the audacity to commandeer wagons from the U.S. Army.[1278]

Baggage wagons would provide a rough ride for men who were already ill, but they would allow Jackson to fulfill his obligation to return every man home. Though Jackson had only limited supplies of food, medicines and funds, at least he finally controlled transportation needed to start the homeward march up the Natchez Trace. At last, he possessed the means to escape Wilkinson's trap. Jackson's skirmish victory over Andrews was not without cost. In addition to exposing himself to charges of mutiny, he was clearly personally liable for the financial costs of transporting the soldiers home.[1279]

Jackson had now proceeded beyond the point of return in his challenge to Wilkinson. Contrary to his friend John Overton's advice, Jackson was no longer playing by the accepted political rules. At best, there was a good possibility that his public career had ended, whatever the outcome. At worst, the already unhealthy major general could die like several of his contemporaries as a public disgrace in a poor house, a prison, or on the wrong side of a firing squad.

Jackson would roll the dice and risk it. He would not abandon a single "son;" he would not surrender his command to Wilkinson; and he would not meekly surrender to a system that had allowed common men of talent to be crowded out by the new ruling class that Wilkinson represented. If the elite prevailed, the country would be strangled by the privileges the aristocratic political leadership created for themselves. Rights that heroes of the Revolution fought for would be lost, and the country would never summon the talent needed for the young nation to gain true independence. If no one else was willing to stand up for the rights of the common citizen as well as his own, Andrew Jackson would.

The Natchez Trace, ancient trail and proving ground, had now become Andrew Jackson's proving ground. Cultures and kingdoms again clashed. Jackson's future, and consequently the future course of the nation, would be altered by the outcome. With a resolve as hard and firm as a hickory tree, the scrappy survivalist Jackson focused all his talents and fought with all the resources he could muster to make sure that his plan succeeded.

CHAPTER EIGHTEEN

OLD HICKORY

"Henceforth, our rights will be respected."

—Andrew Jackson, May 15, 1815

Home waited at the end of the four-hundred-fifty-mile return march for the abandoned Tennessee Volunteers—if they could survive it. Home was the only incentive that could be found to inspire the men for even greater deprivations than they had experienced on the journey to Natchez. Jackson could take some comfort that if he too survived the long return trip on the Natchez Trace, he would finally be out of Wilkinson's trap and back at his Hermitage where he could hope to lick his wounds and regain some control.

No grand speeches were recorded, and no cannons fired to signal the departure. No one shouted "huzzah." Though the men had enjoyed a few days of early spring sunshine, the rainy spring weather even prevented young Mississippi ladies from seeing the men off.

Watching 50 sick military brothers loaded like sacks of flour onto rough baggage wagons did nothing to instill confidence in the troops. One soldier was so ill that the surgeon warned that he could not be moved. Jackson paid no attention. He said that no man who had "life left in him" would be left behind.[1280] It was faint comfort that Jackson had assured the men that if any died on the march, he would bury them with honors of war, and that if he died, he was certain they would extend to him the same honor. The Volunteers had offered their lives and fortunes on Jackson's reputation. Despite the appreciation the men had shown for Jackson's refusal to abandon them, Jackson may have doubted whether Tennesseans would ever follow his call again. The answer depended upon the outcome of the homeward march.

At noon on March 25, with 11 baggage wagons finally under Jackson's control—at least 24 less than he needed—roughly 2,000 men blended together with horses, oxen, and wagons in the best formation possible for the return march. Worn uniforms were noticeable in contrast to the day the soldiers departed from Nashville.

Wet shoes were only one part of the misery as the procession made its way toward the narrowing road into the Wilderness. The spongy mud surface of the road absorbed the wagon wheels and set a painfully slow pace, accompanied by occasional groans from jostled or sick men in the cramped baggage wagons. Some of the healthy grumbled that they had marched 500 miles to do nothing more than eat their country's rations.[1281]

Just when Jackson thought that he had reached the nadir of his career, and possibly his life, the Burr matter resurfaced. A local court officer interrupted Jackson and Coffee from worrying over the final logistics of food, wagons, horses, and fodder to serve them with an attachment for the money they held. Burr's alleged co-conspirator Harman Blennerhassett had asked the Natchez Adams County Court to take money in Jackson and Coffee's possession to pay toward a judgment Blennerhassett had obtained against Burr.[1282] Blennerhassett alleged that Burr had given Jackson and Coffee money for construction of boats for Burr's rebellion and that Jackson still held some of those funds. Blennerhassett's lawyer argued that any money his client paid to Burr could be traced to money Jackson now held. Jackson and Coffee could be compelled to use all funds in their possession to pay Blennerhassett's judgment. Under normal circumstances, evidence that Jackson and Coffee were about to leave the jurisdiction of Adams County might have required the clerk to hold Jackson's money until the matter could be litigated in court.

Those were the only funds Jackson had to buy food and medicines for his men, and he would not willingly lose his last lifeline to satisfy an old Burr debt. It was the last thing Jackson needed to worry about as his troops started north, but he could not afford to have the Burr matter nipping at his heels as he returned on the Natchez Trace. Jackson may have viewed the attempted levy on his funds just prior to his departure as Wilkinson's ace-in-the-hole to keep the Volunteers in Natchez.[1283]

Jackson refused to leave his soldiers even to file his answer. He quickly prepared a response to hand to the magistrate. Jackson's answer avoided the details of the Burr transaction.[1284] As a cautious lawyer, Jackson simply denied that he held any property belonging to Burr. Coffee also said that he held none of Burr's funds, however he admitted that Jackson had endorsed a note for Burr.[1285] That answer might have given the court a basis to hold funds, but Jackson apparently persuaded the magistrate that given the circumstances, Jackson's answer should provide sufficient grounds to litigate the matter another day.

One early biographer wrote that when Wilkinson learned that Jackson was in fact making plans to take his troops from Natchez, the ingratiating façade dropped, and Wilkinson showed his true face and the strategy behind his pleasantries.[1286] The furious Wilkinson promised that Jackson would bear "awful and dangerous responsibility" for his disobedience.[1287]

Jackson spared Reverend Blackman the shared miseries of the return march and relieved him to accompany Hynes in making advance preparations to supply the troops. Before Blackman departed camp, one of the wagon drivers asked Blackman's opinion as to whether wagons would be needed in camp by a certain time. Blackman casually observed that timing did not seem critical.[1288] The teamster waited. When Jackson returned to find that wagons were delayed, he demanded to know who was responsible. When Blackman heard a rumor that he was the target of Jackson' anger, he said a prayer for Jackson—and probably added one for himself.[1289]

The first day's march was critical to set the pace and to establish a high level of morale needed for unexpected challenges ahead. With limited food supplies and funds, the troops needed to travel about 20 miles a day to reach the Tennessee River before all the food had been eaten and meager funds spent and before the Tennessee governor could resupply them.

It soon became apparent that the march was off to a poor start. Soldiers had not traveled far from Camp Jackson before larger numbers began falling ill.[1290] Cold turned to heat, and the extra strain of the march made suffering worse for those weakened from sickness and dehydration. Or perhaps the rotten rations were to blame. Within a short span, so many men became sick that the long lines separated into near confusion as those too weak to walk could go no further, and they could not be carried.

The cavalry was directed to ride ahead to establish an emergency camp at Selsertown, near the large Indian mound about six miles north of Washington.[1291] The troops understood the meaning of the order to halt so soon after departing. They were in trouble.[1292]

Ensign Edmonson sized up the situation and allowed that some of the sick men would probably not recover.[1293] At this pace, food would run out before troops reached the Chickasaw Agency.

The next morning, the infantry renewed the march early to make up lost time from the day before. The day brought new challenges. When companies passed William Ferguson's inn at Union Town, axles on one of the wagons broke and the march had to be halted long enough for the soldiers to repair them.[1294]

As additional men fell ill, even the packed wagons would not hold the sick. Coffee added to Jackson's worries by reporting that his supplies had already been exhausted and the horses would starve if additional forage was not provided soon.[1295] Without horses, the cavalry would have to walk home, and it would not help morale for cavalry officers to watch their horses die from starvation. Coffee asked Jackson to use some of his money to purchase emergency food and fodder supplies. Jackson had traveled only as far north as Greenville. The General said that he had studied all day to find a solution, but he was forced to deny the request.[1296] He needed to save what limited funds he had to take care of the sick. It was too early in the march to tap emergency funds when men were falling ill at a high rate. Worse, rather than adding to Coffee's supplies as requested, Jackson sent a rider ahead to tell Coffee to make his packhorses and 15 bushels of his supply of corn available to Jackson to carry additional sick in the infantry.[1297]

Jackson ordered a subordinate to calculate how many mounted men would need to give up their horses for transportation for the additional men who had fallen ill. He then looked at the three horses he had brought for his own use. All of them would be needed to transport the sick home.

The General dismounted. It was a practical but also a symbolic act. The "old" man gave up his right to ride above the men on a saddle and he joined the ranks of those on foot. No doubt, there were many proffers of horses from the remaining mounted soldiers, but Jackson insisted. He had led the men into this misery, and he would not force any man to walk so that he could ride.

Officers' horses would also be needed to transport the sick. Though cavalry officers and mounted infantry were unaccustomed to marching long distances on foot, several riders would have no choice but to walk back to Tennessee to allow sick men to ride their horses.[1298]

At Jackson's age and in his constant state of poor health, the sacrifice was more than the symbolic gestures he and Benton had demonstrated as they departed Nashville. Not only would Jackson march on the same level as the troops, he would walk every step they took through mud and swamps. Any disgruntlement in the ranks began to thaw. Jackson had refused to abandon the men 450 miles from home, and now he had chosen to endure the same hardships. He was the father of the band of brothers and despite the apparent failure of the mission, the Volunteers would still claim him as their General.

One soldier wrote his friend back in Tennessee:

> "[N]ever were men treated in so shamefull a manner as the Tennessee Volunteers—The general had orders to disband them in this country, but he positively refused to do so—It is well for the honor of our State and the detachment that Jackson had the command—If any other had commanded, we would have been disgraced,—The worthy General has loaned all his horses to the sick and is now on foot—never was there a more feeling man than he is—when he despaired of getting waggons for the transportation of the sick he shed tears: by Heaven I never had my feelings so wrought upon as upon this occasion— To see him, who is worthy to command a nation, reduced to the necessity of quarrelling with petty agents of government, to make them do their duty, was too much to be born with. We have waggons for most of the sick & provisions—all or nearly all our camp equipment is left behind."[1299]

The letter was published in the Nashville *Clarion*, along with a letter from an unnamed Natchez gentleman complimenting Jackson, his officers, his chaplain, and the troops for their conduct in Natchez. He encouraged Tennesseans at home, "They return to Tennessee loaded with honor."[1300] The letters would help to begin laying the groundwork at home for Jackson's justification for what seemed to be a worthless expedition.

Reverend Blackman and Hynes reached Louis LeFleur's two-story log inn French Camp near the center of the Choctaw nation on the Natchez Trace by the 26th. They found the Volunteer's Mr. Coleman already there procuring food for the troops when they arrived. Contractors were being located to supply pork and corn. A portable horse-drawn mill was being set up to grind the corn into meal for the men.[1301] There were no suitable springs that could supply the amount of safe drinking water the men would need, and it may have been during those preparations that the old well known as the "Jackson's Well" was dug just south of French Camp.

Inside the inn, mounted deer heads on the wall and a brightly colored woven rug on the floor gave visitors the feel of home.[1302] It should have been a welcome refuge from the road, but Blackman discovered that Volunteer Thomas Taylor, one of the sick soldiers who had been left south at Pigeon Roost and had been brought back as far as LeFleur's, had become critically ill.[1303] Blackman did what he could to comfort the man. He did not record whether he followed Jackson's instructions on counseling a dying soldier by assuring him that he would improve. Most likely, the parson gave the soldier an honest assessment as he sang spiritual songs to him and prayed for him. Blackman then joined the other men who slept on blankets on the floor.

At about 4:00 a.m., a cornet woke the preacher to advise that Mr. Taylor had died.[1304] Taylor's body was buried alongside the Natchez Trace with other Tennessee Volunteers who did not survive the journey. In another mixing with the Indians, the burying ground for Tennessee Volunteers at French Camp included the grave of LeFleur's wife, Choctaw Princess Rebekah Cravat, the niece of Pushmataha.[1305]

Farther south near Greenville, Jackson struggled to prevent contagious disease from producing mass casualties on the road home. Spring storms replaced the winter hazards the men faced on the southward march. In the valleys, standing water from heavy rains and rising temperatures added to the thick humidity. One soldier became too ill to travel. Sergeant Samuel Goode, who had been one of the mutiny leaders in Nashville, was assigned to stay with the man, nurse him back to health, and catch up with the march as soon as the soldier recovered. Jackson opened access to his limited supply of funds to pay the tavern's tab. Before all soldiers moved north from Greenville, another five men became immobile, but Jackson could spare no more. Sergeant Goode had no choice but to pay for their care from his own limited funds.[1306]

The morning of March 28 began with another hard rain. Even a day's delay would add to the strain on food supplies. Despite spreading disease, the men could not avoid marching in mud up to their ankles in their farm shoes. Some soldiers fell in the mud, prompting the first laughter in several days. Others did not think it proper to laugh at the expense of mud caked brother soldiers, but any form of humor helped break the tension.[1307]

Jackson and his troops reached Big Bayou Pierre at Grindstone Ford to make their temporary camp on the banks. Jackson could recall more pleasant days as a young man near the same area at Little Bayou Pierre with his new bride Rachel. It would be discovered later that Rachel was still legally the wife of another man at the time she and Andrew are said to have been seen "bedding together in the wilderness as man and wife."[1308] The young couple had lived near Little Bayou Pierre in the Bruinsburg area for several months before returning to Nashville. Jackson's critics could see his current misery at the scene of his former indelicacy as just punishment.

Ankle-deep mud of the prior day at first seemed a luxury compared to waist-high water that greeted Volunteers at Bayou Pierre. But Jackson knew that the thick mud could act as a type of quicksand, latching on to the unsuspecting traveler from below. Those who could not extricate their horses from the quagmire had been known to leave them to die. Methodist minister Lorenzo Dow's wife Peggy Dow ignominiously added to the American lexicon by publicizing in her printed journal that travelers called such swamps along the Natchez Trace "hell holes."[1309] The Volunteers trudged ahead through them anyway, with Jackson in the lead.[1310] The march slowed to a crawl and Volunteers were vulnerable. At least there was no sign yet that Wilkinson was sending armed troops to retrieve the wagons transporting the sick.

By March 29, the infantry had reached the southern Choctaw line. Now the Volunteers would enter the Wilderness, and they could expect even more challenging conditions. Slow-moving processions would make the men easier targets for enemy Indians and land pirates. The Choctaw were also in danger. There may have been talk about the travelers who had been attacked in retribution for the Choctaw man's death. A small incident could set off a campaign that Jackson was in no position to pursue. Jackson had prepared his men for the risks of traveling through the Indian nations. He warned:

"Fellow citizens in arms, we have to pass thro savage country. Their rights must be respected and notwithstanding yr humanity is shocked at the unheard of cruelty and murder of our breatheren, still it becomes us untill we are ordered and commanded by the government to withhold our hands of vengeance least we might strike the innocent with the guilty and bring disgrace and guilt upon our heads. It is therefore ordered and commanded that neither the persons or property be disturbed by any officer or solder under my command while returning through that country."[1311]

Ahead in the Chickasaw Nation, conflict among the Indians had heated to the point that James Robertson stopped trying to restrain Jackson. Creek leaders could not control the young Red Stick faction that threatened Chickasaw as well as settlers. Even James Robertson understood that the time for peace had passed. After hearing that Jackson's soldiers would be returning home, Robertson wrote from the Chickasaw Agency begging Jackson to detour from the Natchez Trace at Choate's Stand and march through the Creek Nation to "humble" the Creek hostiles. There was no apology for opposing Jackson's plan months earlier to take the same action. Robertson thought that Choctaw would support the action, but now he was less certain about Chickasaw solidarity. There was new unsupported intelligence that some Chickasaw had participated in attacks on settlers on the Ohio.[1312]

The *Clarion* editor also suggested that Jackson proceed on to the Creek Nation.[1313] He even gave instructions that the villages of the chiefs who had been responsible for some of the attacks could be found on the first road to the right as the Volunteers made their way home. Neither Robertson nor the editor realized that Jackson was doing his best just to keep his men alive.

The weather cleared, and the road began to improve. Choctaw were nowhere to be seen. Unconcerned with the pressures of leadership or logistics, younger soldiers took pleasure in the moment. Ensign Edmonson summed it up succinctly as he wrote in his journal, "Fine road and fine day."[1314]

Jackson's biographer James Parton related the story that as Jackson walked home with the troops on the Natchez Trace, one soldier commented on Jackson's toughness, particularly given his age of 46 that the young men considered "old." As Theodore Roosevelt would later assess, Jackson and his aide-de-camp Benton "cared for a fight simply because it was a fight, and the certainty of a struggle such as would have daunted weaker or more timid men, simply offered them additional inducement to follow out the course they had planned."[1315] Jackson forged ahead through dangers that would have deterred men with ordinary sensibilities, and he did so with a singular focus on overcoming challenges. As Volunteers walked beside the General through the forest and saw Jackson in comparison to the trees around them, one soldier commented that Jackson was "tough as hickory," an especially hard wood tree on the frontier that did not bend and that seemed almost impossible to break. Volunteers knew stories or myths of Jackson's life's adventures, as young soldiers had often selected him as an example of courage. Now, they were witnessing how the accumulation of Jackson's life experiences had apparently hardened the General into a man who would not bend to any challenge. Finally, another referred to Jackson as "Old Hickory."[1316] The name seemed so appropriate that it caught on, and Volunteers soon felt comfortable speaking the name in his presence. Rather than considering it an act of insubordination, Jackson appreciated the boys' badge of respect as the only honor he might be awarded for the expedition.

By March 30, the infantry procession had reached McReaven's Stand. As Jackson would have calculated, news of the Volunteers' return march had now reached Nashville.[1317] Jackson could expect that by this point, Blount should be sending help south on the road, and Jackson would not have to bear the sole responsibility for supplying his troops. With that relief in mind, the financial concerns that had been in the back of Jackson's mind surfaced. Jackson took time to write the Secretary of War to lay the groundwork for reimbursement of the funds he was advancing to return the men home. The General advised that he had followed the secretary's orders as much as possible by returning all the public property that could be spared to the U.S. quartermaster in Natchez. As a not-so-subtle goad, Jackson assured the Secretary of War—whose order directed him to abandon his men 450 miles from home—that he was transporting sick soldiers through the Wilderness in baggage wagons as best he could.[1318]

Jackson did not reveal to the secretary that the march was proceeding slower than he had calculated. In assessing the reason Volunteers were not meeting their distance goals, Jackson found that he was the one slowing the pace. The General had begun the march in poor health, and he quickly began to wear down and slow the lead.

Jackson could not afford to delay any man reaching home as soon as possible. As in the southward march, each additional day only added to demands for food and supplies. Before the Volunteers had departed Camp Jackson, the General had first ordered that everyone should march together for safety through the Indian nations, though the cavalry would ride ahead during each day to set up camp for the arrival of foot soldiers. It was becoming clear that order would be impractical to follow. The cavalry could travel faster on horseback, and there was no need for them to consume additional food for men and forage for horses while waiting for the infantry. Even if dividing the troops put the men at greater risk from possible Indian or bandit attackers, starvation and disease were certain enemies.

Jackson altered marching orders. The cavalry would leave the infantry behind and ride as quickly as possible back to their homes in Tennessee.[1319] Jackson gave Coffee final directions before separating. Coffee could take more confidence in his own ability to lead the march after having led the men south to Natchez, but he would be returning with no illusions of waiting food supplies. It was also a troubling separation, because Coffee knew Jackson's physical condition and mental strain, as well as the risks of traveling on foot. Jackson's assurance that if he died his men would bury him with the honors of war was more than hyperbole. Coffee might never see the General again.

The separation was also troubling for the infantry rank-and-file. Horses enabled a mobile defense force and advanced scouts as well as transportation and a means of escape. Watching cavalry horses ride away made the infantry even more aware that they were on their own in the

Indian nations, surrounded by potential enemies. One of the wisecrackers who heard Jackson's remarks about eating the horses as a last resort may even have joked, "There goes supper" as he watched the horses ride out of sight.

When the cavalry set off, the Choctaw finally appeared, but not as armed enemies. As the infantry approached the Choctaw Agency, they discovered that Choctaw had arrived to receive their yearly allotments from the U.S. government.[1320] Some soldiers no doubt compared their own situation to that of the Choctaw who were being provided for amply by the federal government while federal Volunteers marched through the Wilderness without any support or apparent concern. Such a disparity prompted Jackson to include in his letter to the Secretary of War that he expected to reach Nashville in about a month, at which time, "I expect the proper officers will be furnished with the necessary funds to discharge the detachment under my command."[1321] It was a bold demand from an officer openly disregarding a direct order and still ten- days' march from known sources of provisions. Jackson found a contractor near the agency to purchase six pounds of beef and 20 pounds of hard crackers, which would not feed many men.[1322] The men would need to be reminded of the share-and-share-alike principle as they each took a meager portion.

Choctaw played ball as their families gathered for distributions, but they no doubt stopped their games to gawk at the strange appearance of ragged white troops marching through their nation.[1323] It was not the show of force that Jackson had envisioned. In an act that the Indians considered a shameful badge of defeat, even their general walked with his troops rather than ride proudly on horseback.

Unattached from the procession of wagons and sick troops, Blackman traveled ahead up to 50 miles a day on horseback. By March 25, he had reached Crowder's, a house on the road in the Choctaw Nation near present-day Thomastown, Mississippi. Crowder had married a Choctaw woman, but Blackman found the house dirty and disagreeable. Crowder swore frequently until he learned that Blackman was a preacher. The inn-keeper's newfound awareness of his improper language gave Blackman hope that the Natchez Trace might eventually be tamed.[1324]

The parson thought he would find good shelter for his next stop at John Allen's house. Allen was the son of a British trader, and he had taken an Indian bride and settled in the Indian nations. Allen was not home when Blackman arrived, and Allen's Chickasaw wife refused to speak for fear that Blackman would laugh at her broken English. Blackman pushed on to Levi Colbert's Buzzard Roost about 10 miles south of the Tennessee River. He found Colbert's house more similar to settlers' quarters, calling it a "good house."[1325] Blackman did not record whether he talked with Colbert about the march of the Tennessee Volunteers, but it was common for travelers to bring news to inns, and Colbert's assistance with the march suggests that Jackson's advance riders began laying the foundation for assistance.

Blackman finally reached the widow Cranfield's house in Tennessee, the first settler's house he had seen since he left Grindstone Ford. Any news Blackman provided of the troops' predicament would have spread throughout the Keg Springs community and on to Columbia. On returning to Nashville on Sunday, April 4, Blackman preached at the Methodist Meeting House, the congregation likely enlarged by people anxious for first-hand news of the expedition. The preacher then rode to Jackson's Hermitage to keep his promise to visit the General's family. At Rachel's request, Blackman stayed and prayed with them all night for the soldiers' safe return.[1326]

South on the Natchez Trace, Coffee and the cavalry reached the Chickasaw Agency on April 4, but rather than resting a few days as they had on the march south, the men forged on.[1327] The following day, they began their ride through the swamps known as "Brown's Bottom" and approached Chickasaw Chief James Brown's stand, where they camped among his peach trees. Here the shorter Natchez Trace military highway intersected with the old Piominko Indian trail. There was no question that the cavalry would take the fastest route on the highway.

The men had not rationed their food sparingly and supplies were growing thin. At least the relationship with the Chickasaw had already been confirmed. Coffee wrote Jackson that the men must not starve and that he would arrange somehow to get more food from Colbert as they approached the Tennessee River. Chief Brown agreed to sell Coffee 30 bushels of corn to help him reach Colbert's.[1328]

Before leaving the Choctaw Agency, Jackson found a contractor to sell him another six pounds of beef and 10 pounds of flour to help feed 1,400 men.[1329] It would be stretched vanishingly thin.

With Jackson in the lead, the infantry still plodded more than 100 miles behind the cavalry. Soldiers passed a Choctaw cemetery where long poles had been erected and steps had been built to help the departed climb their way to Heaven. The Choctaw held ceremonies at their burial grounds to let their ancestors know that they were caring for their bones. Mourners who sat near one of the graves paid no attention to the men as they passed.[1330] Instead of abandoning their houses in fear as they had on news of the cavalry's march south, the Choctaw did not even interrupt their activities to acknowledge the passing troops. Runners must have carried advance news that Jackson's troops were harmless.

Near Redbud Springs, French trader or trapper David Choate had taken an Indian wife and opened an inn on the Natchez Trace. He also raised beef cattle along some of the open plains near the Choctaw villages. Cattle had replaced deer hides as a commodity to trade for manufactured goods. Jackson would have met Choate during his travels on the Trace, and he would have known about the springs. Jackson needed food, but he lacked funds to purchase it. Choate was willing to sell Jackson beef on credit, accepting a government receipt that Jackson might personally have to pay. The infantry camped near the springs as they processed the beef for travel.[1331]

Louis LeFleur's French Camp was only a day's march north. Along the way, Volunteers would have been surprised to find another large flowing spring and a waterfall near the foot of a hill that rose over 600 feet in elevation from the Natchez Trace. Compared to the flatter areas along the road in the Choctaw Nation, the hill appeared to be a mountain.

Jackson undoubtedly also knew LeFleur. No matter how Jackson's enemies may have defamed him in Nashville or the federal capital, at least Jackson's credit was still good with his friends on the Natchez Trace. At French Camp, Jackson would have been informed of the details of Mr. Taylor's death and the conditions of any other sick soldiers recuperating at the stand. The soldiers passed by Mr. Taylor's fresh grave along the road as they marched another three miles before making camp near Little Byway Bottom. As in other areas along the road, soldiers took time to record their march by carving their names onto trees.[1332]

Moving north, the infantry neared more swamps. One of their wagons mired down in the mud and they had to strip down, jump in, and pull it out, no doubt taking the sick soldiers off first to lighten the weight.[1333] On one such occasion, a delirious soldier regained consciousness as he was jostled being lifted into a wagon and asked, "Where am I?"

"On your way home," Jackson assured him.[1334]

Choctaw leader David Fulsom's inn Pigeon Roost provided some relief as the next landmark. Soldiers considered it the halfway point on their return.[1335] The cavalry had also left sick troops there on the southbound march, and Coffee had allotted money to care for the troops when it seemed that funds would be plentiful. Now, available food was limited and funds were running low. If Jackson left any sick soldiers behind at the inn, he would also have to rely upon Fulsom's extension of credit to care for them. Jackson gave inn owners vouchers that would later be submitted to the War Department for payment, inadvertently documenting the contribution of Natchez Trace inn owners and Indian nations to the war effort.

Fulsom could give Jackson news on the rising tensions between the Creek and the Chickasaw. Colbert's attempts to pressure Creek leaders to control the Red Stick factions had only resulted in the Creek rebels threatening attacks on Colbert. Colbert and the Chickasaw wanted the U.S. government to support his war with the Creek or Colbert threatened to abandon the ferry operation on the Tennessee River.[1336] At any rate, Tennesseans had counted on Colbert to serve as a buffer between the settlements and the Indian nations and to use his considerable influence to calm the Creek. Jackson and the Volunteers would get a chance to see firsthand how close the Indians were to war. They might also get a chance to participate. Jackson could take some encouragement that the emergency supplies, horses, and wagons he had requested from Governor Blount were expected to meet them soon.

Ensign Edmonson enjoyed his twentieth birthday on the grand adventure. He noted that it was his first trip away from home.[1337] The excitement that Jackson's namesake enjoyed at the milestone in his life may have momentarily diverted Jackson's attention from more serious survival logistics.

Feeling more confident as he neared the anticipated Tennessee supplies, Jackson was 28 miles south of the Chickasaw Agency when he sent another letter to Secretary of War Armstrong. Jackson again reminded the War Department that he was marching through the Wilderness carrying sick soldiers in baggage wagons and on packhorses without the benefit of medical supplies, except those Jackson had purchased himself.[1338]

But Jackson had to be careful how much he revealed about his predicament. If Jackson wanted a new assignment, he could not leave the impression that he or his troops would require a lengthy recuperation. One advantage he could tout was that he already had troops assembled and on the march. Except for the health of the troops, Jackson was in a better position than almost any other commander to march troops to wherever re-enforcements were needed. The General assured the secretary that despite the perilous conditions, the men were healing fast. In one last attempt for an assignment, Jackson implored:

> "Should government have any orders to execute at Malden or its vicinity about the 30th proximo, I shall be happy to execute them at the head of my detachment, provided I can be informed of their wishes about the 25th Inst. at Nashville or before discharged... I have a few standards wearing the American Eagle, that I would be happy to place upon the ramparts of malden."[1339]

Within hours of Jackson's attempt to regain a positive attitude toward the war effort, a southbound Natchez Trace post rider delivered a letter with a report on Jackson's request for emergency supplies. Hynes wrote that Quartermaster William B. Lewis had informed him that Governor Blount had rejected Jackson's request.[1340] The governor claimed that he had no authority to provide additional food or equipment for the returning Volunteers. The post rider may have shared gossip from Nashville that Blount had just taken a new bride, and that he was anxious to leave the press of business for his honeymoon.

Jackson had counted on the emergency food and provisions from Tennessee when he calculated he would have enough supplies for the four-hundred-fifty-mile march. No supplies were waiting for the remaining 1,400 men in his command, and he had nearly exhausted all his resources. Jackson had never entertained a doubt that he could depend upon, if not demand, the loyalty of his old friend Willie Blount. Somehow, Wilkinson must have manipulated one of Jackson's firmest supporters. If Jackson had lost Blount's support, what did that mean for the reception he would receive in Tennessee?

Jackson could not afford to waste a second to obtain food, and if he could not count on support at home out of a sense of friendship, he could attempt to re-instill loyalty with threats. Jackson immediately penned a reply to his quartermaster Lewis as his temper boiled:

"I this moment read a letter by the Post Rider from Major Haynes, who states, you will do nothing or furnish no means for the Conveyance of the sick from the Tennessee to Nashville. This to me is unaccountable, and are these brave men who at the call of their country, rallied around the standard for its defense, be left a prey to the Vultures of the savage wilderness? Is this the reward of a virtuous administration, to its patriotic sons, or is it done by a wicked monster, to satiate the vengeance, of a combination of hypocritical Political Villains, who would sacrifice the best blood of our Country, to satiate the spleen of a villain who their connection with in acts of wickedness they are afraid to offend, and will you lend a helping hand to their wicked machinations of an Armstrong and Wilkinson ___, by withholding from us that which by law we are entitled to? I hope not. Where is the governor? Will he too sit silent and see his own citizens, that he organized that met with his plaudits for their patriotism, thus surrendered as a prey to the wolf in a howling desert"?[1341]

Jackson threatened that when he returned he would publicly name those who made the decision to refuse to rescue Tennessee's sons, and he did not want to include his friend's name among them. He intended to close there, but his anger still poured out on the pages:

"P.S. I have not rode 20 miles, the field and Staff are and have been of foot and the sick mounted on their horses, with hospital stores or medicines for the sick, only what I procured, through my own means; attempted to be dismissed, without pay, 800 miles from home; no provisions for the sick; they are to be stripped of every particle of covering, and left a pray to famine and pestilence."[1342]

Like his friend Butler, Jackson still had heard nothing from his friends in the federal capital when he needed them most. This news only added to doubts whether he would be repaid for advancing money for transportation, food and medicine.

Jackson's fury was not just personal. He was not the only one who had been abandoned. It seemed that the common soldiers who surrounded him had been left to die by unfeeling politicians and bureaucrats who argued that their elite class was better suited to lead the people and command their soldiers. Like the distant federal leaders who had refused to provide protection to settlers on the frontier, this outrageous debacle just confirmed that political aristocrats could become too distanced from the needs of the common citizen who was the backbone of the country.

Quartermaster Lewis knew that he would be the first to face Jackson's wrath when the general returned. The governor had left Nashville for Knoxville, and there would be no one else to give an account to Jackson. Lewis wrote Coffee that he had devised a plan to procure food and supplies for the men, but in the event the plan did not work, he arranged to remain out of Jackson's sight as long as possible. Lewis wrote:

"My dear friend. I regret very much it is out of my power to meet you at Columbia as I intended. Governor Blount says he is not authorized to act in this case, consequently could not authorize me to act. As soon as that information reached me (Gov. Blount is still at Knox.) I set myself about raising money by subscription for the purpose of sending on wagons to transport the sick and their baggage. I have been successful enough to raise about $600, which I hope will be sufficient to afford some alleviation to the unfortunate sick. Any thing I can do to meliorate their situation will be cheerfully accorded."[1343]

Having taken credit for performing above and beyond the call of a duty that the governor had shirked, Lewis reported another problem. Hynes had received a letter from the U.S. Army paymaster Alpha Kingsley that he had no funds to pay the men. Hynes suggested that Coffee dismiss the men to return to their homes as soon as possible.[1344]

Lewis apparently did not know that Andrew Hynes would inform Jackson that Hynes had organized the subscription plan to pay for the wagons, and Hynes had drawn up the paper. Hynes said that Lewis had only followed Hynes's orders in circulating the subscription: "Mr. Lewis carried it around town and almost everybody subscribed to it. There are near one hundred and 60 subscribers. It will be a small portion to each man to pay. Mr. Woods went to Columbia and sent them on with the provisions in them under the care of Mr. Compton. I hope they have reached Tennessee River in proper time."[1345]

At least Jackson still had some friends in Tennessee. Or Tennesseans' support may have arisen only from sympathy for the plight of the men he commanded. He would not know for certain until he returned.

On April 9, the infantry again encountered a day of swamps and high streams, where the bridges had apparently washed out from heavy spring rains. The wagons could move no farther. Troops halted the advance to cut trees and build crude bridges, not uncommon along the old Natchez Road, as wagon trains of settlers sometimes stopped, and all able-bodied men built a bridge for the wagons to cross a high-water stream.[1346]

The infantry arrived at the Chickasaw Agency on April 10 and stopped to eat breakfast.[1347] Strangely, there was no news waiting from

Tennessee or Washington City. The silence continued to prove unsettling. Though the troops were relieved to be surrounded by the comforts that the agency provided in the Wilderness, with no reassuring letters from Tennessee, Jackson could not afford to rest there. The General purchased 15 pounds of flour from a contractor and moved on.[1348]

Jackson ordered the Volunteers to continue the march to James Colbert's inn before they set camp near the large spring at Chickasaw leader Levi Kemp's house. The flow was so great that the spring attracted people from miles around to water their livestock. Locals later called the site "Jackson's Spring." Jackson secured more beef from Colbert's large herds and gave a voucher to the army contractor for 15 pounds of flour.[1349] According to local tradition, Jackson's soldiers hung beef carcasses from two large cottonwood trees overhanging the spring as the meat was stripped and prepared to transport. Without time to cure the meat with salt, the soldiers had to resort to using a quicker method by covering the freshly butchered meat with cold water to remove the heat, placing it in troughs of strong ashes, boiling it, and then hanging it on trees under fires to dry under smoke.[1350] Lower tree limbs were cut for the meat to be hung at 32 feet from the ground, the point above which the Indians believed flies would not go.[1351]

Farther north, the cavalry neared the Tennessee River, and it was time to plan for the long wait to cross. Coffee decided that the first battalion would march to the river to begin the crossing.[1352] The second battalion would wait at Levi Colbert's Buzzard's Roost inn to give the first group time to cross without having all the men and horses compete for the same space and wait in interminable lines. The spring at Buzzard Roost would also provide an ample supply of fresh water for the troops.

George Colbert later submitted an invoice to the government for ferrying 500 of the Volunteers across the river at a charge of $175.[1353] Either the decision was made to limit the cost of Colbert's ferriage or

Coffee or Jackson grew impatient and sent a portion of the men east to cross the river at Muscle Shoals.

As the infantry had arrived at the Chickasaw Agency, the cavalry neared the Tennessee Line. Coffee thought ahead to plan the dismissal of the troops. He ordered:

> "Volunteers we have mainly completed the return march to our native country where it is expected we shall be discharged from further Service. The Col. Commanding have rec'd advices from Major Hynes de-camp to the Maj. Gen.l covering a letter from the paymaster in Nashville stating that there is not funds in hand to pay off the Volunteers, but that application is made for them and it is expected they will be rec'd by the time the Maj. Gen'l will arrive at Nashville or its vicinity with the Infantry. Therefore to save public expense that would be incurred by keeping the troops embodied until Government shall be ready to pay them off, It is ordered that the several companies comprising the Regiment of Cavalry be detached to their respective neighborhoods to break off from the Regiment at the time and place as the Col. Commanding shall direct. The officers commanding companies will be careful to keep their men together and march them in good order until they shall arrive in the neighborhood of their respective homes."[1354]

A day was set to rendezvous the officers at Clover Bottom just southwest of Jackson's Hermitage near Nashville to arrange pay for the men. That appointment assumed that somehow the War Department would provide funds. Otherwise, that was it.[1355] Coffee could only offer words to thank the men for their four months' service without any battles or victories.

Cavalry soldiers returned home with plenty of their own stories to tell their families and neighbors, but their stories were not of conquerors or defenders. Soldiers who had departed Nashville as future heroes had barely survived to return to Tennessee. The danger they faced had not been enemy fire but the lack of support of the commanders in distant cities. Jackson knew that soldiers' stories of hunger and the risks of death on the marches would spread throughout communities hungry for news. He would have no control over how his leadership would be portrayed until he returned. The need to counter criticism from fireside generals added to the incentive to press sick men to march home as quickly as possible.

The infantry was still a two-weeks' march south on the Natchez Trace. So many Chickasaw houses lined a fifteen-mile stretch of the road that travelers called it the "Red Lands."[1356] Ironically, the Red Lands ended just before the mostly abandoned eighteenth century Chickasaw Old Town. Troops marveled at what had been an Indian town of a thousand houses until the Chickasaw and the Creek battled, and the British encouraged Chickasaw to spread out to farms.[1357] Over 5,000 acres had once been under cultivation at Old Town, and now, only one family lived there. The hills of the former long Chickasaw towns gave way to lowland prairies that were now swamps in the spring rains. Marching waist-deep in water most of the way, Jackson and the infantry traveled only a quarter mile an hour. The next day was no better. Volunteers crossed Twenty Mile Creek and camped near Brown's Swamp after taking two hours to cross it.[1358]

On April 14, the infantry stopped briefly at Good Spring, now Tishomingo, Mississippi, and then reached Bear Creek near the old Chickasaw fishing trap ford. During the night, a spring storm dumped more heavy rain and pelted the soldiers with hail.[1359] Levi Colbert's Buzzard's Roost was the destination for April 15. Colbert's inn would provide the landmark that gave some comfort that they were nearing the developed areas they considered civilization.

As cavalry returning to Tennessee brought news that the infantry was still on foot south of the Tennessee River and that supplies were growing thin, anxious parents and friends saw no need to wait for the protocol of a formal return. They gathered up horses and food and rushed south to meet the Volunteers.[1360] Jackson would welcome the supplies and transportation for his men, but the civilians' rescue could be portrayed as humiliating proof that Jackson had been unable to provide adequately for his men as a father or a general. It was not clear how many families would understand that Jackson did not control War Department supplies.

As Carroll marched ahead and dismissed a detachment just north of army hero Meriwether Lewis's grave, he reflected the crush of defeat all Jackson's commanders felt. Stories later spread that Carroll "cried like a baby" at the dismissal.[1361] The commander, who in less than two years would bear the brunt of the British attack at the Battle of New Orleans and who would use his own war-hero status to become Tennessee's longest-serving governor, had not yet earned the troops' respect.

Jackson arrived at the Tennessee River on April 15. While soldiers were waiting to cross, one of the men was bitten by a rattlesnake. Ensign Edmonson offered an opinion that the snake did not appear to do much damage, and he was correct. The man survived.[1362]

Hungry soldiers were elated to see Hynes's supply wagons waiting on the north side of the river. Jackson signed a provisional return for Samuel Thompson, probably an army-contracted wagon driver impressed by Jackson, for using his horse and wagon 21 days in hauling part of the sick from Natchez to Colbert's Ferry, and he dismissed Thompson to return south to Natchez.[1363] Now supplied by the citizens of Nashville and families of the men, Jackson finally no longer had to worry about his men starving. There would be only about a month's reprieve before Jackson would have to worry about the vouchers he had written throughout the journey that he knew the government would refuse to honor.

On April 17, the infantry ate breakfast at Young Factor's inn before moving on north, crossing the Little Buffalo and the Big Buffalo rivers.[1364] Jackson still had to decide how to dismiss the remaining men, what to tell them about their pay, and how to present his case to the Tennessee public.

Edmonson's company finally crossed over the boundary from Chickasaw Territory at Grinder's Stand, where they were served breakfast and then they walked to Meriwether Lewis's grave to pay their respects to the late explorer, governor, and army captain.[1365] Their own expedition had been a much shorter distance, but they now had a greater understanding for what Lewis had accomplished in keeping almost all his men alive on the expedition across the continent. A detachment continued the march north on the Trace and camped at Rhodes's house in the settlement near Dobbins's Stand, where they encountered the first white woman they had seen since Washington.

As Jackson approached Columbia with divisions of infantry on April 19, the War Department had still not given any additional indication whether it would pay the men or reimburse Jackson for his expenses. Jackson was already personally obligated to pay Governor Holmes for the tents used on the return march. He wrote Governor Holmes that funds had not been appropriated to pay the men.[1366] He would need time to arrange payment.

Jackson's men are said to have camped at Ashton Mills on the banks of the Duck River. Like the spring south of Pontotoc, the spring at Columbia that would thereafter be known as "Jackson's Spring."[1367]

Jackson had now reached the point at which he had to dismiss the bulk of the remainder of his troops, and his offer to the War Department to keep his soldiers together and march them toward the front near Canada had not even merited a reply. With no mission to justify keeping his forces intact, the General was now powerless to do anything but prepare to muster out the Second Regiment of Infantry and part of the First Regiment at Columbia.

The moment was more than awkward. Jackson faced the men who had given up the comforts of home to follow him almost 1,300 miles though bitter cold, torrential rains, hail storms, swamps, hunger, disease, and risk of death. It seemed to have been a sacrifice for absolutely nothing. Jackson's final burden was to let his men know that he did not have the funds to pay them for their service, contrary to what they had been promised. He could only ask again for their patience as he attempted to find a source of funds. Edmonson was happy just to be home, and he recorded that seeing his friends and family again was payment enough.[1368]

After dismissing most of his troops at Columbia, Jackson marched the final 40 miles north to Nashville with a few remaining infantry and guards.[1369] On April 22, he called them together on the Nashville Public Square to muster them out, formally concluding his military expedition and beginning what could have been his permanent return to "civilian life" if Wilkinson had his way.

The return to Nashville was not the victory celebration Volunteers had anticipated when they departed with fanfare, and it was far from the rush of good will they felt at their backs as they marched south. Though still full of fury, Jackson was justifiably concerned about how his neighbors would welcome a general who had taken 2,000 men from home, as it turned out, without cause. He worried about whether he would face financial ruin from the funds he had borrowed to get his men home He did not know whether Wilkinson might encourage someone in the War Department to bring charges against him for mutiny and threaten to have him shot. With the future weighing on him, Jackson was uncharacteristically subdued.

Jackson biographer James Parton wrote that unlike the grand departure ceremony that stirred the patriots' hearts, the return ceremony on the Public Square was "a pleasant little ceremonial."[1370] At least it was pleasant.

To the General's great relief, most Nashville citizens were too appreciative that he had not abandoned the Volunteers to criticize the march.

Fresh from his honeymoon, Governor Blount presided. The governor would have to answer Jackson's questions for why he had failed to provide food and supplies for the returning Volunteers, but those discussions would be held in private. In public, everyone made a show of unity and support.

The governor even brought Jackson a souvenir from his Knoxville honeymoon trip. Ladies from East Tennessee had sewn a flag to present to the General on his return to show their appreciation for his leadership, though they had likely anticipated a victory over the British as they sewed it. Stitched into the white satin were the words:

> *Tennessee Volunteers*
> *INDEPENDENCE*
> *Is to be maintained on the battle ground*
> *Of the Republic*
> *The tented field is the post of Honor.*[1371]

It was one of the few highlights of the small public affair, despite the obvious fact that Jackson's only battles had been with General Wilkinson and the disease of the Lower Country. As Governor Blount presented the colors to Jackson, he said: "A few of my female friends of East Tennessee have requested me to present to you, and thro' you to the Patriotic corps of Volunteers, you have the honor to command, the stand of colours which you will herewith receive, and at the same time to express their entire confidence that they will, both by you, and them, be ably supported, on all proper occasions."[1372]

The words "ably supported" must have stung Jackson as he heard them coming from the governor who had refused support for the Sons of Tennessee that he had ordered into the Wilderness. In private, Blount defended that he had asked the quartermaster in Nashville to borrow funds from the Nashville Bank to supply Jackson's soldiers from Colbert's Ferry to their homes, but Blount was forced to admit that the Volunteers instead had been rescued by the citizens.[1373] The fact that Blount made a written apology to Jackson five days after the return ceremony indicates the level of Jackson's lingering anger toward his friend.

As Jackson surveyed the audience that would have included political enemies ready to make the most of Jackson's loss of face, he knew that they would remember the rumor that he had claimed that the country was not big enough for both Wilkinson and Jackson. Here was Jackson returning from a failed mission as general to apparent oblivion at the same time the Nashville newspaper reported that Wilkinson was crossing Lake Pontchartrain for his conquest of Mobile.[1374] The audience would not know that Jackson had won this war with Wilkinson just by surviving, even if he lost several battles along the way.

Momentarily humbled, Jackson demonstrated restraint. He accepted the "victory" flag with gratitude and relief and offered a defense for his service and those of his men, "Although the patriotic corps under my command have not had an opportunity of meeting an enemy, yet they have evinced every disposition to do so."[1375] Revealing his overwhelming preoccupation with the consequences of his return, Jackson probably did not realize that his dismissal remarks essentially quoted from Wilkinson's dismissal letter of March 8.[1376]

Jackson wanted his supporters to know that despite returning home without engaging the enemy, the Volunteers' courage had been tested and not found wanting. *The Nashville Whig* picked up on Jackson's cue and helped protect his reputation by also asking the citizens to consider that the Volunteers' willingness to service their lives for their country was honorable even though they had fought no battles. The Volunteers had acted heroically, and so had the general who led them home.[1377]

On April 24, news arrived in Nashville that the War Department would provide funds to pay the troops. Secretary of War Armstrong said that he had sent written assurances to Jackson on March 22, and that he had expected Jackson to receive the order of dismissal before he left the area of Fort Massac.[1378] From the face of the letter, however, it was clear that Jackson was expected to be near Wilkinson's camp near New Orleans when it was received. It was also argued that the secretary's letter for some reason had been delayed in arriving.[1379] Armstrong wrote a letter of April 10 assuring that he never intended to treat Tennessee Volunteers with disrespect.[1380] The secretary confirmed that the men were to be paid and that they would be entitled to keep their firearms for their service. Jackson apparently did not question whether the letters had been written for the secretary's defense only once it became clear that Jackson would be able to return his troops to Nashville.

Benton at first continued his public fight with Jackson's quartermaster Lewis, even making preliminary arrangements to duel in Kentucky. When Lewis declared that he was too busy accounting for all the equipment from the return of the troops and that his work required a trip from Nashville, Benton publicly branded him a "gold-laced coward."[1381] Benton apologized to newspaper readers that he had allowed himself to get entangled in the dispute with Lewis at the same time his country needed him to use his talents to fight the British.[1382] Eventually, both men met on the dueling field on David McGavock's plantation not far from the place of the Volunteers' departure to Natchez.[1383]

The U.S. war effort did not suffer from the loss of Benton's time as he imagined, but Jackson still needed him for a final mission. The question remained whether Jackson would be reimbursed for expenses for transporting the Volunteers home. The angry Deputy Quartermaster Andrews refused to honor wagon masters' bills authorized by Jackson.[1384] Vouchers that Jackson had signed on the return march began to appear in Nashville along with demands for payment. Jackson was forced to borrow at least $4,000 on short order.[1385]

At Jackson's request, Benton set out for the federal capital to lobby for reimbursement of expenses for Jackson. Jackson provided Benton the incentive of a letter containing a personal recommendation that the War Department consider Benton for a position.[1386] Jackson held out hope that he would have another opportunity to serve as general, but apparently, he and Benton had already determined that Benton would not remain part of Jackson's military family. Referring to Jackson as Benton's rival, an early Tennessee historian noted that Benton, "was exceedingly ambitious, and could not brook the ascendency of his great rival."[1387] Jackson's recommendation also may have been the incentive Benton needed for the moment to move beyond his fight with Lewis.

When Benton arrived in Washington City, he learned that, as anticipated, the War Department had entered a protest of Jackson's claim for reimbursement of travel expenses for returning the soldiers to Tennessee. War Department bureaucrats invited Jackson to file suit if he felt so strongly about his right to incur expenses that had not been authorized. Jackson would be required to bear the full expense of the transportation costs of the return march from his own funds while government solicitors tied him up in court.[1388] Benton used his political and legal skills to diffuse the conflict by arguing that Tennessee citizens were solidly in support of Jackson's actions. If the War Department drove Jackson to ruin, the administration could count on Tennessee supporting the rival party. The political argument worked. Out of the administration's political self-interest, the War Department determined that it would reimburse Jackson.[1389] Now that Jackson had escaped whatever trap Wilkinson had set and had returned to his base of political support, no one wanted to be in his line of fire—politically or literally.

The reimbursement was also a signal that Jackson would suffer no further repercussions for disobeying the secretary's order. Benton reported that people in the federal capital spoke very highly of Jackson's Volunteers and that the president even inquired about Jackson's health.[1390] Jackson's political friends who visited him in Natchez—or possibly Cantonment Washington commander Leonard Covington, who traveled to Washington City in March—sent positive reports of his conduct in Natchez to the War Department, and there was discussion of offering Jackson a position as brigadier general in the U.S. Army when there was an opening. The prospects of that offer may have been calculated to prevent Jackson from riding to the federal city with guns blazing in retribution for his treatment in Natchez.

In the end, the largest gamble to that point of Jackson's life had paid off. Jackson could take further personal satisfaction that the Secretary of War's order to pay his Volunteers was directed to Wilkinson. Quartermasters Schaumburg and Andrews who had ridiculed Jackson and sent him questions to be answered under oath would now have the task of fulfilling the secretary's order.[1391]

With the cloud of prospective financial and political ruin lifted and Tennesseans celebrating his loyalty to their sons, Jackson's mood changed. He wrote Governor Holmes that the government may have neglected the Volunteers, but they had not forgotten them.[1392] Jackson gave Holmes liberal praise in his letters to the newspaper. He was silent about the support of his good friend Willie Blount.

The Nashville Whig proclaimed special recognition to Jackson:

"Long will their general live in the memory of the volunteers of West Tennessee. For his benevolent, humane and fatherly treatment to his soldiers, if gratitude and love can reward him, gen. Jackson has it. It affords us pleasure to say that we believe there was not a man belonging to the detachment but what loves him. His fellow-citizens at home are not less pleased with his conduct. We fondly hope his merited worth will not be overlooked by the government."[1393]

The General could not have summarized his perspective any better.

Taking advantage of just a few words of support from the War Department, Jackson acted quickly to make it clear that he had no intention of returning to civilian life. He published a letter to his Volunteers through the Nashville newspaper to encourage them to stand ready for their next mission.[1394] He assured his military family of his confidence that they would be called to serve in the northern campaign, and that they would plant the flag from the ladies of Knoxville on the northern battlefield at Malden. That assignment would never arrive, but Jackson would not "stay throwed." Within a few months, he would again call his soldiers to the tented fields to march into the Creek Nation.

Jackson worked to quell any stirrings of rebellion that his own harsh words might have caused. He published the War Department's letter in the newspaper so that everyone would know that the federal government had made things right—and more importantly for the General, to make certain everyone knew that it was not Andrew Jackson who had ordered the Natchez Expedition abandoned without first giving the enemy a good fight.[1395]

* * *

Three months after Jackson began his march home from Natchez in seeming defeat, lightning struck again. This time Wilkinson was thunderstruck. Wilkinson received an order from the Secretary of War to leave his post in the South and to report to General Wade Hampton on the Canadian border.[1396] Secretary Armstrong had issued the order just two days after Wilkinson reveled in Jackson's dismissal, and after Senator Crawford had made a push to remove Wilkinson from New Orleans.

Wilkinson was forced to abdicate the fiefdom he had set up in the Southwest, and he would serve under other commanders at what should have been the capstone of his career. He resisted fiercely. He had fought the move years earlier objecting, "my Constitution will not bear a norther Climate, and . . . I do conceive my Rank & Service give me claim to a separate Command."[1397] But he had lost his power to control events. For the first time in his life, Wilkinson had encountered a more determined and unrelenting challenger: Andrew Jackson.

Wilkinson ignored the order at first, remaining on the Gulf Coast until July. Secretary Armstrong prodded Wilkinson to leave his southern post. He portrayed Wilkinson's transfer along with a promotion finally to major general to provide the opportunities for the glories of command in the North. He wrote to Wilkinson, "Why should you remain in the land of cypress when patriotism and ambition equally invite you to one where grows the laurel."[1398]

Wilkinson knew better. His slow relinquishment of his southern command revealed a hope that he could manipulate change as he always had. He could not.

Benton reported to Jackson that he had heard rumors of Wilkinson's transfer when he was in Washington City in June. It was only a bit of gossip, but one that would have been important to Jackson.[1399]

The course of events would shortly prove the true reason for Wilkinson's reluctance to command on the northern front, where the heaviest fighting was taking place. As Jackson had hoped to establish, Wilkinson played the political role of a general, but it was no more than theatrics. He could not command. The battle test of Wilkinson's leadership decisions on the northern front produced disaster. Leonard Covington, the commander at Cantonment Washington who had kept Wilkinson advised of Jackson's actions near Natchez, died under Wilkinson's command in one of those battles at Crysler Fields.[1400] When the post-War of 1812 army was downsized, it was Wilkinson who returned to civilian life.[1401]

Wilkinson turned his attentions again to Mexico and moved to Mexico City. He attempted to use his Spanish connections to collect money from the Mexican government and take advantage of land title controversies. His influence had waned. Wilkinson died in obscurity and poverty. Wilkinson would live long enough to learn of his rival Jackson's success as a U.S. general.

Wilkinson's protector Thomas Jefferson would live long enough to discover that it was Jackson rather than Wilkinson who saved New Orleans from European invasion. It was Jackson who helped assure the United States' control of the Mississippi River and made it possible to fulfill Jefferson's vision for the Natchez Trace and the expansion of the United States across the western continent. Jackson would also help facilitate Jefferson's ideals for the rights of the common citizen to participate in government. After the Battle of New Orleans, Jackson took some satisfaction in news that President Jefferson finally had recognized his worth as a general by attending a banquet in honor of Jackson's victory. Jackson provided the backhanded compliment to the diplomatic president, "I'm glad the old gentleman has plucked up courage enough to at least attend a banquet in honor of battle."[1402]

The Natchez Trace had served as a proving ground for Benton too. He went on to serve again under Jackson's command in the 39th U.S. Infantry, and eventually to the U.S. Senate where he helped prevent a President Jackson from being impeached. Like Jackson, Benton spent his life pushing boundaries. Benton grew up on the border of the United States at Leiper's Fork, and convinced that border would not hold the ambition of the new nation or his own, helped push it to the Pacific Ocean.

Unlike Benton, Wilkinson's conflict with Jackson proved that he was not iron that could be sharpened from conflict. From the time that Wilkinson had failed to honor Jackson's recommendation for clemency for Colonel Thomas Butler, Jackson used his connections in Washington

City to begin a relentless campaign to have Wilkinson removed from command. That campaign intensified during the Burr affair and culminated during the Natchez Expedition. Jackson worked through his well-connected friends: Congressman Felix Grundy and Senator George Washington Campbell of Tennessee, and Senator William Crawford of Georgia. Crawford struck the final blow to demand Wilkinson's removal in a letter to President Madison on March 3, 1813.[1403] Jackson could take some satisfaction that he may have had a role in ultimately saving the nation from General James Wilkinson, the man whom Theodore Roosevelt called the most "despicable character" in American history.[1404] Old Hickory had finally defeated one of his most detested enemies, a privileged and incompetent bureaucrat, politically on the field of bureaucracy, without drawing a pistol.

Though Jackson did not dwell on the mistakes of the Natchez Expedition, it did not escape his memory. Late in Jackson's life, he wrote Amos Kendall that Hynes had possession of his letter book containing his correspondence from 1813 and that Jackson had frequently requested that Hynes return the book to him.[1405]

If Governor Blount had followed Jackson's plan to allow him to oppose the Creek hostiles in mid-1812, and if James Robertson had not undermined Jackson in pursuit of peace, Jackson's plan to bring the hostiles under control might have helped the leadership of moderate Creek chiefs regain control over their nation. The Creek civil war might have been avoided. Jackson's proposed military actions were likely to have proved more surgical, and the wider, devastating Creek War might never have occurred. By early 1813 when Robertson realized that Jackson had been correct and begged him to implement his plan, it was too late. Like tribes west of the Mississippi River, the Southeastern Indian nations still may not have survived the invasion of land-hungry settlers, but given the strong opposition for removal in the U.S., the tribes would have found more support for retaining sovereignty over their homelands. No one gave Jackson credit for having insight on how to avoid a wider conflict. However, Jackson must share the blame. The constant aggressive pronouncements he used to rally support for action undermined confidence that he could be trusted to keep his military incursions limited.

Also, in retrospect, it would seem possible that if Jackson had only delayed his return march to Tennessee until Wilkinson's dismissal order had arrived in the South, he might have negotiated proper arrangements for the return of his Volunteers.[1406] Ten-days' distance from mail in Nashville 20 to 30 days' distance from mail in the federal city, Jackson did not know whether his campaign was bearing fruit. Blount and Jackson had assured Volunteers that they would return home before warm weather threatened disease. When faced with the outbreak of disease without medicines, the general could not afford to remain at Camp Jackson as warmer weather approached. Even if Jackson had waited an additional month in Natchez until Wilkinson lost the southern command, there is nothing to suggest that the War Department would have appointed Jackson to take Wilkinson's place. Jackson had not yet proved himself in command. That test would be completed on his return march to Nashville, which would begin laying the foundation of command experience that Jackson would use finally to achieve his personal and national victory as "Old Hickory."

* * *

In early May 1815, just two years after walking homeward hundreds of miles through mud and swamp water, Jackson again returned to Nashville on the Natchez Trace accompanied by a procession of troops. The forces of war had essentially settled, and everything had changed. In 1815, Jackson rode in a new carriage fit for a general, accompanied by his wife Rachel and his young son Andrew, Jr.[1407] Jackson commanded the United States Southern Military Division, the same position that

Wilkinson had held. More importantly, he was acknowledged as the general who had commanded southern U.S. forces in the stunning victory over the British at the Battle of New Orleans. The man who had been known outside his home state as a backwoods scrapper and a Burr conspirator had been transformed into a defender of the Union and new national hero. As a double honor, Jackson's beloved Hermitage would serve for a time as headquarters of the United States Army Southern Command.

Limbs of trees overhanging the Natchez Trace served as Jackson's victory arch. According to one account, outrider soldiers rode in front of and behind Jackson's carriage to act as guards.[1408] Victory celebrations greeted the General in Natchez, Washington, Greenville, Gibson's Port, Franklin, and Nashville. The public still rewarded their victorious defenders with laurels of political office, and Old Hickory could anticipate that his journeys on the Natchez Trace might eventually lead to the President's Mansion.

Jackson may never have achieved his success without the challenges of the Natchez Expedition. Only a few months after Jackson became "Old Hickory" to his men, the Volunteers' services would be needed again, and then the test would be real. When Jackson issued his next Call to Arms in September 1813, the "foot soldiers" as Davy Crockett called them, who walked with Jackson hundreds of miles on the Natchez Trace, did not hesitate to turn out.[1409] Jackson had already proved that he would stand up even to the Secretary of War, the commanding U.S. general, and the governor to protect every soldier. He had risked personal ruin and possibly his own life to avoid leaving even the poorest soldier behind. That was all his Volunteers needed to know.[1410] Jackson had taken on his own government on their behalf and won. Along with the scar on his head that had been "knighted" by the British soldier, Jackson proudly wore the "Old Hickory" image as a medal bestowed by his soldiers.

Critics like Thomas Hart Benton's brother Jessie would claim that Jackson had acted independently from his superiors to promote his own personal interests and political career. Certainly, Jackson's self-confidence, determination to prove himself in military command, and political aspirations are traits that other successful generals have shared. Though Jackson had never led in battle, as major general of the Tennessee militia, he had borne the responsibility of protecting the frontier from attack for a decade, and he was in a unique position to understand the challenges the militia faced that a distant federal leadership did not. At a time when communication was slow, like other military commanders at distant outposts, Jackson had learned to exercise his own judgment to adjust to situations as he found them.

Jackson may have pushed the limits to earn a command, but his rush prepared his men at a time when the established system would have left civilians needing months to train after the enemy attacked. Jackson realized the advantage by reporting to Secretary Armstrong, "We had taken the field raw and undisciplined with the intention of fighting the Battles of our country and experience had taught me to know that without discipline, courage alone would not do."[1411]

When the call for service went out again, the men were no longer raw recruits, even though they had not faced battle. They had been challenged and tested under severe conditions, and most had survived. Officers had gained experience in command. The men had remained together as a "band of brothers" and they were a more effective team for the effort when they eventually faced their Creek and British enemies. The first march, which at the time seemed a complete waste, provided important leadership experience to Jackson and his officers and hardened the men into disciplined soldiers.

As Jackson dismissed his men at the conclusion of the Natchez Expedition, his first effort at leadership of a military expedition bore the stigma of an embarrassing disaster. He thought that General Wilkinson and his political enemies had tried to crush him. But he would not "stay throwed," and he fought back, as he always had. He took on bureaucrats and politicians in Washington City on his own terms, and he won.

Jackson's decision not to leave a single man behind in Natchez and the risk and personal sacrifice he took to accomplish that mission is one of the more noble chapters of his life. Certainly, Jackson hoped to avoid his own personal disaster by returning his men to Tennessee. However, if he had been a typical politician, he could more easily have sacrificed some of the sick men or cowardly ingratiated himself to the professional military leadership by hiding behind the Secretary of War's order at a time when military leaders considered themselves of a higher class than enlisted men. Jackson was not a typical politician. Because he was not, he would survive the transition from the old norms and eventually lead a new era, the Age of Jackson.

Jackson's influence went beyond just the military. Blackman, who would die a couple years after the Natchez Expedition in a freak drowning accident on the Ohio River,[1412] would never know that his and Reverend Blackburn's ecclesiastical work among these influential frontiersmen would help foster a continued spiritual revival and movement in the old Southwest Territory that would alter the western social landscape when the war had ended.[1413] Jackson's own influence on that religious movement in his choice of chaplains and creation of the environment for the ministers to proselytize community leaders on the expedition also would go unnoticed.

Once again, cultures and leaders had clashed on the ancient Natchez Trace, and the surviving leader began to usher out a political system of aristocratic leadership that had outlived its time. As his rival Senator Benton later conceded, Jackson conquered his own government.

If standing up for his rights to an overpowering British soldier as a fourteen-year-old boy and prisoner of war or his ultimate victory over the British enemy at New Orleans were not enough, Jackson's decision to lead his 2,000 soldiers back to Tennessee against all odds to prevent poor and sick soldiers from dying earned him the respect of his men and his contemporaries. And for that momentous decision in his cold tent far from home without any apparent means of support, Jackson also earned his enduring status as an American hero, regardless of the decisions he would later make as president. The Indians who saved Jackson and the Tennessee Volunteers by providing food and caring for sick soldiers were unsung heroes. Rather than receiving the "applause of the nation" for their partnership and sacrifice as Henderson had suggested, Indians would suffer additional pressure to cede their lands. Though Jackson would show acts of kindness and mercy to a few individual Indians, those who wanted to maintain their own sovereignty would suffer from the same strong will that had saved them from a British invasion. Jackson would never recognize that Indians helped make him "Old Hickory."

Ironically, Secretary of War Armstrong, who upheld Jackson's dismissal in the Natchez Expedition, would finally recognize Jackson's capabilities and arrange his commission as major general in the U.S. Army. Less surprisingly, though Jackson had spent years fighting against the superiority of a regular standing army, he accepted the position without reservation. As it turned out, Jackson only objected to the superiority of a standing army that he did not command.

On Jackson's return home from the Battle of New Orleans in 1815, as he neared Franklin, Tennessee, the townspeople stopped his carriage and asked the General to give a speech about what the victory meant. He put it succinctly: "Henceforth, our rights will be respected."[1414]

Andrew Jackson spoke of American citizens' rights, both at home and abroad. History proved him correct. His battle to defend New Orleans from a British invasion was the last time a foreign army invaded the continental United States. A number of Jackson's contemporaries believed that following his victory at New Orleans, world powers finally respected the rights of the United States as a sovereign nation. Supporters would consider that victory part of the United States' Second War of Independence. As Jackson could only have dreamed when he began his command in the blizzard in Nashville, some even compared Jackson favorably with General Washington.

Jackson also described his own rights as a common man to become a military commander and what it meant for the right of the most talented citizen of any class to rise to the rank of general or president within that nation. Jackson's struggle with Wilkinson helped pave the way for other talented American leaders, particularly those born west of the Appalachians, who were not born to wealthy, privileged, or well-connected families.

For Andrew Jackson, the difficult battle with Wilkinson and his own government during the Natchez Expedition was a life-changing event. It hardened the already combative Jackson to the more politically and militarily astute and determined Old Hickory, who defeated the British at New Orleans. And it gave Jackson a mission that would define his life and place in history. Old Hickory would fight the entrenched eastern political and business leadership to change his own government by giving common American citizens a greater role in their own destinies.

APPENDIX

Maps

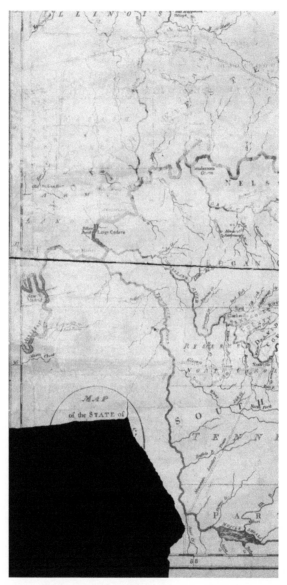

Map of Tennessee and Kentucky published by John Reid, courtesy of Tennessee State Library and Archives.

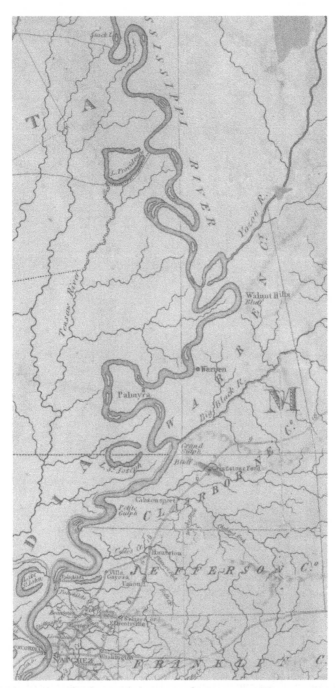

Enlarged section of John Melish Map of Mississippi Territory, 1819, courtesy
Library of Congress.

John Melish Map of Mississippi Territory, 1819, courtesy Library of Congress, shows the Chickasaw and Choctaw nations between Tennessee and the settled areas of the Mississippi Territory near Natchez.

ACKNOWLEDGMENTS

The late Jim Milan, my high school history teacher, asked a group of his students to meet at a section of the Old Natchez Trace one Saturday for extra credit. As he stood us on the remains of the road, one of the intriguing stories he told in his usual compelling style was Andrew Jackson's march on the Natchez Trace during the War of 1812. There was little published information on the subject, and Jim raised questions that I am only now able to answer with the research for this book. I had looked forward to presenting him a copy with thanks for helping instill an interest in history that I enjoy sharing.

I want to thank everyone who provided much needed assistance to tell story of the Natchez Expedition. My developmental editor Dan Crissman provided invaluable advice and chapter organization. The idea for writing this book sparked when Bill Cook described the collection of unpublished War of 1812 journals, documents, and memorabilia that he had donated to the New Orleans Historic Collection, and Rick Warwick of the Williamson County Heritage Foundation presented a copy of one of Jackson's officer's journals that had never been published. Jason Wiese helped guide me through the Cook Collection and other documents at the New Orleans Historic Collection. Others came forward to point toward unpublished resources when they discovered that I planned to write about the Natchez Expedition. I want to thank Bob Duncan of the Maury County, Tennessee Archives, Louise Huddleston of the Collier Library at the University of North Alabama, Dr. Tom Kanon of the Tennessee State Library and Archives, Mimi Miller of the Historic Natchez Foundation, Debra McIntosh of the McCain Archives at Millsaps College, Dr. Elbert Hilliard and Clinton Bagley of the Mississippi Department of Archives and History. Smokey Joe Frank and Adam Gwin of Natchez, Mississippi shared maps and provided tours of the sites where events took place. Nathan Moran of Memphis State University directed me to Zadok Cramer's *The Navigator* and provided insight on the Mississippi River and the 1811 New Madrid Earthquake. Dr. Brad Lieb, Mitch Caver, Raymond Dougherty, Bob Perry, and Bill Duckworth shared research and provided insight into Chickasaw history and culture. The late June Pollard provided copies of maps and excerpts from her lifetime of research on the Choctaw Nation. The late Robert Thrower, Tribal Historic Preservation Officer for the Poarch Band of Creek Indians, provided insight into Creek culture and history. Reverend Von Unruh provided information about Reverend Learner Blackman and Methodism of the period. With the help of Dr. Bryant Boswell and the Natchez Trace Parkway Association Living History group, Steve Abolt and the U.S. 7th Infantry Living History Association, Piqua Shawnee Chief Gary Hunt and Vice-Chief Duane Everhart, Larry Kleusner and the Discovery Expedition of St. Charles, I was privileged to experience re-creations of some of the events at the actual sites where they took pace. One of those experiences included walking at "Andrew Jackson's" (reenactor Grant Hardin's) side in the reenactment of his march through the Old Spanish District in Natchez. Hermitage curator Marsha Mullins showed patience with my many questions about Jackson. Others were generous in taking time to show me additional locations of the sites: Thomas Bowen, Jr, Bruinsburg; Tom Watts, Greenville; Emma Crisler, Port Gibson; John McBride, Brashear's Stand; Bob Heath, sites in Richland, John O'Hear, Choctaw Agency; Donna Holdiness, Redbud

Springs; and Bud Pride and Bob and Annie Perry, Buzzard Roost. Thanks to Dr. Richard Sheridan for sharing his ancestor's letters, William Higgins for sharing his ancestor's recorded insights on Jackson, and the *Lafayette County Times* for allowing me to use Sam Bains's letter they had transcribed in the 1950's. The late Kira Gale generously shared research about General Wilkinson. H. Claude Burkett shared information on Wade Hampton and Fort Dearborn. Jeff Brewer provided insight into the military regulations and customs of the time.

Thanks also to friends who agreed to read rough drafts and provide suggestions and corrections. I also want to acknowledge the good work of my friends at FoxFuel Creative, LLC in Nashville for their work on the cover design and suggestions for completing and marketing the project. Without the help of many, I would never have been able to complete the work.

SELECTED BIBLIOGRAPHY

Primary Sources

Benton, Thomas Hart

— "Journal of a voyage from Nashville (Ten) to New Orleans by the Tennessee Volunteers under the command of Gen. Jackson in the year 1813" printed in the *Clarion,* 9 February 1813, 16 February 1813, and 9 March 1813.

— "Presentation of the Sword of Gen. Andrew Jackson to the Congress of the United States" Delivered In the Senate and House of Representatives, February 26, 1855, Online version, https://archive.org/stream/addressesonprese00united#page/n5/mode/2up.

Blackman, Learner, Journals, 1812-1813, Folder 3, J. B. Cain Archives of Mississippi Methodism and Millsaps College Archives, Millsaps College, Jackson, Mississippi. A portion was transcribed and edited in, Dawson A. Phelps, "The Diary of A Chaplain In Andrew Jackson's Army: the Journal of the Reverend Mr. Learner Blackman, December 28, 1812-April 4, 1813, *Tennessee Historical Quarterly* 12, no. 3 (September 1953): 264-281.

Brown, James Papers, 1765-1867, Library of Congress, MMC-3215, v. 1-3.

William Carroll Orderly Book as recorded by Edmund Dillahunty. In private collection. Copy in Williamson County Archives, Franklin, Tennessee.

Claiborne, W.C.C., *Letter Books of W.C.C. Claiborne*, Mississippi Department of Archives and History, Vol. II, Jackson, Mississippi, 1917.

Claiborne, W.C.C., *Official Letter Books of W.C.C. Claiborne, 1801-1806*, Vol. IV, Jackson, Mississippi: State Department of Archives and History, 1917.

Coffee, John, Letters of General John Coffee to His Wife, 1813-1815, Edited by John H. Dewitt, *Tennessee Historical Magazine*, 2 (December 1915): 264-265.

Col. John Coffee's Orderly Book for 1812-1813, folder 32, the William C. Cook War of 1812 in the South Collection, MSS 557, Williams Research Center, The Historic New Orleans Collection.

Orderly Book of Brig. Genl. John Coffee, 1814-1815, folder 126, the William C. Cook War of 1812 in the South Collection, MSS 557, Williams Research Center, The Historic New Orleans Collection.

Brigadier General John Coffee's Orderly Book for the Creek War, folder 365, the William C. Cook War of 1812 in the South Collection, MSS 557, Williams Research Center, The Historic New Orleans Collection.

Crockett, David, *A Narrative of the Life of David Crockett of the State of Tennessee*, Facsimile Ed., Wright, Nathalia, General Editor, Knoxville, Tennessee: The University of Tennessee Press, 1973.

William Crawford to James Madison, 3 March 1813, https://www.loc.gov/resource/mjm.15_0105_0107/?sp=.

Edmonson, Andrew Jackson, Journal When a Volunteer Under General Andrew Jackson in 1812-1813, Mississippi Department of Archives and History, B E24j.

Ellicott, Andrew, *The Journal of Andrew Ellicott*, Chicago: Quadrangle Books,1962 reprint of 1803 publication.

Hamilton, William S., 12 U.S. Army Order Book, October 1809 - April 1812, William S. Hamilton Papers, George M. Lester Collection, 1789-1899, 1927 and, in the Manuscript and Archival Collection of the Department of Archives, Louisiana State University.

Jackson, Andrew Documents:

Bassett, John Spencer, *Correspondence of Andrew Jackson*, Washington, D.C., Carnegie Institution of Washington, 1926-35.

Andrew Jackson Papers, Online version, https://www.loc.gov/collections/andrew-jackson-papers/about-this-collection/.

Andrew Jackson Papers, Military Papers, Jan 1781- Dec. 1813, Reel 65, TSLA and 3rd Series Letters and Orders, Library of Congress

Papers of Andrew Jackson, Vol. 1, 1770-1803, Samuel B. Smith and Harriet Chappell Owsley, Editors, Knoxville: The University of Tennessee Press, 1980, Second Printing, 1987.

Papers of Andrew Jackson, Vol. II, 1804-1813, Harold D. Moser, Sharon Macpherson, and Charles F. Bryan, Jr., Editors, Knoxville: The University of Tennessee Press, 1984.

Jones, Rev. John G., *A Complete History of Methodism as Connected with The Mississippi Conference of the Methodist Episcopal Church*, South, Vol 1., 1799-1817, (Publishing House of the M.E. Church, South, 1908).

Latour, Arsene Lacarriere, *Historical Memoir of The War in West Florida and Louisiana in 1814-15, with an Atlas*, The Historic New Orleans Collection and University Press of Florida, 1999.

Love, William Calhoun Journal, Recollections Written May 20, 1872, Crittenden County, Arkansas Public Library. Copies courtesy of Dr. Richard Sheridan, a descendant.

Lussatt, Pierre Clement de, *Memoirs of My Life*, Baton Rouge: Louisiana State University Press, 1978.

Marshall, John, *Papers of John Marshall*, Chapel Hill, North Carolina: The University of North Carolina Press. VII., 1993.

McDonald, William Lindsey, Collection, Collier Library, University of North Alabama, Florence, Alabama.

John McKee, Transcribed Journal, University of North Carolina, http://finding-aids.lib.unc.edu/01194/#folder_1#1.

Nashville Reference Room, Nashville Public Library, Nashville, TN. Maps.

Natchez Trace Parkway Collection, McCain Library and Archives, Southern Mississippi University.

Nichol, Reminiscences, Notes in Williamson County, Tennessee Archives, and published 11 January 1923 in the Franklin, Tennessee *Review Appeal*.

Provine, William Alexander, Papers, B18-F1, Tennessee State Library and Archives, 1867-1935 Papers, 1552-1938, TSLA.

Ratified Treaty No. 46, Documents Relating to the Negotiation of the Treaty of July 23, 1805, with the Chickasaw Indians, http://digicoll.library.wisc.edu/cgi-bin/History/History-idx?type=turn&entity=History.IT1805no46.p0002&id=History.IT1805no46&isize=M

Roland, Richard, Letters in private possession.

Stackhouse, Samuel Hastings, Travel Diary, 1811, in private collection.

Tatum, Howell, *Major Howell Tatum's Journal While Acting Topographical Engineer to General Jackson Commanding The Seventh Military District, Smith College Studies in History*, Vol. III, Nos. 1,3, and 3, October 1921 to April 1922, 1-138.

Trimble, M.W., Personal Recollections, Issue of October 27, 1860, Transcribed. Copy at McCain Archives, Millsaps College, Jackson, Mississippi.

Unknown Author, *Old Times in West Tennessee*, Memphis, Tennessee: W.G. Cheeney,1873.

Brigadier General James Wilkinson Trial Transcript, 2 Sept. 1811, Transcribed 1976 from microfilm at the National Archives, by Henry Decker.

War Department Papers.org.

William Winian, Autobiography of William Winian, Millsaps-Wilson Library, Millsaps College, Jackson, Mississippi.

William Winian, Journal, Millsaps-Wilson Library, Millsaps College, Jackson, Mississippi.

Microfilm Records

Blount, Willie, Willie Blount Papers, Governor's Papers, 1803-1815, MF, Tennessee State Library and Archives.

Butler Family Papers, 1778-1975, MSS 102, MF, New Orleans Historic Collection, Williams Research Center, New Orleans, LA.

Robertson, James Robertson, MF, Tennessee State Library and Archives.

Records of the Cherokee Indian Agency in Tennessee, 1801-1824, Correspondence and Misc. Records, 1810-1812, The National Archives, M2809, MF, Roll #5.

Service Records of Chickasaw service members in the War of 1812, MF, M1829, Roll 1, Screen 3, National Archives, Washington, D.C.

Choctaw Trading House Records, The National Archives, MF 305 Amer. Indian Roll 9. Trading House Records 1803-04 Misc. Records 1811-1815.

Secretary of War, Letters Received By the Secretary of War, Registered Series, 1801-1960, National Archives, M21, MF.

Secretary of War, Letters Sent By the Secretary of War, Registered Series, 1800-1899, National Archives, M221, MF.

Service Records of Chickasaw service members in the War of 1812, MF, M1829, Roll 1, Screen 3, National Archives, Washington, D.C.

Legislative Petitions, Rolls 3-4, 1811-1815, TSLA.

Presidential Papers of Andrew Jackson, Reel 61, TSLA.

Correspondence

Sam Baines to Kitty. Undated letter, Transcribed by Elsie Sampson, published in *Macon County Times*, "Cal's Column," Lafayette, TN, 1952. With permission from *Macon County Times*.

William Crawford to James Madison, 5 March 1813, Gilder Lehrman Collection.

Newspapers

Green Mountain Patriot, Peacham, Vermont, Vol. IX, Issue 443, August 12, 1806, page 1.

Nashville Tennessee Gazette and Democratic Clarion, 1807-1813.

Impartial Review, Nashville, Tennessee.

The Nashville Whig, Nashville, Tennessee.

Secondary Sources

Adair, James, *The History of the American Indians*, Forgotten Books Ed., London: Forgotten Books, 2015.

Adams, Henry, *History of the United States, 1801-1809*, Reprinted ed. New York: Library of America, 1986.

Albright, Edward, *Early History of Middle Tennessee*, Gallatin, Tennessee: 1909.

Anton, Mary Sue, *New Madrid: A Mississippi River Town in History and Legend*. Cape Girardeau, Missouri: Southeast Missouri State University Press, 2009.

Atkinson, James R., *Splendid Land, Splendid People: The Chickasaw Indians to Removal*, Tuscaloosa, AL: The University of Alabama Press, 2004.

Bassett, J.S., *The Life of Andrew Jackson,* New York: The Macmillan Company, 1916.

Belt, Gordon T., *John Sevier: Tennessee's First Hero,* Charleston, South Carolina: The History Press, 2014.

Boorean, Hendrix, *Young Hickory: The Making of Andrew Jackson,* Dallas: Taylor Trade Publishing, 2001.

Borneman, Walter R., 1812, *The War that Forged A Nation,* New York:Harper Perrenial, 2004.

Brands, H.W., *Andrew Jackson: His Life and Times,* First Anchor Books Ed., New York: Anchor Books, 2006.

Breazeale, J.W.M., *Life As It Is,* Printed by James Williams at "The Post" Knoxville, TN 1842 reprinted Nashville, TN: Charles Elder: Nashville, TN, 1969.

Brown, Roger H., *The Republic in Peril: 1812,* Paperback Ed., New York: W.W. Norton & Company, 1971.

Buchanan, John, *Jackson's Way: Andrew Jackson and the People of the Western Waters,* New York: John Wiley & Sons, Inc., 2001.

Buell, Augustus C., *History of Andrew Jackson: Pioneer, Patriot, Soldier, Politician, President,* Vol. 1, New York: Chares Scribner's Sons, 1904.

Bunn, Mike and Clay Williams, *Battle for the Southern Frontier: The Creek War and the War of 1812,* Charleston, South Carolina: The History Press, 2008.

Burnstein, Andrew, *The Passions of Andrew Jackson,* New York: Andrew A. Knoff, 2003.

Burt, Jesse C., *Nashville: Its Life and Times,* Nashville: Tennessee Book Company, 1959.

Campbell, Tom W., *Two Fighters and Two Fines: Lives of Matthew Lyon and Andrew Jackson,* Little Rock, Arkansas: Pioneer Publishing Company, 1941.

Carr, John, *Early Times in Middle Tennessee*, Stevenson & FA. Owen 1857, reprinted Nashville: The Parthenon Press, Robert H. Horsley and Associates, 1958.

Chadwick, Bruce, *The First American Army, The Untold Story of George Washington and the Men Behind America's First Fight for Freedom*, Napierville, Illinois: Sourcebooks, Inc., 2005.

Chambers, Henry E, *Mississippi Valley Beginnings*, New York: G. P. Putnam's & Sons, The Knickerbocker Press, 1922.

Cheathem, Mark R., *Andrew Jackson: Southerner*, Baton Rouge: Louisiana State University Press, 2013.

City of Columbia, Tennessee, *Century Review of Maury County, Tennessee, 1807-1907, 1905*. Reprinted, Maury County Historical Society.

Claiborne, J.F.H, *Mississippi, As A Province, Territory and State, Vol. 1*, Jackson, MS: Power & Barksdale, Publishers and Printers, 1880.

Clark, Daniel, *Proofs*, https://ia800203.us.archive.org/30/items/proofsofcorrupti00clar/proofsofcorrupti00clar.pdf.

Clark, Thomas D. and John D. W. Guice, *The Old Southwest: 1795-1830*, Paperback ed. Norman, Oklahoma: University of Oklahoma Press, 1996.

Clayton, W.W., *History of Davidson County, Tennessee*. Philadelphia, J.W. Lewis & Co., 1880.

Clements, Paul, *Chronicles of the Cumberland Settlements: 1799-1796*, Nashville: The Foundation of William and Jennifer Frist and by Paul Clements, 2012.

Colyar, A.S., *Life and Times of Andrew Jackson*, Nashville, Tennessee: Marshall & Bruce Company, 1904.

Corlew, Robert E., *A History of Dickson County: from the earliest times to the present*. Nashville: Dickson County Historical Society and Tennessee Historical Commission, 1956.

Cramer, Zadok, *The Ohio and Mississippi navigator: compromising an ample account of those beautiful rives, from the head of the former, to the mouth of the latter: a particular description of the several towns, posts, caves, ports, harbours &c. On their banks, and accurate directions*, 7th Edition, https://archive.org/details/navigatorcontain1811cram.

Curtis, James C., *Andrew Jackson and the Search for Vindication*, Boston: Little Brown and Company, 1976.

Cusick, James G., *The Other War of 1812*, Athens, GA: The University of Georgia Press, Paperback edition, 2007.

Daniels, Jonathan, *The Devil's Backbone*, New York, McGraw-Hill Book Company, Inc., 1962.

Davidson, Donald, *The Tennessee, Volume One, The Old River: Frontier to Secession*, Southern Classics Series, Nashville: J.S. Sanders & Company, 1946.

Davis, Burke, *Old Hickory: A Life of Andrew Jackson*, The Dial Press, New York, 1977.

Davis, Edwin Adams and William Randolph Hogan, *The Barber of Natchez*, Baton Rouge and London: Louisiana State University, 1954, 1971.

Davis, Louise Littleton, *Nashville Tales*, Gretna, Louisiana: Pelican Publishing Company, 1982.

Davis, William C., *A Way Through the Wilderness*, LSU Press Edition, Baton Rouge, 1995.

Debo, Angie, *A History of the Creek Indians, the Road to Disappearance*, Third Printing. Norman, Oklahoma: University of Oklahoma Press, 1979.

DeConde, Alexander. *This Affair of Louisiana*, New York: Charles Scribner's Sons, 1976.

De Lussat, Pierre Clement, *Memoirs of My Life*, Edited by Robert D. Bush, Louisiana State University Press, 1978.

Dick, Everett, *The Dixie Frontier: A Social History*, Paperback Ed., Norman, Oklahoma: University of Oklahoma Press, 1948.

Drake, Benjamin, *Life of Tecumseh and His Brother the Prophet*, Cincinnati: E. Morgan & Company,1841.

Eaton, John Henry Eaton, and John Reid, The Life of Major General Andrew Jackson, 3d Ed, Philadelphia: McCarthy & Davis, 1828.

Elliott, Lizzie Porterfield, *Early History of Nashville*, Nashville, Copy at Nashville Public Library.

Ellis, Mary H., *Cannonballs and Courage: The Story of Port Gibson*, Virginia Beach, Virginia: The Donning Company Publishers, 2003.

Elting, John R., *Amateurs, TO ARMS!, A Military History of the War of 1812*, Paperback ed., Chapel Hill, North Carolina: Da Capo Press, 1995.

Ethridge, Robbie, *From Chicaza to Chickasaw: The European Invasion and the Transformation of the Mississippian World, 1540-1715*, Chapel Hill, North Carolina: University of North Carolina Press, 2010.

Finger, John R., *Tennessee Frontiers: Three Regions in Transition*, Bloomington and Indianapolis: Indiana University Press, 2001.

Gibson, Arrell M., *The Chickasaws*, Norman, OK: University of Oklahoma Press, 1972.

Gibson, James N., *A War Without Rifles: The 1782 Militia Act and the War of 1812,* Bloomington, Indiana: Archway Publishing, 2016.

Gilbert, Ed, *Frontier Militiaman In The War of 1812.* Oxford, UK: Osprey Publishing Ltd., 2008.

The Goodspeed Histories of Maury, Williamson, Rutherford, Wilson, Bedford & Marshall Counties of Tennessee, 1886. Reprinted Columbia, Tennessee: Woodward & Stinson Printing Co., 1971.

Jane Lucas De Grummond and Ronald R. Morazan, *The Baratarians and the Battle of New Orleans, with Biographical Sketches of the veterans of the Battalion of Orleans, 1814-1815,* Baton Rouge: Legacy Publishing Company, Inc., 1961.

Guild, Jo. C., *Old Times in Tennessee*, Nashville: Tavel, Eastman & Howell, 1878.

Halbert, H.S. and T.H. Ball, *The Creek War of 1813 and 1814,* 1895, reprinted Tuscaloosa: University of Alabama Press, Frank L. Owensby, Editor, 1969.

Hardeman, Nicholas Perkins, *Wilderness Calling: The Hardeman Family In the American Westward Movement, 1750-1900,* Knoxville, Tennessee: The University of Tennessee Press, 1977.

Hawke, David Freeman, *Everyday Life in Early America,* Paperback Ed., New York: Perennial, 1988.

Hay, Thomas Robson and M. R. Werner, *The Admirable Trumpeter: A Biography of General James Wilkinson,* The Scholar's Bookshelf. Cranbury, New Jersey: 2006.

Haynes, Robert V., *The Natchez District and the American Revolution,* Jackson, Mississippi: University Press of Mississippi, 1976.

Heidler, David S. and Jeanne T. Heidler, *Old Hickory's War: Andrew Jackson and the Quest for Empire,* Mechanicsburg, Pennsylvania: Stackpole Books, 1996.

Heller, J. Roderick, III, *Democracy's Lawyer: Felix Grundy of the Old Southwest,* Baton Rouge, LA: Louisiana State University Press, 2010.

Hickey, Donald R., *The War of 1812: A Forgotten Conflict,* Urbana and Chicago: Paperback Ed., University of Illinois Press,1995.

Holland, James D., *Andrew Jackson and the Creek War: Victory at Horseshoe Bend,* University of Alabama Press, 1968.

Howard, Hugh, *Mr. and Mrs. Madison's War: America's First Couple and the Second War of Independence,* New York: Bloomsbury Press, 2012.

Hudson, Angela Pulley, *Creek Paths and Federal Roads: Indians, Steelers, ad Slaves and the Making of the American South,* Chapel Hill, North Carolina, University of North Carolina Press: 2010.

Hunter, Clark, *The Life and Letters of Alexander Wilson,* Philadelphia: American Philosophical Society, 1983.

Inskeep, Steve, *Jacksonland: President Andrew Jackson, Cherokee Chief John Ross, and A Great American Land Grab,* New York: Penguin Press, 2015.

Irving, Washington, *Knickerbocker's History of New York, Vol. II,* Pocket Ed., New York and London: G. P. Putnam's Sons.

Isenberg, Nancy, *Fallen Founder: The Life of Aaron Burr,* Paperback Ed., New York: Penguin Books, 2007.

James, Marquis, *The Life of Andrew Jackson,* The Bobbs-Merrill Company, Part One, 1938.

James, Marquis, *Andrew Jackson: The Border Captain*, Indianapolis: The Bobbs-Merrill Company, 1933.

James, William Dobein, *Swamp Fox: General Francis Marion and his Guerrilla Fighters of the American Revolutionary War*, USA, 2013.

Jenkins, John S., A.M., *The Life of Andrew Jackson*, Buffalo, New York: Derby & Hewson, Auburn, 1847.

Johnson, Timothy D., *Winfield Scott: The Quest for Military Glory*, Lawrence, Kansas: University Press of Kansas, 1998.

Jones, Rev. John G., *A Complete History of Methodism*, Vol. 1, 1799 to 1817, Nashville, TN; Dallas, TX, Publishing House of the M.E. Church South, 1908.

Kane, Harnett T., *NATCHEZ on the Mississippi,* New York: Bonanza Books, 1967.

Kanon, Tom, *Tennesseans At War 1812-1815: Andrew Jackson, The Creek War, and the Battle of New Orleans*, Tuscaloosa: The University of Alabama Press, 2014.

Kincaid, Robert L., *The Wilderness Road: The path of empire in the conquest of the Great West,* Middlesboro, Kentucky: Bobbs-Merrill Company, 1947, reprinted, Mrs. Robert L. Kinkaid, 1973.

Langguth, A.J., *Union 1812; The Americans Who Fought the Second War of Independence,* Paperback ed., New York: Simon & Schuster Paperbacks, 2007.

Latimer, Jon, *1812, War with America,* Paperback Ed., Cambridge, Massachusetts, The Belknap Press of Harvard University Press, 2007.

Lincecum, Gideon, *Pushmataha: A Choctaw Leader and His People,* Tuscaloosa: The University of Alabama Press, 2004.

Linklater, Andro,

—*An Artist in Treason: The Extraordinary Double Life of General James Wilkinson,* New York: Walker Publishing Company, 2009.

—*Measuring America, How An Untamed Wilderness Shaped the United States and Fulfilled the Promise of Democracy,* New York: Walker and Company, 2002.

Livingston, Melinda Burford and Charles A. Rich, *A Treasure on the Trace-The French Camp Story,* Baton Rouge: French Camp Association, 1996.

Logan, John A., *The Volunteer Soldier of America,* R.S. Peale & Company, Chicago and New York, 1887.

Lomask, Milton,

—*Aaron Burr: The Years from Princeton to Vice President, 1756-1805,* Fararr, Straus, Giroux, 1979.

—*Aaron Burr: The Conspiracy and Years of Exile. 1805-1836,* New York: Farrar, Straus, Giroux, 1982.

McCallum, James, *Early History of Giles County,* The Pulaski Citizen, Pulaski, Tenn. 1928.

McDonald, Robert M. S. Ed., *Thomas Jefferson's Military Academy: Founding West Point,* Charlottesville: University of Virginia Press, 2004.

McWhitney, Grady, *Cracker Culture: Celtic Ways in the Old South,* Tuscaloosa: The University of Alabama Press, 1988.

Meacham, Jon, *American Lion: Andrew Jackson in the White House,* New York: Random House, 2008.

Meacham, Jon, *Thomas Jefferson: The Art of Power.* Random House Trade Paperback Ed. New York: Random House 2013.

Monette, John, W., *M.D., History of the Discovery and Settlement of the Valley of Mississippi,* New York: Harper & Brothers, 1846.

Moore, Edith Wyatt, *Natchez Under the Hill,* Natchez, Mississippi: Southern Historical Publications, 1958.

Paige, Amanda L., Fuller L Bumpers, Daniel F. Littlefield, Jr., *Chickasaw Removal,*Ada, Oklahoma: The Chickasaw Press, 2010.

Parton, James,

—*Life of Andrew Jackson*, New York: Mason Brothers,1863.

—*The Life and Times of Aaron Burr*, Vol. 1, Boston: James R. Osgood and Company, 1872.

Pate, James P , *The Reminiscences of George Strother Gaines, Pioneer and Statesman of Early Alabama and Mississippi*, 1805-1843, Tuscaloosa: The University of Alabama Press, 1998.

Polk, Noel, Ed., *Natchez Before 1930*, Jackson, Mississippi: University Press of Mississippi, 1989.

Putnam, A.W., *History of Middle Tennessee; or, Life and Times of Gen. James Robertson, 1859,* Reprint Edition, Arno Press & The New York Times, 1971.

Ratner, Lorman A., *Andrew Jackson and His Tennessee Lieutenants: A Study in Political Culture,* West Port, CT: Greenwood Press, 1997.

Ray, Kristofer, *Middle Tennessee, 1775-1825: Progress and Popular Democracy on the Southwestern Frontier,* Knoxville, TN: The University of Tennessee Press, 2007.

Remini, Robert V.,

—*Andrew Jackson and His Indian Wars,* New York: Viking, 2001.

—*Andrew Jackson and the Course of American Empire 1767-1821,* New York: Harper & Row, 1977.

—*The Life of Andrew Jackson*, New York: Harper & Row, 1988.

Ritten, Louis N., *Fort Adams: Wilkinson County, Mississippi, Forgotten Linchpin of the Lower Mississippi Valley*, Louis N. Ritten, 2013.

Roosevelt, Theodore,

—*American Statesman: Thomas Hart Benton,* Cambridge, Massachusetts: The Riverside Press, 1896.

—*The Winning of the West,* Presidential Ed., New York: G.P. Putnam's Sons, Vol III, 1894.

Ross, James, *Life and Times of Elder Reuben Ross,* https://ia600306.us.archive.org/25/items/lifetimesofelder00ross/lifetimesofelder00ross.pdf.

Rowland, Dunbar Rowland, *Encyclopedia of Mississippi History*, "Fort Dearborn," Vol 1, Madison, WI: Selwyn A. Brant, 1907.

Rowland, Mrs. Dunbar,

—*Mississippi Territory in the War of 1812,* Reprinted from Publications of the Mississippi Historical Society, Centenary Series, Volume IV 1921, Reprinted, Baltimore, MD: Genealogical Publishing Company, 2005.

—*Andrew Jackson's Campaign Against the British, or the Mississippi Territory in the War of 1812: Concerning The Military Operations of the Americans, Creek Indians, British, and Spanish, 1813-1815,* Freeport, New York: Books for Library Press, 1971, Reprint from the 1926 Edition.

—*Mississippi Territory in the War of 1812. 1921. Reprinted from Publications of the Mississippi Historical Society*, Centenary Series, Volume IV, Baltimore: Genealogical Publishing Company, 1968.

Sandlin, Lee, *Wicked River: The Mississippi*, New York: Pantheon Books, 2010.

Sansing, David N., Sim C. Callon and Carolyn Vance Smith, *Natchez, An Illustrated History*, Natchez, Mississippi: Plantation Publishing Company, 1992.

Schlesinger, Arthur M., Jr., *The Age of Jackson*, Konecky & Konecky, Old Saybrook, CT 1945, 1971.

Scott, Winfield, *Autobiography of Lieut-Gen. Winfield Scott*, Sheldon & Company Publishers, New York, 1864, https://ia800500.us.archive.org/15/items/memoirsoflieutge00inscot/memoirsoflieutge-00inscot.pdf.

Skeen, C. Edward, *John Armstrong, Jr., 1758-1843: A Biography*, New York: Syracuse University Press, 1981.

Sparks, W.H., *The Memories of Fifty Years,* Third Edition, Macon, GA: J.W. Burke & Co., 1872. Online. Google Books.

Stewart, David O., *American Emperor: Aaron Burr's Challenge to Jefferson's America,* New York: Simon & Schuster Paperbacks, 2011.

Sugden, John, *Tecumseh, A Life*, Paperback Ed., New York: Henry Holt and Company, 1997.

Syndor, Charles S., *A Gentleman of the Old Natchez Region, Benjamin L.C. Wailes*, Durham, North Carolina: Duke University Press, 1938,

Thomas, Miss Jane, *Old Days in Nashville*. Nashville: Publishing House Methodist Episcopal Church, South, 1897, A Facsimile Reproduction Nashville, TN: Charles Elder.

Vickery, Paul, *Jackson: The Iron-Willed Commander*, Nashville: Thomas Nelson Publishers, 2012.

Waldo, Samuel Putnam, *Civil and Military History of Andrew Jackson late Major-General in the Ar1my of the United States, and Commander-In-Chief of the Southern Division,* P.M. Davis, New York, 1825. Online edition, https://archive.org/details/civilmilitaryhis00waldo.

Watson, Samuel J., *Jackson's Sword: The Army Officer Corps on the American Frontier 1810-1821,* Lawrence, Kansas: University Press of Kansas, 2012.

Watson, Thomas, *The life and times of Andrew Jackson*, Thomson, Georgia: The Jeffersonian Publishing Company, 1912.

Wheelan, Joseph, *Jefferson's Vendetta: The Pursuit of Aaron Burr and the Judiciary,* New York: Carroll & Graf Publishers, 2005.

Wilkinson, James,

—*Burr's Conspiracy Exposed and General Wilkinson Vindicated. 1811*, Online edition https://archive.org/details/burrsconspiracye00inwilk

—*Memoirs of My Own Times*, I. (Philadelphia 1816) Online edition https://ia800201.us.archive.org/22/items/memoirsofmyownti01wilk/memoirsofmyownti01wilk.pdf.

Winston, E.T., *Story of Pontotoc*, Part 1, The Chickasaw, Pontotoc Progress Print, 1931.

Works Progress Administration, *Mississippi: The WPA Guide to the Magnolia State,* New York: Viking Press 1938, reprinted by University Press of Mississippi, 1988.

Yates, W.C., *Tales of a Tennessee Yeoman,* Franklin, TN: W.C. Yates, 1991.

Young, Callie B., Editor, *From These Hills,* Pontotoc County Library.

Tennesseans in the War of 1812 (Nashville: Byron Sister & Associates, 1992).

Periodicals

Boom, Aaron M., "John Coffee: Citizen Soldier," *Tennessee Historical Quarterly* XXII, no. 3 (September1963): 223-237.

Braden, Guy B.,

—,"The Colbert's and the Chickasaw Nation," *Tennessee Historical Quarterly,* pt. 1, XVII, no. 3 (September 1952): 222-249.

—"The Colbert's and the Chickasaw Nation," *Tennessee Historical Quarterly,* pt. 2, XVII, no. 4 (December 1952): 318-335.

Chappell, Gordon T., "The Life and Activities of General John Coffee," *Tennessee Historical Quarterly* I, no. 2 (June 1942):125-146.

Clifton, Frances, "John Overton as Andrew Jackson's Friend," *Tennessee Historical Quarterly* XI, no. 1 (March 1952): 23-40.

Corbitt, D. C. and Roberta Corbitt,

—- "Papers from the Spanish Archives Relating to Tennessee and the Old Southwest, 1783-1800," *The East Tennessee Historical Society's Publications*, no. 9: (1937): 111-142.

—- "Papers from the Spanish Archives Relating to Tennessee and the Old Southwest, 1783-1800," *The East Tennessee Historical Society's Publications* No. 10, (1938) :136-137.

Cotterill, R.S., "The Natchez Trace," *Tennessee Historical Magazine*, Vol. 7, No. 1 (April, 1921) : 27-35.

Ely, James W. Jr., "Andrew Jackson as Tennessee State Court Judge, 1798-1804," *Tennessee Historical Quarterly* XL, no. 2 (Summer 1981): 144-157.

Gower, Hershel, "Belle Meade: Queen of Tennessee Plantations," *Tennessee Historical Quarterly* XXII, no. 3, (September 1963): 203-222.

Guice, John D. W., "Old Hickory and the Natchez Trace," *The Journal of Mississippi History* LXVIX, no. 2 (September 2007):167-182.

Harlan, Louis R., "Public Career of William Berkley Lewis" *Tennessee Historical Quarterly* II, no. 1 (March 1984): 7-8.

Harrell, Laura D.S., "Horse Racing in the Old Natchez District, 1783-1830," *The Journal of Mississippi History* XIII, no. 3 (July 1951):123-137.

Hickey, Donald R., "Andrew Jackson and the Army Haircut: Individual Rights vs. Military Discipline," Tennessee Historical Quarterly, XXXV, no. 4 (Winter 1976): 365-375.

"The United States Army vs. Long Hair: The Trials of Colonel Thomas Butler, 1801-1805." *Pennsylvania Magazine of History and Biography* 101 (October 1977): 462-474.

Howell, R. B., "Early Corporate Limits of Nashville," *Tennessee Historical Magazine* II, no. 2 (June 1916): 110.

Kanon, Tom, "The Kidnapping of Martha Crawley and Settler-Indian Relations Prior to the War of 1812, *Tennessee Historical Quarterly*, (Spring, 2005): 3-23.

Kinard, Margaret, "Frontier Development of Williamson County," *Tennessee Historical Quarterly* VIII, no. 2 (June,1949): 127-153.

Leach, Douglas Edward, "John Gordon of Gordon's Ferry," *Tennessee Historical Quarterly* XVIII, no. 4 (December 1959): 322-344.

"Letters of General John Coffee to His Wife, 1813-1815," *Tennessee Historical Magazine* 2, no. 4 (December 1916): 264-298.

Marshall, Park, "The True Route of the Natchez Trace," *Tennessee Historical Magazine*, 1, no. 3 (September 1915): 173-182.

Owsley, Harriet Chappell, "The Marriages of Rachel Donelson," *Tennessee Historical Quarterly* XXXVI, no. 4 (Winter 1977): 479-492.

Phelps, Dawson A.,

—"The Chickasaw Agency," *The Journal of Mississippi History* XIV, no. 2 (1952):119-137.

—"Stands and Travel Accommodations on the Natchez Trace," *The Journal of Mississippi History* XI, no. 1 (January 1949): 1-54.

—— "The Natchez Trace: Indian Trail to Parkway," *Tennessee Historical Quarterly* XXI, no. 1 (March 1962) :203-218.

Posey, Walter Brownlow, "The Earthquake of 1811 and Its Influence On Evangelistic Methods in the Churches of the Old South," *Tennessee Historical Magazine*, Series II, 1, no. 2 (January 1931): 107-114.

Queener, V.M., "Gideon Blackburn," The *East Tennessee Historical Society's Publication,* 6 (1934): 12-28.

Storm, Colton, Ed., "Up the Tennessee in 1790: The Report of Major John Doughty to the Secretary of War," *The East Tennessee Historical Society's Publications,* 17 (1945):119-132.

Toplovich, Ann, "Marriage, Mayhem, and Presidential Politics: The Robards-Jackson Backcountry Scandal" *Ohio Valley History*, The Filson Historical Society and Cincinnati Museum Center, Volume 5, Number 4, (Winter 2005): 3-22.

Williams, Samuel C., "Tennessee's Frontier Militia Expedition (1803), *Tennessee Historical Magazine*, VIII, no. 3, (October 1924): 179-190.

Young, Rogers W., "Andrew Jackson's Movements on the Lower Natchez Trace During and After the War of 1812," *The Journal of Mississippi History*, X, no. 2, (April 1948): 87-103.

Monographs

Bowers, Laura, "The Choctaw Agency," On file at the Natchez Trace Parkway Headquarters, Tupelo, Mississippi.

Cook, Helen Sawyers, "Rev. Gideon Blackburn," On file at Williamson County, Tennessee Archives.

Cook, Steve, Buddy Palmer, Julian Riley, Historic "Chickasaw Village Locations," 1980. On file at the Lee County Public Library, Tupelo, Mississippi.

Farrell, W. E., "Andrew Jackson, 7th President of the United States and the Jacksons of Ballybay, 1803-1824."

Madden, Robert R., "The History of Grindstone Ford," On file at the Natchez Trace Parkway Headquarters, Tupelo, Mississippi.

Mauldin, Katie Durelle, "Historical Spots In Pontotoc County," Thesis submitted to the University of Mississippi, Oxford, Mississippi, June, 1931. On file at the Pontotoc, Mississippi Public Library.

Phelps, Dawson A., "The Natchez Trace in Colbert County, Alabama." On file at the Natchez Trace Parkway Headquarters, Tupelo, MS.

Sheridan, Dr. Richard C., "Richard Rowland (1791-1872) and His Family," 1975.

Unknown author, Brief Notes on Names and Places, Pontotoc County History, "Of Cate Springs." On file at the Pontotoc, Mississippi Public Library Loose Files.

Unruh, Rev. Von, "Rev. Learner Blackman, Andrew Jackson's Chaplain on the Natchez Expedition, December 1812 - April 1813."

Miscellaneous

Time, Special Edition, *Andrew Jackson, An American Populist*, by Jon Meacham, 11-16.

Higgins, William, Conversation with the author, regarding the journal of his ancestor David Higgins, who served under John Coffee during the Creek War campaign.

NOTE ABBREVIATIONS

Benton, Thomas Hart, "Journal of a voyage from Nashville (Ten) to New Orleans by the Tennessee Volunteers under the command of Gen. Jackson in the year 1813," **Benton Journal**

Blackman, Learner, Journals, Original, Millsaps College, **Blackman Journal**, Transcribed Version, at Millsaps College, **TV**, and version transcribed by Dawson Phelps, cited to the *Tennessee Historical Quarterly*, THQ. (Note that not all the journal was transcribed for the portion published in the THQ).

Coffee John Papers

Coffee, John, Letters of General John Coffee to His Wife, 1813-1815, Edited by John H. Dewitt, Tennessee Historical Magazine, 2 (December 1915) :264-295. **THM**.

Col. John Coffee's Orderly Book for 1812-1813, folder 32, the William C. Cook War of 1812 in the South Collection, MSS 557, Williams Research Center, The Historic New Orleans Collection. **CO**.

Cramer, Zadok, *The Ohio and Mississippi navigator: compromising an ample account of those beautiful rives, from the head of the former, to the mouth of the latter: a particular description of the several towns, posts, caves, ports, harbours &c. On their banks, and accurate directions.* 7th Edition, https://archive.org/details/navigatorcontain1811cram. **Cramer.**

Edmonson, Andrew Jackson, Journal When a Volunteer Under General Andrew Jackson in 1812-1813, Mississippi Department of Archives and History, B E24j. **Edmonson Journal.**

Halbert, H.S. and T.H. Ball, *The Creek War of 1813 and 1814*, 1895, reprinted by University of Alabama Press, Frank L. Owensby, Editor, 1969. **HB**.

Hamilton, William S., 12 U.S. Army Order Book, October 1809 - April 1812, William S. Hamilton Papers, George M. Lester Collection, 1789-1899, 1927 and, in the Manuscript and Archival Collection of the Department of Archives, Louisiana State University. **WSH**

Jackson, Andrew Documents.

Bassett, John Spencer, *Correspondence of Andrew Jackson*, Washington, D.C., Carnegie Institution of Washington, 1926-35. **CAJ I**

Andrew Jackson Papers, Online version, https://www.loc.gov/collections/andrew-jackson-papers/about-this-collection/. **LC**. (These documents can now be found by date; therefore, I have not listed page numbers from earlier indexing that no long applies).

Andrew Jackson Papers, Military Papers, Jan 1781- Dec. 1813, Reel 65, TSLA and 3rd Series Letters and Orders, Library of Congress. **JMP**.

Papers of Andrew Jackson, Vol. 1, 1770-1803, Samuel B. Smith and Harriet Chappell Owsley, Editors, Knoxville, The University of Tennessee Press, 1980, Second Printing, 1987. **PAJ I**.

Papers of Andrew Jackson, Vol. II, 1804-1813, Harold D. Moser, Sharon Macpherson, and Charles F. Bryan, Jr., Editors, Knoxville, The University of Tennessee Press, 1984. **PAJ II**.

James, Marquis, *Andrew Jackson: The Border Captain*, Indianapolis: The Bobbs-Merrill Company, 1933. **MJ**.

Jones, Rev. John G., *A Complete History of Methodism as Connected with The Mississippi Conference of the Methodist Episcopal Church, South*,

Vol 1., 1799-1817, (Publishing House of the M.E. Church, South, 1908). **MIM.**

Linklater, Andro, *An Artist in Treason: The Extraordinary Double Life of General James Wilkinson*, (New York: Walker Publishing Company, 2009). **LL.**

Lomask, Milton,

Aaron Burr: The Years from Princeton to Vice President, 1756-1805, Fararr, Straus, Giroux, 1979. **Lomask 1756-1805**.

Aaron Burr: The Conspiracy and Years of Exile. 1805-1836, New York: Farrar, Straus, Giroux, 1982. **Lomask 1805-1836**.

John McKee, Transcribed Journal, University of North Carolina, http://finding-aids.lib.unc.edu/01194/#folder_1#1. **McKee Journal**.

Nashville *Tennessee Gazette* and *Democratic Clarion*, 1807-1813. ***Clarion***.

Parton, James, *Life of Andrew Jackson*. Mason Brothers, New York, 1863. **Parton Condensed**.

Putnam, A.W., History of Middle Tennessee; or, Life and Times of Gen. James Robertson, 1859, Reprint Edition, Arno Press & The New York Times, 1971. **Putnam**.

Searcy, Robert, apparent writer of journal "Departure from Nashville, A Journal of the Trip down the Mississippi" found in I:CAJ, **Searcy Journal**.

Secretary of War, Letters Received By the Secretary of War, Registered Series, 1801-1960, National Archives, MF, **LR**

Secretary of War, Letters Sent By the Secretary of War, Registered Series, 1800-1899, National Archives, MF, **LS**

Stackhouse, Samuel Hastings, Travel Diary, 1811, in private collection. **Stackhouse Travel Journal**.

Brigadier General James Wilkinson Trial Transcript, 2 Sept. 1811, Transcribed 1976 from microfilm at the National Archives, Historical Society of Fredricksburg, MD. **WCM**.

William Winian, Autobiography of William Winian, Millsaps-Wilson Library, Millsaps College, Jackson, Mississippi. **Winian Autobiography**. William Winian, Journal, Millsaps-Wilson Library, Millsaps College, Jackson, Mississippi. **Winian Journal.**

<<<<>>>

ENDNOTES

1 Parton 1:362. William Winian Journal, Millsaps-Wilson Library, Millsaps College, Jackson, Mississippi.

2 The weather of the day was described in the *Clarion*, 15 December 1812.

3 14 January 1808, as quoted in Henry Adams, *History of the United States, 1801-1809*. Reprinted Library of America, 1986, 975.

4 Adams, Henry, *History of the United States*, 1003.

5 Napoleon to Champagny, November 15, 1807, quoted, Ibid.

6 See Conde De Galvaez to Miro, 20 May 1786 with instructions to give Indian nations weapons under the guise of trade to avoid revealing the true purpose. Additional letters in the series demonstrate support for the Indians to halt advance of U.S. settlement. *Papers from the Spanish Archives Relating to Tennessee and the Old Southwest*, 1783-1800, Translated and Edited by D. C. Corbitt and Roberta Corbitt, *The East Tennessee Historical Society's Publications*, 10 (1938) :136-137.

7 Ibid.

8 Parton Condensed, 29-34. AJ to Amos Kendall 9 January 1844, CAJ VI:253-254, "the sword-point reached my head and has left a mark there as durable as the scull, as well on the fingers," 253. Cheathem, Mark R., *Andrew Jackson: Southerner*, LSU Press, 2013, 11.

9 Mark Cheathem makes the point that Jackson has often been described as growing up on the frontier and that Jackson was shaped

by a different experience where he was raised in the Carolinas than he would have encountered on the frontier west of the Appalachians. Mark R. Cheathem, *Andrew Jackson: Southerner,* Louisiana State University Press, 2013. For purposes of this book, it is suggested that Jackson's survival in the backcountry area of the Carolinas would have provided experiences and challenges similar to those on the western frontier of Tennessee.

10 AJ to Blount, 4 January 1813, CAJ I:254-255, LC. On the deaths of Jackson's mother and brother Robert, see Parton Condensed, 30-34. Parton observed that Jackson was an "orphan of the Revolution," Ibid., 34.

11 *Clarion*, 5 January 1813.

12 Parton 1:362.

13 Parton 1:132.

14 John Coffee, 29 January 1813, CO.

15 John C. Guild, *Old Times in Tennessee*, Nashville: Tavvel, Eastman & Howell, 1878). Guild, 322. For requirement for cavalry to purchase uniforms from Europe, see petition of citizens, Legislative Petitions, 53-2-1812, MF, Roll 4, TSLA.

16 John C. Guild, *Old Times in Tennessee*, 322.

17 Marquis James also used the term "grand adventure" in referencing promises recruiters had made to the young boys in the company. MJ, 158. John Henry Eaton and John Reid mentioned the young ages of the soldiers, *The Life of Major General Andrew Jackson*, 3d Ed, Philadelphia: McCarthy & Davis, 1828, 15.

18 Stackhouse Travel Diary, 16 November 1811.

19 *Clarion*, 12 January 1813.

20 *Clarion*, 15 December 1812. The newspaper stated that soldiers' tents were pitched in the "hills which overlook the town."

21 Veterans of the War of 1812 reunited as part of militia to camp on the commons or Green as part of Nashville's celebration of the visit of General Lafayette in 1825. John C. Guild, *Old Times in Tennessee*, 446.

22 David McGavock's plantation is identified in W.W. Clayton, *History of Davidson County, Tennessee*. Philadelphia, J.W. Lewis & Co., 1880, 196. Edmonson recorded that his regiment under Benton's command camped there, Edmonson Journal, 1.

23 AJ to William Carroll, General Orders, 9 December 1812, LC.

24 *Clarion*, 15 December 1812.

25 Commission as Major General, PAJ I:291-292, and n. 1.

26 *Clarion*, 2 December 1812. As president, Jackson encouraged the government's reliance on "hard money" that had intrinsic value over paper money or bank notes.

27 AJ to the 2nd Division of Tennessee, 8 September 1812, PAJ II:320. Polk suffered from painful kidney stones, Lorman A. Ratner, *Andrew Jackson and his Tennessee Lieutenants*, Westport, CT: Greenwood Press, 1997, 91.

28 *Clarion*, 15 December 1812.

29 Andrew Goff to Robert Preston, 1 February 1813, Williamson County, Tennessee Archives.

30 AJ to William Carroll, 9 December 1812, LC, Parton, "Statement of Certain Tennessee Volunteers who Served under General Jackson in the Creek War," 629.

31 Edmonson recorded in his journal that his camp was on David McGavock's Plantation, Edmonson Journal, 1. *Clarion,* 15 December 1812, reported that soldiers were camped on the hills overlooking the town. The hills were to the west.

32 Camp of Volunteers, *Clarion* 22 December 1812, Camp Necessity, Edmonson Journal, 2, Camp Extortion, Edmonson Journal, 1.

33 The events of the first day of encampment were described in the *Clarion*, 15 December 1812.

34 *Clarion*, 22 December 1812.

35 *The Nashville Whig*, 2 December 1812.

36 *Clarion*, 19 January 1813. Though published after the rendezvous, it reflected the options that had been discussed.

37 It was unclear whether the president as commander in chief of the federal government had the authority to call out state militias. In the Battle of Queenston Heights, U.S. forces lacked militia re-enforcements because it was doubted whether the militia could march beyond the U.S. border. That issue was debated in the Volunteer Bill in 1812, J. Roderick Heller, III, *Democracy's Lawyer: Felix Grundy of the Old Southwest, Louisiana State University Press*, 2010, 100.

38 James Ross, *Life and Times of Elder Reuben Ross*, https://ia600306. us.archive.org/25/items/lifetimesofelder00ross/lifetimesofelder00ross. pdf., 184.

39 William Love Journal, Transcribed version in Crittenden County, Arkansas Public Library, 6.

40 Recited in J. H. Wallace's History of Kosciusko and Attala County, 1916 Attala-countyhistory-geneaology.org

41 AJ to John Armstrong, 1 March 1813, LC. See also Wilkinson Court Martial, 1811.

42 Miss Jane Davis, *Old Days in Nashville*, Publishing House, Methodist Episcopal Church, 1897, Reprinted by Charles Elder, 44.

43 Parton 3:368. Parton noted that the soldiers were drunken, Parton Condensed, 109.

44 Parton made this point, Parton Condensed, 113.

45 Parton Condensed, 105.

46 General Orders, 13 December 1812, CAJ II:247-249. Jackson's model General Washington had used a similar expression.

47 John Henry Eaton and John Reid stated that the boys were sons of Jackson's neighbors and that they were looking to him to protect them, *The Life of Major General Andrew Jackson*, 15. Parton called Jackson a "protector" of his friends. Parton Condensed, 16. Jackson biographer Robert Remini compared him to a rooster who was tender to the hens who clucked around him but a killer to anyone who would threaten. *Andrew Jackson and His Indian Wars*, 15.

48 See note 77 below. It is unclear whether the first cavalry camp was located. From the direction of the march, it appears that it may have been west of Nashville.

49 Regimental Orders, 24 November 1812, JMP.

50 James N. Gibson, *A War Without Rifles*, 83.

51 Eustis to Blount, 21 October 1812, CAJ I:240, n. 5.

52 Parton 1:368.

53 *Clarion*, 15 December 1812.

54 *The Nashville Whig*, 9 December 1813.

55 PAJ II:6, notes.

56 "Letters of General Coffee to his Wife," 1813-1815, THM, 265.

57   Parton seems to refer to the Polly in the letter as Coffee's wife Mary. He may have confused Coffee's wife Mary Donelson with Mary Polly Donelson, wife of Samuel Donelson. The letter seems to make clear that the Polly referred to in the letter lived in Columbia, Tennessee. Parton 1:369-370.

58   Thomas Hart Benton to AJ, 30 January 1812, PAJ II:280-281 and CAJ I:225-226.

59   Theodore Roosevelt, *American Statesman: Thomas Hart Benton*, Cambridge, Massachusetts: The Riverside Press, 1896, 34.

60   Parton 1:362-364.

61   MJ, 160.

62   *Clarion*, 5 January 1813. Lorman A. Ratner, *Andrew Jackson and his Tennessee Lieutenants*, Westport, CT: Greenwood Press, 1997, 66.

63   Reid was to serve as lieutenant and second aide-de-camp but supposedly illness prevented him from traveling with Jackson on the Natchez Expedition. CAJ I:247, n. 2. Reid may have thought he was to be given Benton's position as first aide-de-camp, and he may have chosen to remain behind rather than to serve under Benton. See AJ to John Reid, 11 December 1813 and John Reid to AJ, General Orders, LC. AJ to John Reid, 30 December 1812, CAJ I:251.

64   Jackson's officers are listed in his General Orders, 13 December 1812, CAJ I:247-249.

65   General Orders, 13 December 1813, LC.

66   Edmonson Journal, 2.

67   *Clarion*, 22 December 1812, *The Nashville Whig*, 16 December 1812. *Clarion*, 5 January 1813.

68   Jackson revered Washington the general who won the Revolution, but not Washington the politician who opposed westerner's military actions toward neighboring Indian nations. MJ, 83-84.

69   Order published in *Clarion*, 22 December 1812.

70   *HENRY V*, Act IV, Scene iii, 160-66, William *Shakespeare, The Complete Works,* The Viking Press New York, 1969, Reprinted 1979. For a discussion of the study of military manuals and Washington's usage of the term "band of brothers," see, Don Higgenbotham, "Military Education Before West Point," Robert M. S. McDonald, Ed., *Thomas*

Jefferson's Military Academy: Founding West Point, Charlottesville: University of Virginia Press, 2004, 31-34,47.

71 T.W. Linster, Complaint, 6 April 1813, LC.

72 Timothy D. Johnson, *Winfield Scott: The Quest for Military Glory*, Lawrence, Kansas: University Press of Kansas, 1998, 44.

73 General Orders, 14 December 1812, LC.

74 The larger arsenal was established after the war in Columbia, Tennessee, south of Nashville, but it took decades to implement Jackson's suggestion. The buildings are now part of Columbia Academy.

75 Thomas Hart Benton, Order published in the *Clarion*, 22 December 1813.

76 General Orders, 17 December 1812, LC.

77 16 December 1812, Andrew Jackson, Order No. 8, CO. Edmonson wrote that the second cavalry camp was a few miles south of Nashville. One source listed the distance as six miles. That distance put it near Henry Compton's farm near present-day Tyne Boulevard, W. W. Clayton, *History of Nashville*, 414. According to W.W. Clayton, Compton built flatboats that transported Jackson's troops to New Orleans, and he served as deputy quartermaster. Ibid., 422. A quartermaster was attached to the cavalry.

78 16 December 1812, CO.

79 John C. Guild, *Old Times in Tennessee*, 255.

80 *The Nashville Whig*, 6 January 1813.

81 Recited in J. H. Wallace's History of Kosciuko and Attala County, 1916 Attala-countyhistory-geneaology.org.

82 General Orders, John Reid, 16 December 1813, LC. This Bellview was located in the old town center, as distinguished from the Bellevue west of Nashville that gave name to a Nashville suburb.

83 *Clarion*, 5 January 1813.

84 Ibid.

85 General Orders, To Cantrell and Read, LC.

86 *The Nashville Whig*, 25 November 1813.

87 U.S. Congress, Senate, "Correspondence on the Subject of the Emigration of the Indians" Document 512 23rd Congress, 1st Session. Washington, Government Printing Office, II, 242.

88 Edward Albright, *Early History of Middle Tennessee*, Gallatin, Tennessee, 1909, 64.

89 P. Juzan Report to Spain, 1790, Paul Clements, *Chronicles of the Cumberland Settlements: 1799-1796*. The Foundation of William and Jennifer Frist and by Paul Clements, 2012, 314.

90 John Gordon and others, 1 January 1791, Paul Clements, *Chronicles of the Cumberland Settlements*, 323, 327-328, *United States Chronicle*, 13 August 1791.

91 Putnam, 194-196.

92 W.W. Clayton, *History of Nashville*, 126.

93 Piominko's visit was described in a children's book by Lizzie P. Elliott, *Early History of Nashville* (Nashville, Tennessee: Board of Education 19ll). Her father was a historian and head of the Davidson Academy during the early days of Nashville. A letter from the Red King, remarks prepared by Piominko, 1783, in Paul Clements, *Chronicles of the Cumberland Settlements*, 200, suggests that a new path be formed between the two peoples and seems to reflect the proposal. Though the words of the Red King to create a new path could be taken as symbolic, early Nashville settler John Carr wrote that Piominko made the proposal during the 1783 council and that building of the new path a was literal road or path between Nashville and the Chickasaw Nation that was marked by cutting briars. John Carr, *Early Times in Middle Tennessee*, Stevenson & FA. Owen 1857, reprinted Nashville, The Parthenon Press, Robert H. Horsley and Associates, 1958, 18. Piominko's Trace or Mountain Leader's Trace was likely the first road that became known as the "Natchez Trace" as opposed to the Chickasaw Trace that ran west from Nashville and then turned south on the west side of the Tennessee River.

94 Ibid.

95 Arrell M. Gibson, *The Chickasaws,* University of Oklahoma Press, 1972, 81,88.

96 The Mountain Leader's Trace is referenced on early Tennessee maps, See Map #553 Tennessee State Library and Archives.

97 Putnam, 318. According to one source, the quote was from Sampson Williams who fought alongside Jackson against the Creek Indians who attacked James Robertson.

98 Breazeale, *Life As It Is*, (Printed by James Williams at the office of "The Post", Knoxville, TN 1842), reprinted by Charles Elder, 1969, 101-102.

99 Chief Double Head's threatened attack on the Colberts was reported in the June 1800 edition of the Raleigh *Register*.

100 It has often been written that boatmen could not return north on the Mississippi River (see for example, Henry E. Chambers, *Mississippi Valley Beginnings*, New York: G. P. Putnam's & Sons, The Knickerbocker Press, 1922, 305; however, about half the boatmen returned in pirogues, *Goodspeed History of Maury County, Tennessee*, 754. Rapier's barge company was established in Nashville in 1807 to transport freight in both directions, W.W. Clayton, *History of Nashville*, 203. Jackson encountered northbound boats headed to Nashville on his voyage during the Natchez Expedition. Other references include, John C. Guild, *Old Times in Tennessee*, 324-325. Cramer, *The Navigator*, 1811 Online edition, "Barges, and keel boats, however, may ascend by being rowed or poled," 147.

101 "Spanish Order Closing the Mississippi," 22 December 1792, Carlos De Grandpre. Putnam. 427-428. (Typographical error shows the date of the order as 1802).

102 Andrew Jackson to Daniel Smith, 13 February 1789, as quoted in Paul Clements, *Chronicles of the Cumberland Settlements*, 295. See also, Andrew Jackson to John McKee, 16 May 1794, Paul Clements, *Chronicles of the Cumberland Settlements*, 425. Early Tennessee historians noted that some of the Tennesseans' overtures to the Spanish were simply to encourage their help to prevent Indian attacks, Albright, *Early History of Middle Tennessee*, 153. Lomask made the observation of the effect of Jay's Treaty, Lomask, 1805-1834, 11-12.

103 Marquis James makes this often overlooked point. MJ, 59, 65-66.

104 Oath of Allegiance, 15 July 1789, Andrew Jackson, as quoted in Paul Clements, *Chronicles of the Cumberland Settlements*, 304.

105 See also, Ann, Toplovich, "Marriage, Mayhem, and Presidential Politics: The Robards-Jackson Backcountry Scandal" *Ohio Valley History*, The Filson Historical Society and Cincinnati Museum Center, Volume 5, Number 4, Winter 2005, 3-22.

106 Jackson acquaintance W. H. Sparks claimed in his memoirs *The Memories of Fifty Years* that Rachel divorced her first husband Robards

in the Spanish territory near or at Natchez in 1791. W. H. Sparks., *The Memories of Fifty Years, Third Edition, Macon, GA: J.W. Burke & Co., 1872. Online. Google Books*, 152. Jackson's Bruinsburg trading post and racetrack are mentioned by Marquis James at MJ, 63 and by Thomas E. Watson in, *The Life and Times of Andrew Jackson, Thomason*, Georgia: The Jeffersonian Pub. Co., 1912, 62, though Watson incorrectly concluded that Jackson never lived in Bruinsburg, based upon Parton's statement that Jackson and Rachel returned to Nashville following their wedding. They returned to Nashville after spending a few months in Bruinsburg. See Mrs. Dunbar Rowland, *Andrew Jackson's Campaign Against the British, or the Mississippi Territory in the War of 1812: Concerning The Military Operations of the Americans, Creek Indians, British, and Spanish, 1813-1815.* Freeport, New York: Books for Library Press, 1971, Reprint from the 1926 Edition, 21. Parton mentioned the Bruinsburg cabin where the couple spent their honeymoon, Parton 1:153. For a discussion of whether Rachel Jackson obtained a divorce under Spanish law, see MJ, 383, n.21.

107 James Wilkinson to Governor Gayoso, 3 April 1790, as quoted in Paul Clements, *Chronicles of the Cumberland Settlements*, 310.

108 Parton described the intensity of Jackson's look and presence, Parton Condensed, 43. As to Jackson's defense mechanism, Arthur M. Schlesinger, Jr. concluded that Jackson's "uncontrolled irascibility" was a front that he carefully managed, Arthur M. Schlesinger, Jr., *The Age of Jackson*, Konecky & Konecky, Old Saybrook, CT 1945, 1971, 40.

109 AJ to an Arbitrator, 29 February. 1812, PAJ II:286-289. AJ to an unknown person, 20 March 1812, PAJ II:293. Parton Condensed, 79.

110 John C. Guild, *Old Times in Tennessee*, 255. Parton Condensed, Ibid.

111 *The WPA Guide to the Magnolia State*, Reprint. University Press of Mississippi, 1988, 325. The large plantation house was not built until 1819, and its columns were not added until later.

112 In addition to the 1789 pledge to Spain, Jackson's frequent travel to Natchez was documented at least as early as 1790 when he took swan skins or down to Natchez to sell for Revolutionary War era diplomat James Cole Mountflorence, James Cole Mountflorence to AJ, 23 July 1790, PAJ I:23.

113 Timothy Pickering to Winthrop Sargent, 20 May 1799, copy in Natchez Trace Collection, Box 4, Folder 5.

114 Improvements to make the Natchez Trace a highway for wagon travel—bridges, ramps, causeways—began at least two years prior to similar work on the National Road. Work also began on the Natchez Trace prior to construction of the Federal Road. However, Federal assistance may have improved the Wilderness Road in Virginia and the Cumberland Road between Nashville and Knoxville.

115 Article I, Section 8 of the U.S. Constitution permits the federal government to build roads only for delivery of the mail.

116 Thomas Jefferson to Mr. Granger, 18 July 1806, http://founders.archives.gov. From Granger Papers, LC. The Secretary of War discussed the need to build military roads between posts in his letter to Wade Hampton, 13 August 1811, Territorial Papers, Vol. VI, 213-114. The Natchez Trace wagon highway was also built to lead south of Natchez to Fort Adams.

117 Thomas Jefferson to Congress, 18 January 1803, Thomas Jefferson Papers, Library of Congress Online Edition, www.ourdocuments.gov.

118 Thomas Jefferson to Robert Livingston, 18 April 1802, Thomas Jefferson Papers, Online Edition. Transcription online at Jeffersonwest.unl.edu.

119 Captain James Stirling to the Right Honorable Lord Viscount Melville, 17 March 1813, Louisiana Digital Library, with credit to Jeff Brewer for the reference.

120 MIM, 381.

121 See the draft of Thomas Jefferson to Congress, 2 December 18106, Draft Message to Congress, https://www.loc.gov.

122 For Jefferson's motive to move settlers to the Southwest, see Secretary of War Henry Dearborn to Mississippi Territory Governor W.C.C. Claiborne, 6 December 1802, LS.

123 Chickasaw Treaty, 1801, Articles I and II transcribed in Paul Clements, *Chronicles of the Cumberland Settlements*, 490.

124 George Colbert, *Clarion*, 12 June 1812.

125 By local family lore, George Colbert gave the medal to the member of his family who remained In Alabama, and the family gave the medal to

the Chickasaw Nation. It is currently housed in the Chickasaw Holisso Center in Oklahoma.

126 Creek Indians had similar rights to operate inns on the Federal Road through the southeast; however, they did not exercise the right without pressure from the government. That comparison gives some credence to Colbert's claim that the financial return was not worth the trouble; however, Colbert leveraged the ferry operation into his own town of businesses known as "Georgetown."

127 In Colbert's defense, it took up to five people to pull boats across the wide Tennessee River versus the one or two needed for narrower crossings. The crossing also took more time than required to cross narrower rivers. For Robertson's and Dinsmoor's honest evaluation of Colbert's skills, see Ratified Treaty No. 46, Documents Relating to the Negotiation of the Treaty of July 23, 1805, with the Chickasaw Indians, http://digicoll.library. wisc.edu/cgi-bin/History/History-idx?type=turn&entity=History. IT1805no46.p0002&id=History.IT1805no46&isize=M. A review of the writings of the period reveals that many white writers did not think the Indians capable of competing in the white business structures, and they found it necessary to attribute an Indian's success to dishonesty, luck, or mixed-white blood.

128 The map, sometimes called the "Butler Map" is on record in the National Archives. A copy can be found at the Tennessee State Library and Archives, Map #486. For early construction of the road north of the Chickasaw Nation, see Secretary of War to Brig. Gen. Wilkinson, 11 June 1801, Military Book "A", 83-84, Natchez Trace Collection.

129 Ibid.. Transcription can be found in the Natchez Trace Parkway Survey, Document No. 148, 76th Congress, 3d Session, 81.

130 Henry Dearborn to General James Wilkinson, 18 February 1803, National Archives, Copy on file in the Natchez Trace Parkway collection, McCain Library and Archives, Southern Mississippi University.

131 *Goodspeed History of Maury County, Tennessee*, 755.

132 W.W. Clayton, *History of Nashville*, 98. Overton lobbied the Tennessee Governor and Williamson County, Tennessee commissioners to extend the road into Franklin, Tennessee, arguing that it would improve land values. Overton owned land near the new road. Overton then lobbied the Tennessee Governor to lobby the Secretary of War. John

Overton to Archibald Roane, 11 June 1802. Archibald Roane to Henry Dearborn, 18 June 1802. The Secretary declined, Archibald Roane to John Overton, 7 August 1802, copies in Natchez Trace Collection, Box 4, Folder 5. Nevertheless, the road was improved.

133 See for example, John Overton to Return J. Meigs, 7 March 1802, Copy in Natchez Trace Historical Survey, Natchez Trace Collection, T.S. Butler to John Overton, 9 March 1802.

134 One account states that George and Levi Colbert obtained a flatboat from East Tennessee to use as a ferry boat; however, on 6 December 1803, Secretary of War Dearborn asked Jackson to obtain larger ferry boats for the ferries at Duck River and Tennessee River, Henry Dearborn to AJ, 6 December 1803, PAJ I:406.

135 PAJ, January 1804, n. 6. Also James Irwin to AJ, from Cantonment Tennessee River, 9 February 1805, PAJ II:48 and Silas Dinsmoor to Col. R.J. Meigs, 30 July 1802, referred to the new highway as the "Camp Columbian Road." Box 16, Folder 2, Natchez Trace Papers, McCain Library, Hattiesburg. The Mobile trade route by river intersected with the Natchez Trace at Bear Creek at Underwood's Village a few miles south of Colbert's Ferry.

136 James Wilkinson to Henry Dearborn, 27 October 1801 as quoted in Natchez Trace Historical Survey, 36.

137 Henry Dearborn to Governor Roane, 18 July 1803, Tennessee Governor's Papers, MF, TSLA.

138 John McKee Journal Entry for 1 August 1805, MJ, Stackhouse Travel Journal. 29 November 1815. Henry Dearborn to Silas Dinsmoor, 9 January 1804, Letters Sent, Indian Affairs, National Archives, MF, 417-419.

139 Thomas Jefferson to Robert Livingston, 18 April 1802, as quoted in DeConde, Alexander. *This Affair of Louisiana*, New York: Charles Scribner's Sons, 1976, 113-114.

140 Thomas Jefferson to James Monroe, 13 January 1803, LC, https://www.loc.gov/item/mtjbib012071/.

141 *Natchez Trace Parkway Survey*, 124.

142 DeConde, Alexander. *This Affair of Louisiana*, 147-159. DeConde argued that Napoleon's true purpose was to empower the United States to create a military rival to Britain.

143 Samuel C. Williams, "Tennessee's First Military Expedition," *Tennessee Historical Magazine*, VII (1924):179.

144 Commission as Major General, 1 April 1802, PAJ I:291.

145 William Dickson to AJ, 10 December 1802, PAJ I:317.

146 AJ to Henry Dearborn, 12 November 1803, PAJ I:395-396.

147 Henry Dearborn to AJ, 31 October 1803, PAJ, I:392.

148 Robert Remini, *Andrew Jackson and the Course of American Empire 1767-1821*, 128.

149 Ibid. PAJ I:16, n. 1.

150 Robert Remini, *Andrew Jackson and the Course of American Empire 1767-1821*, 128.

151 Order from Thomas Hart Benton, 18 December 1812, Published in *Clarion*, 29 December 1812.

152 17 December 1812, Address of Governor Willie Blount, Order No. 3, CO, Published in *Clarion*, 29 December 1812.

153 Andrew Jackson, 21 December 1812, Order No. 6, CO and *The Nashville Whig*.

154 Willie C. Blount, Division Orders, 11 November 1812, Published by AJ in the *Clarion* 17 November 1812. Blount assured that solders would be returned home before summer.

155 *Clarion*, 22 December 1813.

156 AJ to Alpha Kingsley, 23 December 1812, PAJ II:345-346.

157 28 December 1812, Coffee Order Book, CO.

158 *Clarion*, 5 January 1813.

159 26 December 1812, Coffee Order Book, CO.

160 *Clarion*, 5 January 1813.

161 *Clarion*, 22 December 1812.

162 *Clarion*, 5 January 1813

163 MIM, 218-219.

164 Ibid.

165 Putnam, 284.

166 Putnam, 518.

167 Ibid. See also, MJ,105.

168 Putnam, 402. Writers of the period spelled Piominko's name "Piomingo," however, Chickasaw now use the "k" to create a sound closer to the original pronunciation.

169   Putnam, 650.

170   26 December 1812, CO.

171   19 December 1812, CO.

172   25 December 1812, CO.

173   25 December 1813. LC.

174   30 December 1812, LC.

175   AJ to Reverend Robert Henderson, General Orders, LC.

176   TV, 12-16. MIM, 120.

177   Transcribed version, Learner Blackman Papers, Folder 3, M30, J.B. Cain Archives of Mississippi Methodism, Jackson, Mississippi. Entry transcribed 3 for journal 10 for the 29th.

178   Blackman Journal, 28 December 1813, and quoted in Dawson A. Phelps, "The Diary of A Chaplain In Andrew Jackson's Army: the Journal of the Reverend Mr. Learner Blackman – December 28, 1812-April 4, 1813," *Tennessee Historical Quarterly* 12, no. 3, September 1953: 264-281, 267.

179   Winian Autobiography, 89.

180   Unruh, 3, citing Blackman Journal, Chapter 5, 1-2. Also, 6, transcribed version, Learner Blackman Papers, Folder 3, M30, J.B. Cain Archives of Mississippi Methodism, Jackson, Mississippi.

181   Blackman Journal, 3, entry immediately predates 25 January 1812.

182   Phelps, Blackman Journal, THQ, 268.

183   AJ to Alpha Kingsley, 23 December 1812, PAJ II:345-346.

184   General Orders, 27 December 1812, LC.

185   *Clarion*, 29 December 1812.

186   General Orders, 26 December 1813, LC, 45. Kingsley also advertised a Notice to Merchants on January 20, that he would accept Bills of Exchange on the government, payable at sight at par value, *The Nashville Whig*, 23 December 1812.

187   Ibid. Jackson also borrowed $1,650 from Nashville Bank director James Jackson, AJ to James Jackson, 30 December 1813, LC.

188   Court Martial, 2 January 1812, LC.

189   General Orders, 30 December 1812, LC.

190   Charges and Specifications, for actions of 31 December 1812, LC.

191   General Orders, 31 December 1812, LC.

192   Sentence, 2 January 1813, LC.

193 General Orders, 31 December 1812, LC.

194 General Orders, 30 December 1812, LC.

195 John Reid to AJ, 30 December 1812, PAJ II:346, AJ to John Reid, 30 December 1812, PAJ II:347. Reid went on to serve under Jackson in the Creek Campaign and at the Battle of New Orleans.

196 Willie Blount to AJ, 31 December 1812, CAJ I:252-253, and LC.

197 AJ to Blount, 4 January 1813, CAJ I:254-255.

198 AJ to the Tennessee Volunteers, 31 December 1812, PAJ II: 348-349.

199 *Clarion*, 19 January 1813. The sale was announced in *The Nashville Whig*, 9 December 1812. Masterson was an ancestor of Batt Masterson. At the time of this writing, the flag is on display in the Smithsonian Museum of American History but identified as a flag presented to the "Nashville Battalion" prior to Jackson's march to the Creek wars.

200 Court Martials, 2 January 1813, 64-67, LC.

201 John Coffee to Mary Coffee, 2 January 1813, THM, 267.

202 Willie Blount to AJ, 3 January 1813, LC.

203 AJ to William B. Lewis, 5 January 1813, LC.

204 Ibid.

205 AJ to Bartholomew Schaumberg. 5 January 1813. Copy from National Archives in the Natchez Trace Collection, McCain Library, Hattiesburg. The letter is referred to in PAJ II:359, n. 2, but it is not published in that volume.

206 Jackson's clerk recorded in his Order book that the letter stated the numbers as fourteen hundred, LC. The letter the deputy quartermaster received stated that the number was 400.

207 Wilkinson would later state that he relied on the lower number, and he could use Jackson's own letter as an excuse for suggesting that Cantonment Washington would accommodate the troops or that he could house them in Baton Rouge. Jackson would not have put it past Wilkinson to change the number on his copies after it was clear that the fort would not hold Jackson's men.

208 AJ to Washington Jackson, LC. James Wilkinson to Secretary of War, 19 February 1813, LR.

209 A bill for $5,069.50 for fodder for the horses was submitted on 18 February 1813 and apparently paid. 18 February 1813, LC.

210 Wilkinson to Armstrong, 19 February 1813, LR.

211 AJ to William Charles Cole Claiborne, 5 January 1813. PAJ II:352.

212 Regimental Order, 8 January 1812, LC and UNA.

213 James Henderson to John Coffee, 14 January 1813, LC.

214 Thanks to Williamson County, Tennessee historian Rick Warwick for his account.

215 Coffee Order Book, 7 January 1813, CO.

216 Blackman Journal, THQ, 268.

217 General Orders, Andrew Jackson, 6 January 1813, CO, LC.

218 JMP, 8 January 1813.

219 General Orders, 5 January 1813, LC.

220 General Orders, 6 January 1813, LC.

221 Coffee Order Book, Order No. 9, 7 January 1813. CO, General Orders, LC.

222 Ibid.

223 Ibid.

224 General Orders, 29 December 1812, LC.

225 AJ to Blount, 9 January 1813, LC.

226 AJ to James Monroe, 4 January 1813, PAJ II:351, General Orders, LC, 76-78. The Order Book shows that the letter was addressed to the Secretary of War in general rather than specifically to Monroe.

227 *Clarion*, 15 December 1812.

228 Ibid.

229 General Orders, Andrew Hynes, 8 January 1813, LC.

230 William Calhoun Journal, Crittenden County Arkansas, Public Library, 23.

231 Ibid.

232 No descriptions or specifications for the boats have been found. In 1804, Jackson contracted with the War Department to build boats 40 feet and 50 feet in length. PAJ II:4-5.

233 Lee Sandlin, *Wicked River: The Mississippi*, New York: Pantheon Books, 2010, Everett Dick, *The Dixie Frontier*, University of Oklahoma Press, 1948 Reprint version, 119.

234 Benton Journal, 12 January 1813, printed *Clarion*, 16 February 1813.

235 Benton's Journal, 7 January 1813, printed *Clarion*, 19 January 1813, reported that the march took place on the 8th. See order General Orders, 6 January 1813, LC, 88-90 to strike tents on the 7th. In Benton's letter

to AJ 9 January 1813, PAJ II:355-356, he reports that the soldiers had already struck their tents and boarded boats by the time he arrived on the 8th, and he gave orders to depart.

236 Ibid.

237 Ibid.

238 *Clarion*, 19 January 1813. Thomas Hart Benton to AJ, 9 January 1813, PAJ II:355-356.

239 Benton Journal, 7 January 1813, printed *Clarion*, 9 January 1813.

240 *The Nashville Whig*, 28 March 1813.

241 W.W. Clayton, *History of Nashville*, 100.

242 Benton to AJ, 9 January 1813. Printed in *Clarion*, 9 January 1813.

243 Ibid.

244 Benton Journal, 7 January 1813, printed *Clarion*, 9 January 1813. Lewis criticized him for the decision, William B. Lewis, 24 April 1813, *The Nashville Whig*, 28 April 1813.

245 Edmonson Journal, 2.

246 General Orders, 6 January 1813, LC.

247 Benton Journal, 7 January 1813, printed 10 February 1813.

248 AJ to Rachel Jackson, 8 January 1813, CAJ I:271, PAJ II:353-354. The letter is incorrectly dated as 18 January in CAJ but corrected in PAJ. Because of the locations described in the letter, it is clear that he was in Nashville when it was written.

249 *Clarion*, 19 February 1813.

250 Searcy Journal, 12 January 1812, CAJ I:257.

251 AJ to William Charles Cole Claiborne, 5 January 1813, PAJ II:352, General Orders, LC.

252 General Orders, 9 January 1813, LC.

253 Benton Journal, for 9 January 1813 printed Clarion, 9 February 1813.

254 Searcy Journal, 10 January 1813, LC, CAJ I:256-257.

255 Edmonson described the Infantry moving their camp to the McGavock's ferry landing, which was two miles north or downriver from Nashville. Benton recorded that Jackson walked two miles below Nashville to board his boat for departure. 10 January 1813, *Clarion*, 9 February 1813. Edmonson Journal, 2.

256 *Clarion*, 9 February 1813.

257 Searcy Journal, 10 January 1813, LC and CAJ I:256-257.

258 Ibid. According to 19th century illustrations of Nashville from the vantage of the Cumberland River, the water level was significantly lower than today. Large bluffs rose from the banks of the river.

259 Benton Journal, 10 January 1813, Printed in *Clarion*, 9 February 1813.

260 Benton Journal, 12 January 1813, Printed in *Clarion*, 16 February 1813.

261 Ibid.

262 The cavalry was ordered to strike their tents on 10 January. General Orders, 7 January 1813, LC. *Clarion*, 19 January 1813, reported that the Cavalry departed January 12th.

263 Piere Clement de Laussat, *Memoirs of My Life*, Louisiana State University Press, 1978, 73.

264 Henry Adams, *History of the United States*, 579.

265 Thomas Robson Hay and M. R. Werner, *The Admirable Trumpeter: A Biography of General James Wilkinson,* The Scholar's Bookshelf. Cranbury, New Jersey: 2006, 2, James Wilkinson, Memoirs of My Own Times, I. (Philadelphia 1816) Online edition https://ia800201.us.archive.org/22/items/memoirsofmyownti01wilk/memoirsofmyownti01wilk.pdf., 8.

266 AJ to Jenkins Whiteside, 10 February 1810, PAJ II:230-232, AJ to John Randolph, 10 February 1810, PAJ II:234-235.

267 James Stirling to Lord Viscount Melville, March 17, 1813. The Louisiana Digital Library. Online URL http://louisdl.louislibraries. org/cdm/ref/collection/AAW/id/509.

268 Timothy D. Johnson, *Winfield Scott*, 35.

269 Ibid, 39.

270 LL, 2.

271 Wilkinson's former business associate published letters suggesting a connection, and additional letters published in the 1850s gave some credence to the allegations, but official documentation from the Spanish removed all doubt.

272 James Parton, *The Life and Times of Aaron Burr*, Vol. 1, James R. Osgood and Company, 1872, 488.

273 Hay and Werner, *The Admirable Trumpeter,* 2.

274 MJ, 30.

275 LL, 10-12 See also, Miro and Navarro to the Minister of the Indies, 25 September 1787, "Papers from the Spanish Archives, 1738-1800," *The East Tennessee Historical Society's Publications*, 12 (1949): 102-106.

276 However, Mark R. Cheathem explains how Jackson learned to emulate southern gentlemen when he was living in Charleston, South Carolina and how he used his network of Tennessee society to gain influence. *Andrew Jackson: Southerner*, Louisiana State University Press, 2013.

277 LL, 183, Hay and Werner, *The Admirable Trumpeter*,181.

278 Testimony of Andrew Ellicott at Wilkinson's 1811 Court Martial, WCM, 1924, Wilkinson denied the allegation.

279 WCM, 1932.

280 The militia system is discussed in detail in John A. Logan, The *Volunteer Soldier of America*, R. S Peale & Company Publishers, 1937.

281 Putnam, 174, Original Version, 1859.

282 Hay and Werner, *The Admirable Trumpeter*, 85.

283 LL, 83-87.

284 James Wilkinson, 22 August 1787 in a Memorial to Spain, as quoted in Paul Clements, *Chronicles of the Cumberland Settlements*, 262.

285 Putnam, 288.

286 Putnam, 292.

287 LL, 106.

288 John Doughty to Henry Knox, 17 April 1790, Paul Clements, *Chronicles of the Cumberland Settlements*, 313. James Wilkinson to Governor Miro, 1 February 1790, Paul Clements, *Chronicles of the Cumberland Settlements*, 310.

289 Henry Knox to George Washington, 7 July 1789, https://founders. archives.go. Lomask concluded that Washington wanted Doughty to obtain approval for construction of a road from Kentucky to New Orleans to avoid the need to transport goods on the Mississippi; however, rivers were used at the time for commerce. A road would have been for military purposes. Lomask, 1805-1834, 18.

290 James Wilkinson to Governor Miro, 3 April 1790, as quoted in Paul Clements, *Chronicles of the Cumberland Settlements*, 310.

291 Colton Storm, Ed., "Up the Tennessee in 1790: The Report of Major John Doughty to the Secretary of War," *The East Tennessee Historical Society's Publications*, 17 (1945):119-132.

292 James Wilkinson to Governor Miro, 29 April 1790, as quoted in Paul Clements, *Chronicles of the Cumberland Settlements*, 314.

293 LL, 117. Linklater referenced Jefferson's notes from the deliberations as to Wilkinson's character.

294 LL, 157.

295 Hay and Werner, *The Admirable Trumpeter*, 118.

296 LL, 135. As further evidence, when Wayne later turned over temporary command of the forces to Wilkinson, there was suddenly no shortage of food or pay to support Wilkinson's Command.

297 LL, 159.

298 LL, 136, Hay and Werner, *The Admirable Trumpeter*, 127.

299 Anthony Wayne to Henry Knox, 29 January 1795, Papers of the War Department, www.wardepartmentpapers.org.

300 LL, 148.

301 LL, 142.

302 LL, 143.

303 Wilkinson to Adams, 20 December 1797, Wilkinson Court Martial, 1975.

304 Ibid.

305 See also, Report of the Spanish Governor at New Orleans, 10 August 1790, McCain Library and Archives, Hattiesburg, MS, Natchez Trace Collection, M249, Box 14, Folder 7.

306 Donald Jackson, Ed., *Letters of the Lewis and Clark Expedition with Related Documents*, 1783-1854, Urbana and Chicago: University of Illinois Press, 1978, 687, relying upon Cook, Warren L., *Flood Tide of Empire: Spain and the Pacific Northwest*, 1543-1819, New Haven, Conn, 1973 to note four attempts to capture Lewis and Clark and noting that the Spanish had received information from additional sources, but acted upon Wilkinson's advice.

307 *Clarion*, 6 June 1804.

308 WSH, General Orders, January 29, 1810, 38.

309 Thomas Butler Order Book, Andrew Jackson Papers, Library of Congress.

310 John Overton to Archibald Roane, 11 June 1802, copy in Natchez Trace Collection, Box 4, Folder 5. Historians writing the Natchez Trace Parkway Survey interpreted the correspondence to reflect that Butler had authority to build the road to Nashville, but not directly through the town of Franklin. Natchez Trace Parkway Survey, 39. Archibald

Roane to John Overton, 31 March 1802 and 7 August 1802, MF, Papers of Archibald Roane, Papers of the Tennessee Governors, TSLA.

311 The portion of the Natchez Trace that soldiers cut was about five miles west of Franklin, but they were withdrawn from improving was known as the "Road Opened by The Federal Troops." Williamson County Minute Book, Vol. 1, 1800-1812, 392, Williamson County, Tennessee Archives. As a result of the troops not improving the road they first cut to Nashville, several routes were known as "The Natchez Trace" into Nashville, though the troops improved one main highway through Franklin to the Chickasaw boundary.

312 Louis N. Ritten, *Fort Adams*, self-published, 49.

313 PAJ II:32-33.

314 Thomas Butler to AJ, 21 October 1804, PAJ II:41-42. See also Don Hickey, Tennessee Historical Quarterly, XXXV, no. 4 (Winter 1976): 365-375, "The United States Army vs. Long Hair: The Trials of Colonel Thomas Butler, 1801-1805." *Pennsylvania Magazine of History and Biography* 101 (October 1977): 462-474., Hay and Werner, *The Admirable Trumpeter* 228-233.

315 PAJ I:353-354, n 1.

316 Hay and Werner, *The Admirable Trumpeter*, 229.

317 Ibid.

318 Tennesseans attacked the Cherokee in the Nickajack campaign in violation of federal orders. Robert Remini, *Andrew Jackson and His Indian Wars*, 35. They also provided military support to the Chickasaw in their defense against the Creeks.

319 Ibid..

320 AJ to Thomas Jefferson, 7 August 1803, PAJ 1:353-356.

321 PAJ II:32-33, n.

322 Thomas Jefferson to AJ, 19 September 1803, PAJ I:365.

323 Washington Irving wrote a satirical piece about the Wilkinson-Butler incident. Irving may have exaggerated when he said the insubordinate officer pulled his hair together so tightly that it disfigured his facial features. Washington Irving, *Knickerbocker's History of New York, Vol. II*, Pocket Ed., New York and London: G. P. Putnam's Sons, 117.

324 AJ to Thomas Jefferson, 3 August 1804, PAJ II:33-35. Butler appealed directly to the Secretary of War, which also angered Wilkinson, and

on 10 October 1804, Wilkinson told Butler to consider himself under arrest. James Wilkinson to Thomas Butler, 10 October 1804, James Brown Papers, Library of Congress.

325 Thomas Butler to AJ, 21 October 1804, PAJ II:41-42.

326 AJ to Thomas Butler 25 August 1804, PAJ II:36-37.

327 AJ to Thomas Jefferson, 3 August 1804, PAJ II:33-35. Ironically, when Jackson became a U.S. general, he directed that no officer could follow an order from the War Department unless he first approved the order. Timothy D. Johnson, *Winfield Scott*, 88.

328 Ibid.

329 Ibid.

330 Thomas Butler to AJ, 31 December 1804, PAJ II:44-45.

331 AJ to Thomas Jefferson et. al., c. December 1804, PAJ II:45-46.

332 Ibid. The petition is reprinted in Hickey, "Andrew Jackson and the Army Haircut," THQ, 370-371.

333 Hickey, Ibid., 372 and note 27.

334 Ibid., AJ to Thomas Jefferson, c. December 1804, PAJ II:45-46.

335 AJ to Thomas Jefferson, 23 September 1805, PAJ II:72-73.

336 Thomas Butler to AJ, 4 March 1805, PAJ II:51-53.

337 Thomas Butler to James Wilkinson, 20 November 1804, James Brown Papers, Library of Congress, Thomas Butler to AJ, 15 July 1805, PAJ II:65-66.

338 Thomas Butler to James Wilkinson, 14 January 1805, James Wilkinson to James Brown, 15 March 1805, James Wilkinson to James Brown, 25 March 1805, James Wilkinson to Col. Thomas Hunt, 31 March 1806, James Brown Papers, Library of Congress, AJ to Thomas Jefferson, 23 Sept. 1805, PAJ II:72-73. See also the James Brown Papers for notes from the Col. Thomas S. Butler court martial. James Brown served as Judge Advocate General.

339 Ibid.

340 C. Edward Skeen, *John Armstrong, Jr. 1758-1843, A Biography* (Syracuse University Press: Syracuse, NY, 1981) 159.

341 Hay and Werner, *The Admirable Trumpeter*, 233, based upon Washington Irving's Knickerbocker's History of New York, II:119.

342 MJ, 139, Cheathem, Mark R., *Andrew Jackson: Southerner*, Louisiana State University Press, 2013, 55, MJ, 139, 144.

343 The electoral vote tie was a result of Burr's innovative political maneuvers to overcome the Federalist's advantage and worked to Jefferson's advantage, Milton Lomask, *Aaron Burr, The Years from Princeton to Vice President, 1756-1805*, 254. The quote "somewhat overstocked" can be found at page 284.

344 *Impartial Review*, 10 January 1807.

345 Lomask 1805-1836, 172, Wheelan, Joseph, *Jefferson's Vendetta: The Pursuit of Aaron Burr and the Judiciary*, New York: Carroll & Graf Publishers, 2005, 253.

346 Ibid.

347 Aaron Burr to AJ, 24 March 1806, PAJ II:91-92.

348 Hay and Werner, *The Admirable Trumpeter*, 223-241, 249.

349 On the Blount conspiracy with the British, see, Lomask, 1805-1834, 20. The quote can be found in Lomask, 1756-1805, 151. Lomask also observed, "No well-known figure of the American past was ever so consistently outsmarted, especially in financial matters, as the subject of this biography." 1756-1805, 117. Burr's fictitious view of the world and his own circumstances is clear in the letters he sent to his daughter from his exile in Europe. Matthew L. Davis, Ed., The Private Journal of Aaron Burr, II, New York 1858.

350 Wilkinson to Burr as quoted in David O. Stewart, *American Emperor: Aaron Burr's Challenge to Jefferson's America*, New York: Simon & Schuster Paperbacks, 2011, 53 and in Lomask, 1805-1836, 27. Quoted as "I think of you always, *mon beau et cher Diable*."

351 David O. Stewart, *American Emperor*, 73. Also described in Lomask, 1756-1805, 359 and in Lomask, 1805-1834, 45.

352 David O. Stewart, *American Emperor*, 84, Lomask, 1805-1836, 71.

353 David O. Stewart, American Emperor, 84, Jefferson wanted Burr's help to stop an impeachment of Supreme Court Justice Samuel Chase, who countered John Marshall's opposition to the Jefferson administration on the Court. Lomask, 1805-1836, 44

354 Hay and Werner, *The Admirable Trumpeter*, 183.

355 See Aaron Burr to AJ, 2 June 1805, PAJ II:59. Jackson did not have the funds to build the two-story brick mansion until 1819.

356 Ibid. According to notes on 58, Burr made four trips between 1805 and 1806.

357 John Coffee and AJ to The Adams County Superior Court, 25 March 1813, PAJ II:398-399.

358 Parton 1:310.

359 LL, 228. It is not clear who created the deception about the mission of the boat. Burr's journal and letters to his daughter Theodosia show that either Burr saw all his circumstances as he wished to see them in a world he constructed for himself, or that he wanted his daughter to see them in that manner. Lomask concluded that Wilkinson was sending the officers south to Fort Adams on a boat owned by Fort Massac Captain Bissell to help shore up the command at Fort Adams. Lomask, 1805-1836, 69.

360 WCM, 1455. Wilkinson suggested that he was discussing the construction of a canal.

361 LL, 229. Lomask, 1805-1834, 78.

362 WCM, 1468.

363 John McKee Journal Entry for 22 August 1805, McKee Journal.

364 WCM, 1468.

365 Henry Adams, *History of the United States*, 759.

366 Joseph Wheelan, *Jefferson's Vendetta,* 250-251.

367 Aaron Burr to AJ, 24 March 1806, PAJ II:91.

368 Ibid. Ironically, Burr's assessment of the capabilities of the West Tennessee militia would prove true at the Battle of New Orleans. However, the forces were not yet the army that could defeat the British.

369 According to John Coffee's account in the *United States Telegraph Extra*, 11, October 1828, cited in n. 4, PAJ II:93, Jackson met with James Robertson and experienced military men to compile the list and sent it on to Burr.

370 Arrangements of Thomas Overton and Hanson Catlet for Duel, 23-24 May 1806, PAJ II:100.

371 PAJ II:104, n.

372 PAJ II:101, comment.

373 AJ to Thomas Eastin, 6 June 1806, PAJ II:101.

374 Statements of Hanson Catlet and Thomas Overton re Duel, PAJ II:104-105.

375 John Overton to AJ, 12 September 1806, PAJ II:108-109.

376 Parton Condensed, 99.

377 Remini, *Andrew Jackson, and the Course of American Empire*, 1767-1821, 147. Also *Tennessee Gazette*, 27 September. 1806, See also, Andrew Jackson to [William Preston Anderson], 25 September 1806, PAJ II:110, and Thomas E. Watson, *The Life and Times of Andrew Jackson*, Thomason, Georgia: The Jeffersonian Pub. Co., 1912, 123.

378 Aaron Burr to AJ, 24 March 1806, PAJ II:91-92.

379 Andrew Jackson to John Overton John McGavock Dickinson Papers, Box 15, No. 9, TSLA.

380 Aaron Burr's account with AJ, PAJ II:113.

381 Parton Condensed, 99-100.

382 AJ to James Winchester, 4 October 1806, PAJ II:110-111.

383 Order to Brigadier Generals of the 2nd Division, 4 Oct. 1806, PAJ II:111-112.

384 Order to Brigade Generals of the 2nd Division, October 4, 1806, PAJ II:111-112, (Two regiments); Andrew Jackson to Thomas Jefferson, c, November 1806, PAJ II:114-115. (Three Regiments).

385 AJ to Winchester, 4 October 1806, PAJ II:110-111.

386 AJ to Thomas Jefferson, c, 5 November 1806, PAJ II:114-115.

387 PAJ II:115,n, AJ to George Washington Campbell, 15 Jan 1807, PAJ II:147-150. Marquis James wrote that Captain John Fort was traveling from New York to join the Burr Expedition and that he mentioned the Burr plot to divide the nation inadvertently. MJ, 128-129 fn. 30, 388-389.

388 AJ to Daniel Smith, 12 November 1806, PAJ II:117-119.

389 Henry Adams, *History of the United States*, 766-768.

390 PAJ II:120, n. 4 to letter of AJ to Daniel Smith, 12 November 1806.

391 AJ to Thomas Jefferson, c. 5 November 1806, PAJ II:114-115.

392 AJ to W.C.C. Claiborne, 12 November 1806. PAJ II:116-117.

393 Parton I:319.

394 AJ to Daniel Smith 12 November 1806, PAJ II:117.

395 PAJ II:115-116, n.

396 Thomas Jefferson to AJ, 3 December 1806, PAJ II:121.

397 Joseph Wheelan, *Jefferson's Vendetta*,250-251.

398 Henry Adams, *History of the United States*, Cabinet Memoranda, cited at page 795. Lomask, 1805-1836, 177.

399 David O. Stewart, *American Emperor*, 166.

400 PAJ II:124-124, n.

401 Ibid. Seth Peas delivered a letter to Jackson from Dearborn, but he was considered to have the job of gathering information on Jackson.

402 *Impartial Review*, 10 January 1807.

403 *Impartial Review*, 3 January 1807. Parton Condensed, 102, John C. Guild, *Old Times in Tennessee*, 485.

404 Parton Condensed, 102.

405 *Impartial Review*, 3 January 1807.

406 *Impartial Review*, 10 January 1807. Robertson reported the action to Jackson, but he did not seek Jackson's approval prior to calling his recruits into service.

407 *Tennessee Gazette*, 21 February 1807.

408 Parton, 1:330.

409 PAJ II:115-116, n., based upon the testimony of John Shaw, commodore of the U.S. Navy.

410 James Wilkinson to a Private, 19 December 1806, PAJ II:126.

411 As quoted in Hay and Werner, *The Admirable Trumpeter*, 16.

412 James Wilkinson to a Private, 19 December 1806, PAJ II:126.

413 Hay and Werner, *The Admirable Trumpeter*, 258-261.

414 *Tennessee Gazette*, 23 February 1807.

415 17 January 1807, reprinting an article from the *Virginia Argus*, 30 December 1806, PAJ II:126. n. 3.

416 Ibid. A John Read also advertised that he planned to publish a patriotic newspaper in Franklin, Tennessee.

417 David O. Stewart, *American Emperor*, 147, quoting Joseph Hamilton Daveiss, *View of the President's Conduct Concerning the Conspiracy of 1806*, Cincinnati: Abingdon Press (1917, original in 1807), 85-87. Daviess and Jackson friend Felix Grundy had defended Jackson from a charge of assault with intent to commit the murder of Samuel Jackson. J. Roderick Heller, *Democracy's Lawyer*, 85.

418 Parton Condensed, 101.

419 PAJ II:124-125, n. 11. To the Adams County Superior Court from John Coffee and AJ, 25 March 1813, PAJ II:398-399. Putnam, 579.

420 When the issue arose again in 1828 in the context of presidential politics, Jackson's friend and defender John Overton wrote that the two boats departed Nashville practically empty. 15 August 1828, John Overton Papers, MF, TSLA. Stokely Donelson Hays kept a journal

of his return up the Natchez Trace after the expedition, but the loose pages that remain mention nothing about Burr. Stokely Donelson Hayes, "Journal of the Road Between Natchez and Nashville, By Sto. D. Hayes, June 20, 1807," LC.

421 *Tennessee Gazette*, 28 March 1807.

422 AJ to Henry Dearborn, 4 January 1807, PAJ II:136-137.

423 PAJ II:164-166, n., and cited by Wilkinson in James Wilkinson, *Burr's Conspiracy Exposed and General Wilkinson Vindicated. 1811*, Online edition, https://archive.org/details/burrsconspiracye00inwilk 44.

424 AJ to Henry Dearborn. 17 March 1807, PAJ II:155-158.

425 J.S. Bassett in, *The Life of Andrew Jackson*, New York: The Macmillan Company, 1916. also noted that the defense went beyond what Dearborn would have expected, 51.

426 AJ to Henry Dearborn 8, January 1807, as quoted in Bassett, J.S., *The Life of Andrew Jackson*, 51. Bassett also noted Jackson's lack of discretion in threatening the Secretary of War when he wanted to serve as general.

427 MJ, 135-136.

428 *Tennessee Gazette*, 4 April 1807.

429 Henry Adams, *History of the United States*, 908.

430 Washington Irving, *A History of New York, in full A History of New York from the Beginning of the World to the End of the Dutch Dynasty*, by Diedrich Knickerbocker.

431 *Tennessee Gazette*, 23 May 1807.

432 Joseph Weelan, *Jefferson's Vendetta*, 182, MJ, 138-139.

433 Henry Adams, *History of the United States*, 920.

434 WCM, 1459. Parton alluded to the rumor, but his reference was vague. Parton, 1:335

435 As cited in Joseph Wheelan, *Jefferson's Vendetta*, 254.

436 Randolph to Nicholson, June 28, 1807 as quoted in Henry Adams, *History of the United States*, 918.

437 Timothy D. Johnson, *Winfield Scott*, 37.

438 Randolph to Nicholson, cited in Joseph Wheelan, *Jefferson's Vendetta*, 169.

439 Yrujo to Cevallos, 28 January 1807, as quoted in Henry Adams, *History of the United States*, 838. Also, Joseph Wheelan, *Jefferson's Vendetta*, 167.

440   W.W. Clayton, *History of Nashville*, 99. Clayton noted that Overton died during Jackson's contentious political campaign for president, and he did not want his correspondence to give support to Jackson's enemies.

441   Parton, I:335, Parton Condensed, 103.

442   WCM, 1459.

443   Parton Condensed, 103.

444   Robert Remini, *Andrew Jackson and the Course of American Empire 1767-1821*, 162. Thomas Hart Benton was the prosecutor of the man who shot Anderson.

445   Parton 1:337, and Parton Condensed, 16.

446   *Clarion*, 14 January 1809.

447   AJ to Jenkins Whiteside, 10 February 1810, PAJ II:230-232.

448   Willie Blount to AJ, 26 February 1811, PAJ II:259.

449   James Wilkinson, *Burr's Conspiracy Exposed and General Wilkinson Vindicated. 1811*, Online edition https://archive.org/details/burrsconspiracye00inwilk, 43.

450   Ibid., 54.

451   A record of the court martial proceedings are in the National Archives, and they have been transcribed by the Historical Society of Fredrickburg, Maryland. The facts set out in this paragraph can be found at 22.

452   John Carr, *Early History of Middle Tennessee*, 1909, 11.

453   HB, Letter from the Harvard Observatory, dated 26 November 1894, and quoted at page 72. For a history of the comet, see "History of the Comet," *Niles Weekly Register* (Baltimore), 7 March 1812, 10-12, available at http://history.hanover.edu/texts/1811.

454   Claiborne, J.F.H, *Mississippi, As A Province, Territory and State*, Vol. 1, 541, n., Lee Sandlin, *Wicked River*, 33.

455   Accounts of Tecumseh's visit often stated that the comet appeared after his return. The Harvard Observatory letter states that the comet traveled closest to Earth in October 1811. John Sugden pointed out the correct timing from historical accounts of the comet. John Sugden, *Tecumseh, A Life*, Henry Holt and Company, 1997, 246-248.

456   John C. Guild, *Old Times in Tennessee*, 174-175. Andro Linklater explains that the concept of parceling up land for ownership and sale was one that Americans introduced to the world, not just to

Indians. People in other nations would also have found the practice objectionable. *Measuring America, How An Untamed Wilderness Shaped the United States and Fulfilled the Promise of Democracy*, New York: Walker and Company, 2002.

457   Ibid.

458   Winian Autobiography, 51.

459   Henry Adams, *History of the United States*, 1021. Benjamin Drake, *Life of Tecumseh and His Brother the Prophet,* Cincinnati: E. Morgan & Company,1841, 101.

460   John Sugden, *Tecumseh, A Life,*189.

461   Benjamin Drake, *Life of Tecumseh and His Brother the Prophet,* 132.

462   Ibid., 141.

463   HB, 41. The accounts of Tecumseh's 1811 campaign for support in the Southeast here are taken almost exclusively from H.S. Halbert and T.H. Ball, *The Creek War of 1812 and 1814,* 1895, reprinted 1985, and their collection of accounts in the late-1800's. That source is quoted and paraphrased liberally in this section. Tecumseh's visit to the Chickasaw Nation and meeting with George Colbert were referenced in the *Clarion* on 17 September 1811, and the letter of J.J. Stuart Stewart to Draper, Vol 10, Series U., 1. Halbert and Ball talked with just one witness who said that George Colbert talked with them about the visit, HB, 57. As shown below, letters from the Chickasaw Agent confirmed that Tecumseh spoke with the Chickasaw King.

464   John Sugden, *Tecumseh, A Life,* 57-60, 69.

465   John Bates and John Kincaid receipts to George Gaines, 31 March 1811, CTH, image #'s. 21, 25 and 220 for hauling 39 kegs of powder and 27 bars of lead from Colbert's Ferry to Ft. St. Stephens.

466   William Calhoun Journal, Crittenden County Arkansas, Public Library, 46.

467   James R. Atkinson, *Splendid Land, Splendid People: The Chickasaw Indians to Removal,* Tuscaloosa, AL: The University of Alabama Press, 2004, 299.

468   Winian Journal, 7.

469   Frank King's recollections as quoted by Guy Braden in "The Colberts and the Chickasaw Nation," 229.

470   Putnam, 525.

471 Tecumseh fought in at least a portion of the battles, Benjamin Drake, *Life of Tecumseh and His Brother the Prophet*, 31.

472 Benjamin Drake, *Life of Tecumseh and His Brother the Prophet*, 118.

473 MIM, 192.

474 Secretary of War Henry Dearborn complained about Colbert's ferriage rates and encouraged the Chickasaw Agent to persuade him to lower them. Henry Dearborn to Samuel Mitchell, 9 July 1803, Letter's Sent, Indian Affairs, MF, No. 15, Roll 3. Dr. William Lindsey McDonald, "George Colbert and His Ferry." Monograph, Dr. McDonald studied local history most of his life and related accounts of Colbert's charity that have not been published except in the Natchez Trace Survey. University of North Alabama Collier Library and Archives.

475 Paul Clements, *Chronicles of the Cumberland Settlements*,357-358.

476 As quoted in HB, 64.

477 *Clarion*, 17 September 1811.

478 (Illegible officer's Name) Assistant Quarter Master to William Eustis, 9 Sept. 1811, LR.

479 J.N. Walton to L.C. Draper, 11 November 1881, Letters on Chief Levi Colbert, Series 10 U, Draper Papers. In the same account, Levi was said to have hid Tecumseh in his cellar until a council could be arranged. That account and a similar account of Tecumseh giving a speech to the Chickasaw near Cotton Gin Port do not seem to match other accounts. It also is unlikely that Tecumseh hid in a cellar.

480 Much of the account of Tecumseh's visit related here is taken from Halbert and Ball's history. Like other accounts of the period from letters or newspapers, it is impossible to know whether the details are accurate. However, they reflect the stories that were conveyed to Tennessee and those upon which Jackson and the settlers formed their decisions.

481 Gideon Lincecum, *Pushmataha: A Choctaw Leader and His People*, Tuscaloosa: The University of Alabama Press, 2004, 43.

482 Ibid., 89, 100.

483 Gideon Lincecum, *Pushmataha: A Choctaw Leader and His People*, 62-63.

484 Ibid.

485 Halbert and Ball said, "Not one Choctaw was disposed to take his talk." HB, 45.

486 Tecumseh gave Hoentubbe an official document sealed in red wax that was suspected to be a British promise of weapons. Tecumseh's party moved south to the Yazoo River, Mokalusha, one of the most populous Choctaw villages, and Chunky Town, or *Chanki Chitto*.

487 Angie Debo, *A History of the Creek Indians, the Road to Disappearance,* Third Printing. Norman, Oklahoma: University of Oklahoma Press, 1979, 76.

488 The speech is quoted by J.H.F. Claiborne, *Mississippi, As A Province, Territory and State,* Vol. 1, 317-318. A similar speech also appears in Claiborne's biography of Sam Dale, *The Mississippi Partisan,* J.H.F. Claiborne, (New York: Harper and Brothers, 1860). Historians suggest that the language is so different from what is known of the Shawnee customs that Dale must have embellished it. J.H.F. Claiborne, *Mississippi, As A Province, Territory and State,* Vol. 1, 317, as quoted in Thomas W. Clark and John D. Guice, *The Old Southwest 1795-1830,* University of Oklahoma Press, paperback edition, 124.

489 H.S. Halbert wrote that Claiborne used Halbert's notes for Tecumseh's visit and that Tecumseh never gave the speech quoted. H.S. Halbert, *Publications of The Mississippi Historical Society,* Oxford, Mississippi, 1898, 102.

490 Benjamin Drake, *Life of Tecumseh and His Brother the Prophet,* 126.

491 J.H.F. Claiborne, *Mississippi, As A Province, Territory and State,* 1:317.

492 Benjamin Drake, *Life of Tecumseh and His Brother the Prophet,*143.

493 According to Davy Crocket, Black Warrior's town was located near what is now Tuscaloosa, Alabama.

494 Benjamin Drake, *Life of Tecumseh and His Brother the Prophet,* 144.

495 HB, 70. Sugden made the connection between the timing of the comet and Tecumseh's appearance and departure in Tecumseh, John Sugden, *Tecumseh, A Life,* 246-248.

496 James Ross, *Life and Times of Elder Reuben Ross,* 201.

497 Ibid.

498 Ibid., 205.

499 Elyza Bryan to Lorenzo Dow, as published by Dow in *History of Cosmopolite, or, Lorenzo's Journal,* Anderson, Gates & Wright, Cincinnati, Ohio 1860), https://archive.org, 344-345.

500 Letter to the Editor of the *New York Evening Post*, 25 December 1813, reprinted in the *Clarion*, 18 February 1813.

501 Moore, Edith Wyatt, *Natchez Under the Hill,* Natchez, Mississippi: Southern Historical Publications, 1958, 73.

502 James Ross, *Life and Times of Elder Reuben Ross*, 208.

503 Ibid.

504 The *Clarion* reported the Indians' beliefs that the earthquake was connected to Tecumseh's prophet's predictions. *Clarion*, 8 December 1812.

505 Louise Littleton Davis, *Nashville Tales*, Pelican, 1981, 85. The earthquake springs near the Hermitage became a resort known as "Fountain Springs."

506 James W. Holland, *Andrew Jackson and the Creek War: Victory at the Horseshoe Bend*, (University of Alabama Press 1968) 7. See also see the Prophet's speech, Clarion, 8 December 1812.

507 MIM, 217

508 "Lexington (Ken.) Decem. 17," *Pittsburg Gazette*, 27 December 1811, 3, available at http://history.hanover.edu/texts/1811.

509 James Ross, *Life and Times of Elder Reuben Ross* 203. Ross found that the Earthquake Christians' interest in religion dissipated as soon as the dangers had past.

510 HB, 71.

511 AJ to Mary Caffrey, 8 February 1812, PAJ II:281-82.

512 *Clarion*, 31 March 1812.

513 James Neely to William Eustis, 29 November 1811, LR.

514 Willie Blount to William Eustis, 12 December 1811, LR

515 George Colbert to Willie Blount 2 February 1812, as copied in Willie Blount to William Eustis, 17 March 1812, LR.

516 Willie Blount to George Colbert, 1 March 1812, as copied in Willie Blount to William Eustis, 17 March 1812, LR.

517 Wilkinson's "Thoughts," enclosed in a letter to Secretary of War, 28 March 1812, LR.

518 Ibid.

519 12 June 1812, Willie Blount Papers, MF, TSLA. Don Higgenbotham, "Military Education Before West Point," Robert M. S. McDonald,

Ed., *Thomas Jefferson's Military Academy: Founding West Point*, Charlottesville: University of Virginia Press, 2004, 37.

520 W.W. Clayton, *History of Nashville*, 75.

521 David Freeman Hawke, *Everyday Life in Early America*, Harper & Row, 1988, Paperback version, Perennial, 1989, 135. John C. Guild, *Old Times in Tennessee*, 322-324. European militia musters also resulted in games of skill and drinking.

522 Margaret Kinard, "Frontier Development of Williamson County, THQ, VII 1949, 133.

523 John A. Logan, *The Volunteer Soldier of America*, 134-152.

524 Ibid.

525 AJ to William Henry Harrison, 28 November 1811, PAJ II:270.

526 Willie Blount to William Eustis, 15 December 1811, LR.

527 Jackson eventually replaced General Harrison as major general in command of the southern U.S. forces.

528 *Clarion*, 30 April 1812.

529 Felix Grundy to AJ, 24 December 1811, PAJ II:274-276.

530 Felix Grundy to AJ, 12 February 1812, PAJ II:283-285.

531 Ibid.

532 Some Alabama historians have written that the James Madison of Virginia who purchased investment land in Alabama in the early 1800's was the president. Other evidence gives credence to that belief. Kira Gale discovered that the Colonel James Van Meter who was robbed of a large amount of silver at James Colbert's stand in 1809 was an agent for President Madison. Land speculation on the frontier was one of the few ways investors from the East made money at the time. No evidence of Madison's ownership of the land has been found in the Madison papers.

533 That strategy also guided a push for settlement of the Mobile and Pensacola areas. *Jackson's Sword*, 84.

534 *The Other War of 1812*, 75-76.

535 Felix Grundy to AJ, 12 February 1812, PAJ II:283-284.

536 AJ to the 2nd Division, 7 March 1812, PAJ II:290-292 and CAJ I:220-222.

537 Ibid.

538 Ibid.

539 Jackson admitted to Governor Blount in November 1812, that he had worked to "excite" the militia to maintain proper attitudes as soldiers. AJ to Willie Blount, 11 November 1812, PAJ II:336-338.

540 AJ to John Coffee, 26 March 1812, CAJ I:224-225.

541 James McCallum in his *History of Giles County, Tennessee*, The Pulaski Citizen, Pulaski, Tenn. 1928 gave the account of his family's reaction to the threatened attack when he was a child. He thought that the event occurred after news of the Fort Mims massacre from 1813; however, the facts more closely match events in 1812.

542 *Clarion*, 28 March 1812 and *The Western Chronicle*, 28 March 1812, on file in the Maury County, Tennessee Archives.

543 AJ to John Coffee, 25 March 1812, PAJ II:294.

544 AJ to John Coffee, 26 March 1812, PAJ, II:295.

545 James McCallum, *Early History of Giles County*, The Pulaski Citizen, Pulaski, Tenn. 1928, 61-62.

546 *Clarion*, 4 April 1812.

547 J. Winchester, *Clarion*, 4 April 1812.

548 Winian Autobiography, 85.

549 Willie Blount to AJ, *Clarion*, 18 April 1812.

550 *Clarion*, 6 April 1812.

551 *Clarion*, 14 April 1812.

552 *Pittsburg Gazette*, 5 June 1812. With thanks to Mitch Caver for the reference.

553 Indians that Colbert questioned told him that the attackers on the Sandy Creek settlement on April 3 were the same who returned to attack the Crawley and Manley families on May 12.

554 *Clarion*, 19 April 1812.

555 Elmore's account and the inquisition was reported in the *Clarion* under the headline "A British Spy," *Clarion*, 24 April 1812.

556 Willie Blount to William Eustis, 1 May 1812, LR.

557 George Colbert to Willie Blount, 9 April 1812, enclosed in letter from Willie Blount to William Eustis, 1 May 1812, LR.

558 Ibid.

559 *Clarion*, 12 May 1812.

560 Details of what has been called the "Duck River Massacre" are taken from Martha Crawley's deposition in CAJ I:22, n. 1, and *Clarion*, 19 May 1812, republished 25 May 1812.

561 Crawley Deposition, CAJ I:22. n.1., LC. See also, James P. Pate, *The Reminiscences of George Strother Gaines, Pioneer and Statesman of Early Alabama and Mississippi, 1805-1843*, Tuscaloosa: The University of Alabama Press, 1998, 53 and Legislative Petition, 1 October 1812, Legislative Petitions, MF, TSLA.

562 *Clarion*, 23 May 1812.

563 Thomas Johnson to AJ, 27 May 1812, PAJ II:298-299.

564 Ibid.

565 AJ to Thomas Jefferson, 20 April 1808, PAJ II:191-192. CAJ 1:186-187.

566 Edmonson Journal, 18. He was referring to reports in the fall of 1813; however, it is illustrative of the type of fear at the time, and the reactions of the youth who became soldiers.

567 *Clarion*, 19 May 1812.

568 *Pittsburg Gazette*, 5 June 1812.

569 James Ross, *Life and Times of Elder Reuben Ross*, 200.

570 Willie Blount to William Eustis, 25 May 1812, LR.

571 Statement of John Bennett, 18 May 1812, Printed in *Clarion*, 19 May 1812.

572 *Clarion*, 19 May 1812.

573 *Clarion*, 23 March 1812.

574 George Colbert to General Isaac Roberts, 22 May 1812 and 24 May 1812, Printed in *Clarion*, 3 June 1812.

575 George Colbert, *Clarion*, 24 May 1812.

576 Ibid.

577 CAJ, 1:225, n. The original copy is on file in the Library of Congress, Andrew Jackson Papers and a digital copy is viewable online.

578 James Neelly to William Eustis, 13 May 1812, LR.

579 James Neelly to Eustis, 24 April 1812, LR.

580 Willie Blount to AJ, 8 June 1812, LC.

581 *Clarion*, 2 June 1812.

582 Willie Blount to William Eustis, 25 June 1812, LC.

583 CAJ 1:225, n.

584 *Clarion*, 12 June 1812. The Chickasaw described the Natchez Trace as the "peace path" to distinguish it from the Creek path toward Nashville they considered a war path, Loose files on "Indians," Alabama Department of Archives and History, files 1-5.

585 George Colbert, 24 May 1812, *Clarion*, 3 June 1812.

586 Blount to AJ, 4 June 1812, JMP, Also Willie Blount to William Eustis 4 June 1812, LR.

587 John Clifford to AJ, 31 May 1812, LC.

588 Thomas Johnson to AJ, 27 May 1812, JMP, MF, TSLA.

589 David Mason to AJ, July 2, 1812. JMP, MF, TSLA.

590 *Clarion*, 8 July 1812. For Jessie Benton's petition for the cost of his horse, see Jessie Benton's Petition 1813, Legislative Petitions, Roll 4, TSLA.

591 Putnam, 598.

592 *Clarion*, 10 June 1812.

593 Ibid.

594 Ibid.

595 Captain McDonald to Col. Return Meigs, 15 June 1812, Records of the Cherokee Indian Agency in Tennessee, 1801-1824, Correspondence and Misc. Records, 1810-1812, The National Archives, M2809, MF, Roll #5.

596 James Neelly to William Eustis, 12 June 1812, LR.

597 Ibid.

598 Ibid.

599 Willie Blount to AJ, 17 April 1812, LC.

600 Robert Remini made this point in *Andrew Jackson and His Indian Wars*. He was criticized by authors who contended that Jackson was only concerned about taking Indian land.

601 George Colbert to James Robertson, 5 June 1812, printed in *Clarion*, 9 June 1812.

602 James Robertson to Mr. Bradford, *Clarion*, 2 June 1812.

603 *Clarion*, 19 May 1812.

604 Notes, PAJ II: 296. AJ to Blount, 4 June 1812, CAJ 1:225-226.

605 AJ to Willie Blount, 4 June 1812, PAJ II:300-301.

606 Willie Blount to William Eustis, 4 June 1812, LR. Blount's report of a conversation with a half-Cherokee was likely Jackson's own conversation.

607 AJ to Willie Blount, 4 June 1812, PAJ II:300-301, CAJ 1:225-226.

608 AJ to John Hutchings, 7 April 1806, PAJ II:93-94.

609 MJ, 9 October 1805, transcribed page 36.

610 AJ to Willie Blount, 4 June 1812, PAJ II:300-301, CAJ I:225-226.

611 Ibid.

612 *Clarion*, 2 June 1812. When Johnson wrote a defense, Jackson supported its publication in the newspaper, *Clarion*, 9 June 1812. A soldier who was part of Johnson's expedition published a contrary view in the *Clarion* on 18 June 1812.

613 AJ to Willie Blount, PAJ II:301-302, CAJ I:226-227.

614 Even in the later Creek war, Jackson only attacked Creek hostiles. Friendly Creek families supported Jackson. It is worth considering whether friendly Creek chiefs could have retained control of the Creek lands if Jackson had been authorized to command a limited strike against the Creek hostiles in 1812 before the hostile Creeks had gained more support and before Fort Mims attack and battles gave Jackson the determination and influence to remove the Creeks. Creek chiefs responded to demands that they stop attacks by the hostiles by pleading that they could not control the young men.

615 AJ to George Colbert, 5 June 1812, PAJ II:302-303, CAJ I: 226-227.

616 Ibid.

617 Ibid.

618 Willie Blount to David Mason, 4 June 1812, included as a copy in letter from Willie Blount to William Eustis, 1 July 1812, LR.

619 Neelly reported that Chickasaw were allowing Creeks wearing white scalps on their waist to dance with them.

620 *Clarion*, 2 June 1812.

621 George Colbert, 5 June 1812, Clarion, 9 June 1812.

622 Ibid.

623 Ibid.

624 These attacks from the Clarksville *Herald were* repeated in the *Clarion* 10 June 1812, and additional attacks in the *Clarion* on 9 July 1812 prompted a defense of Colbert from James Robertson in August.

625 *Clarion*, 10 June 1812.

626 *Pittsburg Gazette*, 5 June 1812.

627 Ibid.

628   *Clarion*, 9 June 1812.

629   *Clarion*, 10 June 1812.

630   Willie Blount to AJ, 14 June 1812, LC.

631   Willie Blount to AJ, 12 June 1812 PAJ II: 303-304.

632   AJ to Willie Blount, 17 June 1812, PAJ II:305-306, CAJ I:227-229.

633   Ibid. Governor John Sevier repeated the phrase often. Jackson did not originate it. Putnam, 500. The territorial government for the territory south of the Ohio even formalized a similar phrase, "Fear, not love, is the only means by which Indians can be governed; and until they are made to feel the horrors of war, they will not know the value of peace…" into a memorandum, and that may be the source of the phrase for Sevier and Jackson's use, Putnam, 501.

634   Roger H. Brown, *The Republic in Peril: 1812*, 101.

635   Ibid., 100-103.

636   Waldo made this point in his 1825 biography of Jackson, Samuel Pitman Waldo, *Civil and Military History*, 17.

637   Ibid.

638   A.J. to Willie Blount, 17 June 1812, PAJ II:305-306.

639   Willie Blount to AJ, 12 June 1812, PAJ II: 303-304.

640   *Clarion*, 19 June 1812.

641   *The Nashville Whig*, 2 December 1813.

642   MIM, 218.

643   *Clarion*, 7 July 1812.

644   *Clarion*, 30 June 1812.

645   John Brahan to William Eustis, 20 June 1812, LR.

646   Willie Blount to W. Eustis, 25 June 1812, LR.

647   Willie Blount to AJ 21 July 1812, PAJ II:315, enclosing copy of letter from William Eustis to Willie Blount, 11 July 1812. A copy of the original with the correction appears on the microfilm version of the Papers of Andrew Jackson, JMP. The term "peculiar satisfaction" is shown in the copy in the Letters Sent letter book, MF, Roll 15, No. 3, LS.

648   *Clarion*, 7 July 1812. August C. Buell in his *History of Andrew Jackson*, wrote that Jackson's former jockey Billy Phillips was in service to President Madison as an express rider and that Phillips delivered the proclamation in Nashville on June 22nd. Buell tied Jackson's division order to the troops and an offer of troops on June 25th to that

pronouncement; however, the division order was issued June 19, and the editor of the *Clarion* wrote in the June 30th edition that there was still no word on whether Congress would declare war. Buell provides other accounts regarding the expedition that have not been published or found in the primary sources, but there are so many known errors that it is difficult to give the unsourced accounts credence.

649 Ibid.

650 Ibid.

651 Putnam, 242. Sappington's son would discover quinine as a cure for malaria.

652 *Clarion*, 8 July 1812.

653 Ibid.

654 Ibid.

655 *Clarion*, 3 July 1812.

656 Willie Blount printed in Clarion, 8 July 1812.

657 Ibid.

658 Thomas Hart Benton to AJ, 4 July 1812, LC.

659 Secretary of War to Willie Blount, 15 May 1812, Letters Sent, Indian Affairs, MF, Roll 15, No. 3. Willie Blount to AJ, 23 June 1812, LC, AJ to Willie Blount, 3 July 1812, PAJ II:307-308. See reimbursement to Eli Hammond, 15 October 1813, Blount Papers, MF, TSLA.

660 AJ, Division Orders, 9 July 1812, *Clarion*, 14 July 1812.

661 *Clarion*, 14 July 1812.

662 Winian Autobiography, 84 and Winian Journal, 9.

663 CAJ 1:225, n.

664 Petition to Legislature, 25 September 1813, Legislative Petitions, Roll 4, TSLA, from citizens of the Mississippi Territory. The Tennessee State Legislature paid Walker $200 for his efforts and to reimburse him for employing up to 20 Indians in the rescue. The citizens stated that Walker risked his "existence to an eminent degree." See also J.F.H. Claiborne, *Mississippi, As A Province, Territory and State*, 1:100-104. See also, Pate, The Reminiscences of George Strother Gaines, Pioneer and Statesman of Early Alabama and Mississippi, 53, 151.

665 Ibid.

666 William Eustis to Willie Blount, 22 June 1812, LC.

667 James Brown to William Eustis, 11 June 1812, LR.

668 Putnam, 594. Like Neelly and many others during the economic conditions created by the embargo, Robertson suffered financial losses, losing his plantation on the Cumberland River. The agent position also offered Robertson a certain income.

669 David Mason to AJ, July 2, 1812. JMP, MF, TSLA.

670 Willie Blount to James Robertson, 28 July 1812, "Correspondence of James Robertson," Garrett, W.R. and John M. Bass, eds. Vol. V, 1900, *American Historical Magazine*, 270-272. Contrary to Blount's assumptions, the Secretary of War still considered the rangers militia, but the secretary gave Blount authority to commission as federal rangers in July 1812. Secretary of War to Blount, 11 July 1812, Secretary of War, Letters Sent, Indian Affairs, MF Roll 15, No. 3, National Archives.

671 W.W. Clayton, *History of Nashville*, 133. Putnam, 595.

672 AJ to the Tennessee Volunteers, 31 July 1812, PAJ 1:317.

673 HB, 45-51.

674 Tom Kanon located the Henry letter in the American State Papers, Indian Affairs 1:814, "The Kidnapping of Martha Crawley and Settler, Indian Relations Prior to the War of 1812," THQ, Spring, 2005: 3-23 at 19, n. 6. Extracts from the letter were printed in the 21 July 1812 edition of the *Clarion*.

675 *Clarion*, 21 July 1812.

676 *Clarion*, 23 July 1812.

677 *Clarion*, 22 August 1812. James Robertson to Mushulatubbe, 25 July 1812, Legislative Petitions, Roll 4, TSLA.

678 James Robertson to Major Bradford, 26 August 1812, published in the *Clarion*, 1 September 1812. See related stories in the *Clarion*, 15 September 1812, 14 October 1812.

679 Letter, 29 October 1812, printed in *Clarion*, 12 January 1813.

680 *Clarion*, 22 August 1812.

681 Ibid. The Choctaw were expected to accept up to the sum of $150 from the U.S. as compensation for the loss of the Choctaw man. 13 November 1812, Secretary of War to James Robertson and Silas Dinsmoor, Secretary of War, Letters Sent, Indian Affairs. MF, No. 15, Roll 3, National Archives.

682 George Colbert, *Clarion*, 21 July 1812.

683   Holmes Message to Legislature, 3 November 1812, Mrs. Dunbar Rowland, *Andrew Jackson's Campaign Against the British, or the Mississippi Territory in the War of 1812: Concerning The Military Operations of the Americans, Creek Indians, British, and Spanish, 1813-1815,* 27. See also, Governor Holmes to James Wilkinson, 7 September 1812, Territorial Papers, VI:320-321, Washington Printing Office, 1938.

684   AJ to Willie Blount, 11 November 1812, PAJ 1:336-338.

685   *Clarion,* 30 June 1812, 1 September 1812. The editor was disturbed that the Chickasaw had not stopped the Creeks from using their nation as a staging area for attacks and that a Choctaw man had just killed the traveler Mr. Haley.

686   *Clarion,* 16 September 1812.

687   Putnam, 601.

688   Ibid.

689   Ibid., 598.

690   Ibid.

691   Talk of Chief Bark, September 1812, Records of the Cherokee Indian Agency in Tennessee, 1801-1835, Correspondence and Miscellaneous, National Archives, M208, Roll 5.

692   Letter dated 29 October 1812, printed in *Clarion,* 12 January 1813, *Clarion,* 19 September 1812.

693   *Clarion,* 3 November 1812.

694   Putnam, 599.

695   *Clarion,* 19 September 1812.

696   AJ to Willie Blount, 11 November 1813, PAJ II:336-337. See also Eustis to Blount, 21 October 1812, CAJ I:240, n 5.

697   Parton Condensed, 107.

698   PAJ II:359, n. 3, referring to a letter from Eustis to Blount, 21 October 1812, and 23 October 1812.

699   Hay and Werner, *The Admirable Trumpeter,* 74.

700   AJ to Willie Blount, 11 November 1812, PAJ II:336-338.

701   Willie Blount to AJ, *Clarion,* 11 November 1812.

702   Ibid.

703   AJ to the Tennessee Volunteers, 14 November 1812, PAJ II: 340-341 and CAJ I:241-242 and published in the *Clarion,* 16 November 1813.

704 V.M. Queener, "Gideon Blackburn," *The East Tennessee Historical Society's Publications,* 6 (1934): 12-28.

705 For authorization to open the school, see Henry Dearborn to Return J. Meigs and Henry Dearborn to Gideon Blackburn, 1 July 1803, Letters Sent, Indian Affairs, MF, No. 15, Roll 3; J.H.F. Claiborne,, *Mississippi, As A Province, Territory and State,* Vol. 1, n, 528. The conflict between Blackburn and the Indians is detailed in Personal Recollections of W. W. Trimble, Issue of October 27, 1860, Transcribed. Copy at McCain Archives, Millsaps College, Jackson, MS.

706 Helen Sawyers Cook, "Reverend Gideon Blackburn," Williamson County Archives. See also *Clarion*, 13 March 1812 for an announcement of Blackburn's work at the academy.

707 *Clarion*, 2 December 1812.

708 Helen Sawyers Cook, "Reverend Gideon Blackburn," Williamson County Archives.

709 AJ to George Washington Campbell, 29 November 1812, PAJ II: 343-344.

710 Thomas Hart Benton to AJ, 9 July 1813, PAJ II:490. See also, Thomas H. Benton to AJ, 25 July 1813, PAJ II:311-314.

711 AJ Memorandum re: Thomas Hart Benton, 13 July 1813, PAJ II:409. Benton had future military aspirations, and he hoped to remove any concerns about insubordination. After Benton and Jackson parted ways in a brawl in Nashville, Benton went on to serve as a regular officer in the U.S. 39th, and he had further correspondence with Jackson as his military subordinate.

712 Memorandum re Thomas Hart Benton's Letter of 9 July 1813, PAJ II:409-410.

713 For needs of horses for military purposes, see Quartermaster's Rules, adopted by the Secretary of War, 6 May 1813.

714 John Sugden, *Tecumseh A Life*, 228.

715 Willie Blount to AJ, 31 December 1812, PAJ, II:349-350.

716 Benton Journal, 12 January 1813, published in the *Clarion*, 16 February 1813.

717 Zadok Cramer, *The Navigator*, 7th Edition, https://archive.org/details/navigatorcontain1811cram.

718 Cramer, 178. Online.

719 Cramer, 13.

720 Ibid

721 Ibid., 130.

722 *The Nashville Whig*, 16 November 1812.

723 *The Nashville Whig*, 18 November 1812. One flatboat maker W. Barrow, advertised just a year earlier that his boatyard eight miles above (east) of Nashville at Pleasant Grove could supply flatboats as short notice, *Clarion*, 11 September 1811.

724 James Wilkinson to William Eustis, 14 December 1812, 20 December 1812, 29 December 1812, LR.

725 Ibid.

726 AJ to George Washington Campbell, 29 November 1812, PAJ II:343-344, and CAJ I:244-245.

727 Ibid.

728 PAJ II:345. n 4.

729 Ibid.

730 James Wilkinson to James Monroe, 29 December 1812, LR.

731 As George Deaderick's friend and lawyer, Jackson honored Deaderick's wish to meet with Deaderick's wife in a contemplated divorce matter to attempt to persuade her to Deaderick's position. Mrs. Deaderick responded by accusing Jackson of making unwanted advances, a rumor that did not gain much traction in Nashville. For the reference to George Washington's Life Guards, see Bruce Chadwick, *The First American Army, The Untold Story of George Washington and the Men Behind America's First Fight for Freedom* (Sourcebooks, Inc., Napierville, IL 2005). 243-244.

732 Lee Sandlin, *Wicked River*, 22.

733 Blackman Journal, 12 January 1813, 268.

734 John Carr, *Early Times in Middle Tennessee*, 67. Carr was one of Jackson's infantry who gave a brief written account of the expedition.

735 Searcy Journal, 10 January 1813, CAJ 1:257.

736 Ibid.

737 Searcy Journal, 11 January 1813, CAJ 1:257. General Orders, LC, 99.

738 Ibid.

739 Ibid.

740 Ibid.

741 Benton Journal, 11 January 1813, printed *Clarion*, 16 February 1813.

742 Ibid.

743 Edmonson Journal, 11 January 1813, 2. General Orders, 15 January 1813, LC.

744 Benton Journal, 12 January 1813, printed *Clarion*, 16 February 1813. Edmonson Journal, 11 January 1813, 2.

745 General Orders, Andrew Hynes, 15 January 1813, LC.

746 Neelly Narrative, Compiled by Grace Parke Renshaw, 1976, Williamson County Public Library, 27.

747 Searcy Journal, 12 January 1813, CAJ II:257-258.

748 Ibid.

749 Benton Journal, 17 January 1813, *Clarion*, 16 February 1813.

750 Order, 12 January 1813, LC.

751 AJ to Cantrell & Read, 14 January 1813, PAJ II:357-358, AJ to William Berkley Lewis, 13 March 1813, PAJ II:381-383.

752 Searcy Journal, 13 and 14 January 1813, CAJ I: 258.

753 Searcy Journal, 14 January 1813, CAJ I:258.

754 AJ to William Berkeley Lewis, 13 March 1813, PAJ II: 381-383.

755 Benton's account claimed that Jackson had ordered the men to forage with bayonets and that they had been "amply supplied" though he admitted that about half the flour was procured after his own command had threatened farmers with the bayonet. Most likely, Jackson did not order use the bayonet or if he did, he did not permit it to the extent that Benton ordered its use. Benton recorded that local merchant Poston helped set the price for flour.

756 General Orders, AJ, 13 January 1813, LC.

757 AJ letter of 4 May 1813, published in the *Clarion*, 25 May 1813.

758 Searcy Journal, 15 January 1813, CAJ I:258.

759 Ibid.

760 Ibid. AJ to William Berkley Lewis, 13 January 1813, PAJ II:356-357.

761 General Orders, 17 January 1813, LC.

762 Searcy Journal, 16 January 1813, CAJ I:258. Hynes' store in Nashville advertised a new delivery of goods on 27 January 1813 in the *Clarion*.

763 Willie Blount to John Armstrong, 25 March 1813, LC, Correspondence, sent to recover payment.

764 Ibid.

765 Historic Clarksville, 1784-2004, 34. Thanks to Eleanor Williams for the citation. Some references suggest that Poston was the subcontractor who should have supplied the quantity of flour Jackson needed. Another contractor frequently mention was Woods. Joseph Woods advertised in the 31 March 1812 *Clarion* that he had moved to Nashville and turned over his business at the mouth of the Cumberland to his brother.

766 Benton told Jackson that he planned to keep a journal of the expedition, CAJ 1:256, n. 1. Bassett speculated that Searcy was the author of the journal from an officer who accompanied Jackson on his headquarters boat. That author was a dinner guest along with Benton at the home of Gen. F. L. Claiborne on 21 February 1813. The author is referred to as "Searcy" in this book, and his journal is referred to as "Searcy Journal."

767 Benton's feud later with quartermaster William B. Lewis revealed that Benton, or someone under Benton's direction, was the real author of the journal that appeared in the Nashville newspapers. *The Nashville Whig*, 28 April 1813. Lewis believed the writings were Benton's.

768 Parton, *Life of Andrew Jackson*, 1:374.

769 William B. Lewis, *The Nashville Whig*, 28 April 1813.

770 *The Nashville Whig*, 28 April 1813, and *Clarion*, 23 February 1813, printing Lewis's letter of 18 February 1813.

771 Ibid.

772 AJ to William Berkley Lewis, 13 March 1813, PAJ II:381-383 and n. 4, *The Nashville Whig*, 24 March 1813, and *Clarion*, 25 May 1813.

773 *Clarion*, 25 May 1813. Lewis's charges suggested that Benton may have traveled overland with Colonel Anderson to Massac and then returned to Clarksville to meet the boats. Benton said that they traveled by river and he did not know that Hayes was still aboard.

774 *Clarion*, 16 February 1813.

775 General Orders, 16 January 1813, LC.

776 Ibid.

777 Searcy Journal, 17 January 1813, CAJ 1:259.

778 Ibid.

779 Ibid.

780 Edmonson Journal, 17 January 1813, 3.

781 Ibid.

782 Tom W. Campbell, *Two Fighters and Two Fines, Lives of Matthew Lyon and Andrew Jackson* (Little Rock, Arkansas: Pioneer Publishing Company, 1941), 122. Lyon later built flatboats to transport Kentucky troops to New Orleans to aid Jackson in the Battle of New Orleans, 122-123.

783 James Wilkinson to William Eustis, 29 December 1812, LR.

784 Ja. Wilkinson to The Officer Commanding the Militia and Volunteers from the State of Tennessee, General Orders Book, LC, Also printed in CAJ I:255. Bassett identified the letter as addressed to Jackson and suggested in note 1 that Wilkinson and Jackson attempted to establish a good relationship; however, the 6 January 1813 letter as copied in Jackson's Order Book does not show that Wilkinson was aware that the recipient would be Jackson. Wilkinson's 22 January 1813 letter was shown as being addressed to "Genl. Jackson or Officer Commanding the Infantry Force From Tennessee", LC, Wilkinson's 25 January 1813 is shown as being addressed to "Maj. Genl Jackson comm. O the Infantry of Tennessee," LC. The address lines seem to reflect Wilkinson's varying state of awareness and certainty on who was commanding the Tennessee Volunteers.

785 James Wilkinson to Secretary of War, 19 January 1813, LR.

786 James Wilkinson to James Monroe, 19 January 1813, LR.

787 The only explanation for the two letters on the same date is that the letter to the secretary already had been sent by the time that Wilkinson learned that Jackson would be leading the troops.

788 James Wilkinson to AJ, 22 January 1813, PAJ II:274.

789 Holmes to Andrews, 16 October 1812, Document No. 1426, Series 488: Administration Papers, 1769, 1788-1817, MDAH digital collection, www.mdah.gov.

790 James Wilkinson to AJ, 22 January 1813, PAJ II:274.

791 Ibid.

792 James Wilkinson to Secretary of War, 19 January 1813, LR.

793 James Wilkinson to AJ, 22 January 1813, CAJ I:274-275, PAJ II:258-359.

794 Ibid.

795 James Wilkinson to James Monroe, 9 February 1813, LR.

796 Ibid.

797 James Wilkinson to AJ, 25 January 1813, PAJ II:359-360.

798 Ibid.

799 Ibid.

800 Edward Albright, *Early History of Tennessee*, 1909, 94-95.

801 Coffee Order Book, Order No 22, 14 February 1813, CO. Camp discipline was easier to enforce outside town. A good second possible campsite is near Spencer Creek.

802 Recollections of Mrs. Jack Nichols. Handwritten notes at Williamson County Archives, used for article in *The Review-Appeal*, Franklin, Tennessee, 11 January 1923 "Reminisces of Franklin in the Earlier Days. Copy at Williamson County Archives.

803 Crockett, Samuel, House, National Register Information System No. 8829.

804 Coffee Order, 18 January 1813, LC, Copy UNA.

805 Order, 18 January 1813, JMP, LC.

806 John Coffee to Mary Coffee, 16 January 1813, THM, 268. Jackson's quote on taking decisions can be found in Arthur M. Schlesinger, Jr., *The Age of Jackson*, Konecky & Konecky, Old Saybrook, CT 1945, 1971, 40, with Schlesinger's discussion of Jackson's certainty in his own wisdom. Jon Meacham refines Jackson's concept of his actions in relation to Providence in his essays in *Time*, Special Edition, *Andrew Jackson, An American Populist*, by Jon Meacham, 11-16. Though from the hours Jackson spent in church services and religious training, like other mortals, Jackson relied less on the certainty of his own abilities and more on God as his body aged and he faced his own limitations and mortality.

807 Parton, *Life of Andrew Jackson*, III:605. Schlesinger discussed this quote in Artur M. Schlesinger, Jr., *The Age of Jackson*, Konecky & Konecky,Old Saybrook, CT 1945,1971, 40.

808 Ibid.

809 With credit to Franklin, Tennessee veterinarian Dr. Monty McInturff for this phrase during an address on the bicentennial of the War of 1812.

810 Regimental Order, 19 January 1813, JMP, 18 January LC.

811 Ibid.

812 Ibid.

813 John Coffee to Mary Coffee, 16 January 1813, THM, 268-269.

814 James Henderson to John Coffee, 20 January 1813, LC.

815 That intersection would prove an important rendezvous point again a few years later during the War for Mexican Independence. A hundred years later, blue phosphate located beneath that ground would be mined to produce explosives for the military in World War I.

816 Coffee Order Book, 23 January 1813, CO.

817 MIM, 178.

818 *Tennessee Gazette*, 18 May 1803.

819 Clark Hunter, *The Life and Letters of Alexander Wilson*, Philadelphia: American Philosophical Society,1983, 360.

820 Coffee Order Book, 23 January 1813, CO.

821 *Natchez Trace Parkway Survey,* 71. MIM, 303.

822 The actual line by treaty in 1813 was near the current Tennessee/Alabama line; however, disputes had prevented the settlers from extending settlements south of Grinder's Tavern, the actual 1805 boundary.

823 AJ to Willie Blount, 25 January 1812, LC.

824 A transcribed copy of the treaty can be found at digital.library. okstate.edu.

825 Dawson Phelps, "Stands and Travel Accommodations on the Natchez Trace," *The Journal of Mississippi History*, XI:1, January 1949, 48.

826 *John Donly vs. Christopher Williams*, In the District Court of Chancery Court of Franklin, Loose Files, Williamson County, Tennessee Archives, Franklin, Tennessee.

827 A.W. Putnam as quoted in Paul Clements, *Chronicles of the Cumberland Settlements*, 252. The river was three-quarters-mile wide when the water was low. Gaines measured it at 1,364 yards.

828 Coffee Order Book, 26 January 1813, CO.

829 Coffee Order Book, Order No. 26 January 1813, CO.

830 Coffee Order Book, Order No. 31, 27 January 1813, CO.

831 Willie Blount to James Robertson, 11 July 1814, James Robertson Papers, Microfilm, TSLA. Colbert abandoned the ferry operation in 1814 when he was threatened by Creek Indian hostiles. Robertson hired Chickasaw men to operate it until the army could relieve them.

832 Coffee Order Book, Order No. 32, 27 January 1813, CO. From the description of soldiers cutting trees for an encampment, Camp Jones was likely located to the east or west of the immediate ferry. A hill on

the river bank east of Colbert's house provided the most commanding view. The National Park Service cleared the hill in the 1960's for the future construction of a lodge to take advantage of the view.

833 Coffee Letters, January 28, 1813, THM, 269.

834 Ibid.

835 John Coffee to Capt. John Donelson, 1 March 1813, "Letters of John Coffee," *American Historical Magazine*, Peabody Normal College, Vol. VI, 1901.

836 John Coffee to Mary Coffee, 29 January 1813, THM, 269.

837 James R. Atkinson, *Splendid Land, Splendid People: The Chickasaw Indians to Removal*, Tuscaloosa, AL: The University of Alabama Press, 2004, 191.

838 Coffee Order Book, Order No 33, 29 January 1813, CO.

839 John Henderson to John Coffee, 31 January 1813, CO.

840 Coffee Order Book, Order No. 33, 29 January 1813, CO.

841 Ibid.

842 *Clarion*, 16 February 1813.

843 George Colbert to *Clarion*, 8 March 1812, published 7 April 1813.

844 *Clarion*, 16 February 1813.

845 James Robertson to William Blount, 7 November 1794, Paul Clements, *Chronicles of the Cumberland Settlements*, 452.

846 Stackhouse wrote that he found the white men in the taverns along the Natchez Trace more threatening than the Indians.

847 Learner Blackman repeated the speculation in his journal at page 16, Blackman Journal.

848 John Coffee to David Holmes, 4 February 1813, NTC, Box 13, Folder 9, (Original in Collection of Historical Society of Pennsylvania).

849 John Coffee to Mary Coffee, 28 January 1813, Coffee Letters, THM, 269.

850 Ibid.

851 *Clarion*, 15 February 1813.

852 James Henderson to John Coffee, 1 February 1813, LC.

853 Ibid.

854 Ibid.

855 John Coffee to David Holmes, 4 February 1813, Natchez Trace Collection, Box 13, Folder 9, McCain Library and Archives, Hattiesburg,

MS (Original in Collection of Historical Society of Pennsylvania) John Henderson provisional return, 29 January 1813, LC.

856 *Clarion*, 16 February 1813.

857 Ibid.

858 John Coffee to Mary Coffee, 28 January 1813, THM, 269.

859 John Coffee to Mary Coffee, 4 February 1813, THM, 370.

860 John Coffee to Mary Coffee, 29 January 1813, THM, 269.

861 James Henderson to John Coffee, 27 January 1813, LC.

862 John Coffee to Mary Coffee, 4 February 1813, THM, 270.

863 Coffee Order Book, Order No. 35, 4 February 1813.

864 James Henderson to John Coffee, 26 January 1813, LC.

865 James Henderson to John Coffee, 22 January 1813, LC.

866 John Coffee to Mary Coffee, 4 February 1813, THM, 270.

867 John Coffee to Mary Coffee, 21 February 1813, THM, 271.

868 John Coffee to Mary Coffee, 21 February 1813, THM 271.

869 Edmonson Journal, 18 January 1813, Searcy Journal, 17 January1813, CAJ I:259.

870 Tom W. Campbell, *Two Fighters and Two Fines*, Pioneer Publishing Company, Second Edition, 1941, 78, 90-91.

871 Lyon's contract for delivery of the mail is referenced in the *Natchez Trace Parkway Survey*, 88, CAJ I:259, note 2.

872 David O. Stewart, *American Emperor*, 98. Lomask wrote that Burr visited with Lyon at Eddyville as he was traveling overland though Kentucky prior to visiting Jackson at the Hermitage. Lomask, 1803-1805, 67.

873 David O. Stewart, *American Emperor*, 102.

874 Searcy Journal, 17 January 1813, CAJ I:259.

875 Searcy Journal, 18 January 1813, CAJ I:259-260.

876 Searcy Journal, 19 January 1813, CAJ I:260.

877 Hay and Werner, *The Admirable Trumpeter*, 81.

878 Benton Journal, 27 January 1813, printed *Clarion*, 9 March 1813.

879 Cramer, *The Navigator*, Online 1811.

880 Ibid.

881 Edmonson Journal, 19 January 1813, 3.

882 Searcy Journal, 19 January 1813, CAJ I:260.

883 Cramer, 4-5.

884 Edmonson Journal, 19 January 1813, 3.
885 Edmonson Journal, 20 January 1813, 3.
886 Edmonson Journal, 20 January 1813, 3.
887 Edmonson Journal, 21 January 1813, 3.
888 Searcy Journal, 20 January 1813, CAJ I:260.
889 General Orders, 21 January 1813, LC.
890 Blackman Journal, 22 January 1813, THQ, 270.
891 Searcy Journal, 22 January 1813, CAJ I: 260-261.
892 Blackman Journal, 22 January 1813, THQ, 270.
893 Searcy Journal,22 January 1813, CAJ I:260-261.
894 Cramer, 10.
895 Searcy Journal, 22 January 1813, CAJ I:260-261.
896 Edmonson Journal, 22 January 1813, 3-4. A John Rogers advertised in *The Nashville Whig* on September 9, 1812, to hire a painter's apprentice and journeymen. It is not known whether there were more than one John Rogers in Nashville at the time.
897 Blackman Journal, 21 January 1813, THQ, 270. Thomas E. Watson, *The Life and Times of Andrew Jackson*, Thomason, Georgia: The Jeffersonian Pub. Co., 1912, 136.
898 General Orders, 23 January 1813, LC.
899 AJ to Captain Thomas Williamson, 23 January 1813, Edmonson, 4.
900 Benton Journal, 22 January 1813, printed *Clarion*, 16 February 1813.
901 Ibid.
902 Ibid.
903 Ibid.
904 Searcy Journal, 24 January 1813, CAJ I:261.
905 Blackman Journal, 24 January 1813, THQ, 271.
906 Ibid.
907 Ibid.
908 Blackman Journal, 24 January 1813, THQ, 271.
909 Ibid.
910 Searcy Journal, 24 and 25 January 1813, CAJ I:261.
911 Benton Journal, 24 January 1813, printed *Clarion*, 9 March 1813.
912 Ibid.
913 Ibid.
914 Ibid.

915 Benton Journal, 23 January 1813, printed *Clarion* 9 March 1813.

916 Benton Journal, 25 January 1813, printed *Clarion*, 9 March 1813.

917 Ibid.

918 Searcy Journal, 22 January 1813, CAJ I:260-361.

919 Court Martial and General Order, 25 January 1813, 29 January 1813, LC.

920 Searcy Journal, 25 January 1813, CAJ I:261, Edmonson Journal, 25 January 1813, 4.

921 Edmonson Journal, 25 January 1813, 4.

922 Benton Journal, 26 January 1813, printed *Clarion*, 9 March 1813.

923 Searcy Journal, 26 January 1813, CAJ I:261.

924 Cramer, 40

925 Thomas Butler Order Book, Andrew Jackson Papers, LC.

926 Edmonson Journal, 26 January 1813, 4.

927 Searcy Journal, 26 January 1813, CAJ I:261, Edmonson Journal, 26 January 1813, 4.

928 Blackman Journal, 26 January 1813, THQ, 271.

929 Benton Journal, 27 January 1813, printed *Clarion*, 9 March 1813.

930 Ibid.

931 Ibid.

932 Ibid.

933 Benton Journal, 23 January 1813, printed *Clarion*, 9 March 2013.

934 Cramer, *The Navigator*, 40.

935 Searcy Journal,27 January 1813, CAJ I:261-262.

936 Cramer, *The Navigator*, 10.

937 William Calhoun Journal, Crittenden County Arkansas, Public Library, 23.

938 Ibid.

939 Searcy Journal, 29 January 1813, CAJ I:262, Edmonson Journal, 29 January 1813, 5.

940 Searcy Journal, 30 January 1813, CAJ I:262-263.

941 Cramer, *The Navigator*, 1811 Online edition, 150.

942 Ibid.

943 Cramer, *The Navigator*, 142, 1814 online version. Archives.org.

944 Searcy Journal, 30 January 1813, CAJ I:262-263.

945 Colonel John Floyd to Colonel William Preston, 5 September 1780, Paul Clements, *Chronicles of the Cumberland Settlements*, 156.

946 Pierre Clement de,Lussatt, *Memoirs of My Life*, 40.

947 Searcy Journal, 30 January 1813, CAJ I:262-263.

948 Searcy Journal, 31 January 1813, CAJ I:263.

949 Edmonson Journal, 31 January 1813, 5.

950 Blackman Journal, 31 January 1813, THQ 273.

951 Everett, Dick, *The Dixie Frontier, A Social History*, (University of Oklahoma Press, Norman and London 1948, reprinted 1993, 316.

952 Searcy Journal, 31 January 1813, CAJ I:263, Edmonson Journal, 5.

953 Searcy Journal, 1 February 1813, CAJ I:263.

954 Blackman Journal, 30 January 1813, THQ, 272, Edmonson Journal, 2 February 1813, 5.

955 Searcy Journal, 2 February 1813, CAJ I:263-264.

956 Ibid.

957 Blackman Journal, 2 February 1813, THQ, 273.

958 Ibid. Blackman said that they were traveling very fast.

959 Searcy Journal, 3 February 1813, CAJ I:264-265.

960 Davy Crockett, *A Narrative of the Life of David Crockett of the State of Tennessee*, 196.

961 Cramer, *The Navigator*, 167, Online.

962 Blackman Journal, THQ, 5 February 1813, 274.

963 John Carr, *Early Times in Middle Tennessee*, 68.

964 Searcy Journal, 4 February 1813, CAJ I:265.

965 Ibid.

966 Searcy Journal, 5 February 1813, CAJ I:265.

967 Blackman Journal, 5 February 1813, THQ, 274

968 Edmonson Journal, 5 February 1813, 5.

969 Searcy Journal, 5 February 1813, CAJ I:265.

970 Blackman Journal, 5 February 1813, THQ, 274.

971 Washington Irving, *Knickerbocker's History of New York*, II:112.

972 John Coffee to David Holmes, 4 February 1813, Natchez Trace Collection, McCain Library and Archives, Hattiesburg, MS.

973 David Holmes to John Coffee, 12 February 1813, Leonard Covington to James Henderson, 13 February 1813, LC.

974 Robert Purdy to John Coffee, 12 February 1813, LC.

975 Coffee Order Book, Order No. 35, 4 February 1813, CO.

976 James Henderson to John Coffee, 1 February 1813, 4 February 1813, LC.

977 I. Smith to John Coffee, 5 February 1813, LC.

978 Coffee Order Book, Order No 87, 7 February 1813, CO.

979 William T. Henderson to John Coffee, 12 February 1813, LC.

980 Edmonson Journal, 6 and 7 February 1813, 5.

981 Searcy Journal, 6 February 1813, CAJ I:266.

982 Searcy Journal, 8 February 1813, CAJ I:266.

983 John Sugden, *Tecumseh, A Life*, 253.

984 Searcy Journal, 7 February 1813, CAJ I:266.

985 Searcy Journal, 8 February 1813, CAJ I:266.

986 William Berkley Lewis to AJ, 8 February. 1813, PAJ II:362.

987 Searcy Journal, 9 February 1813, CAJ I:266-267.

988 Thomas Hart Benton to AJ, 1 February 1813, LC.

989 Searcy Journal, 10 February 1813, CAJ I:267.

990 Cramer, *The Navigator*,1811 Online Edition, 149-150, n. 2., Searcy Journal, 10 February 1813, CAJ I:267.

991 Ibid.

992 Ibid.

993 Searcy Journal, 11 February 1813, CAJ I:267.

994 Ibid.

995 Searcy Journal, 12 February 1813, CAJ I:267.

996 Lee Sandlin, *Wicked River*, 32,37.

997 Blackman, 10 February 1813. THQ, 275-276.

998 James Henderson to John Coffee, 11 February 1813, LC.

999 James Henderson to John Coffee, 7 February 1813, LC. (indexed as Coffee to Henderson).

1000 John, W. Monette, M.D., *History of the Discovery and Settlement of the Valley of Mississippi*, New York: Harper & Brothers, 1846, 389.

1001 Searcy Journal, 13 February 1813, CAJ I:267.

1002 Searcy Journal, 12 February 1813, CAJ I:267.

1003 Searcy Journal, 13 February 1813, CAJ I:267.

1004 Learner Blackman to William Foster, 12 February 1813, LC.

1005 Searcy Journal, 14 February 1813, CAJ I:267-268.

1006 One was the future Methodist preacher Jonathan Jones, whose account of the soldiers outside his farm near Greenville was recorded in MIM, 382.

1007 J.H.F. Claiborne, , *Mississippi, As A Province, Territory and State,* 1:258-260, Mimi Miller, Monograph. Charles S. Syndor, *A Gentleman of the Old Natchez Region*, Benjamin L.C. Wailes, Duke University Press, Durham, North Carolina, 1938, 27-30.

1008 Edmonson Journal, 24 March 1813, 13.

1009 W.C.C. Claiborne to H. Dearborn, 10 September 1802, enclosed in H. Dearborn to James Madison, 10 September 1802, LS, Rowland, Encyclopedia of Mississippi History, I:279.

1010 *The WPA Guide to the Magnolia State*, 333.

1011 Searcy Journal, 15 February 1813, CAJ I:268.

1012 Ibid.

1013 AJ to John Coffee, 16 February 1813, LC.

1014 *Clarion*, 2 March 1813.

1015 John Armstrong to Willie Blount, 8 March 1813, published in *The Nashville Whig*, 17 March 1813.

1016 John, W. Monette, M.D., *History of the Discovery and Settlement of the Valley of Mississippi*, 389.

1017 Felix Grundy, *The Nashville Whig*, 3 March 1813.

1018 Searcy Journal, 15 January 1813, CAJ I:268.

1019 Searcy Journal, 16 February 1813, CAJ I:268.

1020 Ibid.

1021 AJ to William Berkley Lewis, 21 February 1813, LC.

1022 *The Nashville Whig*, 8 January 1813.

1023 Searcy Journal, 16 January 1813, CAJ I:268, B.B. Winn operated a tavern in Nashville, PAJ II:78, n 1. Whether he was related to the owner of Winn's Traveler's Hall that Jackson visited in Natchez is unknown. See also 13 May 1815 Thomas Winn's receipt for Kavenaugh's provisions. Natchez Trace Parkway Survey, Senate. 76th Congress, 2d Session, Doc No. 148, 62.

1024 Wilkinson to AJ, 22 January 1813, CAJ I:273-274.

1025 AJ to James Wilkinson, 16 February 1813, PAJ II:365, LC.

1026 Ibid.

1027 Wilkinson to AJ, 22 January 1813, CAJ I:273-274.

1028 J.H.F. Claiborne, *Mississippi, As A Province, Territory and State,* 1:530. Jackson asked Washington Jackson to borrow a proper saddle and bridle for the purpose of making a good impression as a major general as he entered Natchez, AJ to Washington Jackson, 12 February 1813, LOC.

1029 Searcy Journal, 16 February 1813, CAJ I:268.

1030 Ibid.

1031 Ibid.

1032 Mrs. Dunbar Roland, *Andrew Jackson's Campaign*, 52.

1033 WSH, 19.

1034 AJ to Blount, 21 February 1813, CAJ I:279-280. Jackson admitted that one reason he accepted Wilkinson's command to halt at Natchez rather than following the governor's order was the "prospects of our march to mobile."

1035 Samuel Wilson, Jr., "The Architecture of Natchez before 1830," Noel Polk, Ed., *Natchez Before 1830*, Jackson: University Press of Mississippi 1969, 136-151.

1036 Moore, Edith Wyatt, *Natchez Under the Hill*, 73.

1037 MIM, 165, Mary Susan Anton, *New Madrid*, Southeast Missouri State University Press, 2009.

1038 Edmonson Journal, 19 February 1813, 7.

1039 Moore, Edith Wyatt, *Natchez Under the Hill*, 25, 47.

1040 Searcy Journal, 16 February 1813, CAJ I:268.

1041 Regimental Order, Thomas H. Benton, Edmonson Journal, 6.

1042 General Orders, Andrew Hynes, Edmonson Journal, 16 February 1813, 7, LC.

1043 Ibid., and *Clarion*, 16 February 1813. It was common phrase that was also one of Jackson's Fourth of July toasts in 1805, PAJ II:63-64.

1044 Searcy Journal, 17 February 1813, CAJ I:268-269. Edmonson Journal, 7.

1045 Jackson's liquor bill from Natchez in 1790 was $234.01, a significant sum for the day, according to one bill from a merchant Melling Woolley, MJ, 380, n. 41.

1046 Dunbar Rowland, *Military History of Mississippi*: 1812-1836, 1908, 3-14.

1047 AJ to Willie Blount, 25 January 1812, PAJ, II:277-279.

1048 Searcy Journal, 17 February 1813, CAJ I:268-269.

1049 Edith Wyatt Moore, *Natchez Under the Hill*, 73.

1050 Searcy Journal, 17 February 1813, CAJ I:268-269.

1051 WSH, General Orders, James Wilkinson, 20 November 1809. Latrines were to be placed in the rear of the camp.

1052 Searcy Journal, 17 February 1813, CAJ I:268-269.

1053 Searcy Journal, 18 February 1813, CAJ I:269.

1054 Ibid.

1055 John Coffee to Mary Coffee, 21 February 1813, THM, 270-271.

1056 WSH, November 1, 1809.

1057 AJ to William B. Lewis, 21 February 1813, CAJ I:278-279.

1058 Jackson detailed his assessments of Fort Dearborn in letters to James Wilkinson, 20 February 1813, CAJ I:277, William Lewis, 21 February 1813, CAJ I:278-279, Governor Blount, 21 February 1813, CAJ I:279.-280, John Armstrong, 1 March 1813, CAJ I:283-285.

1059 AJ to John Armstrong, 1 March 1813, CAJ I:283-285, 284.

1060 AJ to Willie Blount, 21 February 1813, CAJ I:279-280.

1061 Searcy Journal, 18 February 1813, CAJ I:269. Governor Holmes requested Andrews to provide seven horsemen's tents and 38 common tents to Henderson for Jackson, Holmes to Andrews, 22 February 1813, Doc. No. 1518, Series 488, Administration Papers, 1769, 1799-1817, MDAH digital archives, www.mdah.ms.gov.

1062 AJ to the Tennessee Volunteers, Division Orders, 31 July 1812, PAJ II:317.

1063 AJ to James Monroe, 4 January 1813, PAJ II:351.

1064 John Armstrong to AJ, 6 February 1813, PAJ II:361, CAJ I:275-276.

1065 Jackson's biographer Bassett would later attribute the difference in the date to a clerk's error. Armstrong claimed that he had been told that the weather had delayed Jackson's march and anticipated that Jackson would receive the letter at Fort Massac shortly after departing Nashville. But the instructions in the order from February to turn over all equipment to General Wilkinson left no doubt about where Jackson would be when the letter was delivered.

1066 Edward C. Skeen, , *John Armstrong, Jr,* 175.

1067 The Secretary of War's Letters Sent log records that the order was sent 8 February 1813. LS.

1068 Similarly, a few months later, when Wilkinson was forced into a rival command with his enemy Major General Wade Hampton, his first order of business was to establish his position that he was in command. C. Edward Skeen, *John Armstrong, Jr*, 160.

1069 AJ to James Wilkinson, 20 February 1813, PAJ II:366-367.

1070 The letter from the unidentified officer dated 22 February 1813 and published in *The Nashville Whig* 3 March 1813 stated that Wilkinson had people watching Jackson's every move. Jackson editor Bassett accepted the polite language between the two generals at face value to conclude that both sincerely attempted to work together. CAJ I:255, n. 1l.

1071 Letter from an officer, possibly Benton, under Jackson's command, published in *The Nashville Whig*, 3 March 1813.

1072 James Wilkinson to John Armstrong, 8 March 1813, LR.

1073 The War Department lacked the ability to assure private contractors would perform, and Jackson's troops would nearly starve under the same system later in the Creek War. Jackson would later help change the system to deposit funds in nearby banks to give commanders power to buy their own food. Evidence that Wilkinson may have taken advantage of the weakness of the system are the facts that General Wayne had accused him of taking such actions and that Henderson had reported to Jackson that he confirmed food deposits.

1074 AJ to James Wilkinson, 8 March 1813, PAJ II:379-381.

1075 Hay and Werner, *The Admirable Trumpeter*, 49. Wilkinson served as a dance master in Philadelphia to provide entertainment for the troops.

1076 *The Nashville Whig*, Letter from Officer, 22 February 1813, published 3 March 1813.

1077 Ibid.

1078 Sam Baines to Kitty. Undated letter, Transcribed by Elsie Sampson, published in *Macon County Times*, "Cal's Column," Lafayette, TN, 1952, with permission from *Macon County Times*.

1079 John Coffee to Mary Coffee, 28 February 1813, THQ. Morning Report, 22 February 1813, JMP. Coffee may have referred to "good health" in relative terms. During the Revolutionary War, it was common for up to one-fourth of the troops to be sick in camp.

1080 AJ to Rachel Jackson, 22 February 1813, PAJ II:369-370.

1081 Coffee Letter, 4 February 1813, published in the *Clarion*, 16 February 1813.

1082 AJ to Wilkinson, 20 February 1813, CAJ I:277-278.

1083 James Wilkinson to James Monroe, 19 February 1813, LR.

1084 Ibid.. Wilkinson complained that Jackson had brought too many soldiers to the Lower Country at the same time he was beginning to worry that he would not be able to recruit new Volunteers from his own sources.

1085 Parton, 1:372.

1086 About 30 boats landed on 16 February 1813. Jackson turned over 25 boats to the deputy quartermaster when he marched from Natchez.

1087 James Wilkinson to AJ, 22 February 1813, CAJ I:273-274, PAJ II:371-372.

1088 AJ to James Wilkinson, 20 February 1813, CAJ I:277-278.

1089 AJ Order, 21 February 1813, LC.

1090 AJ to Wilkinson, 20 February 1813, PAJ II:366-367.

1091 William Berkley Lewis to AJ, 8 February 1813, PAJ II:362-363, CAJ I:276.

1092 AJ to William Berkley Lewis, 21 February 1813, PAJ II:368-369.

1093 *The Nashville Whig*, 13 March 1813, containing an officer's letter dated 22 February 1813.

1094 Jackson reported that the men were in as good health as could be expected to create an impression of strength, AJ to Mrs. Jackson, 22 February 1813, CAJ I:280-281, but the spread of disease would soon be noted in journals.

1095 James Wilkinson to AJ, 22 February 1813, PAJ II:371-372, CAJ I:281-282.

1096 Ibid.

1097 Bartholomew Schaumburg to Robert Andrews, CAJ I:282, n. 1. The schedule of soldiers under the Act of 10 April 1812 allowed a total of 2,500 soldiers from Tennessee. *Clarion*, 30 June 1812.

1098 Searcy Journal, 24-26 February 1813, CAJ I:270.

1099 Searcy Journal, 24 February 1813, CAJ I:270.

1100 WCM, 1471.

1101 Searcy Journal, 27 February 1813, CAJ I:270.

1102 Searcy Journal, 19-20 February 1813, CAJ I:269.

1103 Searcy Journal, 20 February 1813, CAJ I:269, AJ to Contractor, 20 February 1813, LC, 121-122.

1104 20 February 1813, LC. Soldiers were ordered to march on the 21st. Edmonson recorded that rain prevented the march until the 22nd.

1105 General Orders, 21 February 1813, 127.

1106 Ibid. Men were falling ill.

1107 Ibid.

1108 Searcy Journal, 22 February 1813, CAJ I:269.

1109 Edmonson Journal, 22 February 1813, 7.

1110 Searcy Journal, 23 February 1813, CAJ I:269.

1111 Letters of John Coffee, THM,17.

1112 Order, Andrew Hynes, 24 February 1813, Edmonson Journal, 7-8, LC.

1113 Blackman Journal, 20 February 1813, THQ, 277.

1114 Ibid.

1115 Searcy Journal, 24 February 1813, CAJ I:270.

1116 Winian Autobiography, 89-90.

1117 Ibid.

1118 Ibid.

1119 Ibid.

1120 Ibid.

1121 John Coffee to Mary Coffee, 28 February 1813. "Letters of John Coffee to His Wife, THM, 271.

1122 AJ to James Wilkinson, 16 February 1813, CAJ I:276-277.

1123 Order, 26 February 1813, LC.

1124 Bartholomew Schaumburg to Robert Andrews, 25 February 1813, LC. Also, CAJ I:282 n. 1.

1125 Ibid.

1126 General Orders, 21 February 1813, LC, February 1813, LC.

1127 General Orders, 27 February 1813, LC.

1128 General Orders, 25 February 1813, LC. Hewitt was dismissed or cashiered, Edmonson Journal, 9.

1129 Searcy Journal, 27 February 1813, CAJ I:270.

1130 John C. Guild, *Old Times in Tennessee*, 222.

1131 General Orders, 26 February 1813, LC.

1132 See also, John Coffee to Mary Coffee, 1 March 1813, THM, 271-272.

1133 John Coffee to Mary Coffee, 28 February 1813, THM, 271-272.

1134 Searcy Journal, 27 March 1813, CAJ I:270.

1135 Blackman Journal, 28 February 1813, THQ, 278.

1136 AJ to John Armstrong, 1 March 1813, CAJ I:283-284.

1137 AJ to Wilkinson, 1 March 1813, CAJ I:285. General Orders, LC,. Not in PAJ.

1138 AJ to John Armstrong, 1 March 1813, LR, LC.

1139 Ibid.

1140 Many had been mustered in mid-June 1812. On 9 March 1813, Wilkinson wrote that the terms of the 600 Mississippi Territory militia stationed at Baton Rouge would be ending in a few days and not even one of the soldiers would join his forces, James Wilkinson to John Armstrong, 9 March 1813, LR.

1141 James Wilkinson to John Armstrong, 2 March 1813, LC.

1142 Ibid.

1143 Wilkinson to AJ, 1 March 1813, PAJ II:374-375, CAJ I:285-287, LC.

1144 Ibid.

1145 *Clarion*, 2 March 1813.

1146 Ibid.

1147 *The Nashville Whig*, 16 November 1812.

1148 Searcy Journal, 1 March 1813, CAJ I:270-271,

1149 Searcy Journal, 1 March 1813, CAJ I:271. General Orders, LC. For formal appearances, soldiers mimicked the look of powdered wigs by coating their hair in lard and flour.

1150 Searcy Journal, 1 March 1813, CAJ I:270-271.

1151 The editors of the *Correspondence of Andrew Jackson* stated that Jackson used his funds to return his sick and "wounded" back to Tennessee. CAJ I:303 n. 1. They concluded that a note to James Jackson dated 17 October 1813 was drawn for that purpose. Unless there was an unexpected delay in the reimbursement by the federal government, the October note more likely related to the Creek campaign. Jackson through his power of attorney to John H. Smith executed a note to James Jackson in the amount of $1365 on 3 March 1813, LC. The March note was executed in Nashville. If the March note was the note for emergency supplies, Jackson's arrangements for funds would have been requested soon after arriving in Natchez to the end of February to allow time for an express rider to send authorization from Natchez to Nashville. As shown below, Jackson, through his power of attorney, executed several notes upon his return to Nashville, and one of those notes may also have been to memorialize Washington Jackson's commitment. Jackson, who had complained that he had no funds for medicines, wrote that he would buy medicines on March 8, soon after his meeting with Washington Jackson.

1152 Edmonson Journal, 2 March 1813, 9.

1153 Searcy Journal, 2-3 March 1813, CAJ I:271.

1154 Searcy Journal, 2 March 1812, CAJ I:271.

1155 Searcy Journal, 3 March 1813, 271. Searcy's note that the day was set aside for Hughes inspections indicates that Jackson kept up appearances when Hughes did not arrive when scheduled. Edmonson Journal, 8.

1156 Edmonson Journal, 3 March 1813, 9.

1157 Baines Letter.

1158 Searcy Journal, 4 March 1813, CAJ I:271.

1159 Searcy Journal, 5 March 1813, CAJ I:271. A copy of the original in the Library of Congress collection makes it clearer that the page had been torn.

1160 AJ to William Berkley Lewis, 4 March 1813, PAJ II:377-378. Andrews and his superior Shaumberg were just satellites. The "sun" of duplicity Jackson referred to was Wilkinson.

1161 AJ to Robert Andrews, 3 March 1813, CAJ I:287, General Orders, 3 March 1813, LC.

1162 Ibid.

1163 AJ to Andrews, 4 March 1813, CAJ I:288, General Orders, LC.

1164 AJ to William Berkley Lewis, 4 March 1813, PAJ II:377-378.

1165 James Robertson to Capt. John Davis, 9 March 1813, Putnam, 602, n.

1166 Ibid.

1167 Edmonson Journal, 8 March 1813, 9.

1168 James Wilkinson to John Armstrong, 5 March 1813, LR.

1169 James Wilkinson to John Armstrong, 9 March 1813, LR.

1170 AJ to Wilkinson, 8 March 1813, PAJ II:379-381, CAJ I: 289-290.

1171 Ibid.

1172 Letter dated 9 March 1813, published 17 March 1813 in *The Nashville Whig*. Mail normally arrived in Nashville ten days after being sent from

Natchez. Unless the letter was sent by express rider it had probably been written earlier than its date. In either event, the unusual circumstances suggest that it was sent for public purposes rather than as a private letter that was shared with the newspaper as claimed.

1173 John Coffee to AJ, 13 March 1813, LC.

1174 Ibid.

1175 General Orders, AJ, 9 March 1813, LC.

1176 General Orders. 11 March 1813, LC.

1177 General Orders, AJ, 14 March 1813, LC.

1178 Edmonson Journal, 12-13 March 1813, 10.

1179 Parton Condensed, 114, John Henry Eaton and John Reid, *The Life of Major General Andrew Jackson*, 3d Ed, 14.

1180 General Orders, 13 March 1813, LC.

1181 Blackman Journal, 13 March 1813, THQ, 279.

1182 Winian Autobiography, 90.

1183 AJ to William Berkley Lewis, 13 March 1813, PAJ II:381-383.

1184 Lewis said that he was at "no loss to recognize the authority" of Colonel Benton in the production of the journals. By his responses, it was clear that Lewis meant that he thought Benton was the author. *The Nashville Whig*, 28 March 1813.

1185 Wilkinson to Armstrong, 9 March 1813, LR, also cited by Tom Kanon, *Tennesseans At War 1812-1815: Andrew Jackson, The Creek War, and the Battle of New Orleans, Tuscaloosa: The University of Alabama Press, 2014*, 46, citing C. Edward Skeen, *John Armstrong, Jr*, 157.

1186 *Clarion*, 9 March 1813. Wilkinson's copy could have been delivered by ship, but the postal route for New Orleans went down the Natchez Trace from Nashville, then to New Orleans by way of Fort Adams.

1187 Even if the letter had been sent by ship, Winfield Scott wrote that a ship carrying dispatches from New Orleans arrived in Washington City one month after departing in 1812, *Autobiography of Lieut-Gen. Winfield Scott*, Sheldon & Company Publishers, New York, 1864, https://ia800500.us.archive.org/15/items/memoirsoflieutge00inscot/memoirsoflieutge00inscot.pdf., p 47-48. Blount should have received a letter by mail in Nashville 15 to 20 days after it had been sent from Washington City. It is possible that mail delivery was detained; however, it would have raised a question in Jackson's mind.

1188 Letter to Mississippi Territorial Militia Lt. Col. Joseph Carson, 13 March 1813 (the sender's name cannot be deciphered), Document No. 1525, Series 488, Administration Papers, 1769, 1799-1817, MDAH online, www.mdah.ms.gov . For an identification of Carson, see Document Nos. 1498 and 1499, ordering Carson to command the troops and introducing Carson to Wilkinson. See also, Governor Holmes to James Wilkinson, 23 August 1812, *Territorial Papers*, VI:317, Washington Printing Office, 1938, identifying Carson as a member of the legislative council. The secretary later said that he thought the ice had delayed Jackson's march and that he would receive the secretary's letter at Fort Massac, however, Jackson was ordered to turn over his property to General Wilkinson, who was in New Orleans.

1189 Winian Autobiography, 90.

1190 Wilkinson to AJ, 8 March 1813, CAJ I:290-291. Wilkinson referred to Jackson's letter of 1 January. He must have meant 1 March, the date of Jackson's prior correspondence, but that error in connection with the error in the date of the secretary's letter would only have caused greater reason to suspect the authenticity of the secretary's letter.

1191 Winian Autobiography, 90.

1192 Winian Autobiography, 51.

1193 AJ to John Armstrong, 15 March 1813, PAJ II: 383-385.

1194 AJ to Armstrong, 22 March 1813, PAJ II:394.

1195 Parton Condensed, 111-112.

1196 These points were made by John S. Jenkins, *The Life of Andrew Jackson*, Buffalo, New York: Derby & Hewson, Auburn, 1847, 51.

1197 General Orders. 14 March 1813, LC.

1198 Order, 2 January 1813, LC.

1199 AJ to William Berkley Lewis, 15 March 1813, PAJ I:388.

1200 *The Nashville Whig*, 31 March 1813.

1201 John Henry Eaton and John Reid, 23.

1202 *Clarion*, 13 April 1813.

1203 AJ to Willie Blount, 21 December 1812, CAJ I:250-251.

1204 *Clarion*, 30 March 1813. The editor noted the difference one month would make in Jackson's ability to travel and to obtain supplies.

1205 The 31 March 1813 issue of the *Clarion* published that only three men died at the Cantonment at Natchez. The private in Renshaw's Company was at least the fourth.

1206 AJ to Rachel Jackson, 15 March 1813, PAJ II:387.

1207 2 *U.S. Statutes at Large* 671-74 as quoted by Jackson in his letter to Armstrong on 22 March 1813, PAJ II:394-395, n, 5.

1208 Jackson received the Secretary's order on 14 March as he wrote to Blount on 15 March, CAJ I:295. He wrote to Secretary Armstrong in a letter dated 15 March that he received the Secretary's letter that same day. The most logical conclusion is that he wrote several letters in response to the dismissal order into the early hours of the 15th is consistent with what others said about Jackson's angry response and little likelihood that he slept until he wrote those letters.

1209 AJ to James Madison, CAJ I:292-293.

1210 AJ to John Armstrong, 15 March 1813, PAJ II:383-385, CAJ I: 291-292.

1211 Ibid. PAJ II:384, CAJ I:292.

1212 Ibid.

1213 PAJ II:385, n. 3.

1214 Remini, *Andrew Jackson and His Indian Wars*, 38-40.

1215 Jackson fought the fight within the social structure of his time. He did not attempt to change the structure by fighting for vulnerable black slaves or Indians.

1216 Hendrik Booream, *Young Hickory, The Making of Andrew Jackson*, 122-123, citing, in part, James A. McLaughlin to Amos Kendall, 14 February 1843, LC.

1217 AJ to Wilkinson, 15 March 1813, CAJ I:294-295. Not in PAJ.

1218 Ibid.

1219 AJ to Willie Blount, 15 March 1813, CAJ I:295-296. Not in PAJ.

1220 Ibid.

1221 AJ to Felix Grundy, 15 March 1813, PAJ II:385-386.

1222 AJ to Rachel Jackson, 15 March 1813, PAJ II:387, CAJ I:296.

1223 AJ to William Berkley Lewis, 15 March 1813, PAJ II: 388.

1224 Ibid.

1225 James Parton, *Life of Andrew Jackson*, 1:378.

1226 John Henry Eaton and John Reid, *The Life of Major General Andrew Jackson*, 3d Ed, Philadelphia: McCarthy & Davis, 1828, 15.

1227 Benton's comments were reflected in his address upon the presentation of Jackson's sword in 1855. Addresses of the Presentation of the Sword of General Andrew Jackson...26 February 1855, Washington: 1855, 36. Benton admitted that he asked Jackson to soften his letter to the Secretary of War, but he claimed that he supported Jackson's decision.

1228 Winian Autobiography, 91.

1229 *Nashville Gazette*, 12 October 1824. Jessie Benton raised the issues in a pamphlet in the 1824 presidential campaign.

1230 Parton, *Life of Andrew Jackson*, 1:3. Marquis James said that Benton "was not afraid to voice opinions differing from those of his chief," MJ, 159.

1231 John Henry Eaton and John Reid, *The Life of Major General Andrew Jackson*, 3d Ed, Philadelphia: McCarthy & Davis, 1828, 14-16. John S. Jenkins, *The Life of Andrew Jackson*, 51.

1232 General Orders, AJ, 21 March 1813, LC.

1233 AJ to Alpha Kingsley, 21 March 1813, LC, AJ to John Anderson, 21 March 1813, LC.

1234 General Orders, Andrew Jackson, 14-15 March 1813, LC.

1235 AJ to Robert Andrews, 14 March 1813, The Gilder Lehrman Institute of American History.

1236 C. Edward Skeen, *John Armstrong, Jr*, 157, relying upon James Wilkinson to Secretary of War, 15 March 1813, LR.

1237 James Wilkinson to AJ, 15 March 1813, LC.

1238 General Order, James Wilkinson to P Jackson C. Tennessee, 15 March 1813, LC.

1239 Wilkinson to AJ, 16 March 1813, PAJ II:389, CAJ I:296-297.

1240 Blackman Journal, 18 February 1813, THQ, 279.

1241 Robert Andrews to AJ, 23 March 1813, LC.

1242 Wilkinson to AJ, 20 March 1813, PAJ II:392-393. Not in CAJ.

1243 AJ to John Armstrong, 22 March 1813, PAJ II:394-395. CAJ I:297-298.

1244 Ibid.

1245 Ibid. PAJ II:394-395.

1246 AJ to Wilkinson, 22 March 1813, PAJ II:396-397 CAJ I: 298-300.

1247 Ibid.

1248 Ibid.

1249 Claiborne to Jackson, 15 March 1813, Official Letter Books of W.C.C. Claiborne 1801-1816, Mississippi Department of Archives and History: 1917, VI:213, and as quoted in Thomas D. Clark and John D. W. Guice, *The Old Southwest 1795-1830*, University of Oklahoma Press paperback edition 1996, 122.

1250 AJ to Ferdinand Leigh Claiborne, 25 March 1813, PAJ II:397-398.

1251 AJ, General Order, 15 March 1813, LC.

1252 John Henry Eaton and John Reid, *The Life of Major General Andrew Jackson*, 3d Ed, Philadelphia: McCarthy & Davis, 1828, 14-16.

1253 Parton Condensed, 136-137.

1254 AJ to John Armstrong, 15 March 1813, PAJ II: 383-385.

1255 Parton, I: 379. The story was recounted in 1855 on the presentation of Andrew Jackson's sword to Congress. Some of Washington Jackson's family remember that their ancestors put the number at 1,000.

1256 Thomas Hart Benton upon the presentation of Jackson's sword to Congress in 1855, February 26, 1855, Online version, https://archive. org/stream/addressesonprese00united#page/n5/mode/2u.

1257 AJ to David Holmes, 16 March 1813, LC.

1258 AJ to the Tennessee Volunteers, 16 March 1813, PAJ II:390-392.

1259 Winian Autobiography, 91.

1260 Edmonson Journal, 17 March 1813, 12.

1261 John Coffee to Mary Coffee, 15 March 1813, THM, 273-274.

1262 Edmonson Journal, 12.

1263 Ibid.

1264 Baines Letter.

1265 AJ to J. Brandt, Esq., 19 March 1813, General Orders, LC, 199.

1266 J. Brandt to AJ, Ibid., 199-200.

1267 AJ to Robert Andrews, 23 March 1813, CAJ I:300.

1268 Robert Andrews to AJ, 23 March 1814, CAJ I:300-303.

1269 John Coffee, 23 March 1813, LC. Burke Davis concluded that Jackson drew supplies valued at $12,000 from the quartermaster for the return. Burke Davis, *Old Hickory: A Life of Andrew Jackson*, The Dial Press, New York, 1977, 72. He did not cite his source.

1270 Robert Andrews to AJ, 23 March 1814, CAJ I:300-301.

1271 Edmonson Journal, 23 March 1813, 13. Edmonson assumed that wagons rolling into camp meant that the Volunteers would soon be marching.

1272 General Orders. 24 March 1813, CAJ I:301-302.

1273 Andrews' and Schaumburg's concerns were not without merit. On March 25, 1813, Schaumburg was ordered to settle his accounts because of the "vast" sum of his expenditures, though Wilkinson said that Schaumburg economized to starvation, Secretary of War, LS, Roll 6, 413.

1274 AJ to Robert Andrews, 24 March 1813, CAJ I:302-303. LC.

1275 Ibid.

1276 Ibid.

1277 John Henry Eaton and John Reid wrote that Jackson "seized upon the wagons" and "compelled them to proceed to the transportation of his sick," *The Life of Major General Andrew Jackson*, 3d Ed, Philadelphia: McCarthy & Davis, 1828, 16. Parton wrote that Jackson "impressed" the wagons.

1278 Benton also reflected simply that Jackson "impressed" the wagons. He paid a cost of $10 per day per wagon and repaid the U.S. quartermaster at the end of the war. The steep cost for the time, more than a governor's annual salary, shows that Jackson waited until he could take wagons by force, because he lacked funds to pay for them. Parton, 1:379.

1279 The wagons reached Colbert's Ferry 21 days after leaving Natchez on March 25. Based upon Benton's recollection, a roundtrip of 42 days for 11 wagons would have cost Jackson more than $4,600. That cost did not include forage for the horses. The bill for forage in Natchez was over $5,000 in a short period. Jackson also paid for some of the food expenses.

1280 This account was related in John S. Jenkins, *The Life of Andrew Jackson*, 52.

1281 Edmonson Journal, 25 March 1813, 13.

1282 John Coffee and Andrew Jackson to the Adams County Superior Court, 25 March 1813, PAJ II:398-399.

1283 Jackson had received demands for money from Blennerhassett's friends just prior to departing Nashville, and he apparently had ignored them. Jonathan Thompson to AJ, 30 September 1812, PAJ II:322.

1284 To the Adams County Superior Court from John Coffee and AJ, 25 March 1813, PAJ II:398-99.

1285 Ibid.

1286 John S. Jenkins, *The Life of Andrew Jackson*, 51.

1287 Ibid.

1288 Blackman Journal, 45.

1289 Blackman Journal, 50.

1290 Edmonson, 25 March 1813, 13.

1291 Ibid.

1292 NPS Historian Rogers W. Young, wrote, "Andrew Jackson's Movements on Lower Natchez Trace", *The Journal of Mississippi History*, X:2, April 1948, in January 1948 that from the records available, Jackson made his first encampment at Greenville, but he did not have access to Edmonson's journal. With that scare evidence, though, Young correctly surmised that Wilkinson stopped Jackson at Natchez because he feared that Jackson would refuse to subordinate his command. Young also concluded that the quartermaster at Cantonment Washington supplied provisions for 20 days for Jackson's return march, but not medicines, fodder, or for 13 wagons or 26 packhorses. Young did not cite his sources for those numbers.

1293 Edmonson Journal, 25 March 1813, 13.

1294 Edmonson Journal, 26 March 1813, 13.

1295 AJ to Coffee, 26 March 1813, CAJ I:288, (shown as March 6 with a notation that the date is incorrect).

1296 AJ to John Coffee, 26 March 1813. LC, Correspondence. Note that the letter states that it is dated "6 Mach" but it was written from Greenville, apparently after Jackson began the return march on the 25th. From Jackson's statement that he intended to give Coffee funds and push him on and the fact that the letter was sent to Coffee by express mail, it appears that the date of "6" was an error. The facts make "26" more likely.

1297 Ibid.

1298 *The Nashville Whig*, 24 April 1813. The story was also published in the Washington Republican, Washington, Mississippi, Territory, 11 May 1813, as cited in Robert J. Holden, Andrew Jackson and the Tennessee Volunteers on the Natchez Trace, January-April, 1813, Monograph,

February 1978, Natchez Trace Collection, Box 11, Folder 3, J.B. Cain Library and Archives, Mississippi State University.

1299 Extract of a letter from a Tennessee Volunteer to his friend in this place, date 16 March 1813, *Clarion*, 13 April 1813.

1300 Ibid.

1301 B. Coleman to John Coffee, 25 March 1813, LC, Correspondence.

1302 Melinda Burford Livingston and Charles A. Rich, *A Treasure on the Trace-The French Camp Story*, 3.

1303 William T. Henderson to John Coffee, 12 February 1813, LC, Correspondence. Blackman Journal, 26 March 1813, THQ, 280.

1304 Ibid.

1305 Melinda Burford Livingston and Charles A. Rich, *A Treasure on the Trace-The French Camp Story*, 5. 1307 Edmonson Journal, 27 March 1813, 13.

1306 Edmonson Journal, 27 March 1813, 13.

1307 Edmonson Journal, 28 March 1813, 13. Samuel Goode, Petition to Legislature, 25 October 1813, Legislative Petitions, MF, Roll 4, TSLA. Goode was reimbursed $53.50 in 1815.

1308 A. Wright. 1827, as quoted in Paul Clements, *Chronicles of the Cumberland Settlements*, 315.

1309 Lorenzo Dow, *History of Cosmpolite; or Journal of Lorenzo Dow*, Pittsburg, 1849, 648.

1310 Edmonson Journal, 28 March 1813, 13. A reference to horses left to die in the mud can be found in the *Natchez Trace Parkway Survey*, 55.

1311 General Order, 16 March 1813, Jackson Order Book 1812-1813, LC, Mislabeled as being from the Creek Indian War, Florida.

1312 James Robertson to Capt. John Davis, 9 March 1813, Putnam,602. Choate's Stand was located at the intersection of the Natchez Trace and an east-west cross-path.

1313 *Clarion*, 30 March 1813. The path was described a leading east from Choate's Stand. Most likely, it led the village of the Creek chief Oceocehemotla who had asked to live in the Choctaw Nation.

1314 Edmonson Journal, 30 March 1813, 13.

1315 Theodore Roosevelt, *American Statesman: Thomas Hart Benton*, Cambridge, Massachusetts: The Riverside Press, 1896, 114.

1316   The first reference to "Old Hickory" I have found is Waldo's 1825 Jackson biography, which attempted to portray Jackson as a hero, 356. Parton also related the story, Parton Condensed, 114. The nickname does not appear in known contemporaneous journals or letters. Edmonson refers to Jackson as "Old Hickory" in his journal as of September 1814, though his was a recollection written later. (Edmonson Journal, 27). After the Creek War, Davy Crockett, who was not a fan, referred to Jackson as "Old Hickory-face" (David Crockett, *A Narrative of the Life of David Crockett of the State of Tennessee,* 51) and even less adoring soldiers during the Creek War called him "Old Horse Face," Higgins Diary, in private collection. Another writer in 1865 claimed that Jackson was first called "Old Hickory" when some of his soldiers made a small tent for a sick Jackson from hickory bark for warmth and when a drunk soldier kicked the log tent to the ground and was surprised to see General Jackson roll out. *Camden Democrat*, 11 November 1865, Vol. XIX, No. 39, "Old Hickory," with thanks to Mitch Caver for the discovery. In later years, people speculated that Jackson had earned the name foraging off Hickory nuts during the Creek War when food was scarce. J. H. Wallace's *History of Kosciusko and Attala County*, 1916 Attala-countyhistory-geneaology.org. Parton noted that the name "Old Hickory" took some time to gain general use, but he concluded that the fame it brought Jackson was established by the end of the expedition, Parton Condensed, 114,116.

1317   *Clarion*, 30 March 1813 and *The Nashville Whig*, 31 March 1813, printed a letter dated from Camp Jackson written on 16 March 1813.

1318   AJ to John Armstrong, 30 March 1813, CAJ I:303, Not in PAJ.

1319   William Carroll to John Coffee, 26 March 1813, LC.

1320   Edmonson Journal, 1 April 1813,14.

1321   AJ to John Armstrong, 30 March 1813, CAJ I:303. Not in PAJ.

1322   Provision Return, 2 April 1813, LC.

1323   Edmonson Journal, 3 April 1813, 14.

1324   Blackman Journal, 25 March 1813, THQ, 280.

1325   Blackman Journal, 281.

1326   Blackman Journal, THQ, 4 April 1813, 281.

1327   Coffee to AJ, 4 April 1812, LC.

1328   Coffee to AJ, 5 April 1812. CO.

1329 Provision Return, 5 April 1813, LC.

1330 Edmonson Journal, 3 April 1813, 14.

1331 Edmonson Journal, 5 April 1813, 14. *The WPA Guide to the Magnolia State*, 494.

1332 Livingston, Melinda Burford and Charles A. Rich, *A Treasure on the Trace-The French Camp Story*, Baton Rouge: French Camp Association, 1996, 6.

1333 Edmonson Journal, 7 April 1813, 14.

1334 Parton 1:382.

1335 Edmonson Journal, 8 April 1813, 14.

1336 Putnam, 608. Colbert abandoned the ferry in 1814.

1337 Edmonson Journal, 3 April 1813, 14.

1338 AJ to Armstrong, 8 April 1813, CAJ I:303. Not in PAJ.

1339 AJ to John Armstrong, 8 April 1813, CAJ I:303. Jackson had learned of his friend General Winchester's defeat on the northern front, James, 157.

1340 AJ to William Berkley Lewis, 9 April 1813, CAJ I:304-305, PAJ II:401.

1341 Ibid.

1342 Ibid.

1343 William B. Lewis to AJ, 9 April 1813, CAJ I:305. Not in PAJ. See also, William Berkley Lewis to John Coffee, 9 April 1813, LC, Correspondence.

1344 Coffee to AJ, 11 April 1813, with enclosure of letter from Alpha Kingsley to Hynes, 6 April 1813. CO. See also, Andrew Hynes to John Coffee, 7 April 1813, LC.

1345 Andrew Hynes to AJ, 15 April 1813, PAJ II:402, CAJ I:305-306. Louis R. Harlan noted that Lewis was obligated for vouchers he signed as quartermaster and believed that debts of $5,272.84 Lewis paid in the 1820s when Governor Blount settled his accounts with the state related back to Lewis's authorizations of vouchers for the Natchez Expedition, "Public Career of William Berkley Lewis" *Tennessee Historical Quarterly*, II:1, March 1984, 7-8. The author relied up an article in *The Nashville Whig*, August 1, 1829, pg. 2, The article stated that the "cash, to a large extent, was drawn upon the Nashville Bank, not upon the personal responsibility of Major Lewis but 'upon the credit of the government.' Governor Blount as drawer, and Major Lewis as endorser of the bills, might have been held responsible, if they had been protested at the War

Department, but it was the confidence in the Government, and not in reliance upon any contingent responsibility of those individuals, which induced the directors of the Bank to advance the money. Governor Blount has set up a claim against the Government for Commissions on the amount thus raised by means of his draughts." The newspaper said it was true that "Upon the settlement of Governor Blount's account, it was believed that a further sum of $5,000 charged to him should have been charged to Major Lewis. When notified thereof he refused to pay it, unless claims which he held against the government were allowed." The jury rendered judgement against Lewis, which was paid.

1346   Edmonson Journal, 9 April 1813, 14-15.

1347   Ibid.

1348   Provision Return, 11 April 1813, LC.

1349   CAJ I:303, n.

1350   J.W.M. Breazeale, *Life As It Is*, 105-106.

1351   Brief Note on Names and Places, Pontotoc County History, Loose Files, Pontotoc Public Library. The notes relate the oral tradition that Jackson's men camped at the spring on their return from the Battle of New Orleans. The spring would have attracted a camp site in 1813 as well, and the mileage covered roughly coincides with the location of the spring. The Chickasaw Council House was located just a few miles from the spring, which was also located on the southeast-northwest Cotton Gin Road that ran from Fort Pickering to the Cotton Gin Port at Aberdeen and then connected with other trails to Charleston, South Carolina, Pensacola, and Mobile.

1352   John Coffee to AJ, 5 April 1813, LC.

1353   Provisional Return, George Colbert, JMP

1354   Coffee Order, 9 April 1813, CO.

1355   John Coffee to AJ, 11 April 1813. The cavalry may have rendezvoused instead on John Childress' property south of Nashville to collect their pay, because the contractors could not provide enough supplies to Cover Bottom. Andrew Hynes to AJ, 15 April 1813, LC.

1356   Claiborne, J.F.H, *Mississippi, As A Province, Territory and State,* 1:8.

1357   Edmonson Journal, 11 April 1813, 15.

1358   Edmonson Journal, 12 April 1813, 15.

1359   Edmonson Journal, 14 April 1813, 15.

1360 *The Nashville Whig*, 28 April 1813.

1361 Lewis County History of Tennessee (The Goodspeed Publishing Co., 1887) 6. The account suggests that the dismissal occurred after the Battle of New Orleans; however, the circumstances are more consistent with the return of the Natchez Expedition. Decades later, witnesses were more likely to remember the Battle of New Orleans victory than the Natchez Expedition events.

1362 Edmonson Journal, 15 April 1813, 15.

1363 Provisional Return for Samuel Thompson, 16 April 1813, JMP

1364 Edmonson Journal, 17 April 1813, 15-16.

1365 Edmonson Journal, 18 April 1813, 16.

1366 AJ to David Holmes, 24 April 1813, CAJ I:306-307, Not in PAJ.

1367 Turner, *The History of Maury County* (Nashville, Tennessee: The Parthenon Press,1955) 315.

1368 Edmonson Journal, 20 April 1813, 16.

1369 *The Nashville Whig*, 29 April 1813.

1370 Parton, Life of Andrew Jackson, 1:383. Colyar described it as a "great ceremony...Jackson was simply an idol," Colyar 1:88. That view was probably colored by Jackson's subsequent victory at New Orleans. In April 1813, Jackson had earned a place in the men's hearts, but not yet a national hero.

1371 *The Nashville Whig*, 28 April 1813.

1372 Ibid.

1373 Willie Blount to AJ, 27 April 1813, LC. Willie Blount to James White, U.S. Army Contractor at Nashville, 30 March 1813, LC.

1374 *Clarion*, 20 April 1813.

1375 Ibid.

1376 James Wilkinson to AJ, 8 March 1813, CAJ I:290-291. Wilkinson said, "Altho' you have not had an opportunity to render service to the nation, on the field of Battle, you have manifested unequivocally your disposition to do so..."

1377 Ibid.

1378 John A. Armstrong to AJ, 22 March 1813, CAJ I:300.

1379 Ibid.

1380 John Armstrong to AJ, 10 April 1813, CAJ II:305.

1381 T.H. Benton, 24 April 1813, *The Nashville Whig*, 28 April 1813.

1382 *Clarion*, 4 May 1813.

1383 W.W. Clayton, *History of Nashville*,76.

1384 Samuel Butler to Andrew Jackson, 5 May 1813, LC, Correspondence.

1385 Before the reimbursements were paid, Jackson was forced to borrow money. See for example, notes for $1,000 each, AJ to John H. Smith 31 March 1813, 6 June 1813, AJ to John Childress, 13 June 1813, and for $754, AJ to John H Smith 19 May 1813, LC. See also the notice of Jackson's attorney-in-fact W.W. Cooke dated 22 January 1813 to sell 1,300 improved acres belonging to Jackson in *The Nashville Whig*, 10 February 1813.

1386 AJ to John Armstrong, 10 May 1813, CAJ I:307.

1387 W.W. Clayton, *History of Nashville*,100.

1388 Parton, Life of Andrew Jackson, 1:384. Benton's letter to Jackson dated 15 June 1813 suggested only that Armstrong said that the requests would have to proceed through appropriate channels. CAJ I:308.

1389 Thomas Hart Benton to AJ, 15 June 1813, PAJ II:406-407.

1390 Thomas Hart Benton to AJ, 15 June 1813, CAJ I:308-309.

1391 AJ to Robert Andrews, 4 July 1813, LC.

1392 AJ to David Holmes, 24 April 1813, CAJ I:306-307.

1393 *The Nashville Whig*, 28 April 1813.

1394 Ibid.

1395 Ibid.

1396 C. Edward Skeen, *John Armstrong, Jr*, 158. The order arrived in April, but Wilkinson did not receive it until June when he returned to New Orleans from the Mobile mission

1397 James Wilkinson to James Monroe, 9 February 1813, LR, also cited in C. Edward Skeen, *John Armstrong, Jr*, 158.

1398 Secretary of War to Wilkinson, 10 March 1813. Letters Sent, Military Affairs, Roll 6, 424, Letters Sent, also cited in Skeen, C. Edward, *John Armstrong, Jr*, 158 and, as quoted in LL, 300.

1399 Secretary of War to Wilkinson, 10 March 1813. Letters Sent, Military Affairs, Roll 6, 424.

1400 LL, 309.

1401 LL, 317.

1402 As cited in A.J. Languth, *Union 1812*, 379.

1403   William Crawford to James Madison, 3 March 1813, https://www.loc. gov/resource/mjm.15_0105_0107/?sp=1.

1404   Theodore Roosevelt, *The Winning of the West*, Presidential Ed., G.P. Putnam's Sons, New York: 1894, III:124.

1405   AJ to Amos Kendall, 9 January 1844, CAJ 6:253-254. On 12 February 1844, Jackson wrote that the book was in the hands of a Clay Whig (presumably Hynes had become a Whig) and Jackson had given up hope of seeing the book. Ibid., 254, n.

1406   Wilkinson was in West Florida at the time, and he did not receive the order until 19 May 1813. Skeen, C. Edward, *John Armstrong, Jr*, 158.

1407   When Jackson was appointed as U.S. Major General, he told Rachel to purchase a new carriage worthy of a general's lady. The carriage was disassembled and transported by flatboat with Rachel on her trip to join Jackson at New Orleans. Carriages, like modern automobiles, were important status symbols of the day.

1408   W.C. Yates, *Tales of A Tennessee Yeoman* (Franklin, Tennessee: 1991), 18.

1409   David Crockett, *A Narrative of the Life of David Crockett of the State of Tennessee,* Facsimile Ed., Wright, Nathalia, General Editor, Knoxville, Tennessee: The University of Tennessee Press, 1973, 75. Though many of those men abandoned Jackson during the Creek War when their enlistment term expired.

1410   Parton noted that about 1,300 Volunteers eagerly turned out, Parton Condensed, 135. Many refused to remain with Jackson through the Creek Wars when their term of service expired.

1411   AJ to John Armstrong, 24 April 1813, PAJ II:403-404.

1412   Blackman drowned when a horse knocked him off a ferry boat into the Ohio River. John Carr, *Early Times in Middle Tennessee*, 69. Though Blackman's friend Carr wrote that it was thought Blackman was an excellent swimmer, Blackman wrote in his journal that he could not swim. The water route added anxiety for Blackman that he never allowed to slow him from his mission as he and Carr rowed from boat to boat in a small canoe.

1413   John C. Guild, *Old Times in Tennessee*, 450.

1414   *The Nashville Whig*, 15 May 1815. The Battle of New Orleans was fought after the peace treaty had been signed but not ratified; however, Jackson did not initiate the battle. The British invaded. The peace treaty only provided that the countries would return to their status "ante bellum" or before the war. That arrangement would still have left areas vulnerable to British efforts to establish a presence. If the British had won the Battle of New Orleans and moved north, they might not have recognized the treaty as requiring them to relinquish territory. For a discussion of how General Washington sought to emulate European methods by drawing generals from an elite group, see, Don Higgenbotham, "Military Education Before West Point," Robert M. S. McDonald, Ed., *Thomas Jefferson's Military Academy: Founding West Point*, Charlottesville: University of Virginia Press, 2004, 36.

INDEX

sermon to officers after departure 242-243, effect on volunteers 246, collapse of boat roof during sermon 254; speculation as to origin of Indians 274-275, preached to soldiers at stop on Cumberland River 285, insecurity in his abilities but growing confidence 286, ministered to dying soldier Rogers 287, disagreement with AJ on ministering to soldiers 287-288, preached at Fort Massac, view on soldiers as little more than slaves 290, view on ease of war 293-294, speculation as to future of Mississippi River 299, method of preaching to men in boats, took risks 302, at Fort Pickering 303, noticed effects of his work 312, plans to speak in Natchez circuit 315, preached in Washington, MT 348, invited Winian to Camp Jackson 349, found soldiers showing greater interest in sermons 355, proposed West Tennessee Bible societies 365, spoke at funeral 369, grew pessimistic 392, created confusion with wagon drive, rumor of AJ's anger, 407408, ministered to dying soldier at French Camp 411, traveled ahead to Crower's house 417-418, return north on the Natchez Trace 418, preached in Nashville, stayed with Rachel 418, death in a drowning incident 444.

Blennerhassett, Harman, attempted attachment of Jackson's funds 406, friends made demands on AJ, endnote 1284.

Blount, Willie Gov. (selected) ordered call of troops 5, waited with AJ for troops' arrival 8,10, walked through camp with AJ 10, approval of officers 20, review of troops 27, address 52-53, certified commissions and order to march to New Orleans 68, order to obtain supplies for cavalry and to avoid confrontation with Indians 68, issued order to obtain equipment 73,

Warning 79, turned to Nashville Bank for loan 86, participation in departure ceremony 87, comment on Wilkinson 133, reported that Tecumseh was in the area 161, reported Jackson's offer to Secretary of War 164, supported AJ's push to control Indians 172, on witness said to be Simon Gerty, consulted with AJ and gave authority to act 174, gave Jackson authority to investigate attacks 174, reported Crawley attack to Secretary of War 178, sent militia in to Chickasaw Nation 184, called out rangers 184, needed tally of soldiers 188, Colbert asked to call off militia 190, AJ's report of Cherokee intelligence 192, AJ appeal for command 193, public criticism of 200, 206 resisted AJ's pressure 202, gave Jackson limited authority 204, tendered AJ and Volunteer service to War Department 207, War Department encouraged to use diplomacy 215, authorized rangers 217, instructions from War Department on appointment of commander of Volunteers 225, Division Orders to Volunteers 228, Wilkinson criticized lack of notification 236, 255, AJ reported progress to 250, forwarded letters to Wilkinson 255, notified Wilkinson that AJ was in command of Volunteers 259, Colbert criticized for not alerting of Volunteer's march 276, AJ notified of poor conditions at Cantonment Washington 333, Wilkinson claimed exceeded authority 340, AJ blamed 369, forwarded dismissal order to AJ 370, AJ assessment of dismissal order and request for help 385, rejected AJ request for assistance 422, 424, presided at return ceremony 432, apology to AJ 433.

Boats (selected), Jackson's construction in 1803 46, turned over to Colbert 48, Jackson's construction in 1804 50, inspection by Bradley 67, ordered dropped down to wharves in Nashville 67, use to transport tents 74, waiting boat sinking 81, flatboat description 81-82 completion of chimneys 84, Jackson supplied Burr a boat 129, boats for Burr rebellion 118, gunboats to be sent to Mississippi 122, boats Jackson built for Burr 126, passage booked at Colbert's Ferry, 143, Blount's authority to acquire boats 228, recommendations for construction 236, travel north on Mississippi River endnote 100, Colbert's ferryboats endnote 127, 134, size Jackson built in 1804 endnote 232, Lyon built in 1814 endnote 782, numbers in Natchez endnote 1086.

Boatmen, Mississippi River boatmen 38, Jackson's use as merchant 41, returning on Natchez Trace 41, 82, and endnote 100, Wilkinson's boatmen 96, use of Cramer's *Navigator* 235, practice of sheltering in winter 283.

Bradford, Benjamin J., editor of the Clarion, comments on Volunteers' march 8, printed Military Instructor 162, chastened by exaggerations 172, rebuttal to Colbert 200, urging of invasion of Creek Nation 206, urging of rescue of Martha Crawley 211, criticism of Indian annuities 222; urging for Jackson to march into Creek Nation 414.

Bradley, James, Lieutenant Col., Ordered to inspect boats 67, ordered to track down delivery of arms 76-77, 85, took corn from sinking boat 254, led way past Flour Island 301, ordered to inspect rations 344.

Brahan, John, Federal Receiver, 207.

Brandt, John, contractor in Natchez, examination of food 344, requests for wagons 399-400.

Brown's Bottom, swamp, intersection of military road and Piomingo's Trace 46, cavalry crossing and encampment on return march 418, infantry crossing on return march 428.

Brown, James (Chickasaw leader) allegations against Neelly 215, cavalry camped near inn 418, infantry camped near inn 418, sold corn to Coffee 419.

Brown, Joseph, 186.

Bruff, Major James, testified against Wilkinson, 115, warning to federal government 122.

Bruinsburg, Mississippi Territory, AJ's trading post 41, Jackson's cabin fell into river, 297 temporary residence for AJ and Rachel 412.

Buffalo River, Crawley massacre 180, Mason's Rangers scouting 185, as boundary for Chickasaw Nation 268, site of McLeish's Stand 269, Jackson's return across 430.

Burnett, Daniel, inn owner, Grindstone Ford 315.

Burr, Aaron, vice-president, Winfield Scott assessment 100, 1805 first visit to Nashville 109, 113, background 109-110, killing of Hamilton 110, plans for rebellion 110-111, 115,118, 120, 121, 122, 1804 meeting with Wilkinson 112, Jackson assessment 112, 1805 second visit to Nashville 114-115, flattery of Jackson 115, 1806 third visit to Nashville 117, denial of plot 122, hanged in effigy in Nashville 123, arrest 123, trial in Kentucky 125, 1806 fourth visit to Nashville 125-126, departure from Nashville with two boats 126, second arrest 126-127, second trial in Richmond 128-129, correspondence with Wilkinson in code 129, 133, supported Jackson's appointment as general 225, meeting with Lyon 282, meeting with Wilkinson at Fort Massac 282, Blennerhassett judgment 406.

Bush, Oliver Private, Volunteer deserter, 21-22.

Butler, Thomas S. Colonel, (selected) friend of AJ, second in command in U.S. Army, in charge of building Natchez Trace military highway 101, request from AJ and Overton to extend highway through Franklin 101, background 102-102, issue with hair and failure to appear at Fort Adams 102-103, first court martial 104, arrest 104, second court martial verdict and death 106, story of burial 107, orphaned children taken in by Jackson 108, lesson for AJ 120, officers sent to court martial 126, precedent 133, persecution 139, orphaned children taken in by AJ and Rachel, 108, soldiers on Burr boat to court martial Butler 114, pulled soldiers from Fort Massac 293.

Butler, Surgeon, likely son of Col. Thomas S. Butler, 354.

Buzzard Roost, meeting site for Pillows and Roberts 186, Blackman's return 418, infantry's return 426, 429.

Camp Columbian, Jackson commissary 47, fortified 49, taken over by Colbert 143, near Camp Jones 271, endnote 135.

Camp Good Exchange, cavalry encampment in Nashville, 25, 89.

Camp Extortion, encampments in Nashville, 9.

Camp Jackson, second encampment near Natchez, naming 348, movement of AJ's troops to 348, Winian invited to visit and Winian's visit 349-350, arrival of dismissal order 370, arrival of wagons and commandeering 402.

Camp of Volunteers, encampments in Nashville, 9.

Camp Jones, cavalry encampment on south bank of Tennessee River, 271, endnote 832.

Camp Tennessee, cavalry encampment on north bank of Tennessee River, 270.

Campbell, Hugh U.S. Navy Commodore 167.

Campbell, William, Congressman, letter from Jackson 123.

Cantonment Washington, construction and renaming 49, cavalry destination 79, Winfield Scott court martial 100, march of soldiers to Colbert's Ferry 148, Mississippi Territory soldiers rendezvous 221, 324, Wilkinson encouraged Jackson destination 257, quartermasters requested to meet at 305, Henderson arrival 312, description 316, 331, Andrews quartermaster location 390, commander Covington 317, cavalry reached 317, under Wilkinson's command 324, use as a hospital 354-355.

Cantrell & Read, contractors 67,236,251.

Carr, John, Volunteer, 327.

Carroll, William, Volunteer, Captain, (selected) Captain, AJ ordered to study best campsites 4, positioned as muster master 9, background 19, Bush dismissal 22, presented with flag 69, led departure march for Hall's regiment 81, traveled in commandeered boat 89, published notice to settle debts 172, formed parade of militia through Nashville to settle nerves 179, company fired muskets as toasts read 210-211, noticed gambler Hayes 250, distributed

417, Choctaw obtaining annuities, ball play 417, Jackson purchased beef 419.

Choctaw Indians, discovery of Trace 30, warpath 30, treaty for Natchez Trace 45, welcomed Jackson at Choctaw Agency 153, indications for war 173, encamped with hostiles 174, rangers killed Choctaw man and revenge 185-186, attack earlier on Chickasaw 306, plantations 315, receipt of allotments at agency 417, cemetery and burial customs 419.

Choctaw Nation, Choate's Old Field 12, Tecumseh's entry 148, Tecumseh's visit 148-152, allowed Creek warrior to live in nation 182, traveler reported seeing white scalps 201, Tories 202, proposal for justice for rangers 220, council at Itala 223, proposal to join with U.S. efforts 223-224, rumors that Coffee intended to attack Choctaw 278, cavalry's entry on southward march 306, sick soldiers left at Fulsom's 307, infantry reached line on north march 413.

Chunky Town, Choctaw Village, endnote 486.

Claiborne County, Mississippi, 336.

Claiborne, Ferninand L., led soldiers to aid Wilkinson 324, AJ thanked 395, surprise at AJ's dismissal 395.

Claiborne, J.H.C., historian, Tecumseh account, 154-155.

Claiborne, Thomas, Dr., farm as potential camp site, 345.

Claiborne, W.C.C. Gov., AJ's request to use influence 76, appointment as governor 50, AJ lays paper trail 121, Wilkinson requests replacement 124.

Clark, Daniel, U.S. Congressman, part of Mexican Society 114, published book accusing Wilkinson 133.

Clarksville, Tennessee, comet account 157, as stop for boats 247, Jackson's arrival, opening of pork barrels, butchering of meat 248, Jackson's departure 250, provision of additional corn for troops 252.

Clifford, John, ranger scout, 185.

Clover Bottom, AJ store and racetrack near Nashville, 427.

Coffee, John, selection 17, description 17-18, marriage to AJ's niece 18, business operation with AJ 41, ordered to march into Nashville 25, appearance in Nashville parade 27, reluctance for war 64, interests at home 64, in charge of construction of boats for Burr 118, AJ suggested his service in support of Burr 119, told to complete two Burr boats 126, recruitment efforts for AJ 169, vouched for witness in Crawley story 178, Benton accused of fomenting insubordination against Wilkinson 233, orders as to how to approach Indians on march 262, camp at Franklin 263, reflections of command 263, camp at Dobbins's Stand 267, camp at Tennessee River 272, warning of Indians 273, food rations 273, rumors that Coffee intended to assassinate Colbert 274, meeting with George Colbert 276, camp at Chickasaw Agency 278-279, attempts to secure food 305, arrival at Cantonment Washington 317, greeted infantry 332, orders to men in camp at Camp Jackson 348, assessment by Winian 350, use of own funds 367, answer to attachment 406-407, requested to give up horses 409, separation from Jackson 416, reached Chickasaw Agency on north march 418, intent to obtain food from James Colbert 419, suggested to dismiss men in groups due to lack of pay 425, dismissal speech 427.

Cravat, Rebecca, married Louis, LeFleur, Pushmataha niece, 411.

Crawford, William, U.S. Senator, contact with AJ188, role in Wilkinson's dismissal 437, 440.

Crawley, John, Captain, departure from home 175, return to home 176, work for AJ 192.

Crawley, Martha, attack of family 175, influence of story on settlers 178, taken hostage 179, Colbert's account 180, 183, effect on push for war 181, 189, taken into Indian nations, 181, escape 182, AJ's response 192, effect on Creek divisions 198, rumors of being burned at the stake 211, rumors of being paraded and beaten 211, attempt to locate trader 213, encounter with Walker and release 214, nursed by Mrs. Gaines 2214, return to Tennessee 215, effect of release on push for war 218.

Creek Campaign, soldiers shot for mutiny 22.

Creek Indians, Nashville settlers battled 10, British agents armed 11, war whoops 12, most aggressive to settlers 33, Chickasaw warnings 35, attack on Chickasaw 36, AJ's posse 36-37, opposed U.S. expansion 37, attack on Doughty 97, Seekaboo's Creek heritage 141, killed Pushmataha's parents 150, Tecumseh in nation 153-155 response to earthquake 159, divisions 153, grand council 153, first attack on Duck River 172, imaginary attack 170-171, use of Glover's Trace 174, Crawley attack 176, camp from 1808 177, rumors of burning Huntsville 178, attempted to build support for attacks 179, 180, with white scalps 180, 187, rebels escaped 187, rebels ordered home 187, Cherokee rumors of war preparation 191, AJ's plan to attack

rebels 195, AJ ordered Chickasaw to stop Creek travel 195, affect of Crawley abduction 198, stole Chickasaw horses 199, rumors of making special bows and arrows 201, rumor of buying gunpowder 207, Tandy Walker blacksmith 214-215, rebels attempted to persuade Choctaw 218, Henry claimed all were friendly 219, use by British 219, Robertson urged Chickasaw to influence 220, requested to publish letter 220, execution of attackers and resulting divisions 220, friendly chiefs acknowledged failure to control rebels 224, stole whiskey from Blackburn 230, growing conflict with Chickasaw 364, threatened ferry operations 365.

Creek War, 440.

Crockett, Andrew, gunsmith, 263.

Crockett, Davy, drinking habits 59, "boatload of earthquake' 298, Devil's Elbow 301 writings on AJ's foot soldiers 442.

Crockett, James, gun smith, and Mason ranger 263.

Crowder's, Natchez Trace inn, 417.

Crow's Nest Island, Mississippi River, pirate's haven 312.

Cumberland River, bridge and McGavock's plantation 4, fort 33, boats tied at wharfs 67, racetrack 77, first group landed 86, departure ceremony 87, 88,89, Burr's voyage 126, 224, boats ordered taken to 247, Clarksville port 247, Eddyville 281, 282, endnote 258.

Cumberland Road, 48, 76, 85, endnote 114.

Dangerfield, Henry, Mississippi Territory Secretary, Jackson dined at house 245, dining invitation 353,

Darnell, Benjamin, trumpeter, death 368.

Ellicott, Andrew, surveyor and Washington's spy, 93.

Ellicott's Spring, 316, 331.

Ellipororchew, Creek abductor, 184.

Eustis, William Secretary, reports from Neelly 160, 180, 187, report of Jackson of president's acceptance of service 207, reliance upon and blame by Wilkinson for confusion of command 207.

Ferguson's Inn, Natchez Trace inn 408.

Fever, fear of, 56, 106, 107.

Flour Island, Mississippi, River, 330.

Floyd, Colonel R.C. 362.

Forks of the Road, Natchez path intersection, slave market 330.

Fort Adams, Butler's ordered to be transferred 102, 104, Wilkinson's interest in making it the military command 113.

Fort, John, Captain, 120.

Fort Dearborn (see Cantonment Washington) construction 49, Wilkinson's suggestion as quarters for AJ 259, description 316, name change 333.

Fort Greenville, 98.

Fort Hamilton, (Hampton in Alabama), Tennessee River fort, Tennessee militia neared 180, 186, 187,

Fort Jefferson, 449.

Fort Massac, Ohio River fort, Wilkinson left boat 114, AJ fear that Burr had taken control 126, Volunteers waited and Hayes dismissed 252-253, military road connection to the Natchez Trace 274, Volunteers at Massac 287-289, origin of Fort Massac 289, Blackman's assessment 290, reference in dismissal order 374, 393, 434.

Fort Pickering (Memphis, Tennessee) Mississippi River fort, Hunt's illness 114, connection to Chickasaw villages 278, Volunteer's arrival 303, description 303.

Fort Pike, Mississippi River fort 309.

Fort Southwest Point (Kingston, Tennessee), Tennessee River fort, Butler as commander 102.

Fort St. Stephens, Tombigbee River fort, commander Gaines 214, Crawley taken to 214 Big Warrior traveled to 219.

Franklin, Tennessee Presbyterian Church 230.

Franklin, Tennessee, John Reid 19, Andrew Goff 20, AJ raced horses 41, Harpeth Academy 60, Benton and Reid lawyers 68, Natchez Trace 101-102, patriotic meeting 123, Patton Anderson trial 132, alarm 170, rangers sent to massacre site 177, source of supplies and encampment 261-265, victory celebration 442, townspeople requested speech 445.

French Camp, Natchez Trace inn, Henderson procured bacon and Coffee left soldier 306, "Jackson's Well" and cemetery 411, Coleman set up portable mill 411, Mr. Taylor's death 411, AJ's arrival on return march 420.

French Lick, 87.

Fulsom, David, Choctaw leader, Natchez Trace inn owner, attended Tecumseh talk 151, delegated to lead Tecumseh out of Choctaw Nation 152, battle against Creek 153, cavalry arrival at inn on southward march and leaving of soldier in Fulsom's care 306-307, infantry's arrival at inn on return march 420-421.

Gambrill, First Lieutenant, public rebuke 362.

Harrison, William, U.S. General, Tecumseh's meetings 139, opinion of Tecumseh 139, warned by Tecumseh 141-142, product of warning 147, Tecumseh's speeches in presence 155, attacks on 164, military losses and offers from AJ 164, cursing 371.

Hawkins, Benjamin, U.S. Agent to the Creek Indians, attempted to hear Tecumseh's message 153-154, Colbert suggested AJ lodge complaint with for actions of Creek 184, errors and threats 201.

Hay, George 129.

Hayes, Isaiah, notorious gambler, managed to enlist 250, stole chicken from Anderson at Massac 253, Benton accused of allowing to die 253, not known if death reported to AJ 371.

Hayes, Mr., boarder with Crawley, 175-176.

Hayes, Robert, Volunteer muster master 9.

Hayes, Stockley Donelson, AJ nephew, participation in Burr voyage 126.

Henderson, James, Colonel, selection 20, rode ahead to lay out supplies 76, recruitment speech 205, sent messages 266, 272, 273, assured Coffee 275, negotiation with Colbert 276-277, message of rumor that Coffee would assassinate 377, contract with James Colbert 278, 305, 306, arrangement with Fulsom 307, 312, 313, returned to Natchez with Jackson 347.

Henderson, Robert Rev., declined AJ offer 61.

Henderson, cavalry surgeon's mate, assigned to remain with sick soldier at Pigeon's Roost, 301.

Henderson, William, Jackson enemy, cautioned Jefferson against Jackson 50.

Henry, William, led party that returned Martha Crawley 215, reported Crawley not in danger and descriptions of attacks 218.

Hermitage, The, 14, Coffee's wedding 18, Indian attack near 20, Humphrey's Hermitage 41, Blackman's stay 62, Burr's visits 113, 114,119, 125, Fort's visit 120, Jackson sought solace at 132, effects of earthquake 159, Volunteers to Arms 157, 222, Jackson's return after Crawley attack 192, Blackman's return 418, as U.S. Southern Command 442.

Hewlitt, Captain, Volunteer infantry captain, company desertions 67, lack of boats 244, Coffee's intervention for 353.

Hickman County, Tennessee, 176.

Hinds, Thomas, Colonel, Mississippi Territory militia commander 221.

Hobbs, Captain, Nashville militia company commander 209.

Hoentubbe, Choctaw warrior, Tecumseh sought out 148, Tecumseh's council 149, 151, joined party leading Tecumseh out of Chickasaw Nation 152, battle with Creek and shot 153.

Holmes, David, Governor, announced declaration of war 221, also sent request directly to Wilkinson's quartermaster 256, Coffee asked for his help 305, AJ requested use of tents 334, attended dinner at Propinquity 353, AJ asked to retain tents 361, 384, 397, obligated to reimburse 430, AJ praised 436.

Horne, Sergeant, AJ directed to return to Clarksville 254.

Horse racing and training, comparison to AJ's training of soldiers 26, AJ's success 210 AJ raced horses in Franklin 262.

threats to Colbert 190,195, plan to defend against Crawley attackers 193, attempts to obtain command 193-195, 202,204, undermined Johnson 194, promise to defend Colbert 195, Division Orders 204, offer to serve on northern front 207, July 4 lunch to build support 210-211, advanced funds to have arms delivered 212, Robertson's opposition 216, forced to reorganize as Volunteers 217, built public opinion 222-223, opposition by War Department 225, reluctance to serve under Wilkinson 226, officer's organization meeting 229, wrote to have Wilkinson moved 237, supply problems at Clarksville 248, set standards to travel on river 251, delivered blankets to show concern 251, orders for Rogers's burial to show concern 288, concerns over subordination by Benton 310-312, ordered soldiers to wash uniforms to create appearance 314, landing in Natchez 323, decision to halt 324-224, realization that Wilkinson tricked him 332-333, moved camp 346, suggested concessions to Wilkinson 356, obtained funds from Washington and James Jackson 360, receipt of dismissal order 370, decision to return 377-380, accusation of mutiny 388, discovery of mission 403, attachment of funds 406, threatened by Wilkinson 407, decision to give horses to sick men and walk 410, late support for plan for Creek Nation 414, receipt of governor's refusal for emergency supplies 422, dismissal ceremony 432-433.

Jackson, Andrew, Jr. (referred to on 26), 473.

Jackson, James, Nashville merchant and banker, contribution to soldiers 361, endnote 1152.

Jackson, Rachel, niece married Coffee 18, divorce 40, sought religion 62, sent Andrew a locket with her likeness 85, authority to marry AJ 92, as daughter of a Nashville founder 94, took in orphan children 108, refused hospitality to Burr 125, nephew joined Burr 126, AJ reported good health 340, letter from AJ regarding dismissal 386, Bayou Pierre marriage and continued marriage to Robards 412, Blackman promised to report to her 418, accompanied AJ from return from New Orleans in 1815 441.

Jackson's Spring, Pontotoc County, Mississippi 426, Columbia, Tennessee 430.

Jackson, Washington, Natchez merchant, as agent for AJ with quartermaster 75, AJ request for funds and visits to Camp Jackson 360, business transactions with AJ 360, pressured quartermaster 363, provided shoes to Volunteers 396.

Jackson's Well, south of French Camp 411.

Jefferson, Thomas, President, preferred diplomacy to war ix, wax image in Nashville and embargo 4, made Natchez Trace a war road 42, importance of New Orleans 43, Natchez Trace in plans for expansion 43, interest in increasing population on frontier 44, subterfuge of Natchez Trace 45, program to create inns 48, fear of French invasion 49, ordered Tennessee militia to Natchez without AJ 50, rejected AJ's appointment as governor 51, gave information of Lewis and Clark to Wilkinson 100, placed Wilkinson in charge of Natchez Trace construction 101, preferred soldiers cutting hair 102, Jackson's intervention for Burr 103, 104-106, controlled Wilkinson by rewards 107, election 109, marginalized Burr 110, rumor of assassination plot 111,

429, soldiers visited Lewis's grave on return march 430.

Lewis, William B., Volunteer quartermaster, procured cotton for tents 5, remained in Nashville 20, dispute with Benton 252, opened gun crates 310, AJ reported sick soldiers 364, 374, AJ ordered to have provisions for return 387, informed Hynes that Blount rejected request 422, Benton duel 434.

Lexington, Kentucky, Wilkinson opened store 95, newspaper reports of earthquake 159.

Line Islands, Cumberland River 290.

Little Bayou Pierre, as home for AJ and Rachel 412.

Little Byway Bottom, 420.

Little Prairie, Arkansas, 299.

Little Warrior, Creek warrior 198.

Livingston, Robert, Ambassador to France, letter from Jefferson, 43.

Louis Philippe, future king of France, toured by Colbert 145.

Love, William, named one boat the "Barn" 81, description of playing battle 296.

Lyon, Matthew, Colonel, former U.S. congressman, shipbuilder, Eddyville shipyard 255, repaired boat and visit with AJ 281-282, background 282, assessment of AJ and role in Burr scandal 282.

Madison, James President, interest in East Florida 6. 10, orders to recruit soldiers as federal volunteers 75, AJ sent letters showing Wilkinson's involvement with Spain 133, review of Wilkinson's court martial 134, supported East Florida Patriots 166-167, land speculation 166, Crawley massacre's effect on decision for

war 173, bluff to Britain 203, war declaration 205-206 apparent acceptance of AJ's command 210, Jackson supported opponent 225, embargo 249, Congress refused plans 336, Jackson's letter after dismissal 380, AJ threatened Wilkinson with Madison 394, Crawford letter requesting Wilkinson's dismissal 440.

Manley, Jesse, neighbor to Crawley and settler previously atfcked 175, public outrage over massacres 222.

Manley, Mrs., took shelter with Mrs. Crawley 175, description of attack 176, public outrage 222.

Marion, Francis, "Swampfox," 405.

Marshall, Humphrey, former Wilkinson business partner turned critic, 225.

Marshall, John, Supreme Court Chief Justice, presided over Burr trail 128, defined treason 131.

Martin, Captain, Volunteer infantry captain, given charge of boats 82, 84, Benton's boats met 288, experience and decision to save soldiers 300, Blackman preached on boat 312, Bains in company 339.

Mason, David, Ranger Commander, scouts ordered to range 184.

Mason's Rangers, effects of decision to kill Indian man 185, Benton bragged about killing of Choctaw man 212, Crockett served as ranger 263, Blount requested authority to use 174, War Department authorized and scouting 184, ordered to rendezvous 185, killed Choctaw man 185, unable to track down Natchez Trace attacker 187, Blount ordered to assume that all Chickasaw were friendly 196, evidence of New Town 201, newspaper said too few to defend 211.

travel on 274, Chickasaw friendliness to travelers 274, Pontotoc 278, Lyon mail contractor 282, "Devil's Backbone" 305, Propinquity 317, Abijah Hunt mail contractor 317, re-routed through Washington 330, conditions of road in late winter 378, dangerous condition 396, AJ's proving ground 403, French Camp 411, swamps as "hell holes" 413, Choate's Stand 414, 419, AJ walked home 414, Chickasaw Agency 418, Brown's Stand 418, Little Mountain 420, Pigeon Roost 420, building temporary bridges 425.

Natchez Under the Hill, reputation 326, temptations on officers 326, description 352, soldier's view and landing 323-324, Benton's description 362, attraction for Volunteers 344.

Neelly, James, Major, U.S. Agent to the Chickasaw, report of Tecumseh's visit 160, report of Creek attackers in Chickasaw Nation 180, report that attackers have escaped 187, report of council 187, Brown's charges against and dismissal 215-216, comparisons to Robertson 279.

Neelly, William, home as camp site 76.

New Madrid (Missouri), description of earthquake 158, Jackson's soldiers view of earthquake damage 298.

Newsome, Captain, Volunteer captain, command of boats 246.

Newman, Robert, courier for Wilkinson 99.

Newland, Captain, Volunteer, refused to take drowning soldiers onboard 300.

New Orleans, destination for march 10, 66, 68, 73, 74, 75, 79, 80, 228, Spain controlled port 38, Miro in charge 39, goods to AJ's store 40, role in Jefferson's plan 42-43, importance for U.S. defense 44,49, threat to retrocede 49, AJ's letter to U.S. quartermaster at 76, closing of ports 95, Wilkinson's visit 95, Washington's interest in building road 97, Wilkinson's headquarters 102, Butler's court-martial 104-105, 107, Butler's son's home 106, Burr's plan 110, 119, 120, 121, Mexican Society 112, Wilkinson's request to move U.S. military command to 113, Burr's trips 113, 114, 117, AJ's opinion on control of Texas to control 118, destination of Jefferson's courier 122, Wilkinson ordered Burr to be brought to 124, AJ warned of conspiracy in 124, Wilkinson's actions in 124-125, AJ offered to help defend 126, Wilkinson's arrest of plotters 127, as reason for Jefferson's support of Wilkinson 130, Clark's book regarding Wilkinson's actions in 133, role in Wilkinson's defense plan for Gulf Coast 161, war department order 226, boatmen 234, Wilkinson built barracks for Volunteers in 236, 257, proximity to Natchez 257, Wilkinson's description as reason for AJ to halt in Natchez 258, destination for Alexander Wilson 267, not purpose of AJ mission 278, cypress trees floated to 308, keelboat from 311, Natchez provided services for during Battle of New Orleans 325, secretary's order determining need for marching to ended 335, arrival of AJ dismissal order 337, Wilkinson camp 340, Schaumberg as quartermaster in 351, Wilkinson determined to deliver order 370, mail delivery 370, Carroll bore brunt of attack at Battle of New Orleans 429, removal of Wilkinson from 437, AJ's role in saving 439, AJ's return from Battle of New Orleans 445.

Nolan, Philip, Wilkinson agent, 99.

Obion River, 299.

Polk, James K. Col., too sick to muster 8, family as settlers 267.

Pontotoc, Mississippi, trail crossroads 278, Jackson's Spring 438.

Port Gibson, Mississippi, See Gibson's Port, Mississippi Territory.

Preston, Robert, 8.

Propinquity, Covington's home 317, dinner for AJ's officers 353.

Punishments for soldiers, whipping 21, expulsion from camp 22, confinement to camp 61, clean-up 61, riding the wooden horse 67, 368, imprisonment 70, fine of half-pay 70, drumming 285, cobb paddle 292, ball and chain 292.

Purdy, Robert, AJ friend 305.

Pushmataha, Choctaw warrior and chief, background and response to Tecumseh 150-152, 218 self-reputed birth 384, grave of niece at French Camp 411.

Randolph, John, Burr trial 129-130.

Read, John, 125.

Redbud Springs, Kosciusko, MS, "Earthquake Springs," cavalry approached 313, Choctaw plantations appear beyond 315, Choate opened inn nearby 419.

Red Heifer, Nashville tavern, 59, 60.

Red King, red kings war leadership 138, confirmation of approval for Piominko's Trace endnote 93.

Red Lands, area near Pontotoc, Mississippi 428.

Red River, 248.

Reid, John, AJ second aide-de-camp and biographer, selection 19, Nashville parade, dispute with Benton 27, dispute with Benton 68, as biographer 374, 388, endnote 63.

Remini, Robert, AJ biographer 51.

Renfroe Station, 248.

Renshaw, Captain, 278, soldier in company died 494.

Reynolds, Captain, command of companies 73, rescue of boat 315, favored proceeding on voyage 318.

Rhodes house, Tennessee, 430.

Richmond, Virginia, Burr trial 128-131, Wilkinson's description of confrontation with AJ 392.

Ridgeland, Mississippi, location of Choctaw Agency 47.

Roane, Archibald, Gov., Tennessee governor, divided command between Jackson and Sevier 5.

Roberts, General, Tennessee militia general, response to reports of Creek attackers at Bear Creek 186.

Robertson County, Tennessee, 20.

Robertson, James, U.S. Agent to the Chickasaw, description 33-34, meeting with Piominko 33-35, supported Piominko against Creek 35-36, attack by Creeks 37, promoted Spain connection 39, opposed on-site distillation 39, counseled AJ against needless disputes 116-117, organized defense against Burr 123, organized defense against British 162, Colbert's outreach 190, assured Tennesseans of Chickasaw loyalty 190, cautioned against AJ's actions 191, offered to replace Neelly 215-216, re-appointed Chickasaw agent 216, opposed AJ's stirring of war 216, traveled to Gordon's Ferry to deter march into Chickasaw Nation 216,

Colbert's renewed alliance 217, arrival at agency 219, assessment of Indian nations 219, praised council 219-220, attempts to calm Choctaw 220-221, helped convene council at Itala 223, return to Nashville 224, cavalry at agency 278-279, warned of Chickasaw-Creek war 364, reversed position on AJ attacking Creek rebels 414.

Robertson's Landing, destination for infantry 78, march to destination 82, site of meeting of infantry companies 83-84, destination of officers 88, landing of Jackson's boat 244, delivery of arms to 310.

Rogers, John, Private, Volunteer infantry private, death 287, Jackson informed of death and instructions for burial 288, burial 289-290.

Roosevelt, Theodore, opinion of Benton 18, opinion of Wilkinson 414.

Ross, Reuben, Baptist Elder, recollections of comet and earthquake 158-159.

Sandy River, first rebel party attack 172, Crawley attack 175-175, location where Creeks reported taking scalps 180.

Sappington, Dr., Nashville physician, racetrack site of pre-departure service 77, supplied dinner for celebration 210, Sappington's pills 210, 385.

Sappington, Thomas, Franklin inn owner 262.

Searcy, Robert, Volunteer, AJ staff, likely author of voyage journal, (selected) comments on mood of departure ceremony 87, Blackman's prayer 243, opinion of sermon 285, Rogers's burial 200, future of Mississippi River 297, splendor of morning 299, riverbanks crashing 299-300, drowning soldiers 301, Natchez residents 328, attended dinner for AJ 345.

Schaumberg, Bartholomew, U.S. Deputy Quartermaster, allocation of supplies 257, sent express rider to Nashville 344, protested order to reimburse AJ for transportation 321.

Scott, Winfield, description of Wilkinson 92, court martial over Wilkinson statement 100-101, attended Burr trial 14528, opinion that Jefferson saved Wilkinson 130.

Selsertown, Mississippi Territory, meetinghouse 349, emergency camp on return march 408.

Seekaboo, Tecumseh's cousin and prophet, traveled with Tecumseh 141, proselytized Creek rebels 159, suggested that bullets would have no effect 159.

Sevier, John Governor, Tennessee governor and AJ enemy, denied AJ command of expedition and tied in election for militia general 5, command of East Florida campaign 6, passed over AJ for expedition command 50, notified of Creek party passing through area 180, asked to track down Creek attackers 187.

Shakespeare, William, Henry V, 23, 99, Hamlet 99, 226, 318, 371.

Shawnee Indians, Chickasaw defeated on Cumberland River 33, 87, attacked Doughty party 97, sign to attack 137, 138, forced to become nomads 139, traveled through Chickasaw land 143, Colbert fought against, Shawnee victory 144, war dance 149, fight with Tecumseh and Choctaw 152, attacked Kickapoo and Battle of Tippecanoe 164, Battle of St. Clair 174.

Shelton, William, Tennessee Militia company commander, 162.

Simmons, William, U.S. Army Accountant, 114.

Slaves, operated Natchez Trace inns 48, Colbert's slaves worked fields 143, Indians traded slaves 146, Nashville slaves' reaction to earthquake 158, Colbert's slaves operated ferry 270, AJ's trading of slaves 330.

Smith, Captain, Volunteer captain, met boats 217, ordered to provide coin 368.

Smith, Daniel, U.S. Senator, AJ advised to observe Wilkinson 121.

Smithland, Kentucky, passage booked from Colbert's Ferry 143, description 283, Edmonson's assessment 284, landing opposite 284, Benton's arrival 294.

Spanish Kentucky Association, 96.

Squires, Gurdon, Franklin, Tennessee merchant, 262.

St. Catherine's Creek, 317.

St. Catherine's Racecourse, 329.

St. Francis River, 308.

Stirling, John, Captain, British commander 43.

Sumner County, Tennessee, 5.

Swan Creek, bandits killed travelers, prompted Jefferson to build stations 48, settlement 266, stories boys told around campfires 267.

Swartwout, Samuel, Burr trial 131, Wilkinson's claim of role in note 133.

Talbot's Tavern, 53, Burr reception 117.

Taylor, Thomas, Volunteer, became ill 411, grave 420.

Tecumseh, Shawnee warrior, stirred Indian nations to unite 11, used spiritual prophet 77, hoped to be provocation 138, protested U.S. taking of land 138-139, met with Harrison 139, Harrison's assessment 139, Winian's assessment 139, Brit-

ish offer of support 139-140, weakness of plan 141, journey southward 141, warned Harrison 141, prior visits South 142, Battle of St. Clair 144, visit with Chickasaw 141-147, newspaper reports 147, escorted out of Chickasaw Nation 148, visit with Choctaw 148-152, fight with Creek 153, visit with Creek 154-158, Secretary of War reported threat 161, Chickasaw disclaimed association 161, reports of town of disciples in Tennessee 172, 201, rumor of encampment 177, effects of meetings in Southwest 198, opposition by Osage 308.

Tennessee Land Company, 33

Tennessee Line, 1806 Border of Chickasaw Nation 268, Coffee's return march 427.

Tennessee River, crossing of Trace 29, 32, Washington's interest in military installation 32, 97, Creek villages 33, Colbert first ferry operation 37, Colbert second ferry operation 45, AJ built boats 47, road surveyors 48, ferries and boats turned over to Colbert 48, Camp Columbian 49, destination for cavalry 73, 78, Tecumseh's crossing 142, booking passage 143, white settlers' crossing 145, Creek Indians' settlement west of Nashville 172, rangers 174, Creek rebels canoes stashed 179, Tennessee militia crossing 181, 186 ranger scouts 185, cavalry's approach on southward march 270-271, Camp Jones 271, proximity of Buzzard Roost 418, cavalry's approach on return march 426, AJ's approach on return march 429.

Tenskwatawa, the Shawnee Prophet, (selected) stirred Indian nations 11, Tecumseh's use 77, Tecumseh's brother 141, assured Indians the Great Spirit would support 141, proselytized Creek 159, encouraged Indians to take cattle and burn buildings 172, rumor of company at Bear Creek 183, Creek rebels joined 187, reputed British agent 194-195, had influence on Chickasaw 196, Colbert claimed words false 200, converts made inroads 279, reputed prediction of earthquake and comet 313.

Thomastown, Mississippi, 417.

Thompson, Samuel, Natchez wagon driver, 429.

Tishomingo, Mississippi, 428.

Tombigbee River, Tecumseh's crossing and battle 152-153, Crawley abductors 181, Crawley walked toward 213.

Tookabatcha, Tecumseh's visit 156, earthquake and Creek reaction 156.

Tootumastubbe, Choctaw minko 223.

Training, military, muster training time xii, AJ's estimation of need xii, turning recruits into soldiers 20, goals 24, cavalry 25, West Point 26, comparison to training horses 26, rushed 60, created need for action 60, lack of food 84, offers for individual training 204, cavalry parades 348.

Tupelo, Mississippi, Chickasaw settlement 30.

Tuscahootoo, George Colbert's wife 145.

Tuscaloosa, Crawley abductors 182.

Twenty Mile Creek, infantry north march 428.

Underwood's Village, Coffee's southward march 272, endnote 135.

Union Town, Mississippi Territory, Volunteer's northward march 408.

Valley Forge, 102.

Vicksburg, Mississippi, 313.

Walker, Tandy, Blacksmith, Creek Nation, rescue of Martha Crawley 214-223.

Wallace, Captain, Volunteer captain, Blackburn visited boat 287, sinking of boat 300-301, soldier's recollections of sinking boat 302, put memories of boat behind 309, infantry recalled 332.

Walnut Hills (near Vicksburg, Mississippi), infantry southward march 313.

Warrenton, Mississippi, infantry southward march 314-315.

Washington Academy, Washington, Mississippi Territory 348.

Washington City (Washington, D.C.) settler questions support 38, Wilkinson's unexplained actions 99, Butler appealed for support 103, Butler's friends would not come to his aid 106, Burr's meeting with Wilkinson 112, politicians' assessment of AJ 119, cutoff from reports by New Orleans 120, rumors of Burr's plan to attack 122, Senator Adair's arrival 127, AJ's reputation 131, politicians' reports 162, rumors about Wilkinson 166, not prepared 203, no one knew how to deal with threats 203, 204, Blackburn rode to 230, rumor of Jackson's dismissal 318, rumor of Wilkinson's 438, AJ sent letter to by express rider 355, time for mail delivery 370, Benton's lobbying 435, Covington in 436,

Washington, George, model for AJ xii, Benton used as model for AJ 22, role in Von Steuben's manual 162, wanted installation on Tennessee River 32, threat of separation of western territory 39, example of Life Guards, conspiracy to remove 93, offer of cotton gin to Indians 146, spy Ellicott 316, camp moved on birthday 346, comparison to AJ 446.

Washington, Mississippi Territory, site of Cantonment Washington 49, 257.

Waterloo, Alabama 48.

Wayne, Anthony, General, Piominko helped 35-26, dispute with Wilkinson 98-101, Wilkinson's experience in defeating 344.

West, Major, Volunteer infantry major, delivered dispatches for Benton 310.

West Point Academy, 26.

White River, 309.

White's Tavern, Franklin, Tennessee 262.

Whiteside, Jenkins, U.S. Senator, 132.

Williams, John, Colonel, East Tennessee militia marched for East Florida 6.

Williamson, Captain, Volunteer, refused to strike tents, 66.

Wilkinson Cantonment, 49.

Wilkinson, James, General (selected) lost 800 men to disease 13, report on men who signed Spanish roll 40, placed in charge of Natchez Trace wagon highway 45, negotiated treaty for Natchez Trace 45, revealed purpose of road on survey 46, appointed Governor of Upper Louisiana Territory 50, interpreted AJ's order as challenge 75, review of AJ's order 76, prepared for invasion of Mobile 80, description and background 91-93, Revolutionary War service 93, marriage 94, work as army clothier 94, land speculation and store in Kentucky 95, meeting with Spanish governor, promotion of rebellion 95-96, statement of expatriation 95-96, appointment as general 96, providing of intelligence 97, responsibility for killing of U.S. soldiers 97, fight with Wayne 98-100, work as Agent 13 100, intelligence on Lewis and Clark expedition 100, assessment by Winfield Scott 100-101, Butler courts-martial 101-107, role in Burr Conspiracy 111-121, ordered Burr's arrest 124, appearance of defense of New Orleans 124, appearance in Richmond for Burr's trial 129-130, self-reputed insult of AJ 131, AJ continued investigation 132, defense attacking AJ 133, court-martial 134, defense plan for Gulf Coast 161-162, rumors of command of Volunteers 166, critic published attack 225, rumor of appointment as Major General 232, opposition by AJ's officers 232-233, AJ requested transfer 237, letter offering support 255, established territory 256, built barracks for Volunteers in New Orleans 257, tricked AJ into halting at Natchez 257-258, 259, met with Burr at Fort Massac 282, troops at Wilkinsonville 293, sent Pike on expedition 309, delivery of Jan. 22 letter to AJ 319, promised payment and food at Cantonment Washington 320, AJ replied 321, delivery of Jan. 25 letter 322, earlier arrival in Natchez 323, command at Cantonment Washington 324, tombs of soldiers at Cantonment Washington 331, spies 337, reported behaving with prudence 338, AJ replied to Wilkinson's "orders" 340, fear as to AJ 340, AJ anticipated duel 340, suggested AJ to tie boats opposite Natchez 341, AJ begged for help 341, AJ's brag 342, suggested independent commands 342, sent express rider to Nashville 344, consulted with quartermasters to refuse supplies 352, AJ suggested cooperation 355, troops' terms ending and no re-enlistments willing to serve 356, suggested recruitment of some Volunteers 356, flattered AJ, offered support, and threatened to recruit soldiers 357, acknowledged need for Volunteers

ABOUT THE AUTHOR

Tony L. Turnbow has studied the history of the Old Natchez Trace for more than 30 years. He practices law in Franklin, Tennessee. With a Bachelor of Arts and a concentration in southern U.S. history from Vanderbilt University and a Juris Doctorate from the University of Tennessee College of Law, he has continued to use his training to explore unpublished primary sources about the Natchez Trace. He authored "The Natchez Trace in the War of 1812" in *The Journal of Mississippi History*, and he has published articles in the *Tennessee Historical Quarterly* and the Lewis and Clark Trail Heritage Foundation journal "We Proceeded On." He also wrote a full-length play "Inquest on the Natchez Trace" about the mysterious death of explorer Meriwether Lewis. In the course of writing a book about Lewis's death Mr. Turnbow discovered unpublished accounts of Jackson's 1813 Natchez Expedition.

Mr. Turnbow represented the Natchez Trace Parkway Association on the Tennessee War of 1812 Bicentennial Commission, and he was the recipient of the Tennessee Society U.S. Daughters of 1812 "Spirit of 1812" award. He has spoken frequently about his research to meetings of DAR, SAR, Colonial Dames, U.S. Daughters of 1812, General Society of 1812, and historical organizations.